Toward *Samson Agonistes*

Contents

CONTENTS

III
"Lay hold on this occasion": *Samson Agonistes* and Milton's Politics

IV
"Thou hast fulfill'd the work": *Samson Agonistes* and Milton's Ethics

CONTENTS

Appendixes

Preface

In *Areopagitica* the friends of Truth are seen in a warm light, engaged in attractive tasks, "some cutting, some squaring the marble, others hewing the cedar" out of which is made a "spiritual architecture" whose perfection is "that of many moderate varieties and brotherly dissimilitudes that are not vastly disproportional, arises the goodly and graceful symmetry that commends the whole pile and structure." The building is not undertaken by interchangeable workers; neither do ferocious laborers shove away others to jam their bricks into inequivalent spaces. All are distinctively occupied in a collaborative work which culminates in a harmonious unity accepting of differences: "And when every stone is laid artfully together, it cannot be united into a continuity, it can but be contiguous in this world." The activity described is the sort which Milton scholars would hope could characterize their own work, each bringing up his thoughts cheerfully and confidently to be placed side by side as contributions toward the building of a varied, symmetrical edifice.

As one at the building site, I would like to acknowledge here that collaborative Milton scholarship is as Milton described the search for truth in *Areopagitica*, notwithstanding the Nimrod in most of us who looks out now and then from footnotes. I would like, that is, to thank all those whose contiguous labors have assisted my own. My great teacher, William Haller, one of my most brilliant friends, Rosalie Colie, and three of my most magnanimous colleagues, Helen Lockwood, Doris Russell, and Stanley Bennett, are no longer, to my sorrow, to be thanked in person, and yet they were among those to whom I owe most. To my teachers, Paul Oskar Kristeller and Marjorie Hope Nicolson, and to my friends C. A. Patrides, Graham Storey, Ian Jack, John Holloway, Barbara Lewalski, and Muriel Bradbrook, I should like to say that their influence and assistance has gone into my book and their generosity to me has made the writing of it more enjoyable than alarming. I am grateful to my typist, Mrs. Beatrice West, to my copy-editor, Gretchen Oberfranc, and to my proofreader, Mrs. Eleanor H. K. Blayney; together they have done what they could to prevent error. Irene Samuel deserves a special acknowledgment for her detailed criticism of my individual chapters; I greatly enjoyed both her wise conversation and charming letters, so zestfully pursuing both big and little truths. In the dedication of my book to Joan Bennett, I record that it was written to her and for her, and there is not a section of it that has not been improved by her.

Introduction

To EXAMINE any poet's work chronologically makes possible the reading of individual poems in the context of the development of the poet's mind and art. Such a context involves more than the biographical setting of a work within the events of the poet's life. It allows an intellectual and, if I may be forgiven the word, a psychosocial placing. From such a contextual placement a special pleasure results: while the reader may examine the solidity and beauty of individual poems with whatever critical discriminations he chooses, he may at the same time read between the poems, "guessing," as Henry James put it, "the unseen from the seen . . . [tracing] the implications of things . . . [judging] the whole piece by the pattern."[1] This activity is not the same as that of the historical contextualist, who explicates each work, and the poet's *oeuvre*, in terms of the contemporary structure of feeling or thought from which it derives and which it expresses. He accounts for the force of a text or corpus in terms of the social, economic, political, and other pressures exerted upon it by the writer's having lived where and when he did. In contrast, author-contextual reading bridges the gap between the intrinsic or formalistic study of literature and the extrinsic or causal study of literature. Seeking to preserve all the values of practical criticism in its application to individual poems, the contextualist wishes as well to offer insights into the creative process as a continuous and subtly changing activity. How, for example, *Lycidas* differs from the *Epitaphium Damonis* may be a question for the formalist critic; why *Lycidas* differs from the *Epitaphium Damonis* may be a question for the biographer. But what common tendencies or traits may be descried, what trends in the differences which point toward continuing growth in the poet's creativity—these are questions for the contextualist.

Doubtless, author-contextual readings do not provide particular insight into the work of some writers, poets of a happy homogeneity who inherited a secure poetic tradition within which to express their perceptions. These poets may be quite as masterly (Shakespeare comes to mind) as poets of a revolutionary bent; they may be quite as self-conscious (Pope comes to mind) as poets of change; they may be quite as productive (Tennyson or Hardy come to mind) as poets of persistent experimentation. But they do not self-evidently prompt so flex-

---

[1] James, "The Art of Fiction," in *The House of Fiction*, ed. Leon Edel (New York: Mercury Books, 1957), 32.

ible and various a scrutiny as do the continuous breakers of their own molds. The case is different with Milton. Milton frequently expressed his deliberate self-preparation toward writing his major poems. Meanwhile, however, he left few poems which need to be excused as juvenilia. The poems which appear to represent stages of experiment are at the same time finished works of art. Thus, while "At a Vacation Exercise" predicts Milton's future use of his native language in "some graver subject," the poem successfully in itself defends creative play at the expense of scholastic logic. A year later, "On the Morning of Christs Nativity" once more uses the topos of the eager but unready poet preparing for a "hymn, or solemn strein." Yet the Hymn itself successfully celebrates the triumphant arrival of truth and light in the birth of the Son. While Il Penseroso, written two years later, again touches the theme of preparation ("Till old experience do attain / To somthing like Prophetic strain"), it successfully realizes the landscape of the pensive man's mind. And less than a year later, the apparent unripeness of the poet became the very theme of Sonnet 7; but within the sonnet, the movement from the fanciful varied imagery of the octave to the sonorous explicitness of the resolutely unadorned sestet enacts the maturity the poem purports to be anxious about. The analysis of this process of experimental self-conquering could be extended, of course, through Milton's presentation in Arcades of his hopes for a sounder poetry under a more noble government while he yet achieves a graceful compliment, through his quiet emphasis on the growth from immature to transcendent art in Lycidas, and so forth. The progress is by achievement.

For Milton, the years of preparation were followed by nearly two decades in which he expressed his thoughts in the medium of prose. Although much of that prose was polemical—and polemical prose often declares less of what a man thinks than of what he prudently or impatiently finds it expedient to argue—much was not. The amount of prose is considerable; the topics it considers are numerous; its chronology is exactly known. It has been brilliantly edited and well described in our own day. No one need be in reasonable doubt as to what Milton was thinking between 1640 and 1660; the prose exposes it and "records," as Arthur E. Barker succinctly wrote, "the transformation of the Horton poet into the immeasurably greater poet of the last poems."[2] Milton, then, in fifteen years of tremendous creativity, moved from genre to genre, from peak to startlingly different peak. The triad of distinct and brilliant long poems in the last years of his life calls for

[2] Arthur E. Barker, *Milton and the Puritan Dilemma* (Toronto: University of Toronto Press, 1942), xiii.

an order of analysis which moves among them as well as within them.

A context is not, however, a plate or mirror to be slipped behind a poem in order to put it into convenient focus for literary microscopy. A context is not a real entity, and none comes ready-made. The activity of choosing or shaping contexts is the responsibility of the critic. We are still indebted to Coleridge for teaching us that every work of art is in itself an organic contexture, a substantial whole. A poem strikes us as round and not linear, changing and not fixed, durational and not instantaneous, renewing and not to be exhausted by one act of analysis or appreciation. That being so, who can believe that it will yield to a single explanation, or give up its full delight to the reader who stands always on the same spot to look at it or places it always in one setting, clamped into one context? In the pages that follow I shall place Milton's concluding poem, *Samson Agonistes*, alongside selected antecedent works by his hand in six contexts in order to expound its meaning in terms of persistent Miltonic concerns. I shall try to show both how Milton arrived at the ideas brought together in *Samson Agonistes* and what light that final poem throws on its predecessors.

The contexts I have devised for this purpose are intellectual, not historical, generic, or biographical. They are not startling; they are, simply, Milton's logic or dialectic, his conception of history, his politics, his ethics, his theology, and his poetics. I have chosen them because they were prominently indicated by Milton himself as being of special interest to him. I have selected and shaped my contexts under Milton's guidance. As a young student, Milton began keeping a Commonplace Book, a habit itself commonplace in his day. He ordered his entries under indexes which have prompted my division of contexts. Milton's Ethical Index contains 64 entries under 24 topics or headings; his Economic Index, 67 entries under 14 headings; his Political Index, 210 entries under 32 headings. That he kept a further commonplace book, since lost, is clear from six cross-references in the existing notebook to a missing Theological Index. The Economic Index collects ideas about the conduct of domestic life, and modern readers would doubtless see it as a large subsection of the Moral Index, since it contains material about marriage, divorce, and education. The Ethical Index abstracts, along with the traditional topics, some ideas which could as conveniently have been assigned to a separate index, or Poetics Index, under the headings "Of the Knowledge of Literature," "Of Poetry," and "Of Music." The Political Index not only records ideas about government under the expected abstract headings, it also includes ideas derived from Milton's readings of English, Scottish, French, and Italian historians. The Political Index is historical as well as theoretical; it shades into an Historiographical Index, and "the historian" in fact "invades the province of the political writer."[3] Milton recorded ideas in his Commonplace Book. That, of course, was the point of keeping one. It it notable, however, that he recorded no appreciative or critical literary insights. From the beginning, Milton thought of his art in terms of intellectual concepts and of the public good.[4]

Milton's conventional groupings of areas of special concern to him in his youth match the groupings under which he wrote the prose of his productive middle years. The retrospective account he gave of trying to free his countrymen by pamphleteering, in *A Second Defence of the English People*, aligns his prose tracts with the subjects of the Commonplace Book indexes. He described a consistent and systematic application of his gifts to specific intellectual ends: "Since, then I observed that there are, in all, three varieties of liberty without which civilized life is scarcely possible, namely ecclesiastical liberty, domestic or personal liberty, and civil liberty, and since I had already written about the first, while I saw that the magistrates were vigorously attending to the third, I took as my province the remaining one, the second or domestic kind."[5] Milton's Political Index was reflected in the antiprelatical works; his Economic Index, in the divorce tracts; both that and his Ethical Index, in *Of Education*; both those and the topics constituting a Poetics Index, in *Areopagitica*. He continued, "Civil liberty . . . I had not touched upon . . . until the king . . . was pleading his cause as a prisoner before the judges." The Political Index was then further reflected in *The Tenure of Kings and Magistrates*. "When these works had been completed, I turned to the task of tracing in unbroken sequence . . . the history of my country." The historical bent of the Political Index was reflected in *The History of Britain*. In the same period as the writing of *A Second Defence*, Milton composed *De Doctrina Christiana*, for which the lost Theological Index had been preparatory. My point is that Milton thought that the great writer must be a great teacher and transmitter of ideas; he classified his reading under the traditional humanistic branches of learning. In shaping the contexts in which to look at *Samson Agonistes*, it makes sense, I think, to follow the humanistic divisions which pervaded Milton's thinking.

Still a young man, moreover, just returned to England from his hu-

---

[3] Milton to Henry de Brass, July 15, 1657, *The Collected Prose Works of John Milton*, ed. Don M. Wolfe et al. (New Haven: Yale University Press, 1953-), VII, 501 (hereafter cited as *CPW*).

[4] The multiplicity of uses to which Milton put his Commonplace Book is thoroughly explored by Ruth Mohl, *John Milton and His Commonplace Book* (New York: Frederick Ungar, 1969).

[5] *CPW*, IV, pt. 1, 624-27.

manistic Grand Tour, Milton listed in the Trinity Manuscript a number of potential themes or subjects for poetry, together with the drafts, corrected drafts, and fair copies of early poems. For some of the projected tragic subjects on his list, Milton supplied brief plot lines, often noting their sources in Bede, Holinshed, Stow, Speed, and Holy Writ, and he set them forth with his customary intellectual and only intermittently formal emphasis. Where they are developed, Milton's plot suggestions are given intellectual point by such phrasing as "debating what should become," "after much dispute," "where is disputed of a politick religion," "revolted frō the faith and reclaim'd," "for lust depriv'd of his kingdom, or rather by faction of monks," "lie in the contention," "arguments driven home," "discoursing as the world would of such an action divers ways," "it may also be thought," "here is disputed of incredulity of divine judgments and such like matter," "may dispute of love and how it differs from lust," and "it may be argu'd about reformation and punishment illegal." Structural matters are only rarely noted, as in "Beginning from the morning of Herods birth day," or "the oieconomie may be thus," or "the Epitasis whereof may lie." Still rarer are suggestions of tone, diction, or literary analogues, as "ending with alleluiah glory be etc.," "Pastoral. 1 Sam. 25," "A Heroicall Poem may be founded somewhere in Alfreds reigne . . . whose actions are wel like those of Ulysses," "in procession with music and song," or finally, "his agony may receav noble expressions."[6] Usually Milton's own emphasis invites us to examine the intellectual substance of his art. He points toward debate and its resolution in his formulation of subjects for poetry; disputation and argumentation are specified for almost every plot given in any detail. From the beginning, Milton seems to have conceived of his art as composed of conceptual material. The contexts in which to examine it seem inevitably to be those of his ideas. No other English poet known to me so early, regularly, and consistently asks to be read as a thinker. I shall say no more here of the collocation of topics within the individual contexts I have devised. Each of the five parts of my book will begin with a definition of the contexts of Milton's dialectic, conception of history, ethics, politics, theology, and poetics.

The value of a chronological examination within intellectual contexts is nullified, of course, if the chronology adopted is erroneous, and it is nugatory if the chronology is dubious. In the twentieth century, study of the growth and development of Milton's mind and art suffered as dire a check in the fifties and sixties as the critical appreciation of his individual poems suffered in the late twenties and thirties. As some

[6] John Milton, *Poems Reproduced in Facsimile from the Manuscript in Trinity College, Cambridge*, with a transcript (Menston Ilkley: Scolar Press, 1972), 33-39.

critics in the thirties attempted to dislodge Milton himself from his high place in the esteem of readers, prematurely congratulating themselves on their easy success, so some biographers and scholars in the fifties sought to dislodge *Samson Agonistes* from its place as the last testament of the seasoned artist; less rash than the critical dislodgers, they offered this displacement as speculative. They used a true negative discovery—that it is hard to be sure from externally corroborated evidence when the tragedy was written—to hazard a conclusion, that *Samson Agonistes* was probably written long before it was published. (That the play was not written at the date thought correct by almost two centuries of editors and critics is not proved, however, by the failure of this long chain of witnesses to see that external corroboration for the late date is small.) If the detailed discussions of early daters had led to an agreed new date for *Samson Agonistes*, and if they were consistent and also persuasive in themselves, then contextualist readers would not be in an unhappy position. The poem, dislodged from its place as the last work of Milton's creativity and reliably relocated as, say, the sixty-fifth work in his corpus of about one hundred poems, could be read in its new context, where it could shed a clearer light on its surrounding works and could in turn be illuminated by them.[7] The revisionists, however, have not been able to agree on precisely where to reattach *Samson Agonistes*. Instead, as Robert Burton alleged of the earth, the dramatic poem is "tossed in a blanket amongst them, they hoist it up and down like a ball, make it stand and go at their pleasure."[8]

In the final Appendix to this book I have summarized and attacked the arguments for dating *Samson Agonistes* somewhere around 1641, or, alternatively, somewhere between 1646 and 1648, about 1653, or about 1661-1662, instead of between 1667 and 1671. Here I wish only to remark that if it could be proved indisputably by the discovery of a conclusive fact—a lost letter, a contemporary comment by a friend,

---

[7] It is amusing that one of the most strenuous arguers for an earlier date, John T. Shawcross (see "The Chronology of Milton's Major Poems," *PMLA*, 76 [1961], 345-58), in the first edition of his *The Complete English Poetry of John Milton . . . Arranged in Chronological Order* (New York: New York University Press, 1963), placed *Samson Agonistes* between Sonnets 11-14 and *Ad Joannem Rousium, The Fifth Ode of Horace*, Sonnet 12, "On the Forcers of Conscience," and Psalms 80-88. But the second edition of 1971, which supplanted the earlier one, appeared with *Samson Agonistes* back in its old position. Shawcross explained that he had made the change "not because [he] has altered [his] belief, concerning its date of composition, but because its former position isolated some of the minor poems from others, creating a frankly odd arrangement" (*ibid.*, vi). That is to say, if I understand Shawcross, *Samson Agonistes* would spoil the possibility of a contextual reading of the minor poems if it is obtruded among them.

[8] "Diet, etc., Rectified; with a Digression of Air," in Burton, *The Anatomy of Melancholy*, Everyman's Library (London: J. M. Dent and Sons Ltd., 1932), 57.

a draft datable by the known hand of an amanuensis, or the like—that *Samson Agonistes* was of pre-Restoration composition, then at the moment of that discovery every analysis of the tragedy hypothesizing a post-Restoration composition would be false. Clearly, the reverse is also true: external authentication of post-Restoration composition would swiftly deprive a number of books and articles of their standing. That being so, none in our time except absolutely dedicated contextualists who seek to understand Milton's continuous but changing creativity will run the risk of becoming a cautionary tale. Most studies of the drama have been intrinsic and formalist studies; most have hedged their bets to offer a reading not to be impaired or even affected by certainty that the author was thirty-three or thirty-eight, forty or forty-eight, or sixty when he wrote it. I might add here that the preponderant number of twentieth-century critics of *Samson Agonistes* still consider it to have been Milton's last poem, save that they may nevertheless all be wrong—and the security of being among the deluded majority is not a security Milton ever recommended, "truth and wisdom not respecting numbers and bigg names."[9] Where the risk of adopting an hypothesis is high, the reward must be correspondingly rich. The reward for the contextualist is enormous: he is enabled to bring to bear as much as possible of the surrounding circumstances of Milton's thought on an exceedingly complex poem. I have thought it only right, however, to explain why my study can be said to break new ground, since my methodology and techniques are not new. It opens new perspectives by seeking to analyze *Samson Agonistes* in terms of as many as possible of Milton's perpetual concerns. These indicate arc upon arc of the poet's developing thought. And *Samson Agonistes* is the conclusion which embodies the very principle of process itself as the model of its structure and content.

The fullest response to Milton's poetry, I think, comes from interpreting its meaning in relation to its evolution within the corpus of his works. At any point after Milton's death, I would doubt whether the poems can mean more than his richest intuitions about human life had told him—and unless we are careful, they can gradually mean less and less. But the very persistence of a work of art over three centuries is suggestive. Milton's poetry has more than archaeological, anthropological, or historical interest for us because he understood or dreamed or imagined things not dreamed of in the codifications of the abstract writers of his own day. Those meanings continue to move us and to speak to us in our day. We continue to struggle to free ourselves from sterile and narrow conventions and to think new and freely developing thoughts. We have even come to believe that death arrives when

[9] *CPW*, III, 340.

change and growth cease, and that the last charge of energy in the brain, not the last heartbeat, marks its finality.

Samson Agonistes is a poem of growth and change, depicting a hero who achieves late insight superior to his earlier insights. He breaks through clusters of time-encapsulated beliefs to achieve a new synthesis of understanding. The accomplishment of change is attended by pain, loneliness, and remorse, and it commences with a bitter recognition of failure, loss, and waste. Milton is true to his personal experience, true to his historical experience, true to his national experience. In all those aspects of his life—as a blind poet, a defeated republican, a solitary reformer—his experience was of tragic loss and of the agonizing discrepancy between his vision and the realities of his world. No facile optimism about the inevitability of human progress and no self-gratulatory assurance about the easy resolution of contradictory impulses or inconsistent aims can withstand the articulation by Samson himself of his terrible difficulty in facing failure and in seeing and telling the truth. In his last poem Milton gives us a fully tragic vision of reality. Yet the dark steps that descend to take account of loss also reascend into the light of intellectual control. The tragedy *Samson Agonistes* moves and strengthens its audience by leading it toward the recognition that to change and to grow is difficult almost beyond belief but that the human mind may limit and control failure, may compassionately regard the tragic experience of mankind, and may discard the false and harmonize the inconsistent in its own nature.

In Part One of this book I shall treat the tragedy *Samson Agonistes* as a dialectical structure imitating the mind at work for the purpose of attaining balance. My design is to demonstrate that intellectual and psychological change is the internal principle of the drama whose subject is growth and whose mimesis is of a biblical story recording movement from self-destruction to self-transcendence, or from near-death to second birth. In the subsequent sections I shall take up the concept of tragic failure, change, and growth in areas of ever-widening implication. I shall outline in Part Two Milton's progressive discovery that history describes a pattern which can be interpreted as a tragic design. It destroys the possibility of believing in gradual and persistent progress, and equally overturns the impression that all is fortuitous. On the contrary, the pattern of history supports the belief that if human experience is well understood, it will be found to be controllable and rich in purpose. To place *Samson Agonistes* in the context of Milton's understanding of history is to examine the poem in relation to Milton's prose works, since these reveal the stages by which he developed his ideas about time and human endeavor.

In Part Three the context will widen to consider Milton's politics.

The way in which the dramatic poem imitates and proposes tempering and harmonizing as politically crucial activities will be examined in the context of Milton's changing awareness in the realm of politics. Since the tragedy is not overtly political but functions through political analogy and is intended parabolically to diagnose and to alter the political conditions of its time, I shall pay particular attention to other poems likewise not overtly political, but arising from and contributing to public events. In particular, I shall look at *Lycidas* and the sonnets as occasional poems with embedded political force; they recommend the remaking of national life through the remaking of individual free men, upon whom consensual republicanism depends.

Having considered the innermost circle of ideas with which Milton was always wrestling—the human personality, its reason, imagination, emotion, passion, and psychological balance—encompassed by a larger circle—the process of history and the effect of changing circumstances in changing directions in human life—encompassed by a still larger circle—the nature of society and the relation to it of the individual through law, self-realization or self-sacrifice, custom, and the like— I shall look at an even more inclusive area of Milton's thought, the area of moral activities. I hope to show in Part Four how Milton shaped *Samson Agonistes* to reveal his convictions about man's duties and moral choices, how he addressed himself to the larger question of how every man is to live. This question was more vivid in its illuminative power for Milton than even questions about the relationship of an individual to his times or to his nation, for Milton saw the problem of how each human being is to conduct himself as a problem common to all times and all places in the postlapsarian world. In showing how he elicited from the mimesis of his scriptural fable a rule of life enabling change and growth, I shall place *Samson Agonistes* in the context of Milton's psalm translations and psalm interpretations, and of his use of the Psalms and the Book of Job in *De Doctrina Christiana* and *Paradise Regained*. Finally, in Part Five I shall show process and change as the ever-arching principle in the highest realm of Milton's thought, the area of theology, and also show change or modification of sensibility as his aesthetic principle in the most functional realm, the area of poetics. For this purpose I shall juxtapose *Samson Agonistes* with Books III, XI, and XII of *Paradise Lost* and with all of *Paradise Regained* to show that Milton read Scripture and applied it, in the same way that one should read Milton, that is, fully attentive to processive discoveries and progressive relevancies.

If the cessation of intellectual energy, and with that, of the power to grow and change, initiates death, how is it possible for the finished work of a dead poet to triumph over death and chance and time? The endurance of a work of art such as *Samson Agonistes* derives from its incorporation of the principle of change as the very foundation of its permanence. When Milton early spoke of his plans to write something which after ages would not willingly let die, he thought the life of his work would derive from its style, "the stile, by certain vital signes it had, was likely to live."[10] The critics of the thirties who sought to bury Milton thought too that it was the energy of creating in poetry which gave it life and the power to defy the death of its composer. The attack upon Milton's poetry was directed toward proving his style to be inert and dead, demonstrating the "routine gesture," "the inescapable monotony of the ritual," "the sensuous poverty," all of it "as mechanical as bricklaying." The correctness of those implications has so often been attacked that no additional artillery need be brought up against them, nor has any later critic in our generation by so simple a transference blamed the poet for his own unresponsiveness. But if Milton thought that the application of all his art and industry to the adorning of his native language would enable him to "write as men by Leases, for three lives and downward," it was not "to make verbal curiosities the end, that were a toylsom vanity, but to be an interpreter and relater of the best and sagest things among mine own Citizens throughout this Island in the mother dialect." The test of his poetry was to be the assurance of its truth, and the young Milton little doubted that he could fix and immortalize the best and sagest things. Had he never come to know otherwise, his poetry might be a tessellation of ideas dead in their fixity. Our age prides itself upon the discovery of the fictiveness of all our fictions, as though it were the incessantly pleasing playfulness of their unreality rather than the permanence of their effort to produce order that makes fictions live. We often tire ourselves with our own inventiveness. For it is not by the fictiveness of our fictions that we are sustained or disappointed, it is by their incorporation of the fullest resemblance to our lived experience. Milton, too, was of an inventive disposition. In the course of his writing he too "dallied with false surmise" and consoled himself for the shattering of previous certainties by promulgating fictions of stability or final, permanent resolution. At two moments of crisis in *Lycidas*, for example, he invented for that purpose an absolute annihilation of his enemies and an absolute apotheosis of his friend before transcending both with the inclusive conclusion of change, "To morrow to fresh Woods, and Pastures new."

Our reality changes; the poetry which lives for us seeks to uncover in the process of alteration the consistency of the government of flux by adaptive change. Milton's *Samson Agonistes* has triumphed over

---

[10] *Ibid.*, I, 809-13.

death and chance and time, not by eluding the realities of the time of its composition, but by incorporating them through a head-on consideration of his day's historical, political, moral, theological, and aesthetic problems. In those areas the liberation Milton found was not *from* change into fixity but *through* change into growth. *Samson Agonistes* bespeaks the permanence of the human desire for liberation. Because Milton sought to free mankind from the constraints of falsity and inconsistency, so that each individual might achieve a pattern of growth and renewal in himself from which national growth and renewal could follow, the conclusive work of his hand has the vitality today that it had at its conception. My study is of the paradigms of change in the separate works leading to *Samson Agonistes* and then of the poem itself. I seek to show how *Samson Agonistes* invites us "A little onward . . . a little further on" within the corpus of Milton's poetic works.

Labouring thy mind

I

SAMSON AGONISTES AND
MILTON'S DIALECTIC

Introduction

As A total edifice of patterned meanings, *Samson Agonistes* has a coherence, a shape, and a structural design which every reader can recognize at some stage in his reading. Speech and episode follow on speech and episode; the mind registers beginning-exposition, or statement-modification, or image-complication. Then, at a moment which is not very important to fix exactly and which may not be identical for all readers, something more will be recognized than exposition of events through language, rhythm, and imagery. The reader will see a pattern of significance subsuming and arranging within it all the materials of the drama experienced at first one by one. The tragedy is then recognized as a pattern or design which mirrors and organizes a number of converging designs. When the reader makes the shift from the activity of reconstructing experience to that of discovering coherence and perceiving intentions, he is able to realize that the form or structure of which he has become aware was always there; he sees that the beginning implied the end. Or, to put it in terms of growth and process, the reader sees how the writer not only saw a relationship between the parts of his plot but also saw one between content and form. Milton not only imitated purposefully, he also created in form what he perceived was latent in content. The form recognized by the reader is the form discovered by the poet as inherent in the experience for which the chosen fable attracted him. The writer's matter not only conformed to his purpose, it also resolved itself into a structure implicit in the way he experienced that matter.

To put the process schematically, Milton experienced a profound discrepancy between the world he lived in (reality) and the world he wished to live in (dream), which he once optimistically believed he could bring into being. For this he gave his sight and two decades of his life. Samson similarly experienced a terrible discrepancy between the deeds he performed and the effects he intended, for him also resulting in blindness and failure. The English people experienced a profound discrepancy between their achieved Restoration and their promised Revolution. The Greek tragedians experienced a similar discrepancy between the effects of the relationships of men and their expectations in entering into those relationships. The discrepancy in all these cases was a fall, a failure, or a fate; the common experience of it involved a conflict, an opposition, a dialectic; the emotions of that experience contained all the pain and anguish of the struggle to resolve mystery and free oneself from contradiction and conflict, together

3

with the grief, remorse, and loneliness which derive from apparent failure. It follows that the tragic effect of loss necessarily expresses itself through a dramatic structure in which the human mind turns upon itself, through a form which embodies antithetical struggle. Moreover, intellectual conflict and moral antithesis cannot be resolved by inventing an action in which one side triumphs over the other, nor by making a crafty mélange in which each side triumphs. It can only be resolved when the mind sufficiently integrates its own impulses to enable it to go beyond the antithetical mode of thought into a synthetic mode. A man must want beauty *and* truth, sense *and* thought, passion *and* reason, freedom *and* purpose, autonomy *and* fidelity. So long as these present themselves as alternatives, he can achieve neither member of each pair. Only when he can resolve them into something other than pairs in opposition can he achieve inner harmony.[1] Once the pattern of *Samson Agonistes* stands forth as a conclusive design of many designs, a large structure made of many substructures, the tragedy is seen to rest upon a coalescence of form and content of a peculiarly revolutionary sort. It is a didactic drama, resolving the experience of tragic conflict in the mind by imitating the structure of thought itself. It is a poem in which Milton seeks to change the minds of readers by showing them a mind being itself changed in the characteristic way in which the mind can be changed, by dialectic leading to resolution, internal drama leading to integration, conflict leading to harmony.

A long intellectual growth lies behind *Samson Agonistes*, and certain stages of it were crucial to Milton's discovery of an imitative form for the tragedy. Whenever Milton thought about education, there was present to him the idea that the mind can be tempered and harmonized only through debate and dialectic, that argument is the means by which the truth must be reached. Early in his life, in *The Reason of Church Government*, Milton proposed a simple form of education through struggle: "if we but look on the nature of elementall and mixt things, we know they cannot suffer any change of one kind, or quality into another without the struggle of contrarieties."[2] By the time he wrote *Areopagitica* he had found the metaphor for resolved truth which describes the very structural effect discovered in *Samson Agonistes*, that of "spiritual architecture": "the perfection consists in this, that out of many moderat varieties and brotherly dissimilitudes that are not vastly disproportionall arises the goodly and the gracefull symmetry

[1] See Northrop Frye, *Fables of Identity* (New York: Harcourt, Brace and World, 1963), and M. C. Bradbrook, *English Dramatic Form* (London: Chatto and Windus, 1965), for discussions of tragic structure.
[2] *CPW*, I, 795.

that commends the whole pile and structure."[3] Education through dialectic, ethics through wrestling, logic by means of dichotomizing— all show an identical formal pattern which involves discerning and harmonizing polarities, or resolving contrary positions.

Milton's epistemology and psychology both hinge upon the natural tendency of the mind to polarize and then to resolve into harmonious synthesis. In this section, therefore, I shall examine the play *Samson Agonistes* as a large structure composed of debate substructures, which can be best understood in the context of Milton's logic, epistemology, and psychology. In many of Milton's poems the reader attends not to one voice, the voice of the bard,[4] but to two disputants whose dialogue carries the underlying effect of a divided mind which must be integrated. In *Samson Agonistes* the calm of mind at the close of the play rests upon the resolution of disputation rather than the purgation of passion. Passion is not expelled in the drama, it is transformed.

Not all major works of art affirm, celebrate, reassure, or conserve. Some not only use and imitate dialectic but, for educative purposes, actually enter themselves into a disturbing dialectic, shake the preconceptions of the reader, and induce a change of mind. Those revolutionizing works make demands upon the reader, challenge him, and seek to transform him.[5] The experience is often disagreeable. The artist knows that it will be so and needs strong nerves to offer it, as well as confidence that the composure achieved at the end, the better state of mind, will justify the process. He must have the confidence of a physician whose medicine is "sowr against sowr, salt to remove salt humours," for it is to be expected that a reader's instinct will affirm with Keats, "We hate poetry that has a palpable design upon us."[6] The physician-artist with the palpable design to change the reader's mind must discover a form that imitates and encourages thinking itself, its processes and its progression. Milton knew that the life and the mind of man are prone to tragic failure, failure which the mind can limit and control.

[3] *Ibid.*, II, 555. See Michael Lieb, *The Dialectics of Creation: Patterns of Birth and Regeneration in "Paradise Lost"* (Amherst: University of Massachusetts Press, 1970), for a discussion of dialectic and the polarization of creation and degeneration in the epic.

[4] For an exposition of those moments when the reader is listening to that single voice see Anne Davidson Ferry, *Milton's Epic Voice* (Cambridge, Mass.: Harvard University Press, 1963).

[5] Stanley Fish, *Self-Consuming Artefacts: The Experience of Seventeenth-Century Literature* (Berkeley: University of California Press, 1972), describes a number of such prose works.

[6] *The Letters of John Keats*, 2d rev. ed., ed. Maurice Buxton Forman (London: Oxford University Press, 1942), 96.

The story of Samson presented him with a total structure and the necessary substructures to show a mind struggling to understand tragic experience. *Samson Agonistes* is multileveled and complex; it embodies numerous perspectives. Yet it overwhelmingly impresses the reader as a unified, coherent, strongly ordered work of spiritual architecture. The risk of distorting the whole by examining it now from one and now from another perspective is not very great; one is not breaking a butterfly but taking a selection of sightlines upon a great baroque structure.[7] When Milton recast the biblical story of Samson in an adaptation of the form of Greek tragedy, he did so to challenge the preconceptions of his day: the tragedy reconsiders the behavior of man in time and of God in history, the meanings of virtue, freedom, and reason itself. From one perspective it imitates and therefore encourages the life of the mind.

For some readers, however, the play seems to encourage mindlessness. To such readers the tragedy apparently traces the deplorable and abrupt rise from nadir to zenith of a weak-minded, vengeful character. It not only condones, it glorifies a "genocide." Kenneth Burke called it "a wonder-working spell by a cantankerous old fighter-priest who would slay the enemy in effigy."[8] William Empson labeled the hero "unintellectual Samson" and complained that "we do not learn how and why the Fall of Samson occurred, as he is not self-analytical enough to describe it."[9] Arthur Sewall considered that Milton had so far lost faith in reason that "he [turned] to the idea of obedience, away perhaps from the idea of rational cooperation."[10] Irene Samuel considered that although Samson tried to free himself from his fatal flaws, he was nevertheless a monomaniac to the end, encumbered with an obsessive death wish and an ineradicable impulse to violence, a death-dealer whose tragedy was that even though he wrestled more valiantly than all the other characters of the play, he still could not break free enough from pride to eschew public murder.[11] And in the most extreme account of the drama as morally offensive and intellectually negligible, John Carey described Samson as a barbaric foil to the Christ

[7] See Roy Daniells, *Milton, Mannerism and Baroque* (Toronto: University of Toronto Press, 1964), 217-19, for a comparison of *Samson Agonistes* and Bernini's S. Andrea al Quirinale.

[8] Burke, "The 'Use' of *Samson Agonistes*," *Hudson Review*, 1 (1948), 151-67, quoted in *The Poems of John Milton*, ed. John Carey and Alastair Fowler (London: Longmans, 1968), 335.

[9] Empson, *Milton's God* (London: Chatto and Windus, 1961), 227.

[10] Sewall, *A Study in Milton's Christian Doctrine* (London: Oxford University Press, 1939), 213.

[11] Samuel, "*Samson Agonistes* as Tragedy," in *Calm of Mind*, ed. J. R. Wittreich (Cleveland: Case Western Reserve University Press, 1971), 235-57.

of *Paradise Regained*, solemnly emphasizing discarded values, without spiritual development, unwaveringly self-absorbed right up to the repugnant theater-demolition, a lurid finale celebrating savagery.[12] To such readers there seems no necessary connection between Samson's acquiring insight or self-mastery and his pulling down the temple. Samson may be told that he has labored his mind, he may be likened to Jephtha, "who by argument, / Not worse then by his shield and spear / Defended *Israel*," but since Samson himself is nowhere seen to make the transference from the specific issues he debates with Manoa, Dalila, and Harapha to a larger, all-inclusive issue of the relationship between man and God, he cannot be assumed to act because he knows.[13] He despairs, he talks, he no longer despairs, he acts, blind throughout.

Against such readings I would like in this section to show that the larger structure of *Samson Agonistes* was ordered and devised to render what looks like a double catastrophe into a unity, that the apparent double catastrophe has the effect of forcing intellectual effort and a changed mind from the audience, that the movement of the play is a dividing and reconciling movement, that it is composed of a series of substructures (each of which likewise proposes an either-or and resolves it), and that behind the repeated models of disputation within *Samson Agonistes* lie not only very significant earlier treatments of the main ethical struggles in the drama but also an epistemology and psychology to the development of which the drama makes a final contribution. The drama imitates and concludes Milton's own intellectual development; it demonstrates the necessity of mental labor for tempering of the mind and control of the passions. Finally, it is an uncomfortable work; it adapts a revolutionary form and revolutionizes an inherited fable in order to challenge common assumptions. Yet, as all tragedy should, it leaves us freer for our own efforts to free ourselves from our own incompatible passions and disharmonies.

[12] Carey, *Milton* (London: Evans Brothers, 1969), 138-45.

[13] Stanley Fish, "Question and Answer in *Samson Agonistes*," *Critical Quarterly*, 9 (1969), 237-64. See also Paull Franklin Baum, "*Samson Agonistes* Again," *PMLA*, 36 (1921), 354-71, and William Van O'Connor, *Climates of Tragedy* (Baton Rouge: Louisiana State University Press, 1943).

THE IMITATION OF THOUGHT

MILTON wrote little on the structure of tragedy, and what he did write about it has been overlooked in favor of what he wrote about tragic effect. It is worth recalling Milton's prefatory essay to *Samson Agonistes*, "Of that sort of Dramatic Poem which is call'd Tragedy." There his explication of the structure of the drama is introduced with a careful citation of the authority of Martial for an epistle "in case of self defence" or for a work "coming forth after the antient manner, much different from what among us passes for best." Milton states:

> In the modelling therefore of this Poem, with good reason, the Antients and *Italians* are rather follow'd, as of much more authority and fame. . . . Division into Act and Scene referring chiefly to the Stage (to which this work never was intended) is here omitted.
>
> It suffices if the whole Drama be found not produc't beyond the fift Act, of the style and uniformitie, and that commonly call'd the Plot, whether intricate or explicit, which is nothing indeed but such oeconomy, or disposition of the fable as may stand best with verisimilitude and decorum; they only will best judge who are not unacquainted with *Aeschulus, Sophocles*, and *Euripides*, the three Tragic Poets unequall'd yet by any, and the best rule to all who endeavour to write Tragedy. The circumscription of time wherein the whole Drama begins and ends, is according to antient rule, and best example, within the space of 24 hours.

The important points to note are these: The play is deliberately cast in a Greek tragic pattern. Although it does not specify act and scene divisions, it is planned in five act units into which it can be divided.[1] Its plot could have been classified as either simple or complex according to Aristotle's descriptions, but Milton brushed aside this distinction to make a more important point: the ordering of the plot has been made consonant with verisimilitude and decorum rather than shaped to fit either of Aristotle's categories. Readers of Aeschylus, Sophocles,

---

[1] The edition of Euripides that Milton bought in 1634 contains notes by the editor, Paul Stephen, marking the plays into acts and scenes.

and Euripides will notice that the structure consistently reinforces the truth of the thematic material conveyed by the fable, and those dramatists are the best guide to Milton's artistry. And finally, the neoclassical desideratum of unity of time has been met. By brushing aside the distinction between simple (or explicit) and complex (or intricate) plots to establish instead the importance of shaping the action by the principles of verisimilitude and decorum, Milton prepared his audience for an overall structure which is purposive and nothing like so conservative as it might seem in the light of the many studies that have been made of Milton's debts to the Greeks. In fact, his structure consciously modifies several Aristotelian "rules." Milton accepted the Aristotelian principle of structural decorum as formally valuable: *Samson Agonistes* will be a self-contained unit, intelligible without prior knowledge of antecedent or subsequent events; it will treat a complete, serious, important action without the admixture of "Comic stuff" or the introduction of "trivial and vulgar persons"; it will be long enough for the hero to pass from good fortune to bad or bad fortune to good and will "keep within a single revolution of the sun."[2] The ground on which he brushed aside Aristotle's disposition of plots into explicit or intricate is the overriding importance for him of the second concept, verisimilitude. *Samson Agonistes* is structured so that the truth of its shape to its meaning will be clear, not so that it will conform to ancient or Aristotelian precepts.

The Aristotelian distinction between explicit and intricate plot structures is apparently a formal distinction. Simple plots are those in which the change of fortune takes place without *peripety* (sudden reversal) or *anagnorisis* (recognition); complex plots are those in which the change of fortune is accompanied by unexpected reversal, recognition, or both. But Aristotle preferred the complex plot for reasons which are related to content as well as to form. The formal preference arises from the superior coherence in plotting: simple plots are liable to fall into episodic designs where things happen only *post hoc* rather than

---

[2] Milton understood decorum both in a strict and a broad sense. In its strict sense it meant the suitability of speech to speaker; of this he wrote, "we should consider not so much what the poet says, as who in the poem says it. Various figures appear, some good, some bad, some wise, some foolish, each speaking not the poet's opinion but what is appropriate for each person" (*A Defence of the People of England, CPW*, IV, pt. 1, 439). In its broad sense the term *decorum* signified the propriety of the person who speaks, to whom he speaks, of whom or what; the propriety of the time, the place, the purpose, and the propriety of the parts of the work to the total plan. The broad sense was a general agreement that all aspects of the poet's work must suit the "cause and purpose he hath in hand." Thus, to speak of structural decorum is to give the term a meaning quite consistent with Milton's thought.

propter hoc, whereas complex plots create well-developed, unified wholes. The substantive preference arises from the increased suspense and awe and the stronger ethical effect produced by intricate plotting. Here Aristotle draws attention principally to the effects of pity and terror. Pity and terror abound where there is a reversal of expectation or frustration of purpose, an "unexpected catastrophe resulting from a deed unwittingly done,"[3] and where the hero comes to realize the truth earlier concealed from him and to appreciate the full significance of the deed done in error. Both are seen by Aristotle in relationship to *hamartia*, the error which in the *Poetics* bears an aura of significance ranging from passion or violence affecting other human beings to rashness, negligence, or blundering in relation to supernatural beings. The ethical content of the ideal Aristotelian tragedy involves the irony of a hero confronting necessity and becoming conscious of his humanity by discovering the limits of his freedom. Aristotle therefore specifically condemned episodic structure on the grounds of both form and content, since "the episodes do not have to each other the relation of either probability or necessity."[4] He also dismissed another type of simple tragic structure, the double conclusion, which presents a change from bad fortune to good and concludes "in opposite ways for the good and the bad." In form, this structure is indistinguishable from comedy; in content, it flatters the wish of the audience to be reassured.

Without for the moment deciding how far the structure of *Samson Agonistes* can be described as either complex or simple and the catastrophe as either single or double, one might ask how far Milton would have considered himself bound to follow Aristotle in writing "Tragedy . . . after the antient manner" and whether he would have shared Aristotle's preferences in either form or content. When in *Of Education* Milton recommended poetry as the final stage in the educational process and described it as "that sublime art which in *Aristotles poetics*, in *Horace*, and the Italian commentaries of *Castelvetro, Tasso, Mazzoni*, and others, teaches what the laws are of a true *Epic* poem, what of a *Dramatic*, what of a *Lyric*, what decorum is, which is the grand master peece to observe,"[5] he did not help us to be confident as to how he would interpret Aristotle on particular points. Milton's sense of Aristotle's meaning is filtered through Italian humanist commentaries, Castelvetro being particularly important for tragedy. As a scholarly commentator, Castelvetro entered into a dialogue with Aristotle's text,

[3] J.W.H. Atkins, *Literary Criticism in Antiquity*, I (Cambridge: Cambridge University Press, 1934), 91; William K. Wimsatt, Jr., and Cleanth Brooks, *Literary Criticism: A Short History* (London: Routledge & Kegan Paul, 1957), 28-30.

[4] Quotations from Aristotle are taken from the translation by Allan H. Gilbert, *Literary Criticism: Plato to Dryden* (New York: American Book Company, 1940).

[5] *CPW*, II, 404-5.

disputed with it, and annotated it to arrive primarily at a sense of how art and reality are related so that the end of teaching through delight might be achieved. By recommending Castelvetro, Milton implicitly treated Aristotle less as an authority than as a stimulus. Milton's citation of Castelvetro in *Of Education* was not repeated in the preface to *Samson Agonistes* and could not have been, owing to Castelvetro's insistence that tragedy be defined by its effect upon spectators, that is, by reference to the necessities of stage representation, a view equally un-Miltonic and un-Aristotelian. However, Castelvetro's strict distinctions between the genres of tragedy and comedy, and his definition of the unity of time, lie behind Milton's rejection of comic digression and his circumscription of time.

Not only was Milton's Aristotle a palimpsest of the *Poetics* and Italian commentators, it was also a text he felt free to set aside. In the *Reason of Church Government* Milton questioned "whether the rules of Aristotle herein are strictly to be kept, or nature to be follow'd, which in them that know art, and use judgment is no transgression, but an inriching of art." In tragedy as in epic, Aristotelian rules were conditional, subject to appeal to the higher rules of nature, discerned by experience of art and by judgment. In his preface to *Samson Agonistes* Milton added that "the best rule to all who endeavour to write Tragedy" is the practice of "*Aeschulus, Sophocles and Euripides.*" Thus he proclaimed his freedom to devise the structure of the play in accordance with his own sense of natural law and his own choice of tragic models. The preface, therefore, is not a conservative, donnish document in which Milton frigidly turns against the spontaneous and free development of native art to declare autocratically that he knows what most audiences delight in, but will on no account give it to them, as though he were even less accommodating than Jonson, whose "learned Sock" Milton admired, but who after all excused himself from classicizing too strictly since it would prevent general pleasure.[6] Rather, Milton's preface challenges comparison with Greece; in tragedy, too, in the mother dialect Milton wanted to see whether "What the greatest and choycest wits of *Athens, Rome or* modern *Italy*, and those Hebrews of old did for their country, I in my proportion with this over and above of being a Christian, might doe for mine."[7] Of "Gorgeous Tragedy / In Sceptr'd Pall," he had commended as a young poet

---

[6] "Nor is it needful, or almost possible in these our times and to such auditors as commonly things are presented, to observe the old state and splendour of dramatic poems, with the preservation of any popular delight": Jonson's introduction to *Sejanus: His Fall*, in Jonson *The Plays*, ed. Felix E. Schelling, Everyman's Library (London: J. M. Dent and Sons Ltd., 1953), I, 308.

[7] *CPW*, I, 812. See Annette C. Flower, "The Critical Context of the Preface to *Samson Agonistes*," *Studies in English Literature*, 10 (1970), 409-23.

"What (though rare) of later age / Ennobled hath the Buskind stage" (*Il Penseroso*, 101-3). Milton had amused himself in London during his rustication, he declared to Diodati (*Elegia prima ad Carolum Diodatum*, 37-46), by watching Tragedy with streaming hair and rolling eyes brandishing her bloody scepter. He found pleasure in its sadness and especially in the sweet bitterness of the three tragic houses treated in Aeschylus' *Oresteia* trilogy, the *Electra* of Sophocles, and the *Orestes, Electra*, and two Iphigenia plays of Euripides; in Euripides' *Hecuba* and *Trojan Women;* and finally, in Sophocles' two Oedipus plays and *Antigone*, Aeschylus' *Seven against Thebes*, and Euripides' *Phoenician Maidens* and *Suppliants.* (Doubtless he saw some tragedies directly through the "pageantry of the rounded stage," but he probably read more than he saw.) To secure the ends of tragedy, then, Milton did not retreat to a scholarly mode but undertook to revolutionize and modernize the genre.

Although the *Poetics* is descriptive rather than prescriptive in intention and constitutes an inductive work of classificatory criticism rather than a historical or polemical treatise, Aristotle included a few words on the history of tragedy to make the point that once having attained its "natural form" or "full natural stature," tragedy ceases to change. He specifically refused to speculate as to whether it had actually reached the limits of ideal development. Milton clearly considered that it had not and that a modern English Christian poet could give tragedy a further dimension. Within the *Poetics*, in his treatment of examples, Aristotle gave ample indication of his own tragic ideals. Few actual tragedies were wholly acceptable to him, but Aeschylus was praised for firmness of dialogue among a limited number of characters and for a chorus with a proper role, Sophocles' *Oedipus the King* was considered nearest the ideal, and Euripides was commended for preferring the unhappy ending, despite such mismanagements as the omnipurpose, detachable, transferable choral ode and the *deus ex machina*. The evidence of Milton's own allusions in published work earlier than *Samson Agonistes* and of his practice in the play itself shows him to be thoroughly eclectic.[8] Milton, then, came to devise the structure of *Samson Agonistes* in full knowledge of its derivations and its deviations from

---

[8] The fullest account of Milton's taste in classical tragedy and his specific indebtedness is William Riley Parker's *Milton's Debt to Greek Tragedy in "Samson Agonistes"* (Baltimore: Johns Hopkins University Press, 1937), esp. 245-50. See also J. C. Maxwell, "Milton's Knowledge of Aeschylus," *Review of English Studies*, 3 (1952), 366-71; Maxwell, "Milton's *Samson* and Sophocles' *Heracles*," *Philological Quarterly*, 33 (1954), 90-91; Richard C. Jebb, "*Samson Agonistes* and the Hellenic Drama," *Proceedings of the British Academy*, 3 (1908), 341-48; Anthony Low, *The Blaze of Noon* (New York: Columbia University Press, 1974), 13-35, 54-55, 175-79.

Greek norms and Aristotelian precepts, having argued in advance both the diversity of Greek examples and the superiority of decorum and verisimilitude as guides to "the best oeconomy, or disposition of the fable."

The actual structure of *Samson Agonistes* is shaped with both Greek and contemporary practice in mind. The originality of its functional decorum consists in the coalescence of both. Thus the play falls into the following clear parts:

Act I   Exposition (325 lines)
    Minturno: "beginning"; Scaliger: "prologue";
      Aristotle: "arche"

Prologue (1-114)	Samson's soliloquy
Parode (115-175)	Chorus's aside
1st episode (176-292)	Samson and Chorus
1st stasimon (293-325)	Chorus

Act II   Complication (384 lines)
    Minturno: "increase"; Scaliger: "protasis";
      Aristotle: "meson" and "desis"

2nd episode (326-651)	Samson and Manoa
2nd stasimon (652-709)	Chorus

Act III   Apparent settlement (351 lines)
    Minturno: "state"; Scaliger: "epitasis";
      Aristotle: "meson" and "desis"

3rd episode (710-1009)	Samson and Dalila
3rd stasimon (1010-1060)	Chorus

Act IV   New complication (380 lines)
    Minturno: "decline"; Scaliger: "catastasis";
      Aristotle: "lusis"
    Scene 1

4th episode (1061-1267)	Samson and Harapha
4th stasimon (1268-1299)	Chorus

    Scene 2

5th episode (1300-1426)	Samson and Officer
5th stasimon (1427-1440)	Chorus

Act V   Settlement (318 lines)
    Minturno: "end"; Scaliger: "catastrophe";
      Aristotle: "lusis" and "teleute"

Exode (1441-1660)	Manoa, Messenger, Chorus
Dirge or "kommos" (1661-1758)	Manoa, Chorus

The play divides quite naturally into either classical or contemporary units, with well-preserved symmetries in either mode. Milton is unmistakably following Aristotelian principles, but they in no way prevent or inhibit him from taking a series of structural decisions shaping the fable directly toward his independent and highly original ends.

Considered as a five-act structure corresponding both to Aristotelian beginning-middle-end and Renaissance complication-denouement structure, the play offers in each act a substructure composed of thesis-antithesis-synthesis or opposition-resolution. In the middle two acts of complication, the substructure consists of one character who confronts and opposes the protagonist in the presence of the Chorus and elicits from him a resolving definition. The Chorus follows, offering an intermediate synthesis through a direct comment. The case is a little more complicated for the first and two final acts. Act I is composed of the prologue, the parode, the first episode, and the first stasimon. The prologue and parode express Samson's understanding and the Chorus's understanding as two distinct and lyrical statements of despair and pity, in soliloquy and aside, theme and countertheme; the first episode brings them into confrontation; and the first stasimon embodies a minimal agreement. Act IV, containing the crisis of the play, is composed of two scenes, the first of which continues the pattern of Acts II and III—a debate between the protagonist and one other character, concluding in an integrating speech by the protagonist and a choral synthesis. The second scene embodies a confrontation issuing in a "yes" which prompts the anticipated choral synthesis. The fifth act of catastrophe and denouement spreads the task of opposition and reconciliation among the fragmenting and then coalescing characters who remain. The protagonist has departed from the scene but is present in everyone's mind as they describe, attend to, and meditate upon his off-stage action and its meaning.

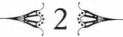
THE DIVIDED MIND

THE DIALECTICAL STRUCTURE OF ACT I

A strong emphasis upon outward stillness and inward movement is created by Milton's disposition of events. Blindness and fetters render Samson motionless once he has dismissed his silent guide, as immobile as Prometheus chained to the rock. He lies "with languish't head un-propt" (Act I); he leans "in low dejected state" (Act II); assailed by unseen visitors, he cannot move away and must ask the Chorus to prevent too close approach, "let [Dalila] not come near me" (Act III); with his "heels . . . fetter'd" he is a fixed and stationary figure whose "manacles remark him, there he sits" (Act IV). Only at the climax, when he becomes aware of "rouzing motions," is Samson enabled to stand, to move, to act. Throughout the morning of the popular feast day which has been called so that Dagon may be magnified "as their God who hath deliver'd . . . *Samson* bound and blind into thir hands," the protagonist-agonist is absolutely still. His self-contempt finds expression precisely in this state: the vilest worm may creep, but he himself is still as a fool in the power of others. He cannot make even the simplest choice of moving or not moving. But while outwardly still, Samson is inwardly restless, assailed by a swarm of disturbing thoughts, thoughts his tormentors armed with deadly stings. His agony is internal but generates a great energy: within himself he struggles with weakness, despair, guilt, pride, self-hatred, and violence. So strong are these interior demons that Samson believes they are only to be buried when he is buried; forsaken by sleep, Samson sees his only cure in death's benumbing opium. He is locked in a self which both feels like a sepulcher and seethes with intellectual pain. His condition is that of hell: enchained, encased in sightless silence, confined to a single bank, enclosed in the dark dungeon of a body, assaulted by numberless inward griefs.

The action of *Samson Agonistes* is composed of encounters which, as debates, are metaphors or metonymies for serious inward change. The Chorus does not speak in interludes which divide sections of the action, it takes full part in the dialogue. The tragedy is stripped of spectacle. The only visual effect from movement available to the mind's eye lies in the approaches of the Chorus, their advance toward Samson and their accompaniment of the other limited number of characters a short distance away from him. They themselves describe the contrast between immobility and movement when they begin the fifth episode by saying:

> This Idols day hath bin to thee no day of rest,
>   Labouring thy mind
> More then the working day thy hands. . . .
>
> (1297-99)

The impression which the overall disposition of the fable gives of having been devised to draw attention to an intellectual conflict within the mind of the protagonist, reflected outwardly in a series of disputations, is at once confirmed by the disposition within each of the smaller units of composition. The prologue simultaneously declares its difference from a hypothetical "average Greek tragedy" and its intentional classical form. Taken as a whole, the prologue is very long, constructed as a soliloquy, and spoken by the protagonist. Among the thirty-two extant Greek tragedies upon which Milton could model his prologue, the longest prologues appear in Euripides. Milton's is nearly double their average length. Nearly half begin with a soliloquy fulfilling an expository function, but such opening soliloquies are usually assigned to a neutral minor witnessing character. In no play of Aeschylus or Sophocles is the prologue spoken by the protagonist; in those plays of Euripides commencing with a soliloquy by the protagonist, the speech is a brief recital of antecedent events. Again, the protagonist opens a certain number of Greek tragedies—two Aeschylean, three Sophoclean, three Euripidean—but in these the practice is for the exposition to be communicated by dialogue. Milton's prologue therefore feels very Greek without being very Greek, conspicuously differing by its inwardness, intellectuality, and personal struggle.[1] The prologue is immediately followed by a parode which is also constructed as a long soliloquy, balancing and echoing the material of the prologue. Each assumes the internal form of debate; placed in juxtaposition, they play off their internal debates as an implicit dialogue which becomes explicit in the first episode.

All Milton's opening adaptations and variations are designed to achieve dialectic. It has often been remarked that *Samson Agonistes* is comparatively free of stichomythia, free not only in comparison with Greek practice but also in comparison with Milton's own practice in *Comus*. William Riley Parker conjectured that stichomythia is omitted

[1] See Parker, *Milton's Debt*, 94-98.

16

because *Samson Agonistes* was not intended for the stage, "thrust and parry in bright monostich" being an obvious stage device.[2] That may well be so, but it is also true that "thrust and parry" is an instrument of debate only between fixed and preestablished positions; it is not an instrument of intellectual discovery.

The internal structure of the prologue again confirms the suggestion of its overall design. The prologue is composed of well-articulated units functional to the exposition before the action commences, that is, functional in presenting the circumstances of time, place, occasion, state of mind, antecedent action, and the like. It is also intensely grieved and grieving: the amount of remorse it conveys and of intense sorrow binds the prologue so painfully into a unity that to separate it into its composite parts seems insensitive. But dissection is necessary in order to show the smaller structures through which Milton stimulates thought. At the center of the prologue is a strongly marked contrast between "Times past, what once I was, and what am now," introduced by two suspended sentences, each of eleven lines, the first hortatory and the second declarative. The opening sentence is addressed to the unnamed silent guiding hand which conducts Samson to the bank with choice of sun or shade before the prison, the quiet bank to which Samson withdraws from popular noise whenever he can. That apparently hortatory sentence nonetheless has the force of prayer. Behind its "lead me" and "leave me" echoes the prayer of the Psalmist: "Judge me, O God, and plead my cause against an ungodly nation; O deliver me from the deceitful and unjust man. / For thou art the God of my strength; why dost thou cast me off? Why go I mourning because of the oppression of the enemy? / O send out thy light and thy truth: let them lead me" (Psalm 43). Behind its "breath of Heav'n . . . with day-spring born" echoes the prophetic benediction of Zacharia: "the dayspring from on high has visited us, to give light to them that sit in darkness and in the shadow of death, to guide our feet into the way of peace." Samson's sense of how shamefully much he needs the help of a hand and how hopelessly far he must travel to emerge from darkness is conveyed, together with all the necessary circumambient conditions of the tragedy. The next, exactly symmetrical declarative sentence begins as though Samson had continued speaking to his outward guide, but in withdrawing from "the popular noise" to "this unfrequented place," the sentence modulates into solitude. It declares *I seek ease to the body and find none to the mind*, the reason being the ceaseless torture of contrasting "what once I was, and what am now."

The main body of the following soliloquy, spoken before Samson becomes aware of being no longer alone, is exactly divided into two

2 *Ibid.*, 64ff.

sections of forty-three and a half lines each, the first looking back at the past, the second lamenting the present. Samson begins as if speaking to himself were a matter of one stable ego alone in self-communion expressed through simple monologue. But the sentence patterns through which the meditation on the past is rendered are not at all patterns with the force of *I tell myself what I know of myself as an integral person*. Two questions ("O wherefore was my birth . . . foretold" and "Why was my breeding order'd"), followed by an exclamation ("O glorious strength") and two imperatives ("Ask for this great Deliverer" and "Yet stay"), lead to a further question ("Whom have I to complain of"), an exclamation ("O impotence of mind"), a question and its answer ("But what is strength" and "God . . . hung it in my Hair"), followed by a final imperative ("But peace"). The last is a command so impossible to obey that in the middle of a line the imperative loses all force and drains into lament ("Would ask a life to wail"). These sentence patterns reveal a human being split within himself into several orders of being, a divided self, one aspect of whom proposes inflexible codes of behavior to the other. Both selves are present as subjects: "if I must die" are the words of a self-solicitous subject; "I must not quarrel" is the comment of a self-denying subject. But the tortured lament also carries a sense of self as object as well as subject:

> Promise was that *I*
> Should *Israel* from *Philistian* yoke deliver;
> Ask for *this* great Deliverer now, and find *him*
> Eyeless in *Gaza* at the Mill with slaves,
> *Himself* in bonds under *Philistian* yoke.
>
> (38-42; emphasis added)

Samson in conflict within himself experiences stress arising from external circumstances, stress from other persons' expectations and judgments impinging upon him, stress from the privately acknowledged contradictions in his own impulses toward duty and comfort. In experiencing the torments of his divided self, he tries to protect his vulnerable core by playing off his private self against a public self and by assuming an external role in public life, the role of laboring fallen hero. Heavy stress upon the contrasting *I* and *him* at the line ends gives the whole game away: Samson protects his innermost "I" by using it to condemn and even to taunt the failed Samson, "him." Within Samson is played an inner drama in which "I" mocks and disowns "him."[3] Until he reintegrates the divisions in his own soul, Samson will be the

[3] See Bradbrook, *English Dramatic Form*, for a general discussion of how external playing imitates internal drama.

objective, tormented fallen hero who reveals a split subjective self, half contemptuously rigorous and half remorsefully self-pitying, and he will be unable to act.

Samson's survey of his present griefs, contained in the next forty-three and a half lines, involves an integration resembling a total withdrawal, but that integration is one which must be put aside. It is subsumed formally under Samson's command to himself to be just to his God, who "Happ'ly had ends above my reach to know," but it swells into a terrible lyric of the grieved "I" expressing its full grief in a way which if it does not call the justice of God into doubt, certainly questions His mercy and goodness. Structured about five apostrophizing O's, it is powerfully reminiscent of Adam's nightlong struggle to justify God's treatment of him, in Book x of *Paradise Lost*. Samson's "O loss of sight," "O worse then chains," "O dark, dark, dark," "O first created Beam," "O yet more miserable" are like Adam's "O miserable of happie," "O voice once heard," "O fleeting joyes," "O welcom hour [of death]," "O thought horrid, if true"—but with the terrible addition that Samson's tolling strokes of despair in this long lamentation identify light and sight with life, and he is dark and blind with death. Yet once again, significantly breaking across the repeated exclamations, come two questions: "Why am I . . . bereav'd" of light and "Why was the sight to . . . th' eye confin'd." The questions are not *why did I* and *now how can I*, questions calling for self-analysis and resolution; they are questions of God's benevolence. They reverse the prayerful quality of the opening sentence of the soliloquy by standing on its head the moral lesson which the Church habitually drew from Samson's blindness. The order of readings for 13 April set as the first lesson the story of Samson from Judges and as the second lesson a passage from Luke which reads in part, "The light of the body is the eye: therefore when thine eye is single, thy whole body is also full of light; but when thine eye is evil, thy body also is full of darkness. Take heed therefore that the light that is in thee be not darkness."[4] The physician Luke denied that sight is confined by God to the easily crushed eyeball, and he specifically affirmed that sight or the light of life *is* diffused in every part. To reverse Luke's assurance is to draw Samson's lament down to the lowest depths. Samson is dark with faithlessness; his loss of faith arises from his loss of sight, just as his loss of sight arose from his loss of faith. His lament is not only devoid of the sublimation Milton himself drew upon for courage in his own personal lyric lament at blindness, it contradicts it. Milton's description of his own case opens Book III of *Paradise Lost*:

[4] This passage is quoted in John Broadbent, *Milton: "Comus" and "Samson Agonistes"* (London: Edward Arnold, 1961), 42.

> Thus with the Year
> Seasons return, but not to me returns
> Day, or the sweet approach of Ev'n or Morn,
> Or sight of vernal bloom, or Summers Rose,
> Or flocks, or herds, or human face divine;
> But cloud in stead, and ever-during dark
> Surrounds me, from the chearful waies of men
> Cut off, and for the Book of knowledg fair
> Presented with a Universal blanc
> Of Natures works to mee expung'd and ras'd,
> And wisdom at one entrance quite shut out.
> So much the rather thou Celestial light
> Shine inward, and the mind through all her powers
> Irradiate, there plant eyes, all mist from thence
> Purge and disperse, that I may see and tell
> Of things invisible to mortal sight.

(III, 40-55)

Here Milton sublimates his loss of sight through the consideration that God may give to the blind a compensatory vision with the inner eye. Milton had been able, although imperfectly and perhaps intermittently, to free himself from an inherited system of harsh theology and could conceive of a relationship with God different from that of taskmaster-servant and nearer that of physician-patient, teacher-pupil, poet-audience. God had not blinded him as punishment, he himself had chosen blindness in fighting for the cause of liberty; God had not deserted him. The severest pain in Samson's lyric lament comes from his shocked and shocking conviction that God has "expos'd, "bereav'd," and "exil'd" him, has left him for dead: "My self, my Sepulcher, a moving Grave."

The last five lines of the prologue signal the speechless approach of the Chorus and underline the fearfulness with which the divided self must receive their advance upon his public personality. Samson's person will be insultingly stared at by enemies, while he remorsefully grieves at the death of his will and faith, tortured by the peremptory commands of the harsh authoritarian who shares his ego. Such an understanding of Samson's psychology is not something which a modern reader retrospectively reads into Milton's lines; it was present in scriptural models upon which Milton drew, present in the sense of loss and dread of the Psalmist—"why hast thou forsaken me. . . . But I am a worm, and no man; a reproach of men, and despised of the people. All they that see me laugh me to scorn. . . . They look and stare upon me" (Psalm 22)—and in the sense of isolation, anxiety, and uneasiness of Job—"That which I am afraid of cometh unto me. I am not at ease, neither am I quiet, neither have I rest; but trouble cometh." The internal symmetries in the prologue bring together such discordant forms of apprehension. Taken as a whole, they achieve a portrait of a tragic hero who makes this kind of statement: *I am alone. I am trying to understand how I came to the fallen state I occupy in spite of all I was meant to be. But I cannot persist in these thoughts because my grief is so great; it appears to me that I was meant to fail.* The structure imitates a mind turning against itself and against God.

To focus, finally, on even smaller units of composition within the parts of the prologue is to discover that Milton's style and his choice of syntax, figures, and rhetorical devices also all tend to promote the impression of thought, internal intellectual struggle, and self-divided debate. Milton has disposed line after line in such a way as to imitate active thought. Apparently, only if Samson were actually to have said to himself in soliloquy *in the first place, in the second place, on the other hand, ergo, hence, therefore,* and *Q.E.D.,* could some readers consent to recognize his intellectual activity. Milton, however, gave him in diction, construction, and variety of ornamentation everything short of that. The diction of *Samson Agonistes* marks the poem as dominantly plain in style. As in *Paradise Regained,* Milton rejected "swelling Epithetes thick laid / As varnish on a Harlots cheek." In the passage in *Of Education* recommending the study of poetics, Milton commends also the organic arts of logic and rhetoric, of which rhetoric can "enable men to discourse and write perspicuously, elegantly and according to the fittest style of lofty, mean, or lowely." The distinction into three levels of style was a commonplace of the period. According to Renaissance theorists, a poet would make his choice of style according to a rigid application of the principles of decorum: tragedies *a priori* would demand the lofty style, for the speaker would concern himself with "the noble gest and great fortunes of Princes and the notable accidents of time. . . ." "All hymnes and histories and Tragedies were written in the high stile," George Puttenham would write.[5] Of course there were some Renaissance theorists unwilling to tie themselves too rigidly to divisions along these lines. Thus Roger Ascham stated, "The trew difference of Authors is best knowne *per diuersa genera dicendi* that euerie one used. And therefore here I will deuide *genus dicendi* not into these three, *tenue, mediocre, et grande,* but as the matter of euri Author requireth, as in *Genus: Poeticum, Historicum, Philosophicum, Oratorium.*"[6] Milton's rejection of the rigidity

---

[5] Puttenham, *The Arts of English Poesie,* in *Elizabethan Critical Essays,* ed. G. Gregory Smith (London: Oxford University Press, 1950), II, 158.

[6] Ascham, "Of Imitation," in *Elizabethan Critical Essays,* ed. Smith, I, 23.

of earlier theories freed him to consider the most appropriate style for tragedy to be that most imitative of discourse. In *Paradise Regained* Milton wrote of

> what the lofty grave Tragoedians taught
> In *Chorus* or *Iambic*, teachers best
> Of moral prudence, with delight receiv'd
> In brief sententious precepts. . . .

The reference to "Iambic" suggests that Milton adopted Aristotle's view of tragedy as employing iambics, since they imitate conversation most aptly. Again, verisimilitude is the stylistic principle that takes precedence over decorum.

This is not to say that Milton's style does not conform to the recommendations of Aristotle, Horace, Tasso, and Castelvetro, for in the most general terms it does. But its dominant qualities arise not from careful reliance upon classical authorities—Parker could find few impressive verbal echoes in the play—but from experimental freedom. In general terms the style answers to Aristotle's recommendations. The diction is clear and not pedestrian; since it imitates speech, it uses those words most natural to conversation ("here I feel amends"; "here leave me to respire"; "I seek this unfrequented place to find some ease"; "why was my breeding order'd"; "if I must dye betray'd, captiv'd, and both my Eyes put out"), but it raises them above the pedestrian by the moderate use of metaphors ("dark steps"; "restless thoughts like a deadly swarm of Hornets"; "breath of Heav'n"; "day-spring"; "charioting his presence"; "my self . . . a moving Grave"), of unfamiliar words, that is, of words used in a sense unusual in English ("popular noise"; "delight annull'd"; "light extinct"; "vacant interlunar cave"; "eye so obvious"; "obnoxious to the miseries of life"), and of ornamental words ("air imprison'd also"; "blaze of noon"; "day-spring"; "Heav'n-gifted"). The drama's most boldly unadorned passages of sheerly conversational writing in plain style occur, as one would expect, when Samson's personal integration is most complete. He engages directly and confidently with an external adversary in poetry which approximates to the condition of prose while it retains a perfection of verse form. Samson achieves that integration in a passage culminating in the triumphant phrase "My self? my conscience and internal peace." That affirmation stands in conscious antithesis to the passage we have been examining, which ends with "My self, my Sepulcher, a moving Grave."[7] But even

---

[7] Interestingly, John Broadbent prints this passage in prose (*Milton*, 36) to display "Milton's eccentric personal talent." The same form would display its conversational plain style.

in the divided and contorted expressions of the prologue, the conversational style is exceedingly plain, very sparingly ornamented.

There are, no doubt, a number of additional reasons for the concentration on plain style in *Samson Agonistes*, beside its suitability for thought, speech, and expression of passion, the authority of classical prescription, and the emerging new taste. One reason is that the play works closely from scriptural sources, and the plain style testifies to the strictly biblical quality of the fable. But beyond all these, the marked stylistic traits are adjustments of the poetry to the conveying of ethical truth through argument and to the characterizing of a speaker wrestling with intellectual problems at every stage in the play.

To begin at the level of words themselves, one notices that the meaning is carried by a series of abstract nouns ("*chance* relieves"; "*superstition* yields"; "*strength* put to the *labour*"; "call in doubt divine *Prediction*"; "*wisdom* bears command"; "*impotence* of mind"; quarrel with the *will* of highest *dispensation*"), as though abstract nouns best display in themselves the vitality of conceptualizing or the energy of thought. Second, a number of single words are used by Samson in a literal sense but, because of the weight of biblical or liturgical significance they bear, are used by Milton in a metaphorical sense, words such as guiding *hand, dark, blind, promise, sight, light, rest, bondage, ransom, deliver,* and *free.*[8] The effect is not only to evoke a pervasive tragic irony as in place after place the reader catches the protagonist unconsciously predicting the final meaning of the play, but also to call forth an effort on the part of the reader to discover these differences and similarities and to interrelate them. In the *Art of Logic*, noting that "the metaphor is a similitude contracted to one word without signs," Milton showed himself sensible of the power of the single word to interrelate two concepts. *Samson Agonistes* is economically spare: one bare word may represent conceptualizing or induce it.

But if the play is exceedingly austere in style, its austerity is variable among the characteristic three kinds of figures which contemporary readers would have considered appropriate for the tragedian to exploit, the kinds of figures which Puttenham, to take a convenient instance, called "auricular," "sensable," and "sententious" or "rhetorical." Auricular figures are perceived by the ear and not by the mind; they are among the most conspicuous and revolutionary devices Milton used, the highest signs of originality in the work and a source of delight to the reader.[9] Sensable figures are perceived intellectually but are appre-

[8] The metaphorical force of isolated words has been noticed by Anne Davidson Ferry in *Milton and the Miltonic Dryden* (Cambridge, Mass.: Harvard University Press, 1968), 155.

[9] Some of the recent studies of auricular figures and their relation to the themes

hended sensuously and include all *tropes* in contradistinction to *schemes*. It is in such figures that *Samson Agonistes* is most restrained, with the effect, of course, of throwing those images that are used into great prominence.[10] Sententious figures are perceived by the ear and the intellect, and they are far and away the most numerous in the play.[11] Individual words are arranged in the prologue as smaller structures within that substructure in a perpetual and arresting series of rhetorical patterns, all requiring that the reader hear and mark how ideas, conceits, and concepts interrelate.

The patterns of parallelism, repetition, antithesis, contradiction, disjunction, paradox, enumeration, continuation, and subordination can all be found within the first eighty lines. Structural patterns (such as: "a little onward . . . a little further on"; "I a prisoner chain'd . . . the air imprison'd also"; "ease to the body some, none to the mind"; "impotence of mind, in body strong"; "what once I was, and what am now"; "scarce half . . . to live, dead more then half"; "deliver . . . Deliverer"; "inferiour to the vilest . . . the vilest here excel"; "dark, dark, dark . . . irrecoverably dark") occur together with word echoes or contrasts across the lines (such as: "light . . . life . . . life . . . light"; "order'd and prescrib'd . . . design'd . . . Betray'd, Captiv'd . . . put out") or at the line ends ("with leave . . . I seek . . . some ease"). The names of the figures for all these relationships and for others were familiar to every contemporary student of the "organic arts" but have passed so out of usage that to revive them would be idle.[12] My point is not simply that

---

of the drama include: Edward Weismiller, "The 'Dry' and 'Rugged' Verse," in *The Lyric and Dramatic Milton*, ed. Joseph H. Summers (New York: Columbia University Press, 1965); Ferry, *Milton and the Miltonic Dryden*; Marcia Landy, "Language and the Seal of Silence in *Samson Agonistes*," *Milton Studies*, 2 (1970), 175-94; Gretchen L. Finney, "Chorus in *Samson Agonistes*," *PMLA*, 57 (1943), 649-64.

[10] John Carey, in his introduction to the play in *Poems of Milton*, effectively answers Christopher Ricks's disappointment with the metaphors because they do not "live along the line" (Ricks, *Milton's Grand Style* [Oxford: Clarendon Press, 1963], 49-56). See also especially Lee Sheridan Cox, "Natural Science and Figurative Design in *Samson Agonistes*," *ELH*, 35 (1968), 51-69; Lynn Veach Sadler, "Typological Imagery in *Samson Agonistes*: Noon and the Dragon," *ibid.*, 37 (1970), 195-210; Duncan Robertson, "Metaphor in *Samson Agonistes*," *University of Toronto Quarterly*, 38 (1969), 319-38; and John Carey, "Sea, Snake, Flower and Flame in *Samson Agonistes*," *Modern Language Review*, 62 (1967), 395-99.

[11] The best modern study of the relationship between tropes and figures of thought is still that of Rosemond Tuve, *Elizabethan and Metaphysical Imagery* (Chicago: University of Chicago Press, 1947).

[12] See Puttenham, *Arts of English Poesie*, chap. 19. See also John B. Broadbent, "Milton's Rhetoric," *Modern Philology*, 56 (1959), 224-42, and Leonard Moss, "The Rhetorical Style of *Samson Agonistes*," *ibid.*, 62 (1965), 296-321.

the prologue, like the entire drama, is artificial while seeming plain, although to be sure it is; nor that its artifice consists in a marked preference for rhythmical effects and rhetorical schemes over poetic tropes, although that too is the case. Rather, the density of artificial arrangements in logical patterns or schemes inevitably and intentionally prompts attention to mental operations. To notice that Samson's speech contains a perpetual and strenuous effort to arrange his thoughts in coherent patterns according to the principles of sententious expressiveness, *because his speech imitates the mind at work*, is to notice half of the force of the small structures in the prologue.

The other half of the prologue's force derives from the imitative syntax: the effort to order thought is expressed by a perpetual disturbance of normal word order. The disturbed syntax reflects intellectual difficulty and prompts intellectual effort. One instance may stand for many. Samson says

> Whom have I to complain of but my self?
> Who this high gift of strength committed to me,
> In what part lodg'd, how easily bereft me,
> Under the Seal of silence could not keep,
> But weakly to a woman must reveal it,
> O'recome with importunity and tears.

(46-51)

The phrases and clauses, if divided, numbered, and rearranged in normal word order, make a pattern of desperate crisscrossing within Milton's poetic order. It is worthwhile taking up the general challenge made by Karl Shapiro, to parse at best this passage.[13] The natural order rearranges Milton's phrases as:

[I] ¹who | could not keep | under the seal of silence | this high gift ⁶of strength | committed ² to me | [and] how easily ⁵ bereft me | [and] in what part [it was] lodged | but | o'recome with importunity and tears | must reveal it | weakly | to a woman.

The sentence seems perhaps to substitute normal Latin word order for normal English word order, but even that, according to Milton's own *Accedence commenct Grammar*, is hopelessly sprung in the middle: the initial copulative relative and the position of the verb are the only clearly Latin elements. The major complication lies in the specifications of what Samson could not keep secret; these have the force of internal exclamations, a lamenting exclamation—"how easily bereft me"—and

[13] Karl Shapiro, *Essay on Rime* (New York: Reynal and Hitchcock, 1945), 8, quoted by Merritt Y. Hughes, *John Milton: Complete Poems and Major Prose* (New York: Odyssey Press, 1957), 539.

a mournful exclamation—"in what part lodg'd." That complication indicates the functional purpose of the irregular syntax. Samson is indicting himself, but the indictment is painful and terrible, not easily spoken, but not to be eluded. He therefore protracts it and underlines it as he postpones it. He produces his self-indictment in thick gasps of two- and three-stress phrases and sweeps into the suspended sentence "who . . . could not keep" not only all the parts of the secret but all the sources of the pain within his total trouble of spirit: his strength was solemnly committed to him so that he knew his responsibility for it; it was strength which could only have been maintained by using his mind; such strength was a contingent high gift so that its efficacy was placed in his hair; he yielded the secret of his strength and of its location and of its contingency, not to a valiant or equal enemy under compulsion, but to a woman; he did so for no better reason than that he was overcome by the sentimental weapons of importunity and tears.

Milton did not interrupt normal word order merely for ornament and variety, as though he enjoyed the effect of backing through a sentence quite as much as going forward. He produced a knotted and contorted phrasing where each element of the thought could sting with its own hornet's attack, sometimes distorting syntax by beginning phrases, clauses, or sentences with adverbs of time ("this day"), place ("a little onward"), manner ("unwillingly this rest"), degree ("but O yet more miserable"), or frequency ("scarce half"; "daily"), as though to give preliminary warning of the quality of the relationship about to be predicated. At other times he distorts syntax by beginning with the object of predication ("whom have I to complain of") or even the verb itself ("suffices that") in order to direct attention and underline emphasis. The smallest units of composition in the prologue are so disposed as to confirm what the larger units suggest: Milton induces intense intellectual concentration by imitating knotty thought both rhetorically and syntactically.

The prologue ends with the blind Samson in a state of dread at the muffled approach of feet, his meditation on death disturbed by their sound. The feet do not march up but stand off; and the parode does not supply reassurance. The Chorus speaks in unison, not voice on voice, and its sixty-one lines function as a symmetrical parallel to the prologue, an objective commentary sometimes complementary and sometimes almost corrective. The prologue contains five logical units, the parode, three. The first of the three identifies Samson in eleven and a half lines ("This, this is he. . . . See how he lies. . . . Can this be hee?"); the second recalls his former greatness in twenty-five lines ("whom no strength . . . could withstand"); the third laments his present state in an equal number of lines ("Which shall I first bewail, thy Bondage or lost

Sight"). The lines which identify Samson parallel the two opening parts of the prologue in which Samson described his coming to the unfrequented bank to seek ease to the body and find none to the mind. Like those lines, they are composed of exclamation ("O change"), imperatives ("let us not"; "see how he lies"), and questions ("do my eyes misrepresent"; "can this be hee"). The passage begins with careful self-imposed quiet in soft sibilants placed in a cadence in which caesural movement forms the primary rhythmical effect almost to the exclusion of stress. It begins with affirmation and ends with pretended doubt. The picture Samson gave of himself was of a man whose external sensations are limited to a change of air. The Chorus in complementary contrast looks at Samson from the outside to observe "how he lies at random, carelessly diffus'd, with languish't head unpropt." To the image of Captive in Samson's speech is added the image of Sufferer. The phrase "with languish't head unpropt" compels visualization and compels it in terms of latent contrast. Samson's posture is so expressive of despair as to constitute an icon of despair in contrast to an imagined posture with hypothetical "upright head propt," which would be an icon of positive thought. Michelangelo's tomb of Lorenzo de Medici comes irresistibly to mind, whether or not Milton visited it on either his first two-month stay in Florence or his second. Lorenzo is depicted as a thinker, upright, resting his well-held head lightly on his right hand; below him recline the two figures of Evening and Dawn. The description of Samson given by the Chorus is precisely that of Evening, leaning heavily slumped on his left elbow as he lies with his head turned down, unsupported, in vacant despair brooding "at random. . . . As one past hope, abandon'd, / And by himself given over." To the picture of the *thought-tormented captive* has been added its complement, the *brooding sufferer*, the man of melancholy.

The passage recalling Samson's former greatness likewise parallels Samson's own account of what he was, complementing Samson's emphasis on the prophecy of his birth and the appropriateness of his early breeding with the choral emphasis upon the deeds of his maturity. Together, the two speeches place all the antecedent action before the reader; where Samson spoke of himself as "design'd for great exploits," the Chorus describes his achievement of them. There is no suggestion in the parode that the Chorus is composed of men divided within themselves or among themselves; they think and speak in coherent accord. And yet Milton contrives to continue the sense of dialogue and debate by giving to the Chorus both affirmative and negative modes of description. They say that Samson's actions were positive and successful, unlike his enemies' negative actions. They communicate Samson's strength by perpetually contrasting it to other, baser uses of strength.

Samson's ways as a warrior were unlike chivalric knightly conquests: he fought victoriously but "unarm'd . . . weaponless . . . in scorn of thir proud arms . . . with what trivial weapon came to hand." Moreover, by employing the same devices of syntactical dislocation and rhetorical patterning in both the prologue and parode, Milton protracts in the parode the themes of past strength and present loss introduced in the prologue in such a way as to imitate and recreate efforts of assessment and thought. A prominent instance of grammatical ambiguity prompting thought by imitation—not of the action described, but of the assessment of that action—is the passage

> But safest he who stood aloof,
> When insupportably his foot advanc't,
> In scorn of thir proud arms and warlike tools,
> Spurn'd them to death by Troops.
>
> (135-38)

Samson made a whole army foolish when he lifted up the support of one foot and insupportably (and punningly) kicked the enemy aside to their doom. In this passage the irresistible advancement of Samson's foot and his individual destruction of platoon by platoon is preceded by the hypothetical cautious withdrawal to safety of a general, "he," whom the Chorus has distinguished and whom the reader must distinguish from the specific Samson with "his foot." This is interlined by the adverbial phrase of manner, which delays the action to communicate its quality. The figurative austerity of Samson's own account of his past also prevails in the Chorus's account. A Scripture-based comparison—"he rent [the lion] as he would have rent a Kid"—and a classical comparison of Samson carrying the gates of Gaza to Atlas— "like whom the Gentiles feign to bear up Heav'n"—are separated by nothing more than two metaphorical adjectives, Chalybean and Adamantean. But once again, schemes abound where tropes do not.

When the Chorus turns to the lamentation of Samson's present state, they again do so initially in the terms Samson himself used. But they *bewail* succinctly what Samson thought "would ask a life to wail," by coalescing and making concentric the two sources of his grief, "Prison within Prison." Although they speak of "inward light" only to dismiss it ("alas [it] Puts forth no visual beam"), they have at least mentioned the countertheme of compensatory illumination, the light of the mind. They conclude their lamentation with an interpretation of Samson's plight. This again is supplementary to the prologue. Samson could do no more than caution himself against attributing his fall to the will of God; the Chorus can describe it: "O mirror of our fickle state, . . . By

how much from the top of wondrous glory, . . . To lowest pitch of
abject fortune thou art fall'n." Their interpretation is close to Aristot-
le's definition of the tragic hero, and so Milton gives the Chorus an addi-
tional five final lines negatively explaining the nature of the true tragic
hero. He is not the prince of noble line raised high by the wheel of
fortune, but the Puritan aristocrat, the man with a talent, the elect
given "strength, while vertue was her mate." With the Chorus's ex-
planation of Samson's fall—that he fell to show how men regularly do
fall—the thesis of Act i has been stated: there is a bleak and fatalistic
meaning in the tragic fall of the great, and it moves those who observe
it to pity. Samson speaks two lines of question, the Chorus moves closer
to address him. Their identification of themselves and their errand
answers the expression of fear with which Samson concluded his pro-
logue, and it initiates the first episode, the dialogue of the first act, the
Aristotelian beginning. They are friends, contemporaries, neighbors,
and they have come to bring, if possible, "Counsel or Consolation" to
Samson's troubled mind.

In the exchanges which follow, two important matters at issue are
left latent, to be resolved in the course of the play. These are the cause
of Samson's fall and the prospect of the remainder of his life. Alone,
Samson dealt with the first to some effect ("O impotence of mind, in
body strong"), but only to reenact it: mind is still powerless, for his
thinking stings and makes no headway against suicidal despair. As for
the second, since he is buried but not exempt thereby from torment
and has desired the oblivion of death, he must be presumed to have
made no progress at all. Alone, the Chorus had not touched on the
cause of the fall but had begun with an estimate of Samson's prospects.
He is to be an example of the irreparable, a mirror of man's fickle
state; his future is fixed in failure. Now, together, they begin to juxta-
pose the cause of the fall and the prospect of the future.

Samson's first speech shows the alteration of mood which an objec-
tive but friendly audience necessarily brings. Samson enters into the
physician-patient relationship which the Chorus offers. His physician
is not wiser nor more experienced in his sort of complaint than he is,
as will shortly be clear, but it can listen and reflect back to Samson
what he can formulate. To formulate and to define is to begin to think
purposefully. As Samson speaks, the divisions within himself are placed
in a new context. He is encouraged to speak of them, and in expressing
them, he can begin the process of readjusting and balancing them
which will lead to their integration. He has said to himself that the most
painful and wounding of his sufferings is his blindness, the symbol of
his powerlessness; he now can say that his shame is an even greater
torture, shame at recognizing himself and being seen by others as a fool.

Stating the shame releases the power to compare his present crushed pride with its former flourishing, and he concludes:

> Immeasurable strength they might behold
> In me, of wisdom nothing more then mean;
> This with the other should, at least, have paird,
> These two proportiond ill drove me transverse.

(206-9)

Milton's version of Samson's *hubris*—proudly exulting in the lesser faculty and taking no thought for the higher faculty—is exactly stated. But when Samson speaks of strength and wisdom as "proportiond ill," he appears to the Chorus to be shifting the responsibility away from himself and onto God, the ultimate disposer of such gifts. They quickly warn him, "tax not divine disposal," before offering him some quite common human comfort, the knowledge that "wisest Men have err'd, and by bad Women been deceiv'd." Ordinary human weakness does not warrant such powerful self-condemnation, their lines continue: "Deject not then so overmuch thy self." Their words carry the implication that since future heroism is impossible, it is better to be a calm failure. That is poor advice; they ought rather to encourage Samson to use his wisdom in the hope of moderating the effects of his failure. But Samson has put a straight question—"do [men] not say, how well / Are come upon him his deserts?"—and the Chorus goes on to give him a true answer: "men wonder / Why thou shouldst wed *Philistian* women." Samson's reply marks the second time the concept of "inner light" appears in the play. He married outside his own tribe because he knew "from intimate impulse" that what he proposed "was of God" in that it provided the occasion to begin the liberation of Israel. He chose Dalila as his second wife in the same manner he chose his first, from among the overlord, unclean, and forbidden tribe, because of the earlier divine guidance and its recognized intention.

The Chorus reminds Samson, however, that "*Israel* still serves," implying that an "intimate impulse" must be judged by its result. In Samson's intelligent but emotional answer there is strong evidence of a potential reintegration of his conflicting impulses. Israel's continued servitude cannot be held to disprove the validity of inner light; as Samson was free to attend to the impulse to offer deliverance, so Israel was free to cooperate or not in the difficult task of realizing it. Samson was not coerced by God, Israel was not coerced by Samson; coercion cannot deliver men into freedom, but their own corruption and sloth can deliver them into servitude. The Chorus responds to the truth in Samson's contention and groups him, as Paul had, with Gideon and

Jephtha as elect saints who were potential, but disregarded, believers. Samson's answer is ambiguous; it is vengeful, yet thoughtful, and it has within it the hinted beginning of integration. When he says, "Mee easily indeed mine may neglect, / But Gods propos'd deliverance not so," he implies both that *it is easy (safe) enough to disregard me, but not so safe to disregard what God proposes* and that *it makes no difference to me if my efforts are disregarded, but it makes a great difference to me if God's are.* The second statement does not invoke God as a self-justifying device but as higher and holier than His self-critical chosen instrument. Samson's scorn of his slavish people is not a form of special pleading for himself; it is directed against them in support of God. Samson is not championing himself but God. Moreover, the lines posit a future as well as a past. If it turns out that the Chorus is right in assuming that a cause must be measured by its effects, perhaps the full effects are not yet known. It may be, however, that God's justice implies that the quality of an act will be judged by the quality of its intention.

The first stasimon attempts a preliminary resolution of the themes on which Samson and the Chorus have touched. God's justice is simply asserted in language recalling both Job and the Psalmist. God is just, but His ways are difficult to understand; He must be trusted even when He seems not only to condone the breach of His own laws but to inspire that breach. The Chorus speaks both to Samson and to themselves, continuing the comforting and cautioning. But the Chorus is not troubled with the most difficult form of attack on God's justice: how is it just to prompt a man to expose himself to continual temptation and neither make him strong enough to resist nor forgive and rescue him if he fail? When they noted earlier that fallen men *are* examples to others of the instability of the human state, they did not say that men fall *in order to be* such mirrors. The question of God's justice remains for them a question of means and causes, not of ends and effects. They ask, did God act fairly? Their stasimon contains a minimal justification of God, a minimal bleak comfort for Samson. The problem that preoccupies them is simply this: if God commands a man to do something He has earlier said is unholy, does God Himself not connive at sin? The Chorus no longer doubts that Samson was prompted by God; they simply define God as above the law He makes and free from all constraint. God can place a "National obstriction" on Jews not to marry Gentiles and can remove that "legal debt" for a particular Nazarite because "with his own Laws he can best dispence," or, as Milton said in *De Doctrina Christiana*, "he is omnipotent and utterly free in his actions."[14] The pains the Chorus takes to absolve God from responsi-

[14] *CPW*, VI, 146.

bility to His own laws are, however, sandwiched between warning men and vindicating God. They begin by asserting the folly of atheism and end by asserting the folly of speculation.

As the first episode ends, the reader has been shown an interior dialogue of a divided mind in the prologue, a balancing attempt to weigh the distance between past and present in the parode, and a series of questions and answers in the first episode, with a preliminary resolution in the first stasimon. Samson fell because he was insufficiently armed by wisdom against the woman he was prompted to marry. The human failure is absolute, yet the divine prompting was just because God is omnipotent and can legitimately do whatever He wills to do. The total structure of Act ɪ is dialectical and traces the following steps: Samson is in a terrifying state, unable to think; he is in a pitiable state, unable to act. How did it happen and what can come of it? He was at fault and nothing can be done. But men must not doubt God in any event; God acts as He wills; it is impious to think He does not. Since God has finished with Samson, human beings can do nothing more than soothe him. His future can only be resigned waiting for death.

SELF-DEFINITION AND OTHER PERSONS IN ACT II

The second episode introduces a more serious challenge to God's justice than the question of the legitimacy of means. The smallest substructures continue to be questions and answers, imperatives implying a harsh voice within the speaker and commanding a fragmented ego, rhetorical schemes predominating over poetical tropes. The total substructure of Act ɪɪ makes an important shift from past and present time to future time. God's ends are to be judged only when complete, since they move forward in time: His timeless ends justify His temporal means. Act ɪɪ also supplies the materials for an important shift from the sense of personal failure through remorse and repentance toward the threshold of understanding and self-acceptance. It supplies those materials only negatively, however; we are shown Samson's descent from a sense of personal failure to loneliness and to despair. With respect to plot structure, Act ɪ functioned as exposition, while Act ɪɪ functions as complication. The complication in theme is inseparable from the complication in plot; the more Samson attempts to think reasonably about his state, the less he appears to be able to control his mood. He sinks down to the death of effort and the death of will: he wishes for oblivion. To die is not unnatural; it is not tragic *that* men die, but *how* they die may be. To die in maturity or even to be overtaken by death in full life is intelligible and may or may not be tragic in effect; to die in the mind and will because no further development is possible, to die in atrophy, is terrible. That seems to be Samson's destiny. The complication in plot is the introduction of the possibility of ransom, of eluding one sort of captivity to settle for another sort, passivity. With the possibility of ransom, Samson's future becomes uncertain. All those who visit him will directly increase the uncertainty: Manoa will propose ransom; Dalila, sensuous compensations for loss; Harapha and the Officer, simple continuance as a cooperative slave. The "middle" of the play is unified by its concern with causes, means, and ends, by Samson's wrestling with his past and future in terms of alternate readings of his fall, and by alternative proposals for what remains of his life.

Act II begins with Manoa rephrasing the Chorus's shocked exclamation, "O change beyond report," in his first words, "O miserable change!" His next words restate Samson's agonized question, "O wherefore was my birth foretold," as "O wherefore did God grant me my request" for a son. He then asks the serious question the whole episode will explore. "Methinks," he says, "whom God has chosen once . . . if he through frailty err, / He should not so o're-whelm." Samson meets the challenge to God's justice himself: it was his own weakness which made him fall ("Sole Author I, sole cause"). Moreover, he has not actually fallen to so debased a condition as he was in before, for though he is now seen to be a slave, he was then, in truth, Dalila's slave:

> The base degree to which I now am fall'n,
> These rags, this grinding, is not yet so base
> As was my former servitude, ignoble,
> Unmanly, ignominious, infamous,
> True slavery, and that blindness worse then this,
> That saw not how degenerately I serv'd.
>
> (414-19)

His words are the highest point of recognition in the second act, their intellectual resolution justifies the claim that Samson is freer in chains than he was before at liberty. Manoa reminds him of his claim of "Divine impulsion" to marry and admonishes him to think that the most shameful matter is not that he has fallen but that he has thereby given the impious Philistines opportunity to exult: "So *Dagon* shall be magnifi'd, and God . . . had in scorn." Samson's answer first shows that the monition was unnecessary—"Father, I do acknowledge . . . that I . . . to God have brought Dishonour"—and then constructs the basis of the intellectual justification of God's ways by reference to His

ultimate designs: "the God of *Abraham* . . . will arise . . . e're long."
Manoa accepts the truth of this concept and properly takes it as "a
Prophecy." Then, because he has accepted God's ends *sub specie
aeternitatis* as it were, Manoa can turn his mind *eheu fugaces* to the
immediate present and ask "for thee what shall be done." His proposal
of ransom is rejected by Samson likewise in terms of a possible re-
demptive future: he must "pay on" his punishment and "expiate, if
possible" his crime. Manoa thinks him so unreasonable that he is driven
to question his motives. Is Samson "self-rigorous . . . over-just, and self-
displeas'd / For self-offence, more then for God offended?" In the
prologue he patently was. His stinging thoughts were proclaimed in an
inner harsh voice of self-flagellation. Now Samson can make no better
answer to this true charge than the self-contemptuous, "like a petty
God . . . swoll'n with pride . . . I fell . . . Softn'd with pleasure and
voluptuous life."

The Chorus is always quick to jump in when the moral code comes
under consideration. In this they are not like a group of moralistic
elders, they are "younger feet" than Manoa; they are rather like men
in their secure and commonsensical maturity, not like old, pious, sen-
tentious men. Seizing on the phrase "voluptuous life," they remind
Samson that, as a true Nazarite, he abstained from wine. Samson
brushes aside such praise because it only emphasizes his sexual intem-
perance. He returns instead to Manoa's offered ransom and rejects it.
God will act in the future, but for himself there can only be "con-
temptible old age," better spent drudging until "oft-invocated death /
Hast'n the welcom end of all my pains." Manoa remonstrates with
him; rather than thereby serve the enemy, it would be better for Sam-
son to lie at home "bed-rid, not only idle." He then tries to comfort
Samson with the hope of a miracle: God can "Cause light again within
thy eies to spring." That is not a regenerative hope, it is a fond
delusion. There was in Samson's self-indictment ("like a petty God")
the possibility of regeneration, which follows upon correct self-
evaluation. Samson could have achieved a whole sense of self in the
discovery of who he really is: not a petty god, but a man whose
freedom is established by his real attempt to serve a real God and to
discard all impulses incompatible with that chosen end. But Samson is
so trapped in the mood of downward-tending despair that Manoa's
wishful fantasy calls forth his death wish. His thoughts portend dark-
ness and death.

Samson's second lyric of suffering and despair is symmetrical to the
first in Act I. "O loss of sight, of thee I most complain" is replaced by
"O that torment . . . must secret passage find / To th' inmost mind."
Of all the torments of spirit, the most tormenting is not now the simple

difference between what he might have been and what he has become, as in Act I, but the "sense of Heav'ns desertion," "now . . . cast . . . off as never known," "left . . . all helpless." Repeatedly, he describes his blindness as irremediable: "these dark orbs no more shall treat with light"; "th' irreparable loss of sight." His mood has such control of his thoughts that no help can come from the possibility of compensatory inner light, and he prays for speedy death. His despair is grounded in total self-rejection as well as in the conviction of God's rejection, and of alienation from family and country.

At this point the Chorus in its second stasimon attempts to achieve synthesis and comprehension by means of a new questioning of God's justice. For the question *Does God respect His own edicts?* they substitute a far more searching question: *Is God just to His own servants? Are God's divine ends compatible with the human beings whom He chooses to enact them?* They question God's disposition of the elect saint, and they extend the definition they gave of the tragic hero, who in the parode was negatively defined as not the man raised by fortune or born high. Tragic heroes are "such as thou hast solemnly elected, / With gifts and graces eminently adorn'd / To some great work, thy glory, / And peoples safety," and who then are cast lower than they once were high: "unseemly falls in human eie." In pain the Chorus concludes,

> Just or unjust, alike seem miserable,
> For oft alike, both come to evil end.

> (703-4)

The punishment exceeds the error. Samson is at his nadir, and the Chorus is baffled to help him.

The stasimon has its own dialectical form, however, which moves from uncertainty and doubt to prayer. It falls into four parts. Part one is a fifteen-line stanza which proposes patience as a heroic tempering of adversity which man himself can achieve when God seems to temper His providence through man's short life unevenly. Yet it acknowledges that patience is impossible without "Some sourse of consolation from above; / Secret refreshings." For Samson patience must involve his role as Judge, not of God, but of himself. He must discover what he is worth, and what is worth dying for. He must rise above his despair to attain sufficient harmony of mind and will to participate in human life. Then he will be patient. The "inner impulse" in him will be a "sourse of consolation" then and not just an imperative command that he cannot obey. Part two of the stasimon consists of a stanza of twenty lines which is an independent hymn of pathos associating Samson with all good men: human beings are not given the easy even lot of angels or animals; the best of men move to the top of fortune's wheel to be cast down. Part three is an eighteen-line stanza which intensifies the pathos. The elect are not simply allowed to slip away to obscurity, they are mysteriously tortured with "causless suffring," without regard to their achievements, irrespective of just or unjust. The stasimon ends with a five-line prayer for Samson: give him peace. It briefly balances the first part: find patience. The Chorus cannot, after witnessing Samson's self-indictment, hope or much believe in God's charity, but they can end with faith.

The next act begins with an answer to the prayer of the Chorus, a stanza of fifteen lines (symmetrical to the fifteen lines of their opening words) announcing the arrival of Dalila. The most important achievements of Act II as a demonstration of the way in which the mind copes with experience are these: Samson has seen that he has imprisoned himself; he is his own jailor, was his own prisoner before he became the Philistines'; the Chorus has seen that mankind itself must make its own terms with experience, tempering within where God apparently has not tempered. The outcome has been predicted in direct prophecy and in ironic prolepsis: God will arise, Samson will struggle toward integration and will find consolation from within and from above. The means has been hinted at: Samson let his secret foe into his mind by the entrance of sensuality; when that has been understood and repulsed in the mature reenactment, he will be in harmony with himself. His secret foe is that which is incompatible with and antithetical to his reasoned, chosen, and willed ends.

The Fit Conversation of Marriage in Act III

It has always been recognized that Samson's exchange with Dalila, Milton's most original invention, contains the high point of the drama. The rhetorical debate in which they engage concludes with the intellectual integration of the hero. In the space of the 351 lines of Act III, words expressive of intellectual processes occur again and again, words such as *foresaw, knew, appease thy mind, instructed, weighed, counterpois'd granting, shewdst the way, interpret'st, saw, design'd, knew, seest impartial, self-severe, determinst, condemning, consented, resolv'd, charge lay'st, sollicited, urged, adjur'd, press'd how just, oppose against powerful arguments, long debate, wisest men . . . grave authority, thought, taught thee, false pretects, argument misguided, not doubting, unwary, wisdom learnt, to gloss upon, count it, was judged, discover'd, conceal'd, musing preferr'd, compar'd capacity, apprehend, value, least confusion.* When Dalila comes to Samson to ask him to forgive her and to return to her house, Milton raises the question of the nature of human relationships, the question of how a man and a woman are related to one another, what purposes their relationship serves, what limitations upon their individual freedom the relationship posits, what satisfaction it offers in compensation, and what that human relationship suggests about how the individual is connected to society, lives purposefully, and achieves fulfillment. To state it at its largest, Milton raises the question of what meaning in human terms there is in the claim that freedom is achieved through responsibility. How and why is freedom identified with responsibility? Of the various proffered answers to the question of why Milton made Dalila Samson's wife and not his harlot, one obviously important one is that the relationship of marriage is the relationship he had particularly studied in connection with the balance of reason and the passions and in connection with the paradox of freedom and responsibility. Act III is about one human relationship, matrimony, as it symbolizes not only a harmonious society but also a well-tempered human soul. But first let us examine the terms of disputation in Act III itself.

Dalila arrives before Samson somewhat penitent, very much self-exculpating, with a specific end in mind, but with a host of subsidiary ends as well. She wants him to pardon her and give her leave to seek his release into her comforting, loving custody.[15] Samson meets her reasoning and triumphs over the temptation she offers. He and Milton have in mind a quite different definition of matrimony from hers: Dalila's is intercourse of body, theirs companionship of mind. She begins in sixteen lines which utter the general proposition, I come from "conjugal affection" "to light'n what thou suffer'st." Tucked within those lines is a parenthesis: "(though the fact more evil drew / In the perverse event then I foresaw)." In eighteen lines which balance hers, Samson answers the particular hint of that parenthesis. Her lines are spoken in a curious falling cadence, six lines ending in unaccented syllables; his reply is couched in strong verbs, not falling nouns, twenty hammer strokes: *break, deceive, betray, submit, beseech, move, confess, promise, try, urg'd, bears, assail, transgresses, submits, reject, forgive, drawn, wear out, entangl'd, cut off*. To her plea of innocent intention, Samson thunders that all false women injure, beg forgiveness, and so reentangle the best men. Dalila initiates the dialectic, which will proceed in three long exchanges, by asking Samson then to *weigh* and *counterpoise* her side of the argument impartially, and she argues in extenuation her human weakness and her protective love. If she was

[15] But see Empson, *Milton's God*, chap. 6, and Samuel, *"Samson Agonistes* as Tragedy," for the two extreme readings of her intellectual competency.

weak in liking to know and tell secrets, as all women are, then Samson was weak first in telling his. The syllogism concludes patly:

Let weakness then with weakness come to parl
. . . .
Thine forgive mine; that men may censure thine
The gentler. . . .

(785-88)

Furthermore, out of love she simply sought to make Samson "Mine and Loves prisoner, not the *Philistines*, / Whole to my self."

To the first argument of weakness, which implies not simply forgiveness but reenactment of weakness, Samson answers her overt point by the decision to forgive her weakness as much as he forgives his own folly, which is not at all. Her latent suggestion that they continue to be weak together he answers with a resolution to be instead fully rational, "Impartial, self-severe, inexorable." To the second argument of love, Samson counters a definition: Dalila was moved by lust, not love, for love does not seek possession or enslavement, it seeks love. The forgiveness she asks for would be a further surrender into her power. Samson has shown no impotence of mind in their exchange. He has arrived at a correct definition of love. More decisively, he has reasoned to the "Impartial, self-severe" conclusion that "All wickedness is weakness." Samson judges himself and his wife equally. He has not withdrawn into a private despair; he has raised his unpropt head to look directly into the truth.

At once Dalila shifts her ground to argue not from their common weakness but from her strength of high purpose: she acted against Samson for good strong reasons of national security, the cloak of crime so familiar in public affairs. The relationship between the first exchange and this one is hard to fix because Dalila's argument carries such a wealth of subsidiary motives. She is presented as desiring several things which are not compatible as goals in a stable ego, but are only too compatible as aspects of a recognizable psychopathic personality. Thus she wishes to attach Samson to her once more in love, but she also wishes to whip him and defeat him; she wishes to seduce him, but also to retain the upper hand; she wishes to master him sexually and demean him so that he may know he is defeated, but no less she wishes to enjoy him. She cannot resist a series of jibes and stings under the cover of her complacent self-criticism ("more strength from me, then in thy self was found"; "though to thy own condemning"; "I leave him to his lot and like my own"). I do not think, however, that the shift from weakness to strength is a shift from deceit to superior candor.[16] Dalila argues throughout that she has simply done what she thought to be right: in the first debate, right in private love; in the second debate, right from public necessity; in the last debate, right to ensure fame. But the standards by which Dalila discovers what she thinks is right are relativistic and self-regardful, disconnected from reality. What she wants is what is right; what is right is what she wants. She has no values external to her own will. She measures her conduct by a variety of inconsistent standards, gives herself too many motives, and sees no inconsistency among them or in the process. Having dramatized herself "wailing thy absence in my widow'd bed" and having acted out the role of the inexhaustible mistress who would "still enjoy thee day and night," she easily passes to dramatizing herself as a warrior maid: she was "girt round" by "sieges" "which might have aw'd the best resolv'd of men"; the princes and priests of Philistia came in person to speak of the honor and glory in defeating Samson; she struggled in silence against their arguments, armed only with love, and finally saw "that to the public good / Private respects must yield." She sounds to herself like an epic heroine renouncing self for cause. She sounds to Milton like Satan, whom "public reason just" compelled and who "with necessitie, the Tyrants plea, excus'd his devilish deeds."

Milton gives to Samson arguments in reply which continue to show an inner logic and consistency and an outer objectivity as well. Dalila has said that she acted patriotically against an enemy and piously against an infidel. Samson counters that he was not an enemy, since by marrying him Dalila chose his country and nation to be her own; that when her country invoked her aid against him, it acted against the law and in violation of the very social ends for which countries come into being and hence was not properly a country but a power-seeking junta; and finally, that gods who require support by ungodly means are not gods but devils. His contradictions of her patriotism and of her piety are fundamental redefinitions of country and of God. A perfect definition, as defined by Milton in the *Art of Logic*, is "nothing else than a universal symbol of the causes constituting the essence and nature of a thing."[17] Only when a predication corresponds to its ideal or proper form and function may it be understood to be real. A country is the ends it serves, not a geographical unit; a priest is what he does for his sheep, not a man anointed by a bishop; a king is a person who fulfills the office of a king, not a man born to that office; and a marriage is the mutual help and fit conversation it contains, not a church- and

[16] See Jon S. Lawry, *The Shadow of Heaven* (Ithaca: Cornell University Press, 1968), 380.

[17] *The Columbia Edition of the Works of John Milton*, ed. Frank A. Patterson et al. (New York: Columbia University Press, 1933), XI, 265.

state-sanctioned arrangement. Dalila's definitions are quite different: a country is what I owe allegiance to, a religion is what I profess to believe, an argument is what I accept. Samson rejects her relativism by making a fully intellectual effort. Samson believes in Jehovah, Dalila in Dagon; Samson is a Jew, Dalila a Philistine; Samson believes in Jehovah because of inner light, it is open to Dalila to say the same of her belief in Dagon. Should either appeal in just those terms to the unprejudiced bystander, there is nothing to choose between them. But say, as Samson does, that Jehovah is God because of His essence and nature, that one answers to His claims not because they are peremptory but because they are value-filled and reasonable, and the unprejudiced bystander faces another sort of question altogether. Dagon requires obedience. But Jehovah? He requires reason and voluntary cooperation.

Dalila acknowledges her defeat in the pettish terms of the inadequate feminist: "a woman ever / Goes by the worse, whatever be her cause" when she argues with a man. And Dalila comes to the proposal which is the theme of their third disputation: she will make recompense for everything "misdone, Misguided" by means of the "many solaces" for "other senses" than sight. Samson is often taken only to recoil passionately. But he does not merely reject her physically, he gives the reason: he is freer in prison than he would be released into bondage to her. He brings to bear his past experience upon his present situation and is able to argue consistently and avoid the mood of romantic sensuality. His integration is complete when he states the theme of inner freedom:

> This Gaol I count the house of Liberty
> To thine whose doors my feet shall never enter.
>
> (949-50)

After Samson's successful practice of reasoned argument, his tempering will be fully accomplished in the following episode when he can state the associated theme of inner light. What Samson has achieved is so integrative of his experience in the play thus far that the three stages fall perfectly into order: he saw that he was blind, alone, and in prison; he learned that his prison was his self; he understood that his self was free, though blind and in prison, when it chose its own action, defined its own ends, and judged its own course. He blames no one now, neither God, nor Dalila, nor the Philistines; he is otherwise occupied, since he has judged and evaluated to such clear purpose almost syllogistically. Dalila is given the last word in the episode to flaunt her subjective criterion of value: she is still right because she thinks she is, and she will be glorious where she wants to be, glory being a local and relative matter when the only absolute is the private will.

As Dalila leaves, the Chorus falls into a very strange reverie in the third stasimon. Beauty experienced through the senses creates strong passions which overthrow reason; reason once subjected is hard pressed to prevent it happening again. Their first reaction seems absolutely right. What they say next is not right but only dramatically apposite as appropriate to Samson's friends: womankind is unstable in love for causes beyond man's ken, but experience teaches that she ruins the best of men. Their intricate free-rhyming lines repeatedly play with the letter *t* in a seeming tut-tut or tsk-tsk within an irony which praises Samson and encourages and joins him in a common masculine plight. At the same time, they so grossly belittle womankind that a residual fear and awe at women's beauty remains. Whatever Milton in his own person might say, his Chorus here expresses a mixture of contempt for and fear of women. They round off the episode with an acceptable "moral" which links the stasimon intellectually with the prayer which concluded the preceding stasimon:

> But vertue which breaks through all opposition,
> And all temptation can remove,
> Most shines and most is acceptable above.
>
> (1050-52)

As they prayed to God to bring Samson to peace, Dalila entered. As Dalila departs, they acknowledge the value of her visit. She was sent as opposition and temptation over which Samson has triumphed. That much of the stasimon performs the reconciling function the Chorus habitually assumes. They then draw another conclusion, signaled by "therefore" and completed by "so." Because true virtue depends upon overcoming difficulties, God *therefore* made a law intended to prevent some foreseeable difficulties, a law giving despotic power to husbands over wives *so* that husbands should "least confusion draw" upon themselves "not sway'd by female usurpation." Because he broke that law, Samson has had to overcome the difficulties arising from female usurpation on his way toward achieving God's other difficult ends. The "law" of despotic power is a biblical "law" and a seventeenth-century "law," and it is useless to discredit the Chorus for having accepted not only its existence but its necessity and its reason. The Chorus is not purblind in arriving at the unexpected conclusion that a man avoids loss of freedom by being coercive over a woman, although the idea is highly conventional and un-Miltonic. The Chorus is not Milton. It is sympathetic with Samson and intends to offer consolation. By this stage, however, it is lagging behind him in moral understanding.

The encounter in Act III needs to be seen in light of Milton's previous writings on marriage. The questions underlying that encounter are not questions affecting particularly the marriage of Samson and Dalila—what are the obligations within mixed marriages, or does the relationship between Samson and Dalila fulfill conditions necessary for divorce—they are questions important to all human beings: Since marriage creates a relationship with another person, is it not symbolic of all such relationships and an image of society itself? Or, since marriage represents a harmonious union between separate beings, is it not symbolic of all such unions and an image of an integrated personality? Or finally, since marriage consists of a contract between unequal members, does it not symbolize the relationship between men and God and consequently become an image of the church?

Milton wrote fully about marriage in the divorce tracts, where he argued for divorce on the grounds of incompatibility in order to annul an ill-sorted union and to make way for a true marriage. In *A Second Defence of the English People*, he gave as his grounds for treating the subject his wish to "advance the cause of true and substantial liberty, which must be sought, not without, but within. . . . Hence I set forth my views on marriage, not only its proper contraction, but also, if need be, its dissolution."[18] Milton's views on the "proper contraction" are set forth in *The Doctrine and Discipline of Divorce*, which opens by affirming "that Man is the occasion of his owne miseries, in most of those evills which hee imputes to Gods inflicting." This is the point Samson reached in Act II. God "in first ordaining of marriage, taught us to what end he did it, in words expressly implying the apt and cheerful conversation of man with woman, to comfort and refresh him against the evill of solitary life." But men interpret God's ordinance of marriage falsely, making it an inseparable bond rather than a useful contract not only terminable but essentially terminated if the ends for which it was ordained are not achieved. Marriage is a "divine institution joyning man and woman in a love fitly dispos'd to the help and comfort of domestic life." "The internal *Form* and soul of this relation, is conjugal love arising from a mutual fitness to the final causes of wedlock, help and society in Religious, Civil and Domestic conversation, which includes an inferior end the fulfilling of natural desire, and specifical increase." Milton not only defines marriage as the means by which man's human loneliness may be assuaged, the only means of solace against the pain of solitude, he goes much further. He holds that the solace of loneliness is the definitive function of mar-

18 *CPW*, IV, pt. 1, 624.

riage, its essential function from which all other of its uses derive their meaning. Animals couple without a meeting of minds; male and female may join bodies without a marriage. A marriage is only accomplished through "likenes, fitnes of mind and disposition which may breed the Spirit of concord, and union between them." Companionship of mind is the essence of marriage for Milton; he is original in his overriding emphasis upon the primacy of this objective.[19] Although he argues that "among Christian writers touching matrimony, there be three chief ends thereof agreed on; Godly society, next civill, and thirdly, that of the marriage-bed," Milton emphasizes an aspect of marriage not explicitly set forth by any previous writer. By marriage Milton means religious companionship, social congeniality, and physical companionship within the dyadic unit.

Marriage has profound symbolic value for Milton under each of these three heads: religious, social, and personal. Each is significant in the Dalila episode. At its best, the spiritual-mental union of an ideal pair in an ideal marriage spreads outward to other states. If a man can bring the relationship of his own faculties into balance, he may be able to balance the relationship of his marriage; if he cannot, he must dissolve it to try again. Possibly, if he can get his marriage in balance, he can help his congregation or church to reach harmony and so assist his society to cohere. The ideal of religious harmony caused Milton to treat in general terms the specific case corresponding to the marriage of Samson and Dalila, the case of a believer marrying a nonbeliever. He juxtaposed the Genesis text, "Therefore shall a man leave his father and his mother, and shall cleave unto his wife," with the

[19] The clearest and most faithful exposition of Milton's views remains that of William Haller, *Liberty and Reformation in the Puritan Revolution* (New York: Columbia University Press, 1955), 78-99, which digests William and Malleville Haller, "The Puritan Art of Love," *Huntington Library Quarterly*, 5 (1941-1942), 235-72. The legal context is helpfully given by C. L. Powell, *English Domestic Relations, 1487-1653* (New York: Columbia University Press, 1917). The political implications of Milton's views on divorce are treated authoritatively by Ernest Sirluck in his introduction to Vol. II of the *Complete Prose Works*; the Reformation background is examined by Roland Mushat Frye in "The Teachings of Classical Puritanism on Conjugal Love," *Studies in the Renaissance*, 2 (1955), 147-59; and the social implications in the New World are studied by Edmund S. Morgan, *The Puritan Family*, rev. ed. (New York: Harper & Row, 1966). Charles H. and Katherine George, *The Protestant Mind of the English Reformation 1570-1640* (Princeton: Princeton University Press, 1961), place Milton's views in a general intellectual context, and John Halkett, *Milton and the Idea of Matrimony: A Study of the Divorce Tracts and "Paradise Lost"* (New Haven: Yale University Press, 1970), specifically examines the relationship between the divorce tracts and the epic, dealing with modifications and enrichments of the earlier positions in the composition of *Paradise Lost*.

Pauline text, "For the unbelieving husband is sanctified by the wife, and the unbelieving wife is sanctified by the husband. . . . But if the unbelieving depart, let him depart." From these texts he deduced that mixed marriage is allowable and that the believer is not defiled by "dwelling in matrimony with an unbeleever," but that desertion by the unbeliever effects a true divorce, as would any desertion.[20] In both *The Doctrine and Discipline of Divorce* and *De Doctrina Christiana* Milton refered to the parallel case of Abraham, who was prompted by God to marry Hagar and then to send away the quarrelsome and "irreligious wife and her son for the offenses they gave in a pious family."[21]

The religious value of marriage, as argued both by Puritan and Anglican divines, consists in the spread of the church, literally through the procreation and education of Christian children and symbolically through the establishing of a community of believers on earth who would become the communion of saints in heaven. Both literally and symbolically, the religious value of marriage was likened in sermons to the mystical marriage of Christ and the Church. On the literal level, Milton was quite traditional. In *De Doctrina Christiana* he summarily noted that "Religious conviction should also be considered to ensure that husband and wife are of one mind in religious matters."[22] On the symbolic level, however, Milton gave to this theme a characteristic individual turn. Marriage symbolizes harmony and concord with the God-given order of the universe. The highest symbolic value in marriage for Milton is that of the well-integrated soul in harmony with all nature. Where others emphasized marriage as the emblem of Christ's authority over the Church, Milton consistently saw it as the emblem of cosmic order. Characteristically, he described it in terms of musical analogies: "true concord"; "all civil and religious concord, which is the inward essence of wedlock"; "discordant wedloc"; "the unchangeable discord of som natures."[23] All nature joins in gratulation at the marriage of Adam and Eve, and Raphael admits that the joys of human love correspond to those of angelic love.

[20] For the fullest study of Milton's reworking of Genesis in his treatment of marriage see Joseph E. Duncan, *Milton's Earthly Paradise: A Historical Study of Eden* (Minneapolis: University of Minnesota Press, 1972), 175-83. See also J. M. Evans, *"Paradise Lost" and the Genesis Tradition* (Oxford: Clarendon Press, 1968), chap. 10; Mary Ann Radzinowicz, "Introduction to Book VIII," in *Milton's "Paradise Lost"* (Cambridge: Cambridge University Press, 1974); and Radzinowicz, "Eve and Dalila: Renovation and Hardening of the Heart," in *Reason and the Imagination: Studies in the History of Ideas, 1600-1800*, ed. Joseph A. Mazzeo (New York: Columbia University Press, 1962).

[21] See *CPW* II, 263, VII, 377.   [22] *Ibid.*, VI, 369.

[23] *Ibid.*, II, 330, 605, 666, 717.

The social value of marriage was widely agreed to consist in the generation of a peaceful, stable community; the institution of marriage preserved society from the chaos which would follow if all men had sexual access to all women so that children were not plainly the parental responsibility of any unit. Milton clearly stated that the "dearest and most peaceable estate of household society" in marriage should result in the "blest subsistence of a Christian family" and not in "household unhappines" or "economical misfortune."[24] He quite traditionally derived all social bonds from the pattern of marriage— "true sourse of human ofspring" by which "all the Charities of Father, Son, and Brother first were known."[25] Yet he also gave to this aspect of marriage his own individualistic emphasis. Marriage is a necessity not so much to society as to the social nature of man himself.[26] In *Colasterion* Milton brushed aside the major social arguments against divorce ("the overturning of all human society") because the society that interested him most was the society of attributes within the human heart as experienced in the social unit of two.

The completeness of Milton's indifference to the traditionally defended social aspect of the marriage contract is testified to, of course, by his heterodox, but not unique, advocacy of polygamy.[27] In *De Doctrina Christiana* Milton established polygamy as scripturally sanctioned, instancing the many holy and polygamous patriarchs and reinterpreting Paul, 1 Cor. 7:2, "Let every man have his own wife." "The text says," he wrote, "that he should have *his own wife*, meaning that he should keep her for himself, not that she should be the only one."[28] Milton's interest in multiple marriages predated his interest in divorce (as witness the entries in the Commonplace Book made before the Italian journey) and continued beyond his own happy second and third marriages.[29] By asserting that no particular form of marriage is necessary to the stability of society but that society arises from the sociability in man which leads to his marrying, Milton gave as strong

---

[24] *Ibid.*, II, 242, 230, 229.   [25] *Paradise Lost*, IV, 750-57.

[26] On this subject John Halkett is the best of the many expositors. See his *Milton and the Idea of Matrimony*, 26-30.

[27] See C. A. Patrides, *Milton and the Christian Tradition* (Oxford: Clarendon Press, 1966), 167. On the polygamous practices of some of the separatists see: George H. Williams, *The Radical Reformation* (Philadelphia: Westminster Press, 1962), 511ff.; Christopher Hill, *The World Turned Upside Down* (London: Temple Smith, 1972), 253; Geoffrey Bullough, "Polygamy among the Reformers," in *Renaissance and Modern Essays Presented to Vivian de Sola Pinto*, ed. G. R. Hibbard (New York: Barnes and Noble, 1966), 5-23; and Leo Miller, *John Milton among the Polygamophiles* (New York: Loewenthal Press, 1974).

[28] *CPW*, VI, 362.

[29] See Mohl, *Milton and His Commonplace Book*, 97-99.

an individualistic twist to the social function of marriage as he had to the religious function.

Milton was equally independent in his emphasis upon the functions which marriage fulfills. The "inward knot" of marriage, its "internal Form and soul," is "conjugal love." Both in *Tetrachordon* and in *Paradise Lost* Milton described in glosses on Gen. 2:18 how God instituted marriage: "And the Lord said, it is not good that man should be alone. I will make him a help meet for him." In *Tetrachordon* God institutes marriage in rational and dialectical form: "Loneliness is the first thing which Gods eye nam'd not good"; "alone is meant alone without woman; otherwise Adam had the company of God himself and Angels to converse with; all creatures to delight him seriously or to make him sport"; and most significantly, as a conclusion from this, "God heer presents himself like to a man deliberating; both to shew us that the matter is of high consequence, and that he intended to found it according to naturall reason, not impulsive command, but that the duty should arise from the reason of it, not the reason he swallow'd up in a reasonless duty." God founded the institution upon the nature of his creatures: "*because* it is not good for man to be alone, I make him therefore a meet help."[30] Man's need is for "delightfull intermissions," "a thousand raptures . . . far on the hither side of carnall enjoyment," "a sociable minde as well as a conjunctive body," "an amiable knot." He needs "another self, a second self, a very self itself."[31] God instituted wedlock not as a command but as a rational ordinance, as indeed God always does: "he advises, and that with certain cautions not commands"; He chooses to present Himself "as if the divine power had bin in some care and deep thought," as a "deliberating God."[32] His ways do not "ever crosse the just and reasonable desires of men." God "requires the observance [of His law] not otherwise then to the law of nature and of equity imprinted in us seems correspondent. And he hath taught us to love and extoll his Lawes, not onely as they are his, but as they are just and good to every wise and sober understanding."[33]

In Book VIII of *Paradise Lost* Milton treated the institution in much the same way both as to dialectical form and rational content. Adam, after hearing what is requisite that he know about creation, engages in a long and fluent conversation with Raphael. At the conclusion of the first third of that conversation, given over to a discussion of astronomy, Adam offers to tell of his own creation and life. He narrates his creation, his first consciousness, his dream of being led to Eden, his awakening, and God's coming to him with the animals in

[30] *CPW*, II, 595. [31] *Ibid.*, 597-600. [32] *Ibid.*, 266, 309, 342.
[33] *Ibid.*, 297-98.

pairs to be named and to pay their fealty. He then shifts from autobiographical narration to dialectic, recounting in the form of a dialogue with God what led to the creation of Eve and the establishment of matrimony. Adam looked at the animals in pairs and questioned God: "with mee / I see not who partakes. In solitude / What happiness . . . (VIII, 363-65). God's reply—"with these [animals] / Find pastime, and beare rule"—had to Adam the force of an imperative: God "seem'd / So *ordering*." Adam asked leave, therefore, to expand his question: "Among unequals what societie . . . harmonie or true delight. . . . [What] fellowship . . . fit to participate all rational delight?" God, "not displeas'd," replied with another question, like a divine Socrates: "Seem I . . . sufficiently possest of happiness . . . who am alone from all Eternitie?" Adam answered that God, in being one, possesses the oneness of unity and universality (like one people, one language), but that the human being is one with the oneness of singularity or aloneness (one solitary man, one single apple, one isolated house). "His single imperfection . . . requires / Collateral love, and deerest amitie." The disputation is resolved when the Father admits that He has given Adam a sort of intelligence test ("Thus farr to try thee, *Adam*, I was pleas'd"), which Adam has passed ("knowing . . . of thy self / Expressing well the spirit within thee free"). God knows that solitude is "not good." But His foreknowledge was in no way compulsory over Adam's self-knowledge. Predestination is adjusted to liberty so that from the human point of view it will always appear that God improvises after the event. And finally, marriage is established between creatures sufficiently equal for "social communication." To end the debate, God promised:

> What next I bring shall please thee, be assur'd,
> Thy likeness, thy fit help, thy other self,
> Thy wish, exactly to thy hearts desire.

Marriage is instituted for mutual solace from loneliness, on the reasonable basis of man's known nature, instituted conditionally or contingently on the compatibility of the nearly equal pair, and instituted so that the satisfaction of reason is more essential than the satisfaction of the senses.

In terms of the ordinance, Samson and Dalila present a classic example of Milton's grounds for divorce.[34] They disagree on the mean-

[34] See Dayton Haskin, "Divorce as a Path to Union with God in *Samson Agonistes*," ELH, 38 (1971), 358ff., for a clear account of the differences between the pair, but with a mystically un-Miltonic suggestion that Samson "divorces" Dalila in order to recover love-unity with God.

ing of love, the importance of sensory gratification in marriage, the grounds for forgiveness, the source of fame, the relative status of conjugal and national loyalty, and much else. Dalila is no fit conversing mate, and worse still, she perpetually drives toward dominance in a relationship for which the natural condition, though not the invariable one,[35] is male dominance. The natural balance of marriage was contained in Paul's complementary words of advice: "Wives be ye subject to your husbands," and, "Husbands love your wives." The reciprocal relationship of love and obedience makes marriage an extremely rich symbol. In addition to representing the spiritual state and the social state, it symbolizes the balanced internal state of man himself, the balance of reason and imagination, of love and obedience, of freedom and responsibility. And Milton saw in the well-adjusted personal functions of matrimony the image of the well-tempered soul. He repeatedly spoke of each partner in marriage as in conversation with his "likeness," "other self," "second self," "other half," and "very self it self." But Samson was ill-married to an incompatible person. His rejection of her therefore actually symbolizes the tempering, reordering, and reharmonizing of his inner personality. The total episode constitutes a dialectic concluding in the reestablishment of personal freedom. Samson could not live with his self at the outset of the play, so divided and fragmented was it. He was "at dreadful variance with [himself]. To [him] nothing was more intolerable than to be, to dwell with [himself]." He defined himself in the contest with Dalila by accurately defining her. The result was so integrative as to release him from dependence upon an incompatible wife by relieving him of his own fragmentation.

Suppose, then, that Samson was right in thinking that God prompted him to marry (while of course leaving him free to marry or not);[36] that he was not unjustified in seeking marriage to an infidel; that their union was one of incompatible persons; but that Samson effectually divorced her and reiterated that divorce in saying "thou and I long since are twain." Suppose that Samson acknowledged his own share

[35] "If she exceed her husband in prudence and dexterity, and he contentedly yeald . . . than a superior and more naturall law comes in, that the wiser should govern the less wise, whether male or female" (*CPW*, II, 589).

[36] This supposition has been generally disallowed, but on no other evidence than that the marriages which resulted from inner impulse turned out badly. Inner impulses are not guarantees against error, however; they are modes of knowing which initiate actions. For the view that Samson's impulse was libido see: Charles Dunster, quoted in Henry John Todd, *The Poetical Works of John Milton*, 5th ed. (London, 1852); Samuel, "*Samson Agonistes* as Tragedy," 249; Arnold Stein, *Heroic Knowledge: An Interpretation of "Paradise Regained" and "Samson Agonistes"* (Minneapolis: University of Minnesota Press, 1957), 178.

in their incompatibility when he acknowledged to her his former romantic love, a love incompatible with the proper functions of marriage and nearer a contemptible *frauendienst*:

> [I] . . . lov'd thee, as too well thou knew'st,
> Too well, unbosom'd all my secrets to thee,
> Not out of levity, but over-powr'd
> By thy request, who could deny thee nothing. . . .
>
> (878-81)

Suppose too that Dalila was "wanton," "not truly penitent," a "sorceress" with a "fair enchanted cup," who by virtue of "feign'd Religion, smooth hypocrisie" was enabled to "cherish . . . hast'n'd widowhood with the gold / Of Matrimonial treason." Samson nevertheless could not overcome her merely because he is right and she is wrong, or because God is with him and against her, or because he is a man and she is a woman. He could overcome her only when he could decisively discover from reasonable criteria what was erroneous in all her wiles and how to meet them.

I earlier showed that within their threefold disputation, Samson countered Dalila's rationalizations with three superior arguments, first of internal logic and consistency in self-judgment, second of objective redefinition of her subjective terms, and third of the application of past experience to a present mood. It will be worthwhile to summarize Samson's personal dialectic in order to see, in light of Milton's views on matrimony, that Samson is not only reasoning to better purpose, he has also brought into harmonious relationship his internal personal dyad, which is symbolized by the external dyad of marriage. On the question of the relationship between freedom and responsibility, Samson has given the decisive internal answer: in a free mind, reason harmonizes the passions and the imagination; no external state of freedom can compensate for the internal chaos and imbalance which arise from passionately pursuing incompatible ends. When the reason in Samson could only fight with his emotions, the chaos of his thoughts tormented him. Moreover, the balance of marriage is not that between a reasonable, active, free man despotically ruling an emotional, passive, dominated woman. Still less is it an uxorious, romantic, yielding man dominated by a masterful, relativistic, sensually aggressive woman. It is the emblem of an integrated state because it freely relates two harmonious beings in a conversation in which their compatibility of mind is reflected in their kindness, spontaneous sexuality, and loving accord. Samson rejects Dalila because he sees what she really is; he is able to see what she really is because he can see what he has been.

Samson defines himself in defining Dalila, and when he does so, discovers that he is at last free.

DEBATE AND INTEGRATION IN ACT IV

To the stable state of apparent settlement achieved in Act III, Act IV supplies plot complication which involves a further dialectic concluding in a perfect synthesis in Samson and a partial synthesis in the Chorus. (It will be the function of the last act to permit the Chorus, and through them the reader, to achieve a synthesis parallel to Samson's.) The complication falls into two parts: Harapha comes to taunt Samson and to threaten him; the Officer comes to summon Samson to Dagon's temple. I will consider them separately before treating them together.

The visit of Harapha is first a provocation. He has come to look at and to measure the limbs of the man of whom so much has been reported. How provocative this is, Samson has already told us when he spoke of his enemies "come to stare . . . to insult, / Thir daily practice." Samson's reply is a riddling invitation to fight—"The way to know were not to see but taste"—which Harapha counters with a professed regret that Samson's blindness debars the taste of battle. In reply to Samson's plainer offer, Harapha feigns disdain. These exchanges are brief and stichomythic, for no points of issue have emerged. But Harapha's disdainful comparison of himself, clean and elegantly armed, with Samson, unwashed, incapable, and blind, prompts Samson to make his own contrast, to compare his type of championship with Harapha's in a fuller description ending in a clear challenge: he "only with an Oak'n staff" will defeat "all thy gorgeous arms." The contempt Samson expresses for the accouterments of chivalric tourney is a contempt for the vanity of all military glory compared with spiritual dedication.

There follows a contest of wills and minds. First, Harapha defends his "glorious arms / Which greatest Heroes have in battel worn" by claiming that Samson fights with magic spells. Samson contradicts him; his strength is not magical, it is God-given. Let Harapha invoke Dagon's aid and he Jehovah's, and in the meeting let the power of their gods be put to test. Samson knows that he is only a man and has no more to hope for in the end than any man, but he serves and trusts the God of Israel. In reply Harapha declares that Samson has been abandoned by his God. Samson denies it, not in terms of his own worth but in terms of the nature of God, "Whose ear is ever open; and his eye / Gracious to re-admit the suppliant." Harapha asserts that no proper god would deign to be championed by a "Murtherer, a Revolter, and a Robber," and he substantiates each charge from the Philistine point of view: Samson is a privateer, a terrorist, and a league-breaker. Samson rejects the imputed criminality and for the third time challenges Harapha. He was not a terrorist, for a conquered nation acts justly when it seeks to free itself ("force with force / Is well ejected when the Conquer'd can"); he was not a privateer "but a person rais'd / With strength sufficient and command from Heav'n"; he was not a league-breaker, for the league was first broken by the hostility of the Philistines "all set on enmity." At the third challenge, Harapha withdraws. The Chorus fears that he has gone to appeal to the Philistine magistrates, but Samson scorns to fear. More important, he knows enough not to fear. His triumph has been by mind and will; he thinks decisively and pithily. Harapha will do no such thing, lest he be maneuvered into an encounter with Samson, which he fears. There is nothing more the Philistines can do against him than they have already done, and if there should be, Samson would willingly face it:

> But come what will, my deadliest foe will prove
> My speediest friend, by death to rid me hence,
> The worst that he can give, to me the best.
> Yet so it may fall out, because thir end
> Is hate, not help to me, it may with mine
> Draw thir own ruin who attempt the deed.
>
> (1262-67)

When the mind is master of itself, threats are of no matter.

The fourth choral stasimon rounds off the scene with exultation and triumphant joy, dancing immortal life just before the onset of death. The Chorus's exhilaration ranges through the sense that God is with Samson either in strong action or in genuine patience, through the acknowledgment that he is free, joyfully free, to their conclusion that his freedom has come through the laboring of his mind, a mind no longer impotent. The dynamics of the scene are a surge upward and forward. Samson devalued himself and felt that all others devalued him; he revalued himself in judging with impartiality his own case and Dalila's. He has been threatened with violence and anger; he has been crossed by Harapha and undervalued again. His present aggressive mood is necessary for the action to come, so that one might say it is fed by the profoundest sources within him of self-preservation. Anger is the natural emotion of the undervalued, threatened man who is invited to undervalue himself again. But Samson has directed his anger into appropriate channels. It is not turned against himself or against the immediate antagonist, Harapha. It is turned against false theatrical heroics, against pride in personal valor, against conflating the physical circumstances of a man with his true inner circumstances. Samson has become tersely indifferent to external pressures: "Or peace or not, alike to me he comes." In the prologue Samson was paranoiac about the approach of his enemies to insult him; he is now indifferent. The integration of the parts of his personality frees him from the necessity of protecting a false public self. He is in isolation, as he was then, but he is not alone: he can hold onto his sense of his own completeness and believe himself related to his God. The way in which he now speaks, so tersely and so honestly, gives the clue to his integration. At the only place where he might be held to speak more than necessary, Samson turns Harapha's provocative words ironically against him. Harapha comes "each limb to survey," and Samson says:

> Cam'st thou for this, vain boaster, to survey me,
> To descant on my strength, and give thy verdit?
> Come nearer, part not hence so slight inform'd;
> But take good heed my hand survey not thee.

(1227-30)

The Chorus contrasts action and patience as alternative courses for man and guesses that Samson will be the patient victor. He is the subject of their thoughts; they do not apply their propositions to themselves. In the event, of course, Samson combines action and patience to the reconciliation of highest fortitude with peace. It is for the Chorus to transfer his tragic and heroic deed into meaning for their own lives. The last act shows them enrolling themselves among those whom "patience finally must crown." All the encounters with external characters symbolize encounters of Samson's own cast of inner personalities. He faced in the Chorus his own self-doubt; in Manoa, his own self-tenderness; in Dalila, his own appetency; and in Harapha, his own aggression. The integrity he achieves is a balance of reason, will, imagination, memory, and the senses.

In the second scene of Act IV, the Officer briefly and peremptorily commands Samson to rise and accompany him to be dressed for a public show of strength to honor Dagon. Samson as briefly refuses on conscientious religious grounds: "Our Law forbids at thir Religious Rites / My presence." Cautioned that his answer "will not content" the Philistine lords, Samson repeats his refusal: let them be entertained by their own "Gymnic Artists." Again warned, "Regard thy self," Samson refuses for the third time and raises himself to the height of his integrity: "My self? my conscience and internal peace." His self *is* his conscience and internal peace, no longer a "moving Grave," not a "second self" oblivious in the love of Dalila. The Officer leaves with Samson's final refusal, saying "I am sorry what this stoutness will produce." Again, Samson prophesies in a terse riddle, "Perhaps thou shalt have cause to sorrow indeed."

The Chorus takes over where the Officer left off. Their burst of joy a few moments earlier gives way to worried caution. They have seen no real future for Samson other than pathetic quiescent submission, as of a broken tool. They believe themselves sensible in warning, "Expect another message more imperious . . . then thou well wilt bear." Samson repeats his refusal to betray God's renewed favor and to prostitute his gift. The Chorus debates that second issue: the gift is already compromised by grinding for the idolatrous Philistines. Samson's answer is again clearly self-evaluative. He uses his strength,

> Not in thir Idol-worship, but by labour
> Honest and lawful to deserve my food
> Of those who have me in thir civil power.
>
> (1365-67)

The Chorus rules that "Where the heart joins not, outward acts defile not," correct enough as a general principle but rejected by Samson because he has not been constrained but only commanded by the Philistines. "If I obey them, / I do it freely; venturing to displease / God for the fear of Man." He concedes, however, that God can waive the prohibition against idolatrous practices: there is no special sanctity in place, and Samson is given freedom from the Law. Now the Chorus feels an absolute dilemma, but during his own speech Samson has penetrated to a further understanding. He has understood that God not only *can* release him from obedience to the Law, He *has* released him. However curtly and abruptly he expresses the *volte face* of his decision to accompany the Officer, the long evolution of Samson's understanding is now complete. He wills death in a different sense and goes willingly to death in a state of mind as far removed as possible from that will to die expressed in his first speech. When the Officer returns, Samson feigns to *him* submission ("Masters commands come with a power resistless") which he really acknowledges to his God, and he pretends to agree with the cyclical view of life the Chorus first expressed in finding him a mirror of man's fickle state: "So mutable are all the ways of men." He takes his leave of the Chorus gently and magnanimously, thoughtful of them in the plangent calmness of all tragic heroes parting from men to meet their destiny—

53

Faustus taking leave of the scholars, Hamlet of Horatio, Oedipus of his children. The final choral stasimon is a blessing on Samson, a benediction weaving together in liturgical cadences the phrases from the Psalmist and Isaiah, culminating in a gradual modulation into the past tense which dismisses him from the earth.

THE TEMPERED PASSIONS

THE MIND IN SICKNESS AND HEALTH

Samson commences his journey toward death, the final short step in the morning's long travail, as an integrated, stable person—a self, a conscience internally at peace. His experiences have been educative. In *Samson Agonistes* Milton casts himself in the role of physician to the soul; the preface to the tragedy makes it clear that he intends Samson's educative experience to be curative to an audience. He perceived the form or structure latent in the action of the play through his own understanding of how the mind acquires knowledge and thinks about experience. His assumptions, buried as well as recognized, led him to discern the patterns in human behavior which patterned the drama. Milton's philosophy of man is not easily distinguished into branches of understanding which resemble modern branches or comprise subordinate disciplines. It is easier to discover and describe what Milton thought about—for example, dreams, laughter, fantasy, or sin—than it is to discern a method of classification which would incorporate dreams and laughter into psychology, fantasy into epistemology, or sin into ethics, and subsume them all into natural and moral philosophy. That he was a poet and not a scientist or philosopher means that it would be unwise to detach what he thought from how he expressed thought. Only a madman would prefer to snip up Milton's works into isolated concepts and convert those into another design by rearranging them in a pattern of universal knowledge. A literary critic can only attend to the design Milton himself made.

There is something else, however, that in my view is worth attempting. Nothing more steadily informed Milton's work than his conviction that a human being has a mind with which to come to terms with experience. In the subsequent chapters of this book I propose to bring to bear on *Samson Agonistes* a series of particular Miltonic convictions: That the actions of individuals throughout history can be rationally examined to yield design (Part Two). That the behavior of social groups at any point within history likewise can be examined rationally to reveal pattern (Part Three). That the activity of individuals in large or small relationships is susceptible to human judgment (Part

Four). That men are related to a cosmic force discernible by the mind. And finally, that men can present in art what they learn from life in such a way as to affect life itself (Part Five). Milton thinks rationally within his poetry about history, politics, ethics, theology, and aesthetics. What, then, did Milton consider thinking itself to be, how did he conceive of the mind as actually working? If we are right in discerning that something has happened to Samson's mind by the end of Act IV, something which is meant to happen to the Chorus's mind in Act V and to the whole audience through Samson and the Chorus, how did Milton believe the mind could be affected by experience and by art?

Simply put, Milton thought that the human mind is a corporeal, rational entity in itself, "its own place," where mental pictures are "seen" and mental voices "heard," into which "evil / May come and go, so unapproved, and leave / No spot or blame behind." Its special activity is "reasoning" with data it receives as "imaging" or "imagining."[1] The mind is housed in a body with which it has a reciprocal relationship; disorder in one affects the other. The bodily forces which can distemper the mind are the four humors; the mental forces which can disease the body are the passions and appetites of the various faculties. When Eve dreamed her "uncouth dream," Adam briefly expounded to her the psychology with which Milton's encyclopedic reading had supplied him:[2]

> But know that in the Soule
> Are many lesser Faculties that serve
> Reason as chief; among these Fansie next
> Her office holds; of all external things,
> Which the five watchful Senses represent,
> She forms Imagination, Aerie shapes,
> Which Reason joyning or disjoyning, frames
> All what we affirm or what deny, and call
> Our knowledge or opinion.
>
> (*Paradise Lost*, V, 100-108)

In cataloging the faculties of the mind, Adam mentioned the faculty of memory, only indirectly in alluding to the fancy in dreams misjoining the data of the senses with "words and deeds long past or late." Otherwise, the process of knowing described by Adam was the common stock of all Renaissance thinkers. Eve was not diseased; Adam

[1] See A. W. Levi, *Literature, Philosophy and the Imagination* (Bloomington: Indiana University Press, 1962), 101.

[2] The fullest discussion of Milton's psychology of dreams is that of Kester Svendsen, *Milton and Science* (Cambridge, Mass.: Harvard University Press, 1956), 36-38, 182-83.

described the normal functioning of the clear mind. He called it "Soule," but there is no indication anywhere in Milton that spirit and mind or that soul and mind are terms to be distinguished. Milton was a materialist whose readings in Scripture and the encyclopedists convinced him that every created being within time and space is entirely composed of matter. "Man is a living being, intrinsically and properly one and individual. He is not double or separable; not, as is commonly thought produced from and composed of two different and distinct elements, soul and body. On the contrary, the whole man is the soul, and the soul the man: a body, in other words, or individual substance, animal, sensitive and rational."[3]

Man has his own special place on the "scale of Nature" relating upper and lower creatures. Yet a diagram which places man on a rung of the ladder does not do much to clarify the way in which Milton related inner and outer forces, even though Raphael resorted to the ladder or tree of life when he instructed Adam in how to think. Adam declared himself satisfied, but he varied the metaphor more illuminatingly:

> Well hast thou taught the way that might direct
> Our knowledge, and the scale of Nature set
> From center to circumference, whereon
> In contemplation of created things
> By steps we may ascend to God.
>
> (*Paradise Lost*, v, 508-12)

What is needed is not so much a ladder as a Venn diagram to encompass all orders of creation in a spherical form.[4]

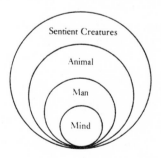

---

[3] *De Doctrina Christiana*, in *CPW*, VI, 318. See Denis Saurat, *Milton, Man and Thinker* (Hamden: Archon Books, 1964), 116-18. See also Lawrence Babb, *The Moral Cosmos of "Paradise Lost"* (East Lansing: Michigan State University Press, 1970), 40-44, and Svendsen, *Milton and Science*, 192-93.

[4] For the suggestion that Milton's epistemology might be described best in a Venn diagram, I am indebted to Brian Weiss, with whom I have discussed Milton's *Art of Logic* to my great profit.

Milton did not take the theological step of coalescing the scale with the circle as, for example, Nicholas of Cusa did, to identify God as the center and circumference of being, the absolute maximum and the absolute minimum, the *coincidentia oppositorum*. That kind of dialectic seemed to him "endless mazes." As a materialist-sensationalist, Milton envisaged thought as occurring when the senses receive impressions (representations) from external objects, convey these impressions to the imagination, or fancy, which in turn perceives the representations and sorts them into such distinctions as similitudes and dissimilitudes. The mind takes those imagings into either the place of reason or the cell of memory; from the cell of memory they can be recalled to the place of reason. (They enter memory by the aid of reason in so far as reason may use a mnemonic logic such as Ramist logic in their storage and their retrieval.) Reason then operates upon the images of fancy or memory so as to inform the will how to act.

Thus far, reason is seen as relating outer stimuli to inner activity. But to reason, Raphael told Adam, is a dual process. The oneness of all life is retained in Raphael's image, within a total theory of knowledge which distinguishes animal, human, and angelic modes of perception, so that every stage contains its own proper function, subsumes a lower stage of functioning, and projects a higher stage to which it sometimes attains.

> So from the root
> Springs lighter the green stalk, from thence the leaves
> More aerie, last the bright consummate floure
> Spirits odorous breathes: flours and thir fruit
> Mans nourishment, by gradual scale sublim'd
> To vital Spirits aspire, to animal,
> To intellectual, give both life and sense,
> Fansie and understanding, whence the soule
> Reason receives, and reason is her being,
> Discursive, or Intuitive; discourse
> Is oftest yours, the latter most is ours,
> Differing but in degree, of kind the same.
>
> (*Paradise Lost*, v, 479-90)

It is possible, therefore, for ideas to be innate and implanted in man, not received through the senses only, but already resident in the mind by intuition. God, as the Savior rebukingly teaches Satan, "sends his Spirit of Truth henceforth to dwell / In pious Hearts, an inward Oracle / To all truth requisite for men to know" (*Paradise Regained*, i, 462-64).

Before the Fall "man was made in the image of God, and the whole law of nature was so implanted and innate in him that he was in need of no command." With the Fall came "the loss or at least the extensive darkening of that right reason, whose function it was to discern the chief good, and which was, as it were, the life of the understanding," although "some traces" remained "in our intellect," as the "wisdom in both word and deed of many of the heathens" shows.[5] But at the moment of the Fall, God "bestows grace on all . . . sufficient to enable everyone to attain knowledge of the truth and salvation." The "mind and will of the natural man are partially renewed and divinely moved towards knowledge of God" when He "restores man's natural faculties of faultless understanding."[6] Discursive reason is "natural logic . . . the very faculty of reason in the mind of man." "It attaches to itself," Milton explained, "four helpers: Sense, observation, induction and experience."[7] Intuitive reason is immediate perception which uses no faculties other than intelligence or reason itself and which relates lower and higher phenomena in the mind. By intuition men discern something in their relationship to each other or to God, but not to external reality. The two modes of reason are complementary and not antithetical. Men normally think discursively, putting together evidence in a logical train of thought and drawing conclusions; but they sometimes know by insight. They characteristically use insight to derive new bases for further discursive thought. Thus Christ at the beginning of *Paradise Regained* first intuitively *knows* and then *thinks*:

> And now by some strong motion I am led
> Into this wilderness, to what intent
> I learn not yet, perhaps I need not know;
> For what concerns my knowledge God reveals.

> (1, 290-93)

And finally, reason delivers judgment to the will.

The will is the part of the rational mind which bridges knowledge and action, its function being volition or choice. Reason forms ideas, opinions, convictions, conclusions; when it concludes that this or that action is good or evil, the will desires the good course, hates the evil, and instructs the body to perform or to shun accordingly. The reasonable will commands the passions. The terminology Milton used makes it clear that he regarded reason and will as twin faculties of mind, and understanding and choice as twin faculties of reason. Ideally, all are in perfect balance: "vertue . . . is reason" (*Paradise Lost*, XII, 98); "Reason . . . is choice" (*ibid.*, III, 108); and "Reason is but choosing" (*Areopagi-*

---

[5] *CPW*, VI, 353, 395, 396, 192. [6] *Ibid.*, 192, 457.
[7] *Art of Logic, Columbia Milton*, XI, 11.

tica). Actions cannot be autonomous or instinctive in a rational being; a man must know in order to will and will in order to act. From Milton's point of view it is absurd to argue, as Samuel Johnson first did and as Stanley Fish recently has, that *Samson Agonistes* has no middle because Samson knows and then acts, with no relation between the two conditions. Samson cannot act until he knows. The question properly put is how and when do we know that he knows. Since knowing is both a matter of discursive and intuitive reason, Milton can comfortably speak of "a double scripture . . . the external scripture of the written word and the internal scripture of the Holy Spirit . . . engraved upon the hearts of believers." He can also speak of a double light. Good conscience (or knowledge) in man therefore "consists . . . of an intellectual judgment of one's own deeds, and an approval of them which is directed by the light either of nature or of grace."[8]

Thus far we have been describing the operations of a mind in a healthy state. "Right reason in self-government and self-control" involves "the control of one's own inner affections . . . love, hate; joy, sadness; hope, and fear and anger."[9] These affections, or appetites, are the same as passions; they exist as pairs requiring temperance. Together they constitute the materials to be ordered by reason, and they are all necessary, not only for the preservation of life itself, but for the creation of virtue. A man does not become virtuous by extirpating his passions but by balancing them: "Wherefore did [God] creat passions within us, pleasures round about us, but that these rightly temper'd are the very ingredients of virtue."[10] But when passions overwhelm reason, man falls from good into evil:

> Reason in man obscur'd, or not obeyd,
> Immediately inordinate desires
> And upstart Passions catch the Government
> From Reason, and to servitude reduce
> Man till then free.
>
> (*Paradise Lost*, XII, 86-90)

The state of being fallen Milton therefore described as a mental storm:

> high Passions, Anger, Hate,
> Mistrust, Suspicion, Discord, . . . shook sore
> Thir inward State of Mind, calme Region once.
>
> (IX, 1123-25)

At the beginning of *Samson Agonistes*, Samson is clearly diseased and incapable of harmonious reasoning. His body-mind balance is

[8] *CPW*, VI, 582, 653. [9] *Ibid.*, 720. [10] *Ibid.*, II, 527.

overturned. He is ill in all parts. The drama enacts his restoration to health.[11] It repairs his ruin of mind by exercising it. When he is cured, he becomes a rational man who thinks and acts in conformity to reason. The course of the play is designed around stages of recognition. We have already noted the points of decisive change in the mind of Samson and the response of the Chorus:

Samson	Chorus
Act I (I know) "My self . . . a moving Grave"	Our human "state" is "fickle"
II "The base degree to which I now am fall'n . . . is not yet so base as was my former servitude"	"Just or unjust, alike seem miserable"
III "This Gaol I count the house of Liberty"	"Vertue which breaks through all opposition . . . most shines"
IV I am "My self, my conscience and internal peace"	After a "Labouring [of] mind," "the Holy One of *Israel*" is our "guide"

When Samson leaves the stage, he goes to do what his will directs in obedience to his reason.

The last act reports what Samson's action was and how it occurred. Buried in the description are phrases indicative of the mental clarity with which positive action was accomplished. "He patient but undaunted . . . perform'd . . . with incredible . . . force. . . . At length . . . with head a while enclin'd . . . he stood, as one who pray'd, / Or some great matter in his mind revolv'd":

> At last with head erect thus cryed aloud,
> Hitherto, Lords, what your commands impos'd
> I have perform'd, as reason was, obeying,
> Not without wonder or delight beheld.
> Now of my own accord such other tryal
> I mean to shew you of my strength, yet greater;
> As with amaze shall strike all who behold.
>
> (1639-45)

"Patient"; "in his mind revolv'd"; "head erect"; "as reason was, obeying"; "my own accord"; "shew you"; "amaze . . . all who behold"—

[11] For comments on disease imagery, medical imagery, and purgative imagery in the play see: Cox, "Natural Science and Figurative Design in *Samson Agonistes*"; Georgia Christopher, "Homeopathic Physic and Natural Renovation in *Samson Agonistes*," *ELH*, 37 (1970), 316ff.; and John Arthos, "Milton and the Passions: A Study of *Samson Agonistes*," *Modern Philology*, 69 (1972), 209ff.

the Chorus is struck with its own appropriate exalted amazement. They understand that God in destroying the Philistines "hurt thir minds"; they were "Insensate left, or to sense reprobate / And with blindness internal struck." Samson in contradistinction, "with inward eyes illuminated," acted "when most unactive deem'd." While the Philistines were irrational and discordant, willing the evil course with unbalanced passion, Samson thought and acted appropriately, having rebalanced the forces of his soul. He began the drama by willing his death, but ended it by dying willingly; he began by lamenting his blindness, but ended by discovering vision in darkness; he began in isolation and alienation, but ended in self-sacrifice with "God not parted from him"; he began as a shame to himself and his nation, but ended in dignity, having returned to "himself and his Fathers house eternal fame." These truths about Samson's life and death seem at first glance to be pure changes from one state into an antithetical state. Looked at more carefully, they all take the form of *both a and b*, rather than the form of *not a but b*. Synthesis and tempering, the knowledge of good through the experience of good and evil, this is the meaning for Samson of the laboring of his mind, to have arrived at the place where antitheses are resolved.

THERAPEUTIC EFFECT UPON THE BYSTANDERS IN ACT V

The last act goes beyond Samson's personal synthesis. It attempts the education of the Chorus and of the audience through the Chorus. Recent reevaluations of the role of the Chorus in this drama abound.[12] The Chorus plays several roles, of course, and it is important to remember that Milton as an artist positively denied that any single char-

---

[12] See for example John Huntley, "A Reevaluation of the Chorus' Role in Milton's *Samson Agonistes*," *Modern Philology*, 63 (1966), 132-45, for the view that the Chorus represents the insensate mass; they begin in darkness and end scarcely beginning to see the light. John T. Shawcross, "Irony as Tragic Effect: *Samson Agonistes* and the Tragedy of Hope," in *Calm of Mind*, ed. Wittreich, 289-305, argues that the Chorus understands that they are to hope when they should understand that hope is the final delusion. Louis L. Martz, "Chorus and Character in *Samson Agonistes*," *Milton Studies*, 2 (1970), 115-34, suggests that the flatly prosing Chorus is meant to contrast with the heroic Samson. Northrop Frye, "Agon and Logos," in *The Prison and the Pinnacle*, ed. Balachandra Rajan (London: Routledge & Kegan Paul, 1975), updates the view that, like Job's friends, the Chorus represents the moral norm but is carried along uncomprehendingly and swept almost unconsciously at the end into eloquence. The best of the reevaluations are those by Jon S. Lawry, *Shadow of Heaven*, where *methexis*, or "participative enactment," gives the Chorus the character both of actor and audience, and by Anthony Low, *Blaze of Noon*, where the Chorus's "new acquist" of experience is carefully examined (pp. 118-35).

acter in a work of art should be regarded as the artist speaking in his own person: in none of the Chorus's roles is the Chorus John Milton. Most of the reevaluations have in common the desire to prevent the reader from making the mistake of taking the Chorus to be Milton's special spokesman. In the context of the educational dialectic in which we have been placing *Samson Agonistes*, the role of the Chorus seems to be especially important in two ways: by remaining onstage to narrate the achievement of Samson's harmony of soul, the Chorus functions as spectator and so, vicariously, as the audience; by attempting to reason upon that spectacle in order to bring their own dialectic of comprehension to a close, the Chorus functions as a reasoning actor and thus as a model for the audience. The first role we have just described. The second role runs through a series of tentative propositions, résumés of earlier stages of understanding, to come to a clear new understanding.

The actual narrative of the Chorus's stages of comprehension begins with their commonsensical misapplied reasonings. Manoa declares that he will bankrupt himself to ransom Samson. His words are interrupted by a shout from offstage. The Chorus simply notes that Manoa and Samson have changed roles in life: fathers budget for sons in the normal event and sons nurse fathers, but Manoa will spend for a son and care for him. The Chorus has easily relapsed into discounting Samson's manhood and individuality, disregarding Manoa's presumptuousness. The effect on Manoa is to flatter him into greater self-flattery: he anticipates a future miracle in which "I perswade me" God will restore Samson's sight. The Chorus complacently and kindly shares his "not ill founded nor vain" hopes, and Manoa acknowledges their sympathy ("I know your friendly minds"). All this is dramatic irony, for a second, more terrible shout interrupts their cheerful mutuality. Nonetheless, Milton has reestablished the Chorus's concern for Samson as one of themselves. When they unheroically and prudently agree not to investigate the noise, "lest running thither / We *unawares* run into dangers mouth," they limit themselves to quick questions and answers among themselves and Manoa, all concerning "fear," "thought," the "incredible," "know, but doubt to think," "tempts Belief."

Into their conjectures the Messenger comes to deliver his account of Samson's last deed. The Chorus's first assessment is that this action was "dearly-bought revenge . . . tangl'd in the fold / Of dire necessity." To this, the first semichorus adds the cosmic note of *dies irae*, "mortal men / Fall'n into wrath divine." The second semichorus contributes the further perception that "vertue giv'n for lost . . . revives," an understanding which corresponds to their earlier discovery that virtue which breaks through opposition most shines above. Manoa adds a fourth stage of insight, including the earlier stages of the Chorus, not simply abolishing their partial insights, but correcting their emphasis, when he raises the question of what action is appropriate for those remaining alive. Thus he notes: "*Samson* hath quit himself. . . . Fully reveng'd" (first stage); "God . . . assisting to the end" (second); and "nothing [here] but what may quiet us in a death so noble" (third). He goes on to resolve, "let us go find the body . . . wash off the clotted gore . . . build him a Monument" (fourth). The Chorus concluded the kommos entirely in the final sense—accepting divine justice, accepting the bleak tragic truth that justice to humanity is paid for by individual suffering.

The final chorus works upon us all, in substructures of pronouns and verbs, in a firm, rational, brief *nunc dimittis*:

> All is best, though we oft doubt,
> What th' unsearchable dispose
> Of highest wisdom brings about,
> And ever best found in the close.
> Oft he seems to hide his face,
> But unexpectedly returns
> And to his faithful Champion hath in place
> Bore witness gloriously; whence *Gaza* mourns
> And all that band them to resist
> His uncontroulable intent,
> His servants he with new acquist
> Of true experience from this great event
> With peace and consolation hath dismist,
> And calm of mind all passion spent.
>
> (1745-58)

The pronouns progress from "we," to "he" (God), to "his faithful Champion" (Samson), to "them" and "all that . . . resist His intent," to *us* again—seen now not subjectively, but objectively as "His servants" dismissed from the experience "with new acquist / Of true experience." The verbs progress from "doubt" to "seems" to "but returns" to "bore witness" to "hath dismist . . . spent," a movement outward into consent and faith. The catharsis of the Chorus, all passion spent, consists in their syncresis. Like Samson and through Samson, they have been educated by God; like Samson and through Samson, like the Chorus and through the Chorus, the reader is so "dismist." The kommos traces a curve from erroneous thought, to unconscious understanding, through personal denial, to objective and impersonal affirmation. Holding the pronouns and verbs together in the rhyming octosyllabic sonnet form of the kommos are two ringing nouns, *dispose* in the octave and *intent* in the sestet. Milton has governed the "oeconomy or disposition of the fable" to assert the justice of the *dispose* of human life, under the *intent* of the tragic poet to figure forth the educative meaning in man's life. The sestet turns finally and decisively away from the past and toward the future to embrace all who might "resist" and, in the emphasis of the rhymes at the line ends, to declare that the "intent" is the "new acquist" of knowledge from a great "event" from which mankind is "dismist" with passion "spent." The preface promised of tragedy that it could "by raising pity and fear . . . purge the mind of those and such like passions—that is, *to temper and reduce them* to just measure." In that sense also the chorus concludes.

In the Seventh Prolusion, Milton, then a gifted undergraduate, extolled the learned human mind, or reason, as the faculty without which there could be no virtue, rather than the human will, which "shines with a borrowed light, even as the moon does."[13] As an experienced schoolmaster Milton indicated in *Of Education* that education could "repair the ruins of our first parents," to fit a man "to perform justly skilfully and magnanimously all the offices both private and publike of peace and war," his right knowledge issuing in right action.[14] In *Aeropagitica* Milton described both the process of acquiring truth and the truth so acquired in dialectical terms. Since the Fall, man has learned to "unite the dessever'd peeces" of truth by "imitating the careful search that Isis made for the mangl'd body of Osiris . . . gathering up limb by limb." "To be still searching what we know not, by what we know still closing up truth to truth as we find it" is the dialectical process Milton metaphorically likened to wrestling and physical exercise: "Knowledge thrives by exercise, as well as our limbs and complexions." Men are "purified by trial"; "the knowledge and survey of vice is necessary to the constituting of human virtue." The value of experience is that through it knowledge accrues when reason is exercised dialectically and man then acts upon his knowledge. Milton was not attracted to pure meditation and was skeptical of the claims of the indifferent stoic, the "Philosophic pride . . . call'd vertue" of "contemning all / Wealth, pleasure, pain or torment, death and life" (*Paradise Regained*, IV, 300-305). Milton over and over cited the experience of art as preeminently suited to the dialectical attainment of knowledge. *Samson Agonistes* achieves its dialectical effect at its close in the minds of the Chorus and in the audience. It has done so by structurally embodying the very principle of intellectual contest which it suggests is the lesson of the tragic human life, prepared for the edification and tempering of men. The tragedy recommends tempering by imitating dialectic to show why God takes the way he does to secure good in the world. Milton has put on the imagined theater of his page an imita-

[13] *CPW*, I, 293.   [14] *Ibid.*, 549.

tion of the working of the theater of the mind, for God has prepared the theater of the world to teach this lesson: "to govern the inner man, the nobler part." Attaining perfect balance is heroic; it is glory attained "without ambition, war, or violence, / By deeds of peace, by wisdom eminent, / By patience, temperance." Through the example of the blind giant, Milton teaches the balanced well-tried man that "who best / Can suffer, best can do."

The structure of *Samson Agonistes* is, therefore, not episodic but fully complex, or intricate, according to the clearest preferred Aristotelian models. It is full of recognitions and reversals. It apparently issues in the double catastrophe which Aristotle disdained, good to the good and evil to the evil. In fact, however, the disputations do not end with a simple victory of one side over the other; they turn always toward synthesis. From "Sun or shade" to "blind of sight . . . With inward eyes illuminated," from "some great act, or of my days the last" to "victorious / Among thy slain self-kill'd"; blind or seeing, light or dark, life or death, patience or action, the fool or the champion— at the close of the play the antinomies are all resolved in synthesis, synthesis and apparent stasis. But the whole drama has shown us what calm of mind means. The development in Milton's understanding of God's "wayes . . . to men" between his last drama, *Samson Agonistes*, and his first, *Comus*, is very great. The masque concludes:

> Or if Vertue feeble were,
> Heav'n it self would stoop to her.

But perhaps the difference is not so very great after all, for *Samson Agonistes* indicates the way in which Heaven stoops—by putting virtue through just that inward dialectic and outward struggle which gives value to integration, dignity to temperance, and peace to conscience. One may not be convinced by Samson's assurance of a cosmic design, yet one cannot but recognize the validity of Milton's imitation of a heroic mind battling with itself and achieving true integration.

Each his own Deliverer

II

SAMSON AGONISTES AND MILTON'S CONCEPTION OF HISTORY

Introduction

Samson Agonistes contains a reading of contemporary events within the framework of Milton's understanding of history. That understanding evolved throughout his life. At each stage of its evolution Milton used the figure of Samson to make a political point connected with his reading of history. Each change was an attempt to understand how human action fitted into divine providence. Finally, in *Samson Agonistes* Milton directly wrestled with the challenge to a providential view of history presented by the failure of the Commonwealth, and he justified God's ways by means of the concept of patience conceived of as what history is meant to teach. Milton did not "doubt, / What th' unsearchable dispose / Of highest wisdom brings about," because in the poetic drama he could show how the Elect themselves had frustrated their election without frustrating God's plan for them. The New Jerusalem they had lost might be retrieved if as individuals they developed a freedom and composure within themselves; though they would not then be delivered from external tyranny by an irresistible movement, each would become his own deliverer into a state of individual liberty from which all could go forward to a new consensus.

Milton had many precedents for his treatment of providential history in the prose works and even in *Paradise Lost* and *Paradise Regained*,[1] but he had no precedents for his treatment of history as Christian tragedy. He continuously strove to understand the events and conditions of his time; his prose works, his epic, and his brief epic reflect his own and the collective reactions of his generation and of his party. As at certain moments in history one man, one great poet, may

[1] See C. A. Patrides, *The Grand Design of God: The Literary Form of the Christian View of History* (London: Routledge & Kegan Paul, 1972), 84-90; William Haller, *Foxe's Book of Martyrs and the Elect Nation* (London: Jonathan Cape, 1963), 238-45; H. R. MacCallum, "Milton and Sacred History," in *Essays . . . Presented to A.S.P. Woodhouse*, ed. M. Maclure and F. W. Watt (Toronto: University of Toronto Press, 1964), 149-68; Mary Ann Radzinowicz, " 'Man as a Probationer of Immortality,' " in *Approaches to "Paradise Lost,"* ed. C. A. Patrides (London: Edward Arnold, 1968), 31-51; Merritt Y. Hughes, "Milton's Treatment of Reformation History in *The Tenure of Kings and Magistrates*," in Hughes, *Ten Perspectives on Milton* (New Haven: Yale University Press, 1965); Michael Langdon, "John Milton's *History of Britain*: Its Place in English Historiography," *University of Mississippi Studies in English*, 6 (1965), 59-76; Irene Samuel, "Milton and the Ancients on the Writing of History," *Milton Studies*, 2 (1970), 131-48; Michael Fixler, *Milton and the Kingdoms of God* (London: Faber and Faber, 1964); and Barbara Lewalski, "Time and History in *Paradise Regained*," in *The Prison and the Pinnacle*, ed. Rajan, 49-81.

see farther than his generation, Milton in *Samson Agonistes* undertook to be a prophet to his times as well as a historian of them. *Samson Agonistes*, rooted in Milton's understanding of history, goes beyond the reflection of public tragedy to the diagnosis of national failure and the prophecy of the conditions necessary for a successful republic.

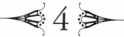

GOD'S DESIGN IN HUMAN HISTORY,
THE RECORD OF THE PAST

MILTON, the young Puritan humanist, saw and reconciled in history patterns both of classical and biblical cast. In response to the events of his own times, his conception of the meaning of history developed through three stages in his prose works and a fourth stage in his epics before he achieved the final synthesis of divine providence, historical pattern, and contemporary events underlying *Samson Agonistes*.

HISTORY AND CHURCH REFORMATION

In his first printed work, Milton came before the people of England as an accomplished historian. The opening sentence of *Of Reformation in England* enunciates the first stage of his vision of history:

> Amidst those deepe and retired thoughts, which with every man Christianly instructed, ought to be most frequent, of *God*, and of his miraculous *ways*, and *works*, amongst men, and of our *Religion* and Worship, to be perform'd to him; after the story of our Saviour Christ . . . I do not know of any thing more worthy to take up the whole passion of pitty, on the one side, and joy on the other: then to consider first, the foule and sudden corruption, and then after many a tedious age, the long-deferr'd, but much more wonderfull and happy reformation of the Church in these latter days.[1]

From retired thoughts about God's ways amongst men—begun at Cambridge and continued at Horton—Milton commenced writing history so as to reveal the continuous presence of God and His special appearance to Englishmen. The classical view he had been taught at school and university was that history is a storehouse of exemplary deeds, in Cicero's formulation, *testis temporum, lux veritatis, vita memoriae, magistra vitae, nuntia vetustatis*.[2] The Christian view, the corner-

---

[1] *CPW*, I, 519.

[2] See Herschel Baker, *The Race of Time: Three Lectures on Renaissance Historiography* (Toronto: University of Toronto Press, 1967) 45-70; Douglas Bush,

stone of biblical exegesis delivered from every Puritan pulpit, added that history progressively reveals God's providence to men through types prefiguring the future.[3] As a boy Milton had loved the "grave Orators and Historians"; as an undergraduate he had praised history for enabling man "to be coeval with time itself" and "wrest from grudging Fate a kind of retrospective immortality"; and as a graduate he had withdrawn to Horton to be "occupied for a long time . . . by history."[4] The first fruits of that research was the view of history contained in *Of Reformation.*

To explain the contrast between the spirit of primitive Christianity and the present corruption of the Church of England, Milton analyzed the forces in English history which had impeded true reformation, "the cawses that hitherto have hindered it." He looked back to the beginning of time; he looked forward to a new beginning; and he characterized the interval as marked by a cyclical "back-sliding" and "stumbling forward." Mankind had been "plodding in the old road," there had been a "sensible decay," a descent "farre lower," "which led the good men into fraud and error." The role of the historian was to prepare a documented narrative of repeated mutation in human affairs.[5] God required only "godliness" of a people, and from that "true florishing of a Land, other things follow as the shadow does the substance." But "if we survey the Story" and see "the shape of our deare Mother England . . . in a mourning weed, with ashes upon her head," then we would agree that "had God beene so minded hee could have sent a Spirit of *Mutiny* amongst us . . . to have made our Funerals." Instead, "when wee least deserv'd," God "sent out a gentle gale, and message of peace."[6] The Christian historian grafted to the recital of recurrent failure the special message of God's presence to redeem history. Permeating the cycle was the apocalyptic promise: "O how much more glorious will those former Deliverances appeare, when we shall know them not onely to have sav'd us from greatest miseries past, but to have reserv'd us for greatest happinesse to come."[7] The most painful question Milton put in *Of Reformation* was how "it should come to passe that England (having had this *grace* and *honour* from GOD to bee the first that should set up a Standard for the recovery of

English Literature in the Earlier Seventeenth Century (Oxford: Clarendon Press, 1962), 209; Harris Francis Fletcher, *The Intellectual Development of John Milton* (Urbana: University of Illinois Press, 1961), II, 322-36.

[3] See Patrides, *Grand Design of God, passim.*

[4] *An Apology for Smectymnuus, CPW,* I, 889; Prolusion VIII, *ibid.,* 297; Milton to Charles Diodati, 1637, *ibid.,* 327.

[5] *Of Reformation, CPW,* I, 520, 524, 540, 545.

[6] *Ibid.,* 571, 585, 596.   [7] *Ibid.,* 615.

lost Truth, and blow the first *Evangelick Trumpet* to the Nations . . .)
should now be last, and most unsettl'd in the enjoyment of the Peace
whereof she taught the way to others."[8] The answer was to affirm
England's special role in God's large design for mankind. The tract's
eloquent concluding prayer summarizes the course of English history
leading to the redemptive present: for the first thousand years the
nation suffered "the impetuous rage of five bloody Inundations"; then
came "intestine warre" in the fifteenth century; with the Tudors, God
"did pitty the sad and ceasles revolution" and did "motion Peace, and
termes of Cov'nant with us." At last, in Milton's time, England was
ready for Millennium.

Milton's conception of history in *Of Reformation* underlies all the
antiprelatical tracts. *The Reason of Church Government,* the fourth
and richest of the five pamphlets and the first one Milton signed, makes
the clearest statement of *how* God covenanted with England to bring
about the perfection of the Reformation. God asked of England one
change, simply a change in the institutions governing the nation. The
tract turns naturally from apocalyptic history to a study of the
scriptural grounds for a church discipline which would promote the
approach of the Kingdom of God. Since "he that hath read with judge-
ment, of Nations and Commonwealths . . . will readily agree that the
flourishing and decaying of all civill societies, all the moments and
turnings of humane occasions are mov'd to and fro as upon the axle of
discipline"—since, that is, the historian considering the cycles of states
will be aware that states rise or fall as they accept or reject discipline—
The Reason of Church Government debates the one true discipline of
the central institution, the church. God has inclined the nation toward
ecclesiastical reform as the sole prerequisite for the stabilizing of a holy
community. The preface sets forth Milton's purpose, to trace from
Scripture the perfect model for church discipline, but the tract itself
argues against prelacy less by reference to Scripture than by reference
to the increasing enlightenment of all men in his nation, that is, by
reference to contemporary history. Christian liberty has increased
greatly in this era, the reasoning runs. Men were children under the
law; under the Gospel they are God's adopted sons, "all sons in obedi-
ence, not in servility."[9] Prelacy cannot conform to God's plan because
it denies the progressive liberation of all believers by forbidding them a
place in the government of the church, which "ought to be free and
open to any Christian man though never so laick, if his capacity, his
faith, and prudent demeanour commend him."[10] Allied arguments for

[8] *Ibid.,* 525-26.
[9] *Reason of Church Government, CPW,* I, 848.
[10] *Ibid.,* 844.

free inquiry, toleration of sects, and persuasion as the only means of securing conformity are all evidence of the optimism of the work. That optimism is grounded in a conviction that the average Englishman is a worthy part of an elect nation with whom God has covenanted: if God's Englishmen reform the Church, He will ensure their social and political stability until the Millennium, when Christ will reign on earth.

In this tract Milton spoke of himself, of his poetic plans, and of Samson. At the end of *Of Reformation*, envisaging all England rising triumphantly to fulfill God's promise, Milton had noted: "Then amidst the *Hymns*, and *Halleluiahs* of *Saints* some one may perhaps bee heard offering at high *strains* in new and lofty *Measures* to sing and celebrate thy *divine Mercies* and *marvelous Judgements* in this Land through all AGES."[11] In *The Reason of Church Government* he asserted the equal responsibility of all who have knowledge to teach and all who have eloquence to write. He began the second book by considering, as each man must, "in what manner he shall best dispose and employ those summes of knowledge and illumination, which God hath sent him into this world to trade with."[12] He predicted his use of his own "one great talent": since his aim was "to be an interpreter and relater of the best and sagest things among mine own Citizens throughout this Iland in the mother dialect," he weighed whether the genre of drama might not be "doctrinal and exemplary to a Nation." Arguing an anti-prelatism which persistently slipped toward total secular individualism, Milton derived from the priesthood of all believers joined to England's special role in history the conviction that "then would the congregation of the Lord soon recover the true likenesse and visage of what she is indeed, a holy generation, a royall Priesthood, a Saintly communion, the household and City of God." To strike away prelacy is to prepare for the irresistible consensus of holy community; it is prelacy which prevents Millennium.

Late in the tract Milton made his first use of the story of Samson:

I cannot better liken the state and person of a King then to that mighty Nazarite *Samson*; who being disciplin'd from his birth in the precepts and the practices of Temperance and Sobriety, without the strong drink of injurious and excessive desires, grows up to a noble strength and perfection with those his illustrious and sunny locks the laws waving and curling about his godlike shoulders. And while he keeps them about him undiminisht and unshorn, he may with the jaw-bone of an Asse,

11 *CPW*, I, 616. Arthur Barker was right to see that "the enthusiastic belief that the completion of England's reformation would bring with it the long-sought release of his poetical powers swept Milton into the ecclesiastical controversy" (*Milton and the Puritan Dilemma*, 17).

12 *CPW*, I, 801.

that is, with the word of his meanest officer suppresse and put to confusion thousands of those that rise against his just power. But laying down his head among the strumpet flatteries of Prelats, while he sleeps and thinks no harme, they wickedly shaving off all those bright and weighty tresses of his laws, and just prerogatives which were his ornament and strength, deliver him over to indirect and violent counsels, which as those Philistines put out the fair, and farre-sighted eyes of his natural discerning, and make him grinde in the prison house of their sinister ends and practices upon him. Till he knowing his prelatical rasor to have bereft him of his wonted might, nourish again his puissant hair, the golden beames of Law and Right; and they sternly shook, thunder with ruin upon the heads of those his evil counsellers, but not without great affliction to himselfe.[13]

As a historian Milton presented the imminent conclusion to the providentially governed cycles of time as arising from reformation, from institutional adjustments aimed at freedom of conscience, and not from revolution, deposition of the king, or any such upheaval. In the same tract, as an orator-historian he allegorized the story of Samson as a type of the just king who could, if shorn of his proper dependence upon national lawfulness, be reduced to a catspaw for a false church discipline until such time as he would have to reassert legal rule at heavy cost. And in the same tract, as a poet Milton promised to write drama exemplary to the elect nation.

HISTORY AND REVOLUTION

Between the antiprelatical tracts and *Areopagitica*, Milton was church-outed a second time, this time by Presbyterian reception of his divorce tracts.[14] He could no longer look to presbyterianism for the realization of his millenarian hopes.[15] His confidence in how history should be read remained unchanged: God had covenanted with the elect nation and would redeem history in Milton's time. What had changed was Milton's understanding of the means to be used. He had became convinced, as he put it retrospectively in "On the new forcers of Conscience under the Long PARLIAMENT," that "*New Presbyter* is but *Old Priest* writ Large." Nevertheless, he still read history apocalyptically by identifying God's means not as institutional reform but as purified consensus. History taught perfectibility, but the necessary precondi-

---

[13] *Ibid.*, 858-59.

[14] Haller, *Liberty and Reformation*, 179.

[15] William Haller, *The Rise of Puritanism* (New York: Columbia University Press, 1938), 362.

tion was not a purified *ecclesia* but a purified *socies*, not reformation but revolution.

Two parts of the quadripartite argument of *Areopagitica* are important to elucidate the second stage of Milton's understanding of history. The first part, historical in method, argues that licensing, which aims at uniformity, is inferior to toleration, which permits growth in purity, because licensing is a tyrannical means invented by the Church of Rome. Part four, rich in texture, opposes the nature of truth itself and the quality of the people of England to coercive means. The historical argument first presents the practice of "ancient and famous Commonwealths": Greece and Rome were free from censorship, except of atheistical, blasphemous, and libelous works; when "the Emperors were become Christians," they were "not more severe"; but "the Popes of *Rome* engrossing what they pleas'd of Politicall rule into their owne hands, extended their dominion" over men's minds. The tyranny of licensing was imposed at the Council of Trent "to no other purpose but to obstruct and hinder the first approach of Reformation," and it is this practice which is now "so il favourdly imitated by our inquisiturient Bishops."[16] The argument from history is selective and jumps over English practice, but it recapitulates Milton's conviction that history repeats itself and that the cooperation of God and man is necessary to prevent the cycle of history from becoming a downward spiral. Books play a liberating role; a man must use his reason to evaluate the evidence of literary texts. Paul himself "thought it no defilement to insert into holy Scripture the sentences of . . . Greek Poets and one of them a Tragedian."[17] God "uses not to captivat under a perpetuall childhood of prescription, but trusts man with the gift of reason to be his own chooser."

From the historicism of part one to that of part four of *Areopagitica* is but a logical step: in part four Milton depicts the people of England themselves trying to fulfill their historic destiny. "Why else was this Nation chos'n before any other, that out of her Sion should be proclaim'd and sounded forth the first tidings and trumpets of Reformation to all Europ" but that this is "a Nation not slow and dull, but of a quick, ingenious and piercing spirit?"[18] Had the prelates not suppressed Wyclif, "the glory of reforming all our neighbours had bin compleatly ours." Yet, "now once again . . . God is decreeing to begin some new and great period in his Church, ev'n to the reforming of Reformation

---

[16] *Areopagitica, CPW*, II, 439, 500, 507.

[17] Milton repeated this point in the preface to *Samson Agonistes*. "The Apostle *Paul* himself thought it not unworthy to insert a verse of *Euripides* into the Text of Holy Scripture, I. Cor. 15.33" (*Areopagitica, CPW*, II, 508, 514).

[18] *Ibid.*, 551-52.

itself: what does he then but reveal Himself to his servants, and as his manner is, first to his Englishmen," "first to us, though we mark not the method of his counsels."[19] What is distinctive in Milton's use of history in *Areopagitica* is the picture of the individual members of the nation engaged in a collaborative search for truth, "sitting by their studious lamps, musing, searching, revolving new notions and ideas wherewith to present, as with their homage and their fealty the approaching Reformation." For Milton, that reformation was approaching as irresistibly in this period of his history-saturated prose as in the first: "the fields are white already."[20] The nation was not "degenerated, nor drooping to a fatall decay"; it would "wax young again." In the midst of a series of images of rebirth—for example, the snake that sloughs its skin, the eagle that rekindles its sight in the sun—Milton pictured the nation as Samson: "Methinks I see in my mind a noble and puissant Nation rousing herself like a strong man after sleep, and shaking her invincible locks."[21] In this new reading of history emphasis shifts from God's election to God's counsel of virtue, for which individuals must wrestle as the precondition for the community of "the Lord's people." The virtue of England would be demonstrated by guaranteeing to each individual the necessary liberty—the liberty God gives and exacts—to achieve perfection and transform society. Samson has become the image for the young, strong, wrestling nation.

The argument of *Areopagitica* is completed in *The Tenure of Kings and Magistrates*, the final work of the second stage of Milton's developing interpretation of history. In order to defend the execution of Charles I as a necessary step toward reformation, Milton began that work with an imaginary historical account of the popular election of the first kings and magistrates, whose power therefore "is only derivative, transferr'd and committed to them in trust from the People, to the Common good of them all, in whom the power yet remains fundamentally, and cannot be tak'n from them without a violation of thir natural birthright."[22] He then argued that popular election implies the right of popular deposition. In the third part he surveyed biblical and classical authorities on the theme of tyrannicide. And the final section abstractly treats the power of a freeborn people, "as oft as they shall judge it for the best, either to choose [a king] or reject him, retain him or depose him though no Tyrant, meerly by the liberty and right of free born Men to be govern'd as seems them best."[23]

The Tenure of Kings and Magistrates does not specifically cite the story or image of Samson. But it once more correlates the Deuterono-

---

[19] *Ibid.*, 553.   [20] *Ibid.*, 554.   [21] *Ibid.*, 558.
[22] *The Tenure of Kings and Magistrates*, CPW, III, 202.
[23] *Ibid.*, 206.

mic message with contemporary events: "as God was heretofore angry with the Jews who rejected him and his forms of Government to choose a King, so he will bless us . . . who reject a King to make him onely our leader . . . if we have . . . the courage to receave what God voutsafes us: wherein we have the honour to precede other Nations who are now labouring to be our followers."[24] Like the Jews, the English had followed "mercenary noise makers . . . false prophets" and had declined from grace into servitude; but God was now calling England "to liberty and the flourishing deeds of a reformed Commonwealth." God had moved some faithful Jews to lead their people out of tyranny, and Milton cites with terse approval a number of biblical tyrannicides: "Among the Jews the custom of tyrent-killing was not unusual."[25] He goes on to specify Ehud slaying Eglon, Samuel slaying Agag, Jehu slaying Jehoram, Mattathias and Judas Maccabaeus overthrowing Antiochus, and Meroz cursed for not supporting Barak against Jabin. Without pause Milton moves from historical biblical example to historical example from the Christian era, and thence to contemporary English example: every period witnesses to God's approval of tyrannicide.

History and the Saving Remnant

In the third stage of his developing conception of history, Milton returned to the story of Samson to give it a further elaboration. The ultimate sanction for tyrannicides that he had invoked in *The Tenure of Kings and Magistrates* was the sovereignty of the people, the right of political choice inherently theirs as free men. But Milton had opened *The Tenure of Kings and Magistrates* by brushing aside the Presbyterians' opposition with the significant words "none can love freedom heartily, but good men."[26] The rights of free men are theirs under natural law, their natural liberty is common to all. Yet some are more clear-eyed than others because to natural liberty they join Christian liberty. In *The Tenure of Kings and Magistrates* Milton saw history as so flowing toward redemption that natural liberty and Christian liberty did not need to be distinguished. The English people enjoyed both and were a community of free wise men; their Commonwealth, not their church, was the model for the New Jerusalem. But the people's revulsion at the execution of King Charles and their reaction to the printing of the King's Book warned Milton against relying on a divinely sanctioned republicanism as the agent by which history would be redeemed. Therefore, in *Eikonoklastes* he initiated a further de-

[24] *Ibid.*, 236.   [25] *Ibid.*, 213.   [26] *Ibid.*, 190.

velopment of his conception of history, which the *First Defence* typi-
fies and *The Readie and Easie Way to Establish a Free Commonwealth*
concludes.

Eikonoklastes was written "in the behalf of Libertie, and the
Common-wealth" to prevent "the retarding of a generall peace."
Milton sent it out "in the world . . . to finde out her own readers; few
perhaps, but those few, such of value and substantial worth, as truth
and wisdom, not respecting numbers and bigg names, have bin ever
wont in all ages to be contented with."[27] The generality of Englishmen,
"imbastardiz'd from the ancient nobleness of thir Ancestors," were
only too "ready to fall flatt and give adoration" to the dead king. Not
because of "the natural disposition of an Englishman" but because of
bad teaching and factional leadership, those who "adhere to wisdom
and to truth" had come to be "so few as to seem a sect or faction."
Charles's identification of the people's welfare with the king's had to
be corrected, for "the happiness of a Nation consists in true Religion,
Piety, Justice, Prudence, Temperance, Fortitude and the Contempt of
Avarice and Ambition. They in whomsoever these virtues dwell emi-
nently, need not Kings to make them happy but are the architects of
thir own happiness."[28] Virtuous men need no king, nor need they be a
majority; a good minority or saving remnant must undertake the se-
curing of political liberty for all. To achieve the good of the English
people they must oppose the popular will. History would then show
God's vindication of those "whom he hath selected as the sole re-
mainder, after all these changes and commotions, to stand upright and
stedfast in his cause; dignify'd with the defence of truth and public
liberties."[29]

In *Eikonoklastes* Milton did not doubt ultimate victory. Nor did
he doubt that the virtuous part of the nation would act so as to liberate
the whole. He confidently invoked success as a historical index of
God's will: "Wee measure not our Cause by our success, but our suc-
cess by our cause. Yet certainly in a good Cause success is a good con-
firmation; for God hath promis'd it to good men almost in every leafe
of Scripture. If it argue not for us, we are sure it argues not against
us: but as much or more for us then ill success argues for them; for
to the wicked God hath denounc'd ill success in all that they take in
hand."[30] Therefore, the reference to Samson in *Eikonoklastes* cites
that part of the story showing the degradation of the unwise leader
rather than the part showing the revival of the people's representative
(as in *Areopagitica*). *Eikon Basilike* had pretended that Charles, like
Samson, was tormented and persecuted by Philistines, that is, Parlia-

[27] *Eikonoklastes, CPW*, III, 340.   [28] *Ibid.*, 344, 348, 542.
[29] *Ibid.*, 348.   [30] *Ibid.*, 599.

ment. *Eikonoklastes* corrects the metaphor: Samson fallen from consecration is like the king shorn of legality. "The words of a King, as they are full of power, in the authority and strength of law, so like Sampson, without the strength of that Nazarites lock, they have no more power in them than the words of another man."[31]

The *First Defence* is another document in the success story of the revolution as Milton tells it. The opening sentence proclaims the victorious theme: "this cause . . . most noble and deserving of eternal remembrance." The subject involves "matters neither small nor mean"; rather, it demonstrates the intervention of God Himself in the affairs of England: "we followed him as our leader," "these great and wondrous deeds performed evidently by almighty God himself."[32] A king who thought himself God's anointed and immune from law was "caught in the meshes of his own laws" and overthrown by a great and noble people. From the opening pages of the tract Milton's theme is seen in the context of contemporary history. In the course of the work, however, Milton must answer Salmasius's charge that "the army with their leaders did this,"[33] not the people of England, that the act is illegal because England is governed by a military junta and not by the people. Milton answers: "why should I not say that the act of the better, the sounder part of the people, was the act of the people"; "only those called Independents knew how to be true to themselves to the end and how to use their victory"; "on our side was an army famous for its loyalty, moderation and courage. With the help of the army, it was possible for us to keep our freedom and save the state"; the English people "cherish one law of great age, passed by Nature herself, which makes all laws, all rights, all civil government depend not on the desire of kings but primarily on the well-being of the better citizens." Salmasius has given "a confused and tasteless account of our history."[34]

The superiority of Milton's own clear and tasteful account of English history is confirmed by "what has been the practice of God's people both Jewish and Christian." God gave Israel freedom. When Israel turned from Him their freedom rebounded against them: they chose, God allowing, to become the slaves of kings. Some among them resisted. Scripture, as an authentic historical record, contains precedents which England has faithfully followed. And once again, as in *The Tenure of Kings and Magistrates*, Milton calls the roll of biblical revolutionaries and tyrannicides. This time Samson is prominent among them:

---

[31] *Ibid.*, 461, 546.
[32] *A Defence of the People of England, CPW*, IV, pt. I, 302-5.
[33] Quoted in Don M. Wolfe's introduction to *CPW*, IV, pt. I, 112.
[34] *CPW*, IV, pt. I, 511-12.

Even the heroic Samson, though his countrymen reproached him say-ing, Judges 15, "Knowest thou not that the Philistines are rulers over us?", still made war single-handed on his masters, and, whether prompt-ed by God or by his own valor, slew at one stroke not one but a host of his country's tyrants, having first made prayer to God for his aid. Samson therefore thought it not impious but pious to kill those mas-ters who were tyrants over his country, even though most of her citi-zens did not balk at slavery.[35]

Samson represented the better part of his nation, not the majority; his action constituted historical precedent for minority action as well as for tyrannicide. He is praiseworthy not just as a killer of tyrants but as a representative of the pious few who acted in the name of the wel-fare of the nation without securing the consent of the nation. "What is most suitable and profitable to a people . . . is something for the wisest men to ascertain."

In *The History of Britain* Milton applied the most careful historical principles to the sources and was unable to arrive at any conclusion other than that England's history is a constant record of the mishan-dling of its election, a constant failure to seize offered freedom. As Milton admonished in the digression "Character of the Long Parlia-ment," England's history teaches the certain lesson that "Libertie hath a sharp and double edge fitt onelie to be handl'd by just and vertuous men, to bad and dissolute it becomes a mischief unwieldie in thir own hands."[36] The overall evolution of Milton's understanding of history was faithfully recapitulated during the process of writing *The History of Britain*. The preparation between 1640 and 1644 coincided with his sense that the history would show how institutional change had brought about irresistible reformation, and the work was intended to be published to greet the consummation of reform. The first stage of writing, between 1646 and 1649, began with his discovery that the consummation was to be brought about by virtuous republican leaders and ended with his sense that they were a minority. In the final stage, after 1655 and until its publication, the history was intended "to relate well and orderly things worth the noting, so as may best instruct and benefit them that read." But where "civility" is always in decline, his-tory teaches: "When God hath decreed servitude on a singul Nation, fitted by their own vices for no condition but servile, all Estates of Government are alike unable to avoid it."

A Second Defence of the English People likewise commenced with the invocation of history, delivered its judgments in terms of history, and offered advice about the next stage of history. It added nothing to

[35] *Ibid.*, 402.   [36] *Ibid.*, v, 449.

Milton's reading of history except his own proud sense that he had recorded a glorious epic achievement in the chronicles of his country. Milton "was born at a time in the history of [his country] when her citizens . . . surpassing all the glory of their ancestors, invoked the Lord, followed his manifest guidance, and . . . freed the state." It was "their purity of life and their blameless character which showed them the one direct road to liberty." They were led by the Independents, "for nothing is more natural, nothing more just, nothing more useful or more advantageous to the human race than that the lesser obey the greater, not the lesser number the greater number, but the lesser virtue the greater virtue, the lesser wisdom the greater wisdom." They succeeded because God was "so unmistakeably at . . . [their] side."[37] Within a few months the first Parliament of the Protectorate would begin. Milton could note that he had redeemed his earlier promise to write a national epic, pointing the way toward future greatness:

> If after such brave deeds you ignobly fail . . . be sure that posterity will speak out and pass judgment: the foundations were solidly laid, the beginnings . . . were splendid, but posterity will look in vain . . . for those who were to complete the work. . . . Yet there was not wanting one who could rightly counsel, encourage and inspire, who could honor both the noble deeds and those who had done them, and make both deeds and doers illustrious with praises that will never die.[38]

The second edition of *The Readie and Easie Way* was written when there was no doubt in Milton's mind that the Good Old Cause had failed; it marked the end of all hope. The urgent tone of resolute optimism—"now is the opportunitie, now the very season, wherein we may obtain a free Commonwealth and establish it forever"; "few words will save us . . . few and easie things now seasonably done"— reflects only the last-ditch stand Milton was making and cannot conceal his profound despair that "what I have spoke, should happen to be the last words of our expiring liberties."[39] To write and publish the tract in its second edition but a few days before the return of Charles II was a brave and defiant act. No printer or bookseller could be found to associate his name with it, and so it came out as "Printed for the author." Again, it retold the history of the Good Old Cause, how the people "magnanimously abolished" kingship, how "thir actions both at home and abroad" became "a glorious rising Commonwealth," how many deeds were "well don both in church and state," how ignominious it would be "after ten or twelve years prosperous warr . . . with tyrannie, basely and besottedly to run their necks again into the yoke." Although Milton deleted from the second edition the confident hope

[37] *A Second Defence, CPW*, IV, pt. 1, 548, 636, 670.
[38] *Ibid.*, 685.   [39] *Ibid.*, VII, 430, 461, 463.

of the first, "since God hath yet His remnant, and hath not yet quenched the spirit of Liberty among us," he steadily opposed the "gentilism" of rule by a "single person." And again he supported republicanism by reference to historical examples among the Jews, Greeks, Romans, and certain Christian states. At the moment that history was pronouncing against the revolution, Milton did not forbear the historical argument bent to his political end: "To make the people fittest to chuse, and the chosen fittest to govern, will be to mend our corrupt and faulty education, to teach the people faith not without virtue, temperance, modestie, sobrietie, parsimonie, justice; not to admire wealth or honour; to hate turbulence and ambition; to place every one his privat welfare and happiness in the public peace, libertie and safetie."[40]

HISTORY AND THE INDIVIDUAL

When Milton in *Paradise Lost* recreated his conception of history (in the fourth stage of its development) in the form of an epic poem, he portrayed in the life of one man the whole span of time, in order to assert the necessity of individual liberty as a precondition for national liberty. History teaches "what reward / Awaits the good, the rest what punishment"; it records "supernal Grace contending / With sinfulness of Men"; and it reveals the lesson of "True patience."[41] Milton pronounced the judgment of history upon his own nation:

> Yet somtimes Nations will decline so low
> From vertue, which is reason, that no wrong
> But Justice, and some fatal curse annext
> Deprives them of thir outward libertie,
> Thir inward lost.
>
> (XII, 97-101)

But he discovered in history itself the means of escape from history: the individual was to apply its lessons

> disciplin'd
> From shadowie Types to Truth, from Flesh to Spirit,
> From imposition of strict Laws, to free
> Acceptance of large Grace, from servil fear
> To filial, works of Law to works of Faith.
>
> (XII, 302-6)

[40] *Ibid.*, 409, 420, 422, 428, 363, 443.
[41] *Paradise Lost*, XI, 709ff. I have written on the probationary aspect of human experience in history as shown in Books XI and XII (see " 'Man as a Probationer of Immortality' "), and I will treat the theological and ethical significance of these books in the chapters below.

Time would continue, and the meaning of history be the teaching of virtue, until Christ would "bring back / Through the worlds wilderness long wanderd man / Safe to eternal Paradise of rest."

To be sure Books XI and XII contain, among other things, a résumé of the history of man from the Creation to the end of time. That history is given a pointed pattern and moral emphasis by Michael:

> so shall the World goe on,
> To good malignant, to bad men benigne,
> Under her own waight groaning, till the day
> Appear of respiration to the just,
> And vengeance to the wicked. . . .
>
> (XII, 537-41)

Even in the most overtly historicist part of this great epic, the poet displays his continuing concern for the political community of individual good men by emphasis on the lessons, not the processes, of history. In the fallen world of *Paradise Lost*, political efforts to achieve reformation or revolution are shown to be intermittent and threatened. Historical hope depends upon seeing the "transient World, this Race of Time" as containing moral lessons for individual men. "All Nations" shall be taught, but the lesson to be learned in their history is that reformation is to come "not by destroying Satan, but his works" in the human heart of each individual. Hence, the historical presentation of Books XI and XII is a focus upon either the individual subverting "worldly strong, and worldly wise" to achieve inner truth or upon the individual failing to understand this "summe of wisdom" and failing as well to add to it "deeds answerable."

What man learned throughout the course of time, Jesus learned likewise within the action of *Paradise Regained*. In the beginning of the poem he conceived his role as national, historical, and kingly; he was

> To rescue *Israel* from the *Roman* yoke,
> Then to subdue and quell o're all the earth
> Brute violence and proud Tyrannick pow'r,
> Till truth were freed, and equity restor'd.
>
> (I, 217-20)

He concluded the first temptation knowing that liberation from outside authority depends upon self-mastery and that to teach this truth is the form of liberation most heroic:[42]

[42] See Fixler, *Milton and the Kingdoms of God*, 249-71; Barbara Lewalski, *Milton's Brief Epic* (Providence: Brown University Press, 1966), 219-55, and also her "Time and History in *Paradise Regained*."

> Yet he who reigns within himself, and rules
> Passions, Desires, and Fears, is more a King;
> Which every wise and vertuous man attains:
> And who attains not, ill aspires to rule
> Cities of men, or head-strong Multitudes,
> Subject himself to Anarchy within,
> Or lawless passions in him which he serves.
> But to guide Nations in the way of truth
> By saving Doctrine, and from errour lead
> To know, and knowing worship God aright,
> Is yet more Kingly, this attracts the Soul,
> Governs the inner man, the nobler part,
> That other o're the body only reigns,
> And oft by force, which to a generous mind
> So reigning can be no sincere delight.
>
> (II, 466-80)

In *Paradise Lost*, in which history teaches escape from history by means of the introversion of all struggle within the individual soul, Samson is presented not as the national figure who dared to defy a majority in acting for the good of his people against tyranny, but as the man whose loss of inner virtue led precisely to his loss of power.[43] He enters the poem only to awake to despair:

> So rose the Danite strong
> *Herculean Samson* from the Harlot-lap
> Of *Philistean Dalilah*, and wak'd
> Shorn of his strength, They destitute and bare
> Of all thir vertue.
>
> (IX, 1059-63)

He is not even mentioned in the prophetic synopsis of Jewish history in the last two books of the epic, "For strength from truth divided and from just / Illaudible, naught merits but dispraise."[44] *Paradise Regained* indicates the way in which true heroism is to be defined: "By deeds of peace, by wisdom eminent, / By patience, temperance"; "who best / Can suffer, best can do."

To recapitulate briefly, in Milton's evolving conception of history God had covenanted with the people of an elect nation in a great cause, the effective spread of liberty of conscience in a purified state.

---

[43] See George M. Muldrow, *Milton and the Drama of the Soul: The Theme of Restoration of Men in Milton's Later Poetry* (The Hague: Mouton, 1970), 243.

[44] See Samuel, "Milton and the Ancients," 146.

The cause depended upon their inner worthiness. If they were obedient to the rule of reason, they would succeed. Success was not just the measure of the goodness of their cause but depended upon their virtue. The way toward success was the way of individual virtue: each man in whom reason ruled could be the architect of his own happiness. As a community, such men could choose fitly those fittest to govern them. They would know truth by wrestling with the mixture of truth and falsehood in the world. Truth could be known by examining history; being known, it could be taught; being taught, it could be heeded. The best instructed nation required the least government by the state; the least government was the best government, for it promoted the most internal government.[45] The ideal of the progressive realization of New Jerusalem on earth could be achieved not by reformations, not by revolutions, not by political movements, but by "plain heroic magnitude of mind." One avenue to knowledge is the spectacle of tragedy, most especially when the tragedy echoes and reechoes with the sounds of contemporary history.

[45] See Haller, *Liberty and Reformation*, 354.

GOD'S PROMISE, THE PROPHECY

OF COMMUNITY

ENGLISHMEN had fought for God's cause and had expected it to prevail. When the cause fell into ruin, they could not but ask themselves whether their defeat was God's condemnation of their cause.[1] History was meaningless and the future hopeless unless, even in the defeat, God worked toward some fulfillment.[2] And could not God work toward fulfillment through tragedy as well as through triumphant pageants, by that mode of teaching which Milton called "the gravest, moralest, and most profitable?" The great tragic questions posed by *Samson Agonistes* are: Why is the good so easily lost? Why is it so mixed with pain? Why does God manage human affairs "not evenly?" It has been usual to read the tragedy as an account of the regeneration of Samson which ends with the vindication of divine providence when the regenerate Samson fulfills his predicted mission of delivering Israel from the Philistines. According to this reading, Samson's fall is another paradoxically fortunate fall, and the tragedy moves beyond tragedy into martyrology and "sings the victorious agonies of . . . Saints."[3] The conventional answer to the question, why is the good so easily lost, is that in *Samson Agonistes* it only appears to be lost and that God works mysteriously His wonders to perform. But Milton knew both Aristotle and the Bible. He knew what tragedy was and he knew that Scripture instanced it. In both *The Reason of Church Government* and the preface to *Samson Agonistes* he referred to Aristotle and commended Paraeus for noticing that Revelation is "a high and stately tragedy." A more Miltonic answer to the tragic mystery of iniquity is that God, like the Aristotelian poet, presents man with the spectacle of life wherein to read tragedy, to learn wisdom by feeling the full impact of the lack of wisdom, to be purged of passion and of evil. God does not annul tragedy but bends it to revelation.

[1] See Christopher Hill, *The Century of Revolution, 1603-1714*, 2d ed. (London: Sphere, 1972), 151.

[2] See Hill, *World Turned Upside Down*, 325-27.

[3] See Samuel, "*Samson Agonistes* as Tragedy," for a strong attack on this reading.

SCRIPTURE AS HISTORY

To Milton, Scripture was neither a collection of apt fables nor a storehouse of sacred metaphor: it was a God-inspired record of historical events predictive of the future and "plain and perspicuous in all things necessary to salvation." Each passage of Scripture has only a single sense, he wrote, though in the Old Testament this sense is often a combination of the historical and the typological.[4] The typical sense of *Samson Agonistes* has been taken to be exhausted when Samson's unconscious prefiguration of Christ's exaltation through humiliation has been marked or "the agony of Samson" seen as "a surrogate for the unbloody sacrifice of the mass."[5] It has been usual in discussing the tragedy to minimize both Milton's interest in history as yielding example and his interest in typology as pointing a continuous prophecy, not merely as presenting Gospel prefiguration. History for Milton taught not only the outcome of the generations of men, it taught the human means efficacious toward a providential outcome. He first conceived of these means as an institutional reform, then as a national coalition of free men, and finally as a consensus of patient virtuous men. At each point, Milton saw Samson as the historical example of how men should conspire with God to bring about New Jerusalem. History also shows the contrary energy, the improvisations of God which deal with the specific evils done by men. Since "God made no absolute decrees about anything which he left in the power of men" but "made his decrees conditional in this way for the very purpose of allowing free causes to put into effect that freedom which he himself gave them," then "it is neither impious nor absurd to say, that the idea of certain things or events might come to God from some other source."[6] God can be seen in history as acting contingently to punish the wicked and redeem the good, to permit suffering to the sinner out of His sense of justice and allow suffering to the saint out of mercy. And through His presentation of prophecy in history He can also be seen as authorizing the conversion of Old Testament history to present uses. The habitual conversion of Old Testament material to contemporary Christian usage need not be justified from theories of biblical exegesis, for it was a commonplace of the Reformation. Rather, the

---

[4] *De Doctrina Christiana, CPW,* VI, 581. See Duncan, *Milton's Earthly Paradise,* for a succinct analysis of Milton's literal exegetical methods. See also MacCallum, "Milton and Sacred History," and his "Milton and Figurative Interpretation of the Bible," *University of Toronto Quarterly,* 31 (1962), 397-415.

[5] See William G. Madsen, *From Shadowy Types to Truth* (New Haven: Yale University Press, 1968), 201-2, and T.S.K. Scott-Craig, "Concerning Milton's *Samson Agonistes,*" *Renaissance News,* 5 (1952), 46-47.

[6] *De Doctrina Christiana, CPW,* VI, 155, 160, 162.

point I wish to make is that for Milton, God wrote more than literal history, typological prophecy, and accommodative theology. Milton's God also wrote tragedy.

In *Samson Agonistes* Milton once more shows his readers "the wayes of God to men." Milton is the Aristotelian tragedian inspired to show that God too works like an Aristotelian tragic poet. God places before men the spectacle of human life, and that spectacle is tragic. The perturbation of mind aroused by human suffering can be assuaged by the imitation of that suffering as shown by a poet such as Milton who is aware of its God-intended value. The imitated suffering is antagonistic to the direct suffering and tempers it, producing quiet of spirit. Milton's contemporaries had been led to "betray a just and noble cause," they were "a scorn and derision to all neighbours," they had "basely and besottedly . . . run their necks again into the yoke." It is the responsibility of the tragic poet to allay the sufferings with which they were afflicted and to purge their passions.[7]

The means by which direct suffering could be dispersed was no other than the imitation of that suffering through the scriptural tragedy recorded in Judges by the greatest teacher-tragedian, God. God Himself was a writer of tragedy. He wrote it through the prophets in Scripture and by means of inspired poets. In *De Doctrina Christiana* Milton had glossed the term *prophet* as applying "not only to a man able to foretell the future but also to anyone endowed with exceptional piety and wisdom for the purposes of teaching."[8] The ancient prophets were to have modern collaborators, amongst whom Milton had repeatedly prayed to be numbered. In *The Reason of Church Government* tragedy was explicitly held to be the mode of instruction in parts of Holy Writ. The effects of tragic instruction were also described there, along with the particular educative effect of each genre to which Milton had been referring. Thus epic inculcates public and private virtue by precept, "to imbreed and cherish in a great people the seeds of virtu, and public civility." Tragedy creates moral reflection by catharsis, "to allay the perturbations of the mind, and set the affections in right tune." Hymns promote the good by panegyric, "to celebrate in glorious and lofty Hymns the throne and equipage of Gods Almightiness, and what he works and what he suffers to be wrought with high providence in his Church." Odes extol the good by inspired example, "to sing the victorious agonies of Martyrs and Saints, the

---

[7] See Arthur E. Barker, "Calm Regained through Passion Spent," in *The Prison and the Pinnacle*, ed. Rajan, 45-48.

[8] *De Doctrina Christiana*, *CPW*, VI, 572. "Thus under the gospel the simple gift of teaching, especially of public teaching, is called prophecy." See Pt. IV below for a discussion of the rationality of this teaching activity.

deeds and triumphs of just and pious nations doing valiantly through faith against the enemies of Christ." All alike serve the especially Miltonic function of sounding a warning "to deplore the general relapse of Kingdoms and States from justice and God's true worship."[9]

Since "Teaching over the whole book of sanctity and virtue" is the intention of all poets, tragedians will depict "whatsoever hath passion or admiration in all the changes of that which is call'd fortune from without, or the wily suttleties and refluxes of mens thoughts from within." In the preface to *Samson Agonistes*, "Of that sort of Dramatic Poem which is call'd Tragedy," Milton succinctly makes the same three points about tragedy made in *The Reason of Church Government*: that Scripture instances tragedy; that tragedy teaches; and that the particular effect of tragedy is to promote a state of mind conducive to reflection by the means of catharsis. As the "gravest, moralest, and most profitable of all other Poems," tragedy is "of power by raising pity and fear, or terror, to purge the mind of those and such like passions, that is to temper and reduce them to just measure with a kind of delight, stirr'd up by reading or seeing those passions well imitated."

By the conjunction of these three central points in both *The Reason of Church Government* and the preface, Milton reaffirms the total complex of aspirations in the earlier works as applicable to the later. *Samson Agonistes* will treat "all the changes of that which is call'd fortune from without," but fortune "is only what is *Fatum*, spoken, by some almighty power," so that tragedy is the educative record of the contingent actions of God within time. It will treat "the wily suttleties and refluxes of mens thoughts from within," but those "refluxes" are free and not necessitated by God. The "freedom of the will always remains uninfringed." Although "God always produces something good and just out of [the evil intentions of sinners] and creates, as it were, light out of darkness," the means by which evil is overcome is not to remove but to apply tragic suffering.[10] The mystery of suffering remains. For Milton, the great tragic mystery is that one knows good by experiencing evil, that one cannot participate in good without evil or enjoy God's mercy without enduring His justice. God is just and merciful, but the ways of His mercy are past man's foreseeing. Man commits iniquity, and it is God's mercy to him to bestow trial upon him, so that by enduring trial he may attain to right knowledge: trial purifies, and trial is by what is contrary. The source of tragic feeling in *Samson Agonistes* is the mystery of iniquity as presented in terms of the tragic inquiry: Why does God dispense His mercy in the

---

9 *Reason of Church Government*, *CPW*, I, 815-17.

10 The glosses upon fortune, psychology, and destiny are all taken from *De Doctrina Christiana*, *CPW*, VI, 131, 330, 333.

way He does? Since man cannot anticipate the balance of mercy and justice in which God's providence is rooted, he must believe in the mercy even whilst the justice strikes him low. For the present, the wicked seem to flourish and the good go to the wall, but that is God's way with His people so that trial may abound. "Prosperity," Bacon noted, "is the blessing of the Old Testament; adversity is the blessing of the New." But Milton made no such distinction, even when agreeing that men were to progress from Law to Gospel, to be disciplined "from shadowie Types to Truth, from Flesh to Spirit." Rather, he claimed for the Old Testament a historicity and authenticity even more reliable than that of the New Testament. With regard to the historical books of the Old Testament,

> Few or none have called in doubt their doctrinal parts. The New Testament, on the other hand, has been entrusted throughout the ages . . . to a variety of hands, some more corrupt than others. . . . I do not know why God's Providence should have committed the contents of the New Testament to such wayward and uncertain guardians unless it was so that this very fact might convince us that the Spirit which is given to us is a more certain guide than Scripture, and that we ought to follow it.[11]

Scripture as Prophecy

Milton acknowledged, then, both the historicity and typicality of the Samson story; he believed that God instructs each generation through the prophets and historians of the past, with whom poet-teachers of the present are to collaborate; and he discerned a pattern in history and contemporary affairs of which the life of Samson was paradigmatic. God collaborated with Samson and improvised from Samson's history of failure a tragedy whose meaning was not cathartic to Samson alone. With the further collaboration of John Milton, Englishman, that history could become both cathartic and educative to Milton's own times.

The play opens by drawing our attention immediately to the disjunction between Samson's destiny and his present fate, between "Times past, what once I was, and what am now." Like the promise made to England—"reserved for greatest happiness to come" when "the congregation of the Lord" would "soone recover the true likeness of . . . a Saintly communion, the household and City of God"—a promise had been made to Samson of a "great act / Or benefit . . . to *Abraham's* race." He was to effect the liberation of his people from the

---

[11] *De Doctrina Christiana, CPW,* VI, 588-89.

tyranny of the Philistines. The Chorus, standing aside for a moment so as not to interrupt Samson's thoughts, recalls the exploits of the formerly "Irresistible *Samson*," who "weaponless himself, / Made arms ridiculous," just as the English people "relying on divine assistance . . . used every honourable exertion to break the yoke of slavery." They then attempt to draw a lesson from his plight; it must be that Samson exemplifies the vanity of human wishes:

> O mirror of our fickle state,
> Since man on earth unparallel'd?
> The rarer thy example stands,
> By how much from the top of wondrous glory,
> Strongest of mortal men,
> To lowest pitch of abject fortune thou art fall'n.
>
> (164-69)

Their formulation is the familiar, desperately cyclical view of human history: things must remain as they have always been, to rise is but to prepare to fall. The inescapable conclusion is the mutability of human life. Their next words importantly link Samson with the English Puritan party: Samson's fall mirrors not simply the general fall of princes and kings, but also the fall of the elect, the man with a talent, the Puritan noble. Like General Fairfax, whose "firm unshak'n vertue ever [brought] / Victory home," or like Cromwell, who "Guided by faith & matchless Fortitude / To peace & truth [his] glorious way [had] plough'd," Samson was a special sort of godly warrior whose private morality guaranteed the success of his public acts:

> For him I reckon not in high estate
> Whom long descent of birth
> Or the sphear of fortune raises;
> But [him] whose strength, while vertue was her mate,
> Might have subdu'd the Earth. . . .
>
> (170-74)

The Chorus is made up of "friends and neighbours not unknown." Samson was chief among them, the representative of the virtuous minority, his special role within the nation being to free it from bondage. Samson, like the Independents, was to fulfill a grand design of God for his nation. The tragic poet will undertake to show how and why he failed and what his self-defeat explains of God's ways toward man.

How short a time earlier the Puritan saints had taken leave of their friends in the place of their execution with God's name on their lips in their defeat! The defeat confronted Milton with the judgment of reason and conscience against his nation—and a most concrete need to justify God's ways. Antichrist had not met his doom on English ground: God's Englishmen had not kept covenant with God. In the figure of Samson was the image of failure, the type of one who had thrown away his great opportunity. In *Samson Agonistes* Milton does not set forth a case against the royalists; it was not the royalists who broke faith. He begins the tragedy with Samson's own explanation of his failure: like a "foolish Pilot" he shipwrecked his vessel; he is proverbed for a fool; he had immeasurable strength but "wisdom nothing more then mean," Milton's version of *hamartia*. The fault was within Samson himself: he married Dalila while "still watching to oppress / *Israel's* oppressours," and could have fulfilled his mission had he not given up his fort of silence. The Chorus cannot but remark "*Israel* still serves with all his Sons," the simple truth in the historical parallel. If Samson can acknowledge his own self-betrayal, however, then the nation too must acknowledge theirs who "not at all consider'd / Deliverance offerd."

The words *deliverer* and *deliverance* sound throughout the play in two senses: delivered from or liberated, and delivered up or enslaved. Four of the five episodes of the plot distinctively manipulate these two senses, only the central episode is silent about them. The first episode, Samson's conversation with the Chorus culminating in the first choral ode, "Just are the ways of God," uses the words seven times to emphasize that the proposed deliverer, the elected deliverer, began his appointed task, "*Israel's* Deliverance, / The work to which [he] was divinely call'd," but that he failed. His failure was his crime, but the crime of his nation was their neglect of "Gods propos'd deliverance," for they "not at all consider'd / Deliverance offerd" and despised "Whom God . . . of his special favour rais'd / As thir Deliverer." The corrupt nation loved "Bondage with ease [more] then strenuous liberty"—and not for the first time. They had also contemned "thir great Deliverer" in arms, Gideon, and in argument "not worse then . . . spear," Jephtha. The proposed deliverer has delivered himself to slavery, and those whom he would deliver have declined deliverance and delivered him to his enemies. The crime of the people was that they "not at all consider'd." What is to eventuate in the tragedy is that they be given again the educative example of Samson's behavior. Samson's tragic end will offer honor and freedom again to Israel, "let but them / Find courage to lay hold on this occasion." The conjunction of strenuousness with consideration, of strength with wisdom, and of power with virtue will be all important in the resolution and application of the tragedy. The second episode of the tragedy, Manoa's visit to his son (concluding with the second choral ode "Many are the sayings of the wise . . . Extolling Patience"), lightly underlines the opposing ironic sense of the word *deliver* in two occurrences: the Philistines celebrate Dagon "who hath deliver'd . . . *Samson* bound and blind into thir hands," but Manoa seeks the means of his "deliverance by ransom."

There are no references to either sense of the word in the pivotal third episode, during which Dalila and Samson pit against each other their opposite ways of reading history. The fourth episode, the encounter with Harapha, builds around four occurrences of the word. Harapha taunts Samson with God's rejection of him: God "delivered up [Samson] into [his] Enemies hand." According to Harapha's reading of history, only success in a power struggle divinely rigged can matter; men are pawns in games played by gods, and when the bigger god is ahead, the feebler god sweeps his own men off the board. Second, Samson dissociates his personal failure from the national failure: his countrymen's "servile minds . . . their Deliverer sent would not receive . . . th' unworthier they; whence to this day they serve." Then the Chorus harmonizes the sense of historical mission Samson had of himself and they had of him with their emerging and corrected sense of the necessary valor. Were God to put "into the hands of thir deliverer . . . invincible might" sanctified by "plain Heroic magnitude of mind," men and nations might be irresistibly saved and liberated for their own good without the concurrence of their will. Thus the people of England might have remained liberated in a ready and easy way, accepting from without the great acts done on their behalf by the Independent saints. But God's ways with men are seldom coercive, and "patience is more oft the exercise / Of saints . . . Making them each his own Deliverer." The Chorus thus reconciles inner peace with action in each individual: the salvation of the individual by inner wisdom is the precondition of deliverance. The Chorus seems to set action against patience as pure alternatives, but the saving deliverance—when each becomes his own deliverer—is the reconciliation of both, the action of self-knowledge and patience.

The final episode focuses on the Chorus and Manoa. Ironically, at the moment of the hideous noise offstage the Chorus is assuring Manoa that it is not "vain" to think of delivering Samson by ransom. The Messenger's announcement of Samson's death forces the shocked and grieving Manoa to declare death the sole delivery. But Samson is not delivered from slavery by death, Samson has delivered himself. And the opportunity of the event has delivered to his people "new acquist of true experience," from which may come their true liberty.

As the first episode concludes, the Chorus can make little of the tragic puzzle of the promised deliverer, who delivered up his might through lack of wisdom, and of those he would have delivered, who not at all considered the offered deliverance. At most, they can only affirm that despite the difficulty of understanding His ways, God is just. They give the very difficulty of understanding God's ways as the grounds for asserting his justice: the justice of men is not the justice of God, "Who made our Laws to bind us, not himself." The spectacle of Samson's failure might cause some men to deny God altogether, those "who think not God at all . . . walk obscure." Still others might charge God with caprice, "not just, / As to his own edicts, found contradicting." Milton had thought history taught that a political solution could be found for all his ethical aspirations. He had staked nearly twenty years of his life on securing consensus of spirit under a light and easy government, on initiating a republicanism which, because of God's covenant with England, would move irresistibly toward the highest cultural achievements. Because he had reasoned upon the historical record of Scripture, it was not open to him to argue that history is meaningless nor to "doubt [God's] ways not just." He could not accept the view that God honors mere success or teaches man the simple historical relativism that to the victor belongs the spoils, that to the defeated remains the option only of a quiet little life of private solaces. In *Paradise Lost* Milton had already glanced at those who "practice how to live secure" and found them "degenerate, all deprav'd":

> The conquerd also, and enslav'd by Warr
> Shall with thir freedom lost all vertu loose
> And feare of God, from whom thir pietie feign'd
> In sharp contest of Battel found no aide
> Against invaders; therefore coold in zeale
> Thenceforth shall practice how to live secure,
> Worldlie or dissolute, on what thir Lords
> Shall leave them to enjoy.

(XI, 797-804)

History could have only relativistic meaning—might equalling right—and there would be no hope for Milton's free and civilized future unless one could believe that God would establish the society which revolution had failed to achieve and would do so in a way that did not violate human liberty but taught the free spirit of man to contemplate past failure and to learn how to achieve a society that would not shatter. At the conclusion of their first ode, the Chorus can do no more than repudiate a reading of events that would conflate God with Dagon, that would suggest that Dagon-God did not fail but that he does not care about individual just men, that he is a god of power and not of reason. Samson has firmly shown the Chorus that his grief and remorse stem from his acknowledged lack of wisdom and faith, not from Israel's plight. To lament most the servitude of Israel would be merely to call into question God's power or the efficacy of Providence. Had Milton's own nation properly "acknowledg'd . . . Deliverance offerd," they would have attended to the effective work done by the minority Rump Parliament and seen how ready and easy was the way forward, they would not have deserted the Good Old Cause nor abandoned such leaders as Cromwell torn from the desecrated grave, Milton driven into hiding, or Vane delivered to the block. Hence Samson exonerates God: his failure was his own. But he exculpates himself from his nation's failure. The Chorus can offer no additional insight into *how* God's justice can include mercy and redeem time; they can but deny God's indifference: "Down Reason then, at least vain reasonings down."

The first episode has proclaimed Samson to be the fallen man and the rejected deliverer. The second episode modulates history as example into history as prophecy. In his conversation with Manoa, Samson carries self-diagnosis a step further: his present experience of blind slavery is

> not yet so base
> As was my former servitude, ignoble,
> Unmanly, ignominious, infamous,
> True slavery, and that blindness worse then this,
> That saw not how degenerately I serv'd.

(415-19)

The moment constitutes a preliminary *anagnorisis*, or recognition; Samson, reconsidering his *hamartia* or fault, applies his mind to the judgment of his inner and outer condition. He does not simply acknowledge his present defeat, he knows that his past false security was worse. He then can take his analysis of God's ways a step further: his unworthiness does not impugn God's providence nor weaken God's power. "All the contest is now / 'Twixt God and *Dagon*," and God "will arise and his great name assert." God may not act through Samson, but God will act.[12] Despairing for himself, Samson does not despair of God's triumph; personal tragedy sets the stage for God's triumph. Manoa seizes upon Samson's suggestion:

[12] Una Ellis-Fermor correctly and sensitively describes this moment as "a sudden leap of the mind forward," "a preliminary climax, a foretaste of exultation" (*The Frontiers of Drama*, 2d ed. [London: Methuen, 1964], 27).

With cause this hope relieves thee, and these words
I as a Prophecy receive. . . .

(472-73)

History transcribed as tragedy becomes prophecy. Manoa, however,
extends the division between God's "prosperous contestation" and
Samson's "miserable loathsom plight." When he asks "But for thee
what shall be done?" Samson can only reply, "Hopeless are all my
evils, all remediless." The episode concludes with the second effort of
the Chorus to understand and to explain the "unseemly [fall] in human
eie."

The Chorus would like to recommend patience to Samson, for they
concede the point he has made: his case does seem remediless; he does
seem to have been discarded by God as an unfit instrument. Patience
is "the truest fortitude." The patience the Chorus considers recom-
mending is only one-half of the traditional and Miltonic dyad of pa-
tience and magnanimity or "Patience and Heroic Martyrdom." The
hero is ideally conceived as patient in adversity and magnanimous in
heroic action.[13] Both qualities are harmonized in his equable tempera-
ment. At this point in the Chorus's intellectual growth, however, they
understand no more than that Samson ought to have patience and that
they ought to recommend it. Yet they are sensitive to a platitudinous
heaviness in the recommendation. The wise have advised patience; to
the afflicted their advice "Little prevails, or rather seems a tune, /
Harsh, and of dissonant mood from his complaint." But now the
Chorus too sounds a prophetic note. Patience can sustain the afflicted
if "he feel within / Some sourse of consolation from above." When
Samson does feel the "consolation from above," then patience and ac-
tion will be in accord within him. For the present, however, the
Chorus can only repeat the bewildering question of Lear and Job:
"God of our Fathers, what is man! / That thou . . . / Temperst thy
providence through his short course, / Not evenly." The elect, "With
gifts and graces eminently adorn'd / To some great work, thy glory, /
And peoples safety, which in part they effect," are cast lower than
they once were exalted. References to the treatment of the Independ-
ent saints and of Milton himself—left to the "prophane" and their

[13] See William O. Harris, "Despair and 'Patience' as 'the truest Fortitude' in
Samson Agonistes," *ELH* 30 (1963), reprinted in *Critical Essays on Milton from
ELH* (Baltimore: Johns Hopkins University Press, 1969), 286-87; see also Paul R.
Baumgartner, "Milton and Patience," *Studies in Philology*, 40 (1963), 203-13, and
Mason Tung, "*Samson Impatiens*: A Reinterpretation of Milton's *Samson Ago-
nistes*," *Texas Studies in Language and Literature*, 9 (1968), 475-92.

"carkasses / To dogs," exposed to the "condemnation of the ingrateful multitude"—culminate in the expression of the mystery of iniquity:

> Just or unjust, alike seem miserable,
> For oft alike, both come to evil end.

> (703-4)

And so the Chorus prays, "turn [Samson's] labours, for thou canst, to peaceful end." Samson has prayed for "speedy death, / The close of all my miseries, and the balm." In answer to both, God sends Dalila, for by trial comes purification.

To Milton's modifications of Greek tragedy glanced at thus far—his transmutation of the hero into the elect saint, of destiny into God's decree of free will, of scriptural history into parallel contemporary history—we can add his modulation of the Chorus from simply "one of the actors, and a part of the whole . . . joining in the action"[14] into a continuously present participating audience. The tragic catharsis will take place within the Chorus quite as much as within the hero. As friends and equals of Samson's tribe, committed to him so far as to think his sufferings "Too grievous for the trespass or omission," the Chorus comes, so they believe, to offer "Counsel . . . Consolation . . . apt words." At the play's opening, exalted by the memory of Samson's past achievement and grieved by his present state, they palliate his offense: "wisest Men / Have err'd, and by bad Women been deceiv'd"; they acknowledge his unique destiny "solemnly elected" in contrast to that of members of the nameless "common rout"; and they reason with Samson, taking up his words to offer explanations prompted by his questions or questions prompted by his self-judgment. Milton's conception of tragedy embodies the mimesis of a human transformation through suffering, the action imitated being true and historical, the hero and the on-stage audience together achieving illumination. The Chorus first sees Samson's tragedy as a piteous spectacle of human disaster, "mirror of our fickle state," then as a terrible, bewildering spectacle, "just or unjust . . . both come to evil end." In both cases they repeat the cyclical view of history, Samson on the wheel of fortune brought down to grind at the mill wheel. As they confront Samson in turn confronting the problem of his fall, however, they grow in understanding and acquire insight along with him.

Louis Martz has found the Chorus's responses at the end of the second episode "ordinary commonplace musings [in] some of the flattest lines and flattest rhymes that Milton ever wrote"; at the end of the third episode, "trite and banal . . . wholly inadequate commentary";

---

[14] Aristotle, *Poetics*, 18.

at the end of the fourth, "completely lacking in insight"; and at the conclusion, "conventional."[15] Similarly, Northrop Frye says that the Chorus is "on the right side but they never fully understand the meaning of the events they are involved in," and he describes them as "old and tired and blinkered by the Law."[16] These readings fail to notice that the Chorus undergoes its own agonistic recapitulation of Samson's agony. In the ode at the end of the second episode the Chorus does not offer facile comfort; they positively hesitate to speak of patience. They echo Samson's despair in a duplicated agony, projecting his particular Hebrew case forward in time to include the lot of the literal audience for whom they are a surrogate, vicarious audience. God's Englishmen watch God's Everymen lament Samson's case with a grief parallel to their grief at God's abandonment of the good men of the Good Old Cause to the hostile sword and to desecration, to "th' unjust tribunals and the condemnation of th' ungrateful multitude." The author and the contemporary audience see their parallel experience in the hero and in the Chorus of his friends, who fear that God has "contrariously" given up His elect to evil. The Chorus prays that this will not be so. In answer to their prayer, Dalila arrives. The false etymology of Samson's name current in Milton's day, "there the second time," underlines the meaning of the episode: regenerative insight comes when, "there the second time" tempted to the old error, the wise man rejects his former folly.[17]

The third episode deals with history's verdict upon nations. Of course it does not deal exclusively with this theme, but it does treat consciously and decisively the question, to what extent is history simply an account of those who have succeeded. Dalila enters to the accompaniment of a choral description using a much-explicated ship

---

[15] Martz, "Chorus and Character in *Samson Agonistes*," 125, 129, 133.

[16] Frye, "Agon and Logos," 159, 163. These views are rapidly hardening into an orthodoxy. Such teaching manuals as Lois Potter's *A Preface to Milton* (London: Longmans, 1971), 127, simply incorporate without challenge the earlier, cruder Frye judgment of the Chorus "standing around uttering timid complacencies in teeth-loosening doggerel." They should surely be corrected by considering carefully the suggestion of John Arthos, *Milton and the Italian Cities* (London: Bowes and Bowes, 1968), 168-85, that the choral declamations have musical parallels. Anthony Low, *Blaze of Noon*, 124-28, has done much to rehabilitate the Chorus, following the lead of Jon Lawry, *Shadow of Heaven*, 346-47, 359-61.

[17] The correct etymology, relating his name to the sun (the Hebrew word for which is *shemesh*), coexisted with the incorrect in Milton's day. By the correct etymology, Samson was a judge who judged his people as God judges Israel and hence was called by one of the names of God in the Psalms, "For the Lord God is a sun and a shield." See Samuel S. Stollman, "Milton's Samson and the Jewish Tradition," *Milton Studies*, 3 (1971), 186, for the correct etymology, and Carey and Fowler, eds., *Poems of Milton*, 330, for the false.

image, one suggestive line of which is "courted by all the winds that hold them play." When she departs, Harapha's entrance to take her place is prefaced by a second, recapitulating reference to subjection to the vicissitudes of wind:

> this another kind of tempest brings. . . .
> Comes he in peace? what wind hath blown him hither
> I less conjecture then when first I saw
> The sumptuous *Dalila* floating this way. . . .
>
> (1063, 1070-72)

History moves in circles like the Philistine mill, men sway in its wake, blown by the contrary winds of fortune. Confident of the triumph of Dagon and Philistia, Dalila finds the triumph a confirmation of her own historical relativism. She has come with "wavering resolution" to "appease [Samson's] mind." She exonerates herself from blame both because she could not anticipate what would come from "the perverse event" of her betrayal and because she acted from the highest motives of "civil Duty / And of Religion."[18] She acted blindly but selflessly, and the righteousness of her act was demonstrated by its success. It was a national triumph:

> at length that grounded maxim
> So rife and celebrated in the mouths
> Of wisest men; that to the public good
> Private respects must yield; with grave authority
> Took full possession of me and prevail'd;
> Vertue, as I thought, truth, duty so enjoyning.
>
> (865-70)

At the precise midpoint of the drama, Milton decisively answers her by redefining the concept of *nation*. His study of history has supplied him with the means. God's election of a nation, a chosen Israel, had once seemed to him irresistible, but the elect nation did not co-operate; it was a nation grown corrupt. Was the promise withdrawn altogether? Dalila taunts Samson with the relativism of fame in history:

> Fame if not double-fac't is double-mouth'd,
> And with contrary blast proclaims most deeds,

---

[18] Dalila has had a variety of defenders, following the original lead of William Empson (*Milton's God*, 211-28). Whereas Empson quotes Dalila's relativistic argument based on the public good to argue that Dalila is civilized and sophisticated, Irene Samuel omits this argument because she wants to defend Dalila as sincere but "bird-brained" ("*Samson Agonistes* as Tragedy," 248).

On both his wings, one black, th' other white,
Bears greatest names in his wild aerie flight.

(971-74)

She exults that "in [her] countrey where [she] most [desires]," she
will enjoy "the public marks of honour and reward / Conferr'd . . . for
the piety / Which to [the] countrey [she] was judg'd to have shewn."
She conceives of country and nation as a power structure. Nothing
succeeds like success.

Samson's conception of *nation* is not of a successful political entity
whose power is the sanction of its action. Such a "nation" acting
"against the law of nature, law of nations" is not a nation but

an impious crew
Of men conspiring to uphold thir state
By worse then hostile deeds, violating the ends
For which our countrey is a name so dear. . . .

(891-94)

Properly conceived, a nation is identified by the ideals it serves, not by
its numbers, nor by its successes. A nation is a community of the well
principled, a society of those dedicated to worthy ends. God will
have purposes beyond the individual's, the tribe's, or the nation's, but
the ends and values implicit in a just God's purposes are the cohesive
force binding man to man within a tribe or nation. Just as Milton saw
history as revealing God's special purposes for an elect nation, then as
allowing time for a wise and good minority to redeem the nation, and
lastly as giving salvation only in spiritual form to the few just men,
so Samson understood his purpose as acting for the whole of his nation.
Their betrayal of him had seemed to him not only to nullify his use-
fulness to God but also to annihilate community. In his clear rejection
of Dalila's conception of self-interest as the cohesive power within a
state and of success as the measure of national rectitude, he argues a
contrary interpretation of the good society, another measure of its
goodness.

The rarer thy example stands

GOD'S CHAMPION AND THE
STATE'S DELIVERER

THE ETHICS OF POWER POLITICS

Ethical and social issues of special concern to thinkers of the Commonwealth are taken up intermittently throughout *Samson Agonistes* in the form of debates embedded within the flow of action and the lyrical expression of passion. In each, usually through Samson but occasionally through the Chorus, Milton insists on right reason while discussing ideals of particular value to his own time. In the course of the tragedy, then, questions of religious, domestic, and civil liberty are debated: the limits of civil obedience to a hostile superior power; the right to divorce a disloyal wife; the relation between outward abstinence and inward temperance; the obligations of a wife to a husband of another country; role differentiation and subordination in marriage; the distinction between command and constraint or between outward submission and inward liberty; the validity of inner impulses of the spirit; dispensation from legal rites; the reasonable man's indifference to the "magic" of a sanctified place; the distinction between inadvertent self-destruction and suicide. All these issues are present because Samson's ability to reason is expressive of the one path toward liberation for Milton's own people.

It has become fashionable to use the Chorus's intricately free-rhyming third ode, its reverie about the power of beauty in women to enslave men's reason to passion, as a model of their intellectual ineptitude. The ideas are commonplaces of another century: most twentieth-century readers consider that there are better ways to promote the triumph of reason over passion than "despotic power over [the] female." Whether the Chorus concludes in a way satisfactory to modern readers or not, they are trying to escape "much inward passion" and to prompt "vertue which breaks through all opposition." The ideals of marriage expressed are Old Testament ideals, seen in Abraham's rule over Sarah. They were likewise the ideals of Milton's day. The significance of the episode is this: whether we like the choral ideas or not,

Samson's power to reason has been restored. The most thoughtful result of the return to that power in the episode itself is the redefinition of *nation* ("countrey") as the ideal that the individuals composing it together serve.

The fourth episode contains a pendant to this theme, and the fourth choral ode reworks the intellectual material of the second ode. Harapha takes up the relativistic interpretation of history precisely where Dalila left off. He admires "prodigious might and feats perform'd," rejects those outside the brotherhood of "glorious arms," and taunts Samson with being no more than a common criminal who "presum'd single rebellion." The last taunt arouses Samson to state again his election:

> I was no private but a person rais'd
> With strength sufficient and command from Heav'n
> To free my Countrey; if their servile minds
> Me their Deliverer sent would not receive,
> But to thir Masters gave me up for nought,
> Th' unworthier they; whence to this day they serve.
>
> (1211-16)

Salvation is of the individual and then through the individual. To serve in gaol with a free mind is less a slavery than to walk about freely with a servile mind. A group of truly free public men could together serve "the ends for which our countrey is a name so dear." Because Harapha and his nation purpose a vicious end, however, their doom may lie precisely in their proud violence. "Because thir end / Is hate . . . it may with mine / Draw thir own ruin to attempt the deed." With this second prophetic utterance in their ears, the Chorus can now confidently balance magnanimity and patience as harmonious alternatives: now patience is to them more than a wise old saw or useless platitude. The "sourse of consolation from above" has manifestly come to Samson in the intellectual clarity with which he beautifully stated his faith in God, beset as he was by boastful threats to his pride:

> All these . . . evils I deserve and more,
> Acknowledge them from God inflicted on me
> Justly, yet despair not of his final pardon
> Whose ear is ever open; and his eye
> Gracious to re-admit the suppliant. . . .
>
> (1168-73)

The Chorus therefore first extols magnanimity, the comely and reviving spectacle of God putting "plain Heroic magnitude of mind / And celestial vigour" in the possession of a deliverer. What defeats "Ammunition / And feats of War" is the awesomeness of inner virtue. This first alternative is in itself a reconciliation of action and inner peace: "the wicked . . . surpris'd / Lose thir defence distracted and amaz'd" at the moral vigor of the hero. Then the Chorus balances magnanimity with patience, "more oft the exercise / Of Saints." Fortitude is conceived of equally and indifferently as "Heroic magnitude" or "patience," but whereas magnanimity delivers other "just men long opprest," patience makes

> each his own Deliverer,
> And Victor over all
> That tyrannie or fortune can inflict. . . .
>
> (1289-91)

The Chorus sets forth two alternatives: violent men who support tyrranic power are overcome either externally and publicly when God raises up one man of plain heroic magnitude (this passage is proleptic; such a one will Samson prove to be), or internally and individually when God exercises each saint in patience and delivers each from outer bondage by means of his own inner peace (this passage is recapitulative; such a one has Samson just proved to be). Balanced and harmonious destinies as the Chorus considers magnanimity and patience to be, either of which might be Samson's lot, they believe that chance may number him "with those / Whom Patience finally must crown." They conclude in quiet and sympathetic respect by noticing

> This Idols day hath bin to thee no day of rest,
> Labouring thy mind
> More then the working day thy hands. . . .
>
> (1297-99)

The lesson of personal responsibility which Samson and the Chorus have worked out in laboring their minds is a lesson equally of public bearing. Defeat and tragedy has become the condition of recovery and deliverance. The fall of the hero carries with it a positive lesson: God does not break covenant; he restores penitents to sufficient inner peace and virtue to permit them to become capable of reconciling thought and action. Samson begins the last episode an integrated man. He has come far from the tormented self-loathing of "My self, my Sepulcher, a moving Grave" when he can say "My self? my conscience and internal peace." He takes leave of the Chorus as one entirely free to act or not to act because he has clearly brought together all the contrary and discomposed forces of his life and identified the core of his being with the honor, purity, and worth expressed in the unity of "Our God, our Law, my Nation, or my self." He does not know whether he will return; he does not know whether he will accomplish his destiny. He does know that he is now capable of "nothing dishonourable, impure, unworthy." The remainder of the tragedy consists of the effort of the Chorus and of Manoa to understand the reported catastrophe. The Messenger reports that the air of the temple, the "spacious Theatre," was rifted with a shout of scorn and derision, into the midst of which Samson came "patient but undaunted," that he stood "with head a while enclin'd . . . as one who pray'd, / Or some great matter in his mind revolv'd," that he proclaimed he would "with amaze . . . strike all who behold," and that he pulled down destruction upon himself and the Philistine lords, "the vulgar only scap'd."

Alone on stage with the Messenger, the Chorus and Manoa wrestle to take in and to apply the significance of what has happened, that is, to achieve and to communicate catharsis.[1] Two distinct modes of catharsis are involved in the conclusion of the play: Samson's catharsis and the catharsis of the on-stage audience. Samson himself consciously figures his action as tragic: it is a spectacle in a theater to amaze all who behold, the natural tragic effect of admiration considered by Renaissance theorists of tragedy as the major test of the genre.[2] Milton set on the title page a passage from Aristotle's *Poetics* in both Greek and Latin, the Greek reading "Tragedy is the imitation of a serious action . . . ," the Latin adding "achieving through pity and fear a purgation of these and similar passions." He glossed the epigraphs briefly in the preface. Tragedy is "said by *Aristotle* to be of power by raising pity and fear, or terror, to purge the mind of those and such like passions, that is to temper and reduce them to just measure with a kind of delight, stirr'd up by reading or seeing those passions well imitated. Nor is Nature wanting in her own effects to make good his assertion: for so in Physic things of melancholic hue and quality are us'd against melancholy, sowr against sowr, salt to remove salt humours." *Lustratio* was the Latin word Milton used for *catharsis; purge, temper*, and *reduce to just measure*, the English words. Milton committed himself to the view that tragedy moderates and does not annihilate the passions, a position consistent with the ethics of *Areopagitica*: "Wherefore did [God] create passions within us, pleasures round about us, but that

---

[1] The fullest and most elaborate statement of Samson's own catharsis is contained in John S. Hill's "Vocation and Spiritual Renovation in *Samson Agonistes*," *Milton Studies*, 2 (1970), 207-9, where the lessons learned are all spelled out: humility, patience, and faith as antidotes to pride, presumption, and doubt.

[2] See Martin E. Mueller, "Pathos and Katharsis in *Samson Agonistes*," *ELH*, 31 (1964), reprinted in *Critical Essays on Milton from ELH*, 249.

these rightly tempered are the very ingredients of virtue." Samson has reduced his own passions to just measure when he is able to attend, in silence and with indifference toward his own fate, to the impulses registering upon his well-tempered spirit:

> If there be aught of presage in the mind,
> This day will be remarkable in my life
> By some great act, or of my days the last.
>
> (1387-89)

Samson's *lustratio* is accomplished at the moment of his *anagnorisis*; tragedy has performed its ethical function, the mimesis of the government of the passions by reason. Reason has arisen through tragedy.

The Politics of the Chastened Nation

The catharsis of the on-stage audience brings into play the remaining aspects of Milton's definition of tragedy. To his concept of the moderation of the passions as the source of tragic value he added the ideas that imitation is the source of tragic delight, that delight accompanies and assists purgation, that the imitation is of the passions, and that purgation is analogous to medical effects in nature. These are the effects not solely upon the hero but upon the audience "reading or seeing those passions well imitated."[3] The value of the tragedy depends upon the completion of tragic effect in the reader or spectator; his passions are likewise tempered. The perturbations of the mind are like the diseases of the body; they are to be tempered by tragedy as the body is to be regulated by medicine. Painful emotions are to be composed by reliving them reasonably with the admixture of pleasure. The emotions cannot be allayed unless understood: what requires understanding is the instrumentality of tragedy itself. Nature, God, and the poet collaborate to present God-intended true experience. The play itself is "this great event," this happening which happens not only to the experiencing agent, the hero, but also to those for whom his experience is surrogate, first on stage and then in the reading.

What happens to Manoa and the Chorus onstage is unambiguous despite a sowr and salt irony. Manoa experiences sheer horror: "O all my hope's defeated . . . death who sets all free / Hath paid his ransom now." He blunders toward *peripeteia* by stages: "A dreadful way thou took'st to thy revenge," followed by "*Samson* hath quit himself like *Samson*," and culminating in the *anagnorisis* of

---

[3] The fullest discussion of Milton's tragic theory is that of John M. Steadman, "'Passions Well Imitated': Rhetoric and Poetics in the Preface to *Samson Agonistes*," in *Calm of Mind*, ed. Wittreich, 175-207.

> To *Israel*
> Honour hath left, and freedom, let but them
> Find courage to lay hold on this occasion,
> To himself and Fathers house eternal fame;
> And which is best and happiest yet, all this
> With God not parted from him, as was feard,
> But favouring and assisting to the end.
> Nothing is here for tears, nothing to wail
> Or knock the breast, no weakness, no contempt,
> Dispraise, or blame, nothing but well and fair,
> And what may quiet us in a death so noble.
>
> (1714-24)

The *anagnorisis* is limited. The application Manoa himself can make is strictly limited. From the correct lesson in the noble death, Manoa proceeds to a less correct: valiant youths are to repair to Samson's monument to inflame their breasts and virgins to mourn his marriages.

The Chorus also strives to understand. As a group they accept the tragic, they do not push it away. Samson *was* "tangl'd in the fold of dire necessity." His enemies were "fond"; "insensate . . . or to sense reprobate," they invited their own ruin. Samson's triumph lies not in their defeat but in himself: "with inward eyes illuminated" he revived, and his virtue reflourished though his body died. The Chorus's final words make a clear contemporary parallel between Gaza and "all that band them to resist / [God's] uncontroulable intent," but they teach again what was implicit in Samson's insight: "God may dispense with me or thee / For some important cause." The Holy One of Israel was Samson's guide as the Chorus had prayed. In their final lines they do not exult in the triumph of a Balshazzar's feast; rather, they speak of witness, example, wisdom overcoming passion, the people made more knowledgeable in the acquist of true experience, and of the catharsis in "calm of mind all passion spent." Samson's spiritual agony has yielded a tempering. The agony is not to be denied, but its fruit was illumination. God has behaved toward Samson like an Aristotelian tragic poet, and that is consistent with God's providence: life is the tragedy He records from human history; He designs the tragedy to effect the purgation. The quiet lesson at the close is the lesson of inner balance. Action is not debarred: Samson could act, but rebellion against the tyranny of passion is the true warfare of the spirit.

Samson has delivered his people by the only means Milton finally considered efficacious in history. He has shown them that each must be his own deliverer. Throughout the tragedy Milton plays on repetitions of the words *example, experience, prophecy, image, test, trial, spectacle, event,* and *occasion*: he links the catharsis on stage with the immediate experience of the audience. In the next stage of their history the chosen people must take the same path Samson took. They must not hope to escape their tragic destiny but to understand it and thence form a true community of the pure.[4] Samson literally failed to execute God's purpose. Philistines died, but Israel was not freed. Milton does not deny Samson's literal failure; he has lived through a similar literal failure of his own nation. In the Book of Judges the account of Samson's life is immediately followed by another story of the Tribe of Dan in which they vanish from history because of their unworthiness. They did not lay hold on the occasion; they did not "fight the good fight of faith, lay hold on eternal life whereunto thou art also called." They vanished from history as Samson might have vanished had he been merely mighty. Milton had no place in history ("sacred memory") for the merely mighty:

> In might though wondrous and in Acts of Warr,
> Nor of Renown less eager, yet by doome
> Canceld from Heav'n and sacred memorie,
> Nameless in dark oblivion let them dwell.
>
> (*Paradise Lost*, VI, 377-80)

But to the Judges picture of Samson as the failed deliverer of others, Paul in the Epistle to the Hebrews gave a different emphasis.[5] He transformed Gideon, Jephtha, and Samson from mere military heroes into elect saints: "Samson . . . who through faith . . . out of weakness was made strong," a true believer distinguished by his faith, one who fought for justice. The Chorus had also held Samson in mind with Gideon and Jephtha, as a scorned deliverer of others whom the people's slothful desire for "ease" made them reject. Living through the collapse of the Good Old Cause, Milton learned the tragic lesson incorporated in the death of Samson: there is no "ready and easy way" to establish a perfect and stable society; there is only a difficult and tragic way. Each must deliver himself from bondage into freedom that all then may reconstitute a nation defined by virtuous ends. The close of the tragedy contains the only hope, a muted and tragic hope, for a political future based on a knowledge of the historical past, for a community based on the consensus of a chastened quieted people.

[4] For a totally dissimilar conclusion see Shawcross, "Irony as Tragic Effect," 302.

[5] See F. Michael Krouse, *Milton's Samson and the Christian Tradition* (Princeton: Princeton University Press, 1949), 130-33.

Lay hold
on this occasion

III

SAMSON AGONISTES AND
MILTON'S POLITICS

Introduction

Two senses in which the figure of Samson communicates Milton's meaning by personifying a type have thus far been noticed in the tragedy. In the first sense Samson is representative of those who learn by tragic experience; in the second, he is the exemplar of God's continuous regulation of human history. Both meanings of type are familiar to most readers of *Samson Agonistes*.[1] The first meaning is still in current usage. It indicates one way in which the particular communicates the universal, and it predicates an intellectual adjustment to the hero's experiences which readers, whether contemporary or modern, make quite naturally: the protagonist enlightens us because he stands for us and undergoes experiences typical of his and our humanity. We learn from this sense of type that tragedy is meaningful and cathartic when our representative discovers for himself the significance of his experience. This sense of Samson's typicality stands outside the stream of time. Since Milton has truly observed the interior psychology of his hero, Samson can "always" communicate a diagnostic and curative rebalancing of the forces within man's heart and mind.

The second sense of type was contemporary to the seventeenth century, an inheritance from reformed theologians' practice of biblical interpretation. Rejecting the Roman Catholic interpretation of Scripture on the four levels of the literal, allegorical, tropological, and anagogical, Protestant theologians insisted that Holy Writ had but one meaning, although that *real* meaning could be the shadow or type of another *real* meaning.[2] Historical Old Testament accounts, according to Protestant hermeneutics, convey meaning to historical New Testament periods by means of figures whose deeds are chronicled in the Old Testament as prophecies or prefigurations of antitypes to come. This

---

[1] But see Pierre Legouis, "Some Remarks on Seventeenth-Century Imagery: Definitions and Caveats," in *Seventeenth-Century Imagery*, ed. Earl Miner (Berkeley: University of California Press, 1971), 192, for a rebuke to those who connive in permitting the word "to drift from its high position in the language of divinity to become an equivalent to 'kind' or 'class' and even to designate a representative of a class."

[2] For full theoretical discussions of typology see Rosemond Tuve, *Images and Themes in Five Poems by Milton* (Cambridge, Mass.: Harvard University Press, 1957), 37-72; Patrides, *Milton and the Christian Tradition*, 128-30; Madsen, *From Shadowy Types to Truth*, 18-35; John C. Ulreich, "The Typological Structure of Milton's Imagery," *Milton Studies*, 5 (1973), 67-82; MacCallum, "Milton and Figurative Interpretation of the Bible"; Northrop Frye, "The Typology of *Paradise Regained*," *Modern Philology*, 53 (1956).

is, of course, the way in which Milton understood the relationship of the Old and New Testaments: "Each passage of scripture has only a single sense, though in the Old Testament this sense is often a combination of the historical and the typological."[3] God makes the meaning of history clear by preserving accounts of certain individuals to whom special abilities and responsibilities were given and of their handling of their election, so that subsequent generations may understand the divine will and behavior throughout time. For the sake of the prophetic or educative force of those individual lives, God covenants with man to protract human history. At the midpoint between Books XI and XII in *Paradise Lost*, Michael instructs Adam in the reciprocal relationship between the actions of man and the reactions of God:

> So willingly doth God remit his Ire. . . .
> Such grace shall one just Man find in his sight,
> That he relents, not to blot out mankind,
> And makes a Covenant never to destroy
> The Earth again by flood, nor let the Sea
> Surpass his bounds, nor Rain to drown the World
> With Man therein or Beast; but when he brings
> Over the Earth a Cloud, will therein set
> His triple-colour'd Bow, whereon to look
> And call to mind his Cov'nant: Day and Night,
> Seed time and Harvest, Heat and hoary Frost
> Shall hold thir course, till fire purge all things new,
> Both Heav'n and Earth, wherein the just shall dwell.
>
> (XI, 885, 890-901)

Samson's life and death in this second sense of type illustrates the coherent meaning of human history recorded in Scripture. God wills a historical course which is redemptive for His human creatures. Neither history itself nor God's intention is annihilated by the failures of typical figures to realize God's intention, for God prophesies through their faith the mode of a future fulfillment. Equally, God does not simply allow senseless cyclical repetitions in history. He responds to man's use or abuse of freedom by intervening within his-

---

[3] *De Doctrina Christiana*, CPW, VI, 581. Milton also thought that "the Holy Scriptures were not written merely for particular occasions, as the Papists teach. They were written for the use of the church throughout all succeeding ages, not only under the law but also under the gospel" (*ibid.*, 575). Thus he believed not only that the New Testament fulfilled the Old Testament typology but that both meanings are exemplary for all historical times beyond the Gospel period. See Part V below for the argument that Milton came to prefer exemplary to typological explanations or dramatizations of Scripture.

tory to restore and augment freedom, for in that way the fate of representative individuals educates future generations. The reference to Samson as a faithful but failing champion of God in the Epistle to the Hebrews showed the relationship between type and antitype.

There is, however, a third sense in which Samson is a type. He is a representative type and a prophetic type; but equally he is an exemplary or parabolical figure who communicates both political and moral ideas. This section will consider *Samson Agonistes* as political teaching and the protagonist as a Commonwealth hero; Part Four will discuss *Samson Agonistes* as moral teaching and the protagonist as a hero purified by trial.

The Representative Hero and His Nation

On the political level, Milton uses the figure of Samson to show the way in which an individual may represent a nation and thereby encapsulate a nation's political existence. *Samson Agonistes* is a drama of the English revolution. It is a revolutionary work, not because it encourages a new political revolution, but because it has a popular hero who can teach Milton's contemporaries a republican truth. It is the work of a nationalist and patriot.

When on August 15, 1666, Milton wrote to Peter Heimbach thanking him for "an admiration of the marriage-union in me of so many different virtues,"[4] he professed himself "alive and well, nor useless yet, I hope, for any duty that remains to be performed by me in this life."[5] The duty accepted so long ago of writing "to celebrate in glorious and lofty Hymns the throne and equipage of God's almightiness, and what he works, and what he suffers to be wrought with high providence,"[6] had been discharged with *Paradise Lost*. Yet the duty might remain "to inbreed and cherish in a great people the seeds of virtue and publick civility" by means of writing "to deplore the general relapses of Kingdom and States from justice and God's true worship." In August 1666, Milton's constancy and his sense of obligation to his country had not vanished. To Heimbach he continued: "virtues are nourished most and flourish most in straitened and hard circumstances; albeit I may say that one of the virtues on your list has not very

---

[4] Heimbach had written, "You have achieved a blending, altogether rare and beyond the deserving of the age, of grave dignity . . . with the most unruffled courtesy, of charity with sound judgment, of piety with policy, of policy with boundless learning, and of a highminded and far from timid spirit (even when younger men were faltering) with a genuine love of peace." Quoted in William Riley Parker, *Milton, A Biography* (Oxford: Clarendon Press, 1968), 599.

[5] *Columbia Milton*, XII, 112-15.

[6] *CPW*, I, 816-17.

handsomely requited to me the hospitable reception she had. For what you call policy, but I would rather have you call loyalty to one's country,—that particular lass, after inveigling me with her fair name, has almost expatriated me, so to speak. The chorus of the rest [of the progeny of the marriage-union of virtues], however, makes a very fine harmony. One's country is wherever it is well with one."[7] The ruefulness of Milton's friendly words reveals the view of politics which enabled him to use *Samson Agonistes* as politically significant, and boldly and simply to relate the individual to his society and nation, so that through the failed representative and enslaved country, seventeenth-century England might discover what to make of its own recent political upheavals. At the time when Milton wrote that a man's country is where it is well with him, he was not entering into voluntary exile from England; although almost expatriated, he was not repudiating the virtue of loyalty. On the contrary, he was saying that a man is bound to his country or nation by ties of love and acceptance. Unlike Hobbes, Milton did not think that political cohesion was founded on self-interest and maintained by fear. For him, human ties are political realities, and a man's country is where he feels at home.

Politics is a network of relationships into which a man enters with other men. In the political sphere the human being, in terms of ends beyond his own, ends for which "our countrey is a name so dear," thinks responsively with his heart.[8] The first three acts of *Samson Agonistes* describe in terms of Samson's failure the failure of the English people. When the forces of Samson's soul are rebalanced, he is able to act for his country as well as for himself, to project his mind into the common future, where his action can be found worthy by standards other than self-interest. Samson names the standards by which worthiness is to be measured, from the highest to the lowest—"Our God, our Law, my Nation or my self." At that point in the drama, the leader reassures his people, shows them what is possible, shows them he will not leave them, makes common cause with them, shows them meaning in their sufferings, and begins a new movement which will go forward toward a more mature state of relationships among them. That

[7] That the ideas of continuing usefulness, of virtue put to the test, of marriage union as a description of well-integrated consciences, of patriotism, and of a chorus are all brought together in a letter written in 1666 is, of course, suggestive, since the ideas were not directly prompted by his correspondent. Too many are crucial to *Samson Agonistes* in this combination not to prompt the thought that Milton was considering a drama on a patriotic theme involving a test of virtue.

[8] But see E.M.W. Tillyard's edition of Milton, *Private Correspondence and Academic Exercises* (Cambridge: Cambridge University Press, 1932), xv, for the view that the letter expresses the extinguishing of patriotism.

movement is completed in the final lines of the drama.

Milton persistently thought in historical terms and allowed his mind to range from the past through the present and toward the future. But in his study of history he learned about current affairs as well. He saw that patterns in human relationships throughout time were identical to patterns in the politics of his own time. Because he had thought out a consistent political philosophy, he could write *Samson Agonistes* "with mortal voice, unchang'd / To hoarce or mute, though fall'n on evil days."[9] His politics had at its basis a conception of the relationship between the individual and the nation and between the nation and the church. Both involve Milton's concept of the representative. His concept of the politically representative enabled him to construct *Samson Agonistes* as a political work and to depict its hero as a political type.

Our understanding of the place of *Samson Agonistes* in Milton's political thinking has been more confused and inadequate, in my view, than our understanding of its relation to any other of its intellectual contexts. The reason is twofold: on the one hand, there is perplexity about whether Milton had any interest at all in politics after the Restoration; on the other hand, there is perplexity about the poetic means by which political concern may become explicit without ceasing to be poetic. A positive reading of the political level in *Samson Agonistes* has been impeded by doubt of Milton's grasp of politics and by mistrust of any reading which considers politics, and hence perhaps propaganda, as one level of a many-layered work of art. A reasonable concern with the stages in Milton's well-documented career in practical politics and the frustration of that political career has hardened recently into a settled conviction that his political beliefs fall into a simple rising and falling or outgoing and recoiling pattern: a period of hopefulness during which he evolved a theoretical libertarianism; a high point in *The Tenure of Kings and Magistrates* and *Areopagitica*, leading to a public post; a period of slow reluctant compromise with the events which whittled down the ideal of Commonwealth to the actuality of Protectorate; and a final, total withdrawal from public life and from patriotic concern for his nation.[10] There is, of course, schematic truth in this perception, but little truth in the corollary that

---

[9] *Paradise Lost*, VII, 24.

[10] Versions of this "simple" pattern can be found in: Stein, *Heroic Knowledge*, 63-77; Don M. Wolfe, *Milton in the Puritan Revolution* (London: Cohen and West, 1963), 337-51; Douglas Bush, *John Milton* (London: Weidenfeld & Nicolson, 1965), 123-30; James H. Hanford, *John Milton, Englishman* (New York: Crown Publishers, 1949), 149-54; and Parker, *Milton*, 589-93. Its currency is clearly suggested by its appearance in Potter, *A Preface to Milton*, 20-29.

Milton's reaction to his party's collapse was a complete retreat from political thinking into pure other- or inner-worldliness.[11] To argue so is to disregard the evidence of *De Doctrina Christiana* and of Milton's last tract, *Of True Religion*.

In the face of this prevailing view, however, doubts about the date of *Samson Agonistes* have been an additional obstacle to considering its political implications. If the tragedy was written in the late forties and early fifties, one could argue that it reflects the dark period when the Presbyterians had turned against the Independents and when a lonely, ill, nearly blind champion emerged to defend his country while his fellow citizens castigated him. This is undoubtedly the picture Milton intended to convey both of himself and of Samson in the *First Defence* of 1651.[12] If the tragedy was written immediately after the Restoration, one could argue that it reflects the even darker period when, without objection from the English people, the faithful leaders of the Good Old Cause were executed and their bodies dishonored, as Samson's countrymen basely gave him over to enslavement in order to save their own skins. Since in either case the tragedy becomes a local political statement by a party politician, literary critics seem to have felt obliged to play down altogether the political aspects of the play.

It is my conviction that *Samson Agonistes* is Milton's last testament in poetry and that it has public purposes consonant with a later date. It is also my conviction that Milton's political thought is not particularly time-serving, even where the emphases and forms of argument are directed toward achieving a difficult immediate consensus among his countrymen. Like his conception of history, Milton's political thought registers development, change, and modification; equally, it displays consistency and a faithful adherence to the overriding concepts of freedom, individualism, and toleration. *Samson Agonistes* is a political

[11] A very much more interesting picture of Milton's political development is drawn by Ernest Sirluck in "Milton's Political Thought: The First Cycle," *Modern Philology*, 61 (1964), 209-24, where the double helix of "formulation, ambivalence, retreat into an alternative theory; restatement, ambivalence, return to the abandoned theory" is presented in the course of its first coil. This picture has had continued support in the analysis of the 1659-1660 tracts made by Barbara Lewalski in *The Prose of John Milton*, gen. ed., J. Max Patrick (New York: Anchor Books, 1967), 439-47, 475-78, 519-27, and in her "Milton: Political Beliefs and Polemical Methods, 1659-60," *PMLA*, 74 (1959). In the remarkably interesting *The Politics of Milton's Prose Style*, Yale Studies in English, 185 (New Haven: Yale University Press, 1975), 101, Keith W. Staveley draws the end of the picture to show the poet "traveling openly through a hostile social landscape, denouncing what cannot be reformed . . . dramatizing the process he witnesses all around him and stating what it means."

[12] *CPW*, IV, pt. 1, 305-7, 402. See Parker, "The Date of *Samson Agonistes* Again," in *Calm of Mind*, ed. Wittreich.

document, not only as it reflects the dominant political concerns of the final phase of Milton's political thought, but also as it reflects consistent and overarching political principles in his works. Milton never failed to translate his own personal needs and discoveries into public terms. What was needful to him—be it a free press, a reformed divorce law, the choice of his pastor from among a brotherhood of preachers, or a disentangling of church from state in immediate disestablishment— he saw not as an exclusive and private need but as a general human need. Politics to him was a matter of arranging public relationships in conformity with private aspirations and fulfillment, for "all citizens equally have an equal right to freedom in the state."[13]

Yet the study of the political aspects of *Samson Agonistes* has been hampered by a kind of *a priori* notion that Milton could not have had "incompatible" ends in mind in writing the play. Thus literary critics who have responded to it as an introspective or religious or ethical work have regularly tried in passing to dispose of the view that it might also be politically orientated.[14] Some critics have taken the identification of political themes and motives in the play to be incompatible with recognition of its psychological verisimilitude, its acqui-

---

[13] *A Second Defence of the English People, CPW*, IV, pt. 1, 679ff. "All citizens of all description should enjoy equal rights and equal laws" in the translation in the *Columbia Milton*.

[14] See, for example, Barbara Lewalski: "Most critics have rightly resisted such explicit allegorical references to the contemporary scene as would make the play a parallel to Milton's political tracts, yet there are many undeniable resemblances in attitude and tone. . . . There is some reason to hear echoes . . . but no basis for reading the play as political allegory of any kind" ("Milton: Political Beliefs," 1061). E. L. Marilla, *Milton and Modern Man* (University: University of Alabama Press, 1968), 69, states: "There are basic fallacies . . . in this conception that *Samson Agonistes* . . . projects an eventual ascendency of Republican ideas . . . as a consummate fulfillment of the author's humanistic hopes and ideals." Arthur E. Barker, in "Calm Regained through Passion Spent," 35, summarized the view he himself repudiates: "We see that it is closet-drama and we conclude that we are to read it in the isolation of our closets, as we think Milton wrote it in the blinded isolation of his closet, despairingly closing the door on all merely mundane and human relations, in favour of a transcendent spiritual and poetic relation to something immutably absolute." David Masson, *The Life of John Milton* (London: Macmillan & Co., 1871-1880), is the source for the simpler sorts of allegorizing. In his interpretation, Harapha becomes a portrait of Salmasius; Samson, a portrait of Milton himself; Dalila, Milton's vengeance upon Mary Powell. Masson's suggestions were amplified by E. H. Visiak in *Milton Agonistes: A Metaphysical Criticism* (London: Werner Laurie, 1923), supported by C. E. Kreipe in *Milton's Samson Agonistes* (Halle, 1922), and refined by E. M. Clark, "Milton's Conception of Samson," *University of Texas Studies in English*, 8 (1928), 88-99. Carole S. Kessner, "Milton's Hebraic Herculean Hero," *Milton Studies*, 6 (1973), 243-58, draws attention to a public political aspect both in Samson and the Herculean hero of 17th-century drama.

escence in God's ways, its emphasis on personal virtue and regeneration, or its magnanimity. Instead, they have preferred to treat any comment on the political strands as reductive. They defend Milton against the charge, as it were, of writing "political allegory" because that would seem to mean that he was not writing something much finer. In my view, however, the dialectical structure of the drama organizes a number of dualities into subsuming harmonies and resolutions. Milton's habit of mind is not that of either/or but of uniting the "dessevered peeces." He saw no incompatibilities in multiple perspective, complex structures, and a spectrum of intentional effects; it is unnecessary to invent incompatibilities for him.[15] He did not find it incompatible to write for "after ages . . . our latest children's children and an age of sounder minds" *and* "to be some way serviceable to the Commonwealth"; "to defend at home and abroad the noble actions of my countrymen" *and* "to deplore the general relapses of . . . states"; "to be an interpreter and relater of the best and sagest things" *and* "to increase the welfare of life and of humankind." *Samson Agonistes* moves dialectically from the individual to the national, first through the figure of the elect hero and then through the chorus of his countrymen at the close of the play. And the tragedy is dialectical in another sense as well, a more frequently employed political sense. It is shaped by the political and social forces in Milton's experience, and Milton meant it, in turn, to act upon those forces.

[15] Galbraith N. Crump offers the telling metaphor of "the photographic process known as holography, from all angles at once" to describe the way in which Milton's "genius forced him into a kind of total engagement which would not allow him to do one thing at a time" (*Twentieth-Century Interpretations of "Samson Agonistes"* [New York: Prentice-Hall, 1968], 10-11).

POLITICAL INTENTION IN MILTON'S
SHORTER POEMS

Lycidas: The Autobiographical Swain
and the Perfected Community

The problem of how to read Milton's poetry as political in import comes into perfect focus with *Lycidas*. It was not the first of Milton's attempts at writing political poetry, but it is the most successful of those in the 1645 poems and the most significant for *Samson Agonistes*. *Lycidas* is self-professedly a timely poem, written for an "occasion" and using that occasion to speak timely words. It is a poem, moreover, which calls itself a monody but nevertheless weaves together other voices, speaking to and through the poet's voice in dialectical progression to make a three-part enactment of the thematic material. At the end a subsuming transforming meaning is achieved which contains topicality within universality. Ironically, the poem has been reproved for that timeliness by being dubbed "a poem *nearly* anonymous," as though the highest form of praise would have been to discover that it is a poem *wholly* anonymous.[1]

Lycidas is, alongside much else, a poem about immediate circumstances in England in the year of its writing, a poem about events and happenings which have meanings for its composer both proximate and ultimate. The poem undertakes to move through time in a structure conceived so that its events and occasion may be perceived as multivalent and its meaning as multivocal. The structure refers the action in an ascending order of universality to the great myths of classical

[1] I shall be referring to the essays collected in *Milton's "Lycidas": The Tradition and the Poem*, ed. C. A. Patrides (New York: Holt, Rinehart and Winston, 1961), supplemented by four other studies: Christopher Grose, *Milton's Epic Process* (New Haven: Yale University Press, 1973); Leslie Brisman, *Milton's Poetry of Choice* (Ithaca: Cornell University Press, 1973); Haller, *Rise of Puritanism*; and Lawry, *Shadow of Heaven*. I do not doubt that my own reading of *Lycidas* is indebted especially to the readings of my two teachers, Marjorie Hope Nicolson and William Haller, and to conversations with my three friends, Rosalie Colie, Irene Samuel, and Joan Bennett. I acknowledge all other specific debts.

literature, of national history, and of religion. Its power derives from the presence within it of a series of direct applications of these myths to the human condition. The poem is perennially moving, not because it is not rooted in any place and time, but rather because it is rooted in local circumstances which are expressed in universal myths. A man has died whose vocation was not unlike the poet's; his death deprived the Church of a faithful pastor in a year in which it had been polarized into two parties by a terrible conflict; the established Church was in fact supported in its ascendancy over the preaching brotherhood by Star Chamber proceedings against dissenters in that very year. These events become the occasion for a triple translation into significant allegory, one part of which the poet signally called attention to in his subsequent headnote, "In this Monody the Author bewails a learned Friend, unfortunately drown'd in his Passage from *Chester* on the *Irish* Seas, 1637. *And by occasion foretels the ruine of our corrupted Clergy then in their height*" (emphasis added).

The poem derives its rich, dense humanity precisely from the great need of the poet to make general sense out of particular pain. It derives its coherence from the device of the retrospective meditation of "the uncouth swain." The swain's monody—later described within the poem as "melodious tear," "Oate," "false surmise," and finally, "Dorick lay" —begins in an apparent present moment whose "Bitter constraint, and sad occasion dear" *compels* the poet to *gather* laurel, myrtle, and ivy and to *sing* for the dead Lycidas. But in a triple series of climaxes in each stage of the poem, when the poet has put to himself a question or heard a question put, the present tense is interrupted by an answering voice which also *speaks* in the present tense but is identified as having *spoken* in the past ("*Phoebus* repli'd, and touch'd my trembling ears"; "He shook his Miter'd locks, and stern bespake"). The interrupting answer having been recorded, the swain continues in the present tense, calling attention each time to his resumption ("That strain I heard *was* of a higher mood: / But now my Oate *proceeds*, / And *listens*"; "*Return Alpheus*, the dread voice *is past* / That *shrunk* thy streams"). Only after the invocation of the Angel Michael and the renunciation of "false surmise" for true ruth (in the lines beginning "Weep no more, woful Shepherds weep no more") does Milton discard the device of the pastoral singer and in his "own" voice place the entire monody in the past: "Thus sung the uncouth Swain." The poem which seemed to narrate encounters as they occurred in the imagination of the poet becomes at its conclusion a commemoration of a cathartic experience, of the harmonizing and interpreting of discordant experiences.

Lycidas is an inclusive, figurative work. On the simplest plot level, it translates the writing of an elegy for a young friend into the imaginary day of a bereaved shepherd whose thoughts from dawn until dusk (from when that "still morn went out with Sandals gray" to when "the Sun had stretch'd out all the hills, / And now was dropt into the Western bay") move back and forth between his own questions and impersonal authoritative answers as he seeks to compose a pastoral elegy. But not all of the poem is included in this plot, for the poem is framed by an editorial headnote written after the event and a final paragraph of *ottava rime* written as if by a spectator at the event of the elegy's composition. The frame calls attention to a distinction between a level of fact and a level of fiction. The factual, literal meaning of the poem embraces the fictive and underlines its existence as fiction. Within each of the poem's three parts further clear distinctions are made between truth and fiction. In the first movement a "melodious tear" or "fond dream" is distinguished from "a higher mood"; in the second movement an "Oate" is distinguished from a "dread voice"; in the final movement "false surmise" is distinguished from "the unexpressive nuptiall Song"; and in the envoi the *Dorick* Lay" itself is dismissed because it has been "replaced" by the possibility of the future ("To morrow to fresh Woods, and Pastures new"). The three movements are bound together by a shared strategy of redefinition and by ever-widening spheres of reference, from the poet in the natural world, to the pastor in the public world, to the microcosmic man in the macrocosmic universe. Moreover, all three are also bound by a consistent building on the truths established in previous movements against the posited fictions.

The dominant concept of the first third of the framed poem is a wrestling with a personal sense of loss. Milton's choice of pastoral elegy is a choice doubly metaphorical and hence doubly meaningful. The movement first presents as a true vision of reality the inescapable fact of the death of poets and the loss of even Orpheus to suggest that no assuagement of grief is possible, save in its expression. That reality is then contested by a truer vision of reality, and the voice of God's judgment is preferred to the expression of man's grief. The most obvious subjects to be dramatized are the psychological state of the grieving young shepherd and the means taken by him to come to terms with the premature death of a friend who showed early promise. Some of the means are delusory, some are more real. The poet to whom the triple crown of victory was to have been extended is offered at the outset a funeral wreath instead. By opening the poem with a cluster of covert quotations or allusions, Milton calls attention to his borrowing of a classical mode for the first delusory answer to bereavement. The reflexive fear of the uncouth swain attempts to include all human life within the inevitable pattern of death by drawing on elegiac poets who made the same point. A dirge like those of Theocritus, Moschus, and Virgil is to be sung for Lycidas because the poet too will die and will himself require a later poet's "lucky words" for his own "destin'd Urn."

At the beginning of the first movement, the poet and Lycidas are shown spontaneously singing their "Rural ditties" to "th' Oaten flute" in delighted response to their beautiful world; in return, Nature herself responds to their song, the trees "Fanning their joyous Leaves to [the] soft layes." The death of Lycidas is then, naturally enough, referred to the most encompassing myth of a poet's death available in common to Milton and the Greek poets, the death of Orpheus, for whom Nature likewise first joyed and then lamented. If it is a fond dream to think that the Muse herself could save her enchanting son, then it is vain to "strictly meditate the thankles Muse." The poet and Lycidas had progressed together from spontaneous to "laborious" creativity, spurred to virtue by the hope of glory. With his friend cut off so suddenly from the possibility of fame, the poet must question the usefulness of either verse or virtue. It is a painful question, and Pheobus alone has an answer.

The first movement, then, asks how to deal with the fact of the death of a poet in the midst of his serious preparations for Orphic poetry. It begins as though the answer were the minimal reassurance of the grief and respect of equally mortal poets: all poets must die, but they will be offered the form of eternity which the dirge may bestow. They die to live forever in verse. The movement concludes by rejecting such "broad rumour" and its circular view of time in favor of an upward movement "aloft" to a final pronouncement of worth "in Heav'n." A cyclical pastoral allegory has been proposed, and the Christian pilgrimage is offered to replace it. One level of allegory yields to a truer level of allegory in "a higher mood." The eternity of duration in human memory gives way to an eternity beyond duration in divine judgment.

The second movement commences with the poet reorienting himself on a more mundane level. It builds upon the same pattern of conjecturing first falsely and then truly. Whereas the first movement employed classical myth and the Orpheus analogy to assuage grief, this movement uses parable to dissipate fear and outrage at injustice. The figure of Orpheus slain gives way to the figure of the Good Shepherd excluded. Again, Lycidas and the uncouth swain are briefly shown together at Cambridge, where the poet remembers Lycidas as the dearest pledge, the most promising postulant. But then the commanding voice becomes that of St. Peter, who contrasts good pastors with "the corrupted clergy then in their height." The hungry sheep look in vain to those who should feed them and protect them from the grim wolf. The good shepherd is gone, and false shepherds have usurped his place.

In this movement the poet himself stands silent "And listens." He supplies nothing of his own, save, as it were, stage directions, first for Camus and then conclusively for Peter, as the movement of the verse circles down to the nadir of human betrayal "and nothing sed." The picture seems one of repetitive corruption of a high profession by hireling unfaithful herdsmen. The silence of the swain testifies to his helplessness in the face of reiterated depravity. Peter alone can sweep away the desperate vision of the continued intrusion of self-seekers encroaching upon the kingdom, the keys to which he carries. He does so in a voice like that of all-judging Jove. The exclusion of good shepherds by bad will not continue: "that two-handed engine at the door, / Stands ready to smite once, and smite no more." Peter tersely announces the judgment upon bad shepherds, the allegory of usurpation is swept aside by a dark allegory of final retribution, and Milton by occasion foretells the ruin of the corrupted clergy. Those who suspect that Milton enjoyed crying doom more than any other poetic activity and took sadomasochistic delight in deploring "the general relapses" should notice that the ascription of doom is to the voice of Peter, that Peter is not given the last word, and that the swain resumes with a note of human remorse, turning from "the dread voice" to the "milde whispers" of valleys to open the last movement.

The last movement builds carefully upon the two preceding movements, once more positing a fictional allegory and replacing it with a real allegory. In no other movement does Milton more carefully draw attention to the contrast. He specifically announces an indulgence in the fictional, "For so to interpose a little ease, / Let our frail thoughts dally with false surmise." At first, in a quiet descriptive vein, the poet offers Lycidas "every flower that sad embroidery wears" from the spring of the year in tribute to his early death. That song is self-deluding, and the poet knows it. Lycidas is denied his "moist vows" by the sounding seas which "wash [his body] far away." There is nothing the poet can do or say to reach the youth who "under the whelming tide / [Visits] the bottom of the monstrous world." A consoling "false surmise" is bluntly suppressed by literal realism: the body of the drowned man is borne to the depths of the Irish Sea by deep tides, either "beyond the stormy *Hebrides*" northward into the Atlantic, or past Lands End southward in the direction toward which St. Michael's Mount looks. There is nothing to balance "sunk." The poet's tearful prayers cannot find their object; the poet can only implore the guardian of St. Michael's Mount himself to melt with ruth. The thought of Michael prompts the poet, however, to invoke the higher allegorical reference of the third movement. The cyclical fiction that man's life is like the star that sinks and rises is quietly dropped in favor of an image of ascending into a final perpetual society of the risen, where all the saints sing the unutterable nuptial song of their true timeless community. This true vision, given through the voice of the poet as a vision intuitively grasped after the earlier levels of truth have been attained, is modulated into greater calm by two couplets enunciating the consolation of the shepherds and their conviction that Lycidas is with them yet to help them, to "be good / To all that wander in that perilous flood."

The three movements are not disjunct treatments of three special areas of human experience; they are progressive stages of enlightenment. In all three, the allegorical seems to be proposed and then withdrawn, but in fact, the new truth itself is a superior form of allegory. The mind discards a false image in favor of a realistic image, which itself contains a true fiction. Variations played upon the theme of singing and song may illustrate both the dialectical nature of the argument and the self-corrective nature of the allegory. The sonnetlike prologue associates the life of Lycidas with "lofty rhyme," the definition at which the poem will finally arrive. Milton was sure that "he who would not be frustrate of his hope to write well hereafter in laudable things, ought himself to be a true poem; that is a composition and pattern of the best and honourablest things; not presuming to sing high praises of heroic men, or famous cities, unless he have in himself the experience and the practice of all that which is praiseworthy."[2]

The association of writing well with living well was instinctive with Milton: the good life was like a good poem, the good poem prompted and celebrated the good life. The first movement begins quaintly, locally, and fictionally: "lucky words" for the singers of "Rural ditties"; the glory of "broad rumour" for poems and lives that "strictly meditate." It ends when the "lofty rhyme" "spreds aloft" to permit a final poem to receive a final criticism, and Jove "pronounces lastly." The second movement treats the pastor-teacher as a poet as well: usurping poet-pastors sing "lean and flashy songs," have grasped power for themselves and reduced their fellows to voicelessness ("nothing sed"). Hirelings have intruded into the fold for personal gain; their songs express their egotism and are as "flashy" as works written "to make verbal curiosities thir end . . . a toylsom vanity."[3] No encompassing song of community can arise from such and they are obliterated. The third movement adds the "I" and "thee" of the first movement to the "worthy bidden guest" of the second movement to create "sweet Societies / That sing, and singing in their glory move." *Lycidas* modu-

[2] *CPW*, 1, 890.   [3] *Ibid.*, 810.

lates in these three treatments of song, from the good singer lost, to the choral community established. The poem commences as monody but ends (before the dismissal, in a last sonnet-like conclusion, when Milton himself sets the rustic singer aside and tells the reader plainly that the poem he has been reading was finished by a completion of reassurance in the poet's own mind and a confidence in the future) as a harmonious polyphony.[4]

The political thought informing *Lycidas* involves a vision of community, a detestation of hirelings, a progressive effort at forward-looking understanding, and a profound concern for Milton's own countrymen. The urgency of the poem arises from its occasion and from the anxiety present in the immediate historical context; the solace of the poem derives from its comprehending a whole society in terms of the progress of a solitary singer toward understanding. The concern of the speaker is for the dangers he and his country face in 1637. What has happened to Edward King may happen to any individual, what he might have been able to do for his nation may by his loss be impossible to achieve. The good is fragile and contingent; the loss of one shepherd affects all shepherds, and the destruction of one teacher and leader affects all who wander in the perilous flood. But the poem concludes with a restored society of singer and shepherds. The poem strikingly prepares for the strategy of *Samson Agonistes*. *Lycidas*, as composed by the uncouth swain, contains the movement from loss in death to triumph in death. Lycidas is given the "recompense" of hear-

---

[4] This reading of *Lycidas* is so indebted to previous readings that the layers of indebtedness are difficult to disentangle. Some, however, are reasonably clear: Arthur Barker, "The Pattern of Milton's Nativity Ode," *University of Toronto Quarterly*, 10 (1941), 167-81, proposed the triple movement of the poem's organization; F. T. Prince, *The Italian Element in Milton's Verse* (Oxford: Clarendon Press, 1962), 71-88, suggested attention to the transitions and repetitions in the poem; John Crowe Ransom, "A Poem nearly Anonymous," *American Review*, 1 (1933), 179-203, first called attention to the multiplicity of voices in the poem; David Daiches, *A Study of Literature* (Ithaca: Cornell University Press, 1948), pointed toward the patriotic strain in the poem; William Madsen, "The Voice of Michael in *Lycidas*," *Studies in English Literature*, 3 (1963), identified one of the voices as that of Michael, an identification which I do not think can stand but is not important to my argument; M. H. Abrams, in *Varieties of Literary Experience*, ed. S. Burnshaw, pointed to the evolution in the thought of the uncouth swain. (All these contributions are included in the collection *Milton's "Lycidas,"* ed. Patrides). Jon S. Lawry drew attention to the dialectic structure of the poem in both *Shadow of Heaven* and in "'Eager Thought': Dialectics in *Lycidas*," *PMLA*, 77 (1963), 27-32. Christopher Grose, *Milton's Epic Process*, commented on the poet's substitution of true fiction for untrue fiction. And Haller, *Rise of Puritanism*, discussed the poem as the expression of the Puritan spirit on the eve of revolution.

ing described his reunion with God, who was not responsible for, but permitted, his death and did not obliterate, but rather established, his usefulness in that death, for Lycidas will now forever exercise his pastoral care for the earthly society he has left by being exemplary to it. The survivor-poet's final lines apply the redefinition of human loss and divine renewal to himself: he can now move forward; he is no longer writing "with forc'd fingers rude . . . before the mellowing year"; and for "tomorrow" he looks forward in hope to an increased service. Similarly, the first four acts of *Samson Agonistes* trace the course of events from death in life to life in death, from the will to die to a willing death. By the fifth act, Samson's seeming self-defeat by defining correctly its element of self-conquest and fair quittal has become a voluntary self-sacrifice fulfilling his vocation. The final act translates the death of Samson into life for his people, if they can "lay hold on this occasion."

Lycidas conveys political meaning in the same manner as *Samson Agonistes*. It expresses the poet's anger that his countrymen should be oppressed, insulted, and tyrannized by Laud's prelates; it expresses his concern for their discontent and gives hope for the future, promising "good to all that wander." *Samson Agonistes* likewise expresses the poet's anger that his countrymen should stand an example to future times of self-defeat, "an ignominy . . . that never yet befell any nation possessed of their liberty." It expresses his grief that some among that nation should be betrayed "far worthier than by their means to be brought into the same bondage." And it expresses his concern for them and his understanding of their oppressed acquiescence, and warns them of a God stern "to all that band them to resist / His uncontroulable intent." Anger does not have the last word in *Lycidas*, and neither grief nor anger have the last word in *Samson Agonistes*. Both poems terminate in reassurance and encouragement.

It would be possible and very agreeable to examine *Comus* also as an occasional poem embodying a political strand. To do so, one need only glance at an action communicated within the framing voice of the Attendant Spirit, the voice of a participant poet-observer. As a poet-prophet, the Attendant Spirit's errand is to "som . . . that by due steps aspire / To lay their just hands on that Golden Key / That ope's the Palace of Eternity." The action begins at the moment when the poet-prophet descends in rustic disguise to

> take the Weeds and likenes of a Swain . . .
> Who with his soft Pipe, and smooth-dittied Song,
> Well knows to still the wilde winds when they roar,

And hush the waving Woods, nor of lesse faith,
And in this office of his Mountain watch,
Likeliest, and neerest to the present ayd
Of this *occasion*.

(84, 86-91)

The occasion the poem recounts is that of a pilgrim lost but essentially not alone. She faces temptation and danger, but led by the radiant light of inner virtue in a persistent journey toward heaven and "attended by a strong siding champion Conscience," she is a pilgrim unmistakably associated with an ideal of republicanism, attracted to a vision of courtesy "sooner found in lowly sheds" and of the just distribution of Nature's goods to all men "In unsuperfluous eeven proportion." When the action of pilgrimage has ended, the voice of the Attendant Spirit "epiloguizes" to such "mortals" as have "true" ears, reminding them that through virtue they too may climb "Higher then the Spheary chime." They too may find that when "Heav'n hath timely tri'd their youth, / Their faith, their patience and their truth," they will triumph as a community "in victorious dance." The moment of most powerful intellectual energy in the work would be seen to be the moment when the mortal spokesman for all the nation rebukes the few who with "swinish gluttony" gorge themselves and blaspheme their feeder. The Lady hates it "when vice can bolt her arguments / And vertue has no tongue to check her pride." Speaking this resonant republicanism with a bravura sense of her own force ("Shall I go on? / Or have I said anough?"), the Lady prophesies the coming political age of true brotherhood and contemptuously leaves to Comus "deer Wit and gay Rhetorick." To her true words "dumb things" and even the "brute Earth" will respond in sympathy.

It would be equally possible and agreeable to look even further back in Milton's life to another "occasional" poem with political significance, a poem which was to comprise the poet's "gifts for the birthday of Christ—gifts which the first light of its dawn brought to me." The occasion was "This . . . Month, and this . . . happy morn," Christmas 1629. To examine this work is to notice once more that the Hymn itself is enclosed within a frame of the contemporary. At the beginning the poet asks the Heavenly Muse to "run" and "prevent" the "Star-led Wisards" with the gift of a "humble ode" to lay at Christ's "blessed feet." At the conclusion, the poet withdraws into the present to imagine that the star has risen which will lead the wizards to the past occasion with their particular gifts to the child. Within the frame, Milton again invents a triple structure, beginning with an apparently naturalistic but highly figurative description of the setting in which the birth occurred, a setting of silence broken only by the shepherds on the lawn "simply chatting." That chatting is set aside in the second movement when angelic music fills the air to unite "all Heav'n and Earth in happier union." The New Testament shepherds hear a "loud and solemn choir," but the contemporary reader of the poem heard instead Milton's extolling of the music of the spheres as containing a power of such irresistible force that it could itself redeem the world and roll time back to a perfection in which "Truth and Justice then / Will down return to men." For three splendid stanzas Milton allows truth to move from mind to mind, "our senses" and "our fancy" perceiving all men swept forward in a Puritan saga of reformation. He recalls abruptly, however, that his theme is the "babe" who "lies yet in smiling Infancy" and that reformation must await the day of judgment, when "at last our bliss true and perfect is." The third section builds again on the vision of a forceful truth spreading from man to man. The former "truth" of "Oracles" is gone, "Nor all the gods beside / Longer dare abide." Each man is now free to enlarge his understanding, unimpeded by fictions offering superseded truths. The "rayes of Bethlehem blind" false seers; true myth is substituted for fictive mythology, and the infant Christ better than the infant Hercules "Can in his swadling bands control the damned crew."

THE SONNETS: THE EXEMPLARY POET AND HIS EVOLVING POLITICS

The most self-evidently occasional poems of political import are the sonnets, some of which constitute the only record in poetry of Milton's public life during the years devoted to prose and politics ending at the Restoration. They can tell us far more about Milton's continuing political ideals and the way he made poetry of them than can the earlier lyric and dramatic works. Milton's sonnets constitute a sequence of individually composed poems, arranged by the poet for the edition of 1673 in an order largely, but not invariably, chronological.[5] The order was fixed by Milton for a contemporary reader, who was given thereby a consistent sequence of sonnets written over a number of years between 1629 and 1658 and now offered as a new whole. They have become the record of a strongly defined and evolving didactic purposiveness having both private and public, or both moral and political, aspects. Looked at individually, the sonnets are isolated occasional poems which repeatedly signal their completeness and individuality by internal ref-

[5] See E.A.J. Honigman, ed., *Milton's Sonnets* (London: Macmillan, 1966), 59-75, for a summary of conflicting dating proposals, and see Appendix A below for a chart of the dates offered by the major modern editors of the sonnets.

erences to their specific times of composition;[6] not one is lacking its *day, hour, now, then, while,* or *when.* Because there are particular literary tasks for which the poet considers the sonnet form to be ideally suited, some sonnets resemble one another. Looked at a little less in isolation, they fall into clusters and subgroups, in which an atomistic topicality becomes subsumed in a linked topicality. Because they employ one consistent form with its own interior dialectical structure and form a consistent dialectical progression, looked at still less near-sightedly, the sonnets take the shape of a self-consistent pattern: the individual occasions and the group topicality both yield to a sequential unity which presents the public and private evolution of the poet as a teacher of his nation.

Three aspects of political and personal exemplary truth are discernible in the sonnets. All three are intentional. Milton intended each sonnet to bear its individual meaning; he grouped the sonnets by interlinked cross-reference and wrote them at distinct periods, often several years apart, so that a thematic meaning emerges within subgroups. He then printed them retrospectively, breaking chronology for other effects, and brought them together so that a final polyphonic harmony would be apparent in them.[7] One chord in the retrospective harmony could not be fully sounded in his own lifetime, that of a commemorative celebration of the republicans Fairfax, Cromwell, Vane, and him-

---

[6] For example: Sonnet 1, "Now timely sing"; 7, "my three and twentieth year"; 10, "the sad breaking of that Parlament"; 11, "was writ of late"; 19, "E're half my days"; 20, "a sullen day"; 22, "this three years day."

[7] My reading of the sonnets in this fashion is a break with the traditional exegesis. Most criticism treats the sonnets as a discontinuous series of poems recording particular events written "during his few spare moments" in a busy public life (e.g., Maurice Kelley, "Milton's Later Sonnets and the Cambridge Manuscript," *Modern Philology,* 54 (1956-1957), 20-25; Lois Potter, *A Preface to Milton,* 129ff.). By such treatment they are best read for the light they throw on Milton's preoccupations in the years of their composition. Some criticism, however, doubts the mere chronological arrangement of the poems and argues subgroupings for aesthetic effect. The earliest criticism to notice thematic sequence is the edition by John S. Smart (Glasgow, 1921), and the fullest consideration is that of E.A.J. Honigman. William McCarthy, "The Continuity of Milton's Sonnets," *PMLA,* 92 (1977), 96-109, also finds in the sonnets "ordering patterns of concern" which "justify regarding them as a sequence," but he does not discuss politics as one of the patterns. The argument that there is no inconsistency between the two critical approaches is my own, as is the argument that Milton retrospectively designed the sequence to bear comprehensive didactic meaning. I believe that Milton gave such retrospective shape to the entire sequence in the same sort of way that he distinctively altered *Paradise Lost* between the 1667 and 1674 editions. For the sonnets, all that was necessary was to reverse the order of composition in four cases. Some sonnets could not be brought forth in 1673. These constitute a subgroup by themselves, linked by theme, strategy, and tone.

self as the defenders of the republic in "*Cyriack*, this three years day."
The four sonnets, 15, 16, 17, and 22, were not printed together until
they appeared at the end of Edward Phillips's preface to Milton's *Letters of State* (1694).

Traditionally, the sonnet is a form in which the poet can express his
personal concerns. For a poet whose most urgent personal concerns
repeatedly involved the appropriate use of his own abilities in adequate
public ways, the sonnet also was traditionally a "heroic" lyric form
which could voice public themes. Milton began writing sonnets in
1629 at the age of twenty-one and ceased in 1658, at the age of fifty.
The extended personal exordia to Books I, III, VII, and IX of *Paradise
Lost* could then give outlet to any of the impulses appropriate to the
sonnet tradition that were not incorporated in the epic itself. The sonnets
begin with one describing a night in spring when the poet enrolls
himself as a servant of the Muse and of Love; they end with another
night, in which the return of day interrupts the blind poet's dream of
the face of his newly dead wife, whom he had never seen in life, a dawn
returning him to "ever during dark." As a coherent whole the sonnets
repeatedly consider two ethical topics: the struggle of virtue toward
purification, and the necessity that the poet be a good man if his poetry
is to be great. Through the use of numerous figurative contrasts—such
as the hill of heavenly truth contrasted with the broad way and the
green; brutal war contrasted with gentle acts; firm unshaken virtue contrasted
with violence and fraud; a tardy poet contrasted with a careful
poet; an impatient taskmaster contrasted with a gracious taskmaster;
slaughtered saints contrasted with bloody Piemontese—the sonnets
show how virtue requires choice and how the soul must be ripened to
dwell with God. Similarly, they repeatedly identify good art with
the good artist, the man who is led by the will of God, who loves
liberty and so "must first be wise and good," whose skill like Lawes's
is associated with worth, whose friends are the virtuous son or daughter
of a virtuous father or the virtuous grandson of a virtuous grandfather.

Individually, many of the sonnets are explicitly autobiographical:
the poet chooses slow poetic self-development; he defends the doors
of his London house against royalist attack; he ironically regrets the
reception of his divorce tracts; he celebrates the fellowship of his
friends; he reveals the thoughts which console him for the loss of sight;
he laments his dead wife. Many others are self-quoting and remind the
reader of a continuous single voice which has sung before.[8] The Mil-

---

[8] For example: "Propitious *May*" half quotes "bounteous *May* that dost inspire";
"when all the woods are still" quotes "dum silet? omne nemus"; "mio cuor
l'humil dono" quotes "lay it lowly at his blessed feet"; "spelling fals" quotes

tonic ethic placed before the reader through the sonnets both autobio-
graphically and occasionally involves exposure to danger and public
disdain; it involves a general relapse of the nation within which is ex-
tolled a pure conscience and a private sense of well-doing consonant
with the approval of God; and it involves submission to tragic experi-
ence and acceptance of the terrible ways in which God deals with His
chosen, recompensing the saints with slaughter, the seer with blindness,
and the loving husband with bereavement. But besides the general co-
herence of the sonnets as didactic poems, there are five clusters of son-
nets which in stages present, in addition to large ethical truths, the po-
litical discoveries of the periods to which they belong. Through these
clusters the poet traces the evolution of his moral and political thought
to arrive at a public truth about God's ways toward men. The sonnets
individually and collectively record a process or struggle which, like
that in *Lycidas* and in *Samson Agonistes*, issues in the poet's offering
his experience to his nation as exemplary.

The five clusters into which the sonnets fall are natural, primarily
chronological, thematic units. The first seven sonnets, written between
1629 and 1632, express Milton's youthful confident sense of the irre-
sistibility of virtue and the certainty of election. They express a prom-
ised destiny (the loss of which darkens the opening of *Samson Ago-
nistes*). In these sonnets Milton is certain, as he wrote in the Seventh
Prolusion that "when universal learning has once completed its cycle,
the spirit of man . . . will reach out far and wide, till it fills the whole
world and the space far beyond with the expansion of its divine great-
ness." He was confident that "one family, one man endowed with
knowledge and wisdom, like a great gift of God, may be sufficient to
reform a whole state." He even ventured to think that he was that
man. Sonnet 1, "O Nightingale, that on yon bloomy spray, / Warbl'st
at eeve," is a simply erotic opening to this group; the poet finds May
propitious for love and poetry and subscribes himself servant to both.
Five Italian sonnets follow, all also erotic but expressive of a particu-
larly Miltonic form of amorousness: the poet loves the *Donna leggiadra*
because she is lofty; he wishes his slow heart were as good soil for
heavenly plants as for the flower of love; he does not mention the
lady's hair, lips, or cheek except to confess to his confidant, Diodati,
that it is not these but her incarnation of an ideal which moves him;
and when he offers her his heart he commends not her value but rather

---

"hard to be spelled"; "and drink thy fill of pure immortal streams" echoes "and
other streams along"; "the paw of hireling wolves" quotes "the grim wolf with
privy paw"; "preventive shears / Clips" quotes "abhorred shears / Slits." Edward
Le Comte, *Yet Once More: Verbal and Psychological Pattern in Milton* (New
York: Columbia University Press, 1953), has studied Milton's self-allusions.

that heart, describing it as faithful, dauntless, and loyal, fair, wise, and good in its thoughts. He elaborates his praise of his own heart in terms which clearly foreshadow the portrait of the Lady in *Comus* as one with "light within her own clear breast":

> When tempest shake the world, and fire the sky
> It rests in adamant self-wrapt around,
> As safe from envy, and from outrage rude,
> From hopes and fears, that vulgar minds abuse
> As fond of genius, and fixt fortitude,
> Of the resounding lyre, and every Muse.[9]

The last sonnet of this early group rounds off the cluster into a single temporal unit. Sonnet 7 has metaphorically transformed "propitious *May*" into a "late spring" which as yet "no bud or blossom shew'th." The octave laments that Milton's "inward ripenes" has not shown forth. The sestet simply and directly records the poet's intention to use his gifts steadily in God's service "soon or slow . . . in strictest measure eev'n." As an occasional poem, this sonnet is the most interesting of the group. The group as a whole has coherence in moving from the subject of poems and love in spring, through the union of love and virtue, to a poem on virtue in late spring. In all seven the latent theme is the poet's true heart. But the "Letter to a Friend" in the Trinity Manuscript makes clear the particular occasion of the capping sonnet. The friend has complained that too much love of learning has kept Milton from putting his gifts to use. Milton answers him in two forms: the letter written because "I think myselfe bound though unask't, to give you account, as oft as occasion is, of this my tardie moving"; and the sonnet enclosed with the letter. He explains "that you may see that I am something suspicious of my selfe, and doe take notice of a certain belatedness in me, I am the bolder to send you some of my nightward thoughts some while since." He pledges himself to be God's servant and declares that the desire to do his best, even at the cost of beginning late, is what keeps him at his studies, notwithstanding his strong impulses to found a family, secure fame, and avoid the "seizing" that befell the man who hid his talent. Milton has not cut himself off from action. He is ambitious "either to defend and be useful to his friends, or to offend his enemies," but he is taking thought to be fit rather than early. The sonnet similarly considers in brief the poet's few achievements to date and then decisively rededicates him to God's service. Of particular interest are the traces of militancy in the letter's

[9] The translation is by William Cowper, *Latin and Italian Poems of Milton Translated into English Verse* (London: J. Johnson, 1808), 101.

reference to defending his friends and offending enemies and the traces of volitional grimness in conceiving of God as a taskmaster.

The capping sonnet of the first group is, as we shall see, to be carefully balanced by an answering sonnet, Sonnet 19, the first in the final cluster. But for the moment, we have seen that the first cluster shows how thoroughly Milton endorsed the domination of his poetic gifts by Puritan didacticism, how perfectly the mood both of the Nativity Ode and of *Comus* is echoed in this group, and with what degree of self-conquest the group ends, issuing as it does in the projection of compulsion onto God the taskmaster and of obedience onto Milton. Milton at this stage has taken the opportunity offered by the dialectical structure of the sonnet form. The octave presents him as he appears, unready, tardy, minimizing his own maturity to pretend that twenty-four is "manhood . . . *near*" rather than present. The sestet, however, presents him as he knows himself to be in reality, decisive, confirmed in his faith, cognizant of the distance between himself and his great Taskmaster but confident and exultant that "soon or slow" he will move across that space "in strictest measure eev'n, to that same lot." The logical form of the sonnet replaces appearance with reality in an individual allegory of pilgrimage.

Ten years elapsed between the writing of the first and second groups of sonnets.[10] Sonnets 8, 9, and 10 were all written in 1642 and 1643 while Milton was exploring in the divorce tracts questions of domestic liberty. In this group, the ethics of purity through election is modulated into an ethics of purification through trial in free choice. From this ethical stance, Milton never deviated; but when he turned from ethics to politics, he moved through three further stages in his thinking. The second and third group of sonnets, separated by two or three years, moved from the treatment of private, active virtue to civil liberty. The third cluster of five sonnets, Sonnets 11, 12, 13, and 14, and "On the new forcers of conscience," considers the public implications of urging liberty of conscience. They grew out of Milton's most revolutionary period, when he was arguing in prose "the liberty and right of freeborn men to be governed as seems them best." The fourth group of sonnets, separated from the previous group by two years, includes Sonnets 15, 16, 17, and 18, written between 1648 and

---

[10] See Appendix A for the chronology of the sonnets' composition according to the major editors and biographers of the last 30 years, together with the chronology and subgroup divisions which seem to me most sensible and coherent. I have not summarized the evidence offered by each authority since a summary can be conveniently found in *A Variorum Commentary on the Poems of John Milton*, ed. Merritt Hughes, Vol. II, ed. Douglas Bush (London: Routledge & Kegan Paul, 1972), pt. 2.

1655, years in which the Puritan revolution gradually fell upon more and more difficult days and Milton conceded in prose that "real and substantial liberty is rather to be sought from within than from without." The fifth group breaches the chronological arrangement to place at its opening a very personal sonnet written two years before the last public sonnet of group four. In the fourth group Milton labored to prevent the revolution from failure; the last five sonnets, written between 1652 and 1658, turn from public movements back to the private individual as the source of political hope. If the state cannot be steadily reformed (second cluster), or remade by successful popular movements (third cluster), or even freed by a resolute minority (fourth cluster), it can be enlightened by privately regenerate men (final cluster), and the moving power of poetry can be turned "to make the people fittest to choose and the chosen fittest to govern."

The second group of sonnets opens with an occasional poem first entitled in the Trinity Manuscript "On his dore when ye Citty expected an assault," then corrected in Milton's own hand to "When the assault was intended to ye Citty." Both titles were deleted for the 1645 edition. The poet guards his door with a poem addressed to any royalist invader, pointing out that as a poet he has the power to confer immortality upon appropriate heroes, those capable of "deed[s] of honour" and "gentle acts," and reminding the "Captain, or Colonel, or Knight in Arms" that military men have hitherto spared as shrines the houses of poets. The two ensuing poems may be taken to express Milton's understanding, arrived at in Sonnet 8, of the role of poetry in peace and war. Each is to "spred . . . o're Lands and Seas" the fame of the Lady Margaret Ley or of the "Lady that in the prime of earliest youth, / Wisely has shun'd the broad way and the green." All three sonnets extol virtuous action. Sonnet 9 is the most fanciful: a lady as dedicated as the Lady of *Comus* (and as open to criticism therefore as "the Lady of Christ's") has borne jibes with "pity and ruth" for her critics; she is assured that the "Bridegroom with his feastfull friends" will join her voice to the nuptial song, for she has chosen wisely to be like Mary and not Martha, Ruth and not Orpah, the wise virgins and not the foolish. She, like Milton in Sonnet 7, has *chosen*. Sonnet 10 honors Lady Margaret Ley for embodying the virtues of her father and by occasion commends her father's devotion to public ideals, a devotion so great that his public service was ended only when "the sad breaking of that Parlament / Broke him"; an act "fatal to liberty" was fatal to him. All three sonnets merely touch public themes, however. The Puritan poet has given general notice that he will take occasion to praise Puritan heroes. Like Tasso, whom he admired, Milton composed love sonnets, heroic sonnets, and moral sonnets. As the earlier love sonnets are erotic in a distinctively Miltonic fashion, so too the heroic sonnets (poems of praise and lamentation) are heroic in a distinctively Miltonic form of didacticism: for every grain of panegyric there will be a gram of advice. The last sonnet of the second group was the final one printed in the poems of 1645. Its resonant lamentation of the "dishonest victory . . . fatal to liberty" broaches the topic with which the third group is concerned.

This third group, Sonnets 11, 12, 13, and 14, and "Ye forcers of Conscience," belongs to the years 1645 and 1646. Sonnets 11 and 12 and "Ye forcers" are vituperative, written by Milton to "offend his enemies"; Sonnets 13 and 14 are complimentary, written to "be useful to his friends." The vituperative three are meant to castigate the people indifferent to the liberty Milton offered them in the divorce tracts and to sting the censors he had attacked in *Areopagitica*; the complimentary pair balances them with forms of praise, the unjust denial of which burned behind the denunciatory group. Lawes's "worth and skill" exempted him "from the throng, / With praise enough for Envy to look wan." Mrs. Thomason's good works spoke the truth about her "on glorious Theams / Before the Judge"; she had a just soul "ripen'd . . . to dwell with God." The instructions in Milton's own hand in the Trinity Manuscript do not make it clear whether he would have wished "Ye forcers" to be published following Sonnet 11 or preceding Sonnet 15, thereby closing off the group.[11] The printed

[11] The Trinity Manuscript does give significant evidence of an order of conscious retrospective realignment of the poems within the group for a particular effect, however. On page 43 of the manuscript, following two drafts of Sonnet 13 in his own hand, Milton entered the title, also in his own hand, "On the detraction which followed on my writing certain treatises." He himself then entered as Sonnet 11 "I did but prompt." On the obverse of that sheet, again in Milton's own hand, is a rough unnumbered draft of the sonnet given the title "On ye religious memory of Mrs. Catherine Thomason," followed by a fair copy of that sonnet with the title deleted and the number 14 supplied. The following manuscript page, number 45, is a small sheet headed in the hand of an amanuensis "those sonnets follow ye 10. in ye printed books. On the detraccon which followed upon my writing certaine treatises." "I did but prompt" appears first on that page, numbered with a figure which may be either 11 or 12 and followed by "A book was writ of late" clearly numbered 12. On the obverse of that small sheet, in the same copyist's hand, Sonnets 13 and 14 are transcribed. The next page, number 47, contains a heavily corrected "A book was writ," written in Milton's hand and clearly numbered 12; below it is a marginal note: "on ye forcers of Conscience to come in heer. turn over the leafe." A copy of Sonnet 15 follows. The note is so placed that it may mean either that "ye Forcers" should follow "A book was writ" or precede "Fairfax, whose name." The 1673 edition altered the manuscript numbering and printed "A book was writ" as 11, "I did but prompt" as 12, and "on ye forcers" out of sequence, altogether separated from the sonnets by the Fifth Ode of Horace and the Vacation Exercise. The

order, however, united the two sonnets against detraction thematically and placed them in a sharpened scale of political applicability to be naturally followed by "Ye forcers."

The first of the group, "On the detraction which followed my writing certain treatises" (Sonnet 11), is a half-haughty and half-humorous snub of "stall-readers," who in their hatred of learning cannot get beyond the hard word on the title page of *Tetrachordon* to come at the work itself—"wov'n close; both matter, form and stile; / The Subject new"—although they have easily mastered both royalist and Presbyterian Scots names. The indirect impersonal discourse incorporating a comic stage direction and colloquial direct speech, as well as the humorous end rhymes, moderate the asperity of this sonnet. Milton wrote for some "good intellects," but his work missed its mark and is "now seldom por'd on." The following sonnet, Sonnet 12, is altogether more serious and stern. Here Milton expostulates in his own voice:

> I did but prompt the age to quit their cloggs
> By the known rules of antient libertie. . . .

He is surrounded by a cackle of ignorant dissent; he has cast his pearls before swine

> That bawle for freedom in their senceless mood,
> And still revolt when truth would set them free.

Their cry for liberty is actually a demand for license, liberty for their own ends, not true liberty; the true lover of liberty "must first be wise and good." The sonnet begins loftily and defensively, and then moves through Milton's clear hatred of his detractors, not conceived of, as some have argued,[12] simply as the unlettered populace of the preceding sonnet who found *Tetrachordon* Greek to them. Rather, his hatred is directed toward those who pretend to extol liberty of prophesying but who actually support the licensing of the press, those for whom

---

Errata of 1673 removed the intruding Vacation Exercise to an earlier chronological position but, oddly, did not remove the intruding Horatian translation. On the authority of Milton's correction, the order of 1673 should stand as the order wished; on the authority of the Trinity Manuscript the order of composition would appear equally clearly to have been 12, 11, 13, 14, "ye forcers." The change from a chronological to a logical order is unimportant in this case but very important in establishing Milton's practice of placing for emphasis when one comes to consider the case of Sonnet 19, as will be made clear below.

12 See Nathaniel H. Henry, "Who Meant Licence When They Cried Liberty?" *MLN*, 66 (1951), 509-13.

liberty is merely a catchphrase that they "bawle . . . in their senceless mood." That is to say, they are the Presbyterian leaders. Milton defends true liberty, of course, both from "Owles" and "Cuckoes," from "Asses, Apes and Doggs"; he dismisses his simpler countrymen in a quick classical comparison: they are like the "Hinds . . . transform'd to Froggs," and his *Tetrachordon* and *Colasterion* are "*Latona's* twin-born progenie." But at the close of the sonnet he aims straight for the learned Presbyterians: it is they who have roved from the mark of true reformation, which demands first that one be "wise and good"; it is they who have *wasted* wealth and *lost* lives without attaining for the nation a true inner liberty. The sonnet closes with a quick elliptical transfer of tone from straightforward indignation toward a compassionate view of the unrewarded sufferings of his nation.

Milton's contempt for those who would seize liberty without being wise and good takes on a still sharper and more direct definition in "Ye forcers," and much of the apparent problem of explicating the "detractors" becomes perfectly clear when the identity of these sonnets as a group is properly seen. In the group as a whole, Milton has cast himself as the champion of liberty; he confronts an enemy and brings it into focus in "Ye forcers," the most directly topical of the group. The poem comments sardonically upon a struggle for dominance within the Puritan party. It does so in the device of a false fiction of the knight saving the lady replaced by a true fiction of Parliament exposing pretended piety. The octave satirically personifies the Presbyterian faction as a church baron breaking free from the previous episcopal control in order to usurp the bishops' rich places, caricatured as a widow'd courtesan, Pluralitie. The Knight Presbyter is a hypocrite who took "stiff Vowes" against his former masters' liturgy but would now cavalierly mount the backs of the English people, using the "Civill Sword" to force their consent. Milton's republican idealism is evident in the satirical caricature of the Presbyterian faction as a kind of Hudibras-Harapha: his target is the double detestations of all idealistic Independents, hire and force, plurality and the civil sword. After the manner of Italian satirical sonnets, the sestet is given two "tails," each of an extra half-line and couplet, to bring it to a resounding aphoristical conclusion. The English people, "Men whose Life, Learning, Faith and pure intent / Would have been held in high esteem with *Paul*," have been branded as heretics by a shallow, self-seeking faction which has "packed" the Westminster Assembly to prevent true reformation. But the English people have a defender: they will be succoured by Parliament when it sees that "*New Presbyter* is but *Old Priest* writ Large."

That the political positions taken in this group of sonnets can be documented thoroughly from the prose works contemporary with it has always been clear.[13] Milton never abandoned those positions. Far from being a narrow elitist, Milton used the occasion of the attacks upon the Independents to write, in his last tracts, most fully of the twin principles of disestablishment and toleration. The sonnets are expressive of a sense of community which Milton never lost.

The third and fourth groups are also separated by two years, and the sonnets of group four, 15, 16, 17, and 18, are also all occasional. To republican heroes and to Protestant martyrs is given the fame worth bestowing only on worthy deeds. In each case the greatness of the hero is not the initial apparent greatness of force of arms but a succeeding intellectual or moral greatness, a "plain heroic magnitude of mind." In all, therefore, the occasion permits Milton to offer political advice in the guise of praise or to celebrate God in the guise of lamentation. To General Fairfax, "whose name in armes through Europe rings" and simply as a name is sufficient, to the delight of the republicans, to "daunt remotest kings," Milton offers in the octave the assurance that his victory at Colchester was gained by "firm unshak'n vertue." In the sestet he is asked to undertake a nobler task in peace, the defense of truth and justice from violence. War intermitted, General Fairfax is reminded of a political responsibility in peace involving a double duty: liberty of conscience remains to be secured and simple fiscal justice to be established.

The same pattern shapes Sonnets 16 and 17. Like Fairfax, who united in himself the two qualities implied by the word *virtue*, prowess and righteousness, and had won in war the right to lead in peace, Cromwell and Vane also receive octaves of praise and sestets of counsel. When Milton came to write the *Second Defence* he offered the same balance of praise and advice and drew on Sonnets 15 and 16 in referring to their subjects.[14] Less than half of the *Second De-*

---

[13] Smart cites *The History of Britain*—"libertie hath a sharpe and double edge fitt onlie to be handl'd by just and virtuous men"—to explain Sonnet 12; Hughes cites the *Doctrine and Discipline of Divorce*—"Honest liberty is the greatest foe to dishonest licence"; Bush and Woodhouse cite *Of Reformation*—"Well knows every wise Nation that their Liberty consists in manly and honest labors, in sobriety . . . and when the people slacken then doo they as much as if they laid downe their necks for some wily Tyrant to get up and ride" to gloss "Ye forcers"; Honigman cites *The Tenure of Kings and Magistrates*—"None can love freedom heartilie but good men; the rest love not freedom, but licence."

[14] In the *Second Defence*, in prose paraphrase, Fairfax is called the man "in whom nature and divine favor have joined with supreme courage supreme modesty and supreme holiness . . . [who] defeated not only the enemy but ambition as well, and the thirst for glory which conquers all the most eminent men" (*CPW*, IV, pt. I, 669). Cromwell, "commander first over himself, victor over himself, [who] had learned to achieve over himself the most effective triumph and so,

fence is in fact a defense; the remainder is a diagnosis of the political crisis in the state. Milton made the best case he could for the English government, but that government was scarcely the "mild and equal . . . magnanimity of a triennial parliament," "the free and humane government" of "a knowing people, a nation of prophets, of sages and of worthies" that he had addressed in *Areopagitica*; nor could its case rest simply on "the liberty and right of freeborn men to be governed as seems them best." In defending the Protectorate Milton was compelled to draw on arguments rather different from those political principles identified in the third group of sonnets, "the known rules of antient libertie" and "our Conscience that Christ set free." He ceased to argue from the will or consent of the people and turned to argue from the welfare of the people, regardless of their own view in the matter, and from the moral superiority of their leaders. "Those who excel in prudence, in experience, in industry and courage, however few they be," the few "animated by the goodness of their cause," must act for the many. The sonnets to both Cromwell and Vane draw upon the changed political principle which confines authority to those who, by virtue, deserve it. Cromwell is depicted as a heroic republican, a "cheif of men" who has "plough'd" through "a cloud" both of war and "detractions rude" to bring down the monarchy placing his foot "on the neck of crowned Fortune proud," being victorious because he "pursu'd" God's work. In the sestet he is warned of new foes to be defeated in peacetime. Vane is depicted as a wise senator in time of war, expert in diplomacy and able "to unfold / The drift of hollow states," expert in naval preparedness and able "to advise how warr may best . . . Move by . . . Iron & Gold / In all her equipage." He is qualified to lead because he can distinguish between the authority of the state and that of the church, "which few have don." This group of sonnets characterizes men raised by merit, not by birth, who are to perform specific public tasks—Fairfax, the cleansing of the conscience of Parliament; Cromwell, the advancing of toleration; Vane, the separation of church from state—for the benefit of all men and for the total community, whom they represent at its best.

The final sonnet of group four, "On the late Massacher in *Piemont*," is the most interesting of all the occasional sonnets from the point of view of the political intention of *Samson Agonistes*. It is a sustained monodic imprecation which becomes multivocal and celebratory in its conclusion. It opens with a prayer for vengeance for the martyred Waldensians, progresses to a prayer for the immortality of the faithful

---

on the very first day that he took service against an external foe, he entered camp a veteran . . . in . . . the soldier's life," is warned likewise in prose paraphrase, "Peace itself will be by far your hardest war" (*ibid.*, 668).

victims and closes with a prayer for their fruitfulness as examples and teachers. At each stage the poem itself supplies the action it requests: the opening eight lines address the God of wrath as the keeper of the Book of Judgment and the strong shepherd of innocent sheep ("Ev'n them who kept thy truth so pure of old") and exhorts Him to "Forget not" and to "record their groanes." Those lines very literally and naturalistically remember and memorialize the Waldensians "whose bones / Lie scatter'd on the Alpine mountains cold," "Slayn by the bloody *Piemontese* that roll'd / Mother with Infant down the Rocks." The direct occasion of the sonnet is described in the plainest of plain words; God appears in metaphor, the martyrs not. God is asked to remember what the lines thereby recall. The beginning of the sestet initiates an upward movement in the poem, from the bones scattered and the bodies rolled down, upward toward Heaven and forward in time. "Their cry came up unto God," and now God is addressed as the sower of good seed; the poet anticipates a good harvest, "that from these may grow / A hunder'd-fold." The harvest is of consciousness and learning as well as warning; it has undertones of the myth of Cadmus and the dragon's teeth. The suggestion it carries of violent literal requital is less strong than the overtone of the providential use God makes of His elect peoples to move the stages of human enlightenment forward by means of those who have "learnt thy way." Milton's final lines ask for an application of the lesson of the massacre to the teaching of God's people, and the lines themselves assure the reader that suffering and agony may enlighten humanity about God's mercy.

The five remaining sonnets composing the final group are personal and introspective; the occasion of each is autobiographical. Sonnet 19 establishes Milton's trust in his kingly maker; Sonnets 20 and 21 record the solace of friendships; Sonnet 22 sublimates the loss of sight; Sonnet 23 ends the sequence with the lament of the blind poet for his lost wife. The two devoted to blindness take the occasion of Milton's own immediate experience to consider retrospectively the course of his prose writing and to pronounce it good; he affords to himself the kind of praise he gave to Fairfax, Cromwell, and Vane. In the octave of Sonnet 22 Milton informs Cyriack Skinner quite simply that for three years he has been unable to see "Sun or Moon or Starre throughout the year / Or man or woman" but that he can "still bear vp and steer / Right onward." (The preceding sonnet had advised his young friend to keep in proper perspective the political issues of the day, "what the *Swede* intend, and what the *French*," remembering "To measure life" and to know "Toward solid good what leads the nearest way." The young friend should not be more severe with himself than God is exacting to him, and "mild Heav'n a time ordains" for recreation.) The sestet commences, also without poetic figure, in the simplest of questions, "What supports me, dost thou ask?" In his answer the poet acknowledges that he has acquitted himself well in the proper work of the Puritan hero: he has defended liberty. His own sense of rectitude and deserved public fame would compensate for his loss of sight even if he were alone in his darkness and had no better guide through it than his moral probity. He has the better guide, however and the close of the sonnet shows Milton himself to be far from the condition of Samson, who at the opening of the tragedy is guided by a human hand but has lost touch with his God and who in place of a calming assurance of his public service is tormented by a sense that he has betrayed his people. The sestet offers the only figure in the poem: the world is a "vain mask" through which the blind champion is led by the best of guides.

Milton's relationship to his "better guide" is the subject of Sonnet 19, the companion piece to Sonnet 7, which was written twenty years earlier and marked the commencement of Milton's dedication to God's service as poet-teacher. The octave weaves together three scriptural parables, two from Matthew (the servant who buried his talent and the laborers who came late to the vineyard) and one from John (the blind man urging us to work while yet it is day, since the night comes wherein no man can work). Those same three parables had been cited in the letter to "a Friend" with which Sonnet 7 had been enclosed, and Sonnet 7 had glanced at both the Matthew parables by referring to God as the great taskmaster. Sonnet 7 was a consideration of delayed service to God; the octave expressed fear of appearing useless and the sestet, resolution to choose the path of appropriate steady development. Sonnet 19 offers a more desperate occasion altogether. The octave gives the occasion in a syntactic irregularity and wrestling which immediately recalls the tortured word order of Samson's opening soliloquy: the poet is blind in a "dark world and wide"; all his will is strained to serve his God, the exacting bestower of the one talent and the judge and keeper of true accounts; the blind poet is not the bad servant who buried his talent, he is the exceedingly anxious good servant whose talent has been buried in him and who fears that his judge will not understand but will "chide" and deal "death" to him. The relationship posited is that of an innocent man and an angry, peremptory God. Anxiety has rendered the man incapable of thought and control; he is on the threshold of blaming God: "Doth God exact day-labour, light deny'd." The challenge to God's goodness resembles Manoa's objection to a Creator capable of giving "with solemn hand / As Graces" those gifts which "draw a Scorpion's tale behind." The sestet halts the downward rush of thoughts toward despair and doubt. At once the syntax clears. The lines move forward with orderly thought. "Patience" cuts through the "murmur" against God and "to prevent" it, substitutes a fuller, truer insight. God's service is not exacted from men by one for whom it is needful: "God doth not need . . . man's work," for His state is kingly and the whole activity of society is governed by Him for whom "Thousands . . . speed / And post o're Land and Ocean without rest." True service does not depend upon particular works, and the true servant need feel no panic of will. It consists in steady readiness: "They also serve who only stand and waite." The sestet assuages the distress expressed in the octave: the poet is not alone in a blank world and God is not an irrational taskmaster.

Sonnet 18 creates a similar mime of agony and also addresses God imperatively: God must avenge the murdered Piedmontese, record their deeds in the Book of Life, and turn the massacre into a greater victory. In this sonnet likewise, so evocative of both *Lycidas* and *Samson Agonistes*, the poet does not merely wait, he records. His own spiritual struggle has led to the conversion of anxiety into assurance, and he foresees that from the "martyr'd blood" of the Waldensians truly faithful and pure Christians "may grow / A hunder'd-fold." He has served; loss has been followed by renewal and rededication, and these are recorded. Milton, like Samson, is full of "conscience and internal peace." His "fond" reaction has been transcended by a purposiveness which grows from a better understanding of his own relationship to God. God has restored freedom to the poet by reestablishing "patience" in him as a "preventing" grace. He is the servant of a benevolent God, not a stern taskmaster. The relationship frees him to make use of all occasions for the service of men, even those tragic occasions of massacre and blindness.

It now becomes clear why Sonnet 19 was moved from its chronological place in the sequence to stand at the beginning of the fifth cluster rather than before Sonnet 18, and why Sonnet 22 should likewise be placed achronologically, three years after Sonnet 19, several months before Sonnet 18, and half a year before Sonnets 20 and 21.[15] The fifth group as a whole records calm of mind and assent to the temporal circumstances of the period of their composition: "time will run / On smoother" for the "not unwise" in Sonnet 20; "mild Heav'n a time ordains" for those not "wise in show" but for those wise in themselves in Sonnet 21; the poet will "argue not / Against heavns hand" because God is his "better guide" in Sonnet 22; the "false surmise" of the dream

15 The argument for dating 18 in 1655, 19 in 1652, 20, 21, and 22 in 1655, and 23 in 1658 is put in *A Variorum Commentary*, II, 442-70. I find the argument conclusive, and it confirms a higher degree of intention in the poet than a strictly chronological ordering would.

of his "late espoused Saint" is surpassed by the "trust to have / Full sight of her in Heaven without restraint," so that even when "day brought back [his] night," the plangent lamentation of Sonnet 23 expresses no loss of faith. But more important, the final sonnets conclude the long process of the full sonnet sequence. Throughout the sequence questions have been raised about writing to serve God and to lead the people; the justification of leadership has been assessed in terms of the leaders' responsibility to virtue; the status of action has been examined in its relationship to human volition and to divine providence; leading, acting, and politics have all been described; and finally, *leading* has yielded to *teaching*, for teaching is conceived now as the highest form of leadership in correspondence with God's known ways with men. The final establishment of trust after defeats and personal disasters is both occasional and prophetic, a trust which looks forward to what time will bring and which prefigures the ideal end in its own harmony. "They also serve who only stand and waite." Milton uses the occasion of recognition of his blindness to make a perceived truth clear. Waiting is an action commended because the poet can foresee its consequences. This is the meaning as well of the sonnetlike conclusion of *Samson Agonistes*. The course of human life is "Ever best found in the close" of poems culminating in acceptance and understanding.

Milton has faithfully championed the causes of liberty and truth throughout the sonnets. He has given his readers "new acquist of true experience" in their course, replacing poems of "semblance" (Sonnet 7), "spleen" (9), "senceless mood" (12), "Death, call'd Life" (14), a less noble "task" (15), an unfinished victory (16), a fond asking (19), an unwise volition (20), an unmeasured life (21), an argument against "heavns hand" (22), and a "fancied sight" (23) with real, substantial truths. He has not made verbal curiosities his end, "a toylsom vanity," but in a period of rapid social change and ceaseless public involvement, Milton has turned his own experience of public and private affairs to the service of his countrymen. A contemporary reader of the complete 1673 sequence would clearly see that politics begins and ends with the self recognizing its selfhood and defining its selfhood in relationship both to a people needing the same freedom he needs, and to a God bestowing time and occasions sufficient for enlightenment.

Milton's political meaning appears in the sonnets as a representation of a sequential or historical process; the sequence illustrates the stages of enlightenment through which individuals or societies must pass on their way toward the achievement of political maturity. The conclusion of the evolution is neither wish-fulfillment nor the projection of an ideal society toward an unidentified future. Milton, as a republican, demanded self-sufficiency in the individual; he was perfectly aware that the price of this might be the isolation of one man seeming to stand alone against all men. He was aware how few dared pay that price. He was certainly no stranger to failure. He might himself, and indeed did, pass through the common reactions to failure—anger, violence, or attempted moral coercion of others—such as would inevitably delay the development of the self-sufficiency that politics was meant to achieve. But he would attempt the new thing nonetheless, would steady himself and could move beyond anger, violence, coercion, and inner perturbation in order to diagnose the cause of failure and prepare for the continuing process of self-liberation. He could, that is, *use* the occasions of failure in the service of political enlightenment. As a political poet, Milton celebrated individualism as the basis of group responsibility. His individualism was not egocentric but allocentric, not exclusive but social, not monadic but multivocal. To take advantage of the occasion to move toward the ideal, Milton used contemporary events to clarify a moral idea and gave account of his own experience to prompt the same spiritual progress in the sequence of experience for others.

POLITICAL INTENTION IN
MILTON'S PROSE

CONSISTENCY AND PROCESS IN MILTON'S POLITICS:
THE FREE INDIVIDUAL AND HIS PEOPLE

Milton's prose tracts were, like so much of his poetry, "occasional." That is not the picture he himself gave of them. He presented them in the *Second Defence* as always consistently motivated pieces of one whole cloth. Casting himself in the role of appointed spokesman for the Commonwealth and Protectorate,[1] the defender both of liberty and of the people,[2] a man speaking to an enormous international audience[3] to whom he was commending "the renewed cultivation of freedom and civic life," and the champion of "the entire human race against the foes of human liberty,"[4] Milton depicted himself as from the beginning to the near end of his political career consistently motivated "by considerations of duty, honour and devotion to [his] country" and consistently occupied with "the liberation of all human life from slavery," with the "cause of true and substantial liberty." He indicated the systematic order in which he took up first ecclesiastical, then domestic, and finally civil liberty, and he made them all but branches of a plan, all parts of one coherent body of thought. He "conceiv'd [himself] . . . as a member incorporate into that truth whereof [he] was pursuaded." He drew his own portrait in idealizing autobiographical terms in all the most important of his political tracts. He minimized changes in his political position and exaggerated his

[1] "It was I and no other who was deemed equal to a foe of such repute and to the task of speaking on so great a theme, and who received from the very liberators of my country this role, which was offered spontaneously with universal consent, the task of defending publicly the cause of the English people and thus of Liberty herself" (*CPW*, IV, pt. I, 549).

[2] "Although they were indeed a multitude in numbers, yet the lofty exaltation of their minds kept them from being a mob" (*ibid.*, 552).

[3] "I . . . speak again to the entire assembly in council of all the most influential men, cities, and nations everywhere" (*ibid.*, 554).

[4] *Ibid.*, 558.

self-consistency. As we have seen in certain of his early poems, how-ever, a far more ubiquitous Miltonic pattern than consistency is the recurrence of occasions involving doubt, difficulty, or suffering, the expression of the difficult elements either overtly or fictionally in a pre-liminary violent resolution, the marshaling of the poet's deepest con-victions toward a true resolution which exorcises the difficulty on a higher level, and a final dismissal of poet and audience with "calm of mind all passion spent."[5] This is the pattern of Milton's political thought taken as a whole, as well as the pattern of his earlier poetry. *Samson Agonistes* participates in that pattern and recapitulates the po-litical development in it.

Milton's most profound political convictions, to which occasional issues were ultimately referred, remained basically constant. He never changed his opinion on the crucial issues of tolerance and disestablish-ment, and he was always convinced that tolerance and disestablish-ment both depended upon making "the people fittest to choose and the chosen fittest to govern," and upon education, than which "noth-ing can be more efficacious . . . in moulding the minds of men to vir-tue (whence arises true and internal liberty), in governing the state effectively, and preserving it for the longest possible space of time."[6] It can be shown that in his occasional tracts Milton increasingly limited true liberty to the Christian and conceived it as possible only to the regenerate. Unlike the Levellers, he did not insist upon the insepara-bility of liberty and equality; he denied it. His specifically political tracts follow the successive stages of the revolution: *Areopagitica* is the most egalitarian and democratic and speaks for the whole people; *The Tenure of Kings and Magistrates* notes that many have fallen away from the Good Old Cause but since the majority remain true, the po-litical principle underlying it is still the consent of the governed; the *Second Defence* observes that still more have deserted, putting the In-dependents in the minority, but "nor for that reason ought the upright citizens to fail in striving against the disaffected and acting bravely, having regard rather for their duty than for their small number,"[7] for politics is "the rule of the man most fitted to rule"; *The Readie and Easie Way* declines to continue an implicit endorsement of rule by the single man, but it no less dismisses the consent of the governed as the basis of politics: "More just it is doubtless . . . that a less number compell a greater to retain . . . their Libertye, then that a greater number . . . compell a less most injuriously to be their fellow slaves." From all

---

[5] See A.S.P. Woodhouse, *The Heavenly Muse*, ed. Hugh MacCallum (Toronto: University of Toronto Press, 1972), 317-18, for analysis and support for this pat-tern.

[6] *CPW*, IV, pt. I, 615.   [7] *Ibid.*, 648.

these occasional works it might seem that Milton cared less and less for the social aspects of political life and finally turned utterly away from his contemporaries to take for himself what they declined to receive from him: "They who seek nothing but thir own just liberties, have alwaies right to winn it and to keep it, whenever they have power, be the voices never so numerous that oppose it." This picture needs the sort of qualification which the close reading of the earlier poems would predict. The authority on which the individual acts in claiming liberty for himself is not merely the authority of one person speaking for many, although Milton claimed that sanction; it is not merely the authority of charity or reason or tradition or experience. Rather, it is the discovery that the freedom which many have repudiated is nonetheless the very law of the universe as created by God. To whom is Christian liberty available? What happens to the man who seeks to free himself by coercing others? What are the ends toward which governments strive? To answer such questions from the occasional tracts is to refer particular problems to universal concerns and to get much closer to the essential nature of Milton's radical politics.

Christian liberty, as Milton understood and defined it, is not an aristocratic or exclusive principle. It does not divide humanity into the regenerate and unregenerate from before all time. On the contrary, it is a state of mind and being which all may attain and which pertains to man's worldly as well as his spiritual existence. As an instinctive individualist Milton found the atoms of society, individual men, rather like the elements of chaos in *Paradise Lost*.[8] They could be viewed as a "mob" and a "rabble"; they could, however, be composed into a "multitude" and a "nation." When they are a mob or rabble, they should be contemptuously dismissed; to castigate a rabble is to work for the ideal of a nation. Like all poets who conceive of their role as legislative, Milton had recourse equally to vituperation and to praise. Decorum of character (by which artistic principle speeches are designed to present a texture of coherent probabilities appropriate to their speaker) did not prevent Milton from singling out in his works persons to whom he might assign his own particular insights.[9] To Christ in *Paradise Regained* Milton gave his own political views in

[8] Curiously, Milton peoples Limbo, located in Chaos, with "all who in vain things / Built thir fond hopes of Glorie or lasting fame, / Or hapiness in this or th' other life; / All who have thir reward on Earth, / . . . here find / Fit retribution, emptie as thir deeds" (*Paradise Lost*, III, 448-54).

[9] "We must not regard the poet's words as his own, but consider who it is who speaks in the play, and what that person says; different persons speak not always the poet's opinion, but what is most fitting to each character" (*First Defence*). But also, "Poets generally put something like their own opinions into the mouths of their best characters."

lines describing the people both as a rabble attracting contempt and as a nation deserving help. As a mob the people are

> a herd confus'd,
> A miscellaneous rabble, who extol
> Things vulgar, & well weigh'd, scarce worth the praise.
> . . . .
> Th' intelligent among them and the wise
> Are few, and glory scarce of few is rais'd.
>
> (III, 49-59)

The mass conceived of as a nation, however, attracts Christ's compassion:

> But to guide Nations in the way of truth
> By saving Doctrine, and from error lead
> To know, and knowing worship God aright,
> Is yet more Kingly.
>
> (II, 473-476)

His role is to teach "The solid rules of Civil Government . . . What makes a Nation happy, and keeps it so." In *Paradise Lost* the decline of nations into a rabble is again described with contempt:

> Yet somtimes Nations will decline so low
> From vertue, which is reason, that no wrong,
> But Justice, and some fatal curse annext
> Deprives them of thir outward libertie,
> Thir inward lost. . . .
>
> (XII, 97-101)

But a single ruler's usurpation of authority over other men is likewise deplored:

> Man over men
> He made not Lord; such title to himself
> Reserving, human left from human free.
>
> (XII, 69-71)

And the arising of true nations from men "as many as offer'd Life / Neglect not" is compassionately viewed.

In *De Doctrina Christiana* Milton defined Christian liberty boldly. "Christian liberty means that Christ our liberator frees us from the slavery of sin and thus from the rule of the law and of men, as if we were emancipated slaves. He does this so that, being made sons instead of servants and grown men instead of boys, we may serve God in charity through the guidance of the spirit of truth." Christian liberty explicity refers to public affairs: "Thus we are freed from the judgments of men, and especially from coercion and legislation in religious matters."[10]

In Milton's definition, Christian liberty is the response of God to the actions of man throughout the course of time. God's providential plan leaves room for a series of divine improvisations within history. The Old Testament recorded the facts of divine improvisations both literally ("historically") and typologically ("obscurely"); the New Testament recorded them "with absolute clarity." The course of history is the process of augmenting freedom:

> So Law appears imperfet, and but giv'n
> With purpose to resign them in full time
> Up to a better Cov'nant, disciplin'd
> From shadowie Types to Truth, from Flesh to Spirit,
> From imposition of strict Laws, to free
> Acceptance of large Grace, from servil fear
> To filial, works of Law to works of Faith.
>
> (*Paradise Lost*, XII, 300-306)

Human history is the history not only of "the one just man" in his day or the "sons of light"; it is the history of groups and nations as well. In the Old Testament period God freed his chosen people by giving them the law and, within the law, typologically prefiguring liberty from that law: "it held a promise of life for the obedient . . . its aim was that all . . . nations should afterwards be educated from this elementary, childish and servile discipline to the adult stature of a new creature; and to a manly freedom under the gospel, worthy of God's sons."[11] In the New Testament period God freed all men by giving them the Gospel. "The Gospel is the new dispensation of the covenant of grace. It is much more excellent and perfect than the law. It was first announced, obscurely, by Moses and the prophets, and then with absolute clarity by Christ himself and his apostles and the evangelists. It has been written in the hearts of believers until the end of the world. It contains a promise of eternal life to all men of all nations who believe in the revealed Christ, and a threat of eternal death to unbelievers."[12] The gospel written in the heart of believers extends beyond the historical period of the New Testament to the end of human history. On the "analogy of faith" which is the postulate of God's consistency, His behavior to man in the past predicts His behavior in the future. The law of that behavior is the law of liberty; the progres-

[10] *CPW*, VI, 537-38.   [11] *Ibid.*, 517.   [12] *Ibid.*, 312.

sion is the interaction of God and man in every phase of human history. Milton described God's ways to man in prehistory in *Paradise Lost*, in the Gospel era in *Paradise Regained*, and in the period of Judges in *Samson Agonistes*. Thus, in an epic, a brief epic, and a tragic reconstruction, he showed God in each era to be augmenting grace and pointing toward increased human understanding in a consistent manner, although the means and the human responses differed as the times prompted. God offers Christian liberty as the form of grace. By grace, both those who fall and those who stand are given renewed freedom throughout the course of time in the moment of the taking of every decision. Historian though he was, Milton was not concerned to reconstruct God's ways with men of the past for the sake of history; he was concerned to speak to his countrymen in their own tongue of what in history might be exemplary to his own nation. It may appear that contemporary history and politics is excluded from Milton's treatment of the life of Adam or Christ or Samson.[13] That is far from true. On the contrary, God's constancy in permitting history to continue for its educative evolution of the law of liberty rendered some historical moments brilliantly apposite to the treatment of contemporary events.

The occasion for the writing of *Samson Agonistes* was the failure of the English people to respond to the offer of liberty made to them through their articulate leaders and poets upon the prompting of God. In the "very season wherein [they might] obtain a free Commonwealth and establish it for ever in the land, without difficulty or much delay," they "pretending the misgovernment of Samuel's sons, no more a reason to dislike their Commonwealth, then the violence of Eli's sons was imputable to that priesthood or religion, clamourd for a king." Warned by Milton not "to be so impetuos, but to keep thir due channell," God's Englishmen took the course of "chusing them a captain back for Egypt."[14] Seven years passed between the warnings of *The Readie and Easie Way* and the preparation for *Samson Agonistes*, years in which the predictions of profligacy in *The Readie and Easie Way* were abundantly fulfilled. The backsliding English all too clearly resembled the Old Testament nation which had been justly enslaved. The English people rejected the proffered liberty and "not

---

[13] See Madsen, *From Shadowy Types to Truth*, 21-22, 36-53; MacCallum, "Milton and Figurative Interpretation of the Bible," 397-99, and "Milton and Sacred History," 159-68; Lynn Veach Sadler, "Regeneration and Typology: *Samson Agonistes* in Relation to *De Doctrina Christiana, Paradise Lost* and *Paradise Regained*," *Milton Studies*, 3 (1971); Haller, *Foxe's Book of Martyrs*, 238-50; Arthur E. Barker, "Structural and Doctrinal Pattern in Milton's 'Later Poems,'" in *Essays Presented to A.S.P. Woodhouse*, 172-79.

[14] *The Readie and Easie Way*, CPW, VII, 430, 450, 463.

at all regarded" the few among them diligently working to establish it. The occasion for *Samson Agonistes* was Milton's discernment that his people were once more fallen but that God was thereby presenting once more the occasion for educating them in His ways. On the theme of God's behavior to the fallen, Milton was writing in *De Doctrina Christiana* with his customary independence in the very period of the writing of *Samson Agonistes*.

The Post-Restoration Revisions in De Doctrina Christiana: The Fallen Man and the Lapsed Nation

In *De Doctrina Christiana* Milton's general view of God's grace and man's failures is explicit: "God rejects none except the disobedient and the unbeliever, he undoubtedly bestows grace on all and if not equally upon each, at least sufficient to enable everyone to attain knowledge of the truth and salvation." Christ "came to save all men, the reprobate and the so-called elect alike"; "All are redeemed, even those who are ignorant of it"; "God did not predestine reprobation at all, or make it his aim." Since all of God's decrees are contingent upon man's behavior within a covenant of grace, God graciously restores to each individual sufficient freedom for choice to be possible: "reprobation lies not so much in God's will as in their own obstinate minds" and is "not so much God's decision as theirs."[15] To those who fail, God restores freedom and uses the occasion of failure for their education. His particular treatment of them is recorded at large in Scripture, which also contains the promise of repeated liberation through grace.

To Milton, nation and church were analogous institutions: "The church might be called a commonwealth and the whole commonwealth a church." In the preface to *De Doctrina Christiana* he wrote: "I had focussed my studies principally upon Christian doctrine because nothing else can so effectually wipe away those two repulsive afflictions, tyranny and superstition."[16] Milton's models of a state and of a church were identical: both were elective associations of individual men drawn together by common ideals and ties of brotherhood. *De Doctrina Christiana* has much to say about both. Writing it was for Milton a protracted process. He began compiling materials for it some time after returning from his Italian trip in 1639; he codified the collected material and prepared a coherent draft during the fifties; that draft was essentially complete by 1658-1660; after the Restoration he revised it carefully but without altering its doctrinal substance.[17] The intention of that "systematic exposition of Christian teaching" was

---

[15] *CPW*, VI, 192, 447., 448, 173.   [16] *Ibid.*, 118.
[17] The evidence for these dates is discussed in Parker, *Milton*, II, 1056-57.

also to make people understand how much it is in the interests of the Christian religion that men should be free not only to sift and winnow any doctrine, but openly to give their opinion of it . . . without this freedom . . . there is no religion and no gospel. Violence alone prevails; and it is disgraceful and disgusting that the Christian religion should be supported by violence. Without this freedom, we are still enslaved; not, as once, by the law of God but, what is vilest of all, by human law, or rather, to be more exact, by an inhuman tyranny.[18]

Whether or not it is appropriate to read *De Doctrina* as a gloss in any way on any work of poetry, it is unmistakably of the greatest possible help in determining Milton's consistency as a prose defender of liberty. It is the least occasional of all his prose works, but since levels of post-Restoration revision can be isolated and examined in it, it likewise reveals the occasional within the constant.[19]

The manuscript of *De Doctrina Christiana* consists of 196 pages in the hand of David Skinner followed by 539 pages in the hand of Jeremie Picard. The first 196 pages were copied after the Picard draft had been made. Four major strata of revisions by four unidentified amanuenses are to be found in the Picard draft and were therefore of post-Restoration composition, dictated at unidentifiable times between 1661 and Milton's death.[20] The revisions do not alter doctrine; they sharpen definition, strengthen argument, and insert proof texts. Not all bear particularly upon *Samson Agonistes* but a significant number do, and of those that have a bearing, most relate to its exemplary political function. It is worth recording those, for they demonstrate Milton's doctrinal emphases in the years in which he wrote his Greek tragedy for the purpose of strengthening his fallen people.[21] Maurice Kelley

[18] *CPW*, VI, 123.

[19] The problems of using *De Doctrina* to establish "what Milton really meant" in his poetry have been canvassed in *Bright Essence: Studies in Milton's Theology* (Salt Lake City: University of Utah Press, 1973) by W. B. Hunter, C. A. Patrides, and J. H. Adamson. Poetry is "truer" than prose; as Milton had it, it is more "simple" (i.e., "unified"), "sensuous" (i.e., "accessible to the whole soul of man"), and "passionate" (i.e., "moving") than prose. *De Doctrina Christiana* does not differ from any of Milton's prose works; none should be used as a "gloss" on the poetry, for the poetry is self-authenticating. Nonetheless, all the prose is illuminative of the ideas with which Milton worked; he was not of two *minds* but of two *gifts*.

[20] See Maurice Kelley's introduction to *CPW*, VI, 13.

[21] Only George M. Muldrow, in *Milton and the Drama of the Soul*, has previously used the revisions for this purpose. He limited himself to one amanuensis to establish Milton's early post-Restoration "mood" and to propose 1660-1661 as the date for the composition of *Samson Agonistes*. My own use of the revisions is dissimilar, as is my dating of *Samson Agonistes* of course, but I have found it enormously encouraging to read his work.

has identified the scribes as Amanuenses A, B, M, and N, and I shall retain his terms for convenience.

Amanuensis A shows Milton to be thinking through again some areas of the tract important to his conception of Samson's role as the unregarded deliverer who failed in his political mission, was punished for that failure, learned enough from it to become at the end God's faithful champion, and was thereby the people's example. The first area concerns the renovation of the natural man. Amanuensis A rewrote the four pages of the Picard draft consisting of Chapter 17, "Of Renovation and also of Vocation," and part of Chapter 18, "Of Regeneration."[22] Chapter 17 states that by renovation man is brought to a state of grace after being cursed and subject to God's anger, renovation being either natural (and affecting only the natural man) or supernatural. Natural renovation includes vocation, the process by which God invites all men to a knowledge of him; men respond by listening and are given thereby the power to act freely, together with the gifts of penitence and faith. In the Picard draft Milton had expounded renovation as either external or internal; the revision substituted the terms *natural* and *supernatural*. The change is not substantive but suggestive, and Milton shaped the character of Samson as the champion of God for the good of God's people during the period in which the change was made. In *De Doctrina Christiana* he described vocation (or calling) as general, the invitation to all mankind, and special, the invitation to particular individuals, such as Abraham described in *Paradise Lost* in specifically social terms: "A Nation from one faithful man to spring." Samson was of the specially called or particularly elect:

> With gifts and graces eminently adorn'd
> To some great work, [*God's*] glory,
> And peoples safety. . . .

(679-81)

When he fulfills his role as champion and liberator, he is a changed, renovated man. Milton wrote in *De Doctrina Christiana*, "As this change is by way of being an effect produced in man, and as it happens in answer to the call, it is sometimes called a hearing or listening." Samson listens to the voice in his mind

> with head a while enclin'd,
> And eyes fast fixt he stood, as one who pray'd,
> Or some great matter in his mind revolv'd.

(1636-38)

[22] See Maurice Kelley, *This Great Argument* (Princeton: Princeton University Press, 1962), 47-49.

Moreover, when renovation is conceived of as natural and supernatural rather than external and internal, the substance is not much changed, but the emphasis is: the scope of renovation becomes man's natural public life on earth as well as his supernatural inner life beyond time.

Amanuensis A also altered Milton's use of the term *elect* to read "the so-called elect." In Milton's view, election is offered to all men; God has given each man a measure of grace sufficient for him to be saved; and a man's final election or salvation is contingent upon his behavior. Amanuensis A sharpened Milton's sense of individual election. Those who respond to the persistent offer of freedom are the "so-called elect," not as the term is taken to mean—some few appointed from all time to be saved despite their own corrupt wills—but all responsive men; as Milton put it in *Paradise Lost*, "Man shall not quite be lost, *but sav'd who will*" (emphasis added). Samson is a hero whose change of will in response to his understanding of God's ways is minutely examined. In the course of the drama he "becomes as it were a new creature," a man "sanctified both in body and soul, for the service of God and the performance of good works." As he goes with the Officer and stands between the pillars of the temple, he has been given "the power to act freely."[23]

Amanuensis A was also responsible for inserting in the chapter "Of Public Duties towards our Neighbors" a specific sharpening of the parallels between contemporary religious persecution in England and past persecution of the Hebrews. The draft reads, "Nowadays, on the other hand, Christians are often persecuted or punished over things which are controversial, or permitted by Christian liberty, or about which the gospel says nothing explicit. Magistrates who do this sort of thing are Christian in name only." Amanuensis A inserted, "And there are plenty of Jewish and heathen magistrates who can be cited as evidence against them . . . ," "also Gamaliel."[24] This insertion explicitly shows that Milton's concern with scriptural history is linked with his concern for contemporary history; it also shows his way of interrelating the two, both by interpreting Scripture and by juxtaposing Scripture to contemporary instances.

Some revisions in the hand of Amanuensis M are also relevant to *Samson Agonistes*. Among numerous changes, he revised a passage dealing with salvation for all, another dealing with the abrogation of Mosaic Law, and another treating good and bad conscience. The first passage read in draft, "Christ has redeemed all transgressors but he

---

23 See John M. Steadman, "'Faithful Champion': The Theological Basis of Milton's Hero of Faith," *Anglia*, 77 (1959), 13-28, for an analysis of the process of renovation.

24 *CPW*, vi, 798.

purifies only the faithful." Amanuensis M deleted "the faithful" and replaced it with "those who are eager to do good works, in other words, believers." The changed emphasis bears directly upon the encounter with Harapha, a much misunderstood part of the play. Samson is willing to pit himself against Harapha not, as some have argued, because he momentarily lapses into his old violent ways[25] and then belatedly recovers to place himself entirely at God's disposal, but because he is numbered among "those who are eager to do good works, in other words believers." His eagerness for action is explicitly linked to his belief. He trusts and despairs not; he therefore wishes to act:

> My trust is in the living God who gave me
> At my Nativity this strength, diffus'd
> No less through all my sinews, joints and bones,
> Then thine, while I preserv'd these locks unshorn,
> The pledge of my unviolated vow.
> For proof hereof, if *Dagon* be thy god,
> Go to his Temple, invocate his aid
> With solemnest devotion, spread before him
> How highly it concerns his glory now
> To frustrate and dissolve these Magic spells,
> Which I to be the power of *Israel*'s God
> Avow. . . .
>
> (1140-51)

He replies to Harapha's disdainful reminder that he is a rejected slave:

> these evils I deserve and more,
> Acknowledge them from God inflicted on me
> Justly, yet despair not of his final pardon
> Whose ear is ever open; and his eye
> Gracious to re-admit the suppliant;
> In confidence whereof I once again
> Defie thee to the trial of mortal fight,
> By combat to decide whose god is god,
> Thine or whom I with *Israel*'s Sons adore.
>
> (1169-77)

Amanuensis M also made revisions to two other chapters, "Of the Manifestations of the Covenant of Grace: also of the Law of God" and "Of the Gospel, and Christian Liberty." Each revision is directed

[25] See Madsen, *From Shadowy Types to Truth*, 190-91; Carey, *Milton*, 144; and Kenneth Fell, "From Myth to Martyrdom: Towards a View of Milton's *Samson Agonistes*," *English Studies*, 34 (1953), 145-55.

toward sharpening and supporting Milton's argument that the Mosaic Law was intended for the Jews alone, was abrogated by the Gospel, and was given so that "all we other nations *should afterwards be educated* from this . . . servile discipline to . . . a manly freedom" (emphasis added). What was formerly offered to a few is now seen as offered throughout time to all and offered as a mode of education. And finally, Amanuensis M clarified the relationship of "good and bad consciences" to "sincerity"; after his revision the relevant passages read: "A good conscience . . . consists of an intellectual judgment of one's own deeds, and an approval of them which is directed by the light either of nature or of grace. By these means we are made absolutely certain of our own inner sincerity"; "An evil conscience means, roughly speaking, the judgment and disapproval of its own evil actions which each individual mind performs by the light either of nature or of grace."[26] Samson comes to his fullest sense of personal identity when he speaks from this awareness of "My self? my conscience and internal peace."

Amanuensis B also made significant amendments which bear upon *Samson Agonistes*. He clarified, for example, the question of the presence of Christians at idolatrous rites. The draft read, "It is often asked . . . whether it is right for someone who professes the true religion to take part in idol-worship if and when the performance of some civil duty makes it necessary. The example of Naaman the Syrian may be taken as proof that this is, in fact allowable." The scribe inserted, "It is however safer, and more consistent with reverence for God, to decline any official duties of this kind, as far as possible, or even relinquish them altogether." Samson's behavior in the second scene of the fourth act reflects both the draft and the correction; the Officer who bids him to Dagon's feast is reminded: "Our Law forbids at thir Religious Rites / My presence; for that cause I *cannot* come." The Chorus, who argue that Samson might go under constraint without sin, is answered:

> who constrains me to the Temple of *Dagon*,
> Not dragging? the *Philistian* Lords command.
> Commands are no constraints. If I obey them,
> I do it freely; venturing to displease
> God for the fear of Man, and Man prefer,
> Set God behind. . . .
>
> (1370-75)

Samson's ultimate position refers the necessity of obedience to the law to the higher principles of obedience to the free spirit of conscience as it understands God's purposes:

[26] *CPW*, VI, 652-53.

Yet that he *may* dispense with me or thee
Present in Temples at Idolatrous Rites
For some important cause, thou needst not doubt.

(1377-79; emphasis added)

At the moment of this speech Samson has gone beyond his own historical era into the Gospel dispensation: he enjoys Christian liberty and is at once aware of "rouzing motions in me which dispose / To something extraordinary my thoughts." His reply changes to "I . . . *will* go along" (emphasis added).

In addition, Amanuensis B strengthened the case for an "undiocest, unrevenued and unlorded"[27] clergy by adding two additional proof texts to a discussion which distinguishes the genuine qualifications to teach given by grace freely to the generality of good men from the pretended false qualifications claimed under the law. "But our modern clergy, if that is the right name for them, who claim the right of preaching as theirs alone, would not have been glad had they seen this grace extended to the laity, as they call them, but would have been more likely to condemn it."[28] The strengthening bears on *Samson Agonistes* as a further instance of the application of conditions "under the law" to times well beyond the Gospel era. It constitutes an anti-elitist position taken in post-Restoration days which reflects the encouragement of his own people that Milton offers at the close of the play. Amanuensis B also inserted a definition of pride—"when a man is more puffed up that he ought to be, with no or insufficient justification, or because of some trifling circumstance"[29]—suggestive of the portrait of Harapha: "tongue-doughty giant"; "vain boaster"; "haughty as his pile high-built and proud."

Those emendations made by Amanuensis N which are particularly significant to *Samson Agonistes* are: an added observation on God's limiting His punishment of man; a further modification to the definitions of the good and evil conscience; and a series of comments on public and private virtue. In the Picard draft Milton had marked the stages of penitence as recognition of sin, contrition, confession, abandonment of evil, and conversion to good (through all of which Samson passes in the course of the first three acts),[30] and he had noted that punishment is often the instrumental cause of repentance. He gave to Amanuensis N an important qualification: "But God sets a limit to his punishment, in case we should be overwhelmed by it. What

[27] This is Thomas Jefferson's paraphrase of Milton's antiprelatical remarks in his own commonplace book, made after the model of Milton's. See Mohl, *Milton and His Commonplace Book*, 29.
[28] *CPW*, VI, 571.   [29] *Ibid.*, 736.
[30] George Muldrow has examined all the corrections of N.

is more he gives us strength to overcome even those afflictions which, as sometimes happens, seem to us to exceed that limit." To both Manoa and the Chorus, Samson's afflictions seem to exceed the limit of human endurance. Manoa protests against what the Chorus calls "unseemly falls":

> Alas methinks whom God hath chosen once
> To worthiest deeds, if he through frailty err,
> He should not so o'rewhelm. . . .
>
> (368-70)

But the Chorus can see at the end of the play how God has supported His faithful servant throughout his chastisement.

> Oft he seems to hide his face,
> But unexpectedly returns
> And to his faithful Champion hath in place
> Bore witness gloriously. . . .
>
> (1749-52)

A number of added proof texts and qualifications made by B concern conscience and bear on Milton's view that "every believer is entitled to interpret the scripture, and by that I mean interpret them for himself. He has the Spirit, who guides truth, and he has the mind of Christ. Indeed, no one else can usefully interpret them for him, unless that person's interpretation coincides with the one he makes for himself, and his own conscience."[31] Milton had the scribe strengthen this position: with one text bearing on the view that "the rule of faith, therefore, is scripture alone" (both that written in the Bible and in the human heart); with three bearing on the view that "Human traditions, written or unwritten, are expressly forbidden"; with one buttressing the view that "The enemies of the church are of various kinds, but they are all doomed to destruction"; with one adding to the view that "The standard of judgment will be the individual conscience itself, and so each man will be judged according to the light which he has received"; and with a final one qualifying his definition of conscience, "Strictly speaking, however, it is correct to give the name 'evil conscience' to one which judges erroneously or by a perverted set of values, and not by the light of nature or of grace at all."[32] This whole area of revision shows how conscious Milton was of the need to affirm the virtue of independent action upon the basis of personal conviction.[33] *Samson Agonistes* is the tragedy of one who did so, whose

---

[31] *CPW*, vi, 583-84.   [32] *Ibid.*, 587, 591, 604, 623, 653.
[33] Muldrow considers that they are highly autobiographical and apply to Mil-

personal consolation would be to quit himself like Samson and whose effect upon his and subsequent times would be to provide "true experience" and a new occasion.

Those revisions of *De Doctrina Christiana* of interest to the reader of *Samson Agonistes* are, in sum, those clustered around the chapters on renovation and election, the manifestation of the covenant of grace and the law of God, the Gospel and Christian liberty, and man's duty toward himself and toward his neighbor. The revisions demonstrate Milton's constancy after the Restoration to the very lines of argument to which he had pointed in the political tracts advocating the Good Old Cause. *The Reason of Church Government* argued the suppression of the priesthood, "that jurisdictive power in the church there ought to be none at all" from "the dignity of God's image" in everyman, "all sons in obedience not in servility"; *The Tenure of Kings and Magistrates* demonstrated the "liberty and right of freeborn Men, to be govern'd as seems them best" from what "God put it into mans heart to find out"; *Areopagitica* argued the necessity of tolerance from the postlapsarian evolution of truth through the ages, "if her waters flow not in a perpetual progression, they sicken into a muddy pool of conformity and tradition"; the *First Defence* proposed to discover "whether the gospel, the heavenly hymn of Liberty, assigns us as slaves to kings and tyrants, from whose limitless power the old law . . . did deliver the people of God"; the *Second Defence* cautioned "You who wish to remain free . . . and if you think slavery an intolerable evil, learn Obedience to reason and the government of yourselfs"; *The Readie and Easie Way* defended the achieving of civil liberty through the inward laws of true religion and pointedly wondered "shall we never grow old enough to be wise, to make seasonable use of gravest authorities, experiences, examples?" From the authority of the "light of nature" and "right reason" given by God to man and restored by His grace or Christian liberty, Milton consistently argued the necessity for every man to work within the particular state of society in which he found himself toward the accomplishment of God's design. The whole ground of evolutionary providence was the law of liberty and the provision of educative instances.

The revisions also provide evidence of another sort. Milton undertook to write *De Doctrina Christiana* when he saw that Christian liberty was not "adequately provided with champions."[34] The post-Restoration revisions are evidence of the effect of occasion upon a

---

ton himself. In my view they are addressed to Milton's contemporaries and "to all in any part of the world."

[34] The translation here is that of Bishop Sumner, not, as elsewhere, of John Carey.

constant theme. The survivors of the Good Old Cause had been in disarray for a number of years, persecuted and harassed by the Act of Uniformity, the exceptions to the Act of Indemnity, the Corporations Act, the Conventicle Act, and the Five Mile Act. They had seen the disinterred bodies of Bradshaw, Cromwell, and Ireton pulled from their coffins, hanged until sunset, decapitated, and thrown into a hole under the gallows; the bodies of some twenty men and women were dug from their graves in Westminster Abbey and thrown into a pit; nearly two thousand nonconformist ministers were forced from their livings; Vane had been executed. The finest republicans, in short, had all been left

> to the hostile sword
> Of Heathen and prophane, thir carkasses
> To dogs and fowls a prey, or else captiv'd:
> Or to the unjust tribunals, under change of times,
> And condemnation of the ingrateful multitude.
>
> (*Samson Agonistes*, 692-96)

All the leaders, and Milton himself, had been caricatured in such books as *The Traytors Perspective-glass, or Sundry Examples of God's just judgments executed upon many Eminent Regicides*.[35] Milton had gone into retirement and had prepared for his nation the great epic examination of God's ways to man in *Paradise Lost* (a complete draft of which Thomas Ellwood had presumably seen in 1665 and which may have been finished as early as 1663). The poem itself is a record of "sundry examples of God's just judgments." It teaches that since Adam's fall each individual was likewise apt to fall, repeating the tragic story of Adam's fall in his own life. But each individual also receives sufficient grace to restore his liberty to stand as "one just man," and upon each individual rests the responsibility of upholding liberty:

> Reason in man obscur'd, or not obeyd,
> Immediately inordinate desires
> And upstart Passions catch the Government
> From Reason, and to servitude reduce
> Man till then free. Therefore since hee permits
> Within himself unworthie Powers to reign
> Over free Reason, *God in Judgement just*
> *Subjects him from without* to violent Lords;
> Who oft as undeservedly enthrall

[35] See Parker, *Milton*, 587; Hill, *A Century of Revolution*, 171-75; Wolfe, *Milton in the Puritan Revolution*, 337-43; Fixler, *Milton and the Kingdoms of God*, 221-26.

His outward freedom: Tyrannie must be,
Though to the Tyrant thereby no excuse.
(*Paradise Lost*, XII, 86-96; emphasis added)

Not only individuals but whole nations recapitulate the process of the fall into self-enslavement:

Yet somtimes Nations will decline so low
From vertue, which is reason, that no wrong,
But Justice, and some fatal curse annext
Deprives them of thir outward libertie,
Thir inward lost. . . .

(XII, 97-101)

To those who might stand when all others sought to restore a Stuart to the throne, to "choose a captain back for Egypt," Milton in *Paradise Lost* offered two forms of consolation familiar to us from *Lycidas* and Sonnet 19: the final judgment of God upon the worthy man, "the day of respiration to the just," and the harmonious reconciliation of God to man in the heart of the believer, "A Paradise within thee happier farr." The times were scarcely propitious or conducive to urging very great social, political, or historical hope in *Paradise Lost*; the more reliable hope was the otherworldly hope, be it afterworldly or innerworldly. Yet too much can be made of the inwardness of *Paradise Lost*. The muted ending of the poem contains a beautifully balanced double mood: grief that man had fallen and maimed the design of God, but faith that enlightenment had been given to him about his nature and destiny and about God's providence through that fall and God's reflexive offer of freedom. To "add deeds answerable" to his understanding was the task given to the new Adam, the newly educated Adam.[36]

In *Samson Agonistes* Milton undertook once more to look at God's "just judgments." The revisions of *De Doctrina Christiana* are revisions of the central positions conducing to a more politically orientated diagnosis. Milton does not at all recede from the belief that by the fall of man

true Libertie
Is lost, which alwayes with right Reason dwells
Twinn'd, and from her hath no dividual being.
(*Paradise Lost*, XII, 82-85)

[36] In my view both Parker and Martz greatly overstress the quietism undoubtedly present in *Paradise Lost* and pass over in silence the many places in the poem presenting the possibilities given to man for heroic struggling and acting.

But he had been sharpening and toughening just those places in *De Doctrina Christiana* which deal with failure or success, loss or restoration, as contingent upon human behavior, places which show the exemplary power of the actions of the elect, the sincerity of good conscience, the power of inner reason, and the limitations set by God on human punishment. The emendations are in the areas in which a single man might see how, by virtue of the Christian liberty given to him, his own behavior can affect the times in which he lives.

THE LAST TRACTS: THE REHABILITATED HERO AND THE PROPHESIED COMMUNITY

Two late pre-Restoration tracts also sound the political note, one against force, *A Treatise of Civil Power in Ecclesiastical Causes*, and one against hire, *Considerations touching the Likeliest Means to remove Hirelings out of the Church*. The first is Milton's fullest discussion and defense of Christian liberty as the primary end of government, and it was addressed to Parliament, who in all their acts *"upon occasion* have profess'd to assert only the true protestant Christian religion"* (emphasis added). The second is its companion piece, printed six months later, when Milton wrote that he was still enjoying "this libertie of writing which I have us'd these eighteen years *on all occasions* to assert the just rights and freedoms both of church and state" (emphasis added). Both are bluntly antielitist, radical documents; both were written as exemplary defenses of freedom when such defenses clearly could be no more than exemplary acts; both use occasions to treat constant truths. In the *Treatise of Civil Power* Milton declares that "any law against conscience is alike in force against any conscience."[37] Church discipline can be exercised on "them only who have wittingly joind themselves in that covnant of union." Since "the church might be calld a commonwealth or the whole commonwealth a church," "a Christian commonwealth may defend itself against outward force in the cause of religion as well as in any other." But no constraint may be used lawfully against free conscience:

> If then both our beleef and practise . . . flow from faculties of the inward man, free and unconstrainable of themselves by nature, and our practise not only from faculties endu'd with freedom, but from love and charitie besides, incapable of force, and all these things by transgression lost, but renewd and regenerated in us by the power and gift

---

The emphasis of Harold Fisch, *Jerusalem and Albion* (London: Routledge & Kegan Paul, 1964), 150-60, is a very necessary counterargument.

[37] *CPW*, VII, 242.

of God alone, how can such religion as this admit of force from man, or force be any way appli'd to such religion, especially under the free offer of grace in the gospel, but it must forthwith frustrate and make of no effect both the religion and the gospel?

Because "to heal one conscience we must not wound another," Milton argues for a "free, elective, and rational worship." His definition of Christian liberty completely segregates church and state, limits the role of the state to guaranteeing the freedom of the church, and makes the analogy between them exactly as strong as the distinction in their roles.[38]

In the *Considerations* Milton denies the need of the people for a learned ministry since free study is the sufficient path toward truth and implicit faith taken from a minister bars the road toward truth. He has something to say too about the clear advantage of abolishing hirelings: it would release economic resources for the education of the people. Milton's model for church government in the *Considerations* is the same as his model for state government in *The Readie and Easie Way*: "the Christian church is universal; not ti'd to nation, dioces or parish, but consisting of many particular churches complete in themselves; gathered, not by compulsion or the accident of dwelling nigh together, but by free consent chusing both thir particular church and thir church-officers." Free and ethically sensitive individuals form themselves into groups by their own decisions in terms of the ends which they wish to serve; their consent creates their community. That community cannot be created for them by men above them, it must arise from within them. Milton shows himself sensitive, therefore, to "how the poore, yea all men may be soone taught," the best means being "to erect in greater number all over the land schooles and competent libraries to those schooles." And he would have leadership rest ultimately upon choice: "ministers elected out of all sorts and orders of men." He concludes with a warning prophecy: "If I be not heard nor beleev'd, the event will bear me witness to have spoken truth: and I in the mean while have borne my witness not out of season to the church and to my countrey."[39]

Both tracts isolate the ultimate law of God's universe—the principle of individual liberty—as the single indispensable principle of religion and politics. The implications of Christian liberty are then boldly and radically sketched: church and state are alike groups of individual parts united solely by their free choice, a choice which each must make;

[38] *A Treatise of Civil Power in Ecclesiastical Causes, CPW*, VII, 249, 254.
[39] *Considerations touching the Likeliest Means, CPW*, VII, 293, 303, 306, 319, 321.

without the individual act of choice there is neither church nor state but only insulting tyranny and violence. Both tracts are founded upon individual liberty and aim at augmenting individual liberty. In both Milton speaks over the heads of the existent church and state, over the heads of the Presbyterians and Parliament, directly to his "countrey," to "every man," to "all sensible and ingenuous men." Both tracts insist on the individual act of bearing witness, the function Milton most resonantly claimed himself to have performed to the bitterest of bitter ends in *The Readie and Easie Way*:

> What I have spoken, is the language of that which is not call'd amiss *the good Old Cause*. . . . Thus much I should perhaps have said though I were sure I should have spoken only to trees and stones; and had none to cry to but with the Prophet, *O earth, earth, earth!* to tell the very soil itself, what her perverse inhabitants are deaf to. Nay though what I have spoke, should happ'n . . . to be the last words of our expiring libertie.[40]

The bearing of witness, the seizing of opportunity and occasion, the proclaiming of the law of liberty—Milton undertook all of these lonely tasks for "som perhaps whom God may raise of these stones to become children of reviving libertie, and may reclaim, though they seem now chusing them a captain back for *Egypt*."[41] At the moment of this, the final pre-Restoration tract, the occasion was thoroughly tragic, and the bitterness of the tragedy finds its way into *Samson Agonistes*. But the meaning of the tragedy was also prepared in public terms: a man who bears witness, a man representative of his nation, might be the means of reclaiming the children of reviving liberty, of teaching them both what the rejection of God's law of liberty would mean and how yet once more to keep faith.

Paradise Lost had given Milton's verdict on the law of liberty when violated and had offered to each man an inner and otherworldly future as well as a worldly future in terms of his selfhood. Action was undoubtedly proposed, but the emphasis was upon individual, not collective, salvation. *Samson Agonistes* moved forward in history to render first a similar but then a distinctive judgment and to propose individual achievement of selfhood as the basis of a regenerative political future. Milton's final tract stands on the other side of the catharsis of *Samson Agonistes*. It is the tersest, plainest, shortest tract Milton ever

[40] *CPW*, VII, 462-63.
[41] *Ibid.*, 463. See my own "*Samson Agonistes* and Milton the Politician in Defeat," *Philological Quarterly*, 44 (1965); James Egan, "Public Truth and Personal Witness in Milton's Last Tracts," *ELH*, 40 (1973), 231-84; and Stavely, *Politics of Milton's Prose Style*, 93-112.

wrote, shorter and plainer even than the tractate *Of Education. Of True Religion, Heresy, Schism, Toleration* is Milton's last testament in prose, as *Samson Agonistes* is that in poetry. It is carefully framed to bring together the free individuals of the nation into a new unity, and it opens with the confident assertion of the consensus and community it wishes to create. The occasion of the work was Milton's discovery that popular support existed for his own profoundest convictions, although that support arose not from pure confidence in toleration but rather was triggered by the public fears of popery. Milton therefore spoke as carefully as he could to strengthen and broaden the possible common ground between himself and Parliament. He began by simply noting that "the greatest part of the nation" was offended by the increase of popery and that "all good men" rejoiced that this was so: "the more their rejoicing, that God hath given a heart to the people, to remember still their great and happy deliverance from popish thraldom, and to esteem so highly the precious benefit of his gospel, so freely and so peaceably enjoyd among them."[42] To all men of good will Milton offered to draw out the implication of their anti-popish uneasiness. That implication was simply the need for toleration of all Protestants by all Protestants. Milton was canny and calm enough not to widen his net to include toleration of all beliefs but to broaden his argument so that the new consensus might establish itself and the direction toward full toleration be adequately plain. He rested his argument on two familiar principles: "that the rule of true religion is the word of God alone"; and that "faith ought not to be an implicit faith." From these it would follow that no Protestant can refuse to tolerate another, nor can he "compel his brother . . . to an implicit faith" which he himself condemns.

In arguing this, Milton has much to say about human failure, and what he says is uniformly magnanimous: "It is a human frailty to err, and no man is infallible here on earth," but where men "use all diligence and sincerity of heart, by reading, by learning, by study, by prayer for illumination of the Holy Spirit . . . they have done what man can do: God will assuredly pardon them." Sectarian conflict, Milton wrote, may well have arisen from "learned, worthy, zealous and religious men, as appears by their lives written, and . . . their many eminent and learned followers . . . holy and unblameable in their lives." Yet it "cannot be imagined that God would desert such painful and zealous laborers in his church, and ofttimes great sufferers for their conscience . . . but rather, having made no man infallible, that he hath pardoned their errors, and accepts their pious endeavours." With-

[42] *Of True Religion, Heresy, Schism, Toleration*, in *The Student's Milton*, ed. Frank Allen Patterson, rev. ed. (New York: F. S. Crofts & Co., 1946), 914.

in an ironic clause Milton does not forbear "to offend his enemies" and to attack the old foe, Roman Catholicism. But significantly, he threatens the newly constituted community of consensus, not with God's chastisement or any two-handed engines, but with His withdrawal. "For God, when men sin outrageously, and will not be admonished, gives over chastising them, perhaps by pestilence, fire, sword, or famine"—such instruments of warning as the plague in 1665, the Fire of London in 1666, the Dutch destruction of the English fleet in the Medway in 1667, and the state bankruptcy (the Stop of the Exchequer) in 1672—"which may all turn to their good, and takes up his severest punishments, hardness, besottedness of heart and idolatry."[43] Disaster and tragedy had served their educative purpose; a new, if muted, hope of a political nature existed. The greatest disaster is not the tragedy of failure but the abandonment of the human struggle to become free. Milton's last words to his countrymen are the words of a teacher consoling and exhorting: there are still "fresh woods and pastures new," the world is still "all before them where to choose."

[43] *Ibid.*, 919.

9

THE POLITICAL SIGNIFICANCE
OF *SAMSON AGONISTES*

MILTON wrote *Samson Agonistes* as an exemplary tragedy for his nation. He took a biblical fable as the subject for his mimesis because he thought that the recorded evidence of how God dealt with man in the past showed how God would deal with man in the present; he intended through that fable to analyze and to lament the failure of his countrymen to establish the rule of God in their own day in their own country; he laid before them the essence of the law of God, that human liberty is the origin and the end of collective life and that violation of it by self-enslavement is the source of tragic failure; and he prophesied a potential political movement through the educative power of the tragedy itself. It was Milton's habit throughout his life to use poetry to contribute thought; a regular pattern in a number of earlier politically directed poems is an agonistic pattern moving through catharsis to harmony. The stages of that pattern regularly consist of a promise of national fulfillment, a vituperative or tragic statement of an inner or outer obstacle to such fulfillment, an expression of a coercive or violent removal of that obstacle, a reconsideration by means of deeper insights, and finally a resolving or harmonizing or "holistic" conclusion. Some of Milton's political pamphlets, considered in their whole course, describe a similar pattern. Milton laid claim to witnessing to and championing liberty throughout his pamphleteering career, and in fact his prose pamphlets were never inconsistent with his fundamental principles. Moreover, the pattern of political response or witnessing in Milton's prose career resembles that in individual poems and in the sonnet sequence. That pattern comprises a hopeful expression of national destiny, a fearful and angry warning of its endangering, a loss of faith in all but the very few, accompanied by denunciations and doubts, a setting of his political vision in the perspective of God's known ways, and a resolving, encouraging, magnanimous conclusion. "Occasion" was significant in his poetry and in his prose, occasion in human life being the instant at which an interchange between God

and man occurs by mutual reaction, God improving the means to re-
new freedom and augment it and man grasping the revelation con-
tained in God's improvisations and taking heart for a renewed effort.
A contingent or flexible politics is one which sees occasions as con-
taining possibilities for fruitful change toward a consensual social fu-
ture. Milton's political thought is of this kind. The emendations to
De Doctrina Christiana, made during the same period in which *Sam-
son Agonistes* was written, show Milton's responsiveness to occasion.
Milton did not abandon either politics or his nation and was never a
quietest or an elitist. The divided heart of the people embittered the
poet whose self-chosen destiny was to lead and teach them and heroi-
cally commemorate them. To concede that, and to concede too that
Milton consoled himself by writing a portrait of Abdiel, who dared
be in the minority and received God's praise, is to discover the source
of the tragic feeling in *Samson Agonistes* and of Milton's strength to
diagnose his countrymen's failure. The consolation that Milton offered
is that of the superiority of heavenly to human judgment. Abdiel
hears the voice of God say,

> Servant of God, well done, well hast thou fought
> The better fight, who single hast maintaind
> Against revolted multitudes the Cause
> Of Truth, in word mightier then they in Armes;
> And for the testimonie of Truth hast born
> Universal reproach, far worse to beare
> Then violence: for this was all thy care
> To stand approv'd in sight of God, though Worlds
> Judg'd thee perverse. . . .
>
> (*Paradise Lost*, VI, 29-37)

This is substantially the consolation offered in *Lycidas* and in Sonnet 22.
And Samson defends himself to Harapha in the same terms, choosing
to be judged by God, not men:

> I was no private but a person rais'd
> With strength sufficient and command from Heav'n
> To free my Countrey; if their servile minds
> Me their Deliverer sent would not receive,
> But to thir Masters gave me up for nought,
> Th' unworthier they; whence to this day they serve.
> I was to do my part from Heav'n assign'd,
> And had perform'd it if my known offence
> Had not disabl'd me, not all your force. . . .
>
> (*Samson Agonistes*, 1211-19)

Moreover, Abdiel is not told to cease the less good fight, having fought the better, but to go on to conquer others as well:

> the easier conquest now
> Remains thee, aided by this host of friends,
> Back on thy foes more glorious to return
> Then scornd thou didst depart, and to subdue
> By force, who reason for thir Law refuse,
> Right reason for thir Law. . . .
>
> (*Paradise Lost*, VI, 37-42)

Neither does Samson reject the use of violence in public terms once he has seen that it is the use of wisdom which is the better and prior necessity. As he tersely comments,

> force with force
> Is well ejected when the Conquer'd can.
>
> (*Samson Agonistes*, 1206-7)

The play is no Balshazzar's Feast, but neither is it the private meditation of an introspective poet who has abandoned politics.

It remains now to document in *Samson Agonistes* the two points I have been stressing. First, Milton accepted that the law of God is the force of individual liberty given to men to fulfill themselves both as private and social beings, to band themselves together against all who opposed that law of liberty, and to become God's chosen people. The law of nations and the law of nature are both derived from the free following of the spirit of truth and reason in the individual. Second, Milton wanted to show how his own nation had erred and betrayed the light of God within them; he wanted to show the responsibility of the English people for their tragic enslavement; and in giving them an instance of God's renewal of freedom, he wanted to dramatize the possibility of recovering liberty, of remaking their national life when they saw occasion. Milton arrived at his final heroic magnanimity only after the fullest expression of anger, remorse, and despair in a tragic drama.

Samson Agonistes explicitly deals with the nature of society and the relation to it of the individual. Samson's self-realization was to have come, we are reputedly told, through a triumphant public role, giving back to his people their lost liberty; it was to have come "from some great act / Or benefit reveal'd to Abraham's race." His destiny corresponded to England's destiny; his failure corresponded to that of the nation called to be the evangelic trumpet to all nations. Samson's rearing and education were intended to prepare him for a public, social, national role. Countless times Milton had warned England of the urgency of a reformed national conduct, education, and culture to accord with its special international role. Samson's "breeding order'd and prescrib'd" was the purest that his race possessed, fit to render him of service to the civilization of which he typified the best. He was one whom "God . . . made choice to rear" by a special cultural code of which an overt sign was his adherence to Nazarite customs (the Chorus, speaks of his eschewing wine, of his leaving uncut his hair, and of his calculated marriage). He was a man inwardly as well as outwardly geared to public life. His private impulses were linked to social purposes; to him, the sole form of self-realization of interest was one having a national context.

Six times in *Samson Agonistes* Milton uses the word *occasion* in connection with the relationship between self-realization and the needs of society. The first two uses are in Act I, the next two in Act II, and the fifth in Act IV; The last, the clearest and most explicit use and that which I have taken as title for this chapter, occurs in Manoa's speech in Act V. In the first use in Act I at line 224, Samson tells the Chorus that he married outside his tribe and nation from an "intimate impulse" "motion'd . . . of God," "that by occasion hence I might begin *Israel's* Deliverance." And the Chorus commends him for "seeking just occasion to provoke the *Philistine*." But the occasion did not lead to the anticipated liberation of his tribe. Rather, it led to the destruction of one form of self-realization and prepared the way for self-sacrifice as the appropriate mode—still a public mode—by which Samson might give to his nation occasion for true freedom. Self-sacrifice as a social act is significant of Milton's politics as opposed to, say, a Hobbesian view, where the motive for self-sacrifice is only private security. The Chorus's commendation ("In seeking just occasion . . . Thou never wast remiss") is instantly followed by their remark, "Yet *Israel* still serves with all his Sons." Milton expressed through the defeated, tormented words of Samson his bitterest disappointment in his own countrymen:

> That fault I take not on me, but transfer
> On *Israel's* Governours, and Heads of Tribes,
> Who seeing those great acts which God had done
> Singly by me against their Conquerours
> Acknowledg'd not, or not at all consider'd
> Deliverance offerd. . . .
>
> (241-46)

"The men of *Judah*," to save their own ease and peace, "gladly yield me / To the uncircumcis'd." Samson, like the Independent leaders, suffered a fate common in public life; "how frequent to desert" their leader are the people and "at last to heap ingratitude on worthiest deeds."

In the second act, Manoa seeks out Samson to recommend a merely private and retired life. He repudiates Samson's account of why he married Dalila:

> thou didst plead
> Divine impulsion prompting how thou might'st
> Find some occasion to infest our Foes.
> . . . this I am sure; our Foes
> Found soon occasion thereby to make thee
> Thir Captive, and thir triumph. . . .
>
> (421-26)

And he suggests that Samson would do well to keep himself out of the public world altogether:

> Wilt thou then serve the *Philistines* with that gift
> Which was expresly giv'n thee to annoy them?
> Better at home lie bed-rid, not only idle,
> Inglorious, unimploy'd, with age out-worn.
>
> (577-80)

The second act ends with the first of the two choral odes on patience, pointedly noting that patience must depend upon "Secret refreshings."

In the first and second acts the reprehension of the slothful people who delivered Samson to his enemies was so bitter that the Chorus offered to extend it to God Himself, who "solemnly elected" Samson "to some great work" and then, like His faithless people, "with no regard of highest favours past . . . or . . . of service," left him "to the hostile sword" and worse. Are there not, however, even in these earlier acts, signs that Samson continues to care for his people and to consider himself their representative leader still? That this is the case becomes clear in the third act: Samson invokes the true law of nature and of nations to deny Dalila's false claim that she betrayed him on the grounds of appropriate patriotism, since "to the public good private respects must yield." He replies that the principle of the greatest good to the greatest number holds only when the public good is the true aim of political action and not otherwise, as when it becomes a mere pretext for self-seeking. As Samson puts it, the Philistines are not a nation seeking public good but

> an impious crew
> Of men conspiring to uphold thir state

By worse then hostile deeds, violating the ends
For which our countrey is a name so dear. . . .

(891-94)

Harrington had made a similar point in *Oceana* when he wrote, "wisdom of the few may be the light of mankind; but the interest of the few is not the profit of mankind nor of a commonwealth." But I think that even in the earlier two acts such half sentences as "the glory late of *Israel*, now the *grief*," or "Friends . . . How counterfeit a coin," or "Brethren and men of *Dan*," or "Friends and neighbours not unknown," show an ambivalence in Samson. A piercing pain amongst all those he suffers is to "have brought scandal / To *Israel*, diffidence of God, and doubt / In feeble hearts." He exhibits this quintessential remorse in the question "To what can I be useful, wherein serve / My Nation?"

The imagery by which Samson is described in the first two acts of the tragedy is predominantly that of physical warfare. That imagery is gradually replaced by imagery of spiritual warfare and spiritual pilgrimage. It is notable that warfaring or wayfaring symbolically so merge in Milton's usage that for the famous *Areopagitica* crux no editor can confidently urge one reading as more Miltonic than another. In writing of the Day of Judgment in *De Doctrina Christiana* Milton said, "This day of judgment, it seems, will not last for one day only but for a considerable length of time, and will really be a reign, rather than a judicial session. The same sense of the word judgment is applicable in the case of Gideon, Jepthah and the other judges who are said to have judged Israel for many years."[1] Samson's self-indulgent people did not support their self-disciplined military leader. He led them not as one ambitious of power but as one determined to provide an example to his people of a purposive active force for freedom. He

Us'd no ambition to commend my deeds,
The deeds themselves, though mute, spoke loud the dooer. . . .

(247-48)

The martial imagery used in the first two acts to describe Samson the military leader showed him to be one who "stood," "ran," "duelled," "on thir whole Host . . . flew," "fell'd their choicest youth." He was a fighter, "that Heroic, that Renown'd, Irresistible *Samson*," who by virtue of his fidelity in his own historical dispensation to the law of God expressed in his inner impulses had achieved "the top of wondrous glory, strongest of mortal men." His personal fall was to be attributed to "wisdom nothing more then mean"; although he was "full of divine

[1] *CPW*, VI, 625.

instinct," he grew "like a petty God . . . swoll'n with pride" and "softn'd with pleasure and voluptuous life"; he did not know how rigorously he must watch over his strength and valor. He undertook warlike activities as the "solemnly elected" agent for the "people's safety," their leader and representative. They were to respond, the imagery of the first two acts suggests, by *counting* his deeds "worth notice," by *considering* "Deliverance offer'd," and by *joining* themselves to him till they "possess'd the Towers of Faith." He would sweep them forward with him into triumphant freedom, for which their consent to his leadership was the necessary precondition. Milton had of course warned the republican leaders of the need to purify manners, widen the basis of rule, and reform English culture as well as to pursue the construction of the Commonwealth. To be a Commonwealthman implied to him an active self-realization. Samson's failure as a leader involved a form of pride, a carelessness about remembering the ends for which he worked.

Political readings of *Samson Agonistes* have often foundered upon the unlikelihood that Milton could charge himself and his party's leadership with uxoriousness or lasciviousness and apparently accept the jibes at his blindness made by royalists who contended that it was God's just judgment upon him.[2] Surely he did not do that, but he did imply criticism both of the Independent leaders and the backsliding people. The error of the Independent leaders was not their self-indulgence so much as their unwise belief that they might sweep the people into freedom, that an "implicit faith" in the Good Old Cause would suffice. The corresponding failure of the English nation was their inability to see how they must apply to themselves the self-discipline, the dedication to cause, the watchfulness and the personal commitment they found in their leaders. On a political level, the Dalila episode attacks the concept of unthinking patriotism. Nations are to be

[2] Jackie DiSalvo, " 'The Lords Battells': *Samson Agonistes* and the Puritan Revolution," *Milton Studies*, 3 (1971), 39-52, has suggested that Samson was a culture hero for the Puritan revolution, taking part in the "Lord's Battels." He undoubtedly was so conceived and is expressive of the ideology and psychology of the republicans. Her further suggestion that he represents in particular the New Model Army is not, I think, correct; she does not see that the imagery of violent physical military warfare is replaced in the course of the poem by imagery still completely and politically significant, but imagery of intellectual and exemplary force, imagery of rising in ideals and thoughts, not of rising in rebellion or arms. See Ruth M. Kivette, "The Ways and Wars of Truths," *Milton Quarterly*, 6 (1972), 81-86, for a discussion of Milton's preference for pilgrimage to military metaphor. See Frank Kermode, "Milton in Old Age," *Southern Review*, 11 (1975), for the role that Milton's token submission to Charles II may have played in his depiction of the agonies God visits upon his elect champions.

judged by the ends which they propose. It is those ends which sanctify their nationhood and not vice versa. I have commented sufficiently on the poem's vituperative condemnation of the ungrateful multitude and the vindictive tone in which they are left to their richly deserved lot in the early acts. The scene with Dalila concludes with Samson's forgiveness of his wife, "At distance I forgive thee, go with that," an ethical stage of development well beyond his earlier intellectually and psychologically remarkable "Such pardon therefore as I give my folly, / Take to thy wicked deed." The resumption of the political education of his people on a higher level in Act IV is subsequent to the rough denunciation of Dalila, giving way to an abrupt, still angry, but now just and terse forgiveness. I do not at all claim that Dalila is an allegorical figure of any contemporary person (such as Mary Powell) or group (such as passive royalists), and it is not my view that Miltonic political teaching consists in such simple identifications. I mean that Samson is now applying a higher and truer morality to his dealings with Dalila, and a consequence is the further renewal of the power in him to reason well and to listen to another sort of prompting impulse than that of violent reprehension.

In the two scenes with Harapha and the Officer in the fourth act of the drama, Milton commences the substitution of a higher representative or exemplary role for Samson than that of military leader. The first stage is the careful contrast of the warrior Harapha and his absurd chivalric pretensions with the individual unarmed ability of Samson; the contrast is between "glorious armes which greatest Heroes have in battel worn" and sheer "trust . . . in the living God," between the power of the military code of the Philistines and "the power of *Israel's* God." The Chorus most explicitly drives that contrast home when they speak of the exaltation which "the Spirits of just men long opprest" feel at the sight of "invincible might" given "to quell . . . the brute and boist'rous force of violent men / Hardy and industrious to support / Tyrannic power." Their language is again explicitly political, and what they praise is a force of mind which overcomes the contrasting force of arms:

> He all thir Ammunition
> And feats of War defeats
> With plain Heroic magnitude of mind
> And celestial vigour arm'd. . . .

> (1277-80)

The Chorus is admiring the kind of spiritual warfare which overcomes mere military might, but they can also admire another kind, the spiritual warfare by which each man becomes "his own Deliverer, / And Victor over all / That tyrannie or fortune can inflict." The Chorus concludes that because of his blindness, Samson's fortitude is more likely to be tested by patience than by action. It is in the occasion to be tested by both. Milton's strategy in framing the final episode to reconcile action with patience and good deeds with sound beliefs is the most complex he ever employed.

The second scene of Act IV sets the stage for patient action. When the Officer comes to command Samson to perform before the "great Assembly," Samson declines:

> Do they not seek occasion of new quarrels
> On my refusal to distress me more. . . .

> (1329-30)

But their "occasion" constitutes Samson's occasion. He has already seen the possibility that this might be so:

> But come what will, my deadliest foe will prove
> My speediest friend, by death to rid me hence,
> The worst that he can give, to me the best.
> Yet so it may fall out, because thir end
> Is hate, not help to me, it may with mine
> Draw thir own ruin who attempt the deed.

> (1262-67)

With the Chorus he takes up the question of how the oppressed minority is to behave under insulting dominion. The Chorus recalls to him once more "Yet with this strength thou serv'st the *Philistines*." Their untimely rebuke recapitulates Manoa's in Act II. Samson's reply is conspicuously different and shows the long pilgrimage he has made toward understanding. To Manoa, Samson had said that he longed for the obliteration of death and felt it near:

> My race of glory run, and race of shame,
> And I shall shortly be with them that rest.

> (597-98)

His reply to the Chorus is a brief program for his people, tersely offered to the saints in the Restoration period as well. Samson is not serving the Philistines "in thir Idol-worship" by working among them, nor do the republicans prefer the rule of Charles II to that of God. What he is in fact doing is "by labour / Honest and lawful to deserve [his] food / Of those who have [him] in thir civil power." Until a new occasion arrives from some contingency which the malice and vindictiveness of the politically mighty may offer, there remains a positive course for Samson, the passive resistance of sojourning among the tyrannical, in a self-disciplined way. Milton no longer expresses his rage and indignation at his own condition by vituperative attacks upon his countrymen; he defends and recommends an interim course. Samson, rid of obsessive guilt, begins to "feel some rouzing motions in me." He accompanies the Officer to the games after a farewell generously expressive of concern for the Chorus, "Brethren farewel, your company along / I will not wish," for "Lords are Lordliest in thir wine." As he leaves, he cites the explicit governance under which he departs:

> of me expect to hear
> Nothing dishonourable, impure, unworthy
> Our God, our Law, my Nation, or my self. . . .
>
> (1423-25)

The English people have been assured through the play that God can free them from "National obligation," that He may allow them to be present at "Idolatrous Rites for some important cause," that the labor of their patient hands under affliction is honorable, that they are not alone and deserted, and that Samson—or every one of their isolated and betrayed republican leaders—continues to concern himself for them. Samson leaves with the completest identification of his innermost self with others, with nation, law, and God.

In Act v new imagery and new forms of expressiveness are invoked (as they are at the close of *Lycidas*) to replace warfaring with wayfaring, falling with rising, self-sacrifice with self-realization. The Messenger's account of the catastrophe comes first. The picture given is of how Samson was "as a public servant" brought to the temple, how "patient but undaunted" he performed quite alone, "none daring to appear Antagonist," how he stood as one who "some great matter in his mind revolv'd," and how he then undertook of his "own accord such other tryal" as seemed to him best. His deed was an act of personal choice, undertaken after listening to the voice of right reason and having full social implications. The first response of the Chorus and of Manoa is given next. Here, of all the emphases open to him of triumph and vindication, Milton chooses to emphasize the conjoint self-realization and self-sacrifice in Samson's act: "Living or dying thou hast fulfill'd / The work for which thou wast foretold / To *Israel*." He follows that by stressing the responsibility of the Philistines for their violent end, they who "drunk . . . regorg'd . . . chaunting . . . set on sport and play . . . importun'd / Thir own destruction to come speedy upon them." (The weight of lines devoted to assessing the role of the Philistines' will has not been adequtaely marked by those critics who are determined to force the drama into an amoral pattern of exultant genocide.) And finally Samson is likened not, as he had been earlier, to Atlas "whom the Gentiles feign" (150), to a "single combatant" (344), to "the sons of *Anac* . . . fearless of danger" (529), to those drawn "forth to perilous enterprises" (804), to Hercules caught "far within defensive arms" by "a cleaving mischief" (1037), nor to Ajax nor Goliath (1121). Rather, blind Samson is likened to figures that imply arising and ascending, first to the "ev'ning Dragon," then to the eagle, then finally, and most tellingly, to the phoenix.

In the first metaphor, out of a night as dark as blindness, a serpent of the ground raises itself against the "tame villatic Fowl." Like a serpent groping his way among the Philistines in his darkness, Samson came among them and they feared his power to rush into their midst. With the change of metaphor to the eagle born of Zeus—the emblem of victory and sovereignty—the destruction the Philistines feared from the ground comes down upon them from above. Samson is seen transmuted into a power rising aloft. In the final image Samson is likened to the resurrection figure of the phoenix itself. Vengeance upon the Philistines drops out of the figure altogether; the final picture is of metaphorical triumph over self. The forms of resemblance between Samson and the phoenix are, as is suitable to triumph, underlined with breathtaking swiftness. Both were "deprest," "overthrown," "embost" (embosked or hunted into dark hiding), but both became "vigorous most when most unactive deemed." Both died in body, leaving their fame to survive; their meaning exists to be applied throughout "ages of lives." With these references to mythologies which directly contradict the military mythologies earlier invoked, Milton has mounted from the public conception of Samson as one "from the top of wondrous glory . . . to lowest pitch of abject fortune . . . fall'n" to the public conception of him as (like Lycidas) one who rises aloft and "revives, reflourishes." His death was not as Manoa first feared, "self-violence"; it was self-fulfillment in self-sacrifice, "victorious among thy slain self-kill'd." His action was exemplary and given to his nation for their encouragement and education.[3]

Manoa attempts the application of the lesson of Samson's life and death. In it is "nothing but well and fair, / And what may quiet us in a death so noble." And Samson

[3] F. T. Prince, in his edition of *Samson Agonistes* (New York: Oxford University Press, 1957), 32, comments on the transitional nature of the imagery from lowly to rising and quotes Masson, *Life of Milton*. See also Lynn Veach Sadler, "Typological Imagery in *Samson Agonistes*," for another reading.

To *Israel*
Honour hath left, and freedom, let but them
Find courage to lay hold on this occasion. . . .

(1714-16)

The nature of "laying-hold" is left for the kommos to clarify. Manoa gives to Samson the consolation possible under the Old Testament dispensation; the kommos shows how that dispensation is exemplary in the new dispensation. To Manoa, Samson will serve to teach "all the valiant youth" "to inflame thir breasts" and all the virgins to bewail "his lot unfortunate in nuptial choice." But to the Chorus the lesson lies in the giving of the lesson. God the Aristotelian tragedian has offered to his people the lesson of tragedy, their own responsibility for fidelity to their wisest, highest impulses and the knowledge that their own experience is instrumental to the providential future:

His servants he with new acquist
Of true experience from this great event
With peace and consolation hath dismist. . . .

(1755-57)

Samson's action at the close of the play is admonitory to "all that band them" against a true response to God's law of liberty. Furthermore, it is doctrinal to the suffering part of his own nation. They are to "lay hold" on cathartic spiritual experience and fight a spiritual pilgrim's fight as agonists like Samson. Manoa echoes 1 Tim., "Fight the good fight of faith, lay hold on eternal life whereunto thou art also called," and it is clear that the good fight is the fight of faith.

In *Samson Agonistes* Milton has measured political loss and found it fully tragic. He has expressed anger, remorse, and grief and gone beyond them. The sole basis on which a political future can become possible is an understanding of God's continuing purposiveness throughout all national eras. One by one, individual Englishmen must remember their inborn freedom—"we are now under Christ a royal priesthood as we are coheirs, kings and priests with him"—and apply the treatment of its loss to their establishment of true community. To the restored Davidic king in epic and mock-epic of Cowley and Dryden, Milton opposed the imaginative portrait of the representative of the people, elected, not born, into leadership. The ideal behavior proposed through Samson's tragedy is a cultural ideal, through which by vocation and self-discipline the old political forms of subordination to kingship might forever be abrogated. The new ideal had not been stable when first announced. The kommos of *Samson Agonistes* prophesies its future stability. Milton's ethics of wrestling give effect to a politics of reconstruction. From the sight of one man freeing himself from despair taught by his own failure to achieve his political destiny, might yet come personal regeneration. Milton anticipated that other men might learn one by one to free themselves for political ends. Tragic catharsis might lead his own people into the stability of a consensus of virtuous men.

Thou hast
fulfill'd the work

SAMSON AGONISTES AND
MILTON'S ETHICS

Introduction

Samson Agonistes belongs to the tradition which assumes that poetry contributes to the education of man, enabling him "to perform justly, skillfully, and magnanimously all the offices, both private and public, of peace and war." This is not the sole English tradition, nor is "the search for truth" the only delight that English poets intended.[1] Even in Renaissance poetics not all verse was expected to be "set high in spirit with the precious taste of sweet philosophy."[2] But Milton, like many of his contemporaries, consistently addressed his poetry to and from "the unpolluted temple of the mind."[3] Like Henry Vaughan he thought nothing of "Idle verse" and "queint folies"; like George Herbert he scorned poetry that could only "wear Venus Livery"; like Richard Crashaw he aspired in poetry "to redeem Vertue to action"; like Andrew Marvell he "no other way could tell / To be ingenious, but by speaking well."[4] With the major English poets of the philosophical tradition, Milton respected the possibilities of "that sublime art" and knew "what religious, what glorious and magnificent use might be made of poetry, both in divine and human things."[5] His poetry is a poetry of knowledge, a poetry arising from and contributing to knowledge; his impulse and end was "to be an interpreter and relater of the best and sagest things among mine own citizens throughout this island in the mother dialect."[6] In *Samson Agonistes* Milton engaged in philosophical wrestling once more to promulgate wisdom and true philosophy, which would make his poetry something after ages would not willingly let die. It should go without saying that Milton's sense of the durability of his art was connected to "both matter, form and stile"; "the stile by certain vital signes it had was likely to live." An "inward prompting" grew in him "that by labour and intent

---

[1] *Of Education, CPW*, ii, 379; *Second Defence, ibid.*, iv, pt. 1, 648. But see also the *First Defence, ibid.*, 304, *Second Defence, ibid.*, 601, *An Apology for Smectymnuus, ibid.*, 1, 890, *The Reason of Church Government, ibid.*, 816-18, and *Defence of Himself, ibid.*, iv, pt. 2, 774, for further statements of Milton's views on the function of poetry. John S. Diekhoff has compiled many of these views in *Milton on Himself* (New York: Oxford University Press, 1939).

[2] Ben Jonson, "Prologue," *Every Man in His Humour.*

[3] *Comus*, l.460.

[4] Vaughan, "Idle Verse," *Silex Scintillans*; Herbert, "Sonnet to his Mother"; Crashaw, "On a Treatise of Charity"; Marvell, "To Mr. Richard Lovelace."

[5] *Of Education, CPW*, ii, 404, 405.

[6] *The Reason of Church Government, CPW*, i, 812.

study . . . joyn'd with the strong propensity of nature" he might become a serious Christian poet for his nation in all times.[7]

The time-honored concerns of classical poets and philosophers were also Milton's, and *Samson Agonistes* reveals his continuing preoccupation with them.[8] Believing that "tragedy hath been ever held the gravest, moralest, and most profitable of all other Poems," Milton composed *Samson Agonistes* in concentric areas of grave and useful thought. Some of these have been the subjects of individual consideration in the preceding chapters: Milton's interest in the innermost circle of thought, in the human personality, its reason, imagination, passion, feeling, and psychological balance was examined in Part One; his interest in the process of history and how time might be thought to bear upon human endeavors, a larger circle, was examined in Part Two; his interest in politics or the nature of society and the relation to it of the individual in terms of law, self-realization, self-sacrifice, and custom, a still larger circle, was treated in Part Three. We come now to an even more inclusive area of Milton's thought, the area of moral activities, to consider how Milton shaped *Samson Agonistes* to reveal his convictions about man's duties and moral choices. The tragedy addresses itself to the question of how each human being is to live, a question more inclusive for Milton than the relationship between the individual and his times or the individual and his nation because he considered it to be a problem common to all times and places in the postlapsarian world. *Samson Agonistes* contains a clear ethical intention as well as a political intention, and it is to the former we now turn.

Milton's ethical task in *Samson Agonistes* was to elicit from his mimesis of a biblical fable a "present rule of life, an insight into how postlapsarian man must face his fallen world, and his own fallen nature, here and now and all the time,"[9] but to elicit that rule in such a way as to enable man to follow it. His formal instruments for achieving this ethical purpose might be thought to have been more difficult to wield than those in *Lycidas* and in *Paradise Lost*. The tragedy makes no use of divine persons advising, consoling, or counselling his charac-

[7] See Robert West, "Milton as Philosophical Poet" in Amadeus P. Fiore, ed., "*Th' Upright Heart and Pure*," Duquesne Studies, Philological Ser., 10 (Pittsburgh: Duquesne University Press, 1967), for a sensible statement of Milton's philosophical limitations. See also William J. Grace, *Ideas in Milton* (Notre Dame, Ind.: Notre Dame University Press, 1968), 152-65, for the view that *Samson Agonistes* is not representative of Milton's highest, richest thought.

[8] See Davis P. Harding, *The Club of Hercules* (Urbana: University of Illinois Press, 1962), 2-4; John Holloway, "*Paradise Lost* and the Quest for Reality," *Forum for Modern Language Studies*, 3 (1967), 12-14.

[9] Holloway, "*Paradise Lost* and the Quest for Reality," 12.

ters, no chorus of angels expounding the correct meaning of the action, no other speaker than a human agent. He did not even employ the voice of a narrator, a poet-personality created by the poem's style and structure to interpose judgments of the image of human life he was presenting or to evaluate the persons, actions, and events being dramatized.[10] In anticipation of that "still time when there shall be no chiding,"[11] Milton analyzed the possibilities of the various literary kinds and listed "that Epick form whereof the two poems of Homer, and those other two of Virgil and Tasso are a diffuse, and the Book of Job a brief model . . . those Dramatick constitutions . . . those magnifick Odes and Hymns." He was in every instance examining the formal properties of the genres to be bent to one end: "teaching over the whole book of sanctity and vertu through all the instances of example."[12] His end was educative and ethical, and the metaphor which struck him as most apt for ethics was that of pilgrimage, "the paths of honesty and good life." He understood that every genre would involve the mimesis of an exemplary action, "to lay the *pattern* of a Christian hero" before England, "to celebrate what [God] *works* and what he suffers to be wrought," or "to sing the victorious agonies of Martyrs and Saints, the *deeds* and triumphs of just and pious Nations doing valiantly." He included in his discussion certain specific formal propositions which seemed to him true: that the single topic for epic recommended by Aristotle is not superior to the digressive epic;[13] that both formally and thematically the "frequent songs throughout the laws and prophets" are superior to "all the kinds of Lyric poesy"; that the functions of the poet could only be served if he were able "with a solid and treatable smoothness to paint out and describe all these things" and if he knew "of that which is the main consistence of a true poem, the choys of such persons as they ought to introduce, and what is morall and decent to each one." He listed succinctly the five functions of the serious national poet—to inculcate virtue by precept and personal example; to purge the passions and harmonize the affections; to celebrate the glory of God; to praise deeds done in God's service; and to deplore the lapses of nations—and he aligned each with its appropriate genre. He enumerated the four prerequisites for great poetry: inspiration; reading and study; observation and ex-

[10] John Berger, *The Allegorical Temper: Vision and Reality in Book II of Spenser's "Faerie Queene"* (New Haven: Yale University Press, 1957), 130-33, contains a discussion of this problem for the poet Spenser.

[11] *An Apology against a Pamphlet, CPW*, I, 892.

[12] *The Reason of Church Government, CPW*, I, 812-18.

[13] "Whether the rules of Aristotle herein are strictly to be kept, or nature followed, which in them that know art, and use judgment is no transgression, but an inriching of art" (*ibid.*, 813).

perience; insight into arts and affairs. He thought that to interpret and relate significant moral truth in *Samson Agonistes* meant knowing the best rule of life under the conditions of man's true state and dramatizing that rule to "temper and reduce to just measure" human passions, not only with "fear, or terror," but with "pity." And he faced the problem of impersonal moral emphasis.

The communication of moral knowledge in an "answerable style" will be the subject of this section, that is, the substance of the Miltonic ethic and the achievement of an ethically apt mode of dramatic expression. In these areas too Milton was a radical innovator; yet once again his ultimate achievement grew out of a lengthy process of testing and molding both thought and instrument. *Samson Agonistes* is successful as an ethical work because Milton discovered the means of incorporating his personal moral insights in an impersonal dramatic form. He enacted his moral theme not only by means of the educative journey of the character Samson but also by means of shading and qualifying linguistic tones which universalize that journey. Debarred from overt comment, he employed instead a richly allusive biblical diction. His fundamental ethical conviction was that the good is discoverable by making a series of rational choices, issuing in actions which limit subsequent options but do not destroy the freedom to choose, upon which the ethical value of action must depend. The good is always contingent, always relative to circumstances, but the individual is free and always capable of renewing virtuous action. Virtue is not an abstract state of mind but an active state involving deeds answerable to insights. Given the contingent nature of good, those deeds can only be measured in relation to alternatives and can only be validated by reference to the motives and insights of the doer. God covenanted with the good man, not to remove painful alternatives from his life, nor even to reward the good with success, but to ensure that the existence of alternatives gave him ground for active faith and fruitful works. On the basis of this sort of ethics, the dramatic form of *Samson Agonistes* and its style follow with a kind of inevitability. The arrangement of incidents was not to be causal, with one incident necessitating the next, but dialectical, with one incident doubling or reenacting the previous one so that a wrestling might be dramatized. The qualities of style were to reflect the interior results of each incident, to suggest the effect of choice upon the thoughts of characters.

My procedure in this section will resemble that in the previous ones. I shall trace Milton's evolving ethics of progressive purification as they issue into the actions of *Samson Agonistes* itself. I shall discuss the rule of life given in the tragedy by reference to the poem which accompanied *Samson Agonistes* in the designedly unified volume of

1671: "*Paradise Regain'd*. Poem. In IV Book. To which is Added *Samson Agonistes*. The Author, John Milton." But first I shall examine Milton's style as appropriate to ethical teaching. The judgments made by characters are not the judgments made upon characters by the poet. The ways of God are just and merciful; the ways of the poet are particularly merciful, and his greatest pity is reserved for the discovery that chastened remorse may be among the purest and least ambivalent responses to life of which the individual is capable. In a tragic view of life, an ethics of action must deal with the mystery of iniquity in such a way as to commend and promote right-living. It is insufficient to judge and to condemn wrong-doing; it is necessary to restore to the tragically failing mortal sufferer a sufficient sense of purpose and a sufficient trust in the value of goodness to enable him to bring the forces of his existence once more under the control of his own will. A tragedy, even one depicting regeneration, cannot commend virtue simply because it is profitable. The triumph of virtue may culminate in success, but the sanction of virtue when it appears in the tragic genre is its truth to the innermost nature of man. Milton meant that truth to be medicinal and fitted his style to that purpose. The stylistic and formal progression in Milton's earlier poetry comes to a culmination in *Samson Agonistes*. Witnessing to high truths was his own role; interpreting them and relating them had heretofore involved uniting his personal voice with his impersonal discoveries. He had learned through *Lycidas* and the sonnets how to dramatize autobiography so as to communicate the process of discovery of impersonal truths. His own mortal voice combined in those poems with the voice of thought, as it did likewise in the poems in *Paradise Lost*. The result was what we have been calling multivocal and dialectic. In *Samson Agonistes* Milton brought his creation of plain style to the highest finish. Having apparently deprived himself of the overt presence of a speaker to modify or emphasize thought, he was nonetheless able to weld together ethical truth and formulaic biblical expressiveness in an instrument that teaches and delights, an instrument of great flexibility and beauty. *Samson Agonistes* was meant to take place in the theater of the mind and to enact the drama of the soul. Milton had learned from his earlier writings to replace false fictions and classical constructs with true fictions and Christian constructs, but he associated this demonstration of truth with Hebrew poetry rather than with "what the Gentiles feign." He wrote *Samson Agonistes* under the dominance of Hebrew poetry, and in particular, under the dominance of the Psalms.

BIBLICAL POETRY AND

MEDICINAL TRUTH

Samson Agonistes is biblical drama, not only in that the mimesis is of a life taken from the period when the Law yielded to the Prophets and external morality began to be replaced by internal freedom, but also in that its style, form, and mood derive from the Psalms. Milton conceived of the Psalms as an account of the spiritual life of the seeking pilgrim or seeking nation, presenting all the stages of pilgrimage, together with their attendant feelings of despair and comfort, hopelessness and hope, remorse and reassurance. *Samson Agonistes* communicates the major stages of Samson's personal growth by reference to groups of psalms particularly applicable to each stage, commencing with psalms of lament, continuing with the didactic psalms of suffering and doubt, and concluding with the hymnic psalms of affirmation and praise. The Chorus follows the course of Samson's growth a step behind him, communicating their understanding first through the psalms of communal lament, then the proverb-linked psalms of wisdom, and finally the psalms of blessing and thanksgiving. Milton quarried the individual groups of psalms for qualifying diction applicable to stages of insight in the consciousness of major characters. In their totality as well as in their individual force the Psalms movingly describe the discovery of an ethical stance. Virtue involves personal discoveries of the nature and the possibility of inner rectitude in the passage through life; God's mercy becomes apparent in the context of his judgment. The Psalms offer a personal and a national journey toward right conceptions of self and God, not a straightforward journey from the bottom of the hill to the peak, but a doubling, repetitive, often backsliding and painful journey, communicated in the five books of the Psalms as a dialectical course rather than as a continuous one. Each of the five books falls into parallel subgroups of psalms; in each the journey is toward light, but in each the traveler errs, requires solace, recalls the stages of his imperfect insight, prays sometimes well and sometimes badly; each closes with a doxology, and that of Psalm 150 closes the whole.

The supposedly amoral and genocidal tendency noticed by some critics of *Samson Agonistes* arises from a partial reading of the play which cuts off the drama before the fullness of the cycle has been recognized. Similar comments on the crudity and moral imperviousness of the Psalms are often made by the supposedly more tender-minded and morally sophisticated twentieth-century reader. But Milton's contemporary Bible-reading audience would not have fallen into either simplicity. To the seventeenth-century reader the Psalm allusions in *Samson Agonistes* would have functioned as an unmistakable guide to its progressive tones, a guide which acknowledges the violence and vindictiveness of men in many of the crises in their lives, and their eagerness to attribute these traits to God, yet sees design in suffering, and insight and assuagement at the end. For Milton the Psalms were a persistent source of allusions in his purpose to make *Samson Agonistes* ethically persuasive because the Psalms reflect and announce God's covenant with man. By responding to that covenant, an ethical life becomes possible: to know, to bear, to understand is the beginning of the ethical journey, to behave well and faithfully is the conclusion. The apt words of the Psalmist take up man's suffering and grief in the most direct way, more closely and nakedly than any other poetry. The expression of pain in the psalms of lamentations shows the Psalmist's psychological insight and also his pity for human suffering. Assuagement through trust in God is what the Psalmist's words can offer, not just to one stricken believer but to all such men.

The Psalms and the 1645 Poems

In *Paradise Regained* Milton has Jesus commend Hebrew poetry above that of the ancients:

> All our Law and Story strew'd
> With Hymns, our Psalms with artful terms inscrib'd,
> Our Hebrew Songs and Harps in *Babylon*,
> That pleas'd so well our Victors ear, declare
> That rather *Greece* from us these Arts deriv'd;
> Ill-imitated . . .
> Remove their swelling Epithetes thick laid
> As varnish on a Harlots cheek, the rest,
> Thin sown with aught of profit or delight,
> Will far be found unworthy to compare
> With *Sion's* songs, to all true tasts excelling,
> Where God is prais'd aright, and Godlike men,
> The Holiest of Holies, and his Saints.

(IV, 334-49)

In writing these lines Milton was returning to some of the very earliest sources of his own creative impulse. The 1645 edition of the shorter poems opens with "On the Morning of Christs Nativity. Composed 1629." Milton placed next the early adaptations of Psalms 114 and 146, with the note "This and the following *Psalm* were don by the Author at fifteen yeers old," the psalm renderings apparently being the first English-language poems Milton saved. They were written in 1624 and preserved as juvenilia, but responsiveness to Sion's songs was to be persistent with Milton. These two psalms of Milton's adolescence are glossed best by reference to "Ad Patrem," a mixed-genre ode, at one and the same time a defense of poetry, an apology for himself, a "slender work of . . . verbal gratitude," and a deliberative encomium.[1] In that poem, written seven years after the paraphrases of the Psalms, Milton recompensed his father for his "liberality" by composing a poetic debate on the theme "Verse is a work divine." The poem is a family affair, but its seven stanzas of sixteen, thirty-nine, eleven, twenty-six, eighteen, four, and six lines alternately interweave personal and impersonal concerns, and they offer a view of the role of poetry and the nature of the poet that was decisive for Milton's early creativity.

The first personal stanza prays that

> for my venerable Father's sake
> All meaner themes renounc'd, my muse on wings
> Of duty borne, might reach a loftier strain.

The higher-lower, meaner-loftier distinction is common in Milton's works, and usually contains a reference to progressive intention. The

---

[1] The discussion of mixed kinds in Rosalie Colie, *The Resources of Kind: Genre-Theory in the Renaissance* (Berkeley: University of California Press, 1973), 114-22, is suggestive of fruitful ways to reconsider Milton's ode. But see Marguerite Little, "Milton's 'Ad Patrem' and the Younger Gill's 'In Natalem Mei Parentis,'" *Journal of English and Germanic Philology*, 49 (1950), 345-51. "Ad Patrem" has attracted two sorts of commentary, that on its date and that on its genre. Douglas Bush and A. B. Giamatti summarize the discussions of its date in *A Variorum Commentary on the Poems of John Milton*, 1, 232-55. If 1631-1632 is correct, and I believe it is, then "Ad Patrem"—a mainly secular, humanistic, and tranquil poem extolling verse of a prophetic cast written by a scholar-poet learned in science, history, and literature—was written not because of anyone's uneasiness about Milton's idleness in writing nothing or his vanity in writing *A Masque* but rather for its face-value concerns. A likable, serious-minded son associates learning, leisure, and high art in his own mind with pleasure in his father's companionship and generosity. Little identifies the genre as a subgenre of the encomium on a conventional subject, the family, a subgenre which authorizes banter and was fit for a young Puritan. In this connection see Barbara Lewalski, *Donne's "Anniversaries" and the Poetry of Praise* (Princeton: Princeton University Press, 1973), 20-41.

second impersonal stanza extols verse "which evinces (nothing more) / Man's heavenly source." The stanza associates poetry with Promethean fire, the harmony of the created world, the music of the spheres, and the song of Orpheus. It concludes by identifying the meaning, not the sound, of verse as the sign of its divine source, and it prepares for the ensuing stress in stanza three upon learning as prerequisite for the poet's work:

> And what avails at last, tune without voice,
> Devoid of matter. . . . Not by chords alone
> Well touch'd, but by resistless accents more
> To sympathetic tears the ghosts themselves
> He mov'd.

The preference of words over song in the second impersonal stanza becomes a harmonizing of both words and song in the unity of one family in the personal third stanza. There, although no evidence within or without the poem suggests that Milton's father was ever inclined to do so, Milton asks him not to make light of poetry:

> thyself
> Art skillful to associate verse with airs
> Harmonious, and to give the human voice
> A thousand modulations, heir by right
> Indisputable of Arion's fame.
> Now say, what wonder is it, if a son
> Of thine delight in verse, if so conjoin'd
> In close affinity, we sympathize
> In social arts, and kindred studies sweet.

The primary activity in which were united the "cognatas artes, studiumque affine" of father and son was the paraphrasing and setting of the Psalms. Stanza four concedes that of course Milton's father does not "despise verse" (stanza two), or "slight the sacred nine" (three), or "hate the gentle Muse" (four). He has not condemned his elder son to "the insipid clamours of the bar," the profession his second son, Christopher, was to follow. Rather, he has bid Milton to "fill [his] mind with treasure," including "Palestine's prophetic songs divine." His father has given him what in *The Reason of Church Government* Milton called "ease and leisure . . . for retired thoughts out of the sweat of other men." Stanza five bonds impersonal to personal: the gift of the sum of knowledge is the highest his father, or any, could give: "What more could Jove himself" or Apollo give a son. In reciprocation Milton promises to persevere in preparing himself to write divine verse and to hold his "place / Among the learned in the laurel grove . . . exempt from the unletter'd throng." The two brief concluding stanzas more modestly declare the poet's inability to "render thanks / Equivalent" to his father's gifts; instead, he intends to record those gifts for future ages. Characteristically, and in a tone the reverse of solemn, he expects of his "voluntary numbers" that they will "by these praises of my sire / Improve the Fathers of a distant age."

The association in "Ad Patrem" of ideas of singing and celebrating high and lofty matters is an association instinctive even in the youthful Milton and remained a characteristic note throughout his life. In *Of Reformation* (1641) "someone may perhaps be heard offering at high strains in new and lofty measures to sing and celebrate thy divine mercies and marvellous judgments"; in *The Reason of Church Government* he resolves "to celebrate in glorious and lofty hymn the throne and equipage of God's almightiness." In the Invocation to Book I of *Paradise Lost* the association receives its fullest expression:

> What in me is dark
> Illumine, what is low raise and support;
> That to the highth of this great Argument
> I may assert Eternal Providence. . . .
>
> (I, 22-25)

In all these places, and in others, the celebration of high truths carries with it a sense that high truths and perfect song come from Sion's Hill.

Milton's psalm paraphrases were written in a household uniformly described by contemporary biographers as pleasant, serious, cohesive, generous, and devoted to the arts. It was a dominantly musical household.[2] Milton's father composed a considerable number of songs: among others, he set two anonymous psalm tunes for Thomas Ravenscroft's collection, *The Whole Book of Psalms* (1621), to serve as music for Psalms 5, 27, 55, 66, 102, and 138, as well as for "A Prayer to the Holy Ghost"; he composed a motet setting for an old Latin hymn for Myriell's *Tristitise Remedium*; and he set the opening sentences of the Order for the Burial of the Dead, "I am the resurrection and the life, saith the Lord." But the Milton household was also markedly literary. Milton's father, in commending a contemporary continuation of Lydgate's *Guy of Warwick*, offered the conventional Renaissance Protestant apology for reading the romances in which he

---

[2] See Ernest Brenneke, Jr., *John Milton the Elder and His Music* (New York: Columbia University Press, 1938), 98-107.

and his son delighted, especially romances authenticated "By Herals' records and each sound antiquary." Romances offered instances of "Love, war and lists quelled by arm heroic" for virtuous imitation:

> To exemplify the flower of chivalry
> From cradle to the saddle and the bier,
> For Christian imitation, all are here.[3]

Thus the Milton family combined verse and voice, and because they united them to the service of religion they were nearly indifferent to whether an extremely gifted son should be pastor or poet so long as voice and verse were biblically inspired and the life of the poet or pastor religiously directed. Milton's modesty about his own poetry, so characteristic of "Ad Patrem"—he speaks of "tenuis sonos" ("trivial songs"), "juvinilia carmina" ("juvenile verses"), *exiguum opus* ("poor attempt")—echoes the self-deprecation in the headnotes to his first psalm versions and "The Passion." "Ad Patrem" was, in my view, written with the consciousness of ineptitudes in his handling of the poetic aspect of the *cognatus artem* shared by the father and son. Milton is not impressed with himself as a psalmist but is profoundly impressed both with the high calling of the poet and the supremacy of psalms among all varieties of poetry.[4]

After paraphrasing Psalms 114 and 146, Milton wrote no English verse until he lamented the death of his sister's "Fair Infant" in a poem deriving from a family sorrow. In the "Vacation Exercise," composed in the same year, he announced a positive turning from his successful writing of Latin poetry to the use of his "native Language" for "some naked thoughts that rove about / And loudly knock to have their passage out." He desired the "chiefest treasure" of the English language:

> Not those new fangled toys, and triming slight
> Which takes our late fantasticks with delight,
> But . . . those richest Robes, and gay'st attire
> Which deepest Spirits, and choicest Wits desire. . . .

The following Christmas he wrote his first important English religious poem, "On the Morning of Christs Nativity." The Nativity Ode is not only generally scriptural, it is Psalm based. The psalms appointed

---

[3] Milton's father's sonnet is printed in Parker, *Milton*, 1, 16.

[4] See R. W. Condee, *Structure in Milton's Poetry* (University Park: Pennsylvania State University Press, 1974), for the pleasantest and fullest treatment known to me of "Ad Patrem" as a poem. Condee has, however, missed the point I am making.

to be read at Christmastime (Psalms 19, 45, 85, 89, 110, and 132, and also 2, 8, and 144) supplied the young poet with a tissue of phrases and concepts for the development of the poem, and Psalm 148, "Let Heaven and Earth Praise the Lord," gave him the incentive to unite all creation and mankind in a chorus of praise. The flight of false gentilish inspiration before the true inspiration of biblical religion constitutes an important aspect of the internal drama of the poem; "Oracles . . . nightly trance and breathed spell" are replaced by what "the holy sages once did sing." The introduction or setting for the hymn "On the Morning of Christs Nativity" makes use of the vision of the Son of God enthroned in heaven in Psalm 2, of the heavenly courts of the tabernacle and the speaking of good matter concerning the King with lips blessed by grace in Psalm 45. Stanza one derives the image of the sun as bridegroom or "paramour" coming forth from his chamber from Psalm 19; stanza two, the image of the clothing or covering of sin from Psalm 85; stanza five, the image of the stilling of the waves from Psalm 89; stanza fifteen, the personification of Truth, Justice, and Mercy, and stanza three, the personification of Peace from Psalm 85; stanza twenty-two, the shrinking horn of the ram god contrasted with the established horn from Psalm 132; stanza twenty-four, the shrouding of the pagan gods with hell likewise from Psalm 132; and stanza twenty-five, the dreaded hand of the Lord from Psalm 144.

The success of the Nativity Ode apparently suggested to Milton a full sequence of Christian poems moving through the year's festivals and the events of the life of Christ.[5] The Book of Psalms had already been adapted for such cyclical worship, of course. He began "The Passion" at the following Easter but left it unfinished, describing it as a failure in a note to the 1645 poems ("This Subject the Author finding to be above the yeers he had, when he wrote it, and nothing satisfi'd with what was begun, left it unfinisht"). Yet he preserved it, like the psalm paraphrases, as another piece of juvenilia.[6] He had once more gone to the Book of Psalms for inspiration and drawn from the Good Friday psalms (22, 40, 54, 69, and 88, and also 64) his major concepts and images. Stanza one derived being swallowed in night from Psalm 22; stanza two, the "dangers, and snares, and wrongs" from Psalm 40;

---

[5] See J. H. Hanford, "The Youth of Milton," in his *Studies in Shakespeare, Milton and Donne* (New York: Macmillan, 1925), 127.

[6] Milton did not, in fact, recur to the subject of the Passion even in his maturity. In Book XII of *Paradise Lost* (393-419), writing of the Atonement, he perforce included the Passion; that is, he devoted seven lines to the subject: "thy punishment / He shall endure by coming in the Flesh / To a reproachful life and cursed death. . . . / For this he shall live hated, be blasphem'd, / Seis'd on by force, judg'd, and to death condemnd / A shameful and accurst, naild to the Cross / By his own Nation."

stanza five, sorrows too dark for day from Psalm 88; and stanza eight, the hurrying on viewless wings from Psalm 55. The following New Year's Day, he tried a further poem upon the life of Jesus, his subject being the Circumcision, which he and his contemporaries regarded as the first event in the Passion.[7]

Between "The Passion" (Easter 1630) and "Upon the Circumcision" (1 January 1633), he wrote "Ad Patrem" and completed the meditations prompted by it, Sonnet 7 (December 1632) and "On Time" (later in December). "At a Solemn Musick" (January-February 1633) followed closely. The four poems—"The Passion," "On Time," "Upon the Circumcision," and "At a Solemn Musick"—Milton printed as a group in both 1645 and 1673.[8] They are linked by their persistent psalmic inspiration and by their discovery of the expressive possibilities of music as a symbol of harmonious, unifying creativity; music converted into words is, in all of them, the image of a harmonious life of ethical endeavor.[9] All very much take their clue from the Nativity Ode and have as their common semidramatic stance the fiction of mortals on earth singing together with the angels a poem about a religious subject. The poet's human song, which moves through the mortal element of time, is an echo and a part of the heavenly song composed in eternity. "The Passion" makes the link with the Nativity Ode explicit in the opening lines: "Ere-while of Musick . . . My muse with Angels did divide to sing . . . now to sorrow must I tune my song." Milton broke off that poem somewhere in the introduction. He had taken up the metrical scheme of "On the Morning of Christs Nativity," had pursued it for eight stanzas, but had not been able to proceed to a Passion hymn; he was trapped inside "my muse," "my song," "my roving vers," "my *Phoebus*," and unable to move beyond writing a poem about himself singing a mournful hymn of "plaining vers" to the accompaniment of "Harpe," "Lute, or Viol," unable to come to the canticle itself.[10] The relationship of the immortal theme and

[7] See Patrides, *Milton and the Christian Tradition*, 145. Patrides quotes Edward Sparke's term for the Circumcision, the "tragick-prologue" to the Passion when Christ "began . . . to take away the sins of the World."

[8] See Bush, *Variorum Commentary*, II, pt. 1, 162-64, 175, for a discussion of the dates of these poems.

[9] See Gretchen L. Finney, *Musical Backgrounds for English Literature: 1580-1700* (Princeton: Princeton University Press, 1961); John Hollander, *The Untuning of the Sky: Ideas of Music in English Poetry, 1500-1700* (Princeton: Princeton University Press, 1961); Winifred Maynard, "Milton and Music," in John Broadbent, ed., *John Milton: Introductions* (Cambridge: Cambridge University Press, 1973); and Lawry, *Shadow of Heaven*, 21-63.

[10] See Northrop Frye in Patrides, ed., *Milton's "Lycidas,"* 208, and Parker, *Milton*, I, 71-72.

the mortal singer so preoccupied Milton that he could not touch the theme of the relationship of the present to the timeless.

"On Time" confidently contrasts the mortal climate of the human being with the immortal state to which it shall return: "When once our heav'nly-guided soul shall clime, / Then all this Earthy grosnes quit." No specific liturgical or calendrical occasion fixed the psalms upon which Milton based "On Time," but even that poem is suffused with imagery drawn from the Book of Psalms: his picture of God's heavenly throne is drawn from Psalms 11 and 27; the joying in God, from Psalm 16; the heavenly guidance of the soul, from Psalms 43 and 48; the streams of gladness or flood of joy, from Psalms 46 and 98; the vanity and falsity of mortal man, from Psalm 39; the balance of loss and gain, from Psalm 62; the shining light in heaven, from Psalm 80; the kiss of eternity and the joining with Truth, Peace, and Love, from Psalm 85; the worldly dross, from Psalm 119; the attiring of man with stars, from Psalm 8; and the perpetuity of the triumph of the saved, from Psalms 138 and 121. With the relationship between time and eternity and between the mortal and immortal voices made clear in "On Time," Milton was able to avoid the breakdown of "The Passion" in his next poem in the projected religious cycle, "Upon the Circumcision."

"Upon the Circumcision" consists of two fourteen-line sentences. The first is an introductory invocation, asking the angelic voices "That erst with Musick, and triumphant song . . . So sweetly sung your Joy the Clouds along" to change their notes to lamentation ("Now mourn, and . . . sad share with us . . . bear") because the Son "who with all Heav'ns heraldry whileare / Enter'd the world, now bleeds to give us ease." The second sentence interprets the meaning of that bleeding of Jesus: "he . . . that great Cov'nant which we still transgress / Intirely satisfi'd." "Upon the Circumcision," like the Nativity Ode and "The Passion," was fashioned from the psalms set for the day: 40, 65, 90, and 103. Milton derived the concept of love exceeding the Law from Psalm 40, of bringing deliverance through dread deeds from Psalm 65, of man as fail dust from Psalms 90 and 103, and of keeping the covenant from Psalm 103.

The final poem in the series, "At a Solemn Musick," recapitulates the uniting of the "harmonious Sisters, Voice, and Vers" into one "undisturbed Song of pure concent" so that "we on Earth with undiscording voice / May rightly answer that melodious noise." The three preceding religious poems or songs are drawn together in the final lines in which living the moral life is seen as the precondition of being restored to the harmony of timeless "pure concent":

> O may we soon again renew that Song,
> And keep in tune with Heav'n, till God ere long
> To his celestial consort us unite,
> To live with him, and sing in endles morn of light.

"At a Solemn Musick" is a prayer which, like the hymns on the Passion and the Circumcision and the companion madrigal on time, creates through its interweaving musical imagery and metrical pattern the harmony which it celebrates.[11] In the prayer, voice and verse are asked to make man pure again, pure as he was before

> disproportion'd sin
> Jarr'd against natures chime, and with harsh din
> Broke the fair musick that all creatures made
> To their great Lord, whose love their motion sway'd
> In perfect Diapason, whilst they stood
> In first obedience, and their state of good.

The occasion for this religious poem is more general than that of the Passion or Circumcision, but it is clearly a religious occasion. The Song (for so Milton called it in heading the two corrected drafts in the Trinity Manuscript before entitling the fair copy "At a Solemn Musick") was to be used for any "solemn" (that is, sacred or religious) musical performance (that is, church service rather than concert).[12] Exactly in the middle of the poem three lines describe redeemed human beings singing in heaven. Seraphim and cherubim on high are pictured together "With those just Spirits that wear victorious Palms, / Hymns devout and holy Psalms / Singing everlastingly. . . ." The imagery is again Psalm based, most of it drawing on the psalms recommended in the Book of Common Prayer for when the themes of worship and the church of God are under consideration. The singing of a blessed song in the courts of God, a new song or renewed song, comes from Psalms 33, 96, 98, and 149, but especially from Psalm 84; the praising with trumpets, harps, and choirs, from Psalms 98, 146, 147, and 149, but especially Psalm 134; the music made by all creatures to their great Lord, from Psalm 122; the singing of God's praise contrasted to the broken harmony in disobedience to His law, from Psalm

---

[11] See Leo Spitzer, *Classical and Christian Ideas of World Harmony* (Baltimore: Johns Hopkins University Press, 1963), 103-7.
[12] This was the sense Milton gave to the word *solemn* in *Samson Agonistes* ("solemn festivals," l.983; "solemn Feast," l.1311) and *Paradise Lost* ("other solemn days," III, 5, 618).

48; the singing in endless morning light in tune with Heaven, from Psalms 51 and 57; the living with God, from Psalm 84; and the union of men into a perfect diapason, from Psalm 132. In all these early works Milton brings together biblical themes and ethical teaching. Voice and verse, with the Book of Psalms as inspiration, are dedicated to reforming and strengthening men in God's service.

THE PSALM TRANSLATIONS OF 1648 AND 1653

What was true of the young Milton was true throughout his life, "David's Psalms were in esteem with him above all poetry."[13] Ten years after his youthful psalm paraphrases, Milton translated Psalms 80 through 88 into rhyming verse, dating them April 1648. He published them in the 1673 volume with the headnote, "Nine of the Psalms done into Metre, wherein all but what is in a different Character, are the very words of the Text, translated from the Original." The headnote so emphasizes Milton's fidelity to the original that accuracy of translation must be taken to be his conscious intention in working on this group. One suggestion as to why Milton undertook to translate these particular psalms is too reasonable to be doubted,[14] namely, that he chose them because the Westminster Assembly had recommended that the Book of Psalms be revised, had appointed a committee to undertake the revision, had enjoined it to use common meter (crossrhyming lines of eight and six syllables, the meter Milton adopted), and, for the convenience of the committee, had divided the Psalms into four groups, group three beginning with Psalm 80, Milton's starting point. Clearly, Milton was trying his hand at a work undertaken for the religious health of the nation, but he may have wished as well to honor his father with the kind of poetry he liked Milton to write.[15] Nonetheless, Milton could have chosen to begin with any of the other three groups, as five years later, in 1653, he did indeed begin with the first eight psalms. But in 1648 it was altogether likely that Milton would be especially interested in the group consisting of the three so-called "judgment" psalms, followed by three prayers for de-

[13] See Thomas B. Stoup, *Religious Rite and Ceremony in Milton's Poetry* (Lexington: University of Kentucky Press, 1968), 3-8, for the suggestion that the young poet intended for the church was particularly sensitive to liturgy.

[14] First proposed by Masson, *Life of Milton*, and supported with full argument by William B. Hunter, "Milton Translates the Psalms," *Philological Quarterly*, 40 (1961), 485-94.

[15] Ernest Brenneke suggested that the translations could have been "a memorial act of filial reverence, for it took place almost exactly on the first anniversary of the scrivener's death." Quoted in Marjorie H. Nicolson, *John Milton: A Reader's Guide to His Poetry* (London: Thomas and Hudson, 1964), 24.

liverance from the wicked and oppressors, one psalm of renewed confidence in God's triumph, and a final psalm of affliction, the most despairing in the Book of Psalms. Protestant commentators, George Wither had noted, interpreted this particular group as treating "the estate of the Church, and Commonwealth of the Messias, distinguishing it into her Politicall, Ecclesiastical and oeconomicke Orders."[16] The group reflects an association of themes—God's displeasure with His chosen people, their longing for Sion, their prayers for renewed grace and divine guidance "in the time of troubles" when "the proud are risen . . . [and] violent men" abound—deriving from the idea of the covenant of God with a national people. The public uncertainties of the spring of 1648 would have made the group particularly apposite to England, and Milton's choice seems securely attached to the contemporary occasion. It is also very probable that Milton did not continue beyond Psalm 88 because that psalm bore such autobiographical reference to his own condition as to constitute a personal relief and consolation, a good staying place.

A major prop to the argument of those who consider *Samson Agonistes* to have been written in 1647 and revised in 1653 has been that these psalms reflect Milton's own troubled sense of his country in danger and his personal despair at the onset of blindness. In mood and tone, so the argument goes, they correspond to Samson's terrible opening soliloquy of grief; moreover, Psalm 88 in particular attracted Milton because, like the Psalmist and like Samson, he himself dreaded being sentenced to mourn in "the lowest pit *profound* . . . Where thickest darkness *hovers round*," cut off from friends and abandoned by God.[17] The political parallels linking England, the Israel of the Psalms, and Samson's nation are undeniable; the autobiographical resemblances between Milton, the Psalmist, and Samson facing or enduring symbolic or real blindness are self-evident. The flaw in the argument is the suggestion that Milton must have experienced simultaneously his own agony, the Psalmist's agony, and Samson's agony. For that there is no evidence, only the supposed probability that similar sentiments point to simultaneous composition and that melancholy moods and melancholy works must be synchronic.[18] Other poets and

---

[16] See Fixler, *Milton and the Kingdoms of God*, 11, 143-44. For a more general study see C. P. Collette, "Milton's Psalm Translations: Petition and Praise," *English Literary Renaissance*, 2 (1972), 243-59.

[17] See Parker, *Milton*, I, 322-25.

[18] Had Milton turned over the Book of Psalms seeking judgment psalms on recalcitrant people, he would have found in Psalms 35, 58, 59, or 79 far stronger words, or could have chosen Psalm 137, for which purpose he cited it in *De Doctrina Christiana* (*CPW*, VI, 604, 755), together with Psalms 37, 54, 91, and 94.

dramatists have not found that to be so, and have referred to the serenity or the joy involved in composing tragic works. What is important to see is that Milton always embodied political circumstances in his poetry, always made it "occasional" and always drew upon the Psalms to discuss God's national covenant and man's ethical response. Psalms 80 through 88 attracted him for their public bearing, and the last consoled him in his private trouble.

Five years later Milton made his third group of psalm paraphrases, translating Psalms 1 through 8 into a great variety of metrical forms. He translated Psalm 1 at an unspecified date in 1653 and Psalms 2 through 8 in the seven days between August 8 and 14. For Psalm 1 Milton supplied the note "Done into Verse," and for Psalm 2, "Terzetti," indicating that metrical experimentation was a dominant intention.[19] The public circumstances in which these psalms were translated differed from those surrounding the translation of Psalms 80 through 88, and so did Milton's private circumstances. He might have considered the state of the nation marginally more secure with the abrupt dissolution of the Rump and the calling together of the Nominated Parliament (which no doubt Milton tried to see as "th' assembly of just men," Psalm 1), but his personal state was less cheerful. Yet he had written the *First Defence* between the two groups of psalm translations, discharging, he considered, a truly epic task, and in Sonnet 19 he had already come to terms with his blindness and could consider God no longer a stern taskmaster but a magnanimous Lord whom "They also serve who only stand and waite." He was, moreover, considering the whole course of his own life in preparing the *Second Defence* at this time, and of that he proudly would claim, "Yet there was not wanting one who could rightly counsel, encourage, and inspire, who could honour both the noble deeds and those who had done them, and make both deeds and doers illustrious with praises that will never die."[20] If he had not yet found apt words with power to suage, he had found an epic stance, midway between lyric and dramatic.

Why Milton chose to translate the first eight Psalms at this juncture has been repeatedly asked. It has been suggested that the times were propitious for psalms "which in general dwell upon God's vindication of the just cause,"[21] that Milton's own sufferings led him to a group which could "voice the conflict of the godly and the ungodly . . . and

---

[19] "When he fled from Absalom" for Psalm 3 and "Upon the words of Chush the Benjaminite against him" are simply abbreviated translations of their superscriptions in Milton's Bible, titles supplied in the pre-Christian era and not, as Parker suggested, Milton's original glosses.

[20] *CPW*, IV, pt. 1, 685-86.

[21] Fixler, *Milton and the Kingdoms of God*, 182.

[reflect] his deplorable condition, a cry from his wounded, thwarted spirit,"[22] that the translating coincided with the composing of *Samson Agonistes* and that Psalm 6 reflected Samson's anguish at his blindness,[23] and even, with unnecessary caution, that "we cannot feel quite certain what elements in these particular Psalms especially appealed to Milton."[24] I have been arguing that Milton persistently drew upon the Psalms in poems not self-evidently indebted to them, that in his view the Book of Psalms contained the record of God's national and individual covenant with Israel and with everyman, and that he read the Book of Psalms as a double depiction of the history of a chosen nation and the pilgrimage of any man through life, admiring not only the beauty of their "artful terms," their "profit or delight," but also their praise of God and godlike men. A cross-check between the psalm citations as proof texts in *De Doctrina Christiana* and their use in *Paradise Lost* and *Paradise Regained* enables the twentieth-century reader to know quite certainly "what elements . . . especially appealed to Milton." Those elements are ethical.

The use of *De Doctrina Christiana* as a gloss upon Milton's poetry is such a vexed subject that a further word about it is perhaps necessary here. *De Doctrina Christiana*, Milton proclaimed in its first chapter, is a compilation "collecting together, as it were, into a single book texts which are scattered here and there throughout the Bible . . . systematizing them under definite headings."[25] The "systematizing under definite headings" consists of a series of axioms arranged into dichotomies according to the Ramist logical method. The axioms are further subdivided into divisions of methodical antinomies. Milton devoted some attention to every subject into which he logically cast his "art of theology" but was free to vary the amount of attention he gave to subjects particularly interesting to him. Under the axioms and subdivisions of his method, Milton subsumed his biblical proof texts. The sustained commentary of the methodical text embodies something like seven thousand scriptural proof texts.[26] When he prepared *De Doctrina Christiana* he set down subject headings, as it were, and arranged under them the complete comprehensive sections of Scripture from which he had melted away local effects unnecessary to doctrine. There is consequently no doubt whatsoever as to Milton's interpretation of any scriptural text contained in *De Doctrina Christiana*. The book is a

[22] M. H. Studley, "Milton and His Paraphrases of the Psalms," *Philological Quarterly*, 4 (1925), 371.

[23] Parker, *Milton*, I, 67-82.

[24] Bush, *Variorum Commentary*, II, pt. 3, 1000.

[25] *CPW*, VI, 127.

[26] Maurice Kelley's estimate in *This Great Argument*, 216.

fluent cross-referencing index to his sense of biblical meaning;[27] any psalm citation in it gives assurance of Milton's understanding of that psalm.

Psalm 1 may be taken as a convenient instance of Milton's ethical use of the Book of Psalms. Milton's paraphrase reads:

> Bless'd is the man who hath not walk'd astray
> In counsel of the wicked, and ith'way
> Of sinners hath not stood, and in the seat
> Of scorners hath not sate. But in the great
> *Jehovahs* Law is ever his delight,
> And in his Law he studies day and night.
> He shall be as a tree which planted grows
> By watry streams, and in his season knows
> To yield his fruit, and his leaf shall not fall,
> And what he takes in hand shall prosper all.
> Not so the wicked, but as chaff which fann'd
> The wind drives, so the wicked shall not stand
> In judgment, or abide their tryal then,
> Nor sinners in th'assembly of just men.
> For the Lord knows th'upright way of the just,
> And the way of bad men to ruine must.

This didactic psalm, introductory to the whole Book of Psalms, contains a conception of the ethically good man, given analytically or discursively in Milton's first six lines (verses 1 and 2 of the original psalm), imagistically in his next five lines (verse 3), and dialectically by contrasts in his last six lines (verses 4-6). The analytic opening contains one image cluster, that of pilgrimage, a man walking a good path and not walking astray or standing or sitting in bad company. Milton cited Psalm 1 in three places in *De Doctrina Christiana*: first in his discussion of predestination, quoting "Jehova knows the ways of the Just" to make the point that "God approves of all [men] in general, if they would believe" and His approval is contingent on their behavior;[28] next in his discussion "Of the Immediate Cause of Good Works," quoting "whose delight is in the law of Jehova" to illustrate "Promptitude or alacrity, the virtue we display when we do good readily and of our own free will";[29] and lastly in his discussion "Of Man's Duty towards his Neighbor, and the virtues connected with this," quoting "Blessed is the man who has no part in the counsel of the wicked" to show the value of

---

[27] See Brian Weiss, "Milton's Use of Ramist Method in His Scholarly Writings" (Ph.D. diss., City University of New York, 1974), ch. 2, pp. 86-95, and Appendix E.

[28] *CPW*, VI, 182.   [29] *Ibid.*, 654.

community or "Brotherly or Christian Charity . . . [which] makes fellow Christians love and help one another."[30] These citations make it clear that Milton thought Psalm 1 constituted a record of a contingent personal covenant entered into by God with the individual, describing the good conduct both in himself and toward others which constitutes the prosperity of the blessed, and clearly distinguishing the right sort of zeal and the right sort of community. In *Paradise Regained* the Son "His holy Meditations thus persu'd":

> my self I thought
> Born to that end, born to promote all truth,
> All righteous things: therefore above my years,
> The Law of God I read, and found it sweet,
> *Made it my whole delight. . . .*[31]

> (1, 204-8; emphasis added)

Some lines later the Son "again revolv'd / The Law and Prophets" and discovered "that my *way* must lie / Through many a hard assay." For Milton, Psalm 1 carries the image of the pilgrimage of life, God covenanting with the believing pilgrim to bring him safely to his end. It is a psalm unhesitatingly to be recommended, not simply because it predicts New Testament fulfillment,[32] but because it is pertinent to all men in all historical dispensations.

Others of the first eight psalms imply covenant in their forms as well as in their themes and images. In them two voices arrive at accord in dialogue. The process is implicit in Milton's translation of Psalm 3:

> Aloud I cry'd
> Unto Jehovah, he full soon reply'd
> And heard me from his holy mount.

He had made it explicit in his translation of Psalm 2:

> Why do the Gentiles tumult, and the Nations
> Muse a vain thing, the Kings of th'earth upstand
> With power, and Princes in their Congregations

---

[30] *Ibid.*, 751.

[31] It is sometimes held that Milton was drawing his own portrait in these lines; see, for example, E.M.W. Tillyard, *Milton*, rev. ed. (London: Chatto and Windus, 1961), 306.

[32] Wither wrote, "there is nothing in the Psalmes . . . written for it owne sake; but all things there, are Types, Figures, Examples, Prophecies, or Parables, to informe or figure out, what should be fulfilled in the New Testament, at the comming of the Messias." Quoted in William Kerrigan, *The Prophetic Milton* (Charlottesville: University Press of Virginia, 1974), 13, 193-94.

Lay deep their plots together through each Land,
　Against the Lord and his Messiah dear.
　Let us break off, say they, by strength of hand
Their bonds, and cast from us, nor more to wear,
　Their twisted cords: he who in Heaven doth dwell
　Shall laugh, the Lord shall scoff them, then severe
Speak to them in his wrath, and in his fell
　And fierce ire trouble them; but I saith hee
　Anointed have my King (though ye rebell)
On Sion my holi' / hill. A firm decree
　I will declare; the Lord to me hath say'd
　Thou art my Son I have begotten thee
This day; ask of me, and the grant is made;
　As thy possession I on thee bestow
　Th'Heathen, and as thy conquest to be sway'd
Earths utmost bounds: them shalt thou bring full low
　With Iron Scepter bruis'd, and them disperse
　Like to a potters vessel shiver'd so.
And now be wise at length ye Kings averse
　Be taught ye Judges of the Earth; with fear
　Jehovah serve, and let your joy converse
With trembling; kiss the Son least he appear
　In anger and ye perish in the way
　If once his wrath take fire like fuel sere.
Happy all those who have in him their stay.

The psalm is spoken by an anointed king in three movements. The first eight lines present in his voice the planned rebellion of the nations and kings of the earth against the irresistible authority of God. (In *Samson Agonistes* they who rebel are "all that band them to resist / His uncontroulable intent" [1753-54].) In the next four lines the earthbound speaker transfers his thoughts from the earthly to the heavenly scene and, to introduce the direct discourse of God, imagines in the future tense how God "shall laugh," "shall scoff." The Psalmist interpolates stage directions, "saith he" and "the Lord to me hath say'd." In eleven lines God then asserts his special relationship to the anointed psalmist-king and transfers power to him. The last seven lines give the didactic conclusion to be drawn from God's words, "now be wise," "be taught." The conclusion incorporates the formula "Happy all those" to complete in the public sphere the formula "Bless'd is the man," which opened Psalm 1. The dialectical process runs from the people musing a vain thing, through God declaring a "firm decree," to the speaker, and concludes, "be taught ye Judges of the Earth." A process of action and reaction on the formal level enunciates a public covenant on the thematic level:[33] the psalm dramatizes an occasion of rebellion to involve a call and a response for their educative value.

Milton repeatedly drew upon this psalm in *De Doctrina Christiana*. He regarded it as decisive for his view that "the Son existed before the creation of the World, but not that his generation was from eternity." It is the psalm "where God the Father is introduced in his own person openly declaring the nature and offices of his Son" and thus showing his "mediatorial office and its threefold function,"[34] which was initiated "from the very beginning of the world" and continues "as long as the world and as long as there is occasion for him to carry out the functions of a mediator."[35] It is a psalm of particular bearing on the historical period of the Samson drama and, of course, of contemporary England. Earthly kings had led their people in rebellion against the true service of God; they were addressed in their own dispensation and required to learn the true nature of God's providential plan and His true service. Milton understood this psalm as a clarification that the covenant God made with man (whereby He promised a liberating mediator) was applicable in the period of the Law, in the Samson period between the Law and the Prophets, in the period of the Prophets, the Gospel, and in all subsequent periods.[36] Milton made similar use of this psalm in *Paradise Lost*, drawing from it God's delight in Sion's holy hill, His contempt at the rebellious angels, His laughter at the curiosity and vanity of Adam and the men of Babel, and His establishment of His Son on a "throne hereditarie" in heaven. The allusions in *Paradise Regained* express both the Messianic expectations of the newly baptized friends and disciples and the Son's own sense of his kingship.

The Book of Psalms is more than the record of a covenant setting forth an ethical program for man in response to a historical and prophetic series of imperatives from God. It is also a mixed-genre anthology representing human responses or insights. And it is a record of misunderstanding, failure, penitence, grief, shame, and despair. Milton himself read the Book of Psalms in this light, as a series of poems all serving an ethic higher than each speaker may have understood, but an ethic very clear in the light of the whole. He used them as a compendium of ethical truths, freely applying their individual verses to all men at all times. The Psalms presented him with a higher vision of the heroic struggle of the human being as a kind of disjunct epic pilgrimage in-

[33] See Fisch, *Jerusalem and Albion*, 59.   [34] *CPW*, VI, 166, 206, 430.
[35] *Ibid.*, 434, 437.
[36] See Arthur E. Barker, "Structural and Doctrinal Pattern in Milton's 'Later' Poems," in *Essays Presented to A.S.P. Woodhouse*, ed. Maclure and Watt, 175-76.

terspersed with hymns, laments, thanksgivings, blessings, curses, and precepts. He read the Book of Psalms as a purgatorial and educative account of personal and national life, offered as exemplary in the main but full of variety and human understanding in its course. This, too, made it particularly apposite to *Samson Agonistes*.

Both the ethical and psychological applicability of the Book of Psalms can be illustrated by brief reference to Milton's translations of the remaining five of the first eight psalms. Psalms 3, 5, and 7 are laments, Psalm 4 is a personal thanksgiving, and Psalm 8 is a hymn. In *De Doctrina Christiana* Milton cited Psalm 3 to show how God uses afflictions to prompt penitence, to warn against "rash judgments about other people's afflictions," and to instance "fortitude . . . when we repel evils or stand against them unafraid."[37] In *Samson Agonistes* Harapha is given a taunt echoing it. Milton cited Psalm 4 to instance God's approval of "right reason in self-government and self-content . . . of one's inner affections" so that "joy . . . is proportionate to excellence."[38] In *Paradise Regained* the Son's composure in the wilderness is expressed in an echo of it. Milton cited Psalm 5 as instancing God's kindness: He never prompts the least sin but commands veracity and denounces duplicity.[39] Milton's translation rendered the Authorized Version's "For thou, Lord, will bless the righteous" as "For thou Jehovah wilt be found / To bless the just man still," and both *Paradise Lost* and *Paradise Regained* establish God's justice in His marks of approbation to the one just man. Milton cited Psalm 6 as a proof text for his mortalist view "that the whole man dies, and . . . each separate part dies."[40] He drew upon its imagery in *Samson Agonistes* to express the grief of isolation from God. Milton cited Psalm 7 to establish the unity of God and the corporality of man, that man is not composed of "two distinct elements, body and soul, but is a body . . . or individual substance, animated, sensitive and rational," and to suggest that all men are born with "a sort of tinder to kindle sin."[41] In both *Paradise Lost* and *Samson Agonistes* this psalm supplies the vision of men's mischief recoiling upon their own heads. Milton cited Psalm 8 to prove that men and angels can be called "by the name 'God' because they were made by Him for a particular end." In *Paradise Lost* and *Paradise Regained* he cited it to extol the strength God gives to weakness.[42] In the citations in *De Doctrina Christiana*, the Psalms yield transposable advice of an ethical nature for contemporary men about how to live in the pilgrimage of their lives; in the major poems, they not only instance God's covenant with men but all the possible human responses to that

37 *CPW*, VI, 470, 674, 738.
39 *Ibid.*, 150, 332, 675, 759, 767.
41 *Ibid.*, 148, 318, 389.
38 *Ibid.*, 721.
40 *Ibid.*, 401.
42 *Ibid.*, 234, 315.

covenant. The same sort of quarrying of Psalms 80 through 88 is evident in *De Doctrina Christiana* and in the major poems.[43] Simply from these citations it is clear that Milton thought of the Psalms as containing an account of a purgatorial and dialectical journey through life in which true private or public heroism is distinguished from apparent heroism.

Milton's impulse to translate psalm groups 1 through 8 and 80 through 88 can be more confidently discussed when it is recognized that the Book of Psalms as a whole was assumed to have ethical dimensions and to be universally applicable. Because he read the Psalms as generally applicable to all ages, recording God's personal and national covenants, they were always fresh and interesting to Milton. They were exceptionally beautiful because they so well united teaching with delight, and they supplied a perfect analogy to Milton's understanding of his own creativity. From the moment in "The Passion" when he described his need to "set my Harp to notes of saddest wo," through the moment in the *Animadversions* when he promised to "take up Harp, and sing thee an elaborate Song to Generations," to the moment in *Paradise Lost* when he swore "never shall my harp thy praise forget nor from thy Fathers praise disjoine," the Psalms as a sequence were crucial to his art. He numbered himself not only with Homer, Tiresias, and Phineus but also with the Psalmist, whose inspiration he invoked repeatedly to assist him. Like the Song of Solomon, which he considered a "pastoral drama" "generally believed to figure the relationship of the Church to Christ," or like the Book of Job, which he thought "a brief epic," or the Book of Revelation, which he considered "a high tragedy" which "soars to prophetic pitch in types and allegories,"[44] the Book of Psalms was understood by Milton to incorporate formal and thematic materials, enjoining or endorsing plain style, ethical teaching, and a dialectical structure. Psalms 1 through 8 were relevant both to Milton's thinking about *how* art can teach by example and

[43] Milton cited Psalm 80 in the chapter on "God's Providence" to prove that God "preserves all created things" (327), and in *Paradise Lost* to introduce the roll call of the heathen gods; Psalm 81 to argue that under some circumstances God "omits to prevent" sin (334, 651, 664), and in *Paradise Regained* to show God allowing his Son to be tested; Psalm 82 to indicate the public and political duties laid on magistrates and kings (213, 234, 794), and in *Paradise Regained* to define Sonship; Psalm 84 to encourage confidence in God's government (658), and in *Paradise Lost* to describe the incomparable beauty of Eden; Psalm 86 to display the connection between God's benevolence and human prayer (118, 669), and in *Paradise Lost* to refer to the Son's compassion; Psalm 88 to spell out man's mortality (101, 674), and in *Paradise Lost* to speak of the nature of grace.

[44] See Austin C. Dobbins, *Milton and the Book of Revelation: The Heavenly Cycle*, Studies in the Humanities, no. 7 (University: University of Alabama Press, 1975).

what it can teach of the true heroism in one private life; Psalms 80 through 88, about the public as well as the private covenant of God with man. These psalms were by no means uniquely formative of Milton's art, and his translation of them was not a necessary preliminary or concomitant to the writing of *Samson Agonistes*. Milton's special responsiveness to the structure, technique, and content of the psalm was lifelong and continuous. However, because the Psalms represented to Milton a repository of human responses to God's covenant they were powerfully influential in the composition of his last poem.

SAMSON AGONISTES AND THE PSALMS OF LAMENT,
WISDOM, TRUST, AND THANKSGIVING

Samson Agonistes is full of direct and concealed references to individual psalms.[45] But Milton not only mined the Psalms for telling images and phrases, he drew upon psalmic structures and brought to bear the repeated patterns of the Psalms in the overall shaping of the drama. The formal structures of four major groups of psalms shape the progressive soliloquies of the hero and pattern the responses of the Chorus. To read the Book of Psalms as a continuously didactic account of the life of the good man interspersed with the typical moods, emotions, and reactions attendant upon religious experience is to mark how the Psalms fall into subgroups of thematic coherence, the most numerous sort being the psalm of lament, both the public or communal lament and the private lament. In the Book of Psalms the lamentations themselves regularly fall into a formal pattern which structures their customary themes so as to control despair and to turn it by remorse in the direction of praise. A typical lament opens with an invocation, proceeds to a mourning, continues with a supplication, an expression of the motives of the mourner, and ends with an affirmation of confidence or a vow to live better. Laments tend to shade into thanksgivings, the next subgroup, and thanksgivings to subsume laments. The typical structure is not, of course, completely present in every lament, but it is common to most and is implicit even where incomplete. The themes organized by this structural pattern include God giving merited judgment, the servant being tested, his confidence affirmed, his integrity avowed, his sins confessed, and the godly and the wicked contrasted. Thanksgiving psalms stand throughout the Book of Psalms as personal expressions of faith. That faith is given a more philosophical or intellectual turn in a third sort of psalm, the hymn, which likewise has a typical shape. It begins with a call to sing the praise of God and pro-

[45] A complete table of Psalm citations in *Samson Agonistes* can be found in Appendix B.

ceeds to the praise itself in a series of propositions (delivered in rhetorical comparisons commencing with *for*) about the nature of God and His providential governance of man for which praise is due to Him. The Psalmist, having described and adored God, sometimes then describes his own relationship to Him before returning to the opening inspiration and restating it. Hymns associate easily with a further subgroup of didactic psalms, psalms offering moral instruction or collective wisdom, as lamentations associate easily with thanksgivings. Milton framed Samson's own lyrics of despair in Acts I and II by drawing particularly upon the psalms of personal lament, not only for figures and themes, but also for patterns. In framing the choral stasimons for the first two acts, he drew upon the communal laments of the Book of Psalms; the confrontation with Dalila incorporates wisdom psalms; the response to Harapha is governed by the pattern of hymnic psalms; and the final act is dominated by hymns and thanksgivings.

Samson begins the drama with a veiled invocation, "A little onward lend thy guiding hand to these dark steps." John Broadbent has seen here a reference to one of the psalms of lamentation, Psalm 43: "O send out thy light and thy truth: let them lead me." There are equally references to other psalms of lamentation, Psalms 25 ("the meek will he guide"), 27 ("lead me in a plain path"), 31 ("into your hand I resign my spirit"), and 143 ("lead me with your good spirit"), for it is a regular feature of the lament to contrast leading and blindness, God's light and man's darkness, God's hand and man's feet. In Samson's prologue the invocation is followed by a brief description of the occasion for the lament, the speaker's broken condition, a device common to the openings of Psalms 32, 38, 69, and 102. At line 22 the remorseful lament itself begins. From lines 22 to 42 Samson contrasts his past promise with his present circumstances in the first phase of a personal outcry. Recollections of the contrast between past grace and present suffering are common in psalms of lamentation, as in Psalms 42, 43, and 143. The circumstances of enslavement, blindness, and isolation are likewise common metaphors for man's desolate and remorseful state of sin. Samson is "made of my Enemies the scorn and gaze" like the Psalmist in Psalm 71 ("Mine enemies speak against me . . . saying, God hath forsaken him, persecute and take him"); he is conscious of the withdrawal of God's promise like the Psalmist in Psalm 77 ("Doth his promise fail forever"); and he is blinded like the Psalmist of Psalms 6 and 38 ("The light of mine eyes is gone from me"). In all these psalms the mourner's personal experiences are woven into a pattern of powerful general application.

The climax of the first cycle of lament comes with Samson's expression of the waste and futility of his having thrown away the good.

From lines 43 to 62 Samson utters what in the lamenting psalms takes the form not of a self-admonition but a supplication which asserts God's justice against his own sin and God's providence against his own ignorance. When Samson twice halts himself at the threshold of blasphemy ("Yet stay" and "But peace . . . highest dispensation . . . Happ'ly had ends above my reach to know"), he distinguishes human nescience from divine omniscience in a form common in lamentations. Among many such might be noticed Psalm 73: "For all the day long have I been plagued, and chastened every morning. If I say, I will speak thus; behold, I should offend . . . So foolish was I, and ignorant. . . . Nevertheless thou shalt guide me with thy counsel." The remainder of the prologue is a renewed lament, broken off with the arrival of the Chorus. This second outburst picks up elements from Psalms 8, 6, 22, 13, 143, 4, and 25. In the first episode, in the presence of the Chorus, Samson continues to express remorse and to define his sin in psalmic formulae, while the Chorus frames their response to Samson's plight under the guidance of communal lament. Conceiving their response to contain "Counsel or Consolation . . . Salve to thy Sores," since "apt words have power to swage" and to give "Balm to fester'd wounds," the Chorus draws their imagery from medicinal psalms such as 38, 91, and 25. Their first stasimon, in their simple assertion of God's righteousness and power against all appearances, briefly prepares for their much richer second stasimon, both choral odes again and again drawing upon the psalms of communal lament.

Because lament psalms have a common structure which organizes their grief and turns it toward responsiveness and faith, implicit in the self-judgment of Acts I and II is the completion of the pattern through a moral awareness that self-judgment is educative. That moral awareness of the purpose of suffering permits the believer to recognize God's mercy even in his troubles. As an arc suggests the total curve, lament reveals covenant. Acts I and II of *Samson Agonistes* are related to Acts IV and V as the two halves of verse 22 in Psalm 31: "For I said in my haste I am cut off from before thine eyes, nevertheless thou heardest the voice of my supplication when I cried unto thee." The first two acts represent the haste of the afflicted; the fourth act opens the possibilities of "nevertheless." The judgments Samson makes of himself are not the judgments the poet finally makes; Samson's remorse and despair in the course of the play issue into a changed mood and a healed heart. When he can recognize both his just remorse and God's comprehensiveness, then the quality of his experience becomes ethically meaningful. Given Milton's thoroughgoing insistence on psalmic patterns, he need not use any sort of narrator-commentator to distinguish between the justice Samson so severely metes out to himself and the potential restorative mercy present in that very harsh justice. Samson's life has an exemplary meaning to communicate in just the way that the Psalms in their total course likewise communicate a moral. The Psalms present the whole pilgrimage of man's life; where part of Samson's path is repeatedly presented in words persistently recalling the Psalms to mind, there the total journey is likewise suggested. The darkest laments become proleptic of the next stage of spiritual growth. The Psalms themselves are often multivocal, containing a dialogue between the self-rebuking and the seeking or self-healing parts of the soul, and they dramatize God as present to the Psalmist and speaking to him. The most interesting characteristic of the Psalms as a unique part of Scripture is their humanity. Parts of the Bible offer themselves as the words of God spoken to men, other parts as the words of inspired men spoken to their people. The Psalms characteristically are the words of men spoken to God, and they record a religious experience with both public and private aspects. They contain implicit theology, they reflect upon history and contain history, but they above all record the spiritual pilgrimage of the human being in his daily life of the mind and heart, a paradigm of the spiritual life passing out of despair and purposelessness and toward remorse and virtue.

Act II, then, continues the strong reliance upon psalms of lament. Manoa's outcries on the vanity of human hopes and the afflictions of those who would serve God but instead fall into the hands of their enemies echo Psalms 60, 62, 108, 89, 79, and 31. Samson's confessed remorse draws upon the penitential Psalms 51, 5, and 41. His brave prophecy that notwithstanding his personal fate God will "arise and his great name assert" interweaves psalmic formulae in 75, 17, 83, 69, and 72, but his despair is so total that for his own case he sees no cure. He abandons himself to that despair at the conclusion of the dialogue with Manoa and expresses his personal desolation in reiterated use of psalms of lament, in particular 22, 88, 31, 27, and 51. Once more in response the Chorus likewise echoes Psalms 39, 22, 8, 144, 75, 43, 49, 89, 44, 79, and 34. Their final prayer draws upon 25, 50, and 85. The Chorus describes the specific afflictions visited by God upon his elect:

> Oft leav'st them to the hostile sword
> Of Heathen and prophane, thir carkasses
> To dogs and fowls a prey, or else captiv'd:
> Or to the unjust tribunals, under change of times,
> And condemnation of the ingrateful multitude.
>
> (692-96)

It is especially notable that this would at the same time remind the contemporary reader both of the public events of his own times and of the painful experiences described in the communal lament of Psalm 79: "The dead bodies of thy servants have they given to be meat unto the fowls of the heaven, the flesh of thy saints unto the beasts of the earth. Their blood have they shed like water round about Jerusalem; and there was none to bury them. We are become a reproach to our neighbours, a scorn and derision to them that are round about us." The three-leveled identification of Samson, the Psalmist, and the seventeenth-century reader is the basis of the ethical teaching in *Samson Agonistes*.

The third act, Dalila's long debate with Samson, shifts from lament to argument. The didactic Psalm 41, which determines the shape of the action and may explain the tone of the concluding choral stasimon as well, marks a turn from reliance on the mood, form, and thematic materials of one group of psalms to those of another group. Samson concluded at the close of Act II that God remains in no relationship with him, is finished with him, but that God is not finished with mankind or with human history. In response, the Chorus has put the bewildering questions of the communal lament. At that low point, that self-despising nadir in Samson's personal life, there comes before him the one human being formerly closest to him, to whom he had bound himself because of his sense of the conjunction of God's will for him and his own desires for himself.[46] Samson's outward confrontation with Dalila forces a renewed inward confrontation of past and present, his former life with her and his present life without her, the climax of which is Samson's clear assertion of present inner freedom—"This Gaol I count the house of Liberty / To thine whose doors my feet shall never enter"—abruptly followed by his unexpected terse and fierce forgiveness of his wife, "At distance I forgive thee, go with that." The very unexpectedness of the forgiveness is of enormous ethical and psychological importance. Less than 150 lines earlier Samson had looked not only at himself but at the way he was looking at himself, to say to Dalila,

> Such pardon therefore as I give my folly,
> Take to thy wicked deed: which when thou seest
> Impartial, self-severe, inexorable,
> Thou wilt renounce thy seeking. . . .

> (825-28)

---

[46] Samson explained his marriage twice, once in terms of lawful "intimate impulse" to "oppress *Israel's* oppressours" and once in terms of loving choice, "I . . . chose thee . . . lov'd thee, as too well thou knew'st, / Too well."

Moral casuists of a Manoa bent[47] could doubtless square these antithetical comments by making much of forgiving the sinner but not the sin. The dialectic, however, strongly enforces another conclusion. Samson's weakness-wickedness—"All wickedness is weakness"—has been confessed; his acknowledgment of it is the source of his acceptance of his present state as not only more nearly free than his former state, not only comparatively free, but as actually free. In the second act Samson had achieved an insight into his relative degree of enslavement when he bitterly, shamefully proclaimed to his father,

> The base degree to which I now am fall'n,
> These rags, this grinding, is not yet so base
> As was my former servitude, ignoble,
> Unmanly, ignominious, infamous,
> True slavery, and that blindness worse then this,
> That saw not how degenerately I serv'd.
>
> (414-19)

To his wife he can now say more. He is not relatively free, he is truly free in himself; his gaol is a very House of Liberty, and he chooses not to resubject himself. To forgive Dalila is at least to encompass the limitless despair of the first two acts and to bring it under control by giving such pardon to his folly in repenting it as he gives to Dalila.

The process of containing despair in the third act points directly to the structure of didactic psalms, which incorporate lament within thanksgiving and use the embedded lament to utter wisdom. Psalm 41 is just such a psalm. It opens with three verses of beatitude: "Blessed is he that considereth the poor: the Lord will deliver him in time of trouble." Milton understood it to proclaim God's mercy to one sorely afflicted. He cited it first in *De Doctrina Christiana* to show that "God sets a limit to punishment." "Indeed, he pities us and seems even to repent his treatment of us; and so he compensates us with a double measure of comfort as if, in his anger, he had inflicted a double dose of punishment for our sins." Hence, "we should not . . . make rash judgments about other people's afflictions," for afflictions provide the occasion for consolation.[48] In making this point, Milton quoted verse 9, "a very evil thing clings tightly to him,"[49] the inspiration for the Chorus's description of Dalila, "far within defensive arms, a cleaving

---

[47] "Repent the sin," Manoa sagely advised, "but if the punishment / Thou canst avoid, self-preservation bids."

[48] *CPW*, VI, 469-70.

[49] The Authorized Version gives this as verse 8, translating it, "An evil disease, say they, cleaveth fast unto him." The Revised Version reads, "A deadly thing has fastened upon him."

mischief." Milton glossed the consolation contained in severe affliction not only from Psalm 41 but also from 2 Cor., "consoling us in all our affliction, that we may be able to console those who are undergoing any kind of affliction by means of that same consolation with which God consoles us." At the end of Act II the Chorus had wished to offer Samson balm to heal his wounds, but he bitterly implored the balm of death:

> Hopeless are all my evils, all remediless;
> This one prayer yet remains, might I be heard,
> No long petition, speedy death,
> The close of all my miseries, and the balm.
>
> (648-51)

The Chorus had acknowledged that the "consolatories writ with studied argument" were useless to "th' afflicted,"

> Unless he feel within
> Some sourse of consolation from above;
> Secret refreshings, that repair his strength,
> And fainting spirits uphold.
>
> (663-66)

Secret refreshings are the subject of Psalm 41. Milton's second citation of it in *De Doctrina Christiana* is as a rebuke to "pretended piety"; he gives as verse 7, "if anyone came to see me, he uttered empty words while his heart gathered mischief; when he went out, he told it abroad."[50] The motives Milton ascribes to Dalila are such pretended piety or, in Samson's words, "feigned Religion, smooth hypocrisie"; when she leaves him, she exults that she will enjoy "the public marks of honour and reward / Conferr'd upon me, for the piety / Which to my countrey I was judg'd to have shewn." Milton's third citation of Psalm 41 appears in a balanced discussion of vengeance, under the heading "Of the special virtues or duties towards ones neighbor." The main force of Chapter 12 is against revenge and in favor of pardoning injuries, but Milton adds one exceptional case, "We are not forbidden to take or to wish to take vengeance upon the enemies of the church," and quotes verses 10-11, "revive me so that I may pay them out."[51] Nowhere does Samson echo this sentiment himself. In the moment between the pillars in the Philistine temple Milton carefully omits to

---

[50] In the Authorized Version this is given as verse 6 and reads "And he comes to see me, he speaketh vanity: his heart gathered iniquity to itself; when he goeth abroad, he telleth it."

[51] As verse 10 in the Authorized Version this reads "Raise me up that I may requite them."

give Samson the prayer he prays in Judges, "O Lord God, remember me, I pray thee, and strengthen me, I pray thee, only this once, O God, that I may be at once avenged of the Philistines for my two eyes." But the Chorus in the fourth stasimon balances a vengeful concept of the conquest of one's enemies and the deliverance of others against a patient concept of self-conquest and self-deliverance. It is "comely and reviving" when God puts might into His champion's hands; it is more usual for His saints to be exercised in patience. Milton's final citation of the psalm is in instancing not vengeance but care for the weak, the helpless, and those persecuted for the sake of religion: "Blessed is the man who cares for the poor, Jehovah will free him in the time of evil."

Psalm 41 opens and closes in the present tense with the Psalmist uttering the largest truth which past bitter experience has taught him and which he wishes to teach others.[52] That truth is gratitude for mercy. The first three verses constitute an ethical beatitude which echoes Psalm 1 and such other didactic psalms as 33, 40, 112, and 128. "Blessed is the man" who like the Psalmist has healing words to give to his congregation; the Psalmist is to the lowly in the congregation a living testimony of God's power and goodness. Rather than describing how God answered his prayers, the Psalmist in verses 4 through 10 repeats the lament he had addressed to God in his past afflictions: "Lord be merciful unto me; Heal my soul, for I have sinned against thee." In this past lament he had enumerated his sufferings, and the bitterest was his helpless exposure to the gloating malice of his enemies and the arrogant dismissal of him by "mine own familiar friend, in whom I trusted, who did eat of my bread." But God had responded to his lament by preventing his enemies from total triumph, and the last three verses of the psalm profess gratitude in a doxology joined by the whole congregation to whom the Psalmist sings. In the section of lament the psalm describes a taunting visit by one formerly loved and reflects in its introduction and conclusion the mastery of the malicious taunter by the afflicted speaker. The psalm has the shape of the confrontation with Dalila, for which no analogue or source has ever been found in the considerable number of literary treatments of the Samson story.[53] Psalm 41 is not the only psalm echoed in the third episode, but the others, like it, are often wisdom psalms.

The choral stasimon which concludes Act III also draws upon didactic psalms. Its misogyny is not psalmic, but its didacticism is. The wis-

[52] The best modern treatment of this psalm is to be found in Artur Weiser, *The Psalms*, 5th ed. (London: SCM Press, 1962).

[53] See Watson Kirkconnell, *That Invincible Samson* (Toronto: University of Toronto Press, 1964).

dom psalms afforded ample instances of workaday proverbs but not much Old Testament marriage guidance. Not only in the third stasimon but elsewhere the Chorus is given to uttering truths of a practical sort, such as "wisest Men / Have err'd, and by bad Women been deceiv'd," or "O madness, to think use of strongest wines . . . our chief support of health." And a number of psalms contain proverbial practical ethics for daily life: Psalms 127 and 133, for example, produce such sensible curt sayings as "it is vain for you to rise up early, to sit up late, to eat the bread of sorrows; for so he giveth his beloved sleep," or "Lo, children are a heritage of the Lord," or "how pleasant it is for brethren to dwell together in unity." The picture the Chorus gives of the ideal marriage under "God's universal law" of male dominance is a thoroughly Old Testament picture. Under the Old Testament dispensation of the Law, the perfect wife is Sarah and the ideal husband Abraham, in whom the Law is vested. So the wise Chorus speaks a sanctioned historical truth in its misogyny. But the ethical force of *Samson Agonistes* does not consist in that kind of rule of life. The drama was not devised to teach men how to preserve themselves under the Law but rather to show how the Law itself is inadequate to establish an appropriate rule of life. Milton's own values accord with the psalms which consider the difficult problems of man's behavior when his role seems futile. *Samson Agonistes* is set in the biblical historical moment when the Law gives way to the prophets of the New Dispensation, the new covenant of Christian liberty. Those psalms which directly consider the problem of suffering and its implications for belief are the crucial psalms for the ethical poet.

God's nature becomes an issue to transient human beings in periods when the self-confidently amoral triumph over the humiliated morally committed. That nature will become fully clear only with the advent of the Son. Nonetheless, psalms of suffering which culminate in trust give evidence of God's mercy. It was widely considered, for example, that Jesus in his agony on the cross spoke the opening lines of Psalm 22—"My God, my God, why hast thou forsaken me"—to recall the trust after doubt in that psalm. The Psalms in their total course reflect a process both in one man's life and in a nation's history. The proverbial wisdom of the Chorus would have been seen by Milton and his audience in the perspective of the processive journey of the Book of Psalms. When they are advising Samson about how God thinks men should treat their wives, the Chorus is wise in their generation; when they pass on to the meaning of personal suffering, they touch on truths valid beyond their own historical moment. When the Chorus tries to explain the significance of Samson's enduring the malice of his serpentlike wife, it suggests,

> But vertue which breaks through all opposition,
> And all temptation can remove,
> Most shines and most is acceptable above.
>
> (1050-52)

The implication that adversity itself can contain a blessing is crucial to the ethical development of *Samson Agonistes*. It is made here for the first time by the Chorus, but in such an odd context that it scarcely has been properly noticed. Psalms 49 and 37, which ask why the ungodly prosper, prepare for the submission and understanding of Psalms 94, 103, and 119, which teach that God tests the godly and that His affliction of them is the sign of covenant and concern. The apparently didactic pat formula of the Chorus derives from that sequence of psalms. The pious wisdom they speak is a popular proverbial pious wisdom, very assured in tone, rather like the wisdom Psalm 37. Appropriately, the Chorus is then given a moment of higher truth, prophetic of Milton's later resolution.

Acts IV and V move steadily toward the final understanding in the poem of the mysterious link between God's mercy and justice upon which the ethical life must be established. They do so still under the governance of the Psalms. The challenging appearance of Harapha before Samson is, like the encounter with Dalila, Milton's own invention. And among all the sources at which critics have asked us to look for the inspiration for both encounters, the Psalms have not heretofore been noted.[54] Nevertheless, Milton read Psalm 53 as treating just such an assault as Harapha's. He cited it in *De Doctrina Christiana*, first in condemning a vain desire for glory—"Why do you boast of your evil, O mighty man"—and second in condemning abuse and disparagement of others, "You promote trouble deliberately with your tongue."[55] He thought it described a confrontation between a vaunting hero who boasted of his own power and position to disdain the true God on the one hand, and a shrewdly ironic believer who impeached the boaster with justifiable sarcasm on the other. The psalm has a dramatic form in itself and aptly suggested to Milton the form of the visit from Harapha. The encounter with Harapha calls forth from

---

[54] For example, E. H. Visiak, *Milton Agonistes*, suggests the mores of the typical Cavalier; George R. Waggoner, "The Challenge to Single Combat in *Samson Agonistes*," *Philological Quarterly*, 39 (1960), 82-92, the romance code of the duel; and Daniel C. Boughner, "Milton's Harapha and Renaissance Comedy," *ELH*, 11 (1944), 297-306, the Italian comic braggart.

[55] *CPW*, VI, 743, 766. These translations are those John Carey makes from Milton's Latin. The Authorized Version reads "Why boasteth thou thyself in mischief, O mighty man," and "Thou lovest all devouring words, O thou deceitful tongue."

Samson not only the thrice-offered challenge to single combat, with its concomitant scorn for the vainglorious, wordy warrior, it also inspires two statements of renewed trust in God:

> I know no Spells, use no forbidden Arts;
> My trust is in the living God who gave me
> At my Nativity this strength, . . .

and

> these evils I deserve and more,
> Acknowledge them from God inflicted on me
> Justly, yet despair not of his final pardon
> Whose ear is ever open; and his eye
> Gracious to re-admit the suppliant. . . .
>
> (1139-41, 1169-73)

These expressions of confidence and trust are profoundly indebted to the psalms of personal faith, which become hymns of praise by working through lament toward thanksgiving. In such psalms the right religious course of ethical human life is described not as leading away from human suffering but as moving straight through suffering until the suffering itself is made the source of insight into God's providential design. God's judgment becomes the efficacious means of His mercy.

In response to Samson's faith the Chorus recurs to the theme of patience, but now in far fuller confidence and resonance than in its tentative, doubtful, and squeamish recommendation of it in the second stasimon.

In the fourth stasimon the Chorus offers two alternative courses of life which exhibit ideal human heroism, courses showing fortitude and patience. The first is marked by might given by God to a deliverer to deliver others; the second, by patience given by God to man to deliver himself from domination by the evils of his life. Both styles of life derive from Psalm 18, which praises God in thanksgiving first by recounting His gift of power and strength to the psalmist-king to achieve victory in battle and then by praising the heroic man for possessing a strength which both delivers his nation and is a good example to it. *De Doctrina Christiana* makes it clear that Milton read Psalm 18 as supporting a theology of works. In denying the Roman Catholic doctrine of imputed righteousness to argue instead his own doctrine of justification "not by faith alone but by works of faith as well," Milton weighed verses 20 and 24 of Psalm 18 ("The Lord rewarded me according to my righteousness"; "The Lord recompensed me according to my righteousness") against verses 19 and 23 ("He delivered me because he delighted in me"; "I was also upright before him and I kept myself from mine iniquity") to conclude that no works other than works of faith "have any inherent justifying power." Milton cited the psalm again, together with Psalms 27, 28, 32, 37, 61, 62, 73, 75, 112, 115, 123, and 130, to expound "confidence" as an "effect of love and a constituent of internal worship." Samson reasserts his faith in echoes of all these psalms. Finally, Milton cited Psalm 18 to display the two virtues "which are exhibited in our repulsion or endurance of evils. These are fortitude and patience."[56] The second style of life offered as an alternative to fortitude by the Chorus in the fourth stasimon is patience. The words of the Chorus concerning patience also draw on the psalms of trust cited in the *De Doctrina Christiana* discussion of confidence because patience is dependent upon faith and shows itself when God's promises are accepted with "confidence in the divine providence, power and goodness,"[57] as well as when sufferings are borne "calmly, as things which our supreme Father has sent for our good." If suffering is understood only as punishment for sin, its effect will not be to inspire virtuous action and fit a man to perform it; to that end, suffering needs to be recognized as a source and concomitant of knowledge.

The encounter with the Officer, which complements the encounter with Harapha in Act IV, is only lightly indebted to the Psalms. This is itself interesting. Throughout the dialogue with the public officer Samson weighs the requirements of the Law against the demands of his conquerors and repeatedly asserts his submission to the Law and his refusal to comply with merely human commands. His assertions of the primacy of the Law as the word of God give way at length to a terse recognition that God may dispense with His own laws "for some important cause." Samson knows himself then to be obedient not to the Law but to God Himself. He may twice announce his compliance with legalistic piety and promise to do nothing "forbidden in our Law" or "unworthy / Our God, our Law, my Nation or my self," but he has rearranged his priorities by the close of the encounter: obedience to God takes precedence over obedience to the Law. The Psalms, save Psalm 119, are notably free of the legalism to

[56] *CPW*, VI, 490-91. "We are justified then, by faith, but a living faith, not a dead one, and the only living faith is a faith which acts. . . . So we are justified by faith without the works of the law, but not without works, though these may be different from the works of the written law." See also *ibid.*, 657, 738, 755. In addition, Milton gave Psalm 18 as a proof text to show that "a cruel enemy should not be spared" (*ibid.*, 802).

[57] *Ibid.*, 662.

which Milton personally took profound exception all his life.[58] The worship of God and His works in nature and man is their theme, rather than the chilly self-righteousness which is the comfort that obedience to the Law may bring. An ethic based upon works of faith and deriving from a covenant theology is not for Milton a legalistic ethic deriving from a law theology. Through *Samson Agonistes* Milton develops further a morality based upon an understanding of the role of reason and liberty for the individual. In freedom man must answer to his own rational understanding of what is truly good. That understanding, like virtue, is not an absolute state of mind; it cannot be upheld by the framework of a rigid law. The Psalms cannot much avail where the Law is Samson's concern, before Christian liberty is shown him.

The Chorus, however, in their brief fourteen-line lyrical fifth stasimon, which sends Samson forth with blessing and prayer, reverts to a very full psalmic texture, touching the notes of one after another of ten hymnlike psalms of trust. Their fair dismissal of Samson is so faithful to the accents of the Psalms that it breathes its source in verse and cadence as well as in language and thought:

> Go, and the Holy One
> Of *Israel* be thy guide
> To what may serve his glory best, & spread his name
> Great among the Heathen round:
> Send thee the Angel of thy Birth, to stand
> Fast by thy side, who from thy Fathers field
> Rode up in flames after his message told
> Of thy conception, and be now a shield
> Of fire; that Spirit that first rusht on thee
> In the camp of *Dan*
> Be efficacious in thee now at need.
> For never was from Heaven imparted
> Measure of strength so great to mortal seed,
> As in thy wond'rous actions hath been seen.

> (1427-40)

The construction by parallelisms, the easy transitions from short lyrical lines to longer meditative units, the freedom from consistent reliance either on blank verse or rhyme, the verbal plainness in conjunction with meditative boldness—all these characterize the source and the

---

[58] "I am not one of those who consider the decalogue a faultless moral code. Indeed I am amazed that such an opinion should have become so widespread. For it is clear that the decalogue is nothing but a summary of the Mosaic law as a whole. . . . It can therefore contain nothing relevant to gospel worship" (*ibid.*, 711).

passage equally.[59] Against the words of the Chorus might be set, for example, verses from Psalm 72:

> I will go in the strength of the Lord God:
> I will make mention of thy righteousness, even
> > > of thine only
> O God, thou hast taught me from my youth:
> And hitherto have I declared thy wondrous works.
> Now also . . . O God, forsake me not;
> Until I have showed thy strength unto this generation,
> And thy power to every one that is to come.
> Thy righteousness also, O God, is very high,
> Who hast done great things:
> O God, who is like unto thee!
> Thou, which hast showed me great and sore troubles,
> Shalt quicken me again . . .
> O thou Holy one of Israel.

The exode of Act v is likewise suffused with psalmic formulae, but one psalm, the seventy-third, is insistently cited. The kommos of Act v is likewise densely psalmic, but insistently draws upon Psalm 103. And the last fourteen lines of the kommos, spoken by the Chorus alone, is again dependent upon hymns of trust, together with prayerful psalms asking for blessing, but draws chiefly on Psalm 104.

Psalm 73 describes a spiritual pilgrimage through trial and suffering into trust not unlike the testing of Job. It begins and ends with a statement of the faith in God which the Psalmist has won after struggle: "Truly God is good to Israel, even to such as are of a clean heart," and "But it is good for me to draw near to God; I have put my trust in the Lord God, that I may declare all thy works." Between these expressions of trust, the Psalmist confesses to experiences which brought him to the edge of despair; he could not believe in God's goodness when he saw the sufferings of the faithful and the prosperity of the wicked. His experiences are presented in a triadic structure: he saw the arrogant prosperity of the ungodly, they wore their pride and violence like gold chains and fine garments (verses 3-12); he himself was stricken all day and woke to punishment in the morning, his religious observations were in vain (13-15); but when he confessed his failure to understand, he gained a new perspective, the things he had ignorantly thought earthly prosperity now seemed to

---

[59] See Harold Fisch, *Jerusalem and Albion*, 141-47; and Frank Kermode, "*Samson Agonistes* and Hebrew Prosody," *Durham University Journal*, 14 (1953), 59-63.

him a dream and the reality of faith alone became trustworthy (17-22). The emotional progression of the psalm is likewise triadic or dialectical: the Psalmist doubted that in his life God was visibly good; he felt that neither his cautious legal faith nor his despair helped him to understand suffering; he came to a halt, ceased to reason to no purpose, and grieved at his envious bitterness, choosing to stand close to God whatever else might fail. Milton read Psalm 73 as a document of the achievement of faithful understanding. In *De Doctrina Christiana* he used several verses of the psalm as proof texts for the axioms that God governs the universe with supreme wisdom and holiness,[60] that the faithful may not understand how good temptations exercise and confirm patience until they think more profoundly,[61] and that the fear of God is a blessing and virtue, whereas carnal security is blinding.[62] Significantly, Milton also referred to Psalm 73 after affirming that it may be right for a man professing the true religion to take part in idol-worship if the performance of a civil duty necessitates it.[63] The shading which the references to this and other psalms of trust gives to Samson's act in quietly accompanying the Officer to the temple of Dagon augments the pathos and the grandeur of the scene.

The exode is spoken in dialogue among the Messenger, Manoa, and the Chorus, to none of whom as yet is full comprehension of the event given.[64] The Messenger can report Samson "patient but undaunted" and register how he concluded his spiritual struggle in such full peace of mind that, after announcing "Now of my own accord such other tryal / I mean to shew you of my strength, yet greater," he performed the deed for which he was consecrated. The Messenger can describe the "choice nobility and flower" of the Philistines carnally secure, can describe Samson's "captive state" and unexpected death. Manoa can acknowledge that "death to life is crown or shame." But to the reader of the Book of Psalms the scene is already colored with the power of good temptations to restore the fallen and raise "the languish't head unpropt" till it be upright. He awaits an explanation of the tragedy which will display both God's justice and His mercy.

In the kommos the Chorus and Manoa arrive at public recognition of the exemplary value of Samson's life. Among the many psalms of communal thanksgiving having exhortatory and didactic overtones

---

[60] *CPW*, vi, 328.   [61] *Ibid.*, 339.   [62] *Ibid.*, 661.   [63] *Ibid.*, 694.

[64] It is not helpful simply to affirm, as does Donald F. Bouchard in *Milton: A Structural Reading* (London: Edward Arnold, 1974), 142, that the Chorus is designed to "mirror and condition our response to the action" by being both actors and spectators of the drama, without stipulating *how* they can do this. I very much agree that the Chorus is not the voice of the poet, but I consider that their movement through stages of Psalmic understanding make them prompt and reflect our movement as well.

upon which Milton now draws, Psalms 103 and 104 are prominent. Psalm 103 is a mixture of hymn and thanksgiving; a suggestion of the antiphonal in its structure may have confirmed Milton's division of his speakers into two semichoruses to give the kommos the effect of dialogue.[65] It opens with a self-dedication to bless the Lord by one who has experienced his grace personally, "so that [his] youth is renewed like the eagle's" (verses 1-5); there follow his meditations on the Lord's acts of grace within human history (6-13) and his perception of the eternal God's compassion toward transient man (14-18); it concludes with a choral glorification of the kingly God. Milton cited Psalm 103 in *De Doctrina Christiana* to prove the axioms that God is supremely kind, governs all creatures, is attended by angels, and deserves gratitude.[66] In modern times Psalm 104 has been conjecturally ascribed to the same poet as Psalm 103;[67] its theme is the manifestation of God's wisdom and glory in the created world, its tone, awe and wonder at God's majesty, which inspires trust. As God's action within time is the concern of Psalm 103, so His action throughout space and eternity is the concern of Psalm 104. Among the most striking images of Psalm 103 is that of the eagle's revival; among the most striking of Psalm 104 is that of God's hiding his face from men and then returning to them. These images of the conquest of death and despair are the self-evident sources of Milton's most convincing pictures in the kommos. But in both psalms the Psalmist's perception of God's grace demands a reciprocal response in man; that response is trusting praise in Psalm 103 and the rejection of the wicked in Psalm 104. What Milton thought the import of Psalm 104 to be is manifested in his citation of it to support the axioms that the sum of all God's attributes is supreme glory and perfection, that the Son is His agent by whom He creates all things, that He also preserves all created things, even the smallest, that the body and soul of man die together and together go down to the grave, and that both stand in need of redemption.[68]

Great and perplexing questions hang over *Samson Agonistes*: Can a god who acts in the way Samson's God acts still be God? Why is the good so easily lost, even by the best of men? Why must the attainment of the good be achieved in such mixture of suffering and

[65] Hans Schmidt, *Die Psalmen* (Göttingen: Vandenhoeck and Rupretcht, 1934), makes the claim that the psalm is antiphonal.

[66] *CPW*, VI, 150, 328, 315, 345, 659.

[67] *The Interpreter's Bible*, Vol. IV, *The Book of Psalms*, ed. W. R. Taylor and W. S. McCullough, 550.

[68] *CPW*, VI, 151, 282, also 324, 316-17, 327, 329, 407. Milton considered Psalm 104 to contain a narration of the creation of the world and cited it repeatedly in Book VI of *Paradise Lost*.

pain? Samson comes to answer these questions, to show his nation and all subsequent nations what kind of god his God is and what man must therefore do to demonstrate his faith. Milton gives to Samson first, and then to the Chorus, just such perceptions of the nature of God and of man as he thought present in the Book of Psalms, interpreted through the spirit given to man after the full revelation of the Gospel. At despairing junctures in his life man doubts not only his own power to succeed but also the purposiveness of his very existence. In acute mental distress he gives utterance to the sort of self-reproach and anxiety that Samson utters in his prologue and to his father, and that Psalms 6, 42, and 43 express. He may wish altogether to deny his God as the Chorus nearly does to conclude Act I, and as Psalms 14 and 53 record. The reproach of God is inhibited, however, by his recollection that he has acted as a free agent, having accepted the gift of life and the good things in it without demur. What has befallen him has been the consequence of his own behavior, and that consideration must come to most as it comes to Samson in Act II and to the Psalmist of Psalms 6, 32, 38, 51, 102, 130, and 143. More important, however, his ability to render a verdict upon his plight is the consequence of his own understanding. He has not only freely acted, he has freely interpreted.

To anticipate the argument of the next chapter, Samson has committed deeds which are irreversible, and it is not open to him to deny his culpability in the face of his behavior. In this he differs from Job. Job can assert his good conscience and his complete sincerity, although Milton will concede of him that he is not "perfect" in the sense of immutably good. Job has not broken the law which was given him by God to constitute the meaning and purpose of his life. Job has correctly understood his mortal significance: his function was to worship God by obeying his laws; goodness was to him nothing more nor less than reasonable and moderate conformity to God's announced definition of goodness. He was to bring all of his forces under the control of his will to perceive the purposive function of God's laws and to abide by them. This he successfully did. Where Job can be said to have failed is in his understanding of God's nature, not of his own function. When he unsuccessfully challenged God to account for His treatment of him, he thereby learned to understand God. The opportunity presented to Job by his sufferings was an opportunity to learn, and a challenge to his free will complementary to the challenge presented to Samson by his failure to obey God and remain faithful to God's purposes for him. Job is free to understand no more than that God is unjust to him; and if that is all he can learn, his sense of his own significance is lost. Samson is free to interpret his own case as involving God's just and utter rejection of him and, if he does so, his life likewise is depleted of all but a cautionary meaning. Job's testing is designed to perfect his understanding of God, to bring him to a truer faith or wisdom. Samson's testing is designed to enable him to perform virtuous deeds, deeds of faith.

In the continuing arc of Samson's experience, however, at the point of his strongest penitence there appears before him the person formerly closest to him, who comes to offer false assuaging words to console him for the knowledge of his own failure. The confrontation of Samson and Dalila, like that of the Psalmist and his friend in Psalm 41, is a "good temptation." Dalila, like the friend, comes to gloat over his fall and to assert against the total uselessness of his existence the relative success of hers in a universe where success or public acclaim is the only yardstick of goodness and all morality is measurable by popular fame. If Samson will confirm her truths—his weakness, her strength—then Dalila will cherish him. Samson's moral standard, however, is the acceptability of his behavior to himself and his God, only. He sees that his present outer enslavement is more consonant with freedom of purpose than his former inner enslavement. Similarly, the confrontation of Samson and Harapha, like that of the Psalmist and the boastful worldling in Psalm 52, constitutes a second good temptation. As Dalila opposes false blame to true freedom, so Harapha opposes false heroism to true service. Steering past these moral barriers, Samson arrives at a new introspective and impersonal conception of the purposiveness of virtue, like that of Psalm 73, which recapitulates the agonized pilgrimage of the believer through pain and incomprehension to trust and quiet; the stage of his former incomprehension is particularly movingly described. Out of the impersonal quiet of a new ordering of his priorities, Samson acts. The explanation of the meaning of his existence and his action falls to his father and the Chorus. They draw upon concepts of revival and renewal, upon concepts of grace developed in Psalms 103 and 104. The God in whom they trust relieves man's grief with a consolation that restores purpose. Samson had thought he was to be one kind of man; he discovered by suffering how to be another kind. Remorse at his inability to act consistently the first kind of role is given psalmic expressiveness. But remorse is also present when he understands that his first sense of role was in itself inadequate. Milton conveys in psalmic terms the complexities of Samson's grief, of Samson's spiritual growth, and of Samson's trust. As *De Doctrina Christiana* communicates the core of Milton's ethics by dissolving drama and narrative from Scripture to rearrange scriptural truths into ethical axioms, so *Samson Agonistes* reverses the process to rearrange a scriptural narrative and subsume under it the emotional cadences of discovery and renewal present elsewhere in scattered form in Scripture —and nowhere more succinctly and movingly than in the Book of Psalms, whose apt words have power to assuage and console.

BIBLICAL POETRY AND

MORAL EXAMPLE

The Ethics of the Companion Poems, Paradise Regained, and Samson Agonistes

At the same time that Milton solved the formal problem of offering medicinal truths in compassionate poetic accents within the detachment of the dramatic genre by drawing upon the accretion of tones in the Psalms, he also achieved consistency between an ethos of faithful works and a tragic view of life. Tragedy was to fit the spectator for new action in his world, not by assuring him that success would crown his works, or that his works were obligatory, but by showing him how his works would express and flow from his enriched understanding or faith. The poet's responsibility was to show that tragic experience did not obliterate, but rather strengthened, the protagonist of his drama to live well; human suffering causes and attends better understanding. *Samson Agonistes* adds to our conception of Milton's mind and art a final term which, without that play, might well have remained obscure. In the sphere of ethics, it does so by building upon earlier works, especially religious poems incorporating the Psalms, as I have shown. It also does so by its relationship to the poem which accompanied it in publication, its companion piece, *Paradise Regained*.

In common with several recent critics,[1] I do not think that Milton paired *Paradise Regained* and *Samson Agonistes* haphazardly or threw the play in with the brief epic as a makeweight. Slenderer volumes of works from his hand were printed after the Restoration so that the case for bringing out either the play or the poem alone would not have been overruled by their length. Rather, I think we may hypothesize from Milton's careful printing practices[2] that he designed a single

[1] See Patrick Cullen, *Infernal Triad* (Princeton: Princeton University Press, 1974), 125-27; Barker, "Calm Regained through Passion Spent," 13-14, 29-35; Kerrigan, *Prophetic Milton*, 268.

[2] The treatment of the poems from the 1645 edition in the 1673 edition would be a case in point; the rearrangement of the sonnets discussed in chapter 7 above would be another.

volume containing two poems, one epic and one dramatic, meant to add complementarily to the rich sum of wisdom given mankind through Adam in the closing scenes of *Paradise Lost*. Adam remained silent a while when Michael completed his apocalyptic vision of human history, but in acknowledgment of the understanding he had been given he at "last reply'd":

> How soon hath thy prediction, Seer blest,
> Measur'd this transcient World, the Race of time,
> Till time stand fixt: beyond is all abyss,
> Eternitie, whose end no eye can reach.
> Greatly instructed I shall hence depart,
> Greatly in peace of thought, and have my fill
> Of knowledge, what this vessel can containe;
> Beyond which was my folly to aspire.
> Henceforth I learne, that to obey is best,
> And love with feare the onely God, to walk
> As in his presence, ever to observe
> His providence, and on him sole depend,
> Merciful over all his works, with good
> Still overcoming evil, and by small
> Accomplishing great things, by things deemd weak
> Subverting worldly strong, and worldly wise
> By simply meek; that suffering for Truths sake
> Is fortitude to highest victorie,
> And to the faithful Death the Gate of Life;
> Taught this by his example whom I now
> Acknowledge my Redeemer ever blest.

(XII, 553-73)

In Adam's words Milton's great reconciliation of God and man was complete. As the sign of its completion he gave to Michael one final charge to Adam, a charge as well to Milton himself, to his nation, and to all men:

> This having learnt, thou hast attained the summe
> Of wisdom; hope no higher, though all the Starrs
> Thou knewst by name, and all th' ethereal Powers,
> All secrets of the deep, all Natures works,
> Or works of God in Heav'n, Air, Earth, or Sea,
> And all the riches of this World enjoydst,
> And all the rule, one Empire: onely add
> Deeds to thy knowledge answerable, add Faith,

Add Vertue, Patience, Temperance, add Love,
By name to come call'd Charitie, the soul
Of all the rest: then wilt thou not be loath
To leave this Paradise, but shalt possess
A Paradise within thee, happier farr.

(XII, 575-87)

The conclusion of *Paradise Lost* concluded everything, but likewise it concluded nothing. In particular, two themes for future treatment are explicit in Adam's submission and in Michael's charge: the example of the "Redeemer ever blest" and his version of heroic fortitude, and the addition of human deeds of faith, virtue, patience, temperance, and love in proportion to the knowledge of God given to any man. The depiction of these two themes was the poet's particular next task so that "what most merits fame" should not be "in silence hid." The first theme, treated in the brief epic, is Milton's version of a New Testament trial of virtue; the second, treated in the tragedy, is his version of an Old Testament trial of virtue. Both end in *anagnorisis* or discovery, both imitate actions exemplary for man, both consist of dialogue and inner debate in an attempt to expound Milton's contingent and progressive ethics. Nor should it be overlooked that the conclusion of *Paradise Lost* is not, like the conclusion of the *Odyssey* and the *Aeneid*, a conclusion of triumph superceding tragic vision. It is a conclusion of controlled intellectual maturity and is therefore supremely ambiguous and open. Everything does not comfortingly turn out all right at the end; no happy fantasy of perfect achievement is offered and no secure nation-state compensates for individual human tragedy. Instead, two human beings are shown entering upon the familiarly difficult experience of existence, and both feel a remorse which turns their despair toward hope.

The ambivalent suspension of verdict in the last scene of *Paradise Lost* is given an authoritative completion in only one work of poetry by Milton's hand, his final work, the tragedy *Samson Agonistes*. Its last lines stand out tellingly in English poetry as lines of a chastened "fare forward." In the last chapter of Book I of *De Doctrina Christiana* Milton concluded everything in a personal vision of the absolute end of the created world. There is no mistaking the boldness and originality of that final vision or the firmness with which Milton there underlined the ethical significance of his *eschata*. "The last judgment," he wrote, "is that at which Christ with the Saints, arrayed in the glory and the power of the father, will judge . . . the whole human race. . . . The standard of judgment will be the individual conscience itself, and so each man will be judged according to the light which he has received."[3] Adam's confessed conversion to Christianity in *Paradise Lost*, his acknowledgment of faith in his redeemer, sets the highest standard of judgment before him, but *Paradise Lost* does not render that judgment prophetically or literally. If, then, in any meaningful sense *Paradise Lost* required a sequel, the ambiguity of its conclusion may be thought to suggest a double sequel: an epic of spiritual triumph or a divine comedy, and a tragedy of human failure encompassing regeneration or redemption. Milton's Protestant maturity directed him firmly to Scripture for mimetic materials for both halves of the double sequel. He turned to the parallels between Job's sufferings and Christ's temptations for one mimesis, and to the parallels between Samson's failure and the Psalms' doubling cycles of lament, thanksgiving, and hymn for the other. Both *Samson Agonistes* and *Paradise Regained* are poems conveying ethics; taken together they celebrate the addition of "deeds" to "knowledge answerable."

In recent criticism, admirers of both poems have seemed perplexed to answer questions about the status of action in each work. There appears to be too much action in *Samson Agonistes* of an unreflective sort and too little in *Paradise Regained*. The problem of where to locate each poem on a scale of activity-passivity or transformation-endurance has lain latent in many recent studies; the question, all but framed in words, has been whether to read them as treating the achievement of identity or the acting out of a chosen self-definition, as treating self-deliverance or the deliverance of others.[4] As with many apparent alternatives in Milton interpretation, the truth seems to me to comprehend both. *Paradise Regained* and *Samson Agonistes* share a common ethics, but they are not identical in their ethical thrust. *Paradise Regained* dramatizes moral choice in the achievement of identity, whereas *Samson Agonistes* unfolds the achievement of integrity through progressive moral choices. The ethos of national action or the value of works of faith is complementarily presented in them. Each variously combines serving and standing.

Several interrelated concepts appear in both works as aspects of their complementary ethics. Prominent among these concepts (and to them I shall shortly turn) are the good temptation, the nature of freedom, and the value of exemplary action. These concepts Milton found mov-

---

[3] *CPW*, VI, 621-23.

[4] See for example: for *Paradise Regained*, Barbara Lewalski, *Milton's Brief Epic*, 133, versus Irene Samuel, "The Regaining of Paradise," in *The Prison and the Pinnacle*, ed. Rajan, 111, 122-28; for *Samson Agonistes*, Lawry, *Shadow of Heaven*, 353, 395-97, versus Shawcross, "Irony as Tragic Effect," 303-4, or Kerrigan, *Prophetic Milton*, 246-47.

ingly expressed in the Psalms; and together with the imagery and
emotional shading which I have been describing, they made the Psalms
for him the greatest poems of his tradition. Milton also found them
exemplified in the Book of Job, which is related to *Paradise Regained*
much as the Book of Psalms is related to *Samson Agonistes*.[5] Milton was,
of course, sensitive to the striking similarities between Job and a number
of the Psalms. The most complete similarity, to which I have already
drawn attention, is to Psalm 73, but Psalms 37 and 39, and 26, 49, and
139 offer analogies to parts of the development of the Book of Job.
Psalm 37, presenting the sufferings of the godly and the prosperity of
the wicked as merely temporary phenomena, defends God's ultimate
retributive-distributive justice in terms of the eventual equation of
suffering with the punishment of sin; that argument is the argument
of Job's comforters. Psalms 39 and 26, depicting the integrity of the
godly under the most severe tests, dramatize a personal probity like
that of Job himself. Psalm 49, showing the inability of the prosperous
to save themselves or others from death, expresses a faith in the im-
mortality of the redeemed souls of the righteous; that faith is the faith
Job achieves after all his trials. Psalm 139 extols the omniscience and
omnipresence of God as embracing every thought and deed of the
Psalmist, preventing any escape from God and reducing man to hu-
mility; its substance is the substance both of Elihu's words and of
Job's final submission to God.[6] All these attitudes are drawn together
in the full course of Psalm 73, which moves from a simple, incorrect
understanding of God's justice, through doubt, to a complex, true
faith. It is not surprising, therefore, that *Samson Agonistes* should
turn to Job as well as to the Book of Psalms in presenting the good
temptation, the nature of liberty, and the value of exemplary suffering,

[5] The plot of *Paradise Regained*, of course, derives from Luke 4:1-13; the plot
of *Samson Agonistes*, from Judg. 13-16. The structure of *Paradise Regained* owes
much to the frame-dialogue pattern of Job, and it has been argued by Barbara
Lewalski, "*Samson Agonistes* and the 'Tragedy of the Apocalypse,'" *PMLA*, 85
(1970), 1050-62, that the structure and tragic significance of *Samson Agonistes*
owes much to Revelations. I am here concerned with ethical teaching rather than
dramatic patterning. For studies of the morality in *Samson Agonistes* see A. B.
Chambers, "Wisdom and Fortitude in *Samson Agonistes*," *PMLA*, 78 (1963),
318-27; A. E. George, *Milton and the Nature of Man* (London: Asia Publishing
House, 1974), chaps. 1-3; Ann Gossman, "Samson, Job and 'The Exercise of
Saints,'" *English Studies*, 45 (1964), 212-24; Burton O. Kurth, *Milton and Chris-
tian Heroism: Biblical Epic Themes and Forms in Seventeenth-Century England*
(Berkeley: University of California Press, 1959); and Camille Slights, "A Hero
of Conscience: *Samson Agonistes* and Casuistry," *PMLA*, 91 (1975), 395-412.

[6] Ivor Armstrong Richards is the most recent of many commentators to re-
mark on this similarity. See his *Beyond* (London: Harcourt Brace Jovanovich,
1974).

nor that *Paradise Regained* should commend not only Job but also the Psalms for their ethical effectiveness:

> In them is plainest taught, and easiest learnt,
> What makes a Nation happy, and keeps it so.

Nor could Milton have been unaware of the significant contemporary tradition which saw the Book of Job as drama, and even as tragedy, although his own view was that it constituted "brief epic."[7]

Wrestling with Temptation

The close and secure interrelatedness of the three concepts which give both *Paradise Regained* and *Samson Agonistes* ethical force makes it difficult to discuss them as isolated units, but since *Paradise Regained* commences with the prologue to a planned series of temptations which will be resisted, and *Samson Agonistes* with the aftermath of succumbing to temptation, which itself initiates a new series, I shall begin with the concept of the good temptation. Milton draws attention to the parallel but antithetical situation of the two heroes at the outset of each work by describing the fallen Samson's mind besieged by "restless thoughts . . . like a deadly swarm / Of Hornets arm'd," the same image he had used to depict the seething of the Son's mind as he considered how to begin his great task as "Saviour to mankind": "O what a multitude of thoughts at once / Awak'nd in me swarm." Both the Son and Samson are in states of intellectual excitment as they enter each upon a series of temptations, the Son eagerly hopeful, Samson despairingly self-indicting. Their temptations are similarly susceptible only to mental conquest, and the temptations are themselves the very material of which virtue is made. The Son at the beginning of his enterprise is hailed by a chorus of angels, "Now entring his great duel, not of arms / But *to vanquish by wisdom* hellish wiles"; Samson near the close of his is comforted by a chorus of friends and neighbors, "This Idols day hath bin to thee no day of rest, / *Labouring thy mind* / More then the working day thy hands." The Son's temptations are the trial of his obedience, "one man's firm obedience fully tri'd / Through all temptations"; Samson's are the test of his virtue, "Vertue which all temptation can remove." Virtue at the end of Samson's life has been "rouz'd / From under ashes into sudden flame":

---

[7] In 1610 Voetius saw an English company in Leyden perform a Job play which may have been Robert Greene's lost *The History of Job* (see Murray Roston, *Biblical Drama in England* [Evanston: Northwestern University Press, 1968], 95-96). The theoretical views of Beza and others are given in Lewalski, *Milton's Brief Epic*, 12-21.

So vertue giv'n for lost,
Deprest, and overthrown, as seem'd,
Like that self-begott'n bird
In the *Arabian* woods embost,
That no second knows nor third,
And lay e're while a Holocaust,
From out her ashie womb now teem'd,
Revives, reflourishes, then vigorous most
When most inactive deem'd. . . .

(1697-1705)

In *Paradise Regained* the Tempter's fears are multiplied at the beginning of the action when he sees "the Womans seed . . . displaying all vertue"; the Father's confidence is firm to venture "his filial Vertue, though untri'd, / Against whate're may tempt." At the end of the Son's human testing in his purely mortal capacities he is found

Proof against all temptation as a rock
Of Adamant, and as a Center, firm
To the utmost of meer man both wise and good.

(IV, 533-35)

The temptations which have revived the virtue of Samson and confirmed that of the Son are good temptations. Good temptations are not the cause of virtue, but they are the stuff from which it is made. Milton was constant to the position he had taken in *Areopagitica*:

Wherefore did he create passions within us, pleasures round about us, but that these rightly tempered are the very ingredients of virtue. . . . This justifies the high providence of God, who, though he command us temperance, justice, continence, yet pours out before us even to a profuseness all desirable things, and gives us minds that can wander beyond all limit and satiety.

Milton defined the good temptation in the eighth chapter of Book I of *De Doctrina Christiana*, a discussion of "God's Providence, or His Universal Government of Things":

Good temptations are those which God uses to tempt even righteous men, in order to prove them. He does this not for his own sake—as if he did not know what sort of men they would turn out to be—but either to exercise or demonstrate their faith or patience, as in the case of Abraham and Job, or to lessen their self-confidence and prove them guilty of weakness, so that they may become wiser and others may be instructed.

233

He introduced the concept of good temptations by noting that they were an aspect of "God's system of providence." The definitive axiom for God's general system of providence Milton gave as: "The general government of the universe is that by which God the Father views and preserves all created things and governs them with supreme wisdom and holiness, according to the conditions of his decree." The axiom was orthodox and conventional among all reformed theologians, but the final qualification—"according to the conditions of his decree" —was not. It arose from Milton's Arminianism. God's decree (predestination) is a conditional decree, a decree of election and not of reprobation, "by which God, before the foundations of the world were laid, had mercy on the human race, although it was going to fall of its own accord, and . . . predestined to eternal salvation . . . those who would in the future believe and continue in the faith."[8] God did not predestine the Fall, but predestined to election such of the fallen as continue in the faith. Their election is contingent upon their faith. It is equally offered to all the fallen. The Fall does not annul contingent election by making it impossible for a man to know or to will the good; rather, "everyone is provided with a sufficient degree of innate reason for him to be able to resist evil desires by his own efforts."[9] Furthermore "when God determined to restore mankind, he also decided unquestionably (and what could be more just) to restore some part at least of man's lost freedom of will."[10] God, in sum, "undoubtedly bestows grace on all, and if not equally upon each, at least sufficient to enable everyone to attain knowledge of the truth and salvation."[11] Good temptations are an aspect of God's providential government of man by means of contingent predestination; man's answering to his knowledge of the good constitutes the condition upon which he will be mercifully saved. The temptations of Job, Christ, and Samson are all good temptations and involve exercise and demonstration of faith or patience; they also involve becoming wiser and instructing others. They vary, of course, in the degree to which they do these things. So Milton added, "But even the faithful are sometimes insufficiently aware of all these methods of divine providence, until they examine the subject more deeply and become better informed about the word of God." Good temptations, that is, are instruments of understanding as well as exercises of will; they depend upon a concept of freedom as the necessary condition for obedience; they issue into exemplary action. God brought into being a universe open and emergent, not causally determined and fixed. The moral man inhabits a cosmos which he must understand and in which he must act, but the

[8] *CPW*, VI, 168. [9] *Ibid.*, 186. [10] *Ibid.*, 187. [11] *Ibid.*, 192.

cosmos and the God who made it do not depend either on his action or his knowledge. At cost he may perfect his nature. The tragic view of life acknowledges both the cost to each man and something of the open and emergent nature of the cosmos in which one man's highest efforts must be superseded by fuller revelations of truth.

The primary function of good temptations is the exercise or demonstration of "faith, or patience." In the second choral stasimon of *Samson Agonistes*, Milton first broached the subject of patience as the "truest fortitude," the virtue by which a man may bear well "all calamities, / All chances incident to [his] frail life." The Chorus asks the bewildering question of Job and of Psalms 8 and 144:

> God of our Fathers, what is man!
> That thou towards him with hand so various,
> Or might I say contrarious,
> Temperst thy providence through his short course,
> Not evenly. . . .

> (667-71)

The unevenness of God's behavior they associate with the distribution of felicity and misery in life:

> Just or unjust, alike seem miserable,
> For oft alike, both come to evil end.

> (703-4)

To consider the circumstances of the equal treatment of the good man and the bad man in life is to create within oneself a "dissonant mood" from that of patience. It is of little use to advise a man to practice patience in order to assuage his personal grief if it be evident to him that, as Milton citing Job put it in *De Doctrina Christiana*, "in this life the fortunes of the good and the bad turn out to be the same"—unless that man already have within himself the prior conviction that his behavior is nonetheless of concern to his God and that his God is somehow loving. That conviction would stand as "some sourse of consolation from above / Secret refreshings that repair his strength." The simplest consideration of justice would humanly posit that God will reward the good and punish the wicked; if the hand of God is indifferent or, worse, "contrarious," and if He is unconcerned to evaluate or approve the deeds of His creatures, then, though He be God indeed, it is a difficult matter to derive a consistent ethics either from His nature or the nature of His creation. Patience can scarcely flow from the experience of mere caprice.

The Chorus and Samson in the first act of the tragedy had seen looming the difficulty of explaining the behavior of an arbitrary God and had withdrawn from it quickly. Only the "heart of the Fool" could deny God's existence, although many might reasonably doubt His goodness, might "doubt his ways not just, / As to his own edicts, found contradicting." They should be reminded that God "made our Laws to bind us, not himself." Beyond that, they were better advised, "Down Reason then, at least vain reasonings down." But if "each man will be judged according to the light which he has received," then it is a matter of great consequence to distinguish between vain reasoning and salvific reasoning. Patience, therefore (and I shall recur to this point later), is a virtue belonging both to understanding as an aspect of wisdom and to will as an aspect of constancy. God must be understood to be just; patience must be chosen by the will with sincerity, promptness, and constancy. The patience which the Chorus would like to commend to Samson is the truest fortitude, but it must be accompanied or activated by a source of consolation from above; they therefore pray that God "turn [Samson's] labours . . . to peaceful end." God's apparent response is the arrival of Dalila, the second in a chain of good temptations which began when Manoa arrived to offer his son ransom and rest. Samson understands that her coming is a testing for him and that what it tests is his patience and well-bearing of all the chances incident to life. She comes, he says, like all such wives, "chief to try / Her husband, how far urg'd his patience bears, / His virtue or weakness which way to assail. . . ."

Patience, Milton wrote, works in two distinct spheres of human life.[12] It is a virtue with respect to man's duty to God and his duty to man. (I shall argue below that it is also a virtue of both the understanding and the will.) Of the first sort of patience he wrote:

> Patience is the virtue which shows when we peacefully accept God's promises, supported by confidence in the divine providence, power and

[12] See Appendix C for an outline summary of Book II of *De Doctrina Christiana* which will be of some help in relating the several parts of his discussion of this and other virtues. Note here II.B.1.(A).(7) and II.B.2.(A).(2).b.ii. My model for this outline is the *synopsis libri* in Brian Weiss, *Milton's Use of Ramist Method in His Scholarly Writings* (Ann Arbor: University Microfilms, 1975), 229-42. See also Lee A. Jacobus, *Sudden Apprehension: Aspects of Knowledge in "Paradise Lost"* (The Hague: Mouton, 1976), for a full discussion of "place-logic," including several logical tables of the sort I have prepared for Book II. Analogous synopses appear in Franklin Irwin, *Ramistic Logic in Milton's Prose Works* (Ann Arbor: University Microfilms, 1941). The utility of such schematic outlines is discussed in Walter J. Ong, *Ramus: Method, and the Decay of Dialogue* (Cambridge, Mass.: Harvard University Press, 1958), and Frances Yates, *The Art of Memory* (Chicago: University of Chicago Press, 1966).

goodness; also when we bear any evils that we have to bear calmly, as things which our supreme Father has sent for our good. . . . Opposed to this is impatience towards God, a sin which even the saints are sometimes tempted to commit.[13]

Among the proof texts of patience are two from Job; among those illustrating impatience are three from Job. Of the second sort of patience, patience as a merely human virtue having to do with one's duty to one's own selfhood, he wrote simply; "Patience is the endurance of evils and injuries. . . . But even holy men sometimes exact compensation for injuries." This aspect of patience Milton illustrated from the Psalms, but he concluded his discussion of it by noting that "sensibility to pain, and complaints and lamentations are not inconsistent with true patience, as may be seen from the example of Job and of other holy men in adversity." Patience in respect to one's own experiences of suffering Milton saw as arising from "righteousness towards [oneself] . . . right reason in self-government and self-control."[14] The good temptation of Dalila's visit arouses Samson's right reason, so that he not only redefines the crucial ethical concepts of right love of persons, places, and God, he also diagnoses the uxoriousness which as an aspect of "impotence of mind" drove him astray: "I . . . lov'd thee . . . Too well . . . who could deny thee nothing." This diagnosis complements, of course, Samson's confession of his *hubris* made to Manoa in the second act of the play: "swoll'n with pride into the snare I fell." The contrition for his own pride and sensuality is a sign of intellectual clarity, and Samson can then make the further assertion that liberty is a state of mind and not of body. But his insight stops there. Patience with respect to personal indignity has been easier for Samson to learn than patience toward God. His verdict upon Dalila's visit is not that it has been an evil "that we have to bear calmly" as something "which our supreme Father has sent for our own good." On the contrary, he is certain she has been sent as a punishment for his past weakness:

> So let her go, God sent her to debase me,
> And aggravate my folly who committed
> To such a viper his most sacred trust
> Of secresie, my safety, and my life.

(999-1002)

Samson's regeneration does not trace a simple curve; like all suffering men, he can and does lapse from new levels of insight back into old positions. Such regressions testify to the painful nature of change and permit change at a pace tolerable to the human psyche.

[13] *CPW*, VI, 662.   [14] *Ibid.*, 720.

The nature of both kinds of patience—patience toward God and patience within oneself—is established in *Paradise Regained*. Christ first uses the word to answer Satan's claim that he collaborates with God, has access to heaven, and has become a friend to man. Satan says:

> I came among the Sons of God, when he
> Gave up into my hands *Uzzean Job*
> To prove him, and illustrate his high worth. . . .
>
> (I, 368-70)

And the Son retorts:

> What but thy malice mov'd thee to misdeem
> Of righteous *Job*, then cruelly to afflict him
> With all inflictions, but his patience won?
>
> (I, 424-26)

Satan, the father of lies, muffled the important clues to the meaning of Job's testing contained in the prose framework of the extended poetic dialogue. The test was proposed not by God but by Satan in asserting that Job's uprightness was purchased by God's favors: "Doth Job fear God for naught? . . . But put forth thine hand now, and touch all that he hath, and he will curse thee to thy face."[15] God permitted the free

---

[15] Satan's muffling of the truth has not been apparent to a number of modern readers. The clearest statement of misreading comes in I. A. Richards's outstandingly interesting book, *Beyond*. Satan "acts as the Lord's agent and executive. The source of Job's afflictions is the Lord himself—though it has taken Satan's theorizing (tauntingly and irritatingly displayed) to bring such action forth. That it is all really the Lord's doing much enhances the significance of the action. And this whether or not we stress as much as I have above the component of his foreknowledge, an aspect that can be separated only by artifice from his omnipotence. (Note: That the Lord knows what will happen because—before Time was—he ordained that it should be so, puts the two aspects into intelligible connection)" (p. 53). The significant separation which Milton insisted upon is not that between omnipotence and foreknowledge; both are attributed to God by him as by every reformed theologian. But the unity of omnipotence and foreknowledge is not, so Milton argued and all Arminians with him, the same as the unity of foreknowledge and necessity. God foreknows without ordaining. Richards believes that the Book of Job is about "What is Justice and why should a man think he is entitled to it" (p. 67). Ironically, he has fallen into a temptation he is perfectly aware of, "the temptation . . . to invent a work for his author to assay, and then to either applaud his achievement or point out how he fails" (p. 70). Milton understood the Book of Job to treat man's knowledge of God, and he denied that God is the necessary author of all human suffering and the source of evil. Richards's argument in the case of Job draws upon Jung. A far finer contemporary psychiatric reading is Jack Kahn's *Job's Illness: Loss, Grief*

testing of Job but set bounds to it: "Behold, all that he hath is in thy power; only upon himself put forth not thy hand"; and later, "Behold, he is in thine hand; but save his life."[16]

The assumption that God had sent Job's afflictions and that they were punishments for Job's secret and unconfessed sins was precisely the error of Job's comforters. They understood God in static, deterministic terms: he was a Father who kept the universe in order by mechanistic equations of good and reward, bad and punishment. In Milton's reading, however, God permitted the testing of Job for the reasons he described under "good temptations." Milton therefore adapted the prose prologue of the Book of Job for the prologue to *Paradise Regained*. There, in a council in middle air, Satan proposes both to assay the nature and undermine the integrity of the Son. He resolves:

> Who this is we must learn, for man he seems
> In all his lineaments, though in his face
> The glimpses of his Fathers glory shine.

(I, 91-93)

On this attempt Milton commented in his own voice:

> Temptation and all guile on him to try;
> So to subvert whom he suspected rais'd
> To end his Raign on Earth so long enjoy'd:
> But contrary unweeting he fulfill'd
> The purpos'd Counsel pre-ordain'd and fixt
> Of the most High. . . .

(I, 123-28)

The "purpos'd Counsel," it should be remembered, is the free redemption of man, "pre-ordain'd" contingently in such a way as to preserve human freedom. The "fixity" of God's purpose is the emergence in time of the full scope of an open universe. That universe will not, however, be chained by man's comprehension of it at some final moment of

---

and Integration (London: Pergamon Press, 1975), which interprets Job as depicting a process of psychological change. Kahn's reading seems to me to be beyond all praise for its delicacy and compassion.

[16] See *De Doctrina Christiana*: "Often punishment is the instrumental cause of repentance, Job v.7. . . . But God sets a limit to his punishment, in case we should be overwhelmed by it. . . . Indeed, he pities us and seems even to repent his treatment of us; and so he compensates us with a double measure of comfort. . . . We should not, then, make rash judgments about other people's afflictions. That was the error of Eliphaz, Job IV and IX.22.23 and of the vilest men, Job xxx" (*CPW*, VI, 469-70).

understanding. Progressive revelation is no sanction for the idea of limitless progress. If that were so, of course, there could be no such genre as Christian tragedy. God, observing the devilish council in mid-air, comments to Gabriel:

> this man born and now up-grown,
> To shew him worthy of his birth divine
> And high prediction, henceforth I expose
> To Satan; let him tempt and now assay
> His utmost subtilty, because he boasts
> And vaunts of his great cunning to the throng
> Of his Apostasie; he might have learnt
> Less over-weening, since he fail'd in *Job*,
> Whose constant perseverance overcame
> Whate're his cruel malice could invent.
>
> (I, 140-49)

The tempting and assaying of the Son, like that of Job, is the act of Satan. Its function is the extempore device and management of God and consists in the establishment and manifestation of the Son's worthiness of divine birth:

> But first I mean
> To exercise him in the Wilderness,
> There he shall first lay down the rudiments
> Of his great warfare, e're I send him forth
> To conquer Sin and Death the two grand foes,
> By Humiliation and strong Sufferance.
>
> (I, 155-60)

Humiliation and sufferance are the consequences and concomitants of patience;[17] the temptations permitted in order to enable the Son to stand are good temptations, and they are so understood by the Son.

The Son's fullest discussion of patience occurs in the "glory" temptation in Book III of *Paradise Regained*. It directly follows upon his definition of true magnanimity in the "riches" temptation in Book II:

> But to guide Nations in the way of truth
> By saving Doctrine, and from errour lead
> To know, and knowing worship God aright,
> Is yet more Kingly, this attracts the Soul,
> Governs the inner man, the nobler part,
> That other o're the body only reigns,

---

[17] See Appendix C, II.B.I.(A), vi-viii, for the interrelationships of these virtues.

> And oft by force, which to a generous mind
> So reigning can be no sincere delight.
> Besides to give a Kingdom hath been thought
> Greater and nobler done, and to lay down
> Far more magnanimous, then to assume.

(II, 473-83)

Magnanimity is a public virtue, a manifestation of one's general duty to all men, and involves humanity, kindness, and pity. Satan abandons the riches temptation swiftly when the Son's magnanimity shows him impervious to material advantages for himself and endowed with kindness, humanity, and pity for others.[18] In the transition to the glory temptation Satan asks ironically, "These God-like Vertues wherefore dost thou hide . . . wherefore deprive / All Earth her wonder at thy acts, thy self / The fame and glory?" He accepts the exemplary aspect of the Son's role in these words quite as much as he hints at an unworthy thrust of ambition in his motives. The Son's ethical vigilance is alert to both the cognitive and volitional traps in Satan's temptation to glory. He deals with understanding first. Dissociating fame from glory, he dismisses public acclaim to argue that true glory consists in the approbation of God and not of men, God praising "the just man," "thus he did to *Job*." The distinction leads to a definition of the kinds of action which deserve fame. Deeds of "peace," "wisdom," "patience," and "temperance" are specified:

> But if there be in glory aught of good,
> It may by means far different be attain'd
> Without ambition, war, or violence;
> By deeds of peace, by wisdom eminent,
> By patience, temperance; I mention still
> Him whom thy wrongs with Saintly patience born,
> Made famous in a Land and times obscure;
> Who names not now with honour patient *Job*?
> Poor *Socrates* (who next more memorable?)
> By what he taught and suffer'd for so doing,
> For truths sake suffering death unjust, lives now
> Equal in fame to proudest Conquerours.

(III, 88-99)

In *De Doctrina Christiana* this sort of patience derives from personal righteousness, or right reason, which pursues good and resists or endures evil.[19] The pursuit of good and resistance of evil are undertaken

---

[18] See Appendix C, II.B.2.(B).i.(a).(i)-(iii); also II.B.2.(B).ii.b.(ii).(a).
[19] See Appendix C, II.B.2.(A).ii.b.(i) and (ii).

for themselves alone, "for truths sake," and not for reward or glory. Patience comes from insight and is a virtue of the understanding. The Son, having noted it of Job and Socrates, the unjust victims of undeserved sufferings, places it in the perspective of that other patience—patience toward God.[20]

The permission given by God for the affliction of His creatures by agents of evil, human or devilish, is not to be understood as a withdrawal by God or a caprice and therefore unjust. It is to be seen as a good temptation:

> What if he hath decreed that I shall first
> By try'd in humble state, and things adverse,
> By tribulations, injuries, insults,
> Contempts, and scorns, and snares, and violence,
> Suffering, abstaining, quietly expecting
> Without distrust or doubt, that he may know
> What I can suffer, how obey? who best
> Can suffer, best can do; best reign, who first
> Well hath obey'd. . . .
>
> (III, 188-96)

The motives or volitional aspects of glorious action also, therefore, need explicit treatment. The Son must answer Satan's sneer that if he be indifferent to glory, his Father is not:

> Think not so slight of glory; therein least
> Resembling thy great Father: he seeks glory,
> And for his glory all things made. . . .
>
> (III, 109-11)

The Son neither accepts this analysis of God's motives and acts nor the easy conflation of divine and human work. He succinctly attributes to God the motive not of glory but of love in creating all things, "to shew forth his goodness, and impart / His good communicable to every soul / Freely." He then distinguishes between human and divine activity, having corrected the false interpretation of the divine will. God acts only to extend being and freedom; He acts under no necessity to complete His being and He enters into no subcontractual relationship with His creatures to perfect His gift of life. The relationship of God and man is nonetheless one which moves in the human element of time to enlarge man's being:

[20] See Appendix C, II.B.I.(A).(7).

But why should man seek glory? who of his own
Hath nothing, and to whom nothing belongs. . . .
Yet so much bounty is in God, such grace,
That who advance his glory, not thir own,
Them he himself to glory will advance.

(III, 134-44)

The point at issue is the basis of merit in good works. What makes the
deeds of the Son, as "th'utmost of meer man," "deeds above heroic"?
The nature and the motive of the deeds are the answer, what they
mean and why they are undertaken. Their value does not reside in
God's need of them.

Standing and Serving

The whole of Book II of *De Doctrina Christiana* treats "good deeds"
and hangs upon a chain of reasoning running through the chapters on
predestination, justification, and the covenant of grace in Book I. Mil-
ton argues there that for any human action to be meritorious it must
be free. It must be willed, that is, for its own value and not for the
possibilities of reward or propitiation it may bring. The point is also
made in *Paradise Lost*, where God is heard to say:

Freely they stood who stood, and fell who fell.
Not free, what proof could they have givn sincere
Of true allegiance, constant Faith or Love,
Where onely what they needs must do, appeard,
Not what they would? what praise could they receive?
What pleasure I from such obedience paid,
When Will and Reason (Reason also is choice)
Useless and vain, of freedom both despoild,
Made passive both, had servd necessitie,
Not mee.

(III, 102-11)

In *De Doctrina Christiana* Milton explains the significance of the
"non-absolute" decrees of God. God makes his decrees conditional
for the very purpose of allowing free creatures to "put into effect
that freedom which he himself gave them."[21] "The matter or object
of the divine plan was that angels and men alike should be endowed
with free will, so that they could either fall or not fall." "God's will
is no less the first cause of everything if he decrees that certain things

21 *CPW*, VI, 156.

shall depend upon the will of man, than if he had decreed to make all things inevitable."[22] So-called "testing," then, is nothing more or less than the offer of freedom to man; and God decrees not the fall but the freedom. When man falls, however, the fall itself is not the end of the story; God does not damn all men in their fall and then arbitrarily save some by special grace. Rather, He gives all men sufficient grace once more to will and to act freely. All men are the elect in potential; some damn themselves by the nature of their persistent free actions.[23]

Thus human works, freely undertaken, are to be assessed in terms of their motives as they relate to human understanding. Adam instinctively understood the significance of work for unfallen men and explained it to Eve:

> other Creatures all day long
> Rove idle unimploid, and need less rest;
> Man hath his daily work of body or mind
> Appointed, which declares his Dignitie,
> And the regard of Heav'n on all his waies;
> While other Animals unactive range,
> And of thir doings God takes no account.
>
> (IV, 616-22)

The moral point made here is one common to the Puritan works ethos: the difference between men and other creatures is that men work, work being the expression of voluntary love and obedience to God. For the unfallen, work is "assigned . . . not strictly impos'd": "For not to irksom toile, but to delight / He made us, and delight to Reason joyn'd . . ." (IX, 242-43). The Son's judgment on Adam after the Fall does not alter the nature of work for fallen men, although it contains the prophecy, "In the sweat of thy Face shalt thou eate Bread." Adam himself sees that, even for the fallen, work is the benevolent gift of God:

> with labour I must earne
> My bread; what harm? Idleness had bin worse;
> My labour will sustain me.
>
> (X, 1054-56)

Samson at the outset of the play conceives of his work as meaningless, "the labour of a Beast, debas't / Lower then bondslave," but comes to see it in just the light in which Adam sees his, "labour / Honest and lawful to deserve my food / Of those who have me in thir civil power."

---

[22] *Ibid.*, 160, 163-64.

[23] For a parallel discussion of the general election of all men see Muldrow, *Milton and the Drama of the Soul*, 246-47.

That kind of work, the labor of sustaining life, is morally neutral and merely human. God is not a stern taskmaster with respect to such work; "God does not need man's work," but man does.

For fallen man the crucial question is whether a particular kind of work achieves his salvation. Milton's answer, as might be anticipated, is both unequivocal and dynamic. Man is saved by faith *and* works, that is, by works of faith, not works of the Law. "Faith has its own works," he wrote in *De Doctrina Christiana*, "which may be different from the works of the law. We are justified then, by faith, but a living faith, not a dead one, and the only living faith is a faith which acts. So we are justified by faith without the works of the law, but not without the works of faith; for a true and living faith cannot exist without works, though these may be different from the works of the written law."[24] Again, Milton's view that the addition of "deeds answerable" to man's understanding is necessary to salvation is a strictly orthodox English Puritan view.[25] But Milton understood man's mortality as proving the existence of a time continuum during which examples proliferate of manly or godlike behavior on the part of those whose death is the gate of life for themselves and whose deeds live on for others "equal in fame to proudest Conquerours." Ethics mature during the dynamic process of history, in Milton's view, although history does not enact a clear progress toward earthly regeneration. Job's friends assert a static God giving static laws according to which He judges man in an immutable fashion—for every eye an eye, for every tooth a tooth, to every good man riches and joy, to every bad man rags and shame. How can you know a good man? Look at how well he makes out.

Milton argued an unfolding revelation. God at first gave to His chosen people the gift of the Mosaic Law. It was a gift indicating God's will that man should be saved. Inadequate of itself to save men, it was nonetheless a step in the salvific, educative course of time, setting forth, as to children, an ideal of behavior, prohibiting evil, and suggesting the potential growth of goodness in time. It was a gift also exactly displaying the need among mortal men for intercessors or help. Who could obey it and be perfect on his own account? The case of Samson fallen is a case in point: given the simplest task (smiting Philistines), the greatest ability (immeasurable strength), the strongest protection (God's own promise), and the firmest guidance (the

[24] *CPW*, VI, 490. See *Paradise Lost*, XI, 63-64, "refin'd / By faith and faithful works," and XII, 426-27, "and the benefit imbrace / By Faith not void of workes."
[25] See Patrides, *Milton and the Christian Tradition*, 188, and E. G. Rupp, *Studies in the Making of the English Protestant Tradition* (Cambridge: Cambridge University Press, 1947), chap. 8.

Nazarite code), Samson nevertheless was unable to govern his passionate nature by the Law. His failure illustrates the inadequacy of legalism. His total stripping down to mere mortal mind and heart by means of the good temptations prefigures the removal of the Mosaic Law and its formalistic grip. Samson's faith in a God capable of converting his errors into goodness, which Samson reveres, is renewed and reformed during his triple testing. He becomes then the benevolent example for which Milton chose him, a hero of faith, a man of good works extending understanding beyond Mosaic legalism. In conceiving of the progressive stages of the revelation of God's will in human history, Milton was orthodox. His view, however, that the entire law, including every particle of Mosaic Law, had been abrogated to be replaced by free deeds of faith is not an orthodox view, and to that we shall return.

Good works, then, are those free deeds of man undertaken "through true faith, to God's glory, the certain hope of our own salvation, and the instruction of our neighbor."[26] They have a double aspect, cognitive and conative, known and willed. The doing of good works is itself a dynamic matter: man is "refin'd / By . . . faithful works." The refinement extends from understanding to willing. The "deeds of peace, by wisdom eminent, / By patience, temperance" manifested by the Son in *Paradise Regained* are presented as deeds "to the utmost of meer man both wise and good" for 1,971 lines of the poem. Then, swiftly, in 99 lines they are shown to derive from a nature greater than that of "meer man," from one who is

> True Image of the Father whether thron'd
> In the bosom of bliss, and light of light
> Conceiving, or remote from Heaven, enshrin'd
> In fleshly Tabernacle, and human form,
> Wandring the Wilderness, whatever place,
> Habit, or state, or motion, still expressing
> The Son of God, with Godlike force indu'd. . . .
>
> (IV, 597-603)

Paradise Regained dramatizes both the understanding and the willing of both human and divine works. The role of the Son is to achieve self-knowledge in relation to a conception of God and to act in conformity to that knowledge. The Son does not begin the process of self-discovery from a position of false understanding and progress toward true knowledge, although Milton reserves for a climactic position in Book IV the fullest articulation of his wisdom. From the commence-

---

[26] *CPW*, VI, 638.

ment of his manhood, the Son conceived himself "Born to promote all truth," not by promulgating or endorsing a system of distributive-retributive justice, but "By winning words [to] conquer willing hearts." He, to be sure, had loved the Law as revealing a good and mighty God, but he had no conception of God as stern taskmaster such as Job had, who sacramentally propitiated Him by "burnt offerings" on behalf of his children, just in case they might perchance have secretly sinned in their hearts.[27]

Although Milton concedes that Job was "righteous" and the "most modest and patient of men," the element of concession in his descriptions of Job is marked in *De Doctrina Christiana*. Job may be perfect but his perfection is emergent, and in Milton's view he is not free from "the sin which each man commits on his own account, quite apart from that sin which is common to all." To the axiom "All men commit sin of this kind," Milton appended two proof texts from Job.[28] Job is subject to death and requires a mediator and redeemer.[29] He must pass through penitence to faith, and in that course his sufferings are instrumental, despite the blame attached to those who simply assert that his afflictions are punishments for secret sins.[30] Although Job is certain of his own inner sincerity, which Milton also called "integrity and good conscience," and although he has hope and confidence, he is tempted to commit the sin of "impatience towards God, a sin which even the saints are sometimes tempted to commit." He makes rash curses: "The godly themselves sometimes fall in this way."[31] His "standards of personal or sexual conduct" are the strictest and he is discriminating about the civilized refinements of life, but he is "too indignant [which] is not praiseworthy," although there is no flaw attached to his "complaints or lamentations."[32] Job need not repent of his deeds, need not confess to secret sins, need not surrender his probity; but he will profoundly repent his failure to know God rightly. His remorse will arise from his inability to free himself from an inadequate inherited theology and see his God, as it were, face to face. The case of Job resembles the case of the Son in that good temptations lead both of them to enriched understanding; the case of Job resembles the case of Samson in that among the forms of wisdom each is to attain are a true understanding of God's ways and a true faith from

---

[27] The Authorized Version reads, "It may be that my sons have sinned, and cursed God in their hearts. Thus did Job continually." See Kahn, *Job's Illness*, 18ff., for an analysis of the obsessional neurosis which he considers the perfectionist Job to display at this stage in his growth and development.

[28] *CPW*, vi, 388.

[29] *Ibid.*, 399, 401, 404, 407, 418.

[30] *Ibid.*, 469, 470.

[31] *Ibid.*, 652-53, 659, 663, 677.

[32] *Ibid.*, 727, 736, 749.

which good works will spring. The case of Job shows the attainment of the highest wisdom under conditions that try the human heart with maximum severity; throughout Job's afflictions his virtue remains constant, while his understanding increases. Job's case is not the same as Samson's, but both were seen by Milton as examples of moral perplexity, the sufferer brought to the verge of despair, followed by moral recovery. Job's case is a different sort of rehabilitative case than that of Samson, but it is a rehabilitative case nonetheless.

On the other hand, Christ's understanding in *Paradise Regained* is free from an aprioristic bias at the very commencement of the action, when he quietly accepts the limitations of his imperfect knowledge and relies on God's prompting:

> And now by some strong motion I am led
> Into this wilderness, to what intent
> I learn not yet, perhaps I need not know;
> For what concerns my knowledge God reveals.
>
> (I, 290-93)

In the course of the brief epic the Son comes to know more of both God and himself; he passes from creative trust and confidence to wisdom. One might instance first his discovery that truth descends from God and resides "In pious Hearts, an inward Oracle / To all truth requisite for men to know" (I, 463-64), and his strictly turning his meditations toward his own task rather than giving them free rein; he

> Into himself descended, and at once
> All his great work to come before him set;
> How to begin, how to accomplish best
> His end of being on Earth, and mission high. . . .
>
> (II, 111-14)

His next perception is that prosperity is not the mark of the goodness of an action. He rebukes Satan for offering him riches and asserts the inner basis of virtuous deeds. Their formal cause is self-government, and they involve the magnanimous help of others:

> For therein stands the office of a King,
> His Honour, Vertue, Merit and chief Praise,
> That for the Publick all this weight he bears.
> Yet he who reigns within himself, and rules
> Passions, Desires and Fears, is more a King;
> Which every wise and vertuous man attains. . . .
> But to guide Nations in the way of truth

> By saving Doctrine, and from errour lead
> To know, and knowing worship God aright,
> Is yet more Kingly, this attracts the Soul,
> Governs the inner man, the nobler part. . . .
> Besides to give a Kingdom hath been thought
> Greater and nobler done, and to lay down
> Far more magnanimous, then to assume.
>
> (II, 463-83)

Thus the Son not only divides good works into the virtues of the understanding and of the will, he also shapes his points about the dichotomy of duties owed to one's self and duties owed to others. These distinctions are incorporated in the scheme of *De Doctrina Christiana*.[33] Subsequently the Son comes to understand and to define the qualities of "the just man," extolling Job's patience and Socrates' sacrifice as acts undertaken to advance truth or God's glory and not their own.[34] But the Son's crowning ethical insight comes in distinguishing true from false understanding and in rejecting inadequate learning:

> Alas what can they teach, and not mislead;
> Ignorant of themselves, of God much more,
> And how the world began, and how man fell
> Degraded by himself, on grace depending?
> Much of the Soul they talk, but all awrie,
> And in themselves seek vertue, and to themselves
> All glory arrogate, to God give none,
> Rather accuse him under usual names,
> Fortune and Fate, as one regardless quite
> Of mortal things.
>
> (IV, 309-18)

True wisdom, "the virtue by which we earnestly search out God's will, cling to it with all diligence once we have understood it, and govern all our actions by its rule,"[35] Milton defined both here and in *De Doctrina Christiana* in opposition to inadequate, false wisdom or folly. He retranslated the *De Doctrina* proof text from Job as "he makes the cogitations of clever men ineffectual," rather than giving the words which the King James Version translates as "he disappointeth the devices of the crafty."[36]

[33] See Appendix C, II.A.1 and 2 and II.B.2.(A), especially i(a); and (B), especially i(a) and (b).
[34] *Paradise Regained*, III, 60-145.
[35] *CPW*, VI, 649.
[36] *Ibid.*, 650. See H. F. Fletcher, *The Use of the Bible in Milton's Prose*, Uni-

Enough has been said to make clear the role of good temptations in *Paradise Regained* as enabling the Son to measure virtue in terms of increased understanding. The brief epic presents the progressive example of widening and deepening understanding, achieved by the one perfect man in his role as "meer man"; its purpose is to show in a sequence of selected incidents the model of meaningfulness in human behavior. At each stage, understanding precedes volition, but the Son then chooses to act in response to his deepening wisdom. The actions of the Son are vicariously undertaken for all men, and the poet narrates them so that all men may understand them and imitate them, having vicariously shared in them. The development of the Son is depicted at a critical stage in his growth; his interpretation of his experience communicates his values to Milton's readers as the poem develops. At the close of the poem the Son is ready to undertake a role to be his alone, the intercessory role which gives restorative grace to fallen men. But the process of the drama has communicated the pattern of existence which Milton considers most fully appropriate or adaptive to the conditions of human life. The Son gives grace to man to live under the guidance of the pattern of behavior which produced that grace.

Samson Agonistes traces a complementary course of communication, and the life chosen for dramatization on the ethical level is a life which retrieves morality in the teeth of tragedy. Again, the Book of Job is helpful in understanding Milton's procedure. The truths Samson learns, the constructions Samson gradually places on the meaning of his experience, are interpretations which the reader shares and whereby he is enlightened. Samson's values change as his interpretation of his sufferings change, and the reader participates in that change. But similarly, what Samson discovers about the scope of his experience, what he learns about his own freedom, alters the volitional possibilities in his life crisis. So long, that is, as he tells himself that the meaning of his life is to be deservedly punished and humiliated, he can only lie quite still under the punishment and wish for its termination by death. When he can tell himself that the meaning of his life is to grow toward knowledge of God, he can will attentiveness to deeper levels of his own being in which his God speaks to him. A more profound faith will then emerge in action. The reader likewise experiences Samson's restoration to liberty. The development of understanding and will in Samson sets patterns of interpretation before the reader. Good tempta-

---

versity of Illinois Studies in Language and Literature, 14 (Urbana: University of Illinois Press, 1929), 64-65, 76-77, for a discussion of Milton's variants in citing the Junius-Tremellius Bible.

tions conduce, within the fabric of Milton's design, to increased knowledge of God and man and to increased scope for virtuous action in the light of that knowledge. The torments of Samson give him further chances to make a true adaptation to his destiny and to fulfill the work for which he was ordained. His life thus becomes exemplary of the acquisition of true knowledge—and that is the work for which he was ordained quite as much as the labor through his strength.

Knowing and Teaching

We are now in a position to take up the stories of Samson and Job where we left Samson last. Samson has made several critically important steps toward understanding the origins of his weakness and failure but has retreated rather than advanced with respect to understanding his God. Dalila's visit came in answer to the Chorus's prayer to "turn his labours . . . to peaceful end" and was a blessing to Samson, but he slumped back into conceiving of it as a punishment, a shame and debasement inflicted on him by a retributive God. His God does not seem to him the creative source of all being but the contemptuous judge of stupid servants. Earlier Samson had prophesied, "all the contest is now / 'Twixt God and *Dagon*. . . . He . . . will arise and his great name assert." That great name was indifferent to Samson himself; but the great name of God at the close of Samson's encounter with Harapha bears a further meaning. His God remains all-powerful, but He is as well the giver of everything good, "who gave me / At my Nativity this strength," and the source of mercy as well as power, "Whose ear is ever open; and his eye / Gracious to re-admit the suppliant." The very fact that Samson speaks out of his sense of a punitive, judgmental God gives him a further chance to examine that view and to discard it: a man cannot replace a false doctrine with a true doctrine without having come to full awareness of the false doctrine. Some men seem to need second or third chances. Our theme now in taking up the stories of Samson and Job is the augmenting of Christian liberty, which comes from freeing oneself from the constraints of false orthodoxy.

Job and Samson alike enjoyed prosperity, power, and felicity, lost them all, and were reduced to despair. Alike they were brought so low as to be unrecognizable to their friends.[37] Job's friends, like the Chorus of Samson's friends, came to share in his sufferings and offer assuage-

---

[37] Book of Job: "Now when Job's three friends heard of all this evil that was come upon him, they everyone came from his own place to mourn with him and comfort him"; *Samson Agonistes*: "We come . . . To visit or bewail thee, or if better, / Counsel or Consolation we may bring."

ment.[38] Milton described Job's comforters in *Of True Religion, Heresy, Schism, Toleration*:

> It is a human frailty to err, and no man is infallible here on earth. But so long as all those profess to set the word of God only before them as the rule of faith and obedience; and use all diligence and sincerity of heart, by reading, by learning, by study, by prayer for illumination of the Holy Spirit, to understand the rule and obey it, they have done what man can do; God will assuredly pardon them, as he did the friends of Job; good and pious men, though much mistaken, as there it appears, in some points of doctrine.

Milton's reading of Job is strikingly subtle and does not make simple scapegoats of the friends. He sees that they mingle with their flatly orthodox "implicit faith" many words of truth but much mistaken doctrine. Milton's use of Jobean proof texts in Book I of *De Doctrina Christiana* winnows from legalistic faith such of their words as reveal God as creator and preserver. The triple confrontation between Job and his friends in which the friends with increasing asperity defend their inherited orthodoxy, their "mistaken . . . doctrine," forces Job to voice with increasing explicitness his own experiences. His presuppositions about the nature and acts of God at the outset do not differ from those of his friends. He too believes that God is to be served by precisely defined external acts, by scrupulous observance of stated laws and rites; he too believes that such service brings God's favor in its turn. It is the shock of experiencing severe torment inconsistent with his own sense of personal scrupulousness which forces from Job the despairing outcries in the first cycle of exchange with his friends. Because God "destroyeth the perfect and the wicked," Job cannot be patient; he cries out for death as the only surcease for moral and physical torment:

> O that I might have my request
> And that God would grant me the thing that I long for!
> Even that it would please God to destroy me.
> What is my strength that I should hope
> And what is my end that I should prolong my life.

His expressed despair recalls Samson's:

[38] Book of Job: "And when they lifted up their eyes afar off, and knew him not, they lifted up their voices and wept"; *Samson Agonistes*: "O change beyond report. . . . Can this be hee?"

His pardon I implore, but as for life,
To what end should I seek it? . . .
Hopeless are all my evils, all remediless;
This one prayer yet remains, might I be heard,
No long petition, speedy death,
The close of all my miseries, and the balm.[39]

The function of the Book of Job as Milton read it was to shatter the "mistaken . . . doctrine" or false orthodoxy of its protagonist without shattering his faith, that is, to replace his inherited theology or implicit faith with an understanding and truer faith that can equip him for the realities of mortal life. The form of the new understanding comprises both a redefinition of himself and a redefinition of God.

It is not possible to sustain human life in the absence of a sense of the purposive. So intrinsic to stability is the purposive that even a negative definition will be brought into service when no positive is available; the truly violent man, the Tamburlaine, will construct a self-definition from his very nihilism and call himself the "scourge of God." Job, under the pressure of redefining his central being to restore a meaning to his existence, resorts to a negative stance and considers himself the "butt and . . . target of God," "a byword in every land, a portent," "one of his enemies." He defines himself not, as formerly, as the blessed servant of God; he sees himself as the special case of the tortured victim. The comforters would make the victim into the villain: were Job truly righteous he could not suffer. Job considers things rather differently with respect to himself, but perfectly similarly with respect to God. He had assumed that he was entitled by his righteousness not to suffer; God owed him prosperity in return for his integrity. For many years he did enjoy God's favor and thought he had earned it by paying the price of his probity. When his probity did not decrease but God's favor was withdrawn, he was indignant and challenged God's justice. But he challenged it from a believer's stance. His uprightness exacted from him continued belief in God's power and presence, and at no point would he call that in question. Rather, he took the line that the universe is God's but that it is unfairly run and God is too arbitrary and "high" to answer his challenges.

---

[39] See Roston, *Biblical Drama in England*, 164-73, for the suggestion that the parallels which can be noted between Samson and Job are rooted in an autobiographical identification Milton made with both, a not unreasonable suggestion, and that the grounds of the identification are too severe punishment for a profaned vocation, a vocation profaned by Milton's sexuality, a less than comprehensive suggestion.

When in the prose prologue to the book his wife required human consistency of him and declared that the evils visited upon him made but one course intelligible, "Curse God and die," his reply was, "Thou speaketh as one of the foolish women speaketh. What? shall we receive good at the hands of God, and shall we not receive evil?"[40] Job *knew* in some half-conscious sense at the outset what he was to *learn* in the course of the book—that both his sense of justice and his grasp on reality were not self-generated, were not his own possessions, that he was not his own creator, that his virtue was not virtue for the purpose of controlling his destiny but virtue with respect to his understanding of God or truth. "In all this Job did not sin with his lips."

The course toward taking conscious possession of a true knowledge of God begins with Job's lament and incorporates his bitterest question, "Why should the sufferer be born to see the light? Why is life given to men who find it so bitter?"[41] Job's first cycle of speeches dwells on his mere mortality and his sense of the impossibility that his situation should change: "O remember that my life is wind: Mine eye shall no more see good. . . . As the cloud is consumed and vanisheth away: So he that goeth down to the grave shall come up no more." His question, "What is man, that thou shouldest magnify him? And that thou shouldest set thine heart upon him? And that thou shouldest visit him every morning, and try him every moment," is the question of the first choral stasimon in *Samson Agonistes*; his conclusion is likewise their conclusion. In the first cycle Job's expression of grief contains the hopelessness of one who cannot get a fair hearing from God, "For he is not a man as I am, that I should answer him, And we should come together in judgment. Neither is there any daysman betwixt us, That might lay his hand upon us both." These definitive statements are eventually to be challenged by Job himself; he is to learn that the progression of time encompassing personal mortal life constitutes a form of immortality; he is to learn that a beneficent intercessor exists; he is to perceive that the desire for justice and wisdom in himself is

[40] New English Bible: "Then his wife said to him, 'Are you still unshaken in your integrity? Curse God and die!' But he answered, 'You talk as any wicked fool of a woman might talk. If we accept good from God, shall we not accept evil?' Throughout all this Job did not utter one sinful word." See Richards, *Beyond*, 56, 64-65, for the possible ambiguities in the final phrase. Richards presses (70-75) the reading which makes Job a rebel ironist to the bitter end and God a bully. In Richards's view the moral superiority of Job to God is self-evident and he does not take up the possibility that Job may have got God wrong.

[41] See *Samson Agonistes*: "Thus exil'd from light; / As in the land of darkness yet in light, / To live a life half dead, a living death, / And buried." Job, Authorized Version: "Wherefore is light given to him that is in misery, / And life unto the bitter in soul."

not his merit but God's creation. In the meantime, however, the despair in the second cycle of speeches is even more intense than in the first, for the comforters presume to undertake God's judgmental role. Job is alone without a defender: "If only there were one to arbitrate between man and God, as between a man and his neighbor! For there are but few years to come before I take the road from which I shall not return. . . . Be thou my surety with thyself, for who else can pledge himself for me?"[42] The only comfort he now asks of his friends is their silence while he opposes their contention that experience must teach the one simple truth that in life the wicked are punished and the righteous prosper, the only possible satisfactory arrangement in justice.[43] Job concludes this cycle with, "One man, I tell you, dies crowned with success, lapped in security and comfort, his loins full of vigour and the marrow juicy in his bones; another dies in bitterness of soul and never tastes prosperity; side by side they are laid in the earth, and worms are the shroud of both." The third cycle resumes after an interval of time—"Even today is my complaint bitter"—and with a consciousness of time and change, before and after, having entered Job's awareness, "O that I were as in months past."[44] Job's burden remains God's refusal to hear him and answer his case: "Behold, my desire is, that the Almighty would answer me." But in the very final statement of his case appear new and significant additions to his descriptions of himself and of God. He continues to assert his integrity, but he confesses now to a relative ignorance:

> Where then does wisdom come from, and where is the source
>   of understanding?
> No creature on earth can see it. . . .
> But God understands the way to it, he alone knows its source;
> For he can see to the ends of the earth and he surveys
>   everything under heaven.
> When he made a counterpoise for the wind and measured out
>   the waters in proportion,
> When he laid down a limit for the rain and a path for the
>   thunderstorm,
> Even then he saw wisdom and took stock of it,

---

[42] King James Version: "O that one might plead for a man with God, As a man pleadeth for his neighbor: When a few years are come, Then I shall go the way whence I shall not return. . . . Lay down now, put me in a surety with thee; who is he that will strike hands with me."

[43] See Kahn, *Job's Illness*, 62-90, for a description of the interaction between Job and his friends presented with striking effectiveness both in dramatic and psychoanalytic terms.

[44] A point made also by Kahn.

He considered it and fathomed its very depths,
And he said to man: The fear of the Lord is wisdom, and to
turn from evil is understanding.

This time, moreover, Job extols virtue while extolling himself for the practice of it and thereby does not so much justify himself as praise goodness. And he affiliates himself with other men: "Did not he who made me in the womb make them? Did not the same God create us in the belly?" These changes set the stage for the crucial intervention of Elihu.

Elihu, in a sense, functions in the Book of Job as the unacknowledged intercessor between Job and God for whom Job has longed, although in a form he could not imagine. But Elihu is also a symbol of the future possibilities of clearer and clearer revelation of God in the universe. He is not fettered by the false doctrine of Job and his comforters. He understands God differently, and the source of his understanding is his inner conviction that "The spirit of God himself is in man, and the breath of the Almighty gives him understanding." Because the very truth and desire for justice in man comes from God, Elihu can speak with God-prompted authority: "My heart assures me that I speak with knowledge, and that my lips speak with sincerity. For the spirit of God made me, and the breath of the Almighty gave me life." But Elihu does not separate himself from Job and the comforters because of his inner light, he does not take the position of a perfect man speaking to an older, ignorant generation (although he makes a considerable point of his youth enabling new truths to be received). Rather, he joins himself in his mortality to Job and the comforters, to group himself with them in a common state: "In God's sight I am just what you are. I too am only a handful of clay." As intercessor he does not defend Job's perfection, but God's. He dismisses Job's ground for complaint. God rules the entire universe with creative goodness; He is Himself neither bettered nor worsened by man's deeds. The effects of human behavior are felt by human beings and establish no claim upon God. "All alike are God's creatures. . . . How does it touch him if you have sinned? However many your misdeeds, what does it mean to him? If you do right, what good do you bring him, or what does he gain from you? Your wickedness touches only men, such as you are; the right that you do affects none but mortal man." Job cannot, therefore, bargain with God and secure his fate by perfectionist observances. But that does not mean that all human deeds are indifferent in God's eyes.

Elihu turns to the implicit question in all Job's demands: what consolation can there be for the mystery of iniquity and why does God employ the means He does to govern his universe? Elihu answers with a double answer. There can be no doubt that God protects the chastened man, speaks to him in dream, in vision, gives regard to disciplining him, allows to him "a messenger, an interpreter, one among a thousand . . . a ransom": "those who suffer he rescues through suffering and teaches them by the discipline of affliction." In the torment of Job lies the possibility of more intelligent belief and renewed growth. The sense of painful but creative change is Elihu's first answer. His second is the comprehensiveness of God's providence, so great that it is not to be marred by man any more than understood by him. God is the guarantor of good, not man; there can be no ultimate destruction of His design by human agents, for that design can include their anger and their protest. In the confidence of God's inclusive eternal design, Job's anger must abate. If Job will consider the creativity of God manifested in the natural world, then he will see suffering and anger contained and converted to universal, energetic good.

The book closes speedily upon God's own words, which contain a description of Creation revealing His power to regulate the universe and a demand made to Job to "stand up like a man." Job's responsibility is for reverent good deeds arising from a true conception of God—not of a bargaining God, not of a limited God who cannot control His creation save by rewarding human agents to do it for Him, not of an indifferent God, but of a progressively self-revealing God. Purpose is restored to Job, assuagement of grief, freedom from ritual obligatory observances and his fearful maneuvers to regulate the whole of creation. Job has a place in the universe. He knows himself and knows how much he can know of God. The prose epilogue describes him as acting once more in his better knowledge and stronger faith: the good deeds he undertakes are an intercession on behalf of his comforters and a resumption of his former patriarchal roles. He has not been, as it were, justified by his good deeds: the impotence of deeds of law to save has been amply shown him. But he has been justified by his understanding or faith and by his motives or humility when they issue into action. The book has depicted a trial of virtue as an aspect first of knowledge and then of volition. Job's new faith acknowledges his ignorance and former belligerence and asserts God's governance:

> I know that thou canst do every thing,
> And that no thought can be withholden from thee,
> Who is he that hideth counsel without knowledge?
> Therefore have I uttered that I understood not,

Things too wonderful for me, which I knew not.
Hear, I beseech thee, and I will speak:
I will demand of thee, and declare thou unto me.
I have heard of thee by the hearing of the ear;
But now mine eye seeth thee:
Wherefore I abhor myself, and repent in dust and ashes.

Milton cited this passage in *De Doctrina Christiana* to describe God's omnipotence.[45] But attendant upon Job's new faith, which contains remorse and patience, is new action. Job prays for his friends that they be excused their erroneous traditional orthodoxy, and he treats their reestablishment of friendship with generosity and magnanimity. Milton cited this passage to illustrate high-mindedness.[46] Only then, when understanding is converted into deeds, is Job freed and restored: "And the Lord turned the captivity of Job, when he prayed for his friends." Job is freed from captivity by a progressive revelation which he not only receives but, by the dramatic communication of the book, transmits.

De Doctrina Christiana supplies evidence of what Milton thought the Book of Job meant. In Book I Milton used Jobean texts to describe the nature and attributes of God. The tractate opens with the axiom, "God has left so many signs of himself in the human mind, so many traces of his presence through the whole of nature, that no sane person can fail to realise he exists." That axiom is "proved" by Job's concluding speech in the first cycle, "Who does not know from all these things."[47] Significantly, Milton's first source of the knowledge of God is the signs of His presence in the human mind itself. That is the crucial discovery Samson makes in his encounter with Harapha, the discovery which both constitutes and enables his regeneration. Milton continues by establishing God's infinity, eternity, omnipotence, purity, and holiness, all from Jobean citations freely drawn from all the speakers in the poem.[48] He next turned to Jobean texts to establish God's use of the Son to make all things and then to define creation.[49] Milton then concerned himself with the narration of the Creation in the Book of Job, the creation not simply of the world and its individual parts—which he nonetheless considered to be "narrated in Genesis and described in Job and in various passages of the Psalms and Prophets"[50] —but the creation of man. Of man, Milton wrote:

We may . . . be absolutely sure . . . that when God breathed that breath of life into man, he did not make him a sharer in anything divine, any

---

[45] *CPW*, VI, 145. [46] *Ibid.*, 735. [47] *Ibid.*, 130.
[48] *Ibid.*, 143, 145, 149, 150. [49] *Ibid.*, 282, 300, 304. [50] *Ibid.*, 315-16.

part of the divine essence, as it were. He imparted to him only some-
thing human which was proportionate to divine virtue. . . . Man is a
living being, intrinsically and properly one and individual. He is not
double or separable; not, as is commonly thought, produced from and
composed of two different and distinct elements, soul and body. On
the contrary, the whole man is the soul, and the soul the man: a body,
in other words, or individual substance, animated, sensitive and ra-
tional.

Samson shares this view and knows its truth at the outset of the poem,
albeit he is tentative in its expression:

> if it be true
> That light is in the Soul,
> *She all in every part.* . . .
>
> (91-93; emphasis added)

The position is important not simply as it distinguishes Milton's doc-
trinal view from that of the Calvinists (who divided body from soul
and considered the soul to lodge in the body as a guest in a house of
clay), or as it leads logically to his materialism and mortalism, but as
it sets the limits to humanity by actually defining a mortal and distinc-
tive individual being whose rationality permits a possible education.
Milton grounds his ethics on this basis.

God, having created this sort of man and not another sort, provi-
dentially "preserves [him in common with] all created things, and
governs them with supreme wisdom and holiness, according to the
conditions of his decree." This axiom Milton likewise "proves" from
Job, as he proves as well the contingency in God's decrees which is
benevolently husbanded by good temptations.[51] God's providence has
reference to the nature of man and the contingent processes of time.
From citing Job in order to establish a true understanding of God,
Milton next moves to citing Job to expound human virtue. He makes
the transition by way of a word about progressive understanding with-
in the individual by which fuller truth and ampler virtue emerges:
"There are striking exhortations to penitence in Job. But all exhorta-
tion would be pointless unless it were addressed to men in whom reno-
vation, at any rate of the natural kind, had to some extent, taken place,
to men, that is, gifted with some powers of judgment and with free
will."[52] Clearly then, Milton read the Book of Job as declaring truths
about the nature of God which in their effects upon men could lead to
growth in virtue.

[51] *Ibid.*, 300, 300n., 327, 328, 329.　　[52] *Ibid.*, 459.

While Milton interpreted the Book of Job as turning upon Job's discovery of his capacity, given by God, to receive God ("gifted with some powers of judgment"), he granted that Job already possessed a good will or conative virtues. Yet Job's good works cannot be of value even as works of faith while they arise from a defective understanding. Good works issue not only from "general virtues which are the properties of the intellect," they arise as well from "those which are properties of the will"—"sincerity, promptitude and constancy." The case of Job is that of the man of "integrity" and "good conscience," which means "pursuing a single good course of action with a sincere and heartfelt desire and sense of purpose." Concessive though Milton was about Job's imperfections, he was not in doubt about his sincerity. The chapter in *De Doctrina Christiana* setting forth the nature of conative virtues are among the most carefully revised of all the chapters, and its final formulation was one of the latest of Milton's additions to the text. Milton was thinking profoundly about the meaning of the Book of Job, that is, at a period after the Restoration. His consideration of that book issued into the double ethical insights of *Paradise Regained* and *Samson Agonistes*.

THE ETHICS OF GOOD WORKS AND THE
TRAGEDY OF EDUCATIVE SUFFERING

THERE is a likeness between the stories of Job and of Samson. For each, the events narrated lead toward full moral awareness; their acts scarcely change. Job interceded with God on behalf of his sons at the opening of the book, and on behalf of his friends at the close. Samson recalled his deeds of prowess and the promise of more at the opening of the tragedy; he executed his final valiant deed to end Act IV. The deeds do not change but their significance does. Job and Samson alike no longer obey the law; they obey the spirit. In this, by the orthodoxy of Milton's times, they prefigure the gift of Christian liberty and are types of the man of faith. Of Christian liberty, Milton wrote, "it means that Christ our liberator frees us from the slavery of sin and thus from the rule of the law, and of men, as if we were emancipated slaves. He does this so that, being made sons instead of servants and grown men instead of boys, we may serve God in charity through the guidance of the spirit of truth."[1] Implicit faith or false doctrine is replaced by true understanding.

> So it is conformity with faith, not with the ten commandments, which must be considered as the form of good works. . . . It is faith that justifies, not compliance with the commandments; and only that which justifies can make any work good. It follows that no work of ours can be good except through faith. . . . Thus we ought to consider the form of good works to be conformity not with the written but with the unwritten law, that is, with the law of the Spirit which the Father has given us to lead us into truth.[2]

And finally, although the external law has been abrogated altogether by Christian liberty in favor of an inward law, in Milton's view "The substance of the law, love of God and of our neighbours, should not, I repeat, be thought of as destroyed. We must realise that only the written surface has been changed, and that the law is now inscribed on believers' hearts by the spirit."[3]

[1] *CPW*, VI, 537.   [2] *Ibid.*, 639-40.   [3] *Ibid.*, 532.

In light of these insights Milton defined the relationship between freedom and obedience, or liberty and service, and showed that Samson learns like Job to obey the God whom he has learned to understand. "Obedience is the virtue which makes us determine to do God's will above all things and to serve him"; yet "What obeys reason is free."[4] Samson's behavior at the close of the play is unconstrained and free because it arises from his most rational inner prompting. We have already seen Samson repudiate human laws which contravene their purposes, specifically, in his rejection of the laws of nations when those nations violate "the ends / For which our countrey is a name so dear." We have seen him repudiate so-called divine laws emanating from ungodly gods, "Less therefore to be pleas'd, obey'd, or fear'd." Samson's discovery of God's mercy enables him to take a further step when the Officer of the Philistines commands his presence at the temple of Dagon. At first he simply refuses on the grounds of his Nazarite vows: God's "Law forbids at thir Religious Rites / My presence; for that cause I cannot come." But the Law is significant not for itself but as declaring God's will to save and govern men. The truer law is that written in the heart of the believer, known to him by "rouzing motions," such as that by which Samson is freed from the Law to obey the spirit of God in him. His inner impulses are the test of his deeds. His second refusal to perform for the Philistines takes account of his inner freedom:

> the *Philistian* Lords command.
> Commands are no constraints. If I obey them,
> I do it freely; venturing to displease
> God for the fear of Man, and Man prefer,
> Set God behind: which in his jealousie
> Shall never, unrepented, find forgiveness.
> Yet that he may dispense with me or thee
> Present in Temples at Idolatrous Rites
> For some important cause, thou needst not doubt.
>
> (1371-79)

Samson is not freed to disobey God, for that, unrepented, is unforgivable, but he is freed from obedience to edicts thought to be emanating from God. He is free to obey only the substance of truth, not the orthodox formulae. Like the consonance of freedom and obedience is the consonance of liberty and service. Samson is brought into the temple of Dagon ostensibly "as a public servant . . . In thir state Livery clad"; he leaves that temple set free by "death who sets all free" to be brought "Home to his Fathers house" as a "faithful Champion," hav-

[4] *Ibid.*, 663.

ing been instructive to all God's "servants . . . with new acquist / Of true experience."

In contrast to free obedience and free service are the concepts of servitude and servility, from which man seeks a deliverer and deliverance. Samson repudiates the view that corporal servitude has broken his spirit:

> Can they think me so broken, so debas'd
> With corporal servitude, that my mind ever
> Will condescend to such absurd commands?
>
> (1335-37)

His countrymen's "servile minds" had not received him as "their Deliverer"; from his own "servil mind" he had fallen into well-earned "servil punishment." He had seen, however, that even this servile punishment was less a servitude than his bond-slavery to his own passions of pride and lust. The course of the drama has brought him to deliverance from servitude of mind. His course is instructive to all, for "each [is] his own Deliverer" who rightly understands his God and practices patience. Neither captive nor slave in mind or will, Samson then "perform'd, as reason was, obeying" the commands of the Philistines. He did so with an inner consciousness of his freedom from outward laws; that is, he knew that there is no particular sanctity in place, no miraculous defilement that could stain him. Having outwardly "obeyed," Samson obeyed his inner imperatives and undertook "of my own accord such other tryal . . . of my strength, yet greater," pulling down "the same destruction" on himself as on his foes (who, by a compassionate interpolation of Milton into the more sweeping Judges text, numbered only the Philistine leaders, "The vulgar . . . scap'd who stood without"). Samson's deliverance of himself fulfills all the conditions of good works. Of it the Chorus says:

> O dearly-bought revenge, yet glorious!
> Living or dying thou has fulfill'd
> The work for which thou wast foretold
> To *Israel*, and now ly'st victorious
> Amongst thy slain self-kill'd
> Not willingly. . . .
>
> (1660-65)

The work was Samson's deed of faith; its value lay in his understanding of his God and his willing not of his own death but of God's glory.

Recalling Milton's definition of good works—"Good works are those which we do when the spirit of God works within us, through true faith, to God's glory, the certain hope of our salvation, and the instruction of our neighbor"[5]—it remains only to speak very briefly of "the instruction of our neighbor," "for a good example leads in good men, to an imitation of that example." The conclusion of *Samson Agonistes* consists of the meditations of Manoa and the Chorus on the significance of Samson's life. This is their effort to make a correct application of Samson's example. Samson's work was not only the deed foretold but the example of the process culminating in that deed. All the visitants to Samson concerned themselves with what Samson should make of his experience. The Chorus proposed him as "the rarer example" of the fickle state of man; Samson thought himself one of the "roul" of "examples" of rejected national deliverers; Manoa thought him the example of "thy Foes derision . . . who now no more canst do them harm"; Dalila found in him "th' example" of weakness who "shewdst . . . the way" to her own weakness; the Philistine Officer wished him to show "public proof" of his mighty strength. In the kommos the Chorus and Manoa make a final attempt to express the illustrative value of Samson's newly completed deed. Their impulse is to validate his ethical significance and to make a moral triumph of his death. It is for Samson's value as evidence that they finally understand him. His deeds of valor before the outset of the play had "spoke loud the doer"; restored at the conclusion to a fuller understanding of his God and a stronger will, Samson once more "hath quit himself / Like *Samson*, and heroically hath finish'd / A life Heroic. . . ." But now his deeds also speak his Maker. God Himself "bears witness" to Samson's faithful championing of God and gives through Samson "true experience" to those observing Samson's tragedy. The fame of his reflourishing virtue survives as the sign of God's nature and as the model for other men. His accomplishment acquits him and bears with it the new acquist of exemplary experience for others. The experience is hard-won and cannot contradict Milton's tragic wisdom of life. But the ethical significance of *Samson Agonistes* is best summarized as seeing God capable of converting every tragedy into a meaning, a God

> in whose look serene,
> When angry most he seem'd and most severe,
> What else but favor, grace, and mercie shon?
>
> (*Paradise Lost*, x, 1095-97)

The exemplary in *Samson Agonistes* illustrates the mercy of God; Samson's final act in effect is to "spread his name / Great among the Heathen round." The knowledge that the "mercy of heaven" may re-

---

[5] *Ibid.*, 638.

side even in a "hideous noise" is the consolation the drama brings. Thus deeds meriting fame are deeds exemplifying knowledge, deeds "to knowledge answerable." Samson lives to learn and dies to educate. Milton's ethics of process in *Samson Agonistes* is an ethics of works of faith deriving from a covenant theology in which a man's pilgrimage toward truth invests his drama with elucidatory value. Milton's ethics of process in *Samson Agonistes* has measured the value of good works entirely without need of an external devil; it has denied no part of the pain and torment of existence, but at the drama's point of maximum violence, vengefulness, and hatred, Milton, through Samson, expresses the quietest trust in the value of confronting reality. Its assuagement of pain is the relieving knowledge that remorse controls grief. The guilt of Samson witnessed not only to his hubristic and violent self but also to the possibilities of a redefined, purposive self. He who was judge of others became judge of himself and could discover in his self-judgment the springs of an inner goodness in himself that could be revived. His purpose was to bear witness by having been acknowledged worthy by his God. He leaves his friends with the motive for his action expressed in terms of being, not doing:

> Happ'n what may, of me expect to hear
> Nothing dishonourable, impure, unworthy
> Our God, our Law, my Nation, or my self,
> The last of me or no I cannot warrant.
>
> (1423-26)

In the event the most violently active of the soldiers of the faith also stood and waited upon the meaningful promptings of conscience, stood not unlike Job at the command of the voice from the whirlwind, or Jesus in despite of Satan's scornful "to stand upright / Will ask thee skill." He

> stood, as one who pray'd,
> Or some great matter in his mind revolv'd.
> At last with head erect. . . .
>
> (1637-39)

The arrangement of Samson's despair, conveyed in the language of Scripture and predicting progressive revelations in time, is a form of consolation apt for tragedy but not annihilative of it. It is an assuagement that enables ethical action.

Th' unsearchable dispose and
New acquist of true experience

SAMSON AGONISTES AND MILTON'S
THEOLOGY AND POETICS

Introduction

A CHRISTIAN tragedy written some time after the completion of a dogmatic theology is likely to reflect or to contribute to that theology, whether implicitly or explicitly. There are distinguished critics who have argued that *Samson Agonistes* does this; others, of similar distinction, contend that it does not. I should like to align myself with the affirmative view and to state that *Samson Agonistes* contains Milton's most advanced theological position. At the same time, it enacts his most revolutionary poetics. Milton's theology and Milton's poetics will be the interlocked subjects of this final section.

It is usual to say that a twentieth-century agnostic may follow Milton's humane meaning with delight while disregarding his theology. But since I believe that in all his work Milton struggled to free himself from rigid theological dogma, and that his major poems embody and communicate his success, I naturally assume that the evolution of Milton's thought within each poem is as intrinsic and vital to it as are diction, imagery, versification, characterization, or any other aspect of the poetry. Hence I shall discuss Milton's materialism, mortalism, Arminianism, and Arianism in the area of theology and also, in the area of aesthetics, his theory of art as the modification of sensibility.

The poet of *Samson Agonistes* can be likened to his protagonist between the pillars, venturing further in theology than he had ventured before and entering into a new freedom:

> Now of my own accord such other tryal
> I mean to shew you of my strength, yet greater;
> As with amaze shall strike all who behold.

In the lines "On Paradise Lost," Milton's friend Andrew Marvell also made an identification of Milton with Samson, fearing what the "other tryal of [his] strength" might do to contemporary religious stability:

> the Argument
> Held me a while misdoubting his Intent,
> That he would ruine (for I saw him strong)
> The sacred Truths to Fable and old Song
> (So Sampson groap'd the Temple Posts in spight)
> The world o'erwhelming to revenge his sight.[1]

[1] It is, I think, clear from the image Marvell gives of "Sampson . . . in spight" groping the pillars that he could not have seen or known or even heard of Milton's

Marvell's reading allayed his fears, however, and not solely by the consideration that Milton had preserved decorum in dealing with theology in the poem:

> things divine thou treatst of in such state
> As them preserves, and thee, inviolate.

His fears were set at rest by a further consideration, that Milton was less like the blind, vengeful, destroying Samson than like the blind prophet:

> Just Heav'n thee like *Tiresias* to requite
> Rewards with Prophesie thy loss of sight.

Unlike Tennyson's Tiresias, Milton was not "to speak the truth that no man may believe" or foretell the future darkly to men who could not understand him. Rather, Milton was to assert that the possibilities of divine intervention in human history had not been exhausted, that although prophetic revelations of the nature and acts of God had been and could be made use of to mislead, as they were by Satan and by false prophets, where they are true and reliable, they are so for the reason that they were prompted by God Himself and arose from a relationship with God. Milton was to show that he himself had looked through and beyond the language of Scripture to discover the inner nature of divine action in relation to human existence, and that upon the basis of that discovery he had written his last works so as to make them further the continuing revelation of God.

Milton did not think that his God was an imaginary God present like any other character within his works of art. God is a "presence divine" both within and without Milton's poems. Michael comforted Adam when he lamented the loss of God's companionship in Eden with the assurance,

> Yet doubt not but in Vallie and in Plaine
> God is as here, and will be found alike
> Present, and of his presence many a signe

Samson Agonistes as a work in progress or as a finished work prior to *Paradise Lost*. Milton's Samson, unlike his biblical source, is no spiteful groper. The probability is strong that had Milton already written *Samson Agonistes* by 1667, when the first edition of *Paradise Lost* came out, Marvell would have known of it. It would then have been too great an impropriety for Marvell to willfully liken Milton to a destructive Samson when Milton had already treated a regenerative Samson. Marvell's poem itself, of course, first appeared as a prefatory compliment in the 1674 second edition but commemorates a first reading.

Still following thee, still compassing thee round
With goodness and paternal Love, his Face
Express, and of his steps the track Divine.

(*Paradise Lost*, XI, 349-54)

Milton's God was to be understood in Milton's poetry as Milton thought He was to be discerned in Scripture, by His "track Divine," not by any final statements of His nature or attributes, not even by what He is made to say at any particular juncture in any single poem. God is not what He says to the Son in Book III of *Paradise Lost*, He is what He shows in His relationship to the Son and to man throughout *Paradise Lost*. His nature is not expressed in fixities but is understood by the kinds of relations He is shown to have had with varying kinds of men during their lives. Those relations are communicated in the plots of Milton's three last works; the works supply paradigms of God's behavior toward man and Creation from which the norms of His dealings can be derived. In addition, the narrator in *Paradise Lost*, progressively describes how God has dealt with him, and that is another model of God's "track Divine." In *Paradise Regained* the Son's relationship with God is an even freer and fuller paradigm of God's customary behavior than Milton showed in Adam's or Christ's relationships in *Paradise Lost*. Moreover, Milton's use of his scriptural sources is freer. *Paradise Lost* had adapted Scripture freshly and transposed Genesis materials boldly, but *Paradise Regained* goes even further. In writing it Milton chose Luke's account of Christ's temptations in the wilderness as indicating more clearly than Matthew's the ways of God to man. In *Samson Agonistes* God's dealings with Samson offer another model of His nature as revealed in relationships. The Chorus observes the relationship that God establishes with Samson and makes the discovery that his most tragic human experience has resulted in a further experience of the Godhead both for him and for them. The discoveries of the Chorus constitute a further model of God's initiating progressive revelation by bringing about a relationship which demands that human beings acknowledge the presence of the transcendent within their own temporal lives. *Samson Agonistes* contains a free and open-ended theology that seems finally to have satisfied Milton. In place of the inconclusive conclusion as a mode of suggesting open-ended transcendence—the mode of *Lycidas* ending "To morrow to fresh Woods, and Pastures new," or of *Paradise Lost* ending "The World was all before them," or of *Paradise Regained* ending "Now enter, and begin"—*Samson Agonistes* offers a conclusive conclusion, the *nunc dimittis* of the achieved prophecy:

His servants he with new acquist
Of true experience from this great event
With peace and consolation hath dismist,
And calm of mind all passion spent.

RATIONAL THEOLOGY AND
PROGRESSIVE REVELATION

SCRIPTURE AND THE KNOWLEDGE OF GOD BY
PRECEPT AND PARABLE

Milton's willingness to speculate freely was instinctive and unremitting, and he thought it no less than a moral obligation.[1] Free speculation in theology could not imperil the soul; indeed, it was the mark of its healthy response to God's intention. As early as the Seventh Prolusion, written when he was at most twenty-four, Milton noted:

God would indeed seem to have endowed us to no purpose, or even to our distress, with this soul which is capable and indeed insatiably desirous of the highest wisdom, if he had not intended us to strive with all our might toward the lofty understanding of those things, for which he had at our creation instilled so great a longing into the human mind.[2]

A Treatise of Civil Power shows him to have been of the same mind on the eve of the Restoration. In the tract he set forth his view that such striving toward highest wisdom, sincerely undertaken and based upon Scripture, could not be "heresy":

He who holds in religion that beleef or those opinions which to his conscience and utmost understanding appeer with most evidence or probabilitie in the scripture, though to others he seem erroneous, can no more be justly censur'd for a heretic than his censurers who but do the same thing themselves which they censure him for so doing.[3]

The Epistle to *De Doctrina Christiana* put the same point positively, affirming that "God offers all his rewards not to those that are thoughtless and credulous, but to those who labor constantly and seek tirelessly after truth," and that since "we are ordered to find out the truth

---

[1] See Thomas Kranidas, "A View of Milton and the Traditional," *Milton Studies*, I (1969), 16-20, and O. J. Hardison, "Written Records and Truths of Spirit in *Paradise Lost*," ibid., 147-48.
[2] *CPW*, I, 291.   [3] *Ibid.*, VII, 251.

about all things," "it is in the interests of the Christian religion that men should be free not only to sift and winnow any doctrine, but also openly to give their opinions of it and even to write about it, according to what each believes."[4] It was Milton's view, from the beginning to the end of his writing life, that opinions differing from received doctrines were not to be considered forbidden and so stamped with the invidious name of heresy. "True religion" he defined in contradistinction to "implicit" rather than to "false religion" in *Of True Religion, Heresy, Schism, Toleration*, the final tract from his hand in the year of his death: "these two points are the main principles of true religion—that the rule of true religion is the word of God only; and that their faith ought not to be an implicit faith, that is, to believe, though as the church believes, against or without express authority of scripture." There he also asserted that "Heresy . . . is a religion taken up and believed from the traditions of men and in addition to the Word of God."[5] Milton consistently sought to free himself from crippling orthodoxies so as to enter into a liberating and expanding truth. The classical statement of both his conviction and his method is found in *Areopagitica*:

> A man may be a heretick in the truth; and if he beleeve things only because his Pastor says so, or the Assembly so determins, without knowing other reason, though his belief be true, yet the very truth he holds becomes his heresie. . . .

> The light which we have gain'd, was given us, not to be ever staring on, but by it to discover onward things more remote from our knowledge. . . .

> To be still searching what we know not, by what we know, still closing up truth to truth as we find it (for all her body is homogeneal, and proportional) this is the golden rule in theology as well as in arithmatic.[6]

Milton matched his insistence upon man's duty to shake off the yoke of received opinion, custom, and traditional orthodoxy with an apparently opposite insistence upon having regard for usable truth ("knowledge within bounds") and avoiding "forbidden knowledge by forbidden means" or "things not reveal'd."[7] It was truths necessary for salvation that concerned him, and by salvation Milton said he meant "regeneration, *growth* and preservation . . . and their effects

---

[4] *Ibid.*, VI, 120-22.   [5] *Ibid.*, VII.   [6] *Ibid.*, 543, 550, 551.
[7] *Ibid.*, VII, 120; *Paradise Lost*, XII, 279; *CPW*, VII, 121.

such as faith, charity and so on for which *man is responsible*."[8] Scripture was plain in matters of salvation: God gave man time in his life to learn all points of religion necessary to salvation and undertook to teach all things necessary to it.[9] Salvation was open only to individuals of faith but God desired it for all men, plainly marked its path, and gave men light to see it.[10] Suggestive is the distinction Milton made between "thoughts" and "truth": "frail thoughts" in *Lycidas*, "troubled thoughts," "vain thoughts," "abstruce thoughts," "perplex'd thoughts," or "thoughts of matters hid" in *Paradise Lost*, and "restless thoughts" in *Samson Agonistes*; but "fair truth," "revealed truth," "spotless truth," and "the light of truth" in *Paradise Lost*, "strong truth" in *Paradise Regained*, and "unimplicit truth" in *Of True Religion*. Thoughts and opinions could be the beginning of truth, but they could on the contrary lead men "in wandering mazes lost" away from the truth. Hence Milton had felt the need to reconcile speculation and free searching with discipline and practice, to free truth from "superstitions and traditions" and yet to attain "the summe of wisdom appropriate to man," the sum *not* surpassing human measure."

The form that Milton's reconciliation of these conflicting impulses took is decisively clear in *Paradise Lost* and in *De Doctrina Christiana*; its application became even clearer in *Paradise Regained* and *Samson Agonistes*. Christian doctrine must be looked for and searched out; it cannot be found "among philosophizing academics, and not among the laws of men but in the Holy Scripture alone and with the Holy Spirit as guide."[11] The derivation of usable truth from Scripture required, as Milton put it in *Paradise Lost*, that the "Spirit, that dost prefer / Before

---

[8] *CPW*, VI, 503.

[9] "It is God only who gives as well to beleeve aright, as to beleeve at all"; "Therefor are the Scriptures translated into every vulgar tongue, as being held in main matters of belief and salvation, plane and easie to the poorest"; "that which makes fit a minister, the scripture can best informe us to be only from above" (*Considerations touching the Likeliest Means to Remove Hirelings out of the Church, CPW*, VII, 276, 303, 316).

[10] "We . . . can have no other grounds in matters of religion but only from the scripture, And these being not possible to be understood without this divine illumination"; "The scripture only can be the final judge of rule in matters of religion, and that only in the conscience of every Christian to himself"; "every true Christian able to give a reason of his faith, hath the word of God before him, the promised Holy Spirit, and the minde of Christ within him" (*A Treatise of Civil Power, CPW*, VII, 246, 247). "God has clearly and frequently declared . . . that he desires the salvation of all and the death of none, that he hates nothing he has made, and has omitted nothing which might provide salvation for everyone" (*De Doctrina Christiana, ibid.*, VI, 174).

[11] *CPW*, VI, 127.

all Temples th' upright heart and pure, / *Instruct . . ."* (i, 17-19, emphasis added). After the Fall in the sad course of human history, truth must be sought where it could be found by the means by which it could be found:

> the truth
> With superstitions and tradition taint,
> Left onely in those written Records pure,
> Though not but by the Spirit understood.
>
> (xii, 511-14)

Milton's strictures against the wrong kind of speculation—"things too high" from which man can "no advantage gaine" (viii, 121-22)—and his injunction to engage in the right kind of speculation—"To ask or search," "things more worthy of knowledg" (viii, 66, and The Argument)—were reconciled by his restricting the seach for divinity to the Bible (that is, by his locating usable theological truth, or "things at hand useful," in "written Records pure") and by his then widening the significance of the "written Records pure" to include their meaning as read by the spirit.[12] Christ expounded the reconciliation in *Paradise Regained*:

> God hath now sent his living Oracle
> Into the World, to teach his final will,
> And sends his Spirit of Truth henceforth to dwell
> In pious Hearts, an inward Oracle
> To all truth requisite for men to know.
>
> (i, 460-64)

To effect the resolution, Milton added a strengthening point in *Paradise Regained*. The Son not only extols Scripture as "from God inspir'd," but revives the claim that all pagan arts, sciences, and literature descended from the Jews, to whom God committed learning in

[12] It goes without saying that we are here considering specifically only Christian truth or theological truth; Milton had a very generous sense of expanding truth in many other spheres and of "things more worthy of knowledg" in an encyclopedic range. I have written of some of these in my edition of *Paradise Lost*, Vol. viii in the *Cambridge Milton for Schools and Colleges*, ed. John Broadbent (Cambridge: Cambridge University Press, 1974), 48-50. Others are the subject of Howard Schultz, *Milton and Forbidden Knowledge* (London: Oxford University Press, 1959); W. C. Curry, *Milton's Ontology, Cosmogony, and Physics* (Lexington: University of Kentucky Press, 1957); Marjorie Hope Nicolson, *The Breaking of the Circle*, rev. ed. (New York: Columbia University Press, 1960); Hugh M. Richmond, *Renaissance Landscapes* (The Hague: Mouton, 1973); Svendsen, *Milton and Science*; and Irene Samuel, "Milton on Learning and Wisdom," *PMLA*, 64 (1949), 708-23.

their Scripture: "*Greece* from us these Arts deriv'd; / Illimitated."[13]

To summarize, Milton thought that human beings are bound to form a personal theology composed of "correct ideas about God." He understood that limitations of human nature would render the "correct ideas" only in a partial and not an absolute form, for "God has revealed only so much of himself as our minds can conceive and the weakness of our nature can bear." God's means are the gift of the Scripture and of the Holy Spirit by which to interpret it. Scripture not only contains abstract concepts deducible from its plain language, it also contains extensive histories of God's habitual practices with individual men. That being so,

> It is safest for us to form an image of God in our minds which corresponds to his representation and description of himself in the sacred writings. Admittedly, God is always described or outlined not as he really is but in such a way as will make him conceivable to us. Nevertheless, we ought to form just such a mental image of him as he, in bringing himself within the limits of our understanding, wishes us to form. Indeed he has brought himself down to our level expressly to prevent our being carried beyond the reach of human comprehension, and outside the written authority of scripture into vague subtleties of speculation.[14]

On the grounds stipulated, Milton found it possible to depict God in Book III of *Paradise Lost* as humanly emotional rather than perfectly impassive. While disclaiming "anthropopathy" as a weak rhetorical classicism (an "ill-imitation," no doubt), he nevertheless took full advantage of God's "accommodation" of Himself to man's understanding.[15] It could not be dangerous to ascribe to God feelings like those of human beings, for God had accommodated Himself to human understanding in Scripture by offering a human analogy. He worked "with scripture as a model." But the dramatization of God is not to be taken as an abstract revelation of God, and "we do not imply by this argument that God, in all his parts and members, is of human form, but that, so far as it concerns us to know, he has that form which he attributes to himself in Holy Writ."[16] God takes accommodative

---

[13] See Schultz, *Milton and Forbidden Knowledge*, 89-95.

[14] *CPW*, VI, 133-34.

[15] See Madsen, *From Shadowy Types to Truth*, 74-82, and the criticism of Madsen in Kerrigan, *Prophetic Milton*, 156-62. I shall attempt to describe Milton's procedure without recourse to either Madsen's "typology" or Kerrigan's "prophesy." The insights in Frederick Plotkin, *Milton's Inward Jerusalem: "Paradise Lost" and the Ways of Knowing* (The Hague: Mouton, 1971), 75-90, deserve considerable attention, as do those in Jacobus, *Sudden Apprehension*, 15-22, 119-66.

[16] *CPW*, VI, 136.

means in order to communicate an understanding of Himself to man as a principle of creative activity, within human time as well as transcending it.

It should not be thought, however, that in asserting that Scripture supplies the "onely . . . written Records pure" giving insight into religious truth, Milton concurred with the contemporary Puritan view set forth in the Westminster Confession, that "The Old Testament in Hebrew . . . and the New Testament in Greek . . . [are] immediately inspired by God, and by his singular care and providence kept pure in all ages."[17] Milton considered the Bible to be a text made by men to whom God committed revelations of Himself. The human mediators of the text—"the prophets, the apostles, and the evangelists"—were "divinely inspired" men who sometimes wrote long after the events they described; and the purpose of the text is not to communicate instant knowledge but to be "useful for teaching . . . even those who are already learned and wise. If studied carefully and regularly, they are an ideal instrument for educating even unlearned readers in those matters which have most to do with salvation."[18] In important matters of faith the Scriptures are "plain and sufficient in themselves" and are not "convey'd obscurely." Hence every believer is individually entitled, indeed enjoined, to interpret Scripture for himself: "He has the spirit, who guides truth, and he has the mind of Christ." (Milton twice used Paul's phrase "the minde of Christ within him" without explaining it further, and I shall try later to say what I think he meant by it.) Milton conceded not only that the Bible is an interpretable text of human making under divine prompting but also that parts of it had been lost, parts corrupted, some parts of oral tradition lost, and other parts given in contradicting or unreliable manuscripts.[19] He was not dismayed by these considerations, however, because he thought that God could "by singular care and providence" have kept the text "pure in all ages" but had not done so for a reason Milton thought he had made out: "I do not know why God's providence should have committed the contents of the New Testament to such wayward and uncertain guardians, unless it was so that this very fact might convince us that the Spirit which is given to us is a more certain guide than scripture, and that we ought to follow it."[20]

[17] See Maurice Kelley in *ibid.*, 589n.

[18] *Ibid.*, 579.

[19] *Ibid.*, 588. Maurice Kelley's "Introduction," *ibid.*, 44-45, is helpful on this point.

[20] *Ibid.*, 589. Howard Schultz argues (*Milton and Forbidden Knowledge*, 151), in order to defend Milton from the charge of subscribing to "the intuitive devotion of Seekers, Quakers, Ranters and the like," that his position was "the ortho-

Persistently a biblicist, Milton simply believed in a double scripture. He distinguished between "the external scripture of the written word and the internal scripture of the Holy Spirit which he, according to God's promise, has engraved upon the hearts of believers."[21] The internal authority is "the pre-eminent and supreme authority . . . internal and the individual possession of each man." It is not a mystical or irrational authority; not only does it require the tools of scholarship, the canons of logic, and the aids of reason in interpreting, it also demands a consistent application of the "analogy of faith," together with a recognition that the truths to be derived by these means pertain "throughout all succeeding ages."[22] The meaning of Scripture cannot simply be distilled once and for all from the text and kept fixed in its original purity. Scripture also contains truth which will be progressively discerned. (This position does not commit Milton to a shallow, optimistic doctrine of progress, for the progressively revealed truth may be held by few and at the expense of great suffering.) Furthermore, it is not the "merely human intellect" which keeps discovering the salvific truth in Scripture, but human intellect together with "the help of the Holy Spirit promised to each individual believer."[23] The progressive discernment of the truth does not imply that human beings may add to the meaning of Scripture but simply that they may progressively discover the truths always latent in the text. Milton read Scripture in the way one should read Milton, attentive to progressive relevancies.

Dogma and the Analogy of Faith

The concept of "the analogy of faith" is crucial to understanding Milton's way of reading Scripture. In *De Doctrina Christiana*, discussing biblical interpretation, Milton wrote:

---

dox reverse of the Quakers' rule which deliberately held the written records secondary to an additive spirit" and that "To Milton, the textual difficulties in [the New Testament] presented a puzzle and a danger." They were, however, a puzzle he thought he could solve. Moreover, although Milton did not speak of the internal spirit in each man as "additive," he did speak of it as "pre-eminent and supreme . . . internal and individual." There is no need to defend Milton from the taint of "enthusiasm" by denying that he saw the possibility of progressive revelation; all that is necessary is to consider the nature of the "pre-eminent and supreme" authority. Milton repeatedly insisted upon its rationality. A.S.P. Woodhouse, *Heavenly Muse*, 140-41, is helpful here.

[21] *CPW*, VI, 587.

[22] *Ibid.*, 582. See also MacCallum, "Milton and Figurative Interpretation of the Bible," 397-415, and Woodhouse, *Heavenly Muse*, 143.

[23] *CPW*, VI, 580.

The requisites are linguistic ability, knowledge of the original sources, consideration of the overall intent, distinction between literal and figurative language, examination of the causes and circumstances, and of what comes before and after the passage in question, and comparison of one text with another. It must always be asked, too, how far the interpretation is in agreement with faith.[24]

Faith, which results from true biblical interpretation arrived at by the comparison of one text with another, is a series of complementary and harmonious propositions.[25] The "analogy of faith" tests any specific interpretation of Scripture against the consistent body of truth that Scripture affords. It is the acknowledgment of scriptural inner consistency. In matters necessary to salvation, that is, in articles of faith, the Bible is self-authenticating and self-consistent. All parts of the Bible do not, however, have the same authority, and some of its teachings are "indifferent" or subordinate to other parts. As Milton put it in *The Doctrine and Discipline of Divorce*: "in the method of religion, and to save the honour and dignity of our faith, we are to retreat, and gather up our selves from the observance of an inferior . . . ordinance, to the strict maintaining of a general and religious command"; "one must compare the words he finds with other precepts, with the end of every ordinance, and with the general analogy of Evangelick doctrine." The opposite of "the direct analogy of sense, reason, law and Gospel" is "the abrupt and Papistical way of a literal apprehension," which Milton deplored in the Preface to *The Judgment of Martin Bucer concerning Divorce*.[26] In *De Doctrina Christiana* one can see Milton using the analogy of faith in a number of places; his discussion of election is a good instance. He prefaces the discussion with the comment: "Two difficult texts remain, which must be explained by reference to many clearer passages which resemble them; for clear things are not elucidated by obscure things but obscure by clear." When Milton divided his theology into "faith or the knowledge of God" and "love or the worship of God," he defined faith not as "the habit of believing, but the things which must be habitually believed." These were clear and accorded with one another; the New Testament proved "almost everything" "by reference to the Old."[27] Milton's hermeneutics sought

[24] *Ibid.*, 582.

[25] "The infallible rule of interpretation of Scripture," according to the Westminster Confession (1647), "is the Scripture itself; and therefore, when there is a question about the true and full sense of any Scripture (which is not manifold but one), it must be searched and known by other places that speak more clearly." See *CPW*, II, 282.

[26] *CPW*, II, 431.   [27] *Ibid.*, VI, 181, 129, 576.

congruences through a logical process, not through an erratic inner light. But Milton's hermeneutics derived from Scripture not only the things which must be habitually believed, but also the patterns of divine action which will be relevant in future times.

Milton's theology in his poems and in *De Doctrina Christiana* is consistent precisely as he thought Scripture consistent when interpreted by "the analogy of faith." The discovery that the language of one sometimes differs from the language of the other should not obscure that. The theology is of the same thrust throughout Milton's two "voices" of prose and poetry despite some quite natural lexical differences. Nor is the intellectual consistency between the two kinds of writing disproved by some readers' feelings that *Paradise Lost* is less heterodox than *De Doctrina Christiana* and other readers' feelings that *De Doctrina Christiana* is less likable or "mature" or "outward-looking" than *Paradise Lost*. That the doctrines advanced in these works are entirely consonant cannot be disputed on the grounds that their tone differs or their effects differ. It remains true, nonetheless, that Milton's poems, as A.S.P. Woodhouse put it, "round out and develop" the "positions reached in the *De doctrina*." The positions reached in both the poetry and prose are biblically derived. The poems present a progressive theology which expands beyond the theology of *De Doctrina Christiana*. Their biblicism is quite as strong as the tract's biblicism, but it is biblicism in a different manner. *De Doctrina Christiana* proceeds by listing "under general headings" biblical texts which illuminate those headings. There Milton wrote of his method:

> Most authors who have dealt with this subject at the greatest length in the past have been in the habit of filling their pages almost entirely with expositions of their own ideas. They have relegated to the margin with brief reference to chapter and verse, the scriptural texts upon which all that they teach is utterly dependent. I, on the other hand, have striven to cram my pages even to overflowing, with quotations drawn from all parts of the Bible and to leave as little space as possible for my own words, even when they arise from the putting together of actual scriptural texts.[28]

Milton searched in Scripture for evidence of abstract ideas; he used the metaphor of winnowing to describe his procedure, and the phrase "putting together of actual scriptural texts" to describe the result. To Milton, Scripture represented God in the way God considered it appropriate to man's nature to know Him; furthermore, Scripture not

[28] *Ibid.*, 122.

only represents God in His nature but more clearly evinces God in His works:

> We know God, in so far as we are permitted to know him, either from his nature or his efficiency. . . .
>
> God by his very nature, transcends everything, including definition, [but] some description of him may be gathered from his names and attributes. . . .
>
> God's efficiency is either Internal or External. God's internal efficiency is that which begins and ends within God himself. His decrees come into this category. . . .
>
> His external efficiency takes the form of the execution of these decrees. By this he effects outside himself something he has decreed within himself. External efficiency subdivides into Generation, Creation, and the Government of the Universe.[29]

God accommodated Himself to man's understanding, and gave to man a variety of modes by which He might be known. *De Doctrina Christiana* abstracts or winnows from scriptural accommodations a total system of technical divinity, rejoining the winnowed parts to make an intellectual outline of theological concepts. This is Milton's first fashion of using Scripture to interpret God.

DRAMA AND THE PARADIGMS OF GOD'S BEHAVIOR

Milton's great poems are likewise built from Scripture. They derive an understanding of God from His efficiency, as Milton called it in *De Doctrina Christiana*, rather than from His names and attributes. *Paradise Lost* and *Paradise Regained* depict God in His efficiency; God appears in person within the poems, and they dramatize both His internal and external efficiency. *Samson Agonistes* depicts God's external efficiency only and does so without His presence on stage. In this second fashion of using Scripture to understand God, Milton treats the Bible as a collection of case histories of human beings and human societies in their relationship to God. The stories of individuals and nations show how God responds to diverse kinds of behavior; He reveals His nature by the quality of His reaction to men or, better, His continuous interacting relationship with men. Of course Scripture is chronologically arranged, and it is perfectly possible to concentrate on the way in which God stages His treatment of man in two main historical contexts, the B.C. and A.D. polarities of the Old and New Testa-

[29] *Ibid.*, 133, 137-38, 205.

ments. The two poems of the 1671 volume seem to ask such special attention to contrasting views of the nature of God in progressive revelation, as though Milton were separately considering the God of the Jews and the God of the Gentiles either to contrast or to synthesize them.

All the careful and detailed work which has recently been done on the significance of the concept of typology and the meaning of prophecy in Milton's thought focuses on this kind of historical discrimination or staging in Holy Writ—looking at Old Testament characters as pictures of men before God revealed Himself in His treatment of Christ, and at New Testament characters as pictures of men after God revealed Himself with maximum fullness in His treatment of Christ,[30] or, as is most frequent in such studies, looking at Old Testament characters to see the presence or absence in them as "types" of what will be fully revealed in Christ as "antitype." Some critics who believe that Old Testament types only or mainly reveal their meaning when the antitype has appeared have made much of Samson's implicit foreshadowing of Christ in explicating the tragedy;[31] others of the same typological bent, but a quite different response to the drama, have seen in Samson a discarded type of Old Testament virtue superceded and made absurd by the advent in the New Testament of an antithetical antitype.[32] The failure of typological criticism to elucidate the relationship between *Paradise Regained* and *Samson Agonistes* lies precisely in this kind of critical conflict. It is difficult to be sure what Samson is a type of and, in terms of typology, inexplicable that Milton should have arranged the two works in his final book so that the "antitype" precedes the "type" and the last word is given to the Old Covenant and not the New. In fact, Milton's particular emphasis in *Paradise Regained* and *Samson Agonistes* is not typological: he nowhere in either poem uses any form of the words *type, shadow, prediction, foreshadowing,* or *prophecy* in a way relevant to typological exegesis; he nowhere makes explicit a typological link between Samson and Christ.[33]

To have relied only upon the contemporary dominance of typo-

[30] I have in mind such studies as Madsen, *From Shadowy Types to Truth*; MacCallum, "Milton and Figurative Interpretation of the Bible"; Barbara Lewalski, *Milton's Brief Epic*; Frye, "The Typology of *Paradise Regained*"; Krouse, *Milton's Samson and the Christian Tradition*; and Sadler, "Typological Imagery in *Samson Agonistes*."

[31] See Madsen, *From Shadowy Types to Truth*, 187.

[32] See, for example, Carey, *Milton*, 138: "Theologians have pretended that the biblical Samson was a foreshadowing of Christ; Milton uses him as a contrast."

[33] See B. Rajan, "To which is added *Samson Agonistes*," in *The Prison and the Pinnacle*, ed. Rajan, 97.

logical reading would have limited Milton to the elucidation of his inherited theology. But he was engaged in freeing himself from that. Milton thought that one might read an Old Testament human drama "with the minde of Christ" and find in it and of itself a significant revelation of God's nature seen in His behavior toward the persons involved, irrespective of the meaning it might bear when reexamined in a New Testament context. Milton clearly used Old Testament characters in this way in the last books of *Paradise Lost*, alongside typological usages. Further, Milton clearly considered that any of the episodes of the life of Christ recounted in the New Testament may also serve to elucidate the nature of God from the nature of His relationship to His human son, irrespective of their antitypical fulfilment of Old Testament typology. The theological difference between *De Doctrina Christiana* and Milton's last poems lies not in the theology in them, but in the means offered for deriving theology. The treatise gives a biblical theology of sifted and reconstituted scriptural doctrines; the poems give a biblical theology through the God-man relationship dramatized in the scriptural narratives of both the Old and New Testaments. *Samson Agonistes* and *Paradise Regained* are theologically related, not as type and antitype (although typological overtones do exist), but because each emphasizes the acquisition of a progressively more correct and full understanding of how God treats every man in terms of the ways He has treated two particular men. Both culminate in a final conviction of the nature of God. Because they reveal that nature through God's response to human beings, a sensible and sensitive reader is meant to modify his own nature so as to prompt a better relationship to a more clearly understood God. Both contain exemplary pressures upon an alert reader; in addition, the tragedy is medicinal.

EXEMPLARY SCRIPTURAL CHARACTERS IN PARADISE LOST

God interacts with a diverse cast of biblical characters in the eleventh and twelfth books of *Paradise Lost*. In preparing to show how *Paradise Regained* and *Samson Agonistes* contribute to our understanding of Milton's theology, it is necessary to glance at several of the narratives in *Paradise Lost*. They are given to Adam to establish and confirm his faith: "That thou mayst beleeve, and be confirm'd . . . I am sent," Michael tells him, "To shew thee what shall come in future dayes." Adam is given a selective preview of the Old Testament. Michael comes before Adam like a scriptural exegete rather than an Old Testament scribe, although God has inspired him, as He inspired his scribes, in charging him to

> reveale
> To *Adam* what shall come in future dayes,
> *As I shall thee enlighten.* . . .

(XI, 113-15, emphasis added)

Michael understands the purpose of his scriptural summary to be to present the prophetic story as an educative drama, teaching Adam both the lesson of the nature of God and of his own need for patience and equanimity. He warns Adam in advance of the intermixed notes of the tragic and the consoling in the account, and also indicates the lesson to be learned:

> good with bad
> Expect to hear, supernal Grace contending
> With sinfulness of Men; thereby to learn
> True patience, and to temper joy with fear
> And pious sorrow, equally enur'd
> By moderation either state to beare,
> Prosperous or adverse. . . .

(XI, 358-64)

In Book XI Michael's narrative and commentary takes the form of a visionary series of tragic masques which traces the history of the world,[34] recapitulating Genesis, beginning with the story of Cain in Gen. 4 and ending with the story of Noah from Gen. 6 through 9. At the beginning of Book XII Milton varies the method of Michael's discourse but not the biblical source (he finishes Genesis and moves selectively and systematically through the remainder of the hexateuch before more abstractly summarizing Judges, Samuel, and Kings) and not the variety of lesson-drawing techniques (he continues to use typology, parable, dialectical discussion, and case history). Dropping the mode of unrolling pageant, Michael proposes a directly described

[34] The insight of Denis Burden in *The Logical Epic* (London: Routledge & Kegan Paul, 1967), 187-97, into the intended tragic effect of the last books supplements the excellent studies of Isabel G. MacCaffrey in *Paradise Lost as Myth* (Cambridge, Mass.: Harvard University Press, 1959), 61-64, and Joseph Summers in *The Muse's Method: An Introduction to "Paradise Lost"* (Cambridge, Mass.: Harvard University Press, 1962), 186-224, to which I have been indebted. For a brief examination of the tragic within Milton's epic vision see Irene Samuel, "Paradise Lost," in *Critical Approaches to Six Major Works: "Beowulf" through "Paradise Lost,"* ed. R. M. Lumiansky and Herschel Baker (Philadelphia: University of Pennsylvania Press, 1968), 209-53. For a full study see John M. Steadman, *Epic and Tragic Structure in Paradise Lost* (Chicago: University of Chicago Press, 1976), 120-41.

series of interlinked summary accounts and their explanation. He marks the shift from vision to description by saying to Adam:

> but I perceave
> Thy mortal sight to faile; objects divine
> Must needs impaire and wearie human sense:
> Henceforth what is to com I will relate,
> Thou therefore give due audience, and attend.
>
> (XII, 8-12)

By "objects divine" Milton means his readers to understand "things of God" and to comprehend God's mode of self-revelation in Scripture as well as His gift of Scripture, that is, objects derived from divine inspiration and objects communicating divinity. Both communicate an understanding of the divine nature through its interchanges with man.[35]

Book XI allows Adam to observe what is in effect one coherent tragedy in a "vision what shall happ'n till the Flood" (XI, The Argument). It is composed of six scenes—five biblical tableaux and one symbolic icon—each pointed, as tragedy always is in Milton's view, toward a cathartic harmonizing effect: "to learn true patience"; "to temper joy with fear." At the conclusion Adam has seen "one World begin and end" in a unified first stage of the revelation of God. Yet the individual scenes within the tragedy are complex.[36] What is common to all six scenes is the presence in each of a part or of the whole pattern of fall and reformation or temptation-fall-repentance-understanding. Typologically or literally, historically or discursively, all convey theological insight in terms of a relationship between God and man in which man describes an arc from fall to rising with God's help and love, or a contrary arc from faith to falling attended by God's sorrow and by human suffering. In all, God is shown as responding to human initiatives rather than coercing them.

Adam is taken to the top of the highest hill in Paradise, a hill offering a panorama of "destined" cities (in contrast, Milton pointedly notes, to the panorama of current cities afforded by the "spectacular Mount" to which Satan bears Jesus in the temptation in the wilder-

[35] See *CPW*, VI, 118: "The only authority I accepted was God's self-revelation." William Chillingworth (1602-44) made the same point in *The Religion of Protestants*: it is a "vain concept that we can speak of the things of God better than in the words of God." Quoted in George N. Conklin, *Biblical Criticism and Heresy in Milton* (New York: Columbia University Press, 1949), 25.

[36] See my "'Man as a Probationer of Immortality,'" 31-52, for a discussion of the ethical teaching of the last two books and a summary of the most recent studies.

ness).[37] There he witnesses a six-act tragedy, some of which his sons will later read in Genesis, some of which his sons will read only in Milton's epic. One, but not the only one, of the principles by which Milton chose the materials for the tragedy is to follow the selection already made by the author of the Letter to the Hebrews of the "cloud of witnesses" representing men of faith who patiently ran the race that was set before them. This roll call of the faithful was the sanction for much typological interpretation in Milton's time and earlier.[38] It accounts for three of the six scenes from Genesis shown to Adam: the dumb-show murder of Abel by Cain (Gen. 4:1-16; *Paradise Lost*, XI, 430-47); the vision of Enoch snatched to safety in a cloud (Gen. 5:21-24; XI, 665-73); and the drama of Noah and the Flood (Gen. 6:9, 9-17; XI, 719-53). Two of the remaining scenes are scriptural but not typological (the sinful generation of Cain and the daughters of Seth; the Giants of mighty bone); the other is neither scriptural nor typological, but rather iconographical and parabolic (the vision of death in the lazar house).

Book XII allows Adam not to see but to hear a Scripture-based summary account of human history "Betwixt the world destroy'd and world restor'd." The Argument to Book XII gives the overview: "The Angel *Michael* continues from the Flood to relate what shall succeed; then, in the mention of *Abraham*, comes by degrees to explain, who that Seed of the Woman shall be which was promised *Adam* and *Eve* in the Fall; his Incarnation, Death, Resurrection, and Ascension; the state of the Church till his second Coming." In the chronology of sacred history, having finished with the Age of Adam, Michael turns to show "Man as from a second stock proceed" (XII, 7), pausing first "as one who in his journey bates at Noone, / Though bent on speed." The pause marks antediluvian time from postdiluvian time. Postdiluvian time, as recounted in Book XII, passes through the five further tradi-

[37] "Not higher that Hill nor wider looking round, / Whereon for different cause the Tempter set / Our second *Adam* in the Wilderness, / To shew him all Earths Kingdomes and thir Glory" (*Paradise Lost*, XI, 381-84).

[38] Heb. 11:4: "By faith Abel offered unto God a more excellent sacrifice than Cain, by which he obtained witness that he was righteous, God testifying of his gifts: and by it he being dead yet speaketh"; 5: "By faith, Enoch was translated that he should not see death; and was not found, because God had translated him: for before his translation he had this testimony, that he pleased God"; 6: "But without faith it is impossible to please him: for he that cometh to God must believe that he is, and that he is a reward of them that diligently seek him"; 7: "By faith Noah, being warned of God of things not seen as yet, moved with fear, prepared an ark to the saving of his house; by the which he condemned the world, and became heir of the righteousness which is by faith."

tional historical periods: the age from the Flood to Abraham; from Abraham to David; from David to the Captivity; from the Captivity to the Nativity; and the Nativity to the Second Coming, the Ascension to the Day of Judgment ("the state of the Church till his second Coming"), encompassing Milton's own era. The traditional schema underlies but does not circumscribe Michael's narrative.[39] Michael's continuous discourse distinguishes God's intervention in human history into sequential stages, and Milton, in order to mark them into assimilable subdivisions, points up some but not all of these conventional historical stages by causing Adam to interpose questions and reactions which mark off the periods.

Michael begins his recital with events of the Age of Noah to show the problems and falling off of Noah's descendants in the story of Nimrod and the Tower of Babel. Adam's shocked moral censure of "Authoritie usurpt, from God not giv'n" (xii, 66) and Michael's careful lesson of individual responsibility for upholding liberty separates this period from the next:

> Thus will this latter, as the former World,
> Still tend from bad to worse, till God at last
> Wearied with their iniquities, withdraw
> His presence from among them, and avert
> His holy Eyes; resolving from thenceforth
> To leave them to thir own polluted wayes.
>
> (xii, 105-10)

But, Michael explains, God's withdrawal from the downward-tending generality of man is only a withdrawal from those who have withdrawn from Him; moreover, it becomes the occasion of the renewal of the covenant made with Noah—now in the form of a new covenant with Abraham—to choose a people of His own for particular care. The next stage in Michael's discourse, therefore, traces the history of that "one peculiar Nation": their settlement in Canaan, their withdrawal to Egypt, their wandering in the desert, Moses leading them back to the Promised Land, and God giving to them the Mosaic Law. At this point Michael's interest in giving a selective account of the remainder of the Book of Genesis, all of Exodus, and some of Deuteronomy appears to be running down: "The rest / Were long to tell, how many Battels fought, / How many Kings destroyd, and Kingdoms won" (xii, 260-62). To mark the conclusion of that stage

---

[39] See the analysis in George Whiting, *Milton and This Pendant World* (Austin: University of Texas Press, 1958), 169-200. See also MacCallum, "Milton and Sacred History."

of human history and the commencement of another, Adam then evinces surprise that a chosen people should require "so many and so various Laws." Michael explains God's progressive and typological way of revealing the truth to mankind: the Law was given to educate mankind away from reliance upon external performances and to move his understanding of God upward as well as onward. That explained, Michael commences the précis of the fourth historical era, when David receives the prophetic promise that of his "Royal Stock . . . shall rise / A Son, the Womans Seed to thee foretold." (This era, placed between the Law and the Prophets, on the threshold of David's psalms, includes the life of Samson.) That stage ends when the people of David's tribe, "Part good, part bad, of bad the longer scrowle . . . so incense God" that he permits them to fall into Babylonian captivity:

> when sins
> National interrupt thir public peace,
> Provoking God to raise them enemies:
> From whom as oft he saves them penitent
> By Judges first, then under Kings.
>
> (XII, 316-20)

Michael's account of this era is the curtest possible treatment of Joshua, Judges, Samuel, and Kings. Adam does not interrupt him as he encompasses in very few lines the fifth period, from the Captivity to the birth of Christ. The announcement of the Nativity leads to a natural break in Michael's discourse before he moves forward to the sixth era with a bleak description of the present age of the world. The angel beholds Adam in tears of joy as he believes he foresees Michael's clear drift: the Messiah's earthly rule must establish forever a millennial reign. Michael corrects him by depicting the darkening stage from the First to the Second Coming of Christ.[40]

Michael's selection of case histories from the Old Testament to be dealt with in Book XII again owes something, but by no means everything, to the selection in Hebrews which greatly influenced typological understanding of the Bible. That roll call encompassed the account of "Abraham, when he was called to go out into a place which he should after receive for an inheritance, obeyed; and he went out, not knowing whither he went." Milton drew on it to show how Abraham

---

[40] See Carey and Fowler, *Poems of Milton*, 1049-50, for a chronological and numerological account of this sacred history, but see also Barbara Lewalski, "Structure and Symbolism of Vision in Michael's Prophecy, *Paradise Lost*, Books XI-XIII," *Philological Quarterly*, 33 (1963), 28-29, for an analysis of the imperfect reflection of this traditional scheme in Michael's account and for another sort of structural explanation.

"straight obeys, / Not knowing to what Land, yet firm believes . . . Not wandring poor, but trusting all his wealth / With God, who call'd him, in a land unknown" (XII, 126-34). It includes Isaac blessing Jacob and Esau, Jacob blessing the sons of Joseph, Joseph prophesying the departure from Egypt; of these Milton makes no mention. It also includes Moses in six contexts, of which Milton uses but one; it does not mention Aaron, Milton does. It specifies of the period of judges, kings, and patriarchs: "And what shall I say more? for the time would fail me to tell of Gideon, and of Barak, and of Samson, and of Jephthah; of David also, and Samuel, and of the prophets: Who through faith subdued kingdoms, wrought righteousness, obtained promises, stopped the mouths of lions, Quenched the violence of fire, escaped the edge of the sword, out of weakness were made strong, waxed valiant in fight, turned to flight the armies of the aliens." Apart from the promises made to David, Milton retains of this only the pressure of time preventing further specification. In *Samson Agonistes* he supplies much of what was here omitted.

The Interpretation of Parable

Samson Agonistes conveys theology and contributes to theology, not indirectly by presenting a type which prefigures the meaning of the antitype, the antitype being the fullest revelation of God, but more obviously by offering a representative figure of one kind of human being who discovers in the course of his life the inadequacy of his own conception of God, who by the experience of his tragic existence learns a more adequate conception, and who, armed with that better understanding, modifies his nature in such a way as to perfect a relationship and thereby also give evidence of God's nature. I do not wish to dispute the existence of typological conceptions in the design of the drama;[41] they enrich and add poignancy to many places. But it is not through them that Milton makes his theology clear in *Samson Agonistes*. Among Milton's Protestant contemporaries typology was the traditional mode of understanding the Old Testament (in addition of course to the literal reading), and Milton struggled to free himself from traditional interpretations. The use he makes of Samson to typify the movement away from inadequate conceptions of God and toward adequate conceptions runs beyond conventional theology. I will instance from *Paradise Lost* the handling of Enoch, Nimrod, and Moses as a preliminary indication of how Milton treated Old Testament bibli-

41 See Kerrigan, *Prophetic Milton*, 244-58, for a fuller discussion of the contradictions between typology and prophecy.

cal characters to show the norms of God's exchanges with man, of how he treated them as exemplary and not typological or proleptic. I will then examine Milton's particularly antimystical treatment of the temptation in the wilderness in *Paradise Regained* to show that Milton's theology determined his handling even of the Messiah as an extreme example of God's active relationship to any man. From that I shall proceed to *Samson Agonistes* itself. But first it will be helpful to point out the pattern which Milton saw in all the single human cases treated in Book XI of *Paradise Lost*, to show that all cases witness to a common "track Divine."

The common pattern begins to be exposed at once with the Cain and Abel story. Horrified at the picture of Abel groaning out his soul, Adam protests in grief to Michael, "Is Pietie thus and pure Devotion paid?" It is a question of the very significance of human life in terms of God's justice. Michael's reply does not make the point, dear to typology, that shameful death in human terms is glorious in divine terms and that Abel's death prefigures the Passion. Instead, Michael draws attention to Cain's motives and judges him in terms of his voluntary act:

> th' unjust the just hath slain,
> For envie that his Brothers Offering found
> From Heav'n acceptance. . . .

(XI, 455-57)

He then offers Adam the assurance that Abel will be consoled in another time or place:

> but the bloodie Fact
> Will be aveng'd, and th' others Faith approv'd
> Loose no reward, though here thou see him die,
> Rowling in dust and gore.

(XI, 457-60)

The next scene, in the "noysom" dark lazar house, specifies eighteen or so painful forms of death (the psychogenic was added in the second edition, when Milton had been considering the irony of the Philistine self-destructive impulses while he was writing *Samson Agonistes*). Adam, again horrified, questions God's justice: "Why is life giv'n / To be thus wrested from us?" The question is even more pointed than it appears: it is directed both at God's power and at His justice; it asks both is it possible and is it just that a creature should be made in a manner susceptible to such degradation. Man's being made or not was not within his will; his debasement likewise comes from without:

291

Can thus
Th' Image of God in man created once
So goodly and erect, though faultie since,
To such unsightly sufferings be debas't
Under inhuman pains? Why should not Man,
Retaining still Divine similitude
In part, from such deformaties be free,
And for his Makers Image sake exempt?

(XI, 507-14)

Again, the answer is given not in terms of all the kinds of bodily humiliation the Son will bear for man, typified in these painful signs of mortality. Rather, it is made in terms of man's own free choice and full responsibility for his own self-degradation:

Thir Makers Images, answerd *Michael*, then
Forsook them, when themselves they villifi'd
To serve ungovern'd appetite, and took
His Image whom they serv'd, a brutish vice. . . .
Disfiguring not Gods likeness, but thir own,
Or if his likeness, by themselves defac't

(XI, 515-22)

The consolation immediately added—that it is in man's power, living well, to "be with ease / Gatherd, not harshly pluckt, for death mature"—is expanded into a lesson which restores omnipotence to God but leaves moral choice to man:

Nor love thy Life, nor hate; but what thou livst
Live well, how long or short permit to Heav'n. . . .

(XI, 553-54)

The third vision, the generations of Cain and Seth engaged in apparently peaceful and congenial activities on the "spacious Plaine," repeats the pattern of a disjunction between Adam's first response and his corrected response. He is relieved to see how "Nature seems fulfilld in all her ends" (XI, 602), but that appearance cloaks a different reality, for natural fulfillment may conceal spiritual poverty. Adam has forgotten that man was not created for human pleasure but "Created . . . to nobler end / Holie and pure, conformitie divine." More important than the pattern of progressive enlightenment or revelation, however, is the iterated pattern of emphasis on man's responsibility for his own fate; his propensity to fall is marked in his choice of sensual pleasure over reason. Adam has seen the pattern of his own fall repeated in the fall of the sons of Cain and the daughters of Seth, seen some who "by thir guise" seemed in "all thir study bent / To worship God aright, and know his works / Not hid" turn from following reason as the law of Nature to "let thir eyes / Rove without rein" and accept the enslavement of reason to passion.[42] Adam's correct response is an educated one:

> O pittie and shame, that they who to live well
> Enterd so faire, should turn aside to tread
> Paths indirect, or in the mid way faint!
>
> (XI, 629-31)

The complementary vision of the subsequent generation engaged in warlike activities introduces the translation of Enoch to which I shall return. But of the vision of the warring giants, Adam delivers a correct assessment: they are "Deaths Ministers, not Men, who thus deal Death / Inhumanly to men." Michael need only supply the analysis of motive and the distinction between the appearance of heroic virtue and the reality of heroic virtue to sharpen the moral:

> For in those dayes Might onely shall be admir'd,
> And Valour and Heroic Virtu call'd;
> To overcome in Battel, and subdue
> Nations, and bring home spoils with infinite
> Man-slaughter, shall be held the highest pitch
> Of Human Glorie, and for Glorie done
> Of triumph, to be styl'd great Conquerours. . . .
> Thus Fame shall be achiev'd, renown on Earth,
> And what most merits fame in silence hid.
>
> (XI, 689-99)

The final scene in Book XI most conforms to Michael's introductory promise to Adam that he will mingle "good with bad" "to temper joy with fear / And pious sorrow." At the Flood, Adam's grief, "comfortless, as when a Father mourns / His Childern, all in view destroyd at once," issues in two questions: "How comes it thus? unfould, Celestial Guide, / And whether here the Race of man will end." The answer Michael gives to the first is to stress once more the voluntary actions of men who "change thir course to pleasure, ease, and sloth," who decide not to adhere to a God who does not materially reward them with prosperity, and who "coold in zeale / Thenceforth shall practice how to live secure." By their choices these men "turn degenerate, all de-

---

[42] See Barbara Lewalski, "Structure and the Symbolism of Vision in Michael's Prophecy."

prav'd." To the second question, he again replies in terms of God's renewal of the possibility of free moral choice, His salvific response to "the onely Son of light / In a dark Age, against example good, / Against allurement, custom, and a World / Offended," the one just man alive. Adam's relief and joy is at the literal meaning of the scene shown him; it teaches him God's benevolence, mercy, and forgiveness:

> Farr less I now lament for one whole World
> Of wicked Sons destroyd, then I rejoyce
> For one Man found so perfet and so just,
> That God voutsafes to raise another World
> From him, and all his anger to forget.
>
> (XI, 874-78)

What it does not teach him is how to play the role of scriptural exegete in typological terms: "But say," he promptly asks, "what mean those coulour streaks in Heavn?" Michael the exegete underscores the typological meaning:

> Such grace shall one just Man find in his sight,
> That he relents, not to blot out mankind,
> And makes a Covenant. . . .
>
> (XI, 890-92)

The waters of the Flood shall not recur until the antitypical fires of the Day of Judgment which they prefigure; Noah, saved by his belief and saving those who believe, prefigures the Son.

It should be clear, then, that Book XI superimposes upon scriptural stories, treated literally and not only topologically, an interpretative pattern with theological as well as moral implications: "what reward / Awaits the good, the rest what punishment" is definitive of man's destiny, and also of God's nature. Milton does not insist upon the historicity of the scenes Adam receives so much as on the normative and archetypal in them; the actors are given no names, and the time signals are minimal, cryptic, and abstract—"in some to spring from thee"; "in his first shape on man"; "another sight"; "a different sort"; "they on the Plain"; "his race who slew his brother"; "another Scene"; "the products of those ill-mated Marriages"; "hee the seventh from thee"; "the face of things quite chang'd"; "those whom last thou sawst."[43] Obviously Milton is playing upon a distinction between the interpreta-

---

[43] An analysis of Milton's narrative devices is contained in Grose, *Milton's Epic Process*, 207-18; an analysis of the reader's response to them, in Stanley Fish, *Surprised by Sin* (London: Macmillan, 1967), 286-300.

tive capacities of Adam and his contemporary readers by making a distinction between those of Adam and Michael. Adam's mistakes on the simplest level yield to more and more correctly official exegesis so that he catches up with Milton's sophisticated Puritan contemporaries in his capacity to read doctrine out of event, to derive spiritual insight from Scripture-based evidence. In Book XII Adam becomes capable of wielding exegetical tools, and yet he continues to eschew the typological. On a more complex level, however, Adam's misconceptions contain assumptions about the nature of God which he believes are shown by God's interactions with him. He first assumed that God could only be known in Eden and by His direct "Presence Divine"; Michael had to show him how to read God in all human affairs, where He is always present. Adam next assumed that God must reward the pious with prosperity and the impious with pain; Abel's death led him to evaluate prosperity and death differently. The lazar house scene depicted forms of death induced by human intemperance and not inflicted by God, enabling Adam to see the course of life as a quiet ripening toward the maturity of a sleeplike death, the gate of another life. Adam next assumed that God designs human existence for delight and that the law of Nature is fulfilled by the joyous use of natural things, but he saw how exploitative and rapacious the search for delight would become, requiring God's extraordinary protection of a truth-teller, the unexplicit lesson being that reason, not pleasure, is Nature's law. He then assumed that history would show God prompting a straightforward human progress where "peace would have crownd / With length of happy days the race of man," but that if God were frustrated of that progress He would have recourse to destruction and would doom the degenerate; instead, Adam learned of God's reluctance to destroy. The design of Book XII continues to exploit the pattern of fall and redemption, to superimpose upon it the pattern of truth emerging from deceptive appearance, and most profoundly, to educate Adam's perceptions so that apparently pious views of God give way to superior views. There is no necessity to labor these interlocked designs by an analysis of all the stages of history in Book XII. It will be sufficient to go back to examine Enoch in Book XI, and then to move forward to Nimrod and Moses in Book XII as paradigms of Milton's treatment of biblical case histories, all less for their typological value than for their exemplary value.

Enoch

In conventional typologies the Enoch episode foreshadows the ascension of Christ and is a miraculous event. Milton very plainly used the incident *not* to be typological and *not* to accept the emphases of traditional or popular mysticism. Enoch was significant to Milton because he had "saving faith" and demonstrated it in saving action, giving an example to men of the courage of faith:

> so beset
> With Foes for daring single to be just,
> And utter odious Truth, that God would come
> To judge them with his Saints. . . .
>
> (XI, 702-5)

In the discussion of saving faith in *De Doctrina Christiana* Milton wrote:

> Thus the ultimate object of faith is not Christ, the Mediator but God the Father. Theologians have been forced to acknowledge this by the clear evidence of the Bible. So it does not seem surprising that there are a lot of Jews, and Gentiles too, who are saved although they believed or believe in God alone, either because they lived before Christ or because, even though they have lived after him, he has not been revealed to them. In spite of this they are saved by means of Christ, for he was given and sacrificed from the beginning of the world even for those to whom he was not known and who believed only in God the Father. Thus those illustrious men who lived under the law, Abel, Enoch, Noah, etc., are honoured with an attestation of their true faith, although it is stated that they believed only in God.[44]

Milton was of course perfectly aware of the typical significance in Enoch's translation and glossed it in the chapter on "complete glorification, also Christ's second coming": "Before the law the type of [complete glorification which must eventually be achieved in eternity] was Enoch, who was taken up into heaven and Elijah." But even in that chapter it is not what Enoch prefigures but what he does and says which really interests Milton: "The coming of the Lord to judgment, when he, with his holy angels, shall judge the world, was prefigured first by Enoch and the prophets and then by Christ himself and his apostles."

Milton was not always of a mind to make a strictly moral and literal use of Enoch rather than a mysterious and typological use. In the course of planning *Paradise Lost* he must consciously have rejected the typological. In the Trinity Manuscript the third draft outline for a drama to be entitled "Paradise Lost" begins: "Moses recounting how

---

[44] *CPW*, VI, 474-75. See also p. 487: "the faithful both before the law and under the law: Abel, Enoch, Noah and many others [are accounted] righteous in the sight of God."

he assum'd his true bodie, that it corrupts not because of his [being] with God in the mount declares the like of Enoch and Eliah, besides the purity of the place that contains pure winds, dues, and clouds praeserve it from corruption whence he hasts to the sight of God. . . ." Here Milton adverted to the seventeenth-century remnants of the medieval view holding that Enoch and Elijah were translated as incorruptible bodies to the terrestrial Eden in the sky on top of the mountain not covered by the waters of the Flood. But Milton lost interest in this kind of speculation. All that remained of it when he wrote *Paradise Lost* was the fanciful metaphorical geography in Book III, where Satan's "far distant" descrying of a staircase to the gates of heaven is likened to the stairs Jacob saw

> *Dreaming by night.* . . .
> Each Stair *mysteriously was meant*, nor stood
> There alwaies, but drawn up to Heav'n somtimes
> Viewless, and underneath a bright Sea flow'd
> Of Jasper, or of liquid Pearle, whereon
> Who after came from Earth, sayling arriv'd,
> Wafted by Angels, or flew o're the Lake
> Rapt in a Chariot drawn by fiery Steeds.
>
> (III, 514-22; emphasis added)

That passage in Book III (following closely on the description of the Paradise of Fools and its "likely habitants," the "Giants" born "of ill-joynd Sons and Daughters," and "the builders . . . of *Babel* on the Plain") looks forward to the literal historical consequences of the Fall as Michael takes them up in Books XI and XII. Milton carefully underscored the metaphorical or fanciful nature of the scenes in Book III. But in Book XI, when he came to treat Enoch as a figure from whom Adam was to learn true doctrine, he noticeably sandwiched the vision between a picture of natural death consonant with his mortalism and a picture of Eden not drawn up by mysterious stairs above the earth but

> moovd
> Out of his place, pushd by the horned floud,
> With all his verdure spoil'd, and Trees adrift
> Down the great River to the op'ning Gulf,
> And there take root an Iland salt and bare,
> The haunt of Seales and Orcs, and Sea-mews clang.[45]
>
> (XI, 830-35)

[45] See Duncan, *Milton's Earthly Paradise*, 190-94, for a discussion of the destruction of Paradise and speculations about the true geographical location of an

In the Enoch episode Milton eschews typology and demythologizes mysticism to make a plain point, "to shew . . . what reward / Awaits the good, the rest what punishment." He stresses the literal teacher in Enoch, not the mysterious prophet, specifying for him an age and demeanor suitable to the didactic role "of middle Age," "eminent in wise deport," who "spake much of Right and Wrong, / Of Justice, of Religion, Truth and Peace, / And Judgement from above."[46] Milton coalesced the scriptural account of Elijah's translation with the cryptic reference to Enoch, so as to paint a picture with credible human details.[47] His emphasis falls throughout on Enoch as an example of a man of faith whose behavior is imitable and hence educative, a person treated by God in a manner illustrative of God's nature.

Book III differs from Book XI in, among other things, the explicitness with which Michael treats covenant. That explicitness seems to throw increased emphasis on the element of typology in each of Michael's accounts of God's entering into relationships with men throughout human history. Such emphasis is present, but not at the expense of the directly exemplary. The charge God had given Michael in sending him to judge and teach the fallen pair had been to

> reveale
> To *Adam* what shall come in future dayes,
> As I shall thee enlighten, *intermix*
> *My Cov'nant in the Womans seed renewed*;
> So send them forth, though sorrowing, yet in peace.
>
> (XI, 113-17; emphasis added)

In his first words to Adam, Michael teaches the doctrine of God's omnipresence: "still compassing thee round / With goodness and pa-

---

historic Eden; see also John Armstrong, *The Paradise Myth* (London: Oxford University Press, 1969), and A. Bartlett Giamatti, *The Earthly Paradise and the Renaissance Epic* (Princeton: Princeton University Press, 1966).

[46] Genesis makes him 365 at his translation, roughly half as old as his son Methuselah at his death. From Jude comes the picture of Enoch as a teacher and interpreter: "And Enoch also, the seventh from Adam, prophesied of these, saying, Behold the Lord Cometh with ten thousand of his saints, To execute judgment upon all, and to convince all that are ungodly among them of all their ungodly deeds which they have ungodly committed, and of all their hard speeches which ungodly sinners have spoken against him." See Carey and Fowler, *Poems of Milton*, 1015-16, for the suggestion that Milton's characterization owes something to parts of the Book of Enoch quoted in patristic writings.

[47] Milton put together 2 Kings 2:11—"And it came to pass, as they still went on, and talked, that, behold, there appeared a chariot of fire, and horses of fire, and parted them both asunder; and Elijah went up by a whirlwind into heaven"—and Gen. 5:24—"And Enoch walked with God: and he was not; for God took him."

ternal Love, his Face / Express, and of his steps the track Divine." He then promises to show him "what shall come in future dayes," without mention of the vital crux, the "Cov'nant in the Womans seed renewd." Throughout the course of Book XI Milton plays down the proleptic aspect of the Old Testament stories to point up instead their exemplary aspect.[48] So too in *De Doctrina Christiana* his discussion of saving faith used the Enoch story to illustrate the evenness in God's grace throughout all periods of time, the faithful being saved through the instrument of Christ's sacrifice before the actual completion of that sacrifice. "From the beginning of the world," God covenanted with man to crush the serpent by the woman's seed; each part of history, the age of the Patriarchs, the Law, and the Prophets, as well as the Christian era, is the recipient of God's covenant, repeatedly renewed. From every part of Scripture, as from one wholly consistent revelation, perspicuous instances of God's nature are derivable in his treatment of men.

Although Michael reserved the promise of the woman's seed for Book XII, it is not then that Adam for the first time hears of it; he heard it from Christ in his judgment upon the fallen pair and the serpent. In one of his major variations on the account in Genesis, Milton specified that Christ, rather than God, came to judge mankind, and he had Christ give the reason:

> Father Eternal, thine is to decree,
> Mine both in Heav'n and Earth to do thy will
> Supream. . . .
>
> (x, 68-70)

The change enabled Milton to define God's nature:

> Easie it may be seen that I intend
> Mercie collegue with Justice, sending thee
> Mans Friend, his Mediator, his design'd
> Both Ransom and Redeemer voluntarie,
> And destin'd Man himself to judge Man fall'n.
>
> (x, 58-62)

Although patriarchal figures were necessarily unaware of Christ's sacrifice, that sacrifice applied to them. Their experiences are relevant to

[48] For a very cogent discussion of the centrality of the protevangelium in Book X of *Paradise Lost* see Georgia B. Christopher, "The Verbal Gate to Paradise: Adam's 'Literary Experience' in Book x of *Paradise Lost*," *PMLA*, 90 (1975), 69-77; see also Irene Samuel, *Dante and Milton* (Ithaca: Cornell University Press, 1966), 221-32.

deducing God's nature because they derived a faith in God from their experiences, without an anachronistic sense of the coming of the Son being prefigured in those experiences. Christ's praise of Socrates in succession to his praise of Job in *Paradise Regained* makes it clear that God's nature is deducible to pre-Christian Gentiles as well as to pre-Christian Jews. Not only the patriarchs but also pious heathens might gather true faith from their experience of God in their own lives. Thus, when in Book x of *Paradise Lost* Christ himself appears in the Garden to judge and commence the salvation of fallen man, he enunciates to the guilty pair the judgment of the serpent containing the protevangelium:

> Between Thee and the Woman I will put
> Enmitie, and between thine and her Seed;
> Her Seed shall bruise thy head, thou bruise his heel.
>
> (x, 179-81)

Simply in terms of his own experience of fall, judgment, and repentance, Adam tried to consider the implications of that promise before Michael arrived to instruct him, "calling to minde with heed / Part of our Sentence, that thy Seed shall bruise / The Serpents head" (x, 1030-32). He got no further than to read it joyfully as "revenge indeed."[49] Nonetheless, Adam's recollection of the promise brings with it a measure of grace, changing his mood so that he can understand God's nature more clearly, even if his own new responsibility seemed cloudy:

> in whose look serene,
> When angry most he seem'd and most severe,
> What else but favor, grace, and mercie shon?
>
> (x, 1094-96)

The merciful fulfillment of "Part of our Sentence" in the constant renewal of the covenant is the burden of Book xii. The sense that God enters into educative relationships with men by which they come to know him was the burden of Book xi. These are complementary mat-

---

[49] It is a weakness in Georgia Christopher's article that she does not indicate that Adam's reading was altogether inadequate until Michael had given his brilliant lessons in biblical exegesis. It is a further weakness, I believe, that her essay denigrates quite unnecessarily the human emotions. Eve's humility does move Adam to relent and to repent; this is not at odds with Adam's learning what the protevangelium means, partly from growing intuition (xi) and partly from instruction (xii). Eve's feelingful behavior moves Adam to a better psychological state from which he can think more energetically. Milton consistently thought that, as he put it in *Areopagitica*, "passions within us, pleasures round about us . . . rightly tempered are the very ingredients of virtue."

ters and Milton does not cancel the exemplary in devoting more attention to the typical in Book XII. By the same token, when the antitype, the Son, is depicted in *Paradise Regained*, the stress falls upon the exemplary rather than the vicarious nature of his salvific struggle, although Milton movingly incorporates typological fulfillments at the close of each of Christ's great exemplary temptations and concludes with a vicarious as well as an exemplary act.

Although the promise had been made earlier, the word *covenant* is heard for the first time in *Paradise Lost* both by Adam and by Milton's readers with respect to the rainbow concluding the Flood, "Betok'ning peace from God, and Cov'nant new." Milton had not used the term, even proleptically, in the dialogue in heaven when he was carefully defining the doctrine of election through the decrees of God and the responses of the Son. Adam takes no account of the *word* itself when he first hears it; he asks instead what is the meaning of the *sign*. Michael repeats the word twice in his explanation: God "makes a Covenant never to destroy / The Earth again by flood," and the rainbow accompanying the clouds will be a sign "whereon to look / And call to mind his Cov'nant." Neither time does Adam pick it up. In Book XII Michael speaks at three further points of the covenant of God. God permitted to be placed in the ark of the tabernacle the records of the covenant under the leadership of Moses, Moses being a type of Christ the mediator and prophet; and God renewed the covenant with David, that of his stock should come a king of endless reign, David being a type of Christ the heavenly king. Between these usages Michael explains the crucial concept of the "better Cov'nant" and the progressive spiritual enlightenment of God's people until the protevangelium is clearly manifested in the prophetic antitype Christ. When Adam knows what act it is which "Shall bruise the head of Satan" and understands "The Womans seed, obscurely then foretold, / Now amplier known thy Saviour and thy Lord" (XII, 543-44), the revelation of God is complete. The yield of that complete revelation is two kinds of knowledge. First is knowledge of God:

> Merciful over all his works, with good
> Still overcoming evil, and by small
> Accomplishing great things, by things deemd weak
> Subverting worldly strong, and worldly wise
> By simply meek. . . .

(XII, 565-69)

The second is Adam's knowledge that he must govern his own nature to bring it into a beneficent relationship to the kind of God he now understands:

301

Henceforth I learne, that to obey is best,
And love with feare the onely God, to walk
As in his presence, ever to observe
His providence and on him sole depend . . .
. . . that suffering for Truths sake
Is fortitude to highest victorie,
And to the faithful Death the Gate of Life.

(XII, 561-71)

These two forms of knowledge have been taught to Adam through Michael's interpreting the "minde of Christ." Adam understands the salvific truth given him to have been exemplary rather than vicarious, "Taught this by his example whom I now / Acknowledge my Redeemer ever blest" (XII, 572-73). As if to underline the persistent need to deduce doctrine from experience in a wrestling for usable truth, rather than to rely upon deriving doctrine primarily from mystical or institutional typology, the first case history Michael shows Adam is the atypological case of Nimrod and the Tower of Babel.

Nimrod

Nimrod is the archetype of the Rebel in the interlinked modes of political and intellectual overreaching, "affecting to subdue / *Rational Libertie*" both by enthralling the "outward libertie" of men and by attempting to "reach to Heav'n." Milton uses the epithet *"Rational Libertie"* not to suggest that Nimrod is a brainless overreacher, but to show that he thinks he has the power to make things mean what he wills them to mean: if he stands on a high platform, that means he is high; if men call him great, that means he is great. The motives of Nimrod and his rebellious crew are, like the motives of the warring giants, to "get themselves a name, least far disperst / In foraign Lands thir memorie be lost, / Regardless whether good or evil fame." Their ambition deserves the direct heavenly rebuke it receives, and the nature of the rebuke defines the particular illegality of their procedure. Adam is meant to derive an understanding of what is improper in seeking their relation to God instead of another sort of relation. The generations of Noah, he has been told, while "the dread of judgement" was "Fresh in thir minds," governed their behavior in fear of God and with "regard to what is just and right." They were not guided by written Law: they governed themselves by the law of Nature, understanding its source to be their Creator. The consequence was a life of "joy unblam'd" and "peace by Families and Tribes / Under paternal rule." The effect of Nimrod's rebellion is to break the known law of

Nature by cutting it off from its source in God and to shatter the concord of men in earth by bringing about something like Hobbes's state of nature. Nimrod's ambitious reasoning did not acquaint him with the coherence of truth as it emerges from the Creator, nor with every man's equal right to it. Michael analyses the building of the tower in these terms:

> one shall rise
> Of proud ambitious heart, who not content
> With fair equalitie, fraternal state,
> Will arrogate Dominion undeserv'd
> Over his brethren, and quite dispossess
> Concord and law of Nature from the Earth. . . .
> . . . as in despite of Heav'n.
>
> (XII, 24-34)

Nimrod's action is illegal by the measure of the law of Nature and the law of nations, reason being the law of Nature and fraternity the law of nations. Nimrod declares himself free from the constraints of both and at once shatters both. Adam's judgment is decisively correct as to the literal crimes committed by Nimrod:

> Man over men
> He made not Lord; such title to himself
> Reserving, human left from human free.
> But this Usurper his encroachment proud
> Stayes not on Man; to God his Tower intends
> Siege and defiance.
>
> (XII, 69-74)

Nonetheless, Michael is made to extend Adam's correct reaction. Milton offers an interpretation of what is wrong in building upward to heaven which makes clear why the punishment is the confusion of tongues and not merely the collapse of the tower. Michael's interpretation has to do with God's omniscience and the absolute nature of transcendent truth as against man's derivative existential knowledge and his tendency to insist that truth is therefore merely relative. (Milton had remarked in *Tetrachordon* that wisdom to God is a high tower of pleasure; relativism is patently shown not to be.)

The episode might seem to direct attention to nothing more than the truth that an omnipotent God punishes all forms of presumption. Michael's first account says much about God's derision and the angels' laughter, as though the ethical force of the scene, teaching humility, were its paramount interest: the presumptuous storm in gabbling tongues because they are being mocked.[50] But the punishment does not simply make ambitious pretenders foolish, it effects the disjunction between words and meanings which was implicit in the denial of the law of Nature or right reason by Nimrod and his crew. God "sets / Upon thir Tongues a various Spirit" because Nimrod's crew have removed from their one language its necessary link to one reality, its dependency upon reason. Their passion for getting themselves a name "regardless whether good or evil fame" introduces disjunction, breaches the rational link between idea and truth, makes the claim that meaning is merely what a man calls meaning and not what reason discovers is meaning. For the first time in human history the arbitrary nature of language is manifest, but its arbitrariness arises from the moral relativism of man, not from the real nature of truth. The "jangling noise of words unknown" results from the claim that meaning or fame is given to words or events by merely human agreement or disagreement. To

---

[50] Enough critics have found Milton distinctly unpleasant on the subject of God's scornful laughter here and elsewhere in *Paradise Lost* to justify perhaps a parenthesis. Two points might be made: first, Milton does more than follow the example of Scripture in assigning to God the human emotion of derision, for the Genesis passage he versifies here contains no such human emotion. If he were merely following Scripture, then his "excuse" would be that which he set forth in *De Doctrina Christiana*: "Let there be no question about it: they understand best what God is like who adjust their understanding to the word of God, for he has adjusted his word to our understanding, and has shown what kind of an idea of him he wishes us to have. In short, God either is or is not really like he says he is. If he really is like this, why should we think otherwise? If he is not really like this, on what authority do we contradict God? If, at any rate, he wants us to imagine him in this way, why does our imagination go off on some other tack?" (*CPW*, VI, 136). Genesis does not inform us that God wishes to be understood in the attitude in which Milton depicted Him. So the question arises, why is Milton sending his imagination off on some other tack? Is he piecing out a deficiency in the text in his own view and thus accommodating his understanding of God to Adam's through Michael? Or is there so much resistance in Milton to the tyrannical picture of a sort of Stuart Nimrod that he desires to mete out to him his own scorn in the form of God's scorn? More likely, I think, the latter. Milton's eye here is less on God than on Nimrod, and he is making less a theological than a political point. But, secondly, Milton shows us here some wicked men on the pinnacle of a tower at whom God and the angels laugh. Other towers of pride have been remarked earlier in *Paradise Lost*, such as those "to swift destruction doomed" on which Abdiel turned his back. And a pinnacle will also be remarked in *Paradise Regained*, on the point of which will stand a good man at whom the angels will marvel. If Milton is making a theological point and we grant that Milton's God unpleasantly laughs because Milton enjoys the fierceness of divine mockery, we must recall that Milton does not always do so. He shows more often and more decisively God's pleasure at goodness than His pleasure at scorning evil.

Nimrod's political tyranny Michael therefore links an intellectual tyranny in order to teach the real meaning of the scene: there is a transcendental truth to be drawn from watching human beings assert that truth is relative to power. One language deriving from one truth by the instrument of reason has been shattered into a multiplicity of languages seeking dominance over other languages by sheer force, asserting the relativity of truth against its unity.

Before the fall of Nimrod's tower, the primacy of reason within men had made each man free in the equal possession of a single true language. Adam *knew* the names of things in the Garden and did not arbitrarily select a sound to signify an object when he gave the animals their names; he had in him the law of Nature, the power of reason, which extracted a single truth in a single word from his experience. (Milton extended to Eve the rational capacity of using experience to name correctly in an extrabiblical flourish, when he allowed her to name the flowers.) Adam's fall involved a loss of inner freedom: his reason became the tool of his will and not its master. Promptly upon deciding to eat the apple, Adam became a linguistic relativist. He rationalized a defense of joining Eve in disobedience; by his rationalization he made words mean what he willed them to mean. He became the world's first bad theologian in the attempt, declaring "Past who can recall, or don undoe? / Not God Omnipotent, nor Fate." The disjunction of *Fate* from *God* is false and constitutes the use of "words unknown." The axiom "what's done is done" is a half truth, as the revelation of the Son's redemptive role must later make clear. Adam's rationalization takes the form not only of imputing to "God Creator wise, / Though threatning" a disinclination to appear at a disadvantage before Satan, a trait for which his experience has supplied no evidence, but also of attributing to God an inability to govern His creation in the medium of time: "all his Works . . . in our Fall . . . needs with us must faile." The mixture of truth and falsehood in Adam's manipulation of words, not to advise his will through reason but to force his reason to serve his will, makes his language a "jangling noise." The picture of the Tower of Babel which Adam sees after Michael's exegesis shows the fall of language imitating his own fall and shows the consequent persistent difficulty subsequent generations will have in communicating transcendent truth through the existential sign. The difficulty will not only affect man's ability to arrive at truth freely and to communicate it clearly, it will also affect his ability to live with other men in political fraternity. Inner liberty, the reasonable capacity to learn truth and communicate it, is the essential precondition of social liberty. Only free men can be brothers; self-enslaved men must either struggle for dominance or slackly yield dominance. Hence Michael's explication of the scene dwells upon the lesson of individual responsibility: on each man falls the burden of upholding reason in himself, liberty in his own state, and the communication of that liberty to other men of equal inner freedom through a language in which *res* and *verba* are united:

> yet know withall,
> Since thy original lapse, true Libertie
> Is lost, which always with right Reason dwells
> Twinn'd, and from her hath no dividual being:
> Reason in man obscur'd, or not obeyd,
> Immediately inordinate desires
> And upstart Passions catch the Government
> From Reason, and to servitude reduce
> Man till then free.
>
> (XII, 82-90)

God may then justly permit the loss of external liberty, which is the natural effect of the moral relativism symbolized in the proliferation of competing tongues. Nimrod's crew declares in effect, *things mean to us what we say they mean and that is what they have to mean to you too*. Nimrod implicitly asserts the relativity of interpretations to Adam, who is trying to learn the literal truth from experience. Condemning Nimrod, God condemns the self-assertive relativism of coercing men into accepting from the mighty their version of truth.

Moses and the Messiah

The last case history to which I would like to draw attention follows intellectually upon the case of Nimrod. Michael has finished describing the leadership of Moses bringing "Laws and Rites" to God's chosen people, and Adam has made the link between the useful, helpful knowledge of God brought by Moses and his own destructive knowledge brought by eating the apple:

> now first I finde
> Mine eyes true op'ning, and my heart much eas'd,
> Erwhile perplext with thoughts what would becom
> Of mee and all Mankind; but now I see
> His day, in whom all Nations shall be blest,
> Favour unmerited by me, who sought
> Forbidd'n knowledge by forbidd'n means.
>
> (XII, 273-79)

Adam knows that his sons will be given access to God's blessing through a legitimate knowledge of God, unlike the illegitimate knowledge he professed to have wrested. Nonetheless, in knowing this Adam knows the reality but not the mode of God's mercy. He knows that God governs human experience in such a way as to enable truth and vision to emerge from the reasonable contemplation of God's presence in it; he does not know that his knowledge will become *higher*, only that it will become plainer in the course of history and that that knowledge will be graciously given and need not be stolen by him. He therefore cannot understand the gift of laws as anything other than a sign of man's increased depravity. The one law, the law of Nature, given by God in the symbolic form of the sole prohibition, seems to him adequate for truth if God but protract time and sustain life long enough for reason to derive truth from experience. Michael reveals a relationship between the temporal and the eternal, or the human and the transcendental when he expounds the Mosaic Law as a second stage in a course of human education, giving way to a higher mode of human understanding:

> So Law appears imperfet, and but giv'n
> With purpose to resign them in full time
> Up to a better Cov'nant, disciplin'd
> From shadowie Types to Truth, from Flesh to Spirit,
> From imposition of strict Laws, to free
> Acceptance of large Grace, from servil fear
> To filial, works of Law to works of Faith.

> (XII, 300-306)

But this explanation has no effect on Adam's perception of meaning, for when Michael, continuing, describes the birth of the Messiah, Adam does not attempt an understanding of the coming of the Son in terms of the higher truth contained in "shadowie Types" nor of the Spirit manifest in the Flesh. He uses none of the terms Michael offers him, neither covenant nor shadow, nor type nor grace, nor the servile/filial distinction, nor the law/faith distinction. He ignores the shift Michael offers from *low* to *high* to concentrate on the continuing movement from *before* to *after*. He simply presses Michael to continue the human history of his race (in contradistinction to developing its spiritual value) to its triumphant historical conclusion: "Say where and when / Thir fight." Michael denies the significance of merely "local wounds"; the destruction of evil he locates not in a place nor at a time but within the heart of man at any time and in any place. The regeneration of man is effected, Michael declares, "Not by destroying *Satan*, but his works / In thee and in thy Seed." Once more Adam has proved more literally apt than spiritually quick; in his response to Michael's second summary he again neglects all of the theological terms

Michael offers him—imputed merit, satisfaction, legal works, ransom, annuls, temporal death—and instead exclaims joyously at the literal conversion of sin into greater good in the historical time of the Messiah. As a biblical literalist, Adam then sensibly and fearfully asks what will happen in the course of real time to the human beings the Deliverer leaves behind him when he ascends to heaven. This gives Michael a final opportunity to spiritualize the literal. He informs Adam that in place of the physical presence of the Son, the faithful will be given "His Spirit within them"; in place of the law of Nature or the ensuing Mosaic Law, the believers shall be given "the Law of Faith / Working through love," written on their hearts "To guide them in all truth"; in place of wolfish, self-seeking teachers, they shall have the "written Records pure" of God's dealings with men, "Though not but by the Spirit understood." With this last prophetic revelation, Adam at last has his "fill of knowledge," taught "by his *example* whom I now / Acknowledge my Redeemer ever blest."

No question has been more repeatedly raised by contemporary critics than the question of how much of a guide to Milton's metaphorical or typological procedures is supplied by Michael's explanation of the Law, taken either to supplement or explicate Raphael's earlier explanation that

> what surmounts the reach
> Of human sense, I shall delineate so,
> By lik'ning spiritual to corporal forms,
> As may express them best, though what if Earth
> Be but the shaddow of Heav'n, and things therein
> Each to other like, more then on earth is thought?
>
> (v, 571-76)

Opinion divides into the opposing schools of the Platonists and the typologists, together with a middle school of eclectic reconcilers. On the one hand stand the Platonist-humanists, who argue that through Raphael, Milton is telling us that the earthly copy of eternal truth is a fleeting shadow but also an accurate analogue of divine reality, that the poet may therefore derive symbols and metaphors from the world of reality and use them to tell truths higher than merely earthly truths. This school argues that since Milton considered that human history, not only in its course but also in its individual events, is the metaphorical vehicle of which the tenor is transcendentally metaphysical, he was free to invent a dialogue in which Raphael delivers an account of the nature of the divine by narrating a fiction of prehistory. Michael's words only show that he is equally free to deliver an account of the nature of the divine through a dialogue about actual history. Truth is revealed by metaphor and fiction because reality is a metaphor or imitation or shadow of truth.[51] On the other hand stand the scripturalist-typologists, who argue that through Michael, Milton is telling us that the knowledge of God is not revealed in an Eternal Now by the correspondence of high and low or spiritual and earthly matters, it is instead revealed only in historical progression in which prehistory prophesies history and Jewish history prefigures Christian history, God progressively revealing His nature more and more fully. They argue that Milton substituted for the doctrine of correspondence a doctrine of progressive revelation, substituted Michael's vision for Raphael's vision, and stripped his poetry systematically of fictional representations to give instead typological revelation.[52] In the middle stand the eclectics, who argue that Milton saw truth revealed both in the book of Nature and of Scripture and that his method is both Platonic and prophetic, so that historical revelations are the graded results of individual struggles to penetrate meaning. They argue that Milton saw history as a redemptive process; the one just man was contained within history to be the vehicle of typological teaching, but he also stood outside history by achieving higher vision than the historical, so as to be himself the vehicle of exemplary teaching. They find therefore that Milton was able to use two inspired narrators, each with vision higher than human, one having free recourse to correspondences and the other to typologies.[53] The controversy over how to read Michael's words in conjunction with Raphael's has implications for the understanding of Milton's metaphorical practice, structural practice, and intellectual habits.

My own view would include the eclectic position, but it is not for that reasoning that Michael's words seem to me important. Michael's

[51] This is representative of the views of James H. Hanford, Merritt Hughes, M. M. Mahood (in *Poetry and Humanism* [New Haven: Yale University Press, 1950]), Marjorie Nicolson, and George W. Whiting. See Leland Ryken, *The Apocalyptic Vision in "Paradise Lost"* (Ithaca: Cornell University Press, 1970), 7-33, for an extended account of the controversy.

[52] This is representative of the views of William Madsen, H. R. MacCallum, Barbara Lewalski, Northrop Frye, F. Michael Krouse, Lynn Veach Sadler, C. A. Patrides, and Christopher Grose.

[53] This is similar to the views of Balachandra Rajan, Arthur E. Barker, A.S.P. Woodhouse, Leland Ryken, and William Kerrigan. An analogous view, more deftly put, that the scenes are exemplary and paideutic can be found in Irene Samuel, "The Purgatorial Way," in her *Dante and Milton*. Boyd M. Berry, *Process of Speech: Puritan Religion Writing and "Paradise Lost"* (Baltimore: Johns Hopkins University Press, 1976), 264-67, also notices how Adam learns not just what Michael speaks but what is appropriate to all men. The Afterword of his book confirms from another stance altogether the existence of an arc of changing theology in Milton.

answer is important because the issue is not a straightforward case of progressive enlightenment and the irresistible betterment of redeemed men becoming clearer in a movement from type to antitype. Nor is it a straightforward case of illumination given to one worthy of it, to one just man. Michael is discussing the profoundly ambiguous case of law given to fallen men to display their fallenness in such a way as to mitigate it. He offers his analysis to a fallen man who has asked how God can endure to live with men so fallen as to require the condemnation of so many of their acts. Adam has put the question not because he is stupid, euphoric, enthusiastic, or any of the faintly downputting things he has sometimes been called by readers who notice his need to know something they think they already know. Milton, that is, did not put into the mouth of Adam a pupil's question to a clever master so that the master could give the official answer due prominence. Adam's question is a real question and a continuing one, more real and more continuing than the angelic theology he is given in reply, for it concerns what can be deduced about God in His interchanges with man. It has implications about how man must alter his behavior in relation to a better understood God, and it is about fallenness and what can be made of it. Adam knows how God has dealt with him, with Noah, with Enoch, with Abraham, and with Moses. It is of enormous concern for him to know how God deals at all times and in all places with men who are confined to the contemporary understanding they may have of God and are seeking a fuller or timeless truth. The period of the Law, Adam learns, contained salvific experience for the people of Moses and also a promise of a higher and more universally available redemption. God's will to save men can be deduced from both the case of Moses and the type of Moses: the important thing is that the people of Moses are shown as instances of reformation. That is the important thing in my view, but it is not what Michael actually says. Michael expresses the double sense of redemption in the Law having been given both for the Jews as a fact and for the Gentiles as a promise in the specifically orthodox Puritan terms of Milton's day—imputed righteousness, justification, better covenant. But Adam is not shown as using that seventeenth-century language of divinity. At the end of the series of visions and descriptions Adam is himself a new Adam and has had revealed to him how the prophecy will be fulfilled in his seed. He is both patriarchal and archetypal. He is exemplary to his sons and has been taught by the perfect example of the perfect Son of his line.

Michael tells Adam that the gift of the Mosaic Law is one from which further gifts will ensue. The Law is saving and will give way to true salvation. Michael expresses seventeenth-century theological deductions from the case histories he shows and describes. The case histories reveal to Adam a more correct view of God than his earlier assumptions contained. Michael makes of them Puritan theology; Adam makes of them a free universal theology. It may be claimed that Milton has merely preserved decorum in restricting Adam's language and insights to the chronological period in which he was presumed to live. Adam's education, however, advances him beyond that period. Milton's contemporary readers would not have understood Adam to learn truths applicable only to Adam while Michael told, over his head as it were, to them truths applicable beyond Adam. They would have seen him to advance in understanding until he could stand upon the same grounds of faith and hold the same concepts of belief as were held as essential matters of faith by their own Puritan generation. Adam is not just patriarch, he is Everyman in the capacity he has to teach every man. It is not simply to avoid anachronism that Milton does not allow to his human speaker the specialist language he hears from Michael or the specialist language Milton himself uses in *De Doctrina Christiana*. Rather, it is to underscore the universality in the Adamic formulations: Adam is the case of the human capacity to think the new. Adam focuses on human needs, contingencies and applications; the angels, whether Raphael the Platonist or Michael the typologist, offer to present larger universal schemes. I by no means intend to suggest that Milton is indifferent to such cosmic subjects, for they figure largely in the first book of *De Doctrina Christiana*. Nor are the views of the angels who stood to be identified and dismissed with the absurd efforts of the angels who fell and

> reason'd high
> Of Providence, Foreknowledge, Will, and Fate,
> Fixt Fate, free will, foreknowledge absolute,
> And found no end, in wandring mazes lost.
>
> (ii, 558-61)

Nor should I be taken to suppose that the just-fallen, much-mistaking Adam represents a superior theology to that of the orthodoxy of the angels, which Milton undercuts in giving Adam less technical terms. I do mean to suggest, however, that what Adam learns exemplifies what all men may learn. Adam stresses the human significance of God's behavior in history; those things are of continuing and primary importance to all men and to Milton. In the end, correct theology is more important as a freeing process than as a codified formula. That this is Milton's effect is clear. That it was his intention can be deduced less within the epic *Paradise Lost* than from the procedure of transforming truth in the last two works from his hand, *Paradise Regained* and *Samson Agonistes*. *Samson Agonistes* is a fully Christian and fully theological poem; moreover, it is an advance even upon the divinity communicated by *Paradise Lost* in being more radically ecumenical and existential than the epic. *Paradise Regained* is transitional both in its mode of communicating Milton's theology and in the theology it communicates. The theology in *Samson Agonistes* shows how "all Nations shall be blest," how "God attributes to place / No sanctitie," and how a man's spiritual country is where it is well with him.

ORTHODOXY AND THE INDIVIDUAL
CONSCIENCE

MILTON'S "HERESIES" AND THEIR DRAMATIC IMPLICATIONS

Milton's so-called heresies, the result both of winnowing abstract concepts from a great variety of didactic scriptural texts and of observing with rational care the biblical cases of God's behavior toward men under every historical dispensation, constitute the last terms in his lifelong effort to free himself from "implicit faith," from the conventional Puritan stances of his inherited theology, in order to discover a free, living, active faith. The heresies are positions Milton took when he recognized coherent new truth. This he believed each man had to internalize and then obey as his inner self-constituted authority. His enduring distaste for "implicit faith" arose from its perpetual connection in his own mind with external authorities. Superstition and force were the twinned powers Milton detested because they prevented human beings from attaining the kind of freedom he valued, not the freedom to feel free to obey or not, but the liberty to answer obediently only to the inner demands of one's conscious beliefs. To Milton, then, freedom was not simply freedom from false concepts, from untried concepts, or from coercion; it was the more important freedom to live and act by reference to and in consistency with an inner conception of reality. True freedom is identical to an obedience and responsiveness to a self-conscious vision of reality; liberty is simply obedience to inner authority and nonsubmission to external authority. Milton, of course, believed that he had abundant evidence of the authenticity of his inner authority. The inner authority was to be believed and acted upon not because it was Milton's personal concoction and he would will to the end his adherence to it; it was to be believed and acted upon because it was the rational internalization of the one real external authority, the spirit of God. Truth was not for Milton the relative validity of one's own inner light or personal impulses. A man could know, could test, could reasonably derive truth from experience, since God put truth into experience, seeded potential knowledge of Himself in the world and in the Bible, and planted in mankind an ability to discover it. In the last two books of *Paradise Lost* Milton showed how one man, Adam, derived his knowledge of God from scriptural extracts in dialogue with an expert teacher who taught him how God would reveal Himself in interrelationships with the men to come, his sons. The manner in which two other men derived their knowledge of God from their experience of God's behavior toward them—Christ in *Paradise Regained* and Samson in *Samson Agonistes*—constitutes two further instances of human beings discovering God's nature in their lives and becoming examples of His divine activity for other men to consider. *Paradise Regained* and *Samson Agonistes*, however, show attentive readers more than patterns of God's ways with man; they give Milton's new convictions about divine truth. They yield specific dogmas derived from human experience.

Milton's theology is a progressive theology, a radical universal theology, and his heresies are signs of augmented free religious speculation. Whatever one may think either about Milton's evidence for any particular heresy, or his success in defending it, his heresies evince both his own capacity to think new things and his effort to commend the struggle to think new things to other men. The heresies, that is, rather than the orthodoxies, enable readers to measure Milton's capacity to move forward. Not everything Milton took into his coherent sense of religious truth was heretical, and the heresies themselves were not all equally startling to his contemporaries.[1] But the argument has far too often been advanced that Milton's heresies do not therefore particularly matter, or are not of much importance in proportion to the nonheretical substance of his faith, since he was, underneath all of them or despite all of them, surely a Christian. Of course he was a Christian. Heresies do not exclude Christians from Christianity; since they can only be the deviant beliefs of believers, they mark, so to speak, subcultures in relationship to the dominant culture. But Milton's heresies remain the clearest available index by which to measure his theological independence, his own continuing answers to the challenge he put before every man, the challenge to internalize one's own concept of divinity in order to make it the sole inner authority for faith. To try to decide whether Milton's doctrine of the Son was the best doctrine of the Son in his times or whether it most resembled the Christology of this or that group of earlier theologians, or, especially, whether it is true or believable or relevant today is both a futile and an altogether unliterary enterprise. It is, however, of enormous interest

[1] See Conklin, Patrides, and Kelley's footnotes in *CPW*, vi, for analyses of Milton's positions in relationship to contemporary thinkers.

to observe Milton's heterodox definitions at work as forces within his last poems and particularly in *Samson Agonistes*, urging the reader to rethink the meaning of human life as Milton has rethought it. Hence, in dealing with Milton's theology I shall focus on his heterodox positions, positions heterodox by the standards of his Anglican and Puritan contemporaries. I shall not retrace the stages of regeneration in *Samson Agonistes* because they were commonly accepted by Puritan divines.[2] Nor shall I take up the triple functions of the Son in *Paradise Regained*, for they were commonly understood by Anglican and Puritan alike.[3] I shall instead consider the relevance of Milton's concepts of election and predestination and of materialism and mortalism in the protagonists' experiences in the last two poems, in particular, showing how *Samson Agonistes* expresses the necessity to follow the truths one discovers, wherever they may lead, and the consolations which come if one must follow them to the grave.

Milton's heresies hold that all men are meant to be redeemed, that none are given over to be lost, that all share the same mark of humanity (they are composed of matter as an indestructible and good constituent element, not only of all creation but of the Creator as well), and that all equally participate in a total mortality bringing to an end their suffering humanity of body and mind and soul in a sleep from which they will awaken to the highest clearest self-fulfillment that their humanity on earth, as probationers of immortality, could enable. Every one of Milton's heresies, then, asserts the brotherhood of man, the community, the equality, and the godlike potentiality of man. None denies the tragedy of the human state, but all see how from it can be derived patience, hope, and the "true experience" of what is otherwise an "unsearchable dispose."

ANTITRINITARIANISM: DE DOCTRINA CHRISTIANA AND PARADISE LOST

One of Milton's most venturesome heresies requires a preliminary notice since it bears upon the conception of *Paradise Regained* and marks the distinctiveness of *Samson Agonistes* as a contribution to divinity. This is the antitrinitarian heresy, which in Milton takes the form of denying that God is one essence existing in three equal and eternal persons or that God is three divine persons interrelated in a paradoxical

---

[2] Moreover, I have glanced at them before in "Eve and Dalila: Renovation and the Hardening of the Heart," and they have been treated by John M. Steadman in " 'Faithful Champion': The Theological Basis of Milton's Hero of Faith."

[3] That has been the subject of books by Barbara Lewalski and Patrick Cullen.

and mysterious unity. This traditional view of the Trinity Milton found totally incompatible with both reason and Scripture.[4] He set forth in *De Doctrina Christiana* both his objections to it and his own formulations of the Father, the Son, and the Spirit, and their relationship to each other. It is his most mature view of the subject, and he held to that view to the end of his life. As a young believer, Milton inherited and assented to the orthodox trinitarian position. "On the Morning of Christs Nativity" (1629) marks the moment at which the "Infant God" lays aside the "Form" in which he appears in "midst of Trinal Unity" to choose a "darksom House of mortal Clay"; *Of Reformation in England* (1640) invokes "one Tri-personall Godhead"; in the same year, in *Animadversions upon the Remonstrants Defence against Smectymnuus*, the Son is addressed in prayer as the "everbegotten light and perfect Image of the Father"; and in *Of Prelatical Episcopacy*, Tertullian is discredited as a useful teacher for having erred in making "an imparity between God the Father and God the Sonne." By the time of *De Doctrina Christiana*, however, Milton had abandoned orthodox trinitarianism. He persisted in his antitrinitarianism until his death; his last work, *Of True Religion*, cites with approval Arians and Socinians for holding that "the terms of trinity, triunity, coessentiality, tri-personality and the like" were "scholastic notions, not to be found in scripture."

What Milton formulated in place of the orthodox view and offered in *De Doctrina Christiana* has variously been called Arian and subordinationist and considered as transparently heterodox and independent, or on the other hand, as identical with that of a respectable but not dominant strain of Protestantism.[5] In the context of my argument, it is immaterial, of course, what label is given to the pigeonhole into which Milton's independent theistic views of the godhead should be placed or how many contemporary thinkers or church fathers share that pigeonhole, or whether Milton's views are more properly called "deviations" or "heresies." What is absolutely crucial and is likewise unmistakable is that Milton in his youth held a view he considered orthodox and in his maturity held a view he considered Scripture-based and unorthodox, and that he defended the latter with particular vigor and attention precisely as an independent and heterodox view. That Milton himself had a strong sense of his own independence in treating the Trinity, whatever present-day critics may judge of the radicalism of his position, is clear from his having inserted in *De Doctrina Christiana*

[4] See Kelley, "Introduction," *CPW*, VI, 47-73.

[5] See C. A. Patrides, *Milton and the Christian Tradition*, 15-25; the articles by Patrides, Adamson, and Hunter in *Bright Essence*; and Maurice Kelley, *This Great Argument*, and his "Introduction," *CPW*, VI.

a special preface to the chapter "Of the Son of God" in order to assert, "I take it upon myself to refute wherever necessary, not scriptural authority, which is inviolable, but human interpretations," adding "since my opponents . . . can lay claim to nothing more than human powers and that spiritual illumination which is common to all men," "what is more just than that they should allow someone else to play his part in the business of research and discussion: someone else who is hunting the same truth, *following the same track*, and using the same method."[6] Milton could the more convincingly urge his independence because he had shown himself capable of changing his mind.[7]

What Milton discovered when he followed the track of God's self-revelation was that the Father is the one true God; that God's first creation was the Son ("not a scrap of real evidence for the eternal generation of the Son can be found in the whole of scripture");[8] that the Son existed before the creation of the world but that his begetting took place within time;[9] that the Father and Son are not one in essence but are one "in love, communion, in agreement, in charity, in spirit and finally in glory";[10] that the Father and the Son have distinct roles, of which the Son's is subordinate and derivative, the Son being God but not the Supreme God and not one with the Father, "the Son's divine nature being something distinct from and clearly inferior to the Father's nature";[11] that the Holy Spirit is a created minister of God, produced voluntarily by God out of His own substance after the Son was made, and is far inferior to the Son;[12] and that Christ was incarnate not as a hypostatic union of two natures in one person, one of those natures being divine, but that he was a "mutual hypostatic union of two na-

---

[6] *CPW*, vi, 214, 204 (emphasis added).

[7] To fix the period of the change is unnecessary to my theme, but since Kelley has left it open in his introduction to Vol. vi of *CPW*, I might hazard the guess that the change can be associated with the considerations of Scripture enjoined upon Milton by writing the divorce tracts. The necessity in *Tetrachordon* of reconciling Old and New Testament comments upon divorce, I think, led Milton toward increased unorthodoxy. In *Tetrachordon* he wrote at length of the sense in which man is an image of God and at length of Christ's limited intention and time-bound language. The latter required a "healing explanation" from John Milton. He advanced the view that Christ left some matters unexplained or unamplified, "Yet did he not omitt to sow within them the seeds of sufficient determining agen the time that his promis'd spirit should bring all things to [the] memory of his [disciples]" (*CPW*, ii, 697). The implication is that there is a distinction of role between the Spirit and Christ; the Spirit acts later in time and in a subordinate manner, Christ functions within an historical context. The direction of Milton's thought is toward his later characteristic anti-trinitarianism.

[8] *CPW*, vi, 204.   [9] *Ibid.*, 209.   [10] *Ibid.*, 220.   [11] *Ibid.*, 273.
[12] *Ibid.*, 289.

tures, or, in other words, of two essences, of two substances and consequently of two persons . . . [with] nothing to stop the properties of each from remaining individually distinct." Christ was incarnate as an actual man with actual flesh and true humanity.[13] These views Milton deduced from Scripture, defended from Scripture, and supported by reason and logic.

Two interlinked considerations depend upon this special kind of monotheism: the distinct role of the Son as divine exemplar; and the manifestation in divine creativity of God's "unsearchable dispose." The primary role of the Son is to manifest the otherwise unmanifested God.[14] The Son is not the "joint cause" of creation;[15] he is the first creation through which subsequent creations occurred, the Son being the "instrumental or less important cause." Milton defined Creation as "the act by which God the Father produced everything that exists by his word and spirit, that is, by his will, *in order to show* the glory of his power and goodness."[16] The purpose of Creation is the revelation of the nature of the Creator; that nature is most clearly exemplified in His "image." It is exemplified by what the Son is and by what he does both in his heavenly and his earthly abode. The subordinationist, role-differentiated Christology abstractly presented in *De Doctrina Christiana* is dramatized in the presentation of the Son as the exemplifying image of the Father in his heavenly guise as God-man; *Paradise Lost* simply prophesies the incarnation of the Son as the exemplifying image of the Father in his human guise as man-God. The historical Jesus of *Paradise Regained*, as the earthly manifestation of the heavenly Son, illuminates the nature of an otherwise unsearchable God in a human manner. Milton's so-called "anthropomorphic God," that is, can be revealed through the Son only if the Father and the Son are not identical. The Son images the Father so that the Father may be understood by men.

In *Paradise Lost*, Milton variously describes the Son as: "The radiant image of [God's] Glory . . . His only Son" (III, 64); "Divine Similitude, / In whose conspicuous count'nance, without cloud / Made visible, th' Almighty Father shines, / Whom else no Creature can behold" (III, 384-87); "Effulgence of [God's] Glorie, Son belov'd, / Son in whose face invisible is beheld / Visibly, what by Deitie [God is], /

[13] *Ibid.*, 424.

[14] See Woodhouse, *Heavenly Muse*, 174, also his *The Poet and His Faith* (Chicago: University of Chicago Press, 1965,), 104-6; and see Roland Frye, *God, Man and Satan* (Princeton: Princeton University Press, 1960), 75.

[15] *CPW*, VI, 302. "For the Father is not only he *by* whom, but also he *from* whom, *in* whom, *through* whom, and *on account of* whom all things are. . . . But the Son is only he *through* whom all things are, and is therefore the less principal cause" (emphasis added).

[16] *CPW*, VI, 300 (emphasis added).

And in whose hand what by Decree [God does], / Second Omnipotence" (VI, 680-84); and "he full / Respendent all his Father manifest / Express'd" (X, 65-67). Milton extended to no other function of the Son quite such prominence as to his role as demonstrating son, praising him as victorious son, viceregent son, judging son, and restoring son as those roles derive from God's decrees and the Son's willing execution of them. The capacities of the Son as victor, ruler, judge, and savior reveal God's nature as well as the Son's free will. The resemblance and the difference between the Son and the Father, two separate beings whom Milton declined to supply with an identity of essence,[17] are the postulates upon which the exemplary capacity of the Son rests. The Son shows what God is like in the way he behaves. He is a different person from the Father and an image of his Father. He thinks his own thoughts, wills his own purposes, and speaks his own understanding; in this he is an independent person. His understanding of the Father is correct and the Father approves it; in this he has been shown to be the image of the Father.

The most vexed question about the dialogue in heaven in *Paradise Lost*—is it dogma or is it drama—is not susceptible to an either/or answer, for the dialogue is necessarily both. The drama contains the dogma of the Father's nature in that the Son expresses, manifests, and thus dramatizes the Father's qualities by revealing his own natural understanding of them. He not only obeys the unexpressed will of the Father, he believes in the unexpressed omniscience and benevolence of the Father. He becomes the occasion of the Father's self-expression before he undertakes the role of savior of men. He does so not only by obedience but also by faith. He is shown in the dialogue taking the step of belief and receiving the reward of his faith, obedient to no external authoritative command of God but obedient to his inner understanding of Him. In the dialogue, the Father prophesies the Fall of man, the Son pronounces the grace to be shown to the penitent; the Father recalls the penalty for disobedience, the Son knows that if grace exists, the means of grace can be found; the Father expresses the need for a vicarious object of punishment, the Son offers to take on man's sins and

[17] See Merritt Hughes, "The Filiations of Milton's Celestial Dialogue," in his *Ten Perspectives on Milton*. The argument of C. A. Patrides, "*Paradise Lost* and the Language of Theology," in *Bright Essence*, that Milton "drastically altered his approach" to the Son in *Paradise Lost*, compared with his treatment in *De Doctrina Christiana*, ignores the evidence of the angelic hymn in Book III of *Paradise Lost*, in which Milton joined. The Son is there hailed as "of all Creation first" (383) and as "second to thee" (409). See John Broadbent, *Some Graver Subject* (London: Chatto and Windus, 1960), 154-55, for an account of the literary effect of Milton's subordinationism; see also his "Milton's 'Mortal Voice' and 'Omnific Word,'" in Patrides, ed., *Some Approaches to "Paradise Lost"*.

be punished for them; the Father warns that the punishment must be even to death, the Son takes on even that. The Son is willing to die for man because he believes

> thou hast givn me to possess
> Life in my self for ever, by thee I live,
> Though now to Death I yeild, and am his due
> All that of me can die, yet that debt paid,
> Thou wilt not leave me in the loathsom grave
> His prey, nor suffer my unspotted Soule
> For ever with corruption there to dwell;
> But I shall rise. . . .
>
> (III, 243-50)

His belief gains for him God's assent to his understanding of Him. God turns to the angels standing round and emphasizes the very difference between Himself and the Son from which the revelation of His nature can be exhibited:

> But all ye Gods,
> Adore him, who to compass all this dies,
> Adore the Son, and honour him as mee.
>
> (III, 341-43)

The Son reveals the nature of the Father even when the Son is depicted exalted on the Father's right hand; he believes in the goodness and justice of the Father; he instances his exemplary faith; and he is made both a witness and an example of God's beneficence.

What John Broadbent describes as "the Son's rhetorical modulations of the Father's theme of grace," Irene Samuel far more accurately and suggestively calls "a dramatic encounter between distinct speakers," noting that the free act of the Son, ignorant of the ultimate design of eternal Omniscience, exalts compassion to work out a plan for man's redemption. Merritt Hughes argues that the scene "synthesizes the thesis of justice and the antithesis of mercy." Elaborating on the insight of both these critics, Antony Low has denied that the dialogue represents any contradiction or opposition between the Father and the Son.[18] Professor Low rightly draws attention to the exemplification of the Father in the Son:

[18] Broadbent, *Some Graver Subject*, 153; Irene Samuel, "The Dialogue in Heaven: Reconsiderations of *Paradise Lost*, III:1-417," *PMLA*, 72 (1957), 167; Hughes, "Filiations of Milton's Celestial Dialogue," 114; Low "Milton's God: Authority in *Paradise Lost*," *Milton Studies*, 4 (1972), 30; see also Joan Webber, "Milton's God," *ELH*, 40 (1973).

The endless love and immeasurable grace which appear in the Son's countenance are the substantial expression of the Father's nature. Here the divine compassion visibly appears, implying that in the Father it is present but invisible. The Son . . . pleads for man. The Father notes in his reply that "All hast thou spoken as my thoughts are, all/ As my Eternal Purpose hath decreed:/ Man shall not quite be lost" (III, 171-73). In other words, the Son is not arguing with the Father, Mercy against Justice; he is expressing what originated from the Father—indeed, what the Father has decreed from all eternity.

I cannot agree, however, with Low's implication that the Father has decreed from all eternity the Fall, or the grace, or the means of grace. Milton makes it clear that the Son does not know everything the Father knows, and because he does not, the dialogue becomes a means for Milton to communicate his dogma.[19] In conformity with his understanding of predestination, Milton depicts God as possessing the wisdom to use contingency in His perfect government of the universe: God's eternal foreknowledge is not only not compulsive upon any created agent—for "neither God's decree nor his foreknowledge can shackle free causes with any kind of necessity"[20]—it is also consistent with temporally acquired knowledge—"For it is neither absurd nor impious to say that the idea of certain things or events might come to God from some other source."[21] Fathers are superior and antecedent to sons, but the behavior of sons and the reactions of fathers reveal truths both to the fathers and about the fathers. How glorious divine creativity *is* appears in how glorious it *becomes*. God is revealed in relationships rather than in static doctrines, and His "unsearchable dispose" is manifested in examples of unfolding events: dogma is drama because the dogma at issue is the doctrine of a creative relationship of free agents; the doctrine is the interaction of Father and Son, Creator and created; the drama reproduces the interaction. *Paradise Regained* and *Samson Agonistes* are both linked to a concept of God the Father as conditionally predestining free agents. That concept in turn is anchored in the supremely revealing instance of God the Father in interaction with the Son.

One last preliminary point to be made about Milton's antitrinitarianism, therefore, is the exceptional stress it places upon the element of freedom in the relationships of parentage, sonship, and human de-

---

[19] See Irene Samuel, "Dialogue in Heaven," on this point, as on the point that conditional predestination is established by the supremely revealing instance of God the Father in interaction with His Son.

[20] *De Doctrina Christiana*, CPW, VI, 166.

[21] *Ibid.*, 164.

scent.[22] In the dialogue in heaven in Book III of *Paradise Lost* the Father signifies His approval of the Son's gracious and faithful offer to become the means of grace by telling the Son truths which the Son does not understand in advance to be implicated in his offer. The Son imagines that efficacious grace will arise from a straightforward exchange of scapegoats, similar to that in the sacrifice of Isaac. He made his offer in those terms:

> Behold mee then, mee for him, life for life
> I offer, on mee let thine anger fall;
> Account mee man.
>
> (III, 236-38)

But the Father has another complex mode of salvation in mind which will perpetuate relationship, not consummate it. The relationship of Father to Son will be internalized in the hearts of all believers and God's Son will thereby become man's father. Milton gives to the Father, who offers it to the Son, a succinct soteriological explanation: Christ will become Jesus Christ, a human father of all Adam's sons, by becoming one of Adam's sons. The manhood in Jesus Christ as the father of Adam's sons will not be a diminution of the godlike in the Son-made-flesh; on the contrary, the godlike will become an inner quality strengthening the manhood of those of Adam's sons who accept the new relationship offered them:

> Thou therefore whom thou only canst redeeme,
> Thir Nature also to thy Nature joyne;
> And be thy self Man among men on Earth. . . .
> . . . Be thou in *Adams* room
> The Head of all mankind, though *Adams* Son.
> As in him perish all men, so in thee
> As from a second root shall be restor'd,
> As many as are restor'd, without thee none.
> His crime makes guiltie all his Sons, thy merit
> Imputed shall absolve them who renounce
> Thir own both righteous and unrighteous deeds,

---

[22] I should here notice that these subjects are those which John Broadbent has identified as obsessive themes in *Paradise Regained* ("The Private Mythology of *Paradise Regained*," in *Calm of Mind*, ed. Wittreich), save that he finds Milton merely to "hammer" and not adequately to mold these themes, a verdict which arises from Professor Broadbent's discovery that Milton cannot penetrate to the true deep significance of his subject—the universal adolescent rites of passage into adulthood—whereas I do not imagine that to be Milton's subject, veiled or otherwise from him.

And live in thee transplanted, and from thee
Receive new life. So Man, as is most just,
Shall satisfie for Man, be judg'd and die,
And dying rise, and rising with him raise
His Brethren, ransomd with his own dear life. . . .
Nor shalt thou by descending to assume
Mans Nature, less'n or degrade thine own. . . .
. . . thy Humiliation shall exalt
With thee thy Manhood also to this Throne;
Here shalt thou sit incarnate, here shalt Reigne
Both God and Man, Son both of God and Man,
Anointed universal King.

(III, 281-317)

All men have a wholly natural father by genetic descent, Adam the patriarch; all men have a wholly divine father by the initial creation of Adam, God the Father; all men have a spiritual brotherhood with the Son, whom God the Father also created. Their spiritual brother, by becoming one of them naturally, is made their spiritual father. Relationships of father and son contain freedom and choice as well as cause and effect; they image strikingly the progressive revelation of truth through generations. Adam, in despair after his fall, had noted that his natural sons might turn against him and not only curse him—"Ill fare our Ancestor impure, / For this we may thank *Adam*" (x, 735-36)—but also rebuke and deny him. He had distinguished between his fatherhood to his sons and God's fatherhood to him in terms of necessity and freedom: God chose to father him in a spiritual fashion; he fathered his sons as effects of natural causes:

> though God
> Made thee without thy leave, what if thy Son
> Prove disobedient, and reprov'd, retort,
> Wherefore didst thou beget me? I sought it not:
> Wouldst thou admit for his contempt of thee
> That proud excuse? yet him not thy election,
> But Natural necessity begot.
> God made thee of choice his own, and of his own
> To serve him, thy reward was of his grace,
> Thy punishment then justly is at his Will.

(x, 759-68)

If all that Adam can give birth to is "propagated curse," then, as Eve suggests, better give birth to nothing and die without issue. But Adam's sons would display more than contempt and pride against Adam if they were to deny their natural father and seek to shake off his corrupting influence or exculpate themselves. Their natural father was the freely chosen creation of a divine Father, who has freely given to them, in order to save them, an eternal-and-temporal father: Christ, the new Adam. Before the Creation, the redemption was willed. Raphael seems to tell us that both were subsequent to an earlier divine plan for an unfallen mankind:

> And from these corporal nutriments perhaps
> Your bodies may at last turn all to Spirit,
> Improv'd by tract of time, and wingd ascend
> Ethereal, as wee, or may at choice
> Here or in Heav'nly Paradises dwell;
> If ye be found obedient. . . .

(v, 496-501)

At every stage and under every description God's creativity intermingles natural relationships and divine truths and preserves human reason and volition. Raphael's exposition of a natural progress in an Edenic paradise was an exposition of contingency: natural growth depended upon rational consent.[23] The postlapsarian "unsearchable dispose" reinstates fallen man in a natural order once more dependent upon rational consent. Milton expounded his Christian faith so as to account for human relationships as well as for salvation. The community of the faithful is the brotherhood of spiritual sons. The loving ties between free men are located in familial interactions, commencing with the interrelationship of father and son at the beginning of time.

ANTITRINITARIANISM: PARADISE REGAINED
AND SAMSON AGONISTES

Both *Paradise Regained* and *Samson Agonistes* confirm Milton's predilection for depicting the relationships of father and son, brother and brother as images of the nature of God and the community of the saved. The dialogue in heaven in *Paradise Lost* looks ahead to the later works in one further sense. Just as Michael's language contained the technical terminology of contemporary theology and Adam's human responses did not, so in the dialogue in heaven the Father's words are overtly theological and technical: *transgress; predestination; decree; grace voutsaft; elect; prayer, repentance, and obedience; conscience; persist-*

---

[23] Jonathan Goldberg, "*Virga Iesse*: Analogy, Typology and Anagogy in a Miltonic Simile," *Milton Studies*, 5 (1973), 177-90.

ing; hard'nd; expiate; rigid satisfaction; merit imputed; transplanted; ransomd; incarnate. The Son's are simply descriptive. The Father's speeches postulate theology in doctrinal nouns. The Son's offer and respond in verbs: *find; visit; comes unprevented, unimplor'd, unsought; seek; lost; indebted and undon; bring; offer; fall; account; leave; put off; die; wreck; lie vanquisht; possess life; yeild; paid; suffer; dwell; rise; subdue; spoild; receive, & stoop; disarm'd; lead; show; bound; pleas'd; look down and smile; raisd I ruin; glut; enter; returne.* In *Paradise Regained* the language even of the Father makes far less use of the contemporary and hence time-bound Puritan or Anglican theological vocabulary than in *Paradise Lost.*

What the Father does say in *Paradise Regained* pointedly emphasizes the perfect humanity of the Son. The Father depicts the Son as tried on a strictly human level, as any man may be tried, and overcoming temptation as any man may overcome it. Speaking to Gabriel in Heaven, God the Father recalls "that solemn message late . . . to the Virgin pure . . . that she should bear a Son / *Great in Renown,* and *call'd* the Son of God," and by preview predicts Satan's failure to tempt that man, "He now shall know I can *produce a man.*" The Son—variously named in the poem "This man of men," "Son of God," "Saviour," "Jesus," and "Messiah" (but only once called "Anointed" and never the synonymic Christ, or Eternal Son, or God of God, Light of Light, or Very God of Very God)—is identified by the Father as "This perfect *Man, by merit* call'd my Son."[24]

When the Son himself first speaks in Book 1 of *Paradise Regained* (Milton economically dividing the exposition amongst Satan in consistory, God in conversation, and the Son in soliloquy), he takes the language of the poem still further toward the natural and conversational. Milton introduces the soliloquy by describing the Son "musing and much revolving in his brest, . . . which way first [to] / Publish his God-like office now mature." The Son's meditation considers his childhood, his study, his idealistic hopes, his important talk with his mother in which she divulged his uniqueness, his renewed study, his baptism, and his present willingness to serve.[25] The Son knows a good deal of his Messianic mission and of the means by which he will fulfill Messianic prediction; it is as Messiah that he defines his role. There is no reason from his words to suppose that he knows anything superhuman

[24] All the emphases have been added.

[25] See Stein, *Heroic Knowledge,* 104-5, for an analysis of the stages of intellectual growth and apprehension in Christ's autobiographical speech. See Walter MacKellar, *A Variorum Commentary,* IV, 73-74, for a summary of Stein's argument.

about a divinity in his nature, even when he turns the blaze of his Messianic self-definition on Satan to conclude the first temptation:

> Why dost thou then suggest to me distrust,
> Knowing who I am, as I know who thou art?
>
> (I, 355-56)

He does not say that Satan knows him to be God, or knows anything more of him than he knows of himself. He knows of himself that he is "the Messiah, to our Scribes / Known partly," that to his mother a special illumination revealed him "no Son of mortal man," that his role is redemptive, liberating, and difficult, and that if he needs to know more, then further knowledge will be given to him.[26]

It seems to me a misreading and a flattening of *Paradise Regained* to minimize Milton's persistent concern in the poem with the theological question of the nature of Christ's sonship by making the divinity of the Son the assumption and not the discovery of the poem, or by assuming that that divinity is "real" to the exclusion of "allegoric."[27] The great duel of the Son with Satan is a "duel, not of arms, / But to *vanquish by wisdom* hellish wiles" (I, 174-75; emphasis added). The strongest source of interest in the brief epic is the interest in the intellectual adequacy of Christ's responses to temptation, not that those responses are appropriate to a mysterious nature, special to the Son and not shared by man, but that those responses triumphantly, generously, and brilliantly place in perspective the reasonable and attractive goals to be gained by accepting the intelligent proposals of Satan. The Son does not answer to temptation in terms of *I may not*; he answers in affirmative terms, *I need not, I would rather not*, and *I have something else in mind*. He will not turn stones to bread because he is not impressed by the "force in Bread," and it is not so attractive to him as "each Word / Proceeding from the mouth of God" (I, 349-50); he will not accept Satan's magical foreknowledge "by presages and signs" because all "pious Hearts [contain] an inward Oracle / To all truth requisite for men to know" (I, 463-64); he will not accept the gifts of the Devil's table because they are "specious gifts no gifts but guiles" (II, 391) and he is well enough without them; he will not ensure kingly power by amassing wealth because poor virtuous men have done mighty things, because self-government is more kingly than ruling headstrong multitudes, and because the finest form of leading is spiritual

---

[26] See MacKellar, *A Variorum Commentary*, IV, 63-64, for the denial of this view supported by the speculations of several critics.

[27] Satan's probing question is very provocative: "A Kingdom they portend thee, but what Kingdom, / Real or Allegoric I discern not" (IV, 389-90).

teaching; he will not seek glory in popular fame as an end because un-
deserved fame often accrues to ignoble violent deeds and true fame be-
longs to grateful magnanimity; he will not seize an active role because
he understands the value of endurance, and thus he will not take up
military alliance with the Parthians to rescue his brethren because those
brethren chose their impenitent lives "distinguishable scarce / From
Gentils" and can only be truly rescued when, penitently and sincerely,
they change their own inner allegiance; nor will he join himself to
imperial Rome and not only gain Roman magnificence but also im-
prove Roman *mores*, because external elegance is tastelessly unattrac-
tive to the mind and the Romans lack the internal liberty from which
external freedom and decency essentially derive; he will not learn
ancient wisdom from Greece as instrumental to his cause for he has
his own "light from above," discerns inadequacy in sophistical and
stoic philosophies, and prefers the inspired wisdom of the Hebrew
writers.

The pleasure Milton proposes to the reader is the pleasure inherent
in intellectual debate, the establishment of the most reasonable position
by the most penetrating analysis. There could be no pleasure of this
sort in the poem if Satan's proposals were not attractive and if the
Son's responses were not intellectually decisive; there is no mental
stimulus in divine impassivity expressing immortal indifference to
merely low stimuli. Beneath the overt intellectual debate lies the latent
contest to define the nature of sonship with God.[28] Milton steadily puts
the question: Is Christ the Son of God by nature or the adopted Son
of God by grace? Or, is Christ the Son of God in a special sense very
different from the sense in which everything God creates and sustains
can be said to be fathered by Him? Or, does the Son save men by dying
for them, or, also and more importantly, by showing them how to live?

Milton so persistently called attention to the question of Christ's
sonship that simply to list the crucial uses of "son deem'd," "man
seems," "attested Son," "by merit call'd," "declar'd the Son," "titl'd
Gods," "False titl'd Sons," "chosen sons," "the father known," "breth-
ren as thou call'st them," would be to cite more than fifty instances of
carefully placed ambiguity in the speeches of God, Christ, Satan, Mary,
Andrew and Simon, and Gabriel.[29] Especially prominent, however, are

[28] For both these points I am grateful for the support of Arthur E. Barker's
important essay "Calm Regained through Passion Spent: The Conclusions of the
Miltonic Effort," in *The Prison and the Pinnacle*, ed. Rajan.

[29] For these and ambiguous uses of *house* and *home* see I, 11, 23, 32, 36, 65, 76,
87, 91, 122, 136, 141, 150, 166, 173, 176, 183, 234, 289, 329, 330, 342, 356,
368, 385, 486; II, 4, 61, 67, 99, 136, 178-79, 192, 225, 303, 377, 414; III, 31, 81,
154, 175, 230-31, 233, 374, 404; IV, 10, 56, 197, 220, 348, 389, 472, 500, 539, 552,
596, 614, 639.

Satan's insistent variations of the attribution and misattribution of sonship. In his opening speech in Book I Satan describes the Son as might Homer, Hesiod, or Virgil depict the typical result of a classical union between an immortal male and a mortal female, placing his birth on the same sort of standing as that of Arcas, son of Zeus and Callisto, or Phaeton, son of Apollo and Clymene, or Dionysius, son of Zeus and Semele, or Amphion and Zethus, sons of Zeus and Antiope, or Bellerophon, son of Poseidon and Eurynome, to say nothing of Hercules, Perseus, Orpheus, or the reverse parentage cases, Aeneas and Achilles, all heroes of Gentile poets. He says:

> out of Heav'n the Sov'raign voice I heard,
> This is my Son belov'd, in him am pleas'd.
> His Mother then is mortal, but his Sire,
> He who obtains the Monarchy of Heav'n,
> And what will he not do to advance his Son?
>
> (I, 84-88)

Satan continues explicitly to distinguish the "Womans seed" produced in this way from God's "first begot" of whom he had experiences recounted in *Paradise Lost*. He knows the Son in heaven: he guesses this is his fabulous half-brother:

> His first-begot we know, and sore have felt,
> When his fierce thunder drove us to the deep;
> Who this is we must learn, for man he seems
> In all his lineaments, though in his face
> The glimpses of his Fathers glory shine.
>
> (I, 89-93)

When Satan returns in changed mood in Book II to "all his Potentates in Council" after the unsuccessful first temptation, however, he reports that the Son's maternal grandsire, "*Adam* first of Men," is "to this Man inferior far":

> If he be Man by Mothers side at least,
> With more then humane gifts from Heaven adorn'd,
> Perfections absolute, Graces divine,
> And amplitude of mind to greatest Deeds.
>
> (II, 136-39)

He therefore asks counsel of his "peers." Belial, the "dissolutest Spirit that fell," advises, "Set women in his eyes and in his walk, / Among daughters of men the fairest found." Satan's contemptuous dismissal of

the suggestion dismisses as well any overeasy attribution of sonship to
all created beings and any loose establishment of parallels between the
generation of fabulous classical heroes by immortal-mortal matches,
and the generation of this "Man by Mothers side at least":

> Before the Flood thou with thy lusty Crew,
> *False titl'd Sons of God,* roaming the Earth
> Cast wanton eyes on the daughters of men,
> And coupl'd with them, and begot a race. . . .
> [You and they delighted] to way-lay
> Some beauty rare, *Calisto, Clymene,*
> *Daphne,* or *Semele, Antiopa,*
> Or *Amymone, Syrinx,* many more
> Too long, then *lay'st thy scapes on names ador'd,*
> *Apollo, Neptune, Jupiter,* or *Pan,*
> Satyr, or Fawn, or Silvan? But these haunts
> Delight not all; among the Sons of Men,
> How many have with a smile made small account
> Of beauty and her lures, easily scorn'd
> All her assaults, on worthier things intent?
>
> (II, 178-95, emphasis added)

Poets, Plato held, slandered the gods by attributing to them human
passions and the generation of half-mortal sons who in turn displayed
immoral appetites.[30] Satan is of the same mind; Belial and his "lusty
Crew"—"False titl'd Sons of God"—have promulgated the lies that
the gods of the heathen begot half-mortal heroic offspring. Fallen
angels have usurped the myths by which the heathen explained divine
nature and corrupted them to cover their own activities. The fabulous
heroes of their generation are distinctly different from the hero "of
more exalted mind, / Made and set wholly on the accomplishment / Of
greatest things." This true hero must be tempted with "*manlier* ob-
jects."[31] Satan challenges Belial as having promulgated a degenerate
concept of an immortal father and a semidivine son. Of the difference
between "real" and "allegoric" in this case of fatherhood and sonship,

---

[30] *Republic,* 389B, in Allan Gilbert's translation: "But let us oblige the poets
either not to attribute these deeds to such men or not to say that they were
sons of gods; they must not combine the two, for by no means can we allow
them to attempt to persuade the young men that the gods do evil deeds and that
the heroes are no better than men. . . . These stories are not holy or true, for . . .
it is impossible for evil to come from the gods."

[31] See Stein, *Heroic Knowledge,* 50-51; MacKellar, *A Variorum Commentary,*
IV, 116-19; and Steadman, *Milton and the Renaissance Hero* (Oxford: Clarendon
Press, 1967), 68-73.

there can be no question even in Satan's mind: Archas, Phaeton, Dionysius are false fictions of semidivine heroes. Milton here simply continues the activity of replacing "false surmises" with "true experience" begun as early as the Nativity Ode. None can know better than the father of lies what is an out-and-out deception, and he exposes that of Belial.

Is Belial really debarred, however, from entitling himself and his crew "Sons of God" as Satan glancingly avers? Satan twice recurs to the subject in Book IV with respect to his own lineage. In the first instance he says:

> Be not so sore offended, Son of God;
> Though Sons of God both Angels are and Men,
> If I to try whether in higher sort
> Then these thou bear'st that title, have propos'd. . . .
>
> (IV, 196-99)

Satan's claim that angels and men bear the title "Sons of God" is biblically justified. Milton noted in *De Doctrina Christiana* that "The name 'God' is, by the will and permission of God the Father, not infrequently bestowed even upon angels and men (how much more, then, upon the only begotten Son, the image of the Father!),"[32] and he supplied the psalmic proof text, "I have said you are gods, and all of you sons of the Highest." Satan goes further in the second instance. He claims to possess constant relationship, to have both the meaning and the name of sonship by right of birth:

> I thought thee worth my nearer view
> And narrower Scrutiny, that I might learn
> In what degree or meaning thou art call'd
> The Son of God, which bears no single sence;
> The Son of God I also am, or was,
> And if I was, I am; relation stands;
> All men are Sons of God; yet thee I thought
> In some respect far higher so declar'd.
>
> (IV, 514-21)

More is involved here even than the "mythological debunking by a puritanical Satan"[33] which Arnold Stein admired in Satan's rebuke of Belial, rejecting the reality of mythical god-human births. A mythological debunking by Milton has been substituted, whether or not Satan believes what he is saying. Milton himself did not believe that any

---

[32] *CPW*, VI, 233.　　　　　[33] Stein, *Heroic Knowledge*, 50.

kind of consubstantial relationship exists between God and any part of Creation, be it angelic or human. In contradiction of a consubstantial relationship he asserted a functional relationship between God and any beings entitled to be called His sons.

In *De Doctrina Christiana* Milton explained the rational and true sense in which angels may be entitled "Sons of God":

> The name of God seems to have been attributed to the angels chiefly because they were sent from heaven bearing the likeness of the divine glory and person and, indeed, the very words of God. . . . This is done to show that angels or messengers, even though they may seem to take upon themselves, when they speak, the name and character of God, do not speak their own words but those specified by God, who sent them.[34]

Before the fallen angels fell, they could have borne the titles "Gods" or "Sons of God" as messengers and not as literal kinsmen of God. They ceased to be thus entitled when they ceased to be messengers or representatives. Belial is "false titl'd" a son of God and so is Satan, who is not sent by God to test Christ but permitted to do so, and who cannot therefore represent God. Looking ahead, one might add that Milton gave to human judges a similar entitlement:

> The name of God is given to judges because, in a way, when they administer justice, they are God's substitutes. The Son, who was a God on both counts, as messenger and as judge, and indeed for a much better reason as well, did not think it foreign to his nature to defend himself along these very lines when the Jews accused him of blasphemy on the grounds that he had made himself a God: John x 34-36: "Jesus replied, Is it not written . . . I have said you are gods? If he called those to whom the word of God came, gods; . . . do you say that I, whom the Father has sanctified, and sent into the world, blaspheme because I have said, I am the Son of God?"—especially when God himself called the judges sons of the Highest.[35]

Furthermore, Milton directly and emphatically repudiated the idea that the relationship between God and created beings could be a substantial relationship: "We may . . . be absolutely sure . . . that when God breathed the breath of life into man, he did not make him a sharer in anything divine, any part of the divine essence, as it were. He imparted to him only something human which was proportionate to divine virtue." What is true of man is true of angels: "The good angels

---

[34] *CPW*, VI, 237. Even more emphatically, "The name . . . is granted in no other sense than . . . as representatives of the divine presence and person and as spokesmen for Jehovah's own words."

[35] *Ibid.*, 238.

stand by their own strength, no less than man did before his own fall, and . . . are call'd 'elect' only in the sense that they are beloved or choice."[36]

In *Paradise Regained* Milton shows that the sonship of Christ is a functional sonship: Christ is son by virtue of his functions "as messenger and judge, and indeed for a much better reason as well," that is, for his function as image. Satan seems to be superstitious and is apprehensive that the "much better reason" for calling Christ the Son has to do with "what more thou art then man, / Worth naming Son of God." The final trial to which he subjects the Son is meant to force him to acknowledge his superhuman, special relationship with the Father. Satan, not Jesus, is either mystically or ironically making the identification of the Son and the Father within the Godhead. Satan rejects the "utmost of mere man" as a sign of the nature of God in itself when, bearing Jesus to the pinnacle, he adds "thus in scorn": "There stand, if thou wilt stand; to stand upright / Will ask thee skill . . ." (IV, 551-52). Satan is sure that mere man cannot "stand" by his own "skill." But as a consubstantial member of a heavenly trinity, the Son can call upon his miraculous nature and his mysterious identity with the Father either to stand or, casting himself down, to be wafted to safety. When the Son rebukes Satan in terms of the universal sovereignty of the Father (whom Satan knew even in denying Him in *Paradise Lost*—"Tempt not the Lord *thy* God") rather than in terms of a Son's divine nature, then "th' exalted man" becomes precisely that. He stands by his own mortal wisdom, which rejects "hellish wiles," "the utmost of meer man"; he stands as "th' exalted man."[37]

Throughout *Paradise Regained* the Son has not been only pretending to be mere man and acting as if he were mere man while discovering gradually, and in the last scene triumphantly, that he is not mere man but is made of divine stuff. In *Paradise Regained* the Son *is* mere man. God predicted that the Son would be "This perfect Man, by merit call'd my Son," and nothing in the poem, until the angelic chorus at the end, adds to the exact terms of the Father's prophecy. John the Baptist's annunciation is treated by Satan as indecisive, as only conferring "Authority . . . deriv'd from Heaven" to the Son to begin his work. Andrew and Simon understand him to be "Messiah" and "Prophet," and the Son concurs with their understanding, save that he under-

---

[36] *Ibid.*, 317.

[37] I am in agreement about the meaning of the final temptation with: Irene Samuel, "The Regaining of Paradise," 111-28; George Williamson, "Plot in *Paradise Regained*," in his *Milton and Others* (Chicago: University of Chicago Press, 1965), 82; John M. Steadman, *Milton and the Renaissance Hero*, 156-60; and Jon S. Lawry, *Shadow of Heaven*, 342-45.

stands that he will fulfill these roles in a manner unexpected by the
Jewish scribes. Mary, to be sure, glances at the mystery of the incarna-
tion, but even Mary prompts the Son to human and preeminently intel-
lectual activity:

> high are thy thoughts
> O Son, but nourish them and let them soar
> To what highth sacred vertue and true worth
> Can raise them, though above example high. . . .

> (I, 229-32)

No one in the poem knows more of the Son than his prophesied Mes-
sianic role. The most "mysterious" recognition in the poem is that the
Son should attain wisdom, elsewhere called by Milton "the minde of
Christ." The "much better reason" for calling Jesus the Son of God
than his activity as messenger and judge is his activity as exemplary
man, teaching the nature of God, most adequately possessing the image
of God possessed by all men until they deface it. The Son prepares for
his work of saving men by instancing the behavior of God to men, by
possessing "the minde of Christ," and by teaching all men to use "the
minde of Christ" in them.

Paradise Regained concludes with an angelic chorus which takes the
meaning of the poem one stage further into theology, but without
weakening the doctrine of the Son's subordination to the Father and
its corollary of the distinctive roles of Father and Son. The angels re-
joice specifically in the Son's "victory over temptation," not in his
manifestation of Godhead; they hail him as "True Image of the Father,"
not as real substance; they treat his action as exclusively and positively
directed toward the salvation of "*Adam* and his chosen Sons," not as
the logos recreating all creation and redeeming the great chain of all
being into a spiritual totality.[38] Their "Heavenly Anthems" say not
only *that* Jesus is the Son of God but *how*: he is the Son because he
expresses the Father as the image of the Father. The suffering servant
who exemplifies God's treatment of all men is heralded by the Chorus
as the historical image of God both on earth and in heaven:

> True Image of the Father whether thron'd
> In the bosom of bliss, and light of light
> Conceiving, or remote from Heaven, enshrin'd
> In fleshly Tabernacle, and human form,

---

[38] See *De Doctrina Christiana*, *CPW*, VI, 345: Angels "desire to contemplate the
mystery of our salvation simply out of love, and not from any interest of their
own. . . . They are not included in any question of reconciliation, and . . . they
are reckoned as being under Christ because he is their head, not their Redeemer."

> Wandring the Wilderness, whatever place,
> Habit, or state, or motion, still expressing
> The Son of God, with Godlike force indu'd
> Against th' Attempter of thy Fathers Throne,
> And Thief of Paradise; him long of old
> Thou didst debel, and down from Heav'n cast
> With all his Army, now thou hast aveng'd
> Supplanted *Adam*, and by vanquishing
> Temptation, hast regain'd lost Paradise,
> And frustrated the conquest fraudulent. . . .

> (IV, 596-609)

To the three and six-seventh books preceding, these lines add a single doctrinal affirmation: Jesus has a transcendental reality in his identity with the heavenly Son of God, true before and after the action which *Paradise Regained* imitates. But the affirmation does not make the point that the Son's divinity has regained lost Paradise. The Son's humanity did that, the "human form," "remote from heaven," "expressing the Son" has regained lost Paradise. The "Heavenly Anthems" therefore conclude,

> Hail Son of the most High, heir of both worlds,
> Queller of Satan, on thy glorious work
> Now enter, and begin to save mankind.

> (IV, 633-35)

Paradise has been regained for all men who follow the example of Jesus, answering freely to an inner authority, choosing to reject the superficially attractive and to embrace the wiser good. Their salvation or damnation is in their own hands since they may follow the enlightening example of one of their kind. The first Adam set a bad example and fathered a line of sons prone to wrong choices; his sin does not damn them if they do not reiterate it in their own choosing. The new Adam sets a good example and fathers a line of spiritual sons; his virtue does not save them if they do not reiterate it in their own free choices. *Paradise Regained* is not about "salvation" so much as about choosing the known good. It ends by predicting salvation as about to begin. But it has shown what mode salvation will take in human life when the vicarious ransom has been effected. The mind of Christ in each man will enable each to be his own deliverer.

As *Paradise Regained* revolves about the question "what *more* [Jesus is] then man, / Worth naming Son of God by voice from Heav'n," there is a sense in which *Samson Agonistes* turns on the question, "God of our Fathers, what *is* man?" Both questions involve explorations of the way in which humanity exemplifies or images divinity. *Paradise*

Regained took up the case of the perfect image manifesting God's ways toward man by portraying the utmost of mere man, both wise and good, in the role of teacher. *Samson Agonistes* takes up the case of a judge, the elect of God, given an earthly mission and special abilities to perform it, failing in his assigned task in the external mode in which he understood it, answering imperfectly to the "minde of Christ" within him, preferring his subjective "intimate impulse" to more rational "intimate impulse," then listening more carefully to what his experiences told him, not about himself, but about his God, "Whose ear is ever open; and his eye / Gracious to re-admit the suppliant," and finally performing the role assigned by heaven of freeing his brethren not from external but from internal enthrallment, if they accept and follow his example as one obedient and responsive in the end to none but an inner authority. On the question of the Son's descent hangs doubt; there is none over Samson's. Samson is a son of Manoa and of Israel; he left his father's house choosing a first and then a second bride who "pleas'd [him] not [his] Parents"; he was betrayed by his "Wife, [his] Traytress," taken from his own "house with chamber Ambushes" to abide in a "loathsom prison-house," blind and "in most things as a child / Helpless," as he had not been when he was God's "nursling once." His father, Manoa, with "a Fathers timely care," wishes to deliver him "By ransom or how else" and keep him "sitting in the house," "idle on the houshold hearth." His wife, Dalila, whom he preferred before "all the daughters of [his] Tribe / And of [his] Nation," likewise wants to bring him "forth from [his] loathsom prison-house," to care for him "with nursing diligence" to an "old age / With all things grateful chear'd." His opponent, Harapha, "of stock renown'd," "Father of five Sons," taunts him with the sneer that his God "hath cut [him] off / Quite from his people." The pitiful concern in Manoa is fatherly. For Samson he will "rather . . . chuse / To live the poorest in [his] Tribe, then richest, / And [Samson] in that calamitous prison left." The Chorus admires Manoa's paternal love:

> Fathers are wont to lay up for thir Sons,
> Thou for thy Son art bent to lay out all;
> Sons wont to nurse thir Parents in old age,
> Thou in old age car'st how to nurse thy Son
> Made older then thy age through eye-sight lost.

> (1485-89)

At the end Samson has brought "eternal fame" "To himself and Fathers house." Manoa resolves to "send for all [his] kindred . . . to fetch him hence . . . Home to his Fathers house."

Samson's parentage is altogether human and well known, but it is implicitly and often explicitly compared to Jesus's parentage. The comparison yields not a type-antitype relationship so much as an even clearer instance of an utterly exemplary overcomer of temptation given providential continued trial of life and experience by God until he deliver himself from evil. In his grief Manoa cries out, "Who would be now a Father in my stead," recalling God's question in Book III of *Paradise Lost*, "Which of ye will be mortal to redeem / Mans mortal crime?" and Mary's "Motherly cares and fears" in *Paradise Regained*, causing her to sigh, "O what avails me now that honour high / To have conceiv'd of God?" Samson is a "person separate to God" as the Son "from . . . consummate vertue [is chosen] / This perfect man." Samson's birth was "foretold twice by an Angel." "A messenger from God fore-told [the Son's] birth," "a glorious Quire of Angels" announced his nativity, and his "Father's voice, / Audibly heard from Heav'n, pronounc'd [him] his" at his baptism. Samson was given "the secret gift of God," what he "motion'd was of God"; he was "divinely call'd" to his work; God had "of his special favour rais'd [him] / As . . . Deliverer"; and to him was "giv'n under pledge" a "mystery of God." The Son's "Authority . . . deriv'd from Heaven," for "deeds / Above Heroic, though in secret done," and he was "th' exalted man" chosen for "the mighty work . . . Of Saviour to mankind." In his "youthful courage and magnanimous thoughts / Of birth from Heav'n foretold and high exploits" Samson also resembled the young Jesus in his "growth . . . to youths full flowr, displaying / All vertue, grace and wisdom to atchieve / Things highest, greatest." The similarities do not only underline differences from Jesus (as is so regularly argued by typological readers), they also ask to be noted for what they are, educative parallels illustrative of God's benevolent government of all Creation, not His peculiar governance of His Son. Further prominent parallels can also be noted for their human meaning: Samson suffers in a "loathsom prison" but is released to do good to man by example; the Son suffers death in a "loathsom grave" from which he arises to do good to man, a scene glanced at in *Paradise Regained* in the Son's acceptance that he

> Be try'd in humble state, and things adverse,
> By tribulations, injuries, insults,
> Contempts, and scorns, and snares, and violence,
> Suffering, abstaining, quietly expecting
> Without distrust or doubt. . . .

(III, 189-93)

Samson is "despis'd and thought extinguish't quite" but roused into life like the phoenix when seemingly overthrown; the Son, when seemingly sure to fall, is raised and upborne "through the blithe Air."

After showing both a transcendent and human father and son in *Paradise Regained* Milton deliberately offered in *Samson Agonistes* an exclusively human father and son. He underscores the sheer domesticity of the household in *Samson Agonistes*, having played off the domestic and the glorious households in *Paradise Regained*. He subordinates Son to Father in *Paradise Lost*, stresses the teaching role of the Son as it illuminates the Father's nature in *Paradise Regained*, and goes even further in *Samson Agonistes*, using the altogether human son as an instrument by which the altogether human father is brought progressively to understand divine paternity, while focusing attention upon the son's progressive illumination. Manoa's concern and care for Samson is profoundly human; readers have had to be taught by constant repetition of the critics to think ill of the disappointed father who tries so repeatedly and anxiously to rescue his self-destructive son.[39] Manoa's merely human fatherly care colors his judgment of God's nature at the outset of the drama. Because of his impatient love for his errant son, whose marriages he cannot praise and whom he thinks conventionally but erroneously to have brought dishonor to God and glory to Dagon, he doubts God's fatherly care or that a continuous concern was promised his son. (In Milton's thought, of course, no one can bring dishonor on God; they honor themselves who honor God, as they dishonor themselves who fail to choose the right. God does not need anything man does and cannot be damaged either by what man does or by what he fails to do.) Milton calls attention to this merely human care in adding, without warrant from Scripture or the Samson tradition,[40] Manoa's attempt to "ransom" his son from the Philistines; *ransom*, used neutrally here, is the most loaded term in the theological vocabulary. Manoa's same fatherly care, however, is the energy which is transmuted in the course of the play into a wiser understanding of God on his part. He begins by doubting God's government of the universe: God "should not so o'rewhelm" "whom [he] hath chosen once." He renews his faith, but in a vengeful, conventionally conceived God: "God . . . will not long defer / To vindicate the glory of his name / Against all competition." He tries to teach Samson to believe in a

---

[39] See Stein, *Heroic Knowledge*, 159, 161; Martz, "Chorus and Character in *Samson Agonistes*," 122; Carey, *Milton*, 145; Bouchard, *Milton*, 154; Don Cameron Allen, *The Harmonious Vision* (Baltimore: Johns Hopkins University Press, 1954), 87; Shawcross, "Irony as Tragic Effect," 298. For alternative readings see: Low, *Blaze of Noon*; Lawry, *Shadow of Heaven*, 347, 367-75, 395; Nancy Hoffman, "Samson's Other Father: The Character of Manoa in *Samson Agonistes*," *Milton Studies*, 2 (1970), 195-209; Thomas Kranidas, "Manoa's Role in *Samson Agonistes*," *Studies in English Literature*, 13 (1973), 95-109.

[40] See Krouse, *Milton's Samson*, 99.

miraculous God: God "can . . . cause light again within thy eies to spring" and will "quit thee all his debt." Half unaware, he answers his own protesting "Who would be now a Father in my stead?" by parenthetically conceiving of a fatherly God, "(Best pleas'd with humble and filial submission)"; he confusedly links divine mercy with human travail, "Mercy of Heav'n what hideous noise was that"; he begins to see that it is presumptuous and dubious to expect miracles or to think "God hath wrought things as incredible." His final true understanding of God's nature comes from his having seen God's constancy to His human saints: God had "not parted from [Samson], as was feard, / But favouring and assisting to the end." The human father learns from the human son's experience what freedom and obedience mean in the divine Father's universe. The major recognition in the drama is Samson's, but Manoa, too, it should be noted, lives through a movement from a constrained and inadequate inherited knowledge of God to a correct experienced knowledge. Milton's rational antitrinitarianism taught him to treat in order of descending humanity; the Son of God as unequal to the Father so as to image and reveal the Father (*Paradise Lost*); the man of men, by merit called God's Son (*Paradise Regained*); and the man of men "on earth unparallel'd," who became "inferiour to the vilest" of men to raise the tragic question "what is man?" (*Samson Agonistes*).

Milton's antitrinitarianism led him to proclaim one God, the Father before all time, of an unknowable nature and an unsearchable will, revealed and known so far as He could be known in Scripture, Who created every subsequent being by His efficiency. God's efficiency is of two sorts, internal and external. His internal efficiency is manifested by His decrees both general and special. The general decree is "that by which he decreed from eternity, with absolute freedom, with absolute wisdom and with absolute holiness, all those things which he proposed or which he was going to perform";[41] the special decrees are the begetting of the Son and the predestining of all believers to be saved. The "first and most excellent special decree of all concerns his Son."[42] The "principal special decree of God which concerns men is called predestination; by which God, before the foundations of the world were laid, had mercy on the human race, although it was going to fall of its own accord, and, to show the glory of his mercy, grace and wisdom, predestined to eternal salvation, according to his purpose or plan in Christ, those who would in the future believe and continue in the faith." God's external efficiency "takes the form of the execution of these decrees" and subdivides into "Generation, Creation, and the

[41] *De Doctrina Christiana, CPW*, VI, 153.
[42] *Ibid.*, 166.

Government of the Universe": Generation begot the Son;[43] Creation produced everything that exists both visible and invisible;[44] and the Government of the Universe, operating "generally according to the conditions of [God's] decree"[45] and specifically upon angels and men, relates to man's prelapsarian and fallen states.[46] The special providence of God concerning the fall of man is seen "in man's sin and the misery which followed it, and also in his restoration." Man's restoration is composed of his redemption and renovation, his redemption being "that act by which Christ, sent in the fulness of time, redeemed all believers at the price of his own blood."[47]

Paradise Lost depicts God's total efficiency; *Paradise Regained* depicts the initial stage in God's external efficiency in the provident government of men by restoration through Christ; *Samson Agonistes* depicts God's external provident special government of men by renovation. These three last works descend from Milton's heretical antitrinitarianism in the exact order in which he expounded it in *De Doctrina Christiana*: God and the created Son, Providence in Christ's nature, renovation in human election. The arrangement of *Paradise Regained* and *Samson Agonistes* in their single volume is neither anticlimactic nor perplexing nor accidental. It is the arrangment of the manifestation of God to man adopted in *De Doctrina Christiana*, an arrangement not arbitrarily reversing the expected typology but one moving purposively toward the exclusively human revelation of God's ways.

ARMINIANISM AND SAMSON AGONISTES

The heresy which *Samson Agonistes* dramatizes most specifically, because it most precisely concerns the tragic but meaningful life of man, is Milton's heresy of contingent predestination, a heresy according to Milton's Puritan and Calvinistic inherited faith. Milton rejected the Calvinistic doctrine of double predestination. He denied that God eternally, arbitrarily, and unchangeably chose a particular and fixed number of men to become objects of His grace, passing over and condemning to damnation all other men. He argued instead that God created all beings with both reason and innate freedom of choice and that, consequently, He decreed nothing absolutely but decreed everything contingently, according each agent the capacity to choose but remaining in relationship with each free agent. God's internal decision to create angels and men with reason and free will was made in the

---

[43] *Ibid.*, 205.   [44] *Ibid.*, 300, 311.   [45] *Ibid.*, 326.   [46] *Ibid.*, 351.

[47] *Ibid.*, 415. The systematic treatment of these subjects in Book 1 of *De Doctrina Christiana* may be seen more clearly in the topical synopsis of this part of the treatise in Appendix D below.

knowledge that some would abuse their freedom, but His foreknowledge in no way impeded their freedom. All events take place as God foresees but not because He foresees;[48] angelic and human beings choose in ignorance of God's foreknowledge. But foreknowing the unnecessitated Fall, God made a special contingent decree concerning man and predestined to eternal or eventual salvation those who were going to believe and continue in their faith during their fallen and falling lives. In doing this, God did not cut Creation off from His constant concern; He covenanted with His creatures to maintain relationship. God did not predestine them to be saved against their free will; rather, He made it possible for fallen men to be saved by enabling them to believe, by restoring both reason and free will to them all, and by strengthening both reason and will progressively in the experience of those who use them to discover His reality. He did not predestine particular individuals but predestined all men to be saved, contingent upon their perfectly possible belief; those who are actually saved are those who use their reason freely to construct an inner belief in God and use their will freely to obey that inner authority and none other. Hence Milton rejected the view that God damns unbelievers or reprobates them or hardens their hearts; unbelievers damn, reprobate, and harden themselves. Election, in Milton's thought, is not the positive pole of a divine activity, of which the negative pole is reprobation. Nor is election the guarantee of perfect spiritual security, for which the saved may collect evidence in their own hearts. Election is general vocation. Milton used the term *elect* in two senses. The elect are those who of their own accord use their restored freedom of mind and will righteously; that is Milton's general sense of the word. Among the general elect some are given special gifts and special tasks to put to the use of informing others of God's nature; that is Milton's particular and frequent second sense of the word. This heretical independent view is fully expounded in the third and fourth chapters of *De Doctrina Christiana*, and it gives to *Samson Agonistes* an additional theological dimension.

Like Milton's "heretical" Arianism or subordinationism, Milton's "heretical" Arminianism was not something he consistently believed in or clearly held throughout his life. On the contrary, he inherited with his early Calvinistic Puritanism a conviction that God specially called and knew a few elect men and nations and specially reprobated the multitude of the damned. As we saw in discussing Milton's concept of history, in his first group of antiprelatical tracts Milton was idealistically convinced as a young polemicist that God had particularly

[48] See Kelley, "Introduction," *CPW*, VI, 82-86.

called his own nation to be saved. The confident message then was that God "hath ever yet had this Iland under the speciall indulgent eye of his providence." More particularly, he held in his early prose works to the concept of the election of particular saints: the "gifts [of the Spirit of God] are promis'd only to the elect."[49] In *Of Reformation* Milton finds "the Pelagians which were slaine by the Heathen for Christ's sake . . . [were] no true friends of Christ." The Arminians are criticized in *An Apology against a Pamphlet* for denying original sin; by *Areopagitica* their leader has become "the acute and distinct Arminius"; and in Milton's last pamphlet, *Of True Religion*, the charge of heresy is specifically withdrawn from them: "The Arminian . . . is condemned for setting up free will against free grace; but that imputation he disclaims in all his writings, and grounds himself largely upon Scripture only."[50] As Milton freed himself from a constraining, inherited theological position, he portrayed Samson similarly altering in the course of the drama his sense of the meaning of election and the nature of his prophesied role. Samson is brought to distinguish his early function (or his election in relationship to men) from his spiritual condition (or his election in relationship to God) and to understand that in exemplifying the latter he will effect the former.

Samson at the outset of the play believes that "Divine Prediction" singled him out for "some great act / Or benefit . . . to *Abraham*'s race" and that his "own default" has utterly destroyed the possibility of his performing it. The Chorus likewise thinks that he was "man on earth unparallel'd," "whose strength, while vertue was her mate, / Might have subdu'd the Earth." Samson defines his "default" as having "divulg'd the secret gift of God / To a deceitful Woman." Because he thought that "*Israel*'s Deliverance" was "the work to which [he] was divinely call'd," Samson had responded to an "intimate impulse" "of God" when he chose to marry into a position from which he could commence that delivering. His "default" is pinpointed exactly to his own and not Dalila's offense, "she was not the prime cause, but I my self." But the Chorus reminds him that if "*Israel*'s Deliverance" was his mission, "*Israel* still serves with all his Sons." Samson therefore sharpens his definition of election and responsibility in further isolating his "default." He is not responsible for Israel's continuing enslavement: his own deeds on Israel's behalf "though mute, spoke loud the dooer," but the leaders of Israel were deaf to them. In this his particular offer and their specific rejection repeats a pattern very common in human experience and not exclusive to him. Samson's deeds are Samson's deeds, performed by a free agent. The reactions of Israel to those deeds are

[49] *An Apology against a Pamphlet, CPW*, I, 941.
[50] *Students Milton*, 916.

341

the reactions likewise of free agents, and God's words about fallen men in *Paradise Lost* exactly fit them:

> they themselves decreed
> Thir own revolt, not I: if I foreknew,
> Foreknowledge had no influence on their fault. . . .
> They trespass, Authors to themselves in all
> Both what they judge and what they choose. . . .
>
> (III, 116-23)

God's special favor is not a guarantee of success or salvation which constrains human agents to a course of action not of their choice, and it cannot properly therefore be considered an "election" in the received Puritan sense of the word. Milton's explanation in *De Doctrina Christiana* elucidates Samson's clearing sense of mission and declines to give it the meaning of an irresistible and gratuitous grace preventing a fall:

> I do not understand by the term election that general or, so to speak, national election by which God chose the whole nation of Israel as his own people. . . . Nor do I mean the election by which, after rejecting the Jews, God chose the Gentiles to whom he wished the gospel should be preached. . . . Nor do I mean the election by which he chooses an individual for some employment . . . , whence they are sometimes called elect who are superior to the rest for any reason . . . which means, as it were, most excellent.[51]

All men are "elect" in the sense that all by their own behavior in relation to God may be saved. Yet to some is given a "special favour":

> If . . . God rejects none except the disobedient and the unbeliever, he undoubtedly bestows grace on all, and if not equally upon each, at least sufficient to enable everyone to attain knowledge of the truth and salvation. I say not equally upon each. . . . For like anyone else, where his own possessions are concerned, God claims for himself the right of making decrees about them as he sees fit. . . . So God does not consider everyone worthy of equal grace, and the cause of this is his supreme will. But he considers all Worthy of sufficient grace, and the cause is his justice.[52]

Milton quietly emphasized the distinction by having Samson described early in the drama with respect to his special mission, "Select, and Sacred, Glorious for a while, / The miracle of men: then in an hour /

---

[51] *CPW*, VI, 172.   [52] *Ibid.*, 193.

Ensnar'd" (363-65), where very little musical advantage is gained by using *select* rather than *elect* to decribe him, and gain in having him described as "chosen once / *To worthiest deeds.*"

Manoa apparently distinguishes between Samson's *being* select and *thinking* himself inspired. He refuses to grant that "divine impulsion" prompted Samson's marriage—"I state not that"—to remind Samson that there is a "rigid score" (like Christ's "rigid satisfaction") to pay for human "fault." Samson agrees about the score and wishes to "pay on my punishment; / And expiate, if possible, my crime" (489-90). Samson considers that his blindness and slavery is "punishment" for the "crime" of publishing God's "holy secret / Presumptuously . . . impiously, / Weakly at least, and shamefully." And he is right, as it constitutes an image of death, the natural punishment for sin. But it is a natural phenomenon and, "strictly speaking," Milton explains in *De Doctrina Christiana*, "God does not either incite or hand over someone if he leaves him entirely to himself, that is, to his own desires and devices. . . . In fact God gives a good outcome to every deed . . . and overcomes evil with good."[53] Samson thinks that expiation is necessary. Milton makes supremely little of expiation beyond recording that the Redeemer makes all necessary expiation "from the beginning of the World, even for those to whom he was not known and who believed only in God the Father."[54] Of the allied notion of a formal penance, Milton is equally dismissive: "I do not see why much trouble should be taken to establish the precise meaning of the word when it does not even occur in the Bible. Certainly penance does not contain any real sign, nor does it seal anything, any more than faith does."[55] Repentance is another matter: it involves "recognition of sin, contrition, confession, abandonment of evil and conversion to good,"[56] all matters of reason and will. When Samson speaks of expiation, it is proper that Manoa should be worried about his state of mind, "self-rigorous . . . over-just, and self-displeas'd / For self-offence, more then for God offended." He warns him away from exacting a "penal forfeit from thy self," advising instead "off'rings, . . . praiers and vows renew'd." The response from Samson is quick and correct: "His pardon I implore."

[53] *Ibid.*, 334-35. See Albert G. Labriola, "Divine Urgency as a Motive for Conduct in *Samson Agonistes*," *Philological Quarterly*, 50 (1971), 99-107, for a contrary argument.

[54] *De Doctrina Christiana, CPW*, vi, 475. In *Paradise Lost*, under the Law the sacrifice of scapegoats is called "shadowie expiations weak" (xii, 291); in *De Doctrina Christiana* likewise, sacrifice and priesthood are called "symbols of expiation" before and during the time of Moses.

[55] *CPW*, vi, 561.   [56] *Ibid.*, 468.

Since the very important essay by John M. Steadman, " 'Faithful Champion': The Theological Basis of Milton's Hero of Faith,"[57] it has been unnecessary to retrace the steps of Samson's gradual process of sanctification, and that is not the process I am now concerned with, although Samson's election is bound up with his regeneration. I wish rather to show that Samson is an elect hero who demonstrates that election is potential for every man and, although dependent upon God's grace through Christ, becomes actual through the acceptance of personal responsibility for one's acts and impulses, and the acceptance of the propriety of one's impulses and choices within God's "unsearchable dispose" of the created universe. While Samson thinks that *once* he was "elect" and "Full of divine instinct" (526) but that *now* he is damned and cannot have or trust "divine instinct," he believes he is useless to God and to himself: "Now blind, disheartn'd, sham'd, dishonour'd, quell'd, / To what can I be useful, wherein serve. . . ."

Since Samson's "thoughts portend" speedy death, "thence faintings, swounings of despair, / And sense of Heav'ns desertion," it is to his thoughts that Milton gives protracted treatment in the "middle" of the drama, especially to the reversal of Samson's view that "I was his nursling *once*." The Chorus distinguishes the condition of the generality of men, "the common rout . . . Heads without name no more rememberd," from that of a particular few, "such as [God has] solemnly elected, / With gifts and graces eminently adorn'd / To some great work, [his] glory, / And peoples safety" (678-81). Among the particular few, they correctly define Samson as "The Image of [God's] strength, and mighty minister." As image and minister, Samson is specially elect, not the people's hero but God's champion. Rebuking Dalila for pretended piety, Samson discovers that God does not *need* man's championship, for He is God and beings unable "to acquit themselves and prosecute their foes / But by ungodly deeds . . . Gods cannot be" (897-99). And yet he considers his God punitive and torturing: "God sent [Dalila] to debase [him], / And aggravate [his] folly." Confronting Harapha, Samson advances from strictly considering that God justly has "inflicted" evils on him, through believing that God is "Gracious to readmit the suppliant," to restating his personal responsibility not only for his fall but for his election—"I was . . . a person rais'd / With strength sufficient and command from Heav'n / To free my Countrey" —to accusing not God but himself of his broken state—"I was to do my part from Heav'n assign'd, / And had perform'd it if my known offence / Had not disabl'd me"—to finally distinguishing what he

---

[57] *Anglia*, 77 (1959), 12-28. See also Franklin R. Baruch, "Time, Body and Spirit at the Close of *Samson Agonistes*," *ELH*, 36 (1969), 319-39.

does for himself from what he does for his God. God is not a task-master who must have Samson's help with the running of the universe, or with proving His might. Samson's final challenge to Harapha is not to pit Jehovah against Dagon in a show of divinity but to "single fight, / *As a petty enterprise of small enforce*" (emphasis added). Now that Samson knows that God does not need a championship of arms, he soon perceives as well that He is not a God of local laws and sanctified places: "he may dispense with me or thee / Present in Temples at Idolatrous Rites / For some important cause." Neither a special place nor a special time affects election or predestination. Samson is given freedom from the Law within his own historical dispensation—as are all men under the Gospel dispensation. His thoughts now portend not death but unusual significance. He expresses the revival of divine impulsion first cautiously,

> If there be aught of presage in the mind,
> This day will be remarkable in my life
> By some great act, or of my days the last,
>
> (1387-89)

although confidently,

> I begin to feel
> Some rouzing motions in me which dispose
> To something extraordinary my thoughts.
>
> (1381-83)

The exact definition of Samson's thoughts is clear. He tells the Chorus, "Commands are no constraints. If I obey them, / I do it freely; venturing to displease / God for the fear of Man," announcing his resolution to answer to nothing but the inner authority of his own sense of God. He tells the Officer,

> Masters commands come with a power resistless
> To such as owe them absolute subjection;
> And for a life who will not change his purpose?
> (So mutable are all the ways of men). . . .
>
> (1404-7)

Samson owes absolute subjection to God, whose power is resistless because it is exerted only by inner constraint. His Master's command is to change his purpose from death to "a life"; the mutability of his own ways is not a denial but an assertion of purposiveness and freedom. Riddling Samson unriddles the meaning of his election, and the Chorus,

345

but not the Officer, catches something of his drift. The fickleness of man that the Chorus marked at the beginning of the drama, and the deceivable and vain in him that Manoa lamented, are discovered to bear another interpretation than the hopelessness of the human condition. In fallen man's mutability within an existence of contingency and change lies the possibility of freedom itself. Who will give up hope for a being that can change? And so the Chorus sends Samson forth:

> Go, and the Holy One
> Of *Israel* be thy guide
> To what may serve his glory best, & spread his name
> Great among the Heathen round. . . .
>
> (1427-30)

They pray that Samson's changed mind and mutable insight be guided to a service through the "efficacious [spirit] in [him]." The service is a human imaging of God's might; it suspends no natural human course: the collapse of the temple of Dagon is the "inevitable cause" of his death, and his mortality is "Of . . . necessity, [the] law in death." The destruction of Philistia is also a strictly human matter: they "importun'd / Thir own destruction to come speedy upon them" and "thir own ruin on themselves [invited]." Samson acted "with inward eyes illuminated," and like the phoenix whose "fame survives . . . ages of lives," he brought "eternal fame" to himself. The ultimate cause was God "favouring and assisting to the end"; the proximate cause was "vertue giv'n for lost" but revived, reflourished. Samson "quit himself like *Samson*," the image of God, and the witnessing to God is his election. God does not appear on stage because God appears rather in human hearts. He is manifested in every time and every place by the behavior of tested men who attest to Him. In His free agent, Samson, He manifests the renewal of freedom to all men. As a final demonstration of the importance of mind and will, the good mind and the good will issue into an exemplary act which teaches how God gives freedom. The "unsearchable dispose" of God is the giving of "new acquist of true experience" to men through the example of purposeful human beings.

Milton's heretical doctrine of election and predestination is most clearly dramatized in the story of the human being who least seemed adequate to an eternal special vocation, whose freedom was strictly limited to an internal movement by his situation, whose life seemed most flawed and maimed by his not having answered to the authority of his God, but who displayed in the close the complex inner nature of that authority. Samson is a special case of God's general election of all men. His humanity is the most fully documented, his forced reliance upon strictly human activities of reason and will is the most clearly displayed, the human strengthening which followed his efforts to reason correctly is the most abundantly clear of all Milton's biblical case histories of God's ways toward men. Samson freed himself from local concerns of a single nation, a law-giving God, a special role in terms of an historical mission, and displayed instead the regenerative power of the experience of tragedy designed by a God offering freedom and life even to the tragic bitter end.

Mortalism and Materialism: The Discarding of Orthodoxy from the 1645 Poems to Samson Agonistes

Milton's remaining two heresies, those of materialism and mortalism, were also positions to which he came late by throwing off inherited conformities. As a young poet Milton clearly did not think either that the universe was created from a preexistent good substance present in God or that man is a single entity of body and soul in every part who dies totally as one whole man. In the Fifth Prolusion, where he was assigned the task of defending an Aristotelian position, that "There are no partial forms in an animal in addition to the whole," Milton simply assumed the body-soul distinction, agreeing with Chrysostom Javello that "The distinction and organization of dissimilar parts must precede the introduction of the Soul." In "On the Platonic Idea as Understood by Aristotle" he was willing, if only sportively, to accept the preexistence of the soul, writing of the "Archetype of Man" "who exists apart in the manner of an individual," either "sitting among the souls that are destin'd to enter human bodies" or wandering "through the tenfold ranks of heaven" or "dwelling on the orb of the moon." In "On the Morning of Christs Nativity" he continued to distinguish between body and soul as separate entities, the body being "a darksom House of mortal Clay." He believed that death annihilates the body and is a sleep of the soul: "to those ychain'd in sleep, / The wakefull trump of doom must thunder through the deep." In *Arcades* the "human mould" and "grosse unpurged ear" of man's flesh prevents the soul from hearing heavenly music. In *Lycidas* the drowned corpse "sleeps" "sunk low" while the Spirit is "mounted high." In *Comus* a chaste soul in dream and vision hears

> things that no gross ear can hear,
> Till oft convers with heav'nly habitants
> Begin to cast a beam on th'outward shape,

347

> The unpolluted temple of the mind,
> And turns it by degrees to the souls essence,
> Till all be made immortal.

Finally, in "On Time" the body is "meerly mortal dross" and "our heav'nly-guided soul shall clime, / Then all this Earthy grosnes quit." In *De Doctrina Christiana*, however, Milton holds, on the contrary, that "God produced all things not out of nothing but out of himself" and that "this original matter was not an evil thing, nor to be thought of as worthless: it was good, and it contained the seeds of all subsequent good."[58] He also argues that man "is not double or separable: not, as is commonly thought, produced from and composed of two different and distinct elements, soul and body. On the contrary, the whole man is the soul, and the soul the man: a body, in other words, or individual substance, animated, sensitive and rational."[59] And when that body dies, "the whole man dies."[60]

These two convictions are present in *Samson Agonistes* and simply underscore the universality of its application to all men in all times. Samson himself confirms the materialism and the indivisibility of body and soul:

> if it be true
> That light is in the Soul,
> She all in every part; why was the sight
> To such a tender ball as th' eye confin'd?
>
> (91-94)

By what he both is allowed and not allowed to say of his son, Manoa confirms the mortalism. He notes positively that Samson's death is a freeing from human bondage, a complete freeing shared by all men, and the final end of life whether it crown it or shadow it:

> but death who sets *all* free
> Hath paid his ransom now and *full* discharge.
> . . . death to life is crown or shame.
>
> (1572-73, 1579, emphasis added)

When Manoa goes to "find the body where it lies" and prepare it for burial, Milton gives him no such consolation as he gave to the mourner of Lycidas or of Damon, that after dying the soul "dwells in the pure ether, and barely walks even on the rainbow . . . [his] bright head haloed in glory." The Chorus calls Samson "victorious / Among thy

---

[58] *CPW*, VI, 310, 318. [59] *Ibid.*, 318. [60] *Ibid.*, 400.

slain self-kill'd" and likens him to the phoenix who "though her body die, her *fame* survives" (1706; emphasis added). The phoenix, engraved on one of Manso's cups to symbolize resurrection in the *Epitaphium Damonis* and prompt the consoling vision of Damon in heaven, is now exactly restricted to symbolizing moral regeneration in a further demythologized use of metaphor.

Milton not only progressed from a conventional theological position to an unconventional one in both these questions, and persisted in the naturalistic and unmysterious position in his final work, he also attempted to reduce the area of controversy in the theological treatise and took for granted the acceptability of both materialism and mortalism in the play. Thus in *De Doctrina Christiana* he wrote that the question of whether only the body die or the whole man die is "a perfectly neutral question answered either way without danger because unconnected to the articles of faith or the practice of religion." "It is a question which can be debated without detriment to faith or devotion, which ever side we may be on. So I shall put forward quite unreservedly the doctrine which seems to me to be instilled by virtually innumerable passages of scripture."[61] On a matter of opinion the better evidenced position is first argued and then simply taken for granted. All men must think what they find to be reasonable.

Samson Agonistes, then, displays a theological hero who annihilates the distance between Old Testament and New Testament revelation, who exemplifies God's ways with man by discovering in his own mind and will the God-intended meaning of his experiences. He instances the progressive awareness which fallen men may have of the purposiveness of their tragic life. He instances the acquisition of freer and more rational conceptions of the nature of God. He instances these through coming to hold and then manifest the minimal theological truths of a heretical rationality which Milton himself came to hold. The reasonableness of Samson's "rouzing motions" is not a seizing of power by an external, even if transcendental, force over a dazzled mind, it is rather an inward prompting to a radical ecumenical faith. Vain reasoning is put down in *Samson Agonistes*, not so that mute obedience may supervene, but so that genuine human rationality may have scope, the rationality of the protagonist as he reasons on the nature of his God, evident in his tragic life and strengthening the rationality of the audience as it reasons on the case history of the fallen "person rais'd."

[61] *Ibid.*, 400.

THE ROLE OF THE POET

THE PROCESS OF SELF-DEFINITION

The arc of Milton's progressive theology, by which he traced God's track in human affairs, runs parallel to the arcs of his progressive psychology, historiography, politics, and ethics. It is therefore not surprising to us to discover that Milton's understanding of the nature and function of poetry should likewise exhibit elements of consistency and yet illustrate change and progress in the same direction toward independence, individualism, and rationality. The process of modification and simplification in Milton's poetics culminates in *Samson Agonistes*. Milton began with the highest possible conception of the role of the poet as the leader and teacher of his nation and subsequent ages, and to that he was consistent throughout his life. He associated himself with a line of poets claiming and manifesting the same high calling, in particular with Orpheus, the Prophets, and the great epic and tragic classical poets. He used the words *inspiration* and *illumination* to describe the inner germination, source, or nearly subconscious energy of poetry throughout his life; he very frequently embodied in his poems preparatory prayers, invocations, and supplications. He thought his genius and his poems were gifts. Sometimes this made him sound exalted and proud, sometimes it made him sound reverent and humble; both were recurrent stances in his poetry. Some critics, however, have gone much beyond this to claim that Milton literally believed from first to last that he was the amanuensis of God,[1] a modern prophet in direct line of descent from Moses and Isaiah,[2] that his own particular Muse was either the Logos[3] or the Holy Spirit[4] or God Almighty,[5]

[1] This is the clamorously asserted argument of William Kerrigan in *Prophetic Milton*, see especially 159-87.

[2] See James Holly Hanford, "'That Shepherd who First Taught the Chosen Seed,'" *University of Toronto Quarterly*, 8 (1939), 403-19.

[3] See Carey and Fowler, *Poems of Milton*, 459n. See also Jackson I. Cope, "Milton's Muse in *Paradise Lost*," *Modern Philology*, 55 (1957), 6-10, and the final chapter, "The Creating Voice," in his *The Metaphoric Structure of "Paradise Lost"* (Baltimore: Johns Hopkins University Press, 1962).

[4] See William B. Hunter, Jr., "Milton's Urania," *Studies in English Literature*, 4 (1964), 35-42.

[5] See Naseeh Shaheen, "Milton's Muse and the *De doctrina*," *Milton Quarterly*, 8 (1974), 72-76.

and that his poetry was an act of mystic worship taking vocal part in the mystic worship of the angels or the music of the spheres.[6] Such critics rebuke many contemporary readers for insisting upon Milton's "Christian humanism" and thereby making too natural and common-place a process which they claim Milton understood as charismatic.

In my view the general case for assigning Milton's poetry to a poetic rapture or heroic fury is weak. Milton did not understand poetry as magical and was profoundly skeptical of magic; he used the word *incantation* in a generally hostile tone and the word *oracle* often in a hostile context; he was uncomfortable about being "rapt beyond the pole" and found himself "more safe standing on earth" and singing in a "mortal voice"; he thought that "God's Secretary" in man was his "conscience,"[7] not a mysterious afflatus; and he never for a moment considered that the response to poetry involved the displacement of reason. Certainly his poetry derived, he thought, from a spirit and light within him in correspondence with a real spiritual truth in the universe. But his views of the Holy Ghost were as guarded as he could make them in view of the "noncommittal" attitude of the "sacred writers."[8] While always confident of the instructive and inspiring power of poetry to elicit from a nation of readers the ethical imitation of his heroic exemplars, in the course of his life Milton changed his conception of the nature and function of poetry in the direction of asserting more fully its plainness, reasonableness, and clarity, and its capacity to teach by affecting man's reason and emotions favorably as well as by offering sound examples for imitation and avoidance. He demythologized the role of the poet, stressing less the prophet than the teacher and even the physician. He increasingly understood the effects of poetry to be a composing and tempering of the passions, clearing the mind and strengthening the reason. And he accepted the likelihood of more modest audiences and more modest effects for poetry as he came to stress more its reasonableness. In all this he was himself like Samson "perswaded inwardly that [his creative impulse] was from God" but that God acts upon man's mind and heart by human means, without coercion.

The argument of some critics that the poet is the literal prophet of God in Milton's poetics may be balanced by the argument in others that the poet is the sage or teacher and his work illuminated by truth or wisdom.[9] From the sheer weight of authoritative writing on either

[6] See David Daiches, "The Opening of *Paradise Lost*," in Frank Kermode, ed., *The Living Milton* (London: Routledge & Kegan Paul, 1960), 60-66; see also Michael Fixler, "Milton's Passionate Epic," *Milton Studies*, 1 (1969), 171-87.

[7] *CPW*, I, 822.   [8] *Ibid.*, VI, 282.

[9] This is the line taken by Grose, *Milton's Epic Progress*, 42; B. Rajan, "Simple, Sensuous and Passionate," *Review of English Studies*, 21 (1945), and by, I take it,

side of this critical divide, it is clear that new evidence to demonstrate the certainty of one or another position cannot be easy to find. My own view is a reconciling one, and my new evidence is the preface "Of that sort of Dramatic Poem which is call'd Tragedy," a contribution as Milton wrote it not simply to genre theory or historical criticism but to poetics.[10] By way of reconciliation I would concede that Milton as a young idealistic poet played enchantedly with the nation that his "deep transported mind" might "soare . . . [to] Heav'ns dore / Look in, and see each blissful Deitie" ("At a Vacation Exercise"), that his "high-rais'd phantasie" might unite him to God's "celestial consort" ("At a Solemn Musick"), that he might be dissolved "into extasies" which would "bring all Heav'n before [his] eyes" to enable his "experience [to] attain / To somthing like Prophetic strain" (*Il Penseroso*). Although he often pointed to the metaphorical level on which his words about inspiration and prophecy should be taken, he did not always do so. Thus in Elegy VI he told Diodati, "the poet is sacred to the gods and is their priest"; and in "Ad Patrem" he told his father, "song retains the sacred traces of the Promethean fire."

During the course of his pamphleteering as well, Milton conceived of his role as prophetic. At first he used prophetic in the sense of uttering as dictated the rebuking, cautionary, corrective warning. In *The Reason of Church Government* he wrote, "when God commands to take the trumpet and blow a dolorous or a jarring blast, it lies not in mans will what he shall say, or what he shall conceal." Even there he went on to qualify, however. God gave him the "ability the while to reason." God "lent" him "those few talents" to utter "A syllable of all that he had read or studied." Later in the pamphlets his role was prophetic in the sense of celebrating victorious deeds done at God's

---

Donald M. Friedman in *"Lycidas*: The Swain's Paideia," *Milton Studies*, 3 (1971), 24-32, who centrally quotes from *Animadversions*—"and therefore Christ left Moses to be the Law-giver, but himself came downe amongst us to bee a teacher" —and who uses the invocations in *Paradise Lost* as prayers for "gifts with which to instruct and solace his fellow men." Kelley takes this view, as do Irene Samuel and Jon Lawry; see also Leon Howard, "The 'Invention' of Milton's 'Great Argument,'" *Huntington Library Quarterly*, 9 (1945), and T.S.M. Scott-Craig, "The Craftsmanship and Theological Significance of Milton's *Art of Logic*," *ibid.*, 17 (1953), 1-16.

[10] Like every student of *Samson Agonistes*, I am so greatly in the debt of John M. Steadman for helpful scholarship that I uneasily record here a difference from his view of the epistle. He takes it that Milton is merely describing tragedy as it used to be written when he says, "Tragedy, *as it was antiently compos'd*, hath ever been held the gravest, moralest, and most profitable of all other Poems." I would emphasize "hath *ever* been" and note that Milton promises that his own tragedy is "coming forth after the antient manner."

prompting, a prophet meant to "send forth a voice and bear witness to the presence of God" (*First Defence*). For this task he required and obtained the assistance of God, "for what eloquence can be august and magnificent enough, what man has parts sufficient to undertake so great a task?" Even there, however, he continued to lay emphasis on his own human gifts as the means of doing God's work, "that the truth . . . should be defended by reason—the only defence which is truly and properly human." Where his pamphleteering course was stormiest, God, he thought, assisted him "unexpectedly." Thus he commenced *The Judgment of Martin Bucer concerning Divorce* with his most thoroughgoing claim, that he wrote at divine prompting and was "no other than a passive instrument under some power and counsel higher and better than can be human," adding that God used Martin Bucer in the same way and made Milton discover him to buttress his work: "God hath unexpectedly raised up . . . more than one famous light of the first reformation to bear witness with me."

But it should also be noted that the general direction of the prose pamphlets is toward the increasingly plain delivery of humanly derived truth, that Milton's last pre-Restoration pamphlet specifically treats the dolorous prophetic role metaphorically and asserts the need of quiet minds to consider what reasonably is to be done. He is urging "the people laying aside prejudice and impatience, [to] seriously and calmly now consider their own good both religious and civil, thir own libertie and the only means thereof."[11] He is speaking "the language of . . . the good Old Cause," and he writes, "Thus much I could perhaps have said though I were sure I should have spoken only to trees and stones; and had none to cry to, but with the Prophet, O earth, earth, earth! to tell the very soil it self, what her perverse inhabitants are deaf to."[12] He is not like that prophet, however, for, he goes on, "I trust I shall have spoken perswasion to abundance of sensible and ingenuous men: to some perhaps whom God may raise of these stones to become children of reviving libertie . . . justly and timely fearing to what a precipice of destruction the deluge of this epidemic madness would hurrie us through the general defection of a misguided and abus'd multitude." He does not literally prophesy; he does nothing more than draw analogies and offer an ironic description, not of a damned rabble, but of a confused majority.

A similar rationality marks the post-Restoration pamphlet *Of True Religion*, a similar cooling of passions, assertion of the values of the tempered mind in achieving consensus, a similar merely metaphorical expression of man's passivity and God's activity in human affairs. "No

[11] *CPW*, VII, 431.   [12] *Ibid.*, 462.

man or angel can know how God would be worshipped and served unless God reveal it; he hath revealed and taught it us in the holy scriptures by inspired ministers, and in the gospel by his own Son and his apostles, with strictest command, to reject all other traditions and additions whatsoever." William Kerrigan draws most of his evidence for Milton's literal assurance that he was a prophet from early pamphlets and in that is correct, but he thinks that in *De Doctrina Christiana* Milton had himself in mind when he described "Extraordinary ministers" as "persons inspired and sent on a special mission by God . . . either through the medium of preaching, or of writing. To this claim belong the prophets, apostles, evangelists and the like." Milton does not say that he is himself an extraordinary minister; he does not say that he is a prophet; he does not imply that prophets differ much from teachers; and he does widen the class to include "the like." He lays stress in the preface to *De Doctrina Christiana* on his "feeling of universal brotherhood and good will," on his advising "every reader, and [setting] him an example by doing the same [himself] to withhold his consent from those opinions about which he does not feel fully convinced, until the evidence of the Bible convinces him and induces his reason to assent and believe."[13] In *A Readie and Easie Way*, Milton similarly asked men to "use all diligence and sincerity of heart, by reading, by learning, by study, by prayer for illumination of the Holy Spirit to understand the rule [of faith] and obey it." Having done that, "they have *done what man can do*." Had Dr. Kerrigan examined *Considerations touching the Likliest means to Remove Hirelings out of the Church*, he would have found Milton arguing that all Gospel laymen are "coheirs, kings and priests" with Christ, proclaiming, "The Levites are ceased," speaking against those who have "miserably Judais'd the church," stressing the "free consent chusing," warning against practices "founded upon the opinion of divine autoritie and that autoritie . . . found mistaken and erroneous," supporting what "the light of reason might sufficiently inform us [of]."[14] In short, he might have seen Milton moving away from an assertion of a passive role in uttering dictated truths and toward the assertion of reason, the tempering of the passions, the superiority of rationality in the saving remnant to whom he would address himself, and the persuasiveness of his consensual message.[15]

---

[13] *Ibid.*, VI, 121-22.   [14] *Ibid.*, VII, 915.

[15] See James Egan, "Public Truth and Personal Witness in Milton's Last Tracts," 231-84, for an analysis of the way in which Milton's prose on the level of style becomes plainer and clearer and more fully addressed to the reason in the directly pre-Restoration period. See also Nathaniel H. Henry, "Milton's Last Pamphlet," in *A Tribute to George Coffin Taylor*, ed. Arnold Williams (Chapel

The Inspired Teacher

Claims for prophetic power in Milton's later poems are qualified claims or prayers, and have to do with efficacious inspiration and not with the great argument itself. In Book III of *Paradise Lost*, for example, he described himself "Taught by the heav'nly Muse to venture down / The dark descent, and up to reascend, / Though hard and rare." The venture is his own action; he prays for teaching. He asks the "Celestial light" to "shine inward, and the mind through all her powers / [to] irradiate," pointing to the mind as the human agency of creative vision. In Book VII, invoking "the meaning, not the Name" of inspiration, a "Heav'nlie" power in contradistinction to Calliope, the mother of Orpheus, who is "an empty dreame," Milton underlined the metaphorical nature of his prayer:

> Into the Heav'n of Heav'ns I have presum'd,
> An Earthlie Guest, and drawn Empyreal Aire,
> Thy tempring; with like safetie guided down
> Return me to my Native Element:
> Least from this flying Steed unrein'd, (as once
> *Bellerophon*, though from a lower Clime)
> Dismounted, on th' *Aleian* Field I fall
> Erroneous, there to wander and forlorne.
>
> (VII, 13-20)

His ascent has been as metaphorical as the horse on which he made it. Moreover, if Urania does "govern" his song and find "fit audience" for it, the audience will yet be few. In Book IX he asks "answerable style" for a "more Heroic" argument,

> Of my Celestial Patroness, who deignes
> Her nightly visitation unimplor'd,
> And dictates to me slumbring, or inspires
> Easie my unpremeditated Verse:
> Since first this Subject for Heroic Song
> Pleas'd me long choosing, and beginning late.
>
> (IX, 21-26)

A collaboration is sought between a chooser of subjects and arguments and a voice speaking within him or inspiring him. Milton offers alternative versions, dictation or inspiration, to describe something so natu-

---

Hill: University of North Carolina Press, 1952), and Keith Stavely, *Politics of Milton's Prose*, esp. 28-34, 57-63, 100-110.

ral or "easie" in his writing as to seem "unimplor'd" and "unpremeditated." He then couples that with something chosen, deliberate, and begun. In Book I he invokes the "aid" of the Heavenly Muse "to [his] *adventrous* Song" that "*intends* to soar"; he asks the spirit to "instruct" him, to "illumine" what is "dark," to "raise and support" what is "low," so that *he* may "assert Eternal Providence." Finally, when the printer S. Simmons secured from Milton for the second printing of *Paradise Lost* the Argument to the poem, he secured as well "a reason of that which stumbled many others, why the Poem Rimes not." That Argument offers as the strongest reason against the barbarous modern custom of rhyme its constraining the poet "to express many things otherwise, and for the most part worse than else [poets] would have exprest them." Milton wished to be free to express things as he wished to express them, without tags or any other constraint. In short, he devised his poem to answer to the truth as he understood it in a consistent process of seeking expressive lucidity.

The case against imagining Milton to have thought himself a passive transmitter of the voice of God is even plainer by the time of *Paradise Regained*. Milton deliberately removed himself from the poem, save pithily to invoke the Spirit which led Christ into the wilderness (Christ called that spirit "some strong motion") to "inspire / As thou art wont, my prompted Song else mute." His song is not dictated or passively received, but he finds it possible to compose it because of inner prompting. Milton further makes in his own voice one or two comments on the action which he is describing as a strictly plain and reasonable poet who feels profoundly and controls his feeling with the clearest, simplest words and tones. "Alas how simple," he notices, "was that crude Apple that diverted *Eve*" compared to Satan's opulent table; or "Ill wast thou shrouded then, O patient Son of God," he comments on the Son's exposure to the tempest. Furthermore, Milton specifically takes up the question of inspired poets and prophets in the Son's rejection of Greek civilization. He causes Christ to extol the sacred songs of Sion because in them "God is prais'd *aright*,"

> and Godlike men,
> The Holiest of Holies, and his Saints;
> Such are from God inspir'd, not such from thee;
> Unless where moral vertue is express't
> By light of Nature not in all quite lost.

> (IV, 348-52)

The "artful terms inscrib'd" on "Hebrew Songs and Harps in *Babylon*" are "to all true tasts excelling" the "ill imitated" works of Greece because God inspired a right understanding of Himself in their composers. Yet some ancient works which express the nature of moral virtue rather than the nature of God are valuable because they arise from a sound "light of Nature." Milton is exact in definition. When he continues through the Son to distinguish Hebrew prophets from Greek orators, the latter are put "far beneath" the former because "our Prophets" write

> As men divinely taught, and better teaching
> The solid rules of Civil Government
> In thir majestic unaffected stile.

(IV, 357-59)

Hebrew prophets were solidly taught solid rules and teach them without affectation, just as Hebrew poets were inspired to derive and express a knowledge of the nature of God. The passage is plainly written, commends plainness, and is far from mentioning as one of the sources of "delight [in] private hours / With Music or with Poem" anything resembling ecstatic, unearthly rhapsodies. If Milton was content to leave so little evidence of himself and of his heavenly inspiration in *Paradise Regained*, it is reasonable to suppose that he was instead seeking what he achieved, the effect of concentration on an intellectual and educative debate.

Samson Agonistes does not supply evidence of divine inspiration obliterating human choice in any form at all. Milton does not claim it, nor does he extol it. Milton praises not an ecstatic possession by God but instead a freeing of oneself from external authority, a composing of the passions and a deliberate effort of the intellect. He even equates prayer and thought by making it indifferent at the moment of catastrophe which activity engages the hero, who "stood, as one who pray'd, / Or some great matter in his mind revolv'd." Milton thought that tragedy is meant to effect in an audience the cure of passions through their tempering, not their exaltation nor their obliteration. The final statement of Milton's poetics is made in the preface to the play. The effect of the play is to remove from the minds of the hero, of Manoa, of the Chorus, and ultimately of the audience a sheerly mental disorder and to isolate that mental disorder, the "spirit of phrenzie" which "hurt thir minds" and the "blindness internal" in the uncomposed minds of the Philistines, affording to Samson, Manoa, the Chorus, and ultimately the audience the "calm of mind" in which a "new acquist" of "true experience" can be possible.[16] That "calm of mind all passion spent" is not a void or blank of mind; it is a vivid, energetic recogni-

---

[16] See Northrop Frye, "Agon and Logos," 143; see also Lynn Veach Sadler, "Coping with Hebraic Legalism: The Chorus in *Samson Agonistes*," *Huntington Library Quarterly*, 66 (1973), 353-69.

tion of a truth. The hero suffered "anguish of the mind and humours black"; these were purged in the course of the play, not into passive compliance, but into "rouzing motions . . . which dispose to something extraordinary [his] thoughts." Manoa brought to the play a sense of the "deceivable and vain" in human activity; he took from the action "what may quiet us in a death so noble." The Chorus sought to bring "apt words . . . to swage / The tumours of [Samson's] troubl'd mind"; they took from the experience their own "calm of mind."

Throughout the course of his writing—either with left or right hand —Milton held, then, to the loftiest conception of his art, believed it inspired by God for a reason, and considered himself obliged to use it in the service of truth. No responsible reader has ever thought otherwise; the point at issue is far narrower. When Milton described himself as a servant of God, did he believe that he was taken over, hallowed, suppressed, and made the passive instrument of a holy force, or did he think that he had been given a power and a role comformable to the best of mere man and a talent it would be death to hide? My argument is simply that the direction and course of Milton's comments upon inspiration is a process of diminishing emphasis upon ecstatic, unearthly music and increasing emphasis upon speaking reason to sensible men. Professor Fixler's view of Milton's poetry as a liturgical act of worship is confirmed for the works he uses to derive it: *The Reason of Church Government*, "Ad Patrem," the prose tracts, and parts of *Paradise Lost*. Professor Hanford's view of Milton as a teacher-prophet in the line of Moses is likewise confirmed for the works from which he derives it. Dr. Kerrigan's position is largely confirmed for Milton as a young pamphleteer,[17] though in *The Reason of Church Government* he confounds a conventional metaphor with Milton's deepest conviction, that the poet is a teacher. The understanding of Milton as rational, deliberate, logical, and steadily answering with full consciousness to a great

---

[17] Dr. Kerrigan, in *Prophetic Milton*, considers the question whether *Samson Agonistes* actually confirms his curious view of Milton the life-long trumpet of God, noticing that apparently it does not since no self-evident "inspired narrator" speaks (204), no "inspired interpreter" comments (201), and "no character fully possesses the gift of prophecy." He resolves the problem of fitting the play to his thesis by identifying the theme as the "relationship between blasphemous and godly play," by seeing Samson as the godly player (209), and by identifying the imagery of birth traumas and defecation as the delivery of "all that vile rebuke." His tasteless analysis of an impotent, windy, constipated Samson undergoing a literal catharsis cannot be confirmed by my analysis of process. I do not think it can be supported by sensitive reading. The play is not about the relationship of godly and blasphemous play, and still less is it about the "good purgation of hatred." The briefest answer to Dr. Kerrigan's cloacal suggestion is contained in the epistle "Of Tragedy." Milton conceived of catharsis as tempering and harmonizing, not as expelling.

plan—an understanding expressed by Burden, Woodhouse, Sirluck, Irene Samuel, and many others—is confirmed by the final poems. What is reconciling and distinctive in my own view, though it has the support I believe of Lawry and Grose, is the recognition of a process in Milton's thought about the role of the poet through which the rhapsode is replaced by the sage.

TRAGIC EFFECT AS THERAPEUTIC:
HARMONY AND ENERGY

Tragic effect, Milton instructs us plainly, is "to temper and reduce (pity and fear, or terror and such like passions) to just measure with a kind of delight, stirr'd up by reading or seeing those passions well imitated." Tragic effect involves contrary motions—calm and delight, composure and emotion, reduction and stirring, stasis and energy. Milton gives the authority of Aristotle and medicine for the description of one part of tragic effect as cathartic.[18] He calls tragic effect "lustratio" in the epigraph from Aristotle given a Latin translation on the title page—*Per misericordian et metum perficiens talium afectuum lustrationes*—and "purge" in the prefatory epistle itself. The other part of tragic effect, delight, he notes arises "from the imitation of the passions." He defines purgation as a harmonizing and moderating rather than an obliteration or extirpation of the emotions. The passions to be harmonized he expands to include passions similar to pity and terror, without specifying the despair or hatred or other such passions he means. He thinks that tempering comes through imitation of the passions themselves, and he draws a medical analogy to clinch his discussion of this tragic effect. Delight he sees as an enlivening and stirring effect to balance the calming and tempering effect of catharsis. In *The Reason of Church Government* Milton gave an extended account of aesthetic pleasure when pursuing the argument that aesthetic pleasure justified poetry by virtue of its beneficial effects upon a reader. He wrote:

[18] The discussion of catharsis has been thoroughly conducted by, among others: Paul Sellin, "Sources of Milton's Catharsis: A Reconsideration," *Journal of English and Germanic Philology*, 60 (1961), 712-30, and "Milton's Epithet *Agonistes*," *Studies in English Literature*, 4 (1964), 136-62; Martin Mueller, "Sixteenth Century Italian Criticism and Milton's Theory of Catharsis," *ibid.*, 6 (1966), 139-50, and "Pathos and Katharsis in *Samson Agonistes*"; Raymond B. Waddington, " 'Melancholy against Melancholy': *Samson Agonistes* as Renaissance Tragedy," in *Calm of Mind*, ed. Wittreich; John M. Steadman, " 'Passions Well Imitated' "; Sherman H. Hawkins, "Samson's Catharsis," *Milton Studies*, 2 (1970), 211-30; Georgia Christopher, "Homeopathic Physic and Natural Renovation"; and Low, *Blaze of Noon*, 139-56.

359

Lastly, whatsoever in religion is holy and sublime, in vertue amiable, or grace, whatsoever hath passion or admiration in all the changes of that which is call'd fortune from without, or the wily suttleties and refluxes of mans thoughts from within, all these things with a solid and treatable smoothness to paint out and describe. Teaching over the whole book of sanctity and vertu through all the instances of example with such delight to those especially of soft and delicious temper who will not so much as look upon Truth herself, unless they see her elegantly drest, that whereas the paths of honesty and good life appear now rugged and difficult, though they be indeed easy and pleasant, they would then appeare to all men both easy and pleasant though they were rugged and difficult indeed.[19]

What was to be derived from painting out and describing with a solid and treatable smoothness human events ("all the changes of that which is call'd fortune from without") and human emotions ("the wily suttleties and refluxes of mans thoughts from within") was "instances of example with such delight." The "passion or admiration" which inhered in human behavior and human psychology is transformed into delight when the events and emotions are well imitated by the poet. The delight which results is a state of mind consonant with calm and incompatible with perturbation. The account in *The Reason of Church Government*, Milton's brief apology for poetry, is generally complemented by that in "Of Tragedy." There too he defends poetry in terms of its effect upon the consciousness of readers when he describes "the gravest, moralest, and most profitable of *all other Poems.*" What applies to "that Epick form" or "those Dramatick constitutions" or "those magnifick Odes and Hymns" discussed in *The Reason of Church Government* applies, the epistle shows, *a fortiori* to tragedy. Thus what Milton says about tragic effect in the preface to *Samson Agonistes* applies not only to the genre tragedy but is an aspect of aesthetic response in general, particularly applicable to tragedy. Notwithstanding the congruence of both texts, however, there are changes of emphasis. In *The Reason of Church Government* the "solid and treatable smoothness" of an apt mimesis is applied like clothing for naked truth to hearten "those especially of a soft and delicious temper" who fearfully think things difficult when they are easy but encouraged and strengthened by their response to art would find things easy when they were difficult. Art changes consciousness in the opinion of the young Milton; art changes consciousness in the opinion of the old Milton. The change is from passion to delight in both texts; the means effecting the change is imitation in both. Nonetheless, a significant shift of em-

[19] *CPW*, I, 817-18.

phasis is effected in "Of Tragedy" in the addition of the words "stirr'd up by reading or seeing those passions well imitated" and the suppression of any metaphorical glancing at "truth elegantly dresst."

Inherent in the direct imitation of human passions is a reduction of those passions, together with the production of an altered state of delight. The later emphasis is upon a strong clearing away of impeding mental experiences to enable the emergence of an energetic healthy mental condition. Nothing oblique, nothing fanciful, nothing delicately adjusted to a delicate audience of men of sensibility is alluded to. Rather, because of the inherent value of the energy of delight, "heretofore Men in highest dignity have labour'd not a little to be thought able to compose a Tragedy." Delight does not come from variety or from "intermixing Comic stuff," which "corruptly . . . [gratifies] the people," or from elegantly dressing truth. Delight derives from the recognition of a true imitation and is the lively state of a mind moving confidently in tune with reason to discover the meaning in God's providential liberating design for his Creation. In the preface Milton does not explicitly make the point that the characters themselves within the drama achieve a harmonizing and tempering of their passions, which is also well imitated and instrumental to the catharsis of the audience. The drama itself, however, fully shows that to have been his view. The application to others of Samson's purgation commences with the Messenger, who has directly witnessed the catastrophe of the tragedy of Samson. The effect on him is the first full response to the event Samson has staged in response to his understanding of the nature of his God—or, if you like, in response to God's staging. That response of the Messenger initiates the new consciousness which ensues after the tempering of passion. The Messenger recoils from the sight in terror and the after image haunts his eyes:

> O whither shall I run, or which way flie
> The sight of this so horrid spectacle
> Which earst my eyes beheld and yet behold;
> For dire imagination still persues me.

> (1541-44)

He has run blindly from terror. Yet his recoil has not been accidental or fortuitous. There is no such thing as accident or fortuity or blind chance in the universe any more than there is fate or compulsion; there is meaningfulness to be discovered. Not all actions need signify profoundly to all men, and some men among the throng "obscurely" stand; but even they participate in God's scenario and act freely in their lesser roles. The Messenger therefore continues:

> But providence or instinct of nature seems,
> Or reason though disturb'd, and scarse consulted
> To have guided me aright, I know not how. . . .
>
> (1545-47)

Milton's equating of providence, natural instinct, and reason is not an offer of pure alternatives; these are synonomous descriptions of the energy or momentum in the universe. The Messenger responds naturally to the force latent in the experience he has seen, not a mindless force, but a rational one.

The Messenger then delivers his own imitation of the passions and actions he has observed. His form of imitation has the expected effect on the audience to whom he delivers it. He does not, as Manoa instinctively feared he would, report Samson "at variance with himself." He reports the action of a man in whose mind balancing and tempering has taken place. He describes first the mood in which he himself attended the "spacious Theatre" of Samson's last performance: "I sorrow'd at his captive state, but minded / Not to be absent at that spectacle." Next, he sketches the emotions and passions of the rest of the audience, their "hearts" filled with "mirth, high chear, & wine," rifting the air with shouts and "clamouring thir god with praise" for making their dreaded enemy their thrall. The excitement of seeing their terrible opponent enter the amphitheater solemnly and triumphantly escorted in the livery of their state, exerting his strength with "incredible, stupendious force," swells and then diminishes for Samson's intermission. The Messenger then tells how Samson filled that silence and cried aloud his second trial of strength, his promise "with amaze [to] strike all who behold." He reports the burst of thunder on the heads of those who sat beneath the roof. He ends in dimenuendo, "The vulgar only scap'd who stood without." The passions of the Philistines, the calmness of the hero, these passions and their harmonizing, the Messenger reports to a new audience of Chorus and Manoa. The complicity of the Philistines in their own destruction, their actual suicidal excitement and impulsive mindlessness, Samson's still consent to his inward energy—all is placed before the little audience to whom the Messenger acts as playwright.

The audience of Chorus and Manoa then exhibits the natural effect of great tragedy. The first semichorus picks up the response they have been guided toward, and in wonder views the Philistines maddened by their excitement and urging on their own death, "So fond are mortal men . . . as thir own ruin on themselves to invite." The emphasis falls on the Philistines' self-induced fate, not upon the instrumentality of external force exerted by Samson. It is not the purgation of violence by violence that we are asked to witness, it is the purgation of mind-lessness by reason. The second semichorus continues the response they have been guided toward; in contrast to the wild Philistines, Samson displays to them the true and delightful energy of revived virtue, re-flourishing and active in the man whose inward eyes were illuminated. Manoa then becomes the third commentator on the drama which the Messenger has restaged for him. His comment reflects his own cathar-sis of doubts and anxieties into its own clear sense of "what may quiet us in a death so noble." The final quatrain of the choral *nunc dimittis* quietly attributes the beneficent action of the tragedy to God,[20] view-ing Him metaphorically as the tragic poet who can restore to His creatures the delight in His dramatic universe which sends them again into their own creative lives:

> His servants he with new acquist
> Of true experience from this great event
> With peace and consolation hath dismist,
> And calm of mind all passion spent.

> (1755-58)

The calm of mind accommodates, of course, as Manoa has shown, an aspect of renewed energy for the future: the residuum in their experi-ence is "honour and freedom." The tragic experience is forward looking: a new energy and delight is acquired, an energy in the harmonizing and tempering of human capacities when the God-intended purposive-ness of those human capacities has been shown. The delight re-leases an energy by which the new creativity may come.[21] When all the shame, loss, bitterness, failure, remorse, and anguish of mind is shown transmuted into self-delivering patience, penitence, pardon, self-acceptance, and reasonable hope, then Milton leaves his largest audience the audience of new generations, to contemplate through the reactions of the interior audience within the drama his final confidence in human life. By how much their earlier confidence was flat, inert, misplaced, and ashy, the removal of it to a new source is progressive and forward looking. It is the truth itself of experience which is the poetic object of delight. The theology of expanding revelations to free men capable of growth is matched in Milton's last great poem by a poetics of changed consciousness. To change men and make it possible for them to think the new and the true is the meaning of human life. This Mil-ton shows in his final work, displaying that capacity not only in the

---

[20] See Jon Lawry, *Shadow of Heaven*, 392-97, for a beautifully given account of this scene.

[21] See Northrop Frye, "Agon and Logos," 163, for a similar line of thought.

heartening example of his biblical hero but in the confidence-inspiring example of his own process of growth and renewal in his understanding of human psychology, of history, of politics, of ethics, of divinity, and of poetry itself.

APPENDIXES

Appendix A

A Table of Suggested Sonnet Datings and the Subgroups into which They Fall

SONNETS	Woodhouse and Bush[1]	Parker[2]	Smart[3]	Honigman[4]	Hughes[5]	Shawcross[6]	Hanford[7]	Carey and Fowler[8]	My dating	My grouping
1. O Nightingale	1628-30	Spring 1629	1629	1629	1630	May 1630	May 1628	1629	1629	Group I
2.-6. Italian	1628-30	1630	1630	1638	1630	1630	1628?	1629	1630	I
7. How soon hath Time	9 Dec. 1632	1632	1631	Dec. 1632	1632	Dec. 1632	1632	Dec. 1631	Dec. 1632	I
8. Captain or Colonel	13 Nov. 1642	1642	Nov. 1642	May 1641	1642	Nov. 1642	1642	Nov. 1642	Nov. 1642	Group II
9. Lady that in the prime	1642-45	1642-early 1643	1642-45	1642	1645	1643-45		1643	1643	II
10. To the Lady Margaret Ley	1642-45	1642-early 1643	1642-45	before Dec. 1641	1645	1643-45		1642	1642	II
11. A Book was writ of late	1645-46	1646	1645-46	1646-47	1646	1647	1647	1647	1646	Group III
12. I did but prompt	1645-46	1645	1645-46	1646-47	1646	Sept. 1645		1646	1645	III
(On the new forcers of Conscience)	1646-47	Jan. 1646	1646	early 1646	1646	Aug. 1646-early 1647	Aug. 1646	Aug. 1646	1646	III
13. Harry whose tuneful Song	9 Feb. 1646	9 Feb. 1646	9 Feb. 1646	9 Feb. 1646	1646	Feb. 1646	Feb. 1646	9 Feb. 1646	Feb. 1646	III
14. When Faith and Love	Dec. 1646	Dec. 1646	Dec. 1646	Dec. 1646	Dec. 1646	Dec. 1646	Dec. 1646	Dec. 1646	Dec. 1646	III

Title	[1]	[2]	[3]	[4]	[5]	[6]	[7]	[8]	Group
	17 Aug. 1648		Aug. 1648	Aug. 1648	Aug. 1648	July-Aug. 1648	Aug. 1648	Summer 1648	IV
16. Cromwell, our cheif of men	May 1652	May 1652	May 1652	May 1652	May 1652	May 1652	May 1652	May 1652	IV
17. Vane, young in yeares	3 July 1652	1652	1652	1652	July 1652	June 1652	June-July 1652	July 1652	IV
18. Avenge O Lord	May-June 1655	1655	1655	1655	1655	May 1655	May 1655	May-June 1655	IV
19. When I consider	1652	1654-55	1652-54	before 9 Dec. 1644 or 1651-52 or 1655	1652	Oct. 1655	1652	Dec. 1652	Group V
20. Lawrence of vertuous Father	1654-56	1654-56	1654	1652	1655	Oct.-Nov. 1655	Winter 1653	Oct. 1655	V
21. Cyriack, whose Grandsire	1654-56	1654-56	1654	1655	1655	Oct.-Nov. 1655	1655	Oct.-Dec. 1655	V
22. Cyriack, this three years day	1654-56	June 1654	1655	1655	1655	Dec. 1655	1655	Jan.-Feb. 1655	V
23. Methought I saw	1658	before 12 Nov. 1656	1658	1658	1658	1656-58	1658	1658	V

[1] A Variorum Commentary on the Poems of John Milton, ed. Merritt Y. Hughes, Vol. II, ed. Douglas Bush and A.S.P. Woodhouse (New York: Columbia University Press, 1970).

[2] William R. Parker, Milton, a Biography (Oxford: Clarendon Press, 1968).

[3] John S. Smart, ed., The Sonnets of John Milton, repr. ed. (Oxford: Clarendon Press, 1966).

[4] E.A.J. Honigman, ed., Milton's Sonnets (London: Macmillan, 1966).

[5] Merritt Y. Hughes, ed., Complete Poems and Major Prose of John Milton (New York: Odyssey Press, 1957).

[6] John T. Shawcross, ed., The Complete English Poetry of John Milton (New York: New York University Press, 1963; 2d ed., 1971).

[7] James Holly Hanford and James Taaffe, eds., A Milton Handbook, rev. ed. (New York: Appleton-Century-Crofts, 1970).

[8] John Carey and Alastair Fowler, The Poems of John Milton (London: Longmans, 1968).

Appendix B

PSALM CITATIONS IN *SAMSON AGONISTES**

Act 1 (lines 1-325) Governed by psalms of private and communal lament.

Prologos (ll.1-114) Private lament; see especially Psalms 6, 22, 42, 43.

ll.1-2　　　A little onward lend thy guiding hand
　　　　　　To these dark steps

　　　　　43:3　　O send out thy light and thy truth: let them lead me

　　　　　31:3　　. . . for thy name's sake lead me and guide me

　　　　　31:5　　Into thine hand I commend my spirit

　　　　　27:11　And lead me in a plain path

　　　　　25:9　　The meek will he guide

　　　　　5:8　　Lead me, O Lord . . . Make thy way straight before my face

　　　　　143:10　. . . lead me into the land of uprightness

ll.19-23　　. . . restless thoughts
　　　　　　. . . rush upon me thronging, and present
　　　　　　Times past, what once I was, and what am now.
　　　　　　O wherefore was my birth . . . foretold

　　　　　43:5　　Why art thou cast down, O my soul? and why art thou disquieted in me?

　　　　　143:4-5　My heart within me is desolate . . . . I remember the days of old

　　　　　42:9　　Why hast thou forgotten me? Why go I in mourning because of the oppression of my enemies?

l.34　　　　Made of my Enemies the scorn and gaze

　　　　　79:4　　A scorn and derision to them that are round about us

　　　　　44:13　Thou makest us a reproach to our neighbours, a scorn and derision to those that are round about us

　　　　　71:10　For mine enemies speak against me; And they that lay wait for my soul take counsel together

* Here, as throughout this study, I have used the 1671 edition of *Samson Agonistes* and the Authorized Version of the Psalms.

368

	22:7	All they that see me laugh me to scorn
	22:17	They look and stare upon me
ll.38, 40		Promise was that I . . .
		Ask for this great Deliverer now
	77:8	Doth his promise fail for evermore?
	33:16	A mighty man is not delivered by much strength
	33:17	Neither shall he deliver any by his great strength
l.46		Whom have I to complain of but my self?
	51:3-4	For I acknowledge my transgressions: And my sin is ever before me. Against thee, thee only have I sinned
l.70		Light the prime work of God to me is extinct
	38:10	As for the light of mine eyes, it also is gone from me
	6:7	Mine eye is consumed because of grief
ll.73-74		Inferiour to the vilest now become
		Of man or worm
	22:6	But I am a worm, and no man; A reproach of men, and despised of the people
ll.98-100		. . . exil'd from light
		. . . in the land of darkness . . .
		To live a life half dead, a living death
	13:3	Lighten mine eyes, lest I sleep the sleep of death
	143:3	He hath made me to dwell in darkness, as those that have been long dead
	97:2	Clouds and darkness are round about him
	23:4	I walk through the valley of the shadow of death
ll.111-13		The tread of many feet . . .
		. . . my enemies who come to stare
		At my affliction, and perhaps to insult
	25:19	Consider mine enemies; for they are many; And they hate me with cruel hatred
	22:17	They look and stare upon me
Parode (ll.115-75)		Communal lament.
l.128		Who tore the Lion, as the Lion tears the Kid
	44:11	Thou has given us like sheep appointed for meat
l.150		. . . the Gentiles feign to bear up Heav'n
	75:3	I bear up the pillars of it

l.169   To lowest pitch of abject fortune thou art fall'n

     44:25   Our soul is bowed down to the dust; Our belly cleaveth unto the earth

     79:8   . . . we are brought very low

     82:7   But ye shall die like men, And fall like one of the princes

     89:44   Thou hast made his glory to cease, And cast his throne to the ground

     22:15   Thou hast brought me into the dust of death

ll.174-75   Might have subdu'd the Earth,

             Universally crown'd with highest praises

     8:5   For thou hast made him a little lower than the angels, And hast crowned him with glory and honor

     89:27   . . . I will make him my firstborn, higher than the kings of the earth

First episode (ll.176-292) Private lament.

ll.191-93   . . . in prosperous days

             They swarm, but in adverse withdraw their head

             Not to be found, though sought

     31:11   I was a reproach among all my enemies, But especially among my neighbours; and a fear to mine acquaintance: They that did see me without fled from me

     69:20   And I looked for some to take pity, but there was none; And for comforters, but I found none

ll.196-97   . . . had I sight, confus'd with shame,

             How could I once look up, or heave the head

     89:45   Thou hast covered him with shame

     44:15   My confusion is continually before me, And the shame of my face hath covered me

     69:7   Shame hath covered my face

     77:4   Thou holdest mine eyes waking: I am so troubled that I cannot speak

l.203   Am I not sung and proverbd for a Fool

     69:11   And I became a proverb to them

ll.206-7   Immeasurable strength they might behold

             In me, of wisdom nothing more then mean

     49:20   Man that is in honour, and understandeth not, is like the beasts that perish

     90:12   So teach us to number our days, that we may apply our hearts unto wisdom

ll.268-69   . . . Nations grown corrupt,
          And by thir vices brought to servitude
          81:11-12 Israel would none of me. So I gave them up
               to their hearts' lust
First stasimon (ll.293-325) Communal lament.
  l.293   Just are the ways of God
          119:137 Righteous are thou, O Lord, And upright are
               thy judgments
  l.298   . . . the heart of the Fool
          14:1   The fool hath said in his heart, There is no
               God
          53:1   The fool hath said in his heart, There is no
               God
ll.307-9   As if they would confine th' interminable,
          And tie him to his own prescript,
          Who made our Laws to bind us
          50:16   What hast thou to do to declare my statutes,
               Or that thou shouldst take my covenant in
               thy mouth?
  l.311   Whom so it pleases him by choice
          115:3   He hath done whatsoever he pleased
          132:6   Whatsoever the Lord pleased, that did he
Act II (ll.326-709) Again dominated by private and communal lament,
  but in the speeches of Samson, increasingly by the penitential psalms.
Second episode (ll.326-651)
ll.348-50   . . . O ever failing trust
          In mortal strength! and oh what not in man
          Deceivable and vain!
          60:11   . . . vain is the help of man
          62:9   Surely men of low degree are vanity, and
               men of high degree a lie: To be laid in the
               balance, they are altogether lighter than van-
               ity
          108:12 . . . vain is the help of man
ll.350-51   . . . Nay what thing good
          Pray'd for, but often proves our woe, our bane?
          34:12   What man is he that desireth life, And loveth
               many days, that he may see good?
  l.358   Why are his gifts desirable
          89:47   Wherefore hast thou made all men in vain?
  l.362   . . . thy nurture holy, as of a Plant
          1:3   And he shall be like a tree planted by the riv-
               ers of water

l.366 Thy Foes derision
   79:4 . . . a scorn and derision
   44:13 . . . a scorn and derision
ll.370-71 . . . as a thrall
   Subject him to so foul indignities
   39:10 Remove thy stroke away from me: I am consumed by the blow of thine hand
   102:9-10 For I have eaten ashes like bread, And mingled my drink with weeping. Because of thine indignation and thy wrath: For thou hast lifted me up, and cast me down
ll.374-76 Nothing of all these evils hath befall'n me
   But justly; I my self have brought them on,
   Sole Author I, sole cause
   41:4 Heal my soul, for I have sinned against thee
   51:4 Against thee, thee only, have I sinned . . . That thou mightest be justified when thou speakest, And be clear when thou judgest
ll.376-77 . . . if aught seem vile,
   As vile hath been my folly
   15:4 In whose eyes a vile person is contemned
l.392 . . . with flattering prayers and sighs
   5:9 They flatter with their tongue
   12:2 With flattering lips and with a double heart do they speak
ll.440-41 . . . God,
   Besides whom is no God
   77:13 . . . who is so great a God as our God?
   71:19 O God, who is like unto thee!
   89:8 O Lord God of hosts, Who is a strong Lord unto thee
l.443 . . . th' Idolatrous rout amidst thir wine
   35:16 . . . with hypocritical mockers in feasts
l.467 . . . [He] will arise and his great name assert
   74:22 Arise, O God, plead thine own cause
   76:1 His name is great
l.471 And with confusion blank his Worshippers
   83:17-18 Let them be confounded and troubled forever . . . That men may know that thou, whose name alone is Jehovah, Art the most High
ll.474-75 . . . [God] will not long defer
   To vindicate the glory of his name

	68:1	Let God arise, let his enemies be scattered
	72:17	His name shall endure forever, His name shall be continued as long as the sun
l.509		God will relent, and quit thee all his debt
	103:9	He will not always chide: Neither will he keep his anger forever
	77:7-8	Will the Lord cast off forever? And will he be favourable no more? Is his mercy clean gone forever? Doth his promise fail forevermore?
ll.529-30		. . . like a petty God I walk'd about admir'd of all and dreaded
	49:12	In Milton's version: "a man who is in an important condition and is not intelligent" (*CPW*, VI, 206-7)
ll.570-71		. . . till length of years And sedentary numness craze my limbs
	102:11	My days are like a shadow that declineth; And I am withered like grass
	90:9-10	For all our days are passed away . . . their strength is labour and sorrow
l.589		Nor shall his wondrous gifts be frustrate thus
	94:14	For the Lord will not cast off his people, Neither will he forsake his inheritance
ll.597-98		My race of glory run, and race of shame, And I shall shortly be with them that rest
	69:19	Thou hast known my reproach, and my shame, and my dishonour
	22:15	And thou hast brought me into the dust of death
l.632		And sense of Heav'ns desertion
	31:22	For I said in my haste, I am cut off from before thine eyes
	89:49	Lord, where are thy former loving-kindnesses
l.636		Under his special eie
	33:18	Behold, the eye of the Lord is upon them that fear him
	51:11	Cast me not away from thy presence
l.641		But now hath cast me off as never known
	89:38	But thou has cast off and abhorred . . . thine anointed
	43:2	. . . why does thou cast me off
	27:9	Leave me not, Neither forsake me

88:5   Like the slain that lie in the grave, Whom thou rememberest no more

Second stasimon (ll.652-709) Governed by the psalms which question man's suffering.

l.656   . . . mans frail life

39:4   That I may know how frail I am

l.660   . . . th' afflicted in his pangs

22:24   For he hath not despised nor abhorred the affliction of the afflicted

ll.664-66   Some sourse of consolation from above;
Secret refreshings, that repair his strength,
And fainting spirits uphold

51:10-12   . . . renew a right spirit within me. . . . Restore unto me the joy of thy salvation; And uphold me with thy free spirit

l.667   God of our Fathers, what is man!

8:4   What is man, that thou art mindful of him?

144:3   Lord, what is man that thou takest knowledge of him?

ll.668-71   . . . hand
. . . contrarious
Temperst thy providence through his short course,
Not evenly

75:7-8   He putteth down one, and setteth up another. For in the hand of the Lord there is a cup, and the wine is red; It is full of mixture; and he poureth out of the same

49:1   Both low and high, Rich and poor together

ll.674, 676   . . . of men the common rout
Grow up and perish, as the summer flie

49:12   Nevertheless man abideth not; He is like the beasts that perish

ll.682,   Yet toward these thus dignifi'd, thou oft
684-85   Changest thy countenance, and thy hand with no regard
Of highest favours past

89:39   Thou has made void the covenant of thy servant

l.690   Unseemly falls in human eie

44:12   Thou sellest thy people for nought

44:14   Thou makest us a byword among the heathen, A shaking of head among the people

ll.692-94 Oft leav'st them to the hostile sword
           Of Heathen and prophane, thir carkasses
           To dogs and fowls a prey
   79:2   The dead bodies of thy servants have they
           given to be meat unto the fowls of the heaven,
           The flesh of thy saint unto the beasts of the
           earth

l.703   Just or unjust, alike seem miserable
   34:19   Many are the afflictions of the righteous
           In Milton's version: "the just man's afflictions
           are many"

ll.708-9   Behold him in this state calamitous, and turn
           His labours, for thou canst, to peaceful end
   50:15   And call upon me in the day of trouble: I will
           deliver thee
   85:4   Turn us, O God . . . and cause thine anger . . .
           to cease
   107:28 . . . they cry unto the Lord in their trouble,
           And he bringeth them out of their distresses

Act III (ll.710-1060) The encounter suggested by Psalm 41:6: . . . if he
come to see me, he speaketh vanity. His heart gathereth iniquity to
itself; When he goeth abroad, he telleth it.
In Milton's version: "If anyone came to see me, he uttered empty
words while his heart gathered mischief; when he went out, he told
it abroad."
The didactic psalms are dominant.
Choral transition (ll.710-24)

ll.714-15 Like a stately Ship
           Of *Tarsus*
   48:7   . . . the ships of Tarshish
ll.720-21 An Amber sent of odorous perfume
           Her harbinger, a damsel train behind
   45:7   All thy garments smell of myrrh, and aloes,
           and cassia
   45:14   The virgins her companions that follow her

Third episode (ll.724-1009)
l.763   Entangl'd with a poysnous bosom snake
   58:4   Their poison is like the poison of a serpent
ll.845-46 . . . what snares besides,
           What sieges girt me round
   64:5   They commune of laying snares privily
   142:3   In the way wherein I walked Have they priv-
           ily laid a snare for me

l.870 Vertue, as I thought, truth, duty so enjoyning

  10:3 For the wicked boasteth of his heart's desire
   In Milton's version: "The wicked man praises
   his own soul"

l.872 ... feign'd Religion, smooth hypocrisie

  12:2 They speak vanity ... With flattering lips
   and with a double heart they speak

ll.885-86 ... for me thou wast to leave
  Parents and countrey

  45:10 Forget also thine own people and thy father's
   house

ll.921-22 ... fetch thee
  Forth from this loathsom prison-house

  142:7 Bring my soul out of prison

l.931 To bring my feet again into the snare

  9:16 The wicked is snared in the work of his own
   hands

l.936 So much of Adders wisdom

  58:4 They are like the deaf adder that stoppeth her
   ear; which will not hearken to the voice of
   charmers, Charming never so wisely

l.997 ... a manifest Serpent by her sting

  140:3 They have sharpened their tongues like a ser-
   pent

Third stasimon (ll.1010-60)

l.1039 A cleaving mischief, in his way to vertue

  91:9 In Milton's version: "A very evil thing clings
   tightly to him"

ll.1050-52 But vertue which breaks through all opposition,
  And all temptation can remove,
  Most shines and most is acceptable above

  94:12 Blessed is the man whom thou chastenest,
   Lord, and teachest him out of thy law

  119:71 It is good for me that I have been afflicted
   that I might learn thy statutes

l.1055 Over his female in due awe

  45:11 For he is thy Lord; and worship thou him

Act IV (ll.1061-1440) Governed by hymnic psalms of trust and thanksgiving.

Scene i (ll.1061-1296)

Fourth episode (ll.1061-1267) This encounter is suggested by Psalm
52, which describes the end of the man who loves violence.

  52:1-3 Why boasteth thou thyself in mischief, O

mighty man. . . . Thy tongue deviseth mischiefs . . . Thou lovest evil more than good; And lying rather than to speak righteousness.

ll.1066-67 . . . a rougher tongue
Draws hitherward

    52:2   Thy tongue deviseth mischiefs; like a sharp rasor

l.1091 The way to know were not to see but taste

    34:8   O taste and see that the Lord is good

l.1104 Boast not of what thou wouldst have done

    52:1   Why boasteth thou thyself in mischief

l.1140 My trust is in the living God

    7:1   O Lord my God, in thee do I put my trust

    42:2   My soul thirsteth for God, for the living God

    56:11   In God have I put my trust: I will not be afraid What man can do unto me

    37:40   He shall . . . save them, because they trust in him

(See also 11:1, 61:4, 62:8, 73:28, 115:11.)

l.1155 . . . whose God is strongest, thine or mine

    77:13   Who is so great a God as our God?

    135:5   For I know that the Lord is great, And that our Lord is above all Gods

l.1157 Thee [thy God] regards not, owns not

    3:2   Many there be which say of my soul, There is no help for him in God

ll.1169-71 . . . these evils I deserve and more,
Acknowledge them from God inflicted on me
Justly, yet despair not of his final pardon

    34:19   Many are the afflictions of the righteous; But the Lord delivereth him out of them all

    32:10   . . . he that trusteth in the Lord, mercy shall compass him about

    25:11   For thy name's sake, O Lord, Pardon mine iniquity

    130:4   But there is forgiveness with thee

ll.1172-73 Whose ear is ever open; and his eye
Gracious to re-admit the suppliant

    130:2   Let thine ears be attentive to the voice of my supplications

    94:9   He that planted the ear, shall he not hear? He that formed the eye, shall he not see?

34:15   The eyes of the Lord are upon the righteous,
And his ears are open unto their cry

ll.1174-75 In confidence whereof I once again
Defie thee

56:11   In God have I put my trust; I will not be
afraid what man can do unto me

37:5   Commit thy way unto the Lord; Trust also
in him
In Milton's version: "Commit your way to
Jehovah, have confidence in him and he will
accomplish it"

l.1176   ... whose god is god

18:31   ... who is God, save the Lord?

ll.1211-12 I was no private but a person rais'd
With strength sufficient and command from Heav'n

89:19,   I have exalted one chosen out of the people

21   ... Mine arm also shall strengthen him

ll.1259-60 ... my labours
The work of many hands, which earns my keeping

128:2   For thou shalt eat the labour of thine hands

ll.1265-67 ... because thir end
Is hate, not help to me, it may with mine
Draw thir own ruin who attempt the deed

37:14-15 The wicked have drawn out the sword. ...
Their sword shall enter into their own heart

139:21 Do I not hate them, O Lord, that hate thee?

Fourth stasimon (ll.1268-1296) Indebted in a general way to the
hymnic thanksgiving in Psalm 18, showing the personal deliver-
ance of one who trusted in God's goodness.

l.1268   Oh how comely it is and how reviving

41:10   ... raise me up, that I may requite them
In Milton's version: "Revive me so that I may
pay them out"

138:7   Though I walk in the midst of trouble thou
wilt revive me

ll.1269-73 To the Spirits of just men long opprest!
When God into the hands of thir deliverer
Puts invincible might
To quell the mighty of the Earth, th' oppressour,
The brute and boist'rous force of violent men

10:18   To judge the ... oppressed, that the man of
earth may no more oppress

18:17   He delivered me from my strong enemy, and from them which hated me

18:39   For thou hast girded me with strength unto the battle: thou hast subdued under me those that rose up against me

18:48   Thou hast delivered me from the violent men

ll.1273,   The brute and boist'rous force of violent men

1275-76   ... raging to pursue

The righteous and all such as honour Truth

86:14   O God, the proud are risen against me, and the assembly of violent men have sought after my soul

ll.1283-85 With winged expedition

Swift as the lightning glance he executes

His errand on the wicked

18:14   Yea, he sent out his arrows, and scattered them; And he shot out lightnings, and discomfited them

(See also 64:7, 147:15, 149:7, 9.)

l.1296   Whom Patience finally must crown

37:7, 9   Rest in the Lord and wait patiently for him. ... those that wait upon the Lord, they shall inherit the Earth

Scene ii (ll.1297-1440)

Fifth episode (ll.1297-1426)

l.1315   ... great Feast, and great Assembly

22:16   The assembly of the wicked have inclosed me

ll.1320-21 Our Law forbids at thir Religious Rites

My presence

81:9   There shall no strange god be in thee; Neither shall thou worship any strange god

ll.1358,   By prostituting holy things to Idols

1362   What act more execrably unclean, prophane?

106:36,   They served their idols. ... thus were they

39   defiled with their own words

ll.1365-66 ... by labour

Honest and lawful to deserve my food

128:2   For thou shalt eat the labour of thine hands

l.1368   Where the heart joins not, outward acts defile not

64:10   ... the upright in heart shall glory

ll.1373-76 ... to displease

God for the fear of Man, and Man prefer,

Set God behind: which in his jealousie
Shall never, unrepented, find forgiveness

16:4   Their drink offerings of blood will I not offer,
Nor take up their names into my lips

56:4   I will not fear what flesh can do to me

106:43   Many times did he deliver them; But they provoked him with their counsel, And were brought low for their iniquity

Fifth stasimon (ll.1427-40)

ll.1427-28 Go, and the Holy One
Of *Israel* be thy guide

78:41   The Holy One of Israel

48:14   For this God is our God forever and ever: He will be our guide even unto death

l.1429   To what may serve his glory best, & spread his name

115:1-2 Not unto us, O Lord, not unto us, But unto thy name give glory

67:2   That thy way may be known upon earth, thy saving health among all nations

(See also 54:6 and 24:7, 10.)

l.1430   Great among the Heathen round

72:11   All nations shall serve him

l.1434   . . . be now a shield

5:12   For thou, Lord, will bless the righteous; With favour wilt thou compass him as with a shield

(See also 59:11 and 84:9.)

Act v (ll.1441-1758) Dominated by Psalm 73, which describes and concludes a spiritual odyssey or pilgrimage not unlike Job's, a psalm of trust and thanksgiving.

Exode (ll.1441-1659)

ll.1461-62 . . . harsh,
Contemptuous, proud, set on revenge and spite

73:6   . . . pride compasseth them about as a chain; Violence covereth them as a garment

ll.1485-86 Fathers are wont to lay up for thir Sons,
Thou for thy Son art bent to lay out all

103:13   Like as a father pitieth his children

ll.1498-99 . . . his purpose
To use him further yet in some great service

119:125, I am thy servant. . . . it is time for thee Lord
126   to work

l.1514   Ruin, destruction at the utmost point

73:18   Thou castedst them down into destruction

73:19   How are they brought into desolation, as in
a moment!

ll.1527-28 . . . (for to *Israels* God

Nothing is hard) by miracle restor'd

72:18   Blessed be the Lord God, the God of Israel,
Who only doeth wondrous things

ll.1572-73 . . . death who sets all free

Hath paid his ransom now and full discharge

73:4   For there are no bands in their death

ll.1612-13 The Feast and noon grew high, and Sacrifice

Had fill'd thir hearts with mirth, high chear, & wine

73:7   Their eyes stand out with fatness: they have
more than heart could wish

l.1647   As with the force of winds and waters pent

147:18   He causeth his wind to blow and the waters
flow

35:5   Let them be as chaff before the wind

124:5   Then the proud waters had gone over our soul

Kommos (ll.1660-1758) Dominated by Psalms 103 and 104.

ll.1661-62 . . . thou has fulfill'd

The work for which thou wast foretold

20:4   Grant thee according to thine own heart, and
fulfil all thy Counsel

ll.1673-74 . . . our living Dread who dwells

In *Silo* his bright Sanctuary

74:7   Thy sanctuary . . . the dwelling place of thy
name

ll.1675-78 Among them he a spirit of phrenzie sent,

Who hurt thir minds,

And urg'd them on with mad desire

To call in hast for thir destroyer

94:23   And he shall bring upon them their own ini-
quity, And shall cut them off in their own
wickedness

ll.1679-81 They only set on sport and play

Unweetingly importun'd

Thir own destruction to come speedy upon them

73:27   Thou hast destroyed all them that go a whor-
ing from thee

ll.1682-84 So fond are mortal men

Fall'n into wrath divine,

As thir own ruin on themselves to invite

7:16   His mischief shall return upon his own head

90:7   We are consumed by thine anger, and by thy wrath are we troubled

l.1689   With inward eyes illuminated

119:18   Open thou mine eyes

ll.1690-91   His fierie vertue rouz'd
From under ashes into sudden flame

104:29-   . . . they die, and return to their dust. Thou
30   sendest forth thy spirit, they are created: and thou renewest

l.1695-96   . . . as an Eagle
His cloudless thunder bolted on thir heads

103:5   . . . thy youth is renewed like the eagle's

ll.1704-5   [Virtue] Revives, reflourishes, then vigorous most
When most unactive deem'd

138:7   Though I walk in the midst of trouble, thou wilt revive me

l.1716   Find courage to lay hold on this occasion

27:4   Be of good courage and he shall strengthen thy heart

ll.1719-20   . . . God not parted from . . .
But favouring and assisting to the end

37:28   For the Lord . . . forsaketh not his saints;
They are preserved forever

ll.1723-24   . . . nothing but well and fair,
And what may quiet us in a death so noble

107:30   Then are they glad because they be quiet; So he bringeth them unto their desired haven

ll.1746-47   . . . th' unsearchable dispose
Of highest wisdom

145:3   Great is the Lord, and greatly to be praised;
And his greatness is unsearchable

l.1749   Oft he seems to hide his face

30:7   Thou didst hide thy face, and I was troubled

27:9   Hide not thy face far from me

104:29   Thou hidest thy face, they are troubled

Appendix C

A SCHEMATIC OUTLINE OF
DE DOCTRINA CHRISTIANA, BOOK II

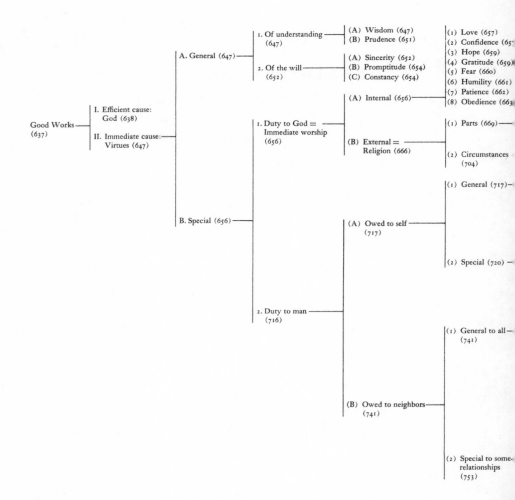

Good Works (637)

I. Efficient cause: God (638)

II. Immediate cause: Virtues (647)

A. General (647)

1. Of understanding (647)
  (A) Wisdom (647)
  (B) Prudence (651)

2. Of the will (652)
  (A) Sincerity (652)
  (B) Promptitude (654)
  (C) Constancy (654)

B. Special (656)

1. Duty to God = Immediate worship (656)
  (A) Internal (656)
    (1) Love (657)
    (2) Confidence (65?)
    (3) Hope (659)
    (4) Gratitude (659)
    (5) Fear (660)
    (6) Humility (661)
    (7) Patience (662)
    (8) Obedience (663)
  (B) External = Religion (666)
    (1) Parts (669) —
    (2) Circumstances (704)

2. Duty to man (716)
  (A) Owed to self (717)
    (1) General (717) —
    (2) Special (720) —
  (B) Owed to neighbors (741)
    (1) General to all — (741)
    (2) Special to some relationships (753)

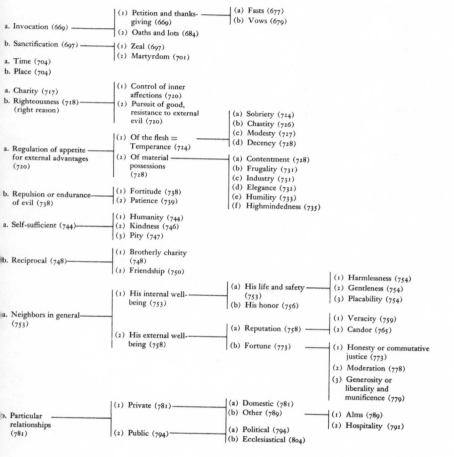

a. Invocation (669) ——
    (1) Petition and thanks- —— (a) Fasts (677)
        giving (669)   (b) Vows (679)
    (2) Oaths and lots (684)

b. Sanctification (697) ——
    (1) Zeal (697)
    (2) Martyrdom (701)

a. Time (704)
b. Place (704)

a. Charity (717)
b. Righteousness (718) ——
(right reason)
    (1) Control of inner
        affections (720)
    (2) Pursuit of good,
        resistance to external
        evil (720)

a. Regulation of appetite
   for external advantages
   (720)
    (1) Of the flesh =
        Temperance (724) ——
            (a) Sobriety (724)
            (b) Chastity (726)
            (c) Modesty (727)
            (d) Decency (728)
    (2) Of material ——
        possessions
        (728)
            (a) Contentment (728)
            (b) Frugality (731)
            (c) Industry (731)
            (d) Elegance (732)
b. Repulsion or endurance
   of evil (738)
    (1) Fortitude (738)
    (2) Patience (739)
            (e) Humility (733)
            (f) Highmindedness (735)

a. Self-sufficient (744) ——
    (1) Humanity (744)
    (2) Kindness (746)
    (3) Pity (747)

b. Reciprocal (748) ——
    (1) Brotherly charity
        (748)
    (2) Friendship (750)

a. Neighbors in general ——
   (753)
    (1) His internal well- ——
        being (753)
        (a) His life and safety ——
            (753)
        (b) His honor (756)
                (1) Harmlessness (754)
                (2) Gentleness (754)
                (3) Placability (754)
    (2) His external well- ——
        being (758)
        (a) Reputation (758) ——
                (1) Veracity (759)
                (2) Candor (765)
        (b) Fortune (773) ——
                (1) Honesty or commutative
                    justice (773)
                (2) Moderation (778)
                (3) Generosity or
                    liberality and
                    munificence (779)

b. Particular ——
   relationships
   (781)
    (1) Private (781) ——
        (a) Domestic (781)
        (b) Other (789) ——
            (1) Alms (789)
            (2) Hospitality (792)
    (2) Public (794) ——
        (a) Political (794)
        (b) Ecclesiastical (804)

Appendix D

A TOPICAL SYNOPSIS OF
DE DOCTRINA CHRISTIANA, BOOK I

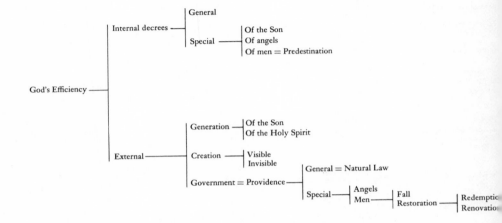

Appendix E

THE DATE OF COMPOSITION OF
SAMSON AGONISTES

FOUR dates for the composition of *Samson Agonistes* have been proposed by twentieth-century Miltonists: 1640-1641, 1647-1653, 1660-1661, and 1667-1670. The four dates, or a combination of some of them, are supported by three kinds of argument: Milton's stylistic practices, especially prosodic and rhyming; his thematic and intellectual preoccupations at several points in his life; and the supposed autobiographical and historical allusions within the play.

The date most often given by modern Miltonists is 1667-1670. A precondition for any dating of *Samson Agonistes* earlier than this is uncertainty about that date in the absence of conclusive objective evidence for it. William R. Parker was the first to show any evidence of uncertainty. He noted a comment by Edward Phillips, Milton's nephew, pupil, and occasional amanuensis, in Phillips's "The Life of Mr John Milton," written twenty years after the poet's death:

> It cannot certainly be concluded when he wrote his excellent Tragedy entitled *Samson Agonistes*, but sure enough it is that it came forth after his publication of *Paradice lost*, together with his other Poem call'd *Paradice regain'd*, which doubtless was begun and finisht and Printed after the other was publisht, and that in a wonderful short space considering the sublimeness of it. . . .[1]

Phillips said he knew that *Paradise Regained* was written after *Paradise Lost* was published; he thought it remarkable that Milton wrote his brief epic in the short space of three years. Had he thought *Samson Agonistes* composed in the same short space, he might have marveled even more. Parker therefore concluded that Phillips thought the play was written sometime before the publication of *Paradise Lost*. Had it been written whenever Phillips was regularly seeing Milton, he would have known its date; hence the writing cannot be ascribed to any period when Phillips was near Milton. The argument depends, of course, on the passage bearing the implication Parker gives it (it might equally bear the implication that *Samson Agonistes* was written before *Paradise Regained*, between the writing of *Paradise Lost* and its publication, or

[1] Quoted in Helen Darbishire, ed., *The Early Lives of Milton* (London: Constable & Co. Ltd., 1932), 75.

even after *Paradise Regained*, and that a tragic poem might not take as long to write as a "sublime" one). It also depends upon two assumptions about Phillips and Milton: that Milton discussed his work in progress with his nephew from Phillips's boyhood to his maturity; and that Phillips had an excellent memory for dates. Parker also requires us to believe that no objective confirmation of the post-Restoration date exists.

Phillips was Milton's pupil in 1639 and boarded with him from 1640 to 1646.[2] About 1647, Milton showed his pupils some lines written for a tragedy on the Fall; many years later Phillips recognized them in *Paradise Lost*.[3] That is Parker's evidence for Milton's confiding in Phillips—but the inference is not that Milton discussed his work in progress with his nephew, only that he used some of his lines for teaching purposes with his boarders on one occasion. Phillips left Milton's household in 1646 or shortly after; he was in Oxford in 1650 for one year and then went to Shrewsbury from 1651 to 1655 upon inheriting property there from his grandmother. He may have visited London occasionally between 1651 and 1655; he moved to London in 1655.[4] When John Aubrey showed him the notes he had prepared for a life of Milton, Phillips inserted his own name and the words "chief amanuensis" after the poem *Paradise Lost*. This might confirm the view that Milton confided in Phillips—if it were not for the fact that Phillips did not repeat the claim in his own life of the poet. Instead, he confined his role to correcting the spelling and punctuation of other scribes.[5] Aubrey, on Phillips's authority, dated the composition of *Paradise Lost* "about 2 yeares before the K[ing] came-in, and finished about 3 yeares after the K[ing]'s Restauracōn." This "was 4 or 5 yeares of his doeing

---

[2] Parker, *Milton*, II, 839.

[3] Darbishire, ed., *Early Lives of Milton*, 72. Phillips said that he saw the lines "several Years before the Poem was begun" and that they were "designed for the very beginning of the said Tragedy." From a conversation with Phillips thirteen years before Phillips wrote his life of Milton, John Aubrey says he learned that "In the 4th Booke of Paradise lost, there are about 6 verses of Satan's exclamation to the Sun, wch Mr E. Ph[illips] remembers, about 15 or 16 yeares before ever his Poëm was thought of, wch verses were intended for the Beginning of a Tragoedie wch he had designed, but was diverted from it by other businesse" ("Minutes of the Life of Mr John Milton," quoted, *ibid.*, 13). The time sequence we are dealing with is the memory of a boy of 12 repeated once by a man of 51 and then retold by a man of 64.

[4] He may or may not have been "the kinsman that was with [Milton] in 1652" (Anonymous Life of Milton, quoted in Parker, "The Date of *Samson Agonistes*: A Postscript," *Notes and Queries*, 203 [1958], 201-2).

[5] Phillips's story of Milton's practice of dictating by parcels to whatever scribe was handy belies his claim, and his is not the hand in the manuscript of Book I, the only manuscript part of *Paradise Lost* we have.

it."[6] Phillips himself wrote that he "had the perusal of it from the very beginning," that after Milton's "Two Answers to *Alexander More* [in 1654 and 1655] . . . he had leisure again for his own Studies and private Designs . . . ," which included the work on the *History of Britain* and a Latin thesaurus, "But the Heighth of his Noble Fancy and Invention began now to be seriously and mainly imployed in a Subject worthy of such a Muse, *viz.* A Heroick Poem. . . ." Phillips added:

> having as the Summer came on, not been shewed any [ten, twenty, or thirty verses at a time, which might possibly want correction] for a considerable while, and desiring the reason thereof, I was answered, That his Vein never happily flow'd, but from the *Autumnal Equinoctial* to the *Vernal*, and that whatever he attempted was never to his satisfaction, though he courted his fancy never so much; so that in all the years he was about this Poem, he may be said to have spent but half his time therein.[7]

Phillips left London in 1663 and did not return until 1672.[8] If Phillips had an excellent memory and was bound to know what Milton was writing, it might follow that *Samson Agonistes* was written before 1642, around 1647-1648 or in 1653. It could also follow that *Samson Agonistes* was written in 1660, when Milton was in hiding out of London, in 1663-1665, when Phillips was out of London, or after 1665, when Milton had moved to Chalfont St. Giles.

Phillips is a dubious witness about matters of dating. He gives only four specific dates in the biography, and three of those are incorrect: the date of Milton's birth; the date of the publication of *Paradise Lost*; and the date of Milton's death. It is reasonable to be skeptical about his memory.[9] Samuel Johnson was only the first to see something improbable in Phillips's picture of the poet mechanically delivering parcels of lines between the autumn and the spring. Moreover, Phillips's surprise is not that Milton composed so much, but that he composed so well in a short period. By Phillips's own account of Milton's composing habits, however, he believed that the poet delivered the 10,565

[6] Quoted in Darbishire, ed., *Early Lives of Milton*, 13.

[7] Quoted, *ibid.*, 72, 73.

[8] He moved first to Deptford to become tutor to John Evelyn's son; in 1664 he moved to Wilton and became tutor to the son of Philip Herbert, fifth earl of Pembroke.

[9] Parker himself comments on "Phillips's chronic inaccuracy, which becomes especially striking in his account of the period 1663-74. . . . There is quite enough inaccuracy, in other words, to warrant our scepticism about any statement of his for which we lack supporting evidence." We lack supporting evidence of others sharing his doubt (if he had it) that *Samson Agonistes* was of post-Restoration composition.

lines of *Paradise Lost* within four or five years, at an annual rate of 2,500 or 2,000 lines. The rate for *Samson Agonistes* and *Paradise Regained*, together totaling 3,828 lines, would have been 960 lines a year.

Thomas Ellwood saw a complete version of *Paradise Lost* in the summer of 1665, two years before its publication, and he thought that he put it into Milton's mind to write *Paradise Regained*. Ellwood thus confirms Phillips's belief that *Paradise Regained* was written after *Paradise Lost*. Yet Parker, Allan H. Gilbert, and John T. Shawcross not only date *Samson Agonistes* as a pre-Restoration work on the basis of Phillips's doubts, they also date *Paradise Regained* as largely pre-Restoration, written before or in the midst of composing *Paradise Lost*, despite Phillips's certainty to the contrary. If Phillips thought that *Samson Agonistes* was written before *Paradise Lost*, nothing prevented him from saying so. In general, inferences from silence are hazardous; but the silence of Andrew Marvell (Milton's valued friend) concerning a tragedy by Milton about Samson strongly suggests that *Samson Agonistes* had not been written by 1667, when Marvell wrote his poem "On *Paradise Lost*." The argument from Marvell's silence is the more compelling since Marvell refers to a blindly destructive "Sampson" quite unlike Milton's Samson.[10]

Phillips's doubt was not shared by the Anonymous Biographer, who stated categorically:

> It was now that hee began that laborious work of amassing . . . a Latin Thesaurus . . .; Also the composing *Paradise Lost* And the framing a Body of Divinity out of the Bible: All which, not withstanding the several Calamities befalling him in his fortunes, hee finish'd after the Restoration: As also the *British history* down to the Conquest, *Paradise regain'd*, *Samson Agonistes*, a Tragedy, *Logica* and *Accedence commenc'd* Grammar and hee begun a Greek Thesaurus.[11]

Parker's identification of the Anonymous Biographer as Cyriack Skinner is now generally accepted,[12] and that identification strengthens his

[10] That Marvell mentioned Samson suggests that, although he cannot have seen the play (Milton's Samson is not of the character Marvell describes), he may have heard of the plan for a tragedy on the subject.

[11] Quoted in Parker, "Date of *Samson Agonistes*: A Postscript," 201-2. When he first proposed to redate *Samson Agonistes*, Parker found this comment "unhelpful." When he returned to the subject, Parker thought the Anonymous Biographer made a distinction between two groups of works, those begun after Milton's blindness and completed after the Restoration and those other six (except for the Greek thesaurus, given as an afterthought) begun at an unspecified time and also completed after the Restoration. I do not think that the words "as also" can be made to bear the meaning "but at a quite different time." See Parker, "The Date of *Samson Agonistes*," *Philological Quarterly*, 28 (1949), 145-66, and "Date of *Samson Agonistes*: A Postscript."

[12] Parker, *Milton*, I, xiv.

evidence. Skinner was close to Milton in 1653, just before the Restoration, again in 1660-1661, and then continuously until 1665, when Milton left London. His identification of *Samson Agonistes* as "finish'd after the Restoration" may stand as objective evidence against Phillips's uncertainty.[13]

Two other pieces of objective evidence for the traditional date should also be noted, the datings by Jonathan Richardson and Thomas Newton.[14] Richardson's life of Milton was the first written by a scholar who did not personally know the poet. In preparing it Richardson consulted Milton's still living kinsmen, friends, and acquaintances, collected relevant official documents bearing on Milton's life, was especially well informed about the post-Restoration years, corrected numerous mistakes in Phillips's account, and, according to Helen Darbishire, added "fresh details that have the stamp of personal knowledge."[15] He affirmed confidently: "His Time was Now Employ'd in Writing and Publishing, particularly *Paradise Lost.* and after That, *Paradise Regain'd*, and *Samson Agonistes*."[16] Richardson's life was published in 1734. Two further lives, by biographers still in a position to acquire data at first hand from the poet's widow, his daughter Deborah, his granddaughter Elizabeth, and from still living friends and acquaintances, were published by Thomas Birch in 1738 and by Newton in 1749. Birch mentioned no uneasiness about the date of *Samson Agonistes*. Newton wrote:

> His *Samson Agonistes* is the only tragedy that he has finished, 'tho' he has sketched out the plans of several, . . . and we may suppose that he was determined to the choice of this particular subject by the similitude of his own circumstances to those of Samson blind among the Philistines. This I conceive to be the last of his poetical pieces. . . . There are also some other pieces of Milton, for he continued publishing to the last. . . . [In 1673] his poems, which had been printed in 1645, were reprinted with the addition of several others.[17]

Parker dismissed the evidence of Newton by implying that Newton merely conjectured that *Samson Agonistes* was late because he thought

---

[13] Quoted in Parker, "Date of *Samson Agonistes*: A Postscript."

[14] See Ernest Sirluck, "Milton's Idle Right Hand," *Journal of English and Germanic Philology*, 60 (1961), 773-80.

[15] Darbishire, ed., *Early Lives of Milton*, xxix-xxx. Richardson, for example, supplied evidence for Milton's brief imprisonment and pardon in 1660. See Parker, *Milton*, II, 1084, 1100, 1119, for reliance on his corrections of Phillips.

[16] Richardson, *Explanatory Remarks on Milton's "Paradise Lost". With the Life of the Author, and a Discourse on the Poem* (London, 1734). Quoted in Darbishire, ed., *Early Lives of Milton*, 275.

[17] Quoted in Sirluck, "Milton's Idle Right Hand," 775-76.

it autobiographical.[18] The first sentence quoted from Newton makes the point that Milton chose the subject of Samson for the reason of its contemporary applicability. The second sentence does not say that for this reason the play is to be considered a post-Restoration work; Newton commences a distinction between composition and publication in Milton's works. His point is that *Samson Agonistes* was the last poem written, although poems written earlier were inserted in editions published later than *Samson Agonistes*. In fact, he confirms Parker's general position that by and large Milton presented his poems in the order of their chronological composition, although he sometimes did not. Richardson and Newton taken together constitute objective confirmation of the conventional date. That it is not altogether naive to argue from order of appearance to order of composition may be inferred from Parker's own tendency to do so. Most readers will draw back from dating *Paradise Regained* before *Paradise Lost*. The evidence of Phillips and Ellwood, together with that of Richardson and Newton, is too strong to be shaken by the improbable concept of simultaneous composition of three great works. Parker's argument in its totality requires that Phillips be disbelieved about *Paradise Regained* but that much be read into his lack of knowledge of *Samson Agonistes*. Those who have accepted the Parker-Shawcross-Gilbert dating of *Samson Agonistes* have passed over in silence its logical consequence with respect to *Paradise Regained*.

ARGUMENTS FROM MILTON'S STYLISTIC PRACTICES AND INTENTIONS

Allan Gilbert, who thought *Samson Agonistes* an unfinished early work dating from 1640-1641, argued that it did not conform to the prologue, "Of that sort of Dramatic Poem which is call'd Tragedy," written when Milton prepared the old play for printing. In "Of Tragedy" Milton condemned "the Poets error of intermixing Comic stuff with Tragic sadness and gravity; or introducing trivial and vulgar persons, which by all judicious hath bin counted absurd." In the drama, Gilbert contended, Milton presents Harapha as the conventional boastful cow-

---

[18] Parker wrote that Newton "not unnaturally, albeit uncritically 'conceives' *Samson Agonistes* to be his last poem. . . . Three years earlier John Upton had considered the drama in an 'allegorical view', in which Samson 'imprisoned and blind, and the captive state of Israel', lively represents our blind poet with the republican party after the restoration." That Milton's contemporaries give authority for seeing the drama as autobiographical and containing historical allusions does not imply that they were uncritical and naive in so doing. See Parker, *Milton*, II, 746, 761, 875.

ard of Plautine comedy and Dalila as a comically overdressed figure of ridicule.[19] Milton's sources for both encounters are not comedies, however, but psalms, and Milton did not consider the Book of Psalms as comic. The Chorus, not Samson, describes Dalila as "bedeckt, ornate and gay" and likens her in an echo of the Psalms to a "stately Ship of *Tarsus*." Samson treats her with utmost seriousness and argues with her, if hotly also gravely. She is not comically overdressed, she is calculatedly scented and arrayed to entrap. Harapha is made the spokesman of a worldly militarism, and Samson answers him in psalm-derived affirmations of a revived faith in God. None of this is at variance with the prologue because it is not a comic intrusion of trivial, vulgar persons. The recognition of the Psalms as source for the scenes with Dalila and Harapha disposes of the view that the prologue could not have been written just after Milton had freshly treated the pair as "comic": Milton neither had his eye on theatrical analogues nor thought these characters trivial.

From Milton's attack on rhyme in the 1668 note "The Verse" supplied for *Paradise Lost*, Parker argued that Milton would never after that date have used rhyme, especially for a tragedy. Milton wrote of "Rime being no necessary Adjunct or true Ornament of Poem or good Verse, in longer Works especially," of rhyme rejected "long since [in] our best *English* Tragedies," and of his "neglect of Rime" as "an example set . . . of ancient liberty recover'd." Parker, reading this as a rejection, denunciation, and damnation, wrote, "*Samson Agonistes* could not have been composed in the years immediately preceding or following this public rejection of rhyme."[20] Milton himself speaks of "neglect of rhyme" in *Paradise Lost* and not of "elimination of rhyme"; he could not have been unaware of the nineteen couplets, the more than four hundred end rhymes separated by one or more lines, and the countless half or internal rhymes in *Paradise Lost* itself.[21] In the second edition of *Paradise Lost* after the so-called damnation of rhyme in 1668, Milton separated Book VII of the 1667 edition into Books VII and VIII of the 1674 edition by adding a quatrain, of which the first and third lines rhyme (Eare/hear) and the second and fourth lines half rhyme (while/repli'd). Milton was rejecting continual couplets ("the

---

[19] Gilbert, "Is *Samson Agonistes* Unfinished?" *Philological Quarterly*, 28 (1949), 98-106.

[20] "The Date of *Samson Agonistes* Again," 166.

[21] See Robert Beum, "So Much Gravity and Ease," in *Language and Style in Milton*, ed. R. D. Emma and John T. Shawcross (New York: Frederick Ungar, 1967), 348-51. See also John S. Diekhoff, "Rhyme in *Paradise Lost*," *PMLA*, 49 (1934), 539-43; J. M. Purcell, "Rime in *Paradise Lost*," *MLN*, 67 (1945), 171-72; Ernest Sirluck, "Milton's Idle Right Hand"; Michael Cohen, "Rhyme in *Samson Agonistes*," *Milton Quarterly*, 8 (1974), 4-6.

jingling sound of like endings"), not occasional rhyme. Rhyme in
Samson Agonistes is virtually limited to the lyrical parts of the play,
occurs in only one-eleventh of it, is usually spoken by the Chorus in
short, irregular lines—no single choral stasimon being regularly rhymed
save the sonnetlike last chorus—and couplets are exceedingly rare in
the play. The unpredictable rhyme in the tragedy is often used to in-
crease lyric impetus, is entirely original to Milton, is never a matter
of continuous couplets, and so need never have come under his general
condemnation.[22] While Milton may have thought he was reproducing
Hebrew prosody in his parallelistic short lines,[23] or may have believed
that near-doggerel suited the frame of mind of a puzzled chorus,[24] he
patently was taking as his models "the Antients and *Italians* . . . as of
much more authority and fame" than "what among us passes for best."
Very probably he recognized the Italian custom of rhyming mono-
strophic choruses and strikingly reduced the frequency of their rhym-
ing practice.[25] Finally, although Parker does not allow that *Paradise
Regained* was written after "The Verse," most critics do, and so it is
worth noting that *Paradise Regained* not only contains an enormous
increase of end stopping over *Paradise Lost*, it also employs much ter-
minal, initial, and medial actual rhyme, identical rhyme, and near
rhyme.[26] Perfect rhymes such as admire/desire, know/foe, ear/hear,
seen/mean, son/none, grace/race, mind/find, try/satisfy, passed/fast/
repast, gained/attained, held/quelled, thou/brow, brought/nought, side/
wide, tree/free, deserve/serve, man/can, hear/ears/years/fear are com-
mon. Half-rhymes, often in long chains, are even more common, such
as light/wide/wiles/try/bright, breast/first/converse, known/found/
gone/doubt/shewn, rear'd/round/herd/loud/brown, high/sire/quire/
might.[27] *Samson Agonistes* could as easily have been written after "The

---

[22] See Appendix B, "On the Verse," in Prince, *Milton: "Samson Agonistes,"* 134.
[23] See Frank Kermode, "*Samson Agonistes* and Hebrew Prosody."
[24] See Louis L. Martz, "Chorus and Character in *Samson Agonistes*," 125, 133.
[25] See Prince, *Italian Element in Milton's Verse*, 155-58.
[26] See Barbara Lewalski, *Milton's Brief Epic*, 349. See also Enid Hamer, *The
Metres of English Poetry* (London: Methuen, 1951), 102; Ants Oras, *Blank Verse
and Chronology in Milton* (Gainesville: University of Florida Press, 1966), and
his "Milton's Blank Verse and the Chronology of His Major Poems," in *SAMLA
Studies in Milton*, ed. J. Max Patrick (Gainesville: University of Florida Press,
1953), 61; S. E. Sprott, *Milton's Art of Prosody* (Oxford: Blackwell, 1953), 126;
John T. Shawcross, "The Chronology of Milton's Major Poems," 345, 349.
[27] One might instance the picture of Christ assailed by the storm in Book IV, ll.
408-25. Between the terminal perfect rhyme of now/thou and terminal half-rhyme
of dreams/peace, come the terminal half-rhymes, now/clouds/round, and pour'd/
abroad; the perfect internal rhymes, sleep/deep; and the internal half-rhymes,
clouds/shrouded/howl'd, ends/heav'n/slept, fell/yell'd, rift/winds/hinges/stiff;

Verse" as the quatrain opening Book VIII or the entirety of *Paradise Regained* was written after it.

Parker further argued that Milton could not have decided to imitate Greek tragedy "after *Paradise Regained* with its attack on Hellenic culture, including Attic drama." But Milton did not attack Attic drama in *Paradise Regained*. Satan recommended to Christ

> what the lofty grave Tragoedians taught
> In *Chorus* or *Iambic*, teachers best
> Of moral prudence, with delight receiv'd
> In brief sententious precepts, while they treat
> Of fate, and chance, and change in human life;
> High actions, and high passions best describing.
>
> (IV, 261-66)

He recommended "Attic drama" in a series of Hellenic arts running: philosophy, odes, epics, tragedy, orators, philosophers. Christ rejected these in a series running: philosophers, the writers of Greek "Fable, Hymn, or Song," "Thir Orators"—omitting mention of tragedy. In place of Hellenic culture he extolled Hebrew hymns, psalms, and songs. Unless Parker thought the lines rejecting "Fable, Hymn, or Song, so personating / Thir Gods ridiculous, and themselves past shame" to refer specifically to tragedy, which they do not, he simply read into Christ's words something that is not there. But more importantly, in "Of Tragedy" Milton in his own voice uttered something of Christ's grounds for preferring Hebrew to Greek culture; he emphasized the the biblical sanction for tragedy as Christ had emphasized the Hebrew priority in the arts.[28] Ralph Condee argues that Milton's adaptation of Greek tragedy is much too close to Hellenic models to be a late poem. Unlike *Paradise Lost*, which offers a critique of the classical epic and triumphs over it into a Christian epic, he claims, *Samson Agonistes* presents a skillful, uncritical parallel to classical tragedy; the slavishness of the imitation of his models is the mark of an immature Milton.[29] To unite current English history with an Old Testament fable within the inherited genre, however, and to conclude with God's justice and mercy extolled rather than with fate or nemesis or divine power re-

---

to say nothing of the assonances, horrid/rift/mixt/winds/hinges/stiff/ill/wilderness, or fierce/lightning/fire/pines/environ'd/fiery, and many others.

[28] "*Paraeus* commenting on the *Revelation*, divides the whole Book as a Tragedy," and "The Apostle *Paul* himself thought it not unworthy to insert a verse of *Euripides* into the Text of Holy Scripture."

[29] Condee, *Structure in Milton's Poetry*, 123-52.

affirmed, was Milton's quite un-Hellenic intention. Even Parker has been unable to pinpoint any single play or group of plays upon which Milton based *Samson Agonistes*.

Still drawing on "Of Tragedy," Parker glossed the sentence, "Division into Act and Scene referring chiefly to the Stage (to which this work never was intended) is here omitted." In Parker's opinion the use of the imperfect tense in the parenthesis implies, "When I wrote *Samson Agonistes* the theatres were closed so that I could not have intended a theatrical production; now they are open and I am belatedly publishing my tragedy, but I still have not divided it for a production because that wasn't the way I planned it." Were that the probable sense of the parenthesis, it would follow, as Parker argues, that *Samson Agonistes* must have been written between 1642, when the theaters were closed, and 1660, when they were reopened. The parenthesis, however, bears two other possible, opposite meanings. In *The Reason of Church Government* Milton wrote, "Dramatick constitutions [can be] doctrinal . . . to a Nation" if "our Magistrates . . . would take into their care . . . the managing of our publick sports, and festival pastimes . . . and the procurement of wise and artfull recitations . . . in Theatres, porches, or what other place." He believed in a purified and elevated stage, not in the existing commercial stage. He planned to write for a reformed theater. The imperfect tense of the parenthesis does not suggest composition completed far in the past when Milton could not have been writing for the stage; for this Milton would have used the pluperfect tense. It could mean, "The commercial stage being what it has been and now again is in England was never the intended goal of this tragedy." Or it could mean, "When the theatres were closed in 1642 I planned tragedies for a reformed theatre which the magistrates would shortly reopen, I hoped. After 1660 when the actual theatre was reopened, I could not write for it; hence this play was never planned for the stage." The second reading is that given by Anthony Low.[30] He believes that Milton did give *Samson Agonistes* act and scene divisions but did not indicate them, thus preparing an actable play which he knew could not achieve dramatic production in his lifetime because of the loss of a potential national audience by the downfall of the Commonwealth. The crucial word to Low is *never*, not *was*. In the 1640s Milton did plan dramas and give them stage directions in the Trinity Manuscript. He was hopeful then of a correction in the manners of the theater. *Samson Agonistes* could not have been written in the 1640s if it *never* was intended for the theater since the projected tragedies of the forties *were* intended for the theater.

[30] *Blaze of Noon,* 226.

Finally, Parker considered that his view that both *Paradise Regained* and *Samson Agonistes* were written before *Paradise Lost* had been confirmed by "detailed analysis of prosody . . . the frequency of strong pauses (terminal or medial), run-on lines, feminine endings, pyrric endings," and the like. Statistical analyses of such things as these have been made by two Miltonists, both assuming that "the employment of a specific prosodic technique must increase as development of it occurs, and correspondingly an opposing technique will decline."[31] That assumption should not, of course, be assented to unreservedly, and many will think it more likely if confined to prosodic practices *in the same genre*. Thus, if within the genre of the sonnet a poet progressively extends his use of medial pauses, he will probably decrease his use of terminal pauses, and one would not expect late sonnets to revert to earlier practices. But if a poet were to end-stop in a drama, move away from end-stopping in two epics, and then return to drama, it would not be surprising to find him end-stopping rather more again for the purpose of strengthening verisimilitude in dialogue. Of this sort of functional patterning, the similarity between *Comus* and *Samson Agonistes* in part consists. Moreover, few stylistic procedures are unaffected by the poet's sense of decorum: speeches meant to characterize their speakers may bear stylistic marks of the personality uttering them rather than of the date of their composition. It would be hard to date *Samson Agonistes* and *Paradise Regained* from stylistic elements without noting that both works contain contrasts of styles between different speakers.[32] Finally, no single prosodic device gives us the signature of a poet. Edward Weismiller, for example, thinks that Milton's use of accentual trochees in connection with pauses and also his elisions, compressions, and contractions are vital prosodic features requiring analysis. To the list of as yet unquantified elements, S. E. Sprott, James Whaler, and Wheeler add multilinear patterns, integral lines (both slow and fast paced), and the inversion of feet.

Since it would only be possible to date from stylistic features if all relevant stylistic traits were accurately computed, while all stylistic traits linked to genre or decorum were omitted, Parker's confidence that the matter has been settled cannot be shared. Even to confine ourselves to the competing views of Ants Oras and John Shawcross, however, is not to arrive at the necessary overturning of the conventional chronology, but rather to confirm the impossibility of deciding the

---

[31] John T. Shawcross, "Chronology of Milton's Major Poems," 345.

[32] See Louis L. Martz, "*Paradise Regained*: The Meditative Combat," *ELH*, 27 (1960), 223-47; Anne Ferry, *Milton and the Miltonic Dryden*, 41-93, 138-77; Weismiller, "A Review of Studies of Style and Verse Form of *Paradise Regained*," in *A Variorum Commentary*, IV, 362-63.

case by the prosodic tests hitherto applied. Where Shawcross uses Oras's figures for ten variables, he concludes against Oras's reading of them by the process of averaging the indices. Thus, for example, he notes, "*Samson Agonistes* precedes *Paradise Regained* II in 5 . . . tests, is even with it once, and follows it four times." But when he comes to summarize his findings, he writes, "We discover for the final form of these works a statistical ordering . . . *Samson Agonistes, Paradise Regained* II, IV, III, *Paradise Lost* VIII, IX, I, III, XII, XI, *Paradise Regained* I, *Paradise Lost* V, VII, IV, II, VI." By his own statistics, there is exactly as good a chance that *Paradise Regained* II preceded as followed *Samson Agonistes*. Shawcross also concedes, "Parts of *Paradise Lost* and *Paradise Regained* I may date in an earlier position than indicated in this ordering, and parts of *Samson Agonistes* and *Paradise Regained* may date later through revision."[33]

What picture of the composing practices of the blind poet dependent upon amanuenses emerges from Shawcross's survey? In place of the "uncritical" and "naive" view of the poet writing his poems one at a time and from beginning to end, we now have a critical and sophisticated view of the poet restlessly turning from one to another and back again. The speculation that *Paradise Regained* was originally composed as a "drama" (in contradistinction to the customary view that it was a "wise and artful recitation" or Platonic dialogue) is necessary to preserve the probability that it was written just after *Samson Agonistes* and just before *Paradise Lost* and in the order II, IV, III, I. Since Shawcross is indifferent to Milton's biblicism, he has not noticed that his version of the composing must postulate an original poem following Matthew's order of Christ's temptation in the wilderness, a change to Luke's order, and a final bracketing of Luke's account within a Jobean framework. Work on the deep structure of *Paradise Regained* and of *Samson Agonistes* makes that kind of restructuring of the profoundest logic of both works highly unlikely.[34]

In answering Shawcross in 1966 Oras considered more fully two practices discussed in the original analysis but excluded in Shawcross's reexamination of it: Milton's handling of sounded and unsounded *-ed* forms, and his use of adjectives and adjectival participles of the "supreme throne-divine property" and "throne supream-lineaments divine" form. Oras also added one practice not previously discussed, that of word length and the position of long and short words within the pentameter line. By giving all his studies in graph form, Oras is able to move beyond simple averages with all their misleading possibilities. He concludes:

[33] Shawcross, "Chronology of Milton's Major Poems," 357.
[34] See Patrick Cullen, *Infernal Triad*, xiii-xxv, 125-81.

After largely Elizabethan beginnings, Milton created his own idiosyncratic, highly individual epic style, emphatically a high style, heroic and soaring, rather consistently sustained throughout somewhat more than the first half of *Paradise Lost*. Then a change set in, gradually developing and persisting, with modifications, through all the rest of Milton's poetic career. A more austere style, less orotund, less reverberant and ornamental, briefer in its rhythms, shorter in the words it used, took Milton's poetry farther and farther away from the Elizabethan.[35]

A host of formal analysts—among them Masson, Symonds, Raleigh, Broadbent, Tillyard, Robson, Menzies, Marjorie Nicolson, Baum, Blondel, Martz, Woodhouse, Hanford, Stein, Barbara Lewalski, and Havens[36]—has seen a similar tendency in Milton's poetry. It runs parallel to a discernible movement toward plain style in his prose, also often commented upon. The shift is one marked in numerous poets within the century. No one is surprised to have the impression of a trend toward a less figurative style in Milton's poetry confirmed by Oras's new counts of quantifiable traits. To these, Seymore Chatman has added a further feature in his analysis of Milton's participial style, which also points toward a progression in which *Samson Agonistes* has a late date.[37]

Not many Miltonists have been attentive to possible dating evidence in the formal practices of Milton's contemporaries. Two exceptions should be noted: his relationship to Abraham Cowley and to John Dryden. The work of Weismiller on the versification of the choruses in *Samson Agonistes* disposes of Parker's argument that the choral odes must have been written at the same time that the Latin "To John Rouse" (1647) was written because both were explained in similar terminology and used similar stanza forms. Milton wrote of the Latin Ode, "the strophes and antistrophes do not perfectly correspond either in the number of verses or in divisions which are strictly parallel . . . a poem of this kind should perhaps more properly be called monostrophic. The metres are in part regularly patterned and in part apolelymenon" (that is, free from the restraint of correlation). He wrote of *Samson Agonistes*, "The measure of Verse us'd in the Chorus is of all sorts, call'd by the Greeks *Monostrophic*, or rather *Apolelymenon*, without regard had to *Strophe*, *Antistrophe* or *Epod* . . . or being divided into Stanza's or Pauses, they may be call'd *Allaeostropha*." Parker held, therefore,

---

[35] Oras, *Blank Verse and Chronology in Milton*.

[36] See Weismiller, "A Review of Studies," 308-17.

[37] See Chatman, "Milton's Participial Style," *PMLA*, 83 (1968), 1286-97; considered in Low, *Blaze of Noon*, 223.

that the ode and the choruses were of contemporary composition. Weismiller has shown that Milton's admiration of "those magnific odes of Pindar" was as early and persistent as his admiration of the Psalms. He studied Pindar in the seventh form at Saint Paul's School in 1620;[38] referred to him in the sixth elegy written to Diodati in 1629, in *The Reason of Church Government* in 1642, and in Sonnet 8 in the same year; and experimented with Pindaric irregular stanzas in "On Time," "At a Solemn Musick," and *Lycidas*. In 1656 Cowley published a number of "Pindarique Odes, Written in Imitation of the Stile and Maner of the Odes of Pindar." Weismiller has shown that "In the Pindarique Odes we find English syllabic lines in most of the extraordinary variety of different lengths and sequences in which they are to be found, later, in the choral odes of *Samson Agonistes*."[39] Cowley was one of Milton's favorite poets. Edward Phillips, in *Theatrum Poetarum*, made three suggestive comments: of Pindaric verse, "that which we call the Pindaric hath a nearer affinity with the Monostrophic, or Apololymenon, used in the Choruses of Aeschylus his Tragedies"; of tragedy, "for the Verse, if it must needs be Rime, I am clearly of the opinion that way of Versifying, which bears the name of Pindaric, and which hath no necessity of being divided into Strophs or Stanzas would be much more suitable for Tragedy then the continued Rhapsodie of Riming Couplets"; of Cowley, "the most applauded Poet of our Nation was the inventor of Pindaric verse in English."[40] The versification of the choruses in *Samson Agonistes* is thus linked with Cowley's verse, Greek tragedy, and spare rhyming. The evidence points not to the period of the "To John Rouse" but to a firmly post-1656 date. The death of Cowley in 1667 attracted universal mourning.

Finally, the argument that Milton's "The Verse" debarred him from using rhyme in *Samson Agonistes* fails to take cognizance of the irony of the paragraph and the contemporaneity of its argument. Claude Wells has shown that within the 250 or so words of explanation "why the Poem Rimes not" there occur at least fifteen ingenious and absurd rhymes, parodic of the practice of Milton's post-Restoration contemporaries.[41] Morris Freedman has shown that the preface takes part in the controversy between Sir Robert Howard and Dryden over rhyme and that Milton, Howard, and Dryden were consciously conducting

---

[38] See Donald L. Clark, *John Milton at St. Paul's School* (New York: Columbia University Press, 1948), 109-26.

[39] Weismiller, "The 'Dry' and 'Rugged' Verse of *Samson Agonistes*," 139.

[40] Quoted, *ibid.*, 146, 148. Phillips would more naturally have discussed his efforts at literary criticism with Milton than Milton would have confided in Phillips, of course.

[41] Wells, "Milton's 'Vulgar Readers' and 'The Verse,'" *Milton Quarterly*, 9 (1975), 67-69.

a critical debate in which the Englishness and modernity of rhyme were specific issues.[42] Milton argued that modern poets rhymed because they were "carried away by Custom"; Marvell made the same point in his couplets, that rhyme was a contemporary fashion like the "tags" on clothes. Milton denied that it is delightful, denied that it is essentially English, and gave notice that he would free his times and nation from its constraints. Phillips, in *Theatrum Poetarum*, forgave Dryden for having "indulg'd a little too much to *the French way* of continued Rime." "The Verse" is a satiric thrust at a clear target conducted with tongue-in-cheek curtness, in no way constraining Milton himself. Milton was not writing in vacuo about general principles.

ARGUMENTS FROM MILTON'S THEMATIC AND INTELLECTUAL CONCERNS

Since the place of *Samson Agonistes* in Milton's intellectual development is the subject of my book, I shall confine myself here to examining the several refutations which others have made of thematic arguments for an early date for *Samson Agonistes*.[43] It has been said that *Samson Agonistes* is "devoid of theology" and that therefore the writing of it preceded *De Doctrina Christiana*; that it stresses the concepts of election, divinely prompted intuition, and a saving remnant, themes exclusive to the sonnets and prose of the early fifties; that it is nationalistic and deeply despairing in presenting a hero of faith not authorized by the Bible and exclusively Milton's invention; and finally, that it contains many verbal echoes of prose works written before 1653 and none of works written after that date.[44]

The impressionistic argument that *Samson Agonistes* is "devoid of theology" has proved particularly vulnerable. George Muldrow, working with the evidence of Maurice Kelley about the layers of composition of *De Doctrina Christiana*, has decisively shown that many of the most crucial concerns of the drama—vengeance and anger, chastisement and repentence, atheism and idolatry, good conscience and sincerity, liberty of interpretation and the primacy of Scripture—are subjects which post-Restoration amanuenses revised in *De Doctrina Christiana*.[45] John M. Steadman has shown how Samson systematically moves through the stages of repentence set forth in *De Doctrina Chris-*

[42] Freedman, "Milton and Dryden on Rhyme," *Huntington Library Quarterly*, 24 (1961), 337ff.

[43] I shall not repeat arguments against the supposed link between translating the Psalms and writing *Samson Agonistes*, since I have examined them fully in Part IV.

[44] Parker, *Milton*, II, 907, 910-17.

[45] Muldrow, *Milton and the Drama of the Soul*, 254-62.

tiana: "the psychic drama follows a moral pattern already set forth in the *De doctrina*."[46] F. Michael Krouse has further shown that the interpretation of Samson as a hero of faith was not peculiar to Milton and isolated in one period of the poet's thought, but was an accepted typological reading in the customary Protestant mode.[47] Anthony Low has shown that "no other single prose work . . . or even perhaps all of them together, proves as widely relevant to the understanding of the play as the *Christian Doctrine*."[48] My own analysis of the development of Milton's theology through *De Doctrina Christiana*, *Paradise Lost*, and *Paradise Regained* to the ecumenical and universalist theology of *Samson Agonistes* confirms the findings of Muldrow, Steadman, Krouse, and Low.

It is true that Milton was concerned with the themes of election, inspiration, and the saving remnant in the late forties and the early fifties, and his choice of Samson to represent the elect champion of God in a great national cause is apparent in the *Second Defence*. Milton was equally concerned with these themes after 1653.[49] His understanding of election, however, underwent changes in the final pre-Restoration tracts, and especially in *The Readie and Easie Way*. The new doctrine of election was ultimately embodied in *Samson Agonistes*. The election of Samson in the tragedy is preeminently to the performance of an exemplary role: he comes to show not how God's will is exerted through the single hero as the instrument of divine public purpose, but to show instead that individual faith is the precondition of public service and that the community of the regenerate can only come about by the gathering together of morally well-tried believers. Samson is an elect saint, not an elect general. The studies in Samson's recovery of faith and acquisition of patience, as well as the studies in both prophetic and exemplary concepts of heroism, work against the 1653 date.[50]

---

[46] Steadman, " 'Faithful Champion,' " 13.

[47] F. Michael Krouse, *Milton's Samson and the Christian Tradition*, 130-31.

[48] Anthony Low, *Blaze of Noon*, 222-25.

[49] See Jackie DiSalvo, " 'The Lord's Battells': *Samson Agonistes* and the Puritan Revolution," pp. 39-92. Dr. DiSalvo's understanding of Milton as elect warrior rather than elect saint leads her to reinforce an early date. Her study is a useful supplement to our understanding of the New Model Army and Milton's triumphant glorification of it in the *Second Defence* but she has not established a necessary conjunction between the Samson of the *Second Defence* and the Samson of the fourth act of the play.

[50] See Harris, "Despair and 'Patience as the Truest Fortitude' in *Samson Agonistes*," 119-20; Ann Gossman, "Samson, Job, and 'The Exercise of Saints' "; Kenneth Fell, "From Myth to Martyrdom": Towards a View of Milton's *Samson Agonistes*"; see my own "*Samson Agonistes* and Milton the Politician in Defeat"; Anthony Low, *Blaze of Noon*, 86-87; Muldrow, *Milton and the Drama of the Soul*, 250; Kerrigan, *Prophetic Milton*, 201-58.

The political and national concern in *Samson Agonistes* is self-evident. The political lesson of the drama, however, is not what may happen to a society which breaks faith, but what can happen to educate and redeem a society which has already broken faith. The "new acquist" of "true experience" directs our attention not to the middle prose tracts in which a puissant Samson warns the multitude to keep faith with the Good Old Cause but rather to the post-Restoration *Of True Religion*, in which the emergently tolerant nation is counselled.[51] Hence, although merely verbal echoes from prose to poetry are profoundly suspect and far too many of the so-called echoes in *Samson Agonistes* of pre-Restoration tracts turn out to be echoes in each of their common sources in the Psalms, it is not surprising to discover verbal echoes of *Samson Agonistes* in *Of True Religion*, echoes of the foolishness of atheism, the forbidding of idolatry, the readiness of God's pardon for His servants, His reluctance to desert them, the revival and reawakening of virtue, the banding together of holy and unblameable men, the refusal of the intelligent to run again into former yokes, the hope of deliverance, and the like. The work of both Edward Le Comte and of A.S.P. Woodhouse on deep patterns and recurrent image clusters in Milton's late poems shows how persistent self-quoting was throughout Milton's total corpus.[52] That *Samson Agonistes* contains verbal echoes from early and middle prose works could only serve to date it contemporaneously with them, if it contained no verbal echoes of even earlier or of later works and if the habit of verbal echoing was unusual in Milton and particularly noticeable in the tragedy. None of these conditions exist.

ARGUMENTS FROM AUTOBIOGRAPHICAL AND HISTORICAL REFERENCES

Ambivalent attitudes have been present in the attempt to date *Samson Agonistes* by means of references to datable allusions to the poet's private or public experiences within the play. On the one hand, early daters have made much of the theoretical positions of the "new critics," who deny that the relationship between life and art is demonstrable or valuable. (They wrote too early to take whatever advantage they might from the structuralists' view that a text is an exclusive interdependence of objective elements and that the structure of interdepend-

---

[51] See William Haller, "The Tragedy of God's Englishman," in *Reason and the Imagination*, 201-12.

[52] Le Comte, *Milton's Unchanging Mind* (Port Washington: Kennikat Press, 1973), 35-54; Woodhouse, *Heavenly Muse*, 176-80.

ence constitutes its meaning.)[53] Critical purists have maintained that the poet's intention, if he had one, cannot be calculated, only inferred or misinferred, and is irrelevant anyway, being necessarily extraliterary. Thus Parker wrote of the "autobiographical fallacy," echoing Wimsatt on the intentional fallacy and a host of others on the genetic fallacy. We are wisely warned by Richard Ellmann of the opposite danger, the "parthenogenetic fallacy that the text is a virgin birth without human intervention." He reminds us of Goethe declaring that all his works were "fragments of a great confession," of Flaubert affirming, "Madame Bovary, c'est moi," of George Eliot admitting that Casaubon was written from her own heart, of T. S. Eliot confessing that *The Waste Land* was "only the relief of a personal and wholly insignificant grouse against life," of Yeats speaking of his poetry as "personal utterance."[54] Doubtless it was once necessary for critical formalists to discourage us from identification of the personal life of the poet with his creative work. More than that, contemporary critics increasingly refuse to acknowledge. The modern position sees the work of art not as an autotelic object but as the convergence of energies which come from the individual, from society, and from the literary tradition, where life and art interfuse and interact. Hence a modern Miltonist searches for the autobiographical parable, not the overt simple reference which illuminates the poem.

On the other hand, the same early daters who cried "fallacy" at those who sought to detect Milton's mature experience in *Samson Agonistes* have undertaken their own explanations from the earlier private and public experience of the poet against the drift of their theoretical argument. Another man's fallacy was their "total picture of Milton's intellectual and artistic development."[55] Naturally, a critic who would never "contaminate" his reading of a poem by seeking to uncover the consciously and semiconsciously parabolic use the artist makes of his own experience would never accept dating by internal evidence; naturally, a critic who conceives of poetic process and development as of enormous interest will not seek simply to date but to explicate through the interpenetration of life and text. Early daters should not try to have it both ways. The core of the early dating by means of analogy to Milton's personal and public experience rests on the demonstration that

[53] Even so, the only "structuralist" reading of Milton so far to have appeared posits the conventional date and observes structural patterns of intelligibility which confirm the order *Paradise Lost, Paradise Regained, Samson Agonistes*. See Donald F. Bouchard, *Milton: A Structural Reading*, 148-50, 157-60, 173.

[54] See Ellmann, "Love in the Catskills," *New York Review of Books*, Feb. 5, 1976, 27-28.

[55] Parker, *Milton*, II, 906.

"our picture of Milton in the years 1647-8" fits the drama and that political and personal allusions do not "point definitely to a period later than 1662."[56]

Parker has counted thirteen passages containing supposed autobiographical allusions and nine containing further current political allusions which, some commentators have argued, demonstrate a late date; he has then attempted to overthrow them. A single example may stand for many. Parker wrote, "Samson eyeless in Gaza is an allusion to the once victorious republican party, after the Restoration. (But the Puritans had actually succeeded in overturning monarchy for more than a decade, as Samson had not.)."[57] In fact, Samson judged (that is, governed) Israel successfully for twenty years and had commenced its full deliverance when his people, preferring "bondage with ease" before "strenuous liberty," betrayed him; they chose in effect a captain back from Egypt, and the Samson parallel points to a post- and pre-Restoration date. The political reference is not shaken by Parker's misreading.[58] One could simply leave the quarrel in midair with the early daters' case not proved, as Ants Oras does, noting that while references in the drama may be to the experiences of a man undergoing the approach of blindness and fearing the future defection of his nation from God's willed destiny for it, they may refer even more naturally to the recollection of a blind poet diagnosing his nation's lapse after it had taken place. Parker died before a number of further explorations of biographical and historical allusions had been made, leaving us a picture of Milton having finished composing before 1665 and sitting idle from that moment to his death, a picture of a man with much too much on his plate for twelve years and much too little on his plate in the last twelve. The tracing of datable allusions has continued since Parker's death, and most of them tend to support the traditional order.

Frank Kermode, in "Milton in Old Age,"[59] has directed attention to Milton's ceremonial submission to Charles II as explicative of Samson's persistent defensiveness and worry about his "intimate impulse." Christopher Hill has argued that Samson's self-betrayal, the perversion of his public role, reflects Milton's diagnosis of the perversion of the Good Old Cause by its ambitious and avaricious generals.[60] Edward Le Comte has shown that although Milton carefully refers to Samson as

[56] *Ibid.*, 907.

[57] "The Date of *Samson Agonistes* Again," 174.

[58] See Barbara Lewalski, "*Samson Agonistes* and the 'Tragedy of the Apocalypse,'" 1050-62. Professor Lewalski rejects the earlier date because of the patent links between *Samson Agonistes* and *The Readie and Easie Way.*

[59] *Southern Review*, 11 (1975), 513-29.

[60] *World Turned Upside Down*, p. 326. Christopher Hill's *Milton and the Eng-*

in the "flower of youth," references to his "old age" keep intruding, suggestive of an aging poet, presenting as the hero of his tragedy an elderly man who bursts out into action from under ashes, one who dies in action, his last work his greatest.[61] Hugh Richmond sees Milton's development as a movement from depicting heroes in archetypal roles in Adam and Christ to depicting a hero in a psychologically realistic role in Samson, and he interprets the confrontation between Samson and the Officer as treating "the nature of the obligation of the autonomous individual to the forms of the society in which he finds himself." He finds both the realism and the individualism "an imperceptible conditioning of English awareness," enabling the nation in but a few years to overthrow the Stuart monarchy without a blow, Milton having pointed the way toward a tolerant consensus in the tragedy. By Richmond's analysis, the calm and plangent tone of the exode prepares and reflects a national movement toward community.[62] Lawrence W. Hyman, who discerns in Samson an *unwilling* martyr, offers an interpretation stressing the very powerful human pain in the hero's suffering. He sees Samson as the most overtly personal and problematical of all Milton's heroes and the drama as "based not only on Milton's faith but also on his doubt in God's justice." Although I do not agree with Hyman's assessment of the conclusion of the play, his description of the feelings it communicates up to, but not I think through Act IV, is masterly. Hyman's reading posits a Samson-Milton pattern of similarity pointing in its deep humanity beyond the Christ-Milton aspects of similarity; his reading is incompatible with an early dating from autobiographical evidence.[63] Along the same lines of identification of the revived hero of Israel with the blinded poet, Jon Lawry sees Milton as quitting himself in his final role with strength comparable to Samson.[64] Both M. M. Mahood and George Williamson concur in finding Samson a "pattern-hero" for Milton, noting that the action begins long after the typical Fall of the earlier epics and traces the pattern of the general believer moving from fallen and blinded Adamic sinfulness toward upright internal sight, from which both the hero and the poet are dismissed quietly from their

---

lish *Revolution* (London: Faber and Faber, 1977) appeared when my own study was in page proofs. He argues in that book even more fully for a post-Restoration but not necessarily post-*Paradise Regained* date.

61 *Milton's Unchanging Mind*, 45-6, 67.

62 *The Christian Revolutionary* (Berkeley: University of California Press, 1974), 176-92.

63 *The Quarrel Within: Art and Morality in Milton's Poetry* (Port Washington: Kennikat Press, 1972), 94-95.

64 *The Shadow of Heaven*, 350.

duties in life.[65] Murray Roston also accepts the conventional date of composition for the tragedy, noting the philosemitism of the Puritan party in the late 1650s and the revival of pseudobiblical drama at the reopening of the theaters as suggesting a later date.[66] And finally, Boyd Berry links *Samson Agonistes* with the movement toward humane optimism and Puritan demystification which increasingly broadened the concept of salvation in the late 1650s, arguing a late date on the grounds of Milton's spiritual autobiography.[67] Among critics who treat works of art as written by a particular person in a particular place and time, and are not anxious about psychological or historical criticism, *Samson Agonistes* seems a late work. Of course, none of the newer critics crudely identify Samson and Milton but they do discern latent patterns pointing toward a poem of Milton's old age.

In summary, objective evidence is not lacking for the late date; artistic practices and theories do not militate against it; thematic links between *Paradise Regained* and *Samson Agonistes* confirm it; and the existence of allusions from autobiography and current affairs points so strongly to the late date that early daters have to expend heroic effort to discredit intentional and biographical readings in general before mounting their own claim that in *Samson Agonistes* Milton was anticipating in dread what late daters abundantly see him as already having undergone.

[65] Mahood, *Poetry and Humanism*, 211; Williamson, *Milton and Others*, 101.
[66] *Biblical Drama in England*, 161, 169.
[67] Berry, *Process of Speech*, 270-71.

Bibliography

Allen, Don Cameron. *The Harmonious Vision*. Baltimore: Johns Hopkins University Press, 1954.

———. *Mysteriously Meant*. Baltimore: Johns Hopkins University Press, 1970.

Arthos, John. *Milton and the Italian Cities*. London: Bowes and Bowes, 1968.

———. "Milton and the Passions: A Study of *Samson Agonistes*." *Modern Philology*, 69 (1972), 209-21.

Ascham, Roger. "Of Imitation." In *Elizabethan Critical Essays*, ed. Smith.

Atkins, J.W.H. *Literary Criticism in Antiquity*. Cambridge: Cambridge University Press, 1934.

Atkinson, M. "The Structure of the Temptations in Milton's *Samson Agonistes*." *Modern Philology*, 69 (1972), 289-91.

Axton, Marie, and Williams, Raymond, eds. *English Drama: Forms and Development*. Cambridge: Cambridge University Press, 1977.

Babb, Lawrence. *The Moral Cosmos of "Paradise Lost."* East Lansing: Michigan State University Press, 1971.

Baker, Herschel. *The Race of Time: Three Lectures on Renaissance Historiography*. Toronto: University of Toronto Press, 1967.

Baldwin, T. W. *Shakespeare's Five-Act Structure*. Urbana: University of Illinois Press, 1947.

Barker, Arthur Ernest. "Calm Regained through Passion Spent: The Conclusions of the Miltonic Effort." In *The Prison and the Pinnacle*, ed. Rajan.

———. *Milton and the Puritan Dilemma*. Toronto: University of Toronto Press, 1942.

———. "The Pattern of Milton's Nativity Ode." *University of Toronto Quarterly*, 10 (1941), 167-81.

———. "Structural and Doctrinal Pattern in Milton's 'Later' Poems." In *Essays Presented to A.S.P. Woodhouse*.

Baruch, Franklin R. "Time, Body and Spirit at the Close of *Samson Agonistes*." *ELH*, 36 (1969), 319-39.

Baum, Paull Franklin. "*Samson Agonistes* Again." *PMLA*, 36 (1921), 354-71.

Baumgartner, Paul. "Milton and Patience." *Studies in Philology*, 40 (1963), 203-13.

Berger, John. *The Allegorical Temper: Vision and Reality in Book II of Spenser's "Faerie Queene."* New Haven: Yale University Press, 1957.

Berry, Boyd M. *Process of Speech: Puritan Religious Writing and "Paradise Lost."* Baltimore: Johns Hopkins University Press, 1976.

Beum, Robert. "The Rhyme in *Samson Agonistes*." *Texas Studies in Language and Literature*, 4 (1962), 117-82.

Beum, Robert. "So Much Gravity and Ease." In *Language and Style in Milton*, ed. Emma and Shawcross.

Bouchard, Donald F. *Milton: A Structural Reading*. London: Edward Arnold, 1974.

——. "Samson as Medicine Man: Ritual Function and Symbolic Structure." *Genre*, 5 (1971), 257-70.

Boughner, Daniel C. "Milton's Harapha and Renaissance Comedy." *ELH*, 11 (1944), 297-306.

Bradbrook, Muriel Clara. *English Dramatic Form*. London: Chatto and Windus, 1965.

Brenneke, Ernest, Jr. *John Milton the Elder and His Music*. New York: Columbia University Press, 1938.

Brisman, Leslie. *Milton's Poetry of Choice*. Ithaca: Cornell University Press, 1973.

Broadbent, John B. "Milton's 'Mortal Voice' and 'Omnific Word.'" In *Some Approaches to "Paradise Lost,"* ed. Patrides.

——. "Milton's Rhetoric." *Modern Philology*, 56 (1959), 226-37.

——. "The Private Mythology of *Paradise Regained*." In *Calm of Mind*, ed. Wittreich.

——. *Some Graver Subject*. London: Chatto and Windus, 1960.

——, ed. *John Milton: Introductions*. Cambridge: Cambridge University Press, 1973.

——, ed. *Milton: "Comus" and "Samson Agonistes."* London: Edward Arnold, 1961.

Brooks, Cleanth, and Hardy, John Edward. *Poems of Mr. John Milton*. New York: Harcourt, Brace and Company, 1951.

Bullough, Geoffrey. "Polygamy among the Reformers." In *Essays Presented to Vivian de Sola Pinto*, ed. Hibbard.

Burden, Denis. *The Logical Epic*. London: Routledge & Kegan Paul, 1967.

Burke, Kenneth. "The 'Use' of *Samson Agonistes*." *Hudson Review*, 1 (1948), 151-67.

Burton, Robert. *The Anatomy of Melancholy*. Everyman's Library. London: J. M. Dent and Sons Ltd., 1932.

Bush, Douglas. *English Literature in the Earlier Seventeenth Century, 1600-1660*. 2d ed. rev. Oxford: Clarendon Press, 1962.

——. *John Milton*. London: Weidenfeld & Nicolson, 1965.

Carey, John. *Milton*. London: Evans Brothers, 1969.

——. "Sea, Snake, Flower and Flame in *Samson Agonistes*." *Modern Language Review*, 62 (1967), 395-99.

Carson, Barbara Harrell. "Milton's Samson as Parvus Sol." *English Language Notes*, 5 (1968), 171-76.

Chambers, A. B. "Wisdom and Fortitude in *Samson Agonistes*." *PMLA*, 78 (1963), 318-27.

Chatman, Seymour. "Milton's Participial Style." *PMLA*, 83 (1969), 1386-99.

Christopher, Georgia. "Homeopathic Physic and Natural Renovation in *Samson Agonistes*." *ELH*, 37 (1970), 361-73.

———. "The Verbal Gate to Paradise: Adam's 'Literary Experience' in Book x of *Paradise Lost*." *PMLA*, 90 (1975), 69-77.

Clark, Donald L. *John Milton at Saint Paul's School*. New York: Columbia University Press, 1948.

Clark, E. M. "Milton's Conception of Samson." *University of Texas Studies in English*, 8 (1928), 88-99.

Cohen, Michael. "Rhyme in *Samson Agonistes*." *Milton Quarterly*, 8 (1974), 4-6.

Colie, Rosalie. *The Resources of Kind: Genre-Theory in the Renaissance*. Berkeley: University of California Press, 1973.

Collette, C. P. "Milton's Psalm Translations: Petition and Praise." *English Literary Renaissance*, 2 (1972), 243-59.

Condee, Ralph W. *Structure in Milton's Poetry*. University Park: Pennsylvania State University Press, 1974.

Conklin, George N. *Biblical Criticism and Heresy in Milton*. New York: Columbia University Press, 1949.

Cope, Jackson I. *The Metaphoric Structure of "Paradise Lost."* Baltimore: Johns Hopkins University Press, 1962.

———. "Milton's Muse in *Paradise Lost*." *Modern Philology*, 55 (1957), 6-10.

Cox, Lee Sheridan. "Natural Science and Figurative Design in *Samson Agonistes*." *ELH*, 35 (1968), 51-74.

Crump, Galbraith N., ed. *Twentieth-Century Interpretations of "Samson Agonistes*." New York: Prentice-Hall, 1968.

Cullen, Patrick. *Infernal Triad: The Flesh, the World, and the Devil in Spenser and Milton*. Princeton: Princeton University Press, 1974.

Curry, W. C. *Milton's Ontology, Cosmogony, and Physics*. Lexington: University of Kentucky Press, 1957.

Daiches, David. *Milton*. London: Hutchinson University Library, 1957.

———. "The Opening of *Paradise Lost*." In *The Living Milton*, ed. Kermode.

———. *A Study of Literature for Readers and Critics*. Ithaca: Cornell University Press, 1948.

Daniells, Roy. *Milton, Mannerism and Baroque*. Toronto: University of Toronto Press, 1964.

Darbishire, Helen, ed. *The Early Lives of Milton*. London: Constable & Co. Ltd., 1932.

Davie, Donald. "Syntax and Music in *Paradise Lost*." In *The Living Milton*.

Diekhoff, John. *Milton on Himself*. New York: Oxford University Press, 1939.

———. *Milton's "Paradise Lost": A Commentary on the Argument*. New York: Columbia University Press, 1946.

———. "Rhyme in *Paradise Lost*." *PMLA*, 49 (1934), 539-43.

BIBLIOGRAPHY

Diekhoff, John. "Terminal Pause in Milton's Verse." *Studies in Philology*, 32 (1935), 235-39.

DiSalvo, Jackie. "'The Lords Battells': *Samson Agonistes* and the Puritan Revolution." *Milton Studies*, 3 (1971), 39-52.

Dobbins, Austin C. *Milton and the Book of Revelation: The Heavenly Cycle.* Studies in the Humanities, no. 7. University: University of Alabama Press, 1975.

Dryden, John. *Preface to the Fables* and *Essay on Satire.* In *"Of Dramatic Poesy" and Other Critical Essays.* Edited by George Watson. Everyman's Library. London: J. M. Dent and Sons Ltd., 1962.

Duncan, Joseph E. *Milton's Earthly Paradise: A Historical Study of Eden.* Minneapolis: University of Minnesota Press, 1972.

Egan, James. "Public Truth and Personal Witness in Milton's Last Tracts." *ELH*, 40 (1973), 231-84.

Ellis-Fermor, Una. *The Frontiers of Drama.* 2d ed. London: Methuen, 1964.

Ellman, Richard. "Love in the Catskills." *New York Review of Books*, February 5, 1976.

Elyot, Thomas. *Bibliotheca Eliotae.* Edited by Thomas Cooper. London, 1559.

Emma, R. D., and Shawcross, John T., eds. *Language and Style in Milton.* New York: Frederick Ungar, 1967.

Empson, William. *Milton's God.* London: Chatto and Windus, 1961.

Evans, J. M. *"Paradise Lost" and the Genesis Tradition.* Oxford: Clarendon Press, 1968.

Fell, Kenneth. "From Myth to Martyrdom: Towards a View of Milton's *Samson Agonistes.*" *English Studies*, 34 (1953), 145-55.

Ferry, Anne Davidson. *Milton and the Miltonic Dryden.* Cambridge, Mass.: Harvard University Press, 1968.

———. *Milton's Epic Voice.* Cambridge, Mass.: Harvard University Press, 1963.

Finney, Gretchen L. "Chorus in *Samson Agonistes.*" *PMLA*, 57 (1943), 649-64.

———. *Musical Backgrounds for English Literature: 1580-1650.* New Brunswick: Rutgers University Press, 1962.

Fiore, Amadeus P., ed. *"Th' Upright Heart and Pure."* Duquesne Studies: Philological Series, 10. Pittsburgh: Duquesne University Press, 1967.

Fisch, Harold. *Jerusalem and Albion.* London: Routledge & Kegan Paul, 1964.

Fish, Stanley. "Question and Answer in *Samson Agonistes.*" *Critical Quarterly*, 9 (1969), 237-64.

———. *Self-Consuming Artefacts: The Experience of Seventeenth-Century Literature.* Berkeley: University of California Press, 1972.

———. *Surprised by Sin.* London: Macmillan, 1967.

Fixler, Michael. *Milton and the Kingdoms of God.* London: Faber and Faber, 1964.

———. "Milton's Passionate Epic." *Milton Studies*, 1 (1969), 171-87.

Fletcher, Angus. *Allegory: The Theory of a Symbolic Mode.* Ithaca: Cornell University Press, 1964.

Fletcher, Harris Francis. *The Intellectual Development of John Milton.* Urbana: University of Illinois Press, 1961.

———. *The Use of the Bible in Milton's Prose.* University of Illinois Studies in Language and Literature, 14. Urbana: University of Illinois Press, 1929.

Flower, Annette C. "The Critical Context of the Preface to *Samson Agonistes.*" *Studies in English Literature*, 10 (1970), 409-23.

Freedman, Morris. "Dryden's 'Memorable Visit' to Milton." *Huntington Library Quarterly*, 18 (1955), 10-21.

———. "Milton and Dryden on Rhyme." *Huntington Library Quarterly*, 24 (1961), 337-42.

Friedman, Donald M. "*Lycidas*: The Swain's Paideia." *Milton Studies*, 3 (1971), 24-32.

Frye, Northrop. "Agon and Logos." In *The Prison and the Pinnacle*, ed. Rajan.

———. *Fables of Identity.* New York: Harcourt, Brace and World, 1963.

———. *The Return of Eden.* Toronto: University of Toronto Press, 1965.

———. *The Stubborn Structure.* London: Methuen, 1970.

———. "The Typology of *Paradise Regained.*" *Modern Philology*, 53 (1956), 227-38. (Revised in *The Return of Eden.*)

Frye, Roland Mushat. *God, Man and Satan.* Princeton: Princeton University Press, 1960.

———. "The Teachings of Classical Puritanism on Conjugal Love." *Studies in the Renaissance*, 2 (1955), 147-59.

George, A. E. *Milton and the Nature of Man.* London: Asia Publishing House, 1974.

George, Charles H. and Katherine. *The Protestant Mind of the English Reformation 1570-1640.* Princeton: Princeton University Press, 1961.

Giamatti, A. Bartlett. *The Earthly Paradise and the Renaissance Epic.* Princeton: Princeton University Press, 1966.

Gilbert, Allan H. "Is *Samson Agonistes* Unfinished?" *Philological Quarterly*, 28 (1949), 98-106.

———. *Literary Criticism: Plato to Dryden.* New York: American Book Company, 1940.

———. *On the Composition of "Paradise Lost."* Chapel Hill: University of North Carolina Press, 1947.

Goldberg, Jonathan. "*Virga Iesse*: Analogy, Typology and Anagogy in a Miltonic Simile." *Milton Studies*, 5 (1973), 177-90.

Gossman, Ann. "Samson, Job and 'The Exercise of Saints.'" *English Studies*, 45 (1964), 212-24.

Grace, William. *Ideas in Milton*. Notre Dame: Notre Dame University Press, 1968.

Grenander, M. E. "Samson's Middle: Aristotle and Dr. Johnson." *University of Toronto Quarterly*, 24 (1955), 377-89.

Grose, Christopher. "Milton on Ramist Similitude." In *Seventeenth-Century Imagery*, ed. Miner.

———. *Milton's Epic Process*. New Haven: Yale University Press, 1973.

Halkett, John. *Milton and the Idea of Matrimony: A Study of the Divorce Tracts and "Paradise Lost."* New Haven: Yale University Press, 1970.

Haller, William. *Foxe's Book of Martyrs and the Elect Nation*. London: Jonathan Cape, 1963.

———. *Liberty and Reformation in the Puritan Revolution*. New York: Columbia University Press, 1955.

———. "Milton and the Protestant Ethic." *Journal of British Studies*, 1 (1961).

———. *The Rise of Puritanism*. New York: Columbia University Press, 1938.

———. "The Tragedy of God's Englishmen." In *Reason and the Imagination*, ed. Mazzeo.

———, and Haller, Malleville. "The Puritan Art of Love." *Huntington Library Quarterly*, 5 (1941-1942), 235-72.

Hamer, Enid. *The Metres of English Poetry*. London: Methuen, 1951.

Han, Pierre. "Vraisemblance and Decorum: A Note on the Baroque in *Samson Agonistes* and *Berenice*." *Seventeenth Century News*, 29 (1971), 67-68.

Hanford, James Holly. *John Milton, Englishman*. New York: Crown Publishers, 1949.

———. "*Samson Agonistes* and Milton in Old Age." In *Studies in Shakespeare, Milton and Donne*. New York: Macmillan, 1925.

———. " 'That Shepherd who First Taught the Chosen Seed.' " *University of Toronto Quarterly*, 8 (1939), 403-19.

———. "The Temptation Motive in Milton." *Studies in Philology*, 15 (1918), 176-94.

———. "The Youth of Milton." In *Studies in Shakespeare, Milton, and Donne*. New York: Macmillan, 1925.

———, and Taaffe, James. *A Milton Handbook*. Rev. ed. New York: Appleton-Century-Crofts, 1970.

Harding, Davis P. *The Club of Hercules*. Urbana: University of Illinois Press, 1962.

Harding, D. W. *Experience into Words*. London: Chatto and Windus, 1963.

Hardison, O. J. "Written Records and Truths of Spirit in *Paradise Lost*." *Milton Studies*, 1 (1969), 147-66.

Harington, Sir John. "A Brief Apology for Poetry." In *Elizabethan Critical Essays*, ed. Smith.

Harrington, James. *Oceana*. Edited by S. B. Liljegren. Heidelberg: Carl Winter, 1924.

Harris, William O. "Despair and 'Patience as the Truest Fortitude' in *Samson Agonistes*." *ELH*, 30 (1963). Reprinted in *Critical Essays on Milton from ELH*. Baltimore: Johns Hopkins University Press, 1969.

Haskin, Dayton. "Divorce as a Path to Union with God in *Samson Agonistes*." *ELH*, 38 (1971), 358-69.

Hawkins, Sherman H. "Samson's Catharsis." *Milton Studies*, 2 (1970), 211-30.

Henry, Nathaniel H. "Milton's Last Pamphlet." In *A Tribute to George Coffin Taylor*, ed. A. Williams.

———. "Who Meant Licence When They Cried Liberty?" *Modern Language Notes*, 66 (1951), 509-13.

Hibbard, G. R., ed. *Renaissance and Modern Essays Presented to Vivian de Sola Pinto*. New York: Barnes and Noble, 1966.

Hill, Christopher. *The Century of Revolution, 1603-1714*. 2d ed. London: Sphere, 1972.

———. *The World Turned Upside Down*. London: Temple Smith, 1972.

Hill, John S. "Vocation and Spiritual Renovation in *Samson Agonistes*." *Milton Studies*, 2 (1970), 149-74.

Hoffman, Nancy. "Samson's Other Father: The Character of Manoa in *Samson Agonistes*." *Milton Studies*, 2 (1970), 195-210.

Hollander, John. *The Untuning of the Sky: Ideas of Music in English Poetry, 1500-1700*. Princeton: Princeton University Press, 1961.

Holloway, John. "*Paradise Lost* and the Quest for Reality." *Forum for Modern Language Studies*, 3 (1967), 1-14.

Honig, Edwin. *Dark Conceit: The Making of Allegory*. London: Faber and Faber, 1959.

Howard, Leon. "The 'Invention' of Milton's 'Great Argument.'" *Huntington Library Quarterly*, 9 (1945), 149-74.

Hughes, Merritt Y. *Ten Perspectives on Milton*. New Haven: Yale University Press, 1965.

Hunter, William B. "Milton Translates the Psalms." *Philological Quarterly*, 40 (1961), 485-94.

———. "Milton's Urania." *Studies in English Literature*, 4 (1964), 35-42.

Hunter, W. B., Patrides, C. A., and Adamson, J. H. *Bright Essence: Studies in Milton's Theology*. Salt Lake City: University of Utah Press, 1972.

Huntley, John. "A Revaluation of the Chorus' Role in Milton's *Samson Agonistes*." *Modern Philology*, 63 (1966), 132-45.

Hyman, Lawrence W. "Belief and Disbelief in *Lycidas*." *College English*, 33 (1972), 532-42.

———. "Milton's Samson and the Modern Reader." *College English*, 28 (1966), 39-43.

———. *The Quarrel Within: Art and Morality in Milton's Poetry*. Port Washington: Kennikat Press, 1972.

———. "The Unwilling Martyrdom in *Samson Agonistes*." *Tennessee Studies in Literature*, 13 (1968), 91-98.

Jacobus, Lee A. *Sudden Apprehension: Aspects of Knowledge in "Paradise Lost."* The Hague: Mouton, 1976.

James, Henry. *The House of Fiction.* Edited by Leon Edel. New York, Mercury Books, 1957.

Jebb, Richard C. *"Samson Agonistes* and the Hellenic Drama." *Proceedings of the British Academy,* 3 (1908), 341-48.

Jonson, Ben. *The Plays.* Edited by Felix E. Schelling. Everyman's Library. London: J. M. Dent and Sons Ltd., 1953.

Kahn, Jack. *Job's Illness: Loss, Grief and Integration.* London: Pergamon Press, 1975.

Kelley, Maurice. "Milton's Later Sonnets and the Cambridge Manuscript." *Modern Philology,* 54 (1956-1957), 20-25.

———. *This Great Argument.* Princeton Studies in English. Princeton: Princeton University Press, 1941.

Kermode, Frank. "Milton in Old Age." *Southern Review,* 11 (1975), 513-29.

———. *Renaissance Essays.* London: Routledge & Kegan Paul, 1971.

———. *"Samson Agonistes* and Hebrew Prosody." *Durham University Journal,* 14 (1953), 59-63.

———. *The Sense of an Ending.* London: Oxford University Press, 1968.

———, ed. *The Living Milton.* London: Routledge & Kegan Paul, 1960.

Kerrigan, William. *The Prophetic Milton.* Charlottesville: University Press of Virginia, 1974.

Kessner, Carole S. "Milton's Hebraic Herculean Hero." *Milton Studies,* 6 (1975), 243-58.

Kirkconnell, Watson. *That Invincible Samson.* Toronto: University of Toronto Press, 1964.

Kivette, Ruth M. "The Ways and Wars of Truth." *Milton Quarterly,* 6 (1972), 81-86.

Kranidas, Thomas. "Dalila's Role in *Samson Agonistes." Studies in English Literature,* 6 (1966), 124-37.

———. *The Fierce Equation.* The Hague: Mouton, 1965.

———. "Manoa's Role in *Samson Agonistes." Studies in English Literature,* 13 (1973), 95-109.

———. "A View of Milton and the Traditional." *Milton Studies,* 1 (1969), 15-29.

———, ed. *New Essays on "Paradise Lost."* Berkeley: University of California Press, 1969.

Kreipe, C. E. *Milton's "Samson Agonistes."* Halle, 1922.

Krouse, F. Michael. *Milton's Samson and the Christian Tradition.* Princeton: Princeton University Press (for the University of Cincinnati), 1949.

Kurth, Burton O. *Milton and Christian Heroism: Biblical Epic Themes and Forms in Seventeenth-Century England.* Berkeley: University of California Press, 1959.

Labriola, Albert C. "Divine Urgency as a Motive for Conduct in *Samson Agonistes*." *Philological Quarterly*, 50 (1971), 99-107.

Landy, Marcia. "Language and the Seal of Silence in *Samson Agonistes*." *Milton Studies*, 2 (1970), 175-94.

Langdon, Michael. "John Milton's *History of Britain*: Its Place in English Historiography." *University of Mississippi Studies in English*, 6 (1965), 59-76.

Lawry, Jon S. " 'Eager Thought': Dialectics in *Lycidas*." *PMLA*, 77 (1963), 27-32.

———. *The Shadow of Heaven*. Ithaca: Cornell University Press, 1968.

Le Comte, Edward S. *Milton's Unchanging Mind*. Port Washington: Kennikat Press, 1973.

———. *Yet Once More: Verbal and Psychological Pattern in Milton*. New York: Columbia University Press, 1953.

Levi, A. W. *Literature, Philosophy and the Imagination*. Bloomington: Indiana University Press, 1962.

Lewalski, Barbara K. *Donne's "Anniversaries" and the Poetry of Praise: The Creation of a Symbolic Mode*. Princeton: Princeton University Press, 1973.

———. "Milton: Political Beliefs and Polemical Methods, 1659-60." *PMLA*, 74 (1959), 191-202.

———. *Milton's Brief Epic*. Providence: Brown University Press, 1966.

———. "*Samson Agonistes* and the 'Tragedy of the Apocalypse.' " *PMLA*, 85 (1970), 1050-62.

———. "Structure and Symbolism of Vision in Michael's Prophecy, *Paradise Lost*, Books XI-XII." *Philological Quarterly*, 33 (1963), 25-35.

———. "Time and History in *Paradise Regained*." In *The Prison and the Pinnacle*, ed. Rajan.

Legouis, Pierre. "Some Remarks on Seventeenth-Century Imagery: Definitions and Caveats." In *Seventeenth-Century Imagery*, ed. Miner.

Lieb, Michael. *The Dialectics of Creation: Patterns of Birth and Regeneration in "Paradise Lost."* Amherst: University of Massachusetts Press, 1970.

———, and Shawcross, J. T., eds. *Achievements of the Left Hand*. Amherst: University of Massachusetts Press, 1974.

Little, Marguerite. "Milton's 'Ad Patrem' and the Younger Gill's 'In Natalem Mei Parentis.' " *Journal of English and Germanic Philology*, 49 (1950), 345-51.

Low, Anthony. "Action and Suffering: *Samson Agonistes* and the Irony of Alternatives." *PMLA*, 84 (1969), 514-19.

———. *The Blaze of Noon*. New York: Columbia University Press, 1974.

———. "Milton's God: Authority in *Paradise Lost*." *Milton Studies*, 4 (1972), 19-38.

———. "Tragic Pattern in *Samson Agonistes*." *Texas Studies in Language and Literature*, 11 (1969), 915-30.

Lumiansky, A. M., and Baker, Herschel, eds. *Critical Approaches to Six Major English Works: "Beowulf" through "Paradise Lost."* Philadelphia: University of Pennsylvania Press, 1968.

BIBLIOGRAPHY

MacCaffrey, Isabel G. *"Paradise Lost" as Myth.* Cambridge, Mass.: Harvard University Press, 1959.

MacCallum, H. R. "Milton and Figurative Interpretation of the Bible." *University of Toronto Quarterly*, 31 (1962), 397-415.

———. "Milton and Sacred History." In *Essays Presented to A.S.P. Woodhouse*, ed. Maclure and Watt.

McCarthy, William. "The Continuity of Milton's Sonnets." *PMLA*, 92 (1977), 96-109.

Maclure, M., and Watt, F. W., eds. *Essays in English Literature from the Renaissance to the Victorian Age. Presented to A.S.P. Woodhouse.* Toronto: University of Toronto Press, 1964.

Madsen, William G. *From Shadowy Types to Truth: Studies in Milton's Symbolism.* New Haven: Yale University Press, 1968.

Mahood, M. M. *Poetry and Humanism.* New Haven: Yale University Press, 1950.

Marilla, E. L. *Milton and Modern Man.* University: University of Alabama Press, 1968.

Martz, Louis L. "Chorus and Character in *Samson Agonistes.*" *Milton Studies*, 2 (1970), 115-35.

———. "*Paradise Regained*: The Meditative Combat." *ELH*, 27 (1960), 223-47.

———. *The Paradise Within.* New Haven: Yale University Press, 1964.

Masson, David. *The Life of John Milton.* London: Macmillan & Co., 1871-1880.

Maxwell, J. C. "Milton's Knowledge of Aeschylus." *Review of English Studies*, 3 (1952), 366-71.

———. "Milton's *Samson* and Sophocles' *Heracles.*" *Philological Quarterly*, 33 (1954), 80-91.

Maynard, Winifred. "Milton and Music." In *John Milton: Introductions*, ed. Broadbent.

Mazzeo, Joseph A., ed. *Reason and the Imagination: Studies in the History of Ideas, 1600-1800.* New York: Columbia University Press, 1962.

Miller, Leo. *John Milton among the Polygamophiles.* New York: Loewenthal Press, 1974.

Milton, John. *Cambridge Milton for Schools and Colleges.* Edited by John Broadbent. Cambridge: Cambridge University Press, 1974. Vol. VIII, *Paradise Lost*, edited by Mary Ann Radzinowicz.

———. *The Columbia Edition of the Works of John Milton.* Edited by Frank Allan Patterson et al. New York: Columbia University Press, 1940.

———. *The Complete English Poetry of John Milton.* Edited by John T. Shawcross. New York: New York University Press, 1963. 2d ed., 1971.

———. *The Complete Poems and Major Prose of John Milton.* Edited by Merritt Y. Hughes. New York: Odyssey Press, 1957.

———. *The Complete Prose Works of John Milton.* Edited by Don M. Wolfe et al. New Haven: Yale University Press, 1953-.

———. *Latin and Italian Poems of Milton Translated into English Verse.* Translated by William Cowper. London: J. Johnson, 1808.

———. *Milton's Sonnets*. Edited by E.A.J. Honigman. London: Macmillan, 1966.

———. *The Poems of John Milton*. Edited by John Carey and Alastair Fowler. London: Longmans, 1968.

———. *Poems Reproduced in Facsimile from the Manuscript in Trinity College, Cambridge*. Menston Ilkley: Scolar Press, 1972.

———. *Private Correspondence and Academic Exercises*. Translated from the Latin by Phyllis B. Tillyard. With an introduction and commentary by E.M.W. Tillyard. Cambridge: At the University Press, 1932.

———. *The Prose of John Milton*. Edited by J. Max Patrick. New York: Anchor Books, 1967.

———. *Samson Agonistes*. Edited by F. T. Prince. New York: Oxford University Press, 1957.

———. *The Sonnets of John Milton*. Edited by John S. Smart. Reprint ed. Oxford: Clarendon Press, 1966.

———. *A Variorum Commentary on the Poems of John Milton*. Edited by Merritt Y. Hughes. New York: Columbia University Press, 1970.

Miner, Earl, ed. *Seventeenth-Century Imagery*. Berkeley: University of California Press, 1971.

Mohl, Ruth. *John Milton and His Commonplace Book*. New York: Frederick Ungar, 1969.

Mollenkott, Virginia R. "Relativism in *Samson Agonistes*." *Studies in Philology*, 68 (1970), 89-102.

Morgan, Edmund S. *The Puritan Family*. Rev. ed. New York: Harper & Row, 1966.

Moss, Leonard. "The Rhetorical Style of *Samson Agonistes*." *Modern Philology*, 62 (1965), 296-301.

Mueller, Martin, E. "Pathos and Katharsis in *Samson Agonistes*." *ELH*, 31 (1964), 156-74. Reprinted in *Critical Essays on John Milton from ELH*.

———. "Sixteenth-Century Italian Criticism and Milton's Theory of Catharsis." *Studies in English Literature*, 6 (1966), 139-50.

———. "Time and Redemption in *Samson Agonistes* and *Iphigenie auf Tauris*." *University of Toronto Quarterly*, 41 (1972), 227-45.

Muldrow, George N. *Milton and the Drama of the Soul: The Theme of Restoration of Men in Milton's Later Poetry*. The Hague: Mouton, 1970.

Murrin, Michael. *The Veil of Allegory*. Chicago: University of Chicago Press, 1969.

Nicolson, Marjorie H. *The Breaking of the Circle*. Rev. ed. New York: Columbia University Press, 1960.

———. *John Milton: A Reader's Guide to His Poetry*. London: Thames and Hudson, 1964.

Nuttall, A. D. *Two Concepts of Allegory*. London: Routledge & Kegan Paul, 1967.

O'Connor, William Van. *Climates of Tragedy*. Baton Rouge: Louisiana State University Press, 1943.

BIBLIOGRAPHY

Ong, Walter J. "Logic and the Epic Muse." In *Achievements of the Left Hand*, ed. Lieb and Shawcross.

———. *Ramus: Method and the Decay of Dialogue*. Cambridge, Mass., Harvard University Press, 1958.

Onuska, John T. "The Equation of Action and Passion in *Samson Agonistes*." *Philological Quarterly*, 52 (1973), 69-84.

Oras, Ants. *Blank Verse and Chronology in Milton*. Gainesville: Florida University Press, 1966.

———. "Milton's Blank Verse and the Chronology of His Major Poems." In *SAMLA Studies in Milton*, ed. Patrick.

Parker, William Riley. "The Date of *Samson Agonistes*." *Philological Quarterly*, 28 (1949), 145-66.

———. "The Date of *Samson Agonistes* Again." In *Calm of Mind*, ed. Wittreich.

———. "The Date of *Samson Agonistes*: A Postscript." *Notes and Queries*, 203 (1958), 201-2.

———. *Milton, a Biography*. Oxford: Clarendon Press, 1968.

———. *Milton's Debt to Greek Tragedy in "Samson Agonistes."* Baltimore: Johns Hopkins University Press, 1937.

Patrick, J. Max, ed. *SAMLA Studies in Milton*. Gainesville: Florida University Press, 1953.

Patrides, C. A. *The Grand Design of God: The Literary Form of the Christian View of History*. London: Routledge & Kegan Paul, 1972.

———. *Milton and the Christian Tradition*. Oxford: Clarendon Press, 1966.

———, ed. *Approaches to "Paradise Lost."* London: Edward Arnold, 1968.

———, ed. *Milton's "Lycidas": The Tradition and the Poem*. New York: Holt, Rinehart and Winston, 1961.

Phillips, Edward. *The Life of Mr. John Milton*. In *Early Lives of John Milton*, ed. Darbishire.

———. *The New World of English Words*. 4th ed. London, 1678.

———. *Theatrum Poetarum*. London, 1675.

Plotkin, Frederick. *Milton's Inward Jerusalem: "Paradise Lost" and the Ways of Knowing*. The Hague: Mouton, 1971.

Potter, Lois. *A Preface to Milton*. London: Longmans, 1971.

Powell, Chilton L. *English Domestic Relations, 1487-1653*. New York: Columbia University Press, 1917.

Prince, F. T. *The Italian Element in Milton's Verse*. Oxford: Clarendon Press, 1962.

Purcell, J. M. "Rime in *Paradise Lost*." *Modern Language Notes*, 67 (1945), 171-72.

Puttenham, George. *The Art of English Poesie*. In *Elizabethan Critical Essays*, ed. Smith.

Radzinowicz, Mary Ann. "Eve and Dalila: Renovation and Hardening of the Heart." In *Reason and the Imagination*, ed. Mazzeo.

―――. " 'Man as a Probationer of Immortality.' " In *Approaches to "Paradise Lost*," ed. Patrides.

―――. "Medicinable Tragedy: The Structure of *Samson Agonistes* and Seventeenth-Century Pathology." In *English Drama: Forms and Development*, ed. Axton and Williams.

―――. "*Samson Agonistes* and Milton the Politician in Defeat." *Philological Quarterly*, 44 (1965), 454-71.

Rajan, Balachandra. "Jerusalem and Athens: The Temptation of Learning in *Paradise Regained*." In *Th' Upright Heart and Pure*, ed. Fiore.

―――. *The Lofty Rhyme*. London: Routledge & Kegan Paul, 1970.

―――. "*Paradise Lost" and the Seventeenth-Century Reader*. London: Chatto and Windus, 1947.

―――. "Simple, Sensuous and Passionate." *Review of English Studies*, 21 (1945), 289-305.

―――, ed. *The Prison and the Pinnacle*. London: Routledge & Kegan Paul, 1975.

Ransom, John Crowe. "A Poem nearly Anonymous." In *"Lycidas*," ed. Patrides.

Richards, Ivor Armstrong. *Beyond*. London: Harcourt Brace Jovanovich, 1974.

Richmond, Hugh M. *The Christian Revolutionary*. Berkeley: University of California Press, 1974.

―――. *Renaissance Landscapes*. The Hague: Mouton, 1973.

Ricks, Christopher B. *Milton's Grand Style*. Oxford: Clarendon Press, 1963.

Rivers, Isabel. *The Poetry of Conservatism, 1600-1745: A Study of Poets and Public Affairs from Jonson to Pope*. Cambridge: Rivers Press, 1973.

Robbins, Harry F. *If This Be Heresy*. Urbana: University of Illinois Press, 1963.

Robertson, Duncan. "Metaphor in *Samson Agonistes*." *University of Toronto Quarterly*, 38 (1969), 319-38.

Robson, W. W. "The Better Fortitude." In *The Living Milton*, ed. Kermode.

Roston, Murray. *Biblical Drama in England*. Evanston: Northwestern University Press, 1968.

Rupp, E. G. *Studies in the Making of the English Protestant Tradition*. Cambridge: Cambridge University Press, 1947.

Ryken, Leland. *The Apocalyptic Vision in "Paradise Lost*." Ithaca: Cornell University Press, 1970.

Sadler, Lynn Veach. "Coping with Hebraic Legalism: The Chorus in *Samson Agonistes*." *Huntington Library Quarterly*, 66 (1973), 353-69.

―――. "Regeneration and Typology: *Samson Agonistes* in Relation to *De doctrina Christiana, Paradise Lost* and *Paradise Regained*." *Milton Studies*, 3 (1971), 141-56.

―――. "Typological Imagery in *Samson Agonistes*: Noon and the Dragon." *ELH*, 37 (1970), 195-210.

Safer, Elaine B. "The Socratic Dialogue and 'Knowledge in the Making' in *Paradise Regained.*" *Milton Studies*, 8 (1975), 215-26.

Samuel, Irene. "The Dialogue in Heaven: Reconsiderations of *Paradise Lost*, III: 1-417." *PMLA*, 72 (1957), 601-11.

———. *Milton and Dante.* Ithaca: Cornell University Press, 1966.

———. *Milton and Plato.* Ithaca: Cornell University Press, 1947.

———. "Milton and the Ancients on the Writing of History." *Milton Studies*, 2 (1970), 131-48.

———. "Milton on Learning and Wisdom." *PMLA*, 64 (1949), 708-23.

———. "*Paradise Lost.*" In *Critical Approaches to Six Major English Works*, ed. Lumiansky and Baker.

———. "The Regaining of Paradise." In *The Prison and the Pinnacle*, ed. Rajan.

———. "*Samson Agonistes* as Tragedy." In *Calm of Mind*, ed. Wittreich.

Saurat, Denis. *Milton, Man and Thinker.* Repr. ed. Hamden: Archon, 1964.

Schmidt, Hans. *Die Psalmen.* Göttingen: Vandenhoeck and Rupretcht, 1934.

Schultz, Howard. *Milton and Forbidden Knowledge.* London: Oxford University Press, 1959.

Scott-Craig, T.S.K. "Concerning Milton's *Samson Agonistes.*" *Renaissance News*, 5 (1952), 45-53.

———. "The Craftsmanship and Theological Significance of Milton's *Art of Logic.*" *Huntington Library Quarterly*, 17 (1953), 1-16.

Seaman, John E. *The Moral Paradox of "Paradise Lost."* The Hague: Mouton, 1971.

Sellin, P. R. "Milton's Epithet *Agonistes.*" *Studies in English Literature*, 4 (1964), 137-62.

———. "Sources of Milton's Catharsis: A Reconsideration." *Journal of English and Germanic Philology*, 60 (1961), 712-30.

Sewall, Arthur. *A Study in Milton's Christian Doctrine.* London: Oxford University Press, 1939.

Shaheen, Naseeh. "Milton's Muse and the *De doctrina.*" *Milton Quarterly*, 8 (1974), 72-76.

Shapiro, Karl. *Essay on Rime.* New York: Reynal and Hitchcock, 1945.

Shawcross, John T. "The Chronology of Milton's Major Poems." *PMLA*, 76 (1961), 345-58.

———. "The Date of Milton's *Ad Patrem.*" *Notes and Queries*, 204 (1959), 358-59.

———. "Irony as Tragic Effect: *Samson Agonistes* and the Tragedy of Hope." In *Calm of Mind*, ed. Wittreich.

Shumaker, Wayne. *Unpremeditated Verse: Feeling and Perception in "Paradise Lost."* Princeton: Princeton University Press, 1967.

Sidney, Sir Philip. *An Apologie for Poetrie.* In *Elizabethan Critical Essays*, ed. Smith.

Sims, James H. *The Bible in Milton's Epics.* Gainesville: Florida University Press, 1962.

Sirluck, Ernest. "Milton's Idle Right Hand." *Journal of English and Germanic Philology*, 60 (1961), 749-85.

——. "Milton's Political Thought: The First Cycle." *Modern Philology*, 61 (1964), 209-24.

——. *"Paradise Lost": A Deliberate Epic*. Cambridge: W. Heffer and Sons, 1967.

Slights, Camille. "A Hero of Conscience: *Samson Agonistes* and Casuistry." *PMLA*, 91 (1975), 395-412.

Smith, G. Gregory, ed. *Elizabethan Critical Essays*. London: Oxford University Press, 1950.

Spingarn, J. E. *Critical Essays of the Seventeenth Century*. London: Oxford University Press, 1908.

Spitzer, Leo. *Classical and Christian Ideas of World Harmony*. Baltimore: Johns Hopkins University Press, 1963.

Sprott, S. E. *Milton's Art of Prosody*. Oxford: Blackwell, 1953.

Staveley, Keith W. *The Politics of Milton's Prose Style*. Yale Studies in English, 185. New Haven: Yale University Press, 1975.

Steadman, John M. *Epic and Tragic Structure in "Paradise Lost."* Chicago: Chicago University Press, 1976.

——. " 'Faithful Champion': The Theological Basis of Milton's Hero of Faith." *Anglia*, 77 (1959), 13-28.

——. *The Lamb and the Elephant*. San Marino: Huntington Library, 1974.

——. " 'Men of Renown': Heroic Virtue and the Giants of Genesis 6.4 (*Paradise Lost* XI:638-99)." *Philological Quarterly*, 30 (1961), 580-89.

——. *Milton and the Renaissance Hero*. Oxford: Clarendon Press, 1967.

——. *Milton's Epic Characters*. Chapel Hill: University of North Carolina Press, 1968.

——. "Milton's Rhetoric: Satan and the Unjust Discourse." *Milton Studies*, 1 (1969), 67-92.

——. "*Paradise Regained*: Moral Dialectic and the Pattern of Rejection." *Philological Quarterly*, 31 (1962), 416-30.

——. " 'Passions well Imitated': Rhetoric and Poetics in the Preface to *Samson Agonistes*." In *Calm of Mind*, ed. Wittreich.

Stein, Arnold. *Answerable Style: Essays on "Paradise Lost."* Minneapolis: University of Minnesota Press, 1953.

——. *Heroic Knowledge: An Interpretation of "Paradise Regained" and "Samson Agonistes."* Minneapolis: University of Minnesota Press, 1957.

Stollman, Samuel S. "Milton's Samson and the Jewish Tradition." *Milton Studies*, 3 (1971), 185-200.

——. "Milton's Understanding of the 'Hebraic' in *Samson Agonistes*." *Studies in Philology*, 69 (1972), 334-47.

——. "Samson as Dragon and a Scriptural Tradition." *English Language Notes*, 7 (1970), 186-89.

Stoup, Thomas B. *Religious Rite and Ceremony in Milton's Poetry*. Lexington: University of Kentucky Press, 1968.

Studley, M. H. "Milton and His Paraphrases of the Psalms." *Philological Quarterly*, 4 (1925), 364-72.

Summers, Joseph H. "Milton and the Cult of Conformity." *Yale Review*, 46 (1957), 511-20.

———. *The Muse's Method: An Introduction to "Paradise Lost."* Cambridge, Mass.: Harvard University Press, 1962.

———, ed. *The Lyric and Dramatic Milton*. New York: Columbia University Press, 1965.

Svendsen, Kester. *Milton and Science*. Cambridge, Mass.: Harvard University Press, 1956.

Taylor, Dick. "Grace as a Means of Poetry." *Tulane Studies in English*, 4 (1954), 57-90.

Taylor, E. W. "Milton's Samson: The Form of Christian Tragedy." *English Literary Renaissance*, 3 (1973), 306-21.

Taylor, W. R., and McCullough, W. S., eds. *The Book of Psalms*. Vol. IV of *The Interpreter's Bible*.

Thorpe, James. "On the Pronunciation of Names in *Samson Agonistes*." *Huntington Library Quarterly*, 31 (1967), 65-74.

———, ed. *Milton Criticism: Selections from Four Centuries*. London: Routledge & Kegan Paul, 1950.

Tillyard, E.M.W. *Milton*. Rev. ed. London: Chatto and Windus, 1961.

Tung, Mason. "*Samson Impatiens*: A Reinterpretation of *Samson Agonistes*." *Texas Studies in Language and Literature*, 9 (1967), 475-92.

Tuve, Rosemond. *Allegorical Imagery: Some Medieval Books and Their Posterity*. Princeton: Princeton University Press, 1966.

———. *Elizabethan and Metaphysical Imagery*. Chicago: University of Chicago Press, 1947.

———. *Images and Themes in Five Poems by Milton*. Cambridge, Mass.: Harvard University Press, 1957.

Ulreich, John C. "The Typological Structure of Milton's Imagery." *Milton Studies*, 5 (1973), 67-82.

Visiak, E. H. *Milton Agonistes: A Metaphysical Criticism*. London: Werner Laurie, 1923.

Waddington, Raymond B. " 'Melancholy against Melancholy': *Samson Agonistes* as Renaissance Tragedy." In *Calm of Mind*, ed. Wittreich.

Waggoner, George R. "The Challenge to Single Combat in *Samson Agonistes*." *Philological Quarterly*, 39 (1960), 82-92.

Watkins, W.B.C. *An Anatomy of Milton's Verse*. Baton Rouge: Louisiana State University Press, 1955.

Webber, Joan. "Milton's God." *ELH*, 40 (1973), 514-31.

Weinkauf, Mary. "Dalila: The Worse of All Possible Wives." *Studies in English Literature*, 13 (1973), 135-47.

Weiser, Artur. *The Psalms*. 5th ed. London: SCM Press, 1962.

Weismiller, Edward. "The 'Dry' and 'Rugged' Verse of *Samson Agonistes*." In *The Lyric and Dramatic Milton*, ed. Summers.

———. "A Review of Studies of Style and Verse Form of *Paradise Regained*." In *A Variorum Edition of the Poems of John Milton*, Vol. IV.

Weiss, Brian. *Milton's Use of Ramist Method in His Scholarly Writings*. Ann Arbor: University Microfilms, 1975.

Wells, Claude E. "Milton's 'Vulgar Readers' and 'The Verse.'" *Milton Quarterly*, 9 (1975), 67-69.

West, Robert. "Milton as a Philosophical Poet." In *Th' Upright Heart and Pure*, ed. Fiore.

Whiting, George W. *Milton and this Pendent World*. Austin: University of Texas Press, 1958.

———. *Milton's Literary Milieu*. Chapel Hill: University of North Carolina Press, 1939.

———. "*Samson Agonistes* and the Geneva Bible." *Rice University Studies*, 38 (1951), 16-35.

Wilkes, G. A. "The Interpretation of *Samson Agonistes*." *Huntington Library Quarterly*, 26 (1963), 363-79.

Williams, Arnold, ed. *A Tribute to George Coffin Taylor*. Chapel Hill: University of North Carolina Press, 1952.

Williams, George H. *The Radical Reformation*. Philadelphia: Westminster Press, 1962.

Williamson, George. *Milton and Others*. Chicago: University of Chicago Press, 1965.

Wimsatt, William K., Jr., and Brooks, Cleanth. *Literary Criticism: A Short History*. London: Routledge & Kegan Paul, 1957.

Wittreich, Joseph A. *The Romantics on Milton: Formal Essays and Critical Asides*. Cleveland: Case Western Reserve University Press, 1970.

———, ed. *Calm of Mind*. Cleveland: Case Western Reserve University Press, 1971.

———, ed. *The Line of Vision*. Madison: University of Wisconsin Press, 1974.

Wolfe, Don M. *Milton in the Puritan Revolution*. London: Cohen and West, 1963.

Woodhouse, A.S.P. *The Heavenly Muse: A Preface to Milton*. Edited by Hugh MacCallum. Toronto: University of Toronto Press, 1972.

———. "Milton, Puritanism and Liberty." *University of Toronto Quarterly*, 4 (1935), 485-513.

———. "Notes on Milton's Early Development." *University of Toronto Quarterly*, 13 (1943), 85-108.

———. *The Poet and His Faith*. Chicago: University of Chicago Press, 1965.

———. "*Samson Agonistes* and Milton's Experience." *Transactions of the Royal Society of Canada*, 3d Ser., 43 (1949), 169-75.

———. "Tragic Effect in *Samson Agonistes*." *University of Toronto Quarterly*, 28 (1959), 205-22.

Index

INDEX

Library of Congress Cataloging in Publication Data

Radzinowicz, Mary Ann.
  Toward Samson Agonistes.

  Bibliography: p.
  Includes index.
    1. Milton, John, 1608-1674. Samson Agonistes.
  2. Milton, John, 1608-1674—Criticism and
  interpretation.   I. Title.
  PR3566.R3   821'.4   77-85559
  ISBN 0-691-06357-5